THINKING ABOUT
GENDER

A Historical Anthology

THINKING ABOUT
GENDER
A Historical Anthology

JANET McCRACKEN

Lake Forest College

Under the general editorship of

ROBERT C. SOLOMON

The University of Texas, Austin

HARCOURT BRACE COLLEGE PUBLISHERS

Fort Worth   Philadelphia   San Diego   New York   Orlando   Austin   San Antonio
Toronto   Montreal   London   Sydney   Tokyo

PUBLISHER	*Christopher P. Klein*
SENIOR ACQUISITIONS EDITOR	*David C. Tatom*
DEVELOPMENTAL EDITOR	*J. Claire Brantley/Susan Petty*
PROJECT EDITOR	*Betsy Cummings*
PRODUCTION MANAGER	*Lois West*
SENIOR ART DIRECTOR	*Melinda Welch*

Cover: Jean Ranc, Vertumnuis and Pomona, c. 1710–20. Oil on canvas, 170 × 120 cm. Musee Fabre, Montpellier, Photo: Giraudon/Art Resource, New York.

ISBN: 0-15-502495-7

Library of Congress Catalog Card Number: 96-76122

Copyright © 1997 by Harcourt Brace & Company

Harcourt Brace College Publishers may provide complimentary instructional aids and supplements or supplement packages to those adopters qualified under our adoption policy. Please contact your sales representative for more information. If as an adopter or potential user you receive supplements you do not need, please return them to your sales representative or send them to:

Attn: Returns Department
Troy Warehouse
465 South Lincoln Drive
Troy, MO 63379

Address for Editorial Correspondence: Harcourt Brace College Publishers, 301 Commerce Street, Suite 3700, Fort Worth, Texas 76102.

Address for Orders: Harcourt Brace & Company, 6277 Sea Harbor Drive, Orlando, Florida 32887-6777. 1-800-782-4479, or 1-800-433-0001 (in Florida).

Printed in the United States of America

6 7 8 9 0 1 2 3 4 5   090   0 9 8 7 6 5 4 3 2 1

PREFACE

Over the past few years, American educational institutions have faced a seemingly contradictory pair of demands. On the one hand, there is a demand for diversity in education, a need to speak to students' political concerns, including sexism and other "-isms." On the other hand, there is a demand for renewed commitment to classical liberal arts education and its ideals. Many teachers face these conflicting demands as they plan their classes, either wanting to teach traditional courses and feeling that they are out of touch with their profession, or wanting to teach less traditional courses and feeling the pressure not to overlook basic texts. Many students, asked from the beginning of their college careers to criticize a canon of works with which they are not yet familiar, face conflicting demands for both precise scholarly rigor and broad political speculation. This anthology provides a set of readings on gender through which some of these conflicts may be resolved.

Most collections that deal with the issue of gender either assume a familiarity with the basic texts of western culture or offer feminist perspectives as a comment upon the passages of the great thinkers that comprise their bulk. This book is intended both to fill a gap in the set of texts available for classes on gender and to help open the field of gender studies beyond contemporary feminist critiques. My goal here has been to provide and elucidate significant treatments of the question of gender by authors whose work is within what has become known as the traditional Western canon. In this way, I hope to avoid the superficial progressivism with which many contemporary students approach their college courses. I believe many of the extant texts in gender studies do little to counteract this belief that the present generation has nothing of value to learn about contemporary problems from the thinkers of earlier ages. I also hope to avoid the opposite problem—the sort of scholarly veneration of texts within the traditional canon that can establish habits of reading these books in uncritical, static, or impersonal ways. The selections in this anthology demonstrate that the question of gender is a longstanding and difficult one, to which many different answers have been posed, even within the Western tradition. Just as the collection demonstrates the perennial importance of traditional Western thought, however, it also brings these texts into a contemporary conversation of urgent personal and political concern, making them answerable for their legacy to today's students.

While this collection has a literary as well as a philosophical bent, it is first and foremost philosophical. It aims to challenge, clarify, and sharpen students' ideas about femininity and masculinity rather than to inform them widely of current scholarship on the topic or to reorient their sympathies about it. On this account, I have tended to isolate the issue of gender rather than to link it to other political and moral issues, such as race, culture, or class. Many academics believe that work on these issues gains momentum from their association, and they may be right. Still, it seems to me that good thinking on any question requires two different movements of thought: one that interconnects the question with other issues in a larger context and one that contemplates it in itself. There are many anthologies available that bring the issue of gender together with other important topics. I believe, however, that textbooks that facilitate our thinking about gender per se are underrepresented in the market; here, I have tried to keep it logically distinct.

By presenting basic texts for consideration and discussion on their own terms, but with a philosophical approach, I believe I leave open the questions of what the Western tradition is, what constitutes gender, and what we should take as moral and political goods with regard to this or any issue. By offering the vast array of positions available within these widely read and accepted texts, this collection demonstrates that even this supposedly narrow tradition is far from monolithic. By their juxtaposition the claims made in these readings challenge, question, and complement each other in a variety of ways while encouraging readers to do the same. As an editor, I have sought to make available for investigation at least some of the presuppositions with which contemporary readers might come armed; yet, I have striven never to do disrespect to the authors of the pieces herein or to readers. The principle of charity is observed throughout as an example for students and as a professional obligation for teachers.

USING THIS BOOK: FOR INSTRUCTORS

My orientation, as the organization of the book makes clear, is always philosophical and historical. However, philosophy classes with a problems orientation could also make fruitful use of this textbook, as could women's studies classes or interdisciplinary humanities courses on gender.

The parts of the book are designated by numbers and descriptive titles; these are organized around the broad historical trends in the treatment of gender, which roughly parallel the historical divisions in the tradition philosophy course: pre-Socratic, Ancient, Early Modern, Nineteenth Century, Twentieth Century, pre-WWII, and post-WWII. I have devoted a separate section to pre-Socratic works, normally included with the ancients, because of the special importance of their prereflective images of gender. Each author within each part is designated with a number; each selection is titled separately and includes both original text and my comments. My commentary has three intentions: (1) to provide necessary background for texts where some knowledge of context is required for an adequate understanding, (2) to point out some interesting or important lines of thought in the excerpts, and

(3) simply to break up long passages of text to allow students moments for reflection as they read. The commentary is designed to set an example for the students; there is far more to be done with each passage in the classroom than could be indicated in any one textbook. The commentary merely gives an idea of how one might proceed in regarding a thick and perhaps obscure text and should not be taken as the only interpretation. It is meant to provide students with access to a work so that they can critically analyse it in their own terms. The amount of commentary differs from selection to selection, depending on the amount required by the particular reading. In general, I have found that students relate much better to works with historical sensibilities closer to their own, even when they are conceptually very difficult. Hence the length of my commentary generally diminishes as the parts progress chronologically.

Some classes may be well served by confining themselves to two or three parts of the book while others will use portions of all the parts. A nonhistorical syllabus might well begin with Part 6. Instructors may pick and choose from the available readings to best match their course and their goals. Here are two sample syllabi for nonhistorically organized courses.

COURSE I: 14 WEEKS

WEEKS 1–4: GENDER IDENTITY

Part 6	Irigarary, Cixous
Part 5	Freud, De Beauvoir
Part 1	Hesiod *Theogony*
Part 2	Aristotle *Generation of Animals*
Part 3	Rousseau *Emile* "Sophy," Wollstonecraft *A Vindication of the Rights of Woman* "On Sexual Character"
Part 4	Nietzsche selections

WEEKS 5–8: NATURE VS. NURTURE

Part 6	Ortner
Part 5	Mead
Part 1	Old Testament *Genesis*
Part 2	Sophocles *Oedipus Rex*, Plato *Symposium*
Part 3	Milton or Descartes, Hobbes, Rousseau *Discourses on the Origins of Inequality*, *Emile* "Natural Sex Differences and Education"
Part 4	Hegel, Mill *The Subjection of Women* Chs. 1 and 2

WEEKS 9–12: MEN'S AND WOMEN'S WORK

Part 1	Hesiod *Works and Days*, Homer *Illiad*, Old Testament *Ruth*
Part 2	Plato *Republic*, Aristotle *Politics*, St. Paul
Part 3	Shakespeare *Macbeth*, Locke
Part 4	Mill *The Subjection of Women* Ch. 3, Marx *1844 Manuscripts*
Part 5	Gilman, Woolf, De Beauvoir

WEEKS 13–14: MARRIAGE AND RELATIONSHIPS

Part 1   Homer *Odyssey*
Part 2   Aeschylus *Agamemnon*, Aristotle *Nicomachean Ethics*
Part 3   Shakespeare *The Taming of the Shrew*, Milton "Adam and Eve"
Part 4   Engles, Kierkegaard
Part 5   Horney "The Dread of Woman"

COURSE II: 14 WEEKS

WEEKS 1–5: GENDER AND ETHICS

Part 6   Gilligan
Part 5   Horney "The Flight from Womanhood," "The Overvaluation of Love"
Part 1   Hesiod *Works and Days*, Old Testament *Ruth*
Part 2   Sophocles *Antigone*, Plato *Republic*, St. Paul
Part 3   Hobbes, Locke, Rousseau, Wollstonecraft
Part 4   Mill, Marx *1844 Manuscripts*
Part 5   Gilman, Sartre, De Beauvoir
Part 6   Millett

WEEKS 6–11: IMAGES OF GENDER

Part 1   Hesiod *Theogony*, Pythagoreans, Old Testament *Genesis*
Part 2   Sophocles *Oedipus Rex*, Plato *Theaetetus* and *Symposium*, Aristotle
          Generation of Animals
Part 3   Shakespeare *Macbeth*, Milton, Descartes
Part 4   Shelley, Kierkegaard, Nietzsche
Part 5   Freud, Woolf, Jung
Part 6   Ortner, Irigaray, Cixous

WEEKS 12–14: GENDER IN HISTORY & SOCIETY

Part 6   Foucault
Part 4   Hegel, Engles
Part 2   Aeschylus *Eumenides*, Aristotle *Politics*
Part 5   Horney, Mead

USING THIS BOOK: FOR STUDENTS

One of the blessings of textbooks like this one, which edit great works into manageable pieces for students, is that such books help rid us of our reverence for the printed word. You can't hope to understand an author's theory if you believe it to be up on a pedestal, far away from you and unimpeachable. This book is a tool for your use. Get everything you can out of it. Use it at your own pace. Feel free to disagree with the various authors, add to their theories along their same lines, and argue with or defend the authors of the readings included. Write your responses in the margin; don't confine yourself to highlighting their sacred words. Mark passages that you want to ask your teacher about or return to when you write your own essays. Read passages that bother or perplex you to your friends and get their input. A devoted student always loves a puzzle; what is difficult or confusing is always an opportunity to learn.

The issue of gender provides the student with a wealth of such opportunities. It is hard work to think about gender, and the best use of this textbook is to exercise your mind. In philosophy, the most important ways to exercise our minds are by *inquiring* and *arguing*. To inquire in a philosophical way, you should try to formulate specific questions about the material you read. For instance, in the Plato section from the *Republic*, Socrates makes an analogy between gender and hair color in order to argue that employers should not discriminate on the basis of gender. You might ask in the margin alongside this passage, "I'll agree that we shouldn't pick a shoemaker based on her hair color, but why shouldn't we?" The more specifically and clearly you can state your question, the more opportunity you provide yourself to pursue a clear line of thought on the issue. To argue in a philosophical way, you should try to give all the relevant reasons for any claim you assert. For instance, if you wanted to claim against Rousseau that women are no more naturally gifted at dressing nicely than men, you should try to list examples of women who dress poorly and men who dress well by the standards of good dressing that Rousseau lays out. You might also give specific reasons why his standards are wrong and why the right standards apply to men as well as women.

Inquiring and arguing well can not only form a foundation for good work in your course on gender, they are ultimately valuable skills in themselves, and can help you approach any material responsibly and fruitfully. If, after reading this book, you ask better questions about gender and argue about the subject better than you did before, then you have achieved something of immeasurable value even if all your arguments are eventually countered and all your questions go unanswered.

ACKNOWLEDGMENTS

This book would not have gotten off the ground without the help and support of many people. The original idea that I put together a collection on gender was suggested to me by Lou Lombardi, the chair of the philosophy department at Lake Forest College. I thank him heartily. I am also grateful to the various students in my PHL 200 class, "Philosophy and Gender," who have genially allowed me to test certain reading selections. I would also like to thank the reviewers who looked over early drafts of manuscript and provided useful comments and constructive criticism; thanks to Marcia Baron, University of Illinois at Urbana—Champaign; Cynthia Freeland, University of Houston; Elton A. Hall, Moorpark College; Karen Hanson, Indiana University; Christine Holmgren, Santa Monica College; Leslie Huntress Hopkins, College of Lake County; and Rhoda Hadassah Kotzin, Michigan State University.

Robert C. Solomon, University of Texas at Austin and philosophy series editor for Harcourt Brace College Publishers, checked in on my progress regularly and kept me both on track and in good spirits. I am very grateful to David Tatom, Senior Acquisitions Editor at Harcourt Brace, for continuing his support of this project even when it seemed like a risky one. Leanne Winkler was first in charge of developing the book, and I thank her for her graciousness. I am quite indebted to J. Claire Brantley, Developmental Editor, for her tireless and cheerful efforts to improve and facilitate my work. Project Editor Betsy Cummings, Senior Art Director Melinda Welch, and Production Manager Lois West worked on different aspects of producing this book, and I thank them all for their professionalism.

Heather Brown, Doug Ehrman, Geoffrey McNeil, and Alicia Witten—all students at Lake Forest College—were an enormous help in the preparation of the manuscript. They served as test-readers of commentary and Ms. Witten, especially, offered very useful suggestions. Kathleen Higgins, University of Texas at Austin, also provided welcome insight about procedure and content, and I thank her. My friend Jennifer O'Brien, professor of psychology at Lake Forest College, was gracious enough to help with all the little things all the time, especially the index. Finally, I must thank my husband Chad, who not only assisted greatly in the preparation of the manuscript and provided valuable criticism and suggestions, but who also kept a stoic bearing while I put this together.

CONTENTS

WHAT ARE MASCULINITY AND FEMININITY, ANYWAY?

THINKING ABOUT GENDER

In Plato's *Theaetetus* (174b), Socrates describes the philosopher of human nature in the following way:

> *He not only doesn't notice what [his neighbor] is doing; he scarcely knows whether he is a man or some other creature. The question he asks is, What is Man? What actions and passions properly belong to human nature and distinguish it from all other beings? This is what he wants to know and concerns himself to investigate.[1]*

Socrates' point is that the philosopher is radically unbiased—so much so that he or she can put aside even the fact that he or she is a human being, in order to consider fairly and fully what the word "human" really means. In this book, although we will look at some texts from disciplines other than philosophy, we will try to consider gender in the same profoundly unbiased way that Socrates describes. This book asks you to put aside, to the best of your abilities, your attachments to your own body (and so, to your own sex) and to your experiences with men and women, in order to explore as thoroughly as possible whether masculinity and femininity really exist, and if so, what masculinity and femininity really are, how they inform your life and the lives of others.

---

[1] Plato, *Theaetetus.* Translated by M. J. Levett, revised by Myles Burnyeat, edited by Bernard Williams. (Indianapolis: Hackett, 1992), p. 44.

1

These days, in the media, in the courts, in our workplaces, in our classes, even in our homes, we do an awful lot of arguing over issues that could roughly be described as gender-related. The value of Hillary Clinton's contribution to public policy, the moral characters of Clarence Thomas and Anita Hill, the constitutionality of abortion, the propriety of military combat for women, etc., are exemplary cases around which we fashion our general worldviews. On this account, whether one is a feminist or not is by many today considered to be central and definitive of one's moral perspective.

But many of these arguments with which we are so often occupied, and many of the actions they seek to promote or censure, are ones in which the philosopher, in Socrates' sense, has little to say. Particular questions about men's and women's actions, or about public policy regarding men and women, tell us relatively little about the nature of gender. In fact—and importantly—the judgments we make about these particular cases really should depend upon a philosophical view about the nature of gender which they presuppose. For instance, until we know for sure that aggression is masculine—as has often been suggested—and that men always have more of what is masculine than do women, we cannot decide whether it would be good or bad, fair or unfair, to let women serve in combat in the military, where aggression may be a prerequisite. Without knowledge of these underlying issues, any judgment we might make about specific policies can only be based on bald speculation, hunch, or fashion.

Our concern here, then, is not whether, but *why* and *to what extent* we would consider a particular person masculine or feminine; not how, but *why* and *to what extent* we would judge such a person on this account. Our concern will not be with making particular judgments but with establishing the underlying *criteria* on which to base them. Our concern, in Socrates' terms, is with what "actions and passions properly belong" to femininity and masculinity, what distinguishes them from each other, how they affect individual human beings, and in each case, with how we know it. Each of the reading selections which follows explores or argues, in its own way, these abstract but fundamental questions.

"FEMININITY" AND "MASCULINITY"

The questions above may seem trivial—it might, on the face of it, seem obvious that a particular person is, say, a man, and that being a man makes him masculine. But the issue is far more complicated. Do we not sometimes call a particular man "feminine" or a particular woman "masculine"? Can we ever be right to do so? How would this be possible? Let us take as an example of this point, the color, blue. Just as in the case of gender, it may seem obvious that the sky is blue and that this is what makes us see the color blue when we look at the sky on a clear day. But blueberries are blue, too, yet they are not the same color as the sky. Cornflowers, sapphires, gas flames, some people's eyes, window cleaner, and robins' eggs are all different colors, yet we call them all blue. Why? What *is* blue, that we should apply its name to all these very different colors?

THE PROBLEM OF DEFINITION OR TRUTH IN GENERAL

We might try defining "blue" as light of a certain wave-frequency. Indeed, this is one of its dictionary definitions: the light which falls between green and violet in the spectrum of frequencies. But the dictionary also defines "blue" as "a blue thing," as well as simply "the color of the sky."[2] But a blue thing—say, a blueberry—isn't a frequency of light at all, and so the two definitions are incompatible with each other. They aren't just two different ways of the saying the same thing—they cannot both be true at the same time. And a definition *ought* to be true *always* about the thing it defines.

If the word "blue," then, doesn't mean anything *but* "the color we call the sky," then "blue" might seem to be *just* a word—i.e., whatever we happen to *call* "blue" *is* blue. The case of gender is analogous. Being intuitive, having XX chromosomes, having a curvy body, being domestic, being able to bear children, etc., are all very different from one another, and yet many people would want to call all of them "feminine." And yet whenever anybody does define one or another of these things as feminine, somebody is likely to disagree. For instance, say we decided that having a curvy body is feminine. Many would object by offering up the example—called a "counterexample" to the definition—of a particular person with square, flat features, who is nonetheless very feminine. Or, to avoid that problem, we might simply define as "feminine" the set of all women and what they do. Some feminists, for instance, claim something like this in order to avoid stereotyping. But in this case there can be no such things as masculine women (or feminine men), and many people might offer up their own "counterexamples" of women with masculine characteristics and men with feminine ones.

Indeed, one objection to this last definition—that what is feminine is whatever women are or do, or similarly with what is masculine—is that it may be difficult in many cases to decide whether a particular person is a woman or a man, just as we get in arguments over whether a particular color is blue or green. For instance, consider the case of someone in the middle of the lengthy preparations for a sex-change operation (taking hormones, etc.). We might describe such a person as a man or a woman, as *between* a man and a woman, as *both* a man and a woman, etc. Or consider the rare case of a person born with both sets of genitals, or with Klinefelter's syndrome, (i.e., a person with XXY chromosomes). In these cases, our decision about what constituted a man or a woman, instead of helping us define masculinity and femininity, would just put us in a vicious circle. Examples like these, similarly to the ones we raised in the case of color, could be interpreted as evidence that gender *is nothing but* a name, that we just happen to categorize some things as women, some as men, some things as feminine, some as masculine, for convenience's sake—that masculinity and femininity are nothing but words.

---

[2] From *The American College Dictionary*. Edited by C. L. Barnhart. (New York: Random House, 1966).

This is one way to close the question. Indeed, many philosophers do believe something like this, and some of them are included in this book. Perhaps, ultimately, you will wind up believing something like this about gender yourself; but keep in mind, as we indicated above, that if anything is blue that we choose to call "blue," then we can never be wrong about the color blue; there would then be no legitimate arguments—no good counterexamples—against a person who claims that, say, the sun is blue. Similarly, if we could call "feminine" anything we like, then the word "femininity" is always rightly applied by anybody who uses it, and we can never argue against someone who, say, claims that Arnold Schwartzenegger is feminine. If we go this route, we might have to abandon, ultimately, any belief that there is really such a thing as gender at all that grounds our application of gender terms.

In this way, our search for a definition of gender ties in with what we believe in general constitutes truth, or in other words, with how we believe language in general gets its meaning in the first place. For instance, some people will claim when asked (even if they've never thought about it before) that masculinity and femininity are things that exist in the world independently of us—perhaps as physical characteristics of animals, or perhaps as concepts—and that therefore our definitions of these words will refer to real things. Not surprisingly, then, people who believe that truth is derived this way are called *realists*. Others will claim that a "true" understanding of the concepts "masculinity" and "femininity" will consist, not as a realist would claim, in a correct reference to the existent things that the words pick out, but instead in any understanding that meets the standards set by our society or our scientific method. Still others might claim that "masculinity" and "femininity" mean whatever it is most efficacious for them to mean in any particular time period or culture. Whether we believe that language gets its meaning from things that exist in the world or from human conventions of speaking and reasoning will shape the way we go about clarifying our thoughts on gender.

GENDER, SEX, AND MEN AND WOMEN

Perhaps we can save the view that gender is nothing but words against the objections we raised above; you might already have thought of some arguments you could use in its defense, and you'll get a chance to use them later on. But for now, let us pursue the possibility that there is something to which gender terms refer by returning to the color analogy. The problem with our first definition of "blue" was that some things we wanted to call blue didn't fit the definition; some blue things are not frequencies of light. Still, it seemed like a pretty good definition, and we might not want to let it go entirely. One way we can save our first definition, while recognizing its inadequacy, is to make a *distinction* between different *senses* of the word "blue."

For instance, we might make a distinction between blue *light*, blue *pigment*, and blue *things*, each of which is called "blue" in a different sense. For instance, we could use our original definition—"light with a wave frequency between that of green and violet"—as the definition of "blue *light*." Even already, we could account for a range of frequencies, and hence for a range of shades we could call "blue."

Then, we could define "blue *pigment*" as "that material in a thing which reflects blue light and absorbs all other colors of light such that, when we look at the thing, it looks blue to us." Blue pigment, then, because of its dependence on reflection and on human perception, yields weaker and less precise uses of the word "blue" than our original definition; we could find people disagreeing about what things had blue pigment, and having to send things off to a lab to establish their blueness. Lastly, we could define "blue *things*" as those things whose pigmentation is all or mostly blue. This is the least precise sense of "blue" so far; we could easily disagree about how much blue pigment was enough to make something blue, and even things with plenty of blue pigment might not look blue when viewed under different light, etc. There might seem to be very little upon which to resolve such disagreements besides who yelled the loudest.

On analogy, we could define *masculine* and *feminine characteristics* as sets of characteristics of people and animals (or maybe even of inanimate objects) which together constitute the most precise and proper meaning of the terms "masculinity" and "femininity," perhaps along the lines of our list of possible feminine characteristics above. It would be very hard to establish this list definitively—in fact, a great number of the arguments included below center on whether or not a particular characteristic really belongs to the gender with which it has been associated. However difficult such a list may be to construct, we could call the items we would include on it "gender characteristics" for now and distinguish them from sex and sexuality.

We can distinguish from these sets of characteristics male and female *chromosomes* (or perhaps we could use male and female *genitalia,* or male and female *hormonal structures* equally well, or perhaps even male and female *socialization* or *upbringing* would do the same work [see the section on "nature vs. culture", below]. Whatever mark we choose, we could make it something which, analogously to pigment, is whatever it is in things or people that makes them masculine or feminine, respectively. We could call this category "sex"—i.e., *male and female*—and it would be a weaker terminology. For instance,we can imagine having a disagreement about which people had female chromosomes or hormonal makeup and which people male chromosomes or hormonal makeup, and having to send off to a lab for a judgment. In addition, because of things like borderline cases—people with XXY chromosomes, or with both sets of genitals, transsexuals, etc.—it may be very difficult to decide just what it is in us that makes us masculine or feminine.

Lastly, we could distinguish from both of the above, male and female *individuals* (men and women, ganders and geese, rams and sheep, etc.) This would be the weakest use of gender terms, as we saw in the cases we described above; it can be very difficult, for instance, to make judgments about whether transsexuals, people with hormonal or genetic abnormalities, or even people with a lot of characteristics or behaviors or skills of both sexes, are men or women. Indeed, it is really this last group of people—people of the male sex who may strike us as "feminine" for some reason, or people of the female sex who seem "masculine"—who present the most common occasions for philosophical inquiry into gender.

So we could make several distinct senses of "gender," different realms in which we may talk about the issue of gender—1) gender characteristics themselves, 2) the male and female sexes, and 3) men and women. It may be useful to keep these senses separate in your mind as you read the selections below, because the discussions often turn subtly upon them. For instance, the gender of a female divinity in a scriptural or ancient work, since she doesn't have a mortal body like human beings, is likely not well interpreted merely as a woman. Her chromosomal makeup or genitalia or upbringing are moot points in our discussion. Similarly, an argument that cites statistics about tendencies among women, or that cites anecdotes about particular real women, cannot tell us much about the nature of femininity in the abstract. We may interpret these data as *guides* to establishing our criteria for what is feminine and what is masculine (and would do so, if we decided, as we indicated above might be possible, that gender was nothing but words we applied to the world). Talk about women by itself, however, can't tell us whether chromosomes or socialization *should* count as the standard female sex-typing, or whether we should consider "feminine" whatever may be the trends among the majority of women. In other words, these distinctions may be important in interpreting certain works. On the other hand, as we discussed above, many thinkers about gender would advocate not making these distinctions at all. One might argue, for instance, that the application of gender terms is in general nothing but a bad habit, and that we should only take up the question of the application of gender terms on a case-by-case basis. Our decisions about how to understand gender terms will be made in the larger context of our beliefs about the basis of truth, the purpose of inquiry, the limits of human knowledge.

Consider, for instance, the androgynous *Saturday Night Live* character, Pat, whose body shape, style of hair and dress, voice, and lifestyle are all sexually ambiguous. Her/his perplexed acquaintances tend to be of the opinion that if they could just find out what genitalia were attached to her/his body, they would then know if Pat is a man or a woman. Would that really close the question, though? Suppose we found out that Pat had male genitals. Would that really make us comfortable in the knowledge of Pat's gender? Even if we knew Pat's genital equipment, the decision whether Pat was a man or woman would depend on whether we considered *sex* an adequate criterion upon which to base a judgment about the *gender* of an individual, and so we would have another vicious circle.

As in the case of color, correct application of the terms "female" and "woman," (or "male" and "man") may only beg the question of what "femininity" or "masculinity" really are. If we knew for sure the set of all the characteristics we would consider feminine (or masculine), then all we'd have to do is make a check-list for particular individuals and add up the preponderance of evidence to decide whether each had female or male sex, whether each was a man or a woman. But even establishing these lists, as we mentioned above, may not be an easy task. It seems, at least on the face of it, that we would depend on things like statistics about women and on the biological capabilities of the female sex in order to establish the list. Is it possible to avoid a vicious circle?

MORE PROBLEMS WITH DEFINITIONS

Though making the distinctions above may turn out to be helpful to us in understanding gender, there are still problems that making such distinctions will not be able to solve. Consider, for instance, in our analogy to color, a person who is blue-green colorblind. Despite this person's inability to distinguish it from green light, blue light does strike the receptors in the eye, and the person is able to see the things that others call blue. In other words, the colorblind person sees the blue light, but does not see it *as blue.* The colorblind person sees the blue light but not its blueness. This shows that the blue light and its blueness are not conceptually the same. This is true, however, even for non-colorblind people. Because it is a shade of light, and subject to the physical environment, no shade in the range of blue light—not even the central shade of the blue spectrum—will look the same to everyone. Under certain conditions, it may not even look blue.

To make the analogy to gender, suppose that an alien lands on Earth. On the alien's home planet, there are one hundred different sex types, able to effect reproduction in a variety of combinations. Our own males and females present an aberration to the alien's sense, and it finds itself "sexblind" on our planet, just as we do on the alien's planet when we go there to visit. Like the colorblind person, the alien sees (and hears and touches, etc.) the same characteristics, instantiated in the same bodies, as we do; the alien just can't perceive them *as* male or female. In other words, the alien would perceive the same characteristics we called "gender characteristics" above, but the alien would not perceive them *as gendered.* How do we want to think about the "sexblind" alien? Is the alien perceiving our world wrongly, or is the gender-language of the alien's planet just as good as ours?

The question of gender then, for a philosopher, is like a question of whether we and the alien can have a meaningful discussion together about gender. For instance, if we could translate the alien's seven characteristics of sex-type number five, plus two of the eight characteristics of sex-type number twenty-two, etc., as "masculine" in our sense of the term, then we would have a very nice beginning on our list of masculine characteristics. Still better, if we could come up with a formula for making the translation—some sort of rules for a "sexual grammar" for the alien and us—we would have a good start on defining masculinity and femininity for ourselves. We still might decide that gender does not exist independently of the 102 types of bodies with which we had now become familiar; but the words would mean something different to us than just those bodies.

We hardly need to imagine life on another planet to recognize this problem: we could very easily designate a hundred different types of human bodies right here on earth, right now. For many purposes, we do so already: doctors and lawyers sometimes categorize people physically by reference to their blood types, coaches and sports recruiters by reference to their heights and weights, physical anthropologists and biologists by reference to the configurations of their skeletons. We could very easily classify each of the sexually ambiguous cases we listed above (transsexuals, androgynes, Klinefelter's syndrome cases, etc.) as a separate sex-type. We can imagine a whole history of making such multitudinous classifications, such that we ourselves did not think in terms of male and female at all. Why isn't this what happened? One way we might solve the problem of gender would be to figure out what it is that makes us tend to put individual bodies into two categories when we think about gender, and to evaluate our habit once we found its cause. If we could explain our concepts of "femininity" and "masculinity" to someone who was "sexblind," then we might better understand our own uses of these terms. If we could not, then maybe we could not establish that gender is a definable "thing" at all.

Femininity and masculinity themselves (whatever we ultimately decide about them) are called by philosophers "universals," and feminine and masculine things—however abstract they may be, such as gentle or aggressive characteristics—are called "particulars." Some philosophers believe that universals really exist, i.e., by themselves independently of particulars, and some philosophers believe that universals are just abstract concepts through which we understand the particular things we find in the world (i.e., that universals, like masculinity and femininity, are just *words*). If we decide that femininity and masculinity are nothing more than the set of characteristics which we agree to call "feminine" and "masculine" respectively, then we can say that the universals, femininity and masculinity, don't exist independently of our particular men's and women's bodies.

ABSOLUTISM VS.RELATIVISM ABOUT GENDER

In *Through the Looking Glass,* the character Humpty Dumpty instructs Alice in his theory of language: "'When *I* use a word,' Humpty Dumpty said, in a rather scornful tone, 'it means just what I choose it to mean—neither more nor less. . . .'" The question, he claims, is "which is to be master, that's all."[3] Where do we get these universal notions through which we understand and analyze our world? Do we construct them from our experience of the world, as tools, or do they make us interpret the world as we do? Deciding which is a question of *absolutism* vs. *relativism.* Humpty Dumpty is a rather radical relativist.

The absolutist believes that there is a single true definition for each of the words that we use, even if he or she doesn't claim to know what that definition is in any particular instance. To the absolutist, then, this single truth is the "master" over our use of language. We can be wrong in our use of terms, and we correct ourselves by finding out the truth of the matter. Thus, for the absolutist, the term "femininity"—whether or not the thing it refers to exists independently of men and women—will *always and everywhere mean the same thing,* and the same will be true for "masculinity." This true meaning is the single correct criterion for our application of the terms. In any disagreement, according to the absolutist, someone must be wrong.

The relativist, on the other hand, believes that there may be many truths, maybe even infinitely many, changing from society to society, or year to year, or even from individual to individual. Thus, according to the relativist, we are the "masters" of language, because we (or our societies) make words mean what we want them to. For the relativist, then, we can never use words wrongly, except relatively to our social or historical or individual norms. For instance, while in our society it would be wrong, in a relative sense, to call blue baby clothes "feminine," it might be perfectly correct to do so in another country or era. The relativist would maintain that,

---

[3] Lewis Carroll, *Through the Looking Glass.* (New York: Random House, 1946), p. 94.

say, "femininity" meant a wholly different thing in sixteenth-century China than in twentieth-century America and would be comfortable to leave it at that.

Pushed to the level of universals, some people—in an effort to find the "absolute truth"—will try to describe "femininity" and "masculinity" by referring to characteristics of the genders (different from our list of abstract particulars, the gender characteristics) that distinguish them from each other. Some might pick out two principles, like action and passion, and interpret all the masculine and feminine particulars (such as the characteristics on our lists, or different individuals) as deriving their character as masculine or feminine, from these principles. Along this line, one might think of femininity as distinct from masculinity in the same way as a morality of caring is distinct from one of justice, as an attitude of slavishness is distinct from one of mastery, as a narcissistic (or self-loving) sexual style is distinct from an anaclitic (or other-loving) sexual style, etc. While few such thinkers would claim to have given a definitive answer to the truth of gender, they are involved nonetheless in a basically absolutist enterprise—they believe that there is a single truth to be found, and that their studies point us in its direction.

Other people faced with a demand to define "femininity" and "masculinity" will handle the question through wholly hypothetical, sociological, or practical means. For instance, many relativists about gender would be satisfied that what is feminine has XX chromosomes, and would be comfortable with undecidable cases like the Klinefelter's syndrome case mentioned above. Some others would claim that what is feminine is what a particular society treats in a certain way, thereby deferring the problem of definition to the level of determining cultural norms. Still others, as we have mentioned, would shun this issue entirely, regarding it as distracting from the practical economic and political concerns of women and men, and would simply make do with these concrete particulars. All of these are quite different sorts of relativist answers to the gender question.

In fact, it is very difficult indeed to define something absolutely, and it is very difficult to conceptualize something very abstract—maybe it is even impossible. This is one reason why some philosophers claim that universals do not exist independently of particulars, and why we tend to rely so heavily on scientific definitions or on concrete imagery in our understanding of gender. Indeed, in our scientific and technological age, we tend also to be relativists. It is very hard to maintain an absolutist stance in the face of so many different norms of language use. Many philosophers insist, nonetheless, that relativism is untenable. In the readings in this collection, you will find arguments for both absolutist and relativist views of gender.

BINARY OPPOSITIONS

The attempt to describe masculinity and femininity by picking out distinct masculine and feminine principles or traits is very common among thinkers about gender (and, actually, among thinkers about a lot of other things). A popular school of philosophy and literary criticism today, called "deconstruction," associated with some contemporary feminism, has called this way of defining gender universals "binary thinking." Deconstructionists, following the French philosopher, Jacques Derrida, have criticized Western philosophy as founded in binary oppositions, such as the one between masculinity and femininity. Passages from the work of some thinkers in this school appear in Part Six.

To understand masculinity and femininity according to the opposition of action and passion, or master and slave, or according to any binary opposition, may limit the wealth of interpretations of our world of which we are intellectually capable and delegate real men and women to behave or to be understood in certain ways. In addition, it may be impossible to apply binary oppositions fairly: one of the opposites is likely always to be valued more highly than the other. Thus, deconstructionists for instance, might claim that the understanding of gender in terms of binary oppositions contributes to sex discrimination. Attention to binary oppositions may be useful in forming a definition of gender because, if masculinity and femininity are indeed definable in themselves, chances are they will be opposed to each other. The pay-off of "binary thinking" may be that we can come close to defining things like masculinity and femininity. The cost may be that in defining them through opposing principles, we may evaluate one or the other unfairly.

There is no question that the ancient Greek thinkers, particularly before Socrates, did indeed interpret the natural world in terms of binary oppositions, as we will see, and there is little disagreement that ancient Greece is the intellectual foundation of Western culture. The history of philosophical thought, however, sometimes seems like a game of telephone, in which a long series of interpreters garble an original message—the details of our ancestors' intentions may remain obscure to us, even while they form the foundation of our own thought. Thus, it will be useful to us to take from deconstructionists and other contemporary critics the notions that masculinity and femininity may only be definable through a set of binary oppositions, and that an evaluation of gender accompanies these oppositions. But it is important that we go back to the original texts and read them with complete freedom, in order to interpret them as we believe is right.

As an ongoing exercise, it might be useful to begin a table of those characteristics or principles that you associate with masculinity and femininity—your own list of binary oppositions, if you will. Perhaps you can keep it in the front of the notebook in which you make your reading notes on this book. Is masculinity an active principle? Is femininity passive? Do you recognize any traits of the opposite gender in your own behavior or physique? How is that possible? In the last column of the table, note down your reflections on why you think that such-and-so opposition represents the opposition between masculinity and femininity. Did you get this impression from your parents' behavior? From T.V.? From something you've read? From your boyfriends and girlfriends? Then, as you go along in your reading, turn back to your list from time to time and update it according to your reflections on the passages. In the case of changes, note down which authors inspired you to change your mind.

MIND AND BODY, THOUGHT AND MATTER

One binary opposition of ongoing interest to philosophers (one finds it again and again, from before Socrates to the present day) is the distinction between *mind and body* or *thought and matter.* When we investigate the world, we are struck immediately by two seemingly very different things: we find ourselves thinking— i.e., we perceive "thought-stuff"—and we also find ourselves moving, taking up space, having weight, etc.—i.e., we perceive "matter-stuff." These experiences seem on the face of it to be quite distinct from each other, and even opposed. (Some philosophers—called *dualists*—have claimed, because of this, that the universe is actually composed of these two, fundamentally different, kinds of things.) Descartes, whose work is excerpted in Part Four, was a dualist of this sort.

Some recent thinkers, including some feminist deconstructionists, have claimed that philosophers in the Western tradition tend to associate the opposition between mind and body with the opposition between masculinity and femininity, where mind is masculine and body is feminine. Some of these thinkers believe that this association is pernicious and that femininity is as much to be associated with thinking as is masculinity. Some of these philosophers would claim, on the other hand, that the association is right and good and that the feminine association with the body is a political and moral asset for women, i.e., that Western culture tends to value the intellect far too much, anyway.

Questions about the nature and content of thought—i.e., questions about what constitutes knowledge and how knowledge is distinguished from things like fiction, belief, and myth—are called by philosophers *epistemology.* Thus, questions about the gender-content of certain types and ways of thinking might be called an "epistemology of gender." Some recent feminist philosophers of science have argued that modern scientific method—which is considered by most scientists and many philosophers to be the only legitimate foundation of knowledge—is masculine. Thus, abstract thoughts with clean truth content, like mathematical thinking, might be thought to be masculine, too. It may be possible that different sorts of thoughts line up in a binary opposition with gender content, parallel to that between mind and body: perhaps all concrete, more "material" images are feminine in character.

Perhaps we may decide—one way or another—that thinking about men's and women's bodies, or the bodies of animals or plants, has some kind of gender content, but that thinking about very abstract principles like Justice or Number or God does not. Perhaps there are *some* mental and psychological gender differences, therefore, yet perhaps not all mental or psychological differences have gender content. Thus, we may decide that men and women think differently without resorting to an absolute binary distinction, either between men and women or between mind and body, thus allowing for a distinction while avoiding dualism; as in our example of the alien, above.

Are there any psychological differences between men and women at all, or are our bodies the only gender differences we have? Many thinkers in the modern liberal tradition would claim that a person's sex is wholly irrelevant to his or her psychological makeup or intellect (indeed, even Plato, the ancient Greek philosopher, would be included among those who make such a claim). On the other hand, the entire careers of many psychologists have been spent in the investigation of psychological sex differences, including differences in the intellectual styles and capacities of the sexes. The thinkers whose works appear in this book will argue many sides of this question. In reading them, we shouldn't be limited in our understanding of gender by its seeming intimacy or physicality, nor should we necessarily be limited in our understanding of the nature of the world, or of ultimate truths, by our embodiment as individuals of one or another sex.

NATURE VS. NURTURE

Even if we did decide, after reflection, that gender differences did really exist, there would remain the question of why and how this is the case. Gender may be a "given" of the natural world. On the other hand, maybe gender is a social or cultural phenomenon, something we are "nurtured" into; a quality that we bestow upon ourselves and the world through cultural norms or habits. Obviously, we could question the origin of any concepts to establish whether they are given in the world or invented by us. We could return to our old analogy of color and ask whether blue is given in nature or a construct of human perception. But this concern is of particular importance with regard to concepts like gender because such concepts inform our treatment of one another, our political systems, our family structure, and other human activities. Philosophers call the study of how we should act (especially towards one another) and why *ethics,* and the question of whether gender originates in *nature* or in *culture* is an important one for ethical questions about gender.

Because of their ethical objection to the traditional treatment of women, many feminists have argued against the claim that gender is natural. They have claimed, instead, that it is cultural, something we have invented and can therefore reinvent. Obviously, it doesn't follow from the claim that gender is natural, by itself without any other premises, that there is anything at all natural or unchangeable in the suppression of women. There is nothing in the pure claim that femininity and masculinity are natural to imply that they are unequal, nor is there anything to imply that human institutions should imitate that nature. But ethical arguments for equality of the sexes may find strength in disassociating gender from nature. Like mind and body, nature and culture together form a binary opposition of interest to contemporary thinkers, including feminists. Some, for instance, might argue that if culture is masculine, and gender is culturally based (i.e., it is not natural) then it might follow that gender itself is a masculine invention. If that were true, then the (in this case, false) *claim* that gender is natural, and the universally unfair treatment of women which such a claim might be used to bolster, may all just be a masculine myth.

SOCIALIZATION AND GENDER ROLE

Whether we decide that the foundation of gender is natural or cultural—or some combination of the two, there can be no denying that one component of gender difference, at least, is cultural—one's gender role in his or her household, community, or nation. Even if one believes that one's social role is an outgrowth of one's nature—as many thinkers in this book will claim—the role itself is a cultural phenomenon. One's role is one's social position with regard to other people. It is the result of legal or social traditions. Thus, whether or not we decide that gender differences are natural, we still have to face the questions of whether the socialization or education that a community provides to its members about these gender differences is right or true, whether the roles into which it puts men and women are fair and good, and for whom—the individual or the society as a whole, or both.

For some philosophers—for instance, some of those who claim that gender differences are all culturally based—socialization and role are the dominant concerns in the study of gender. Many thinkers would claim that while some social distinctions of role are necessary to the functioning of a community, these roles need not be defined along gender lines. Further, some claim that attaching role to gender has had damaging effects—limiting individual freedoms and inhibiting the progress of society in which individual initiatives would result. Margaret Mead, for instance, whose work is represented in Part Five, argued that gender roles varied greatly from culture to culture, and that much of the necessary social organization achieved through roles could be achieved without attaching these roles to gender.

Other thinkers—for instance, some deconstructionists and other twentieth-century thinkers mentioned above—might claim that all social roles are repressive and debilitating to society as well as to individuals, and that gender roles are merely one pernicious example. Some thinkers might argue that everyone is capable of playing an enormous—perhaps infinite—variety of roles, and that both individuals and society would be better off if everyone were free to do so all the time. For instance, Nietzsche, Sartre, and Foucault, passages of whose work appear in Parts Four, Five and Six, are sometimes interpreted as claiming something like this, as is—less often—Freud's notion that everyone is naturally bisexual.

Even if one believed that sex differences were natural, one might still want society to overcome this natural difference through socialization or role; or, on the other hand, one might want society to exaggerate or bolster the difference. For instance, if one believed that women were naturally physically weaker than men, one might want to argue that women should be educated like men anyway, to exhibit physical strength. Plato (whose work is excerpted in Part Two) and Mary Wollstonecraft (see Part Three) both argue something like this, advocating equal education for women and men despite admitting natural differences between them. Based on a similar assumption that women are naturally physically weaker than men, however, Jean-Jacques Rousseau (some of whose work appears in Part Three) argues the contrary point. He claims that women's socialization and role should further refine their natural differences from men, exaggerating what he considers their beautiful frailty.

Suppose, for instance, that we, as political consultants, visited the home planet of the alien we met above. How would we divide labor in the alien's society? To whom would we assign childrearing? To whom would we assign bricklaying? If there were really one hundred different genders in the alien's world, each one defined by a different set of characteristics, then we might be able to design an extremely efficient society there, picking for each social task only those who were distinctly suited to it. On the other hand, the assignment of social roles in such a society might be so complicated that it would be counterproductive, with thousands and thousands of different sets of courtesies and different social units for each possible combination of genders. Perhaps it would be impossible to organize such a society at all. Perhaps out of a sense of practicality and fairness, we would simply advise anarchy; or perhaps we would have to devise an arbitrary categorization of aliens into four or five groups in the interests of a functional society.

No matter what their opinion about the natural or cultural basis of gender roles, or about the rightness or wrongness of men's and women's socialization into them, most modern and contemporary thinkers agree that women's traditional roles in Western civilizations have been socially and politically subordinate to men's. Some have claimed that women's subordination is proper and fair, some that it is unjust and vicious. Some have claimed that women make up for their social inequality through their dominance in the household and family, some that women are subordinated at home as well. Whatever your conclusions on this issue, it is well to add this new category—social role—to our distinctions above. Many of the works that appear in this book will focus on this issue, and their arguments will turn on the distinction between an individual and his or her role.

GENDER AND HISTORY

Why is this an historical anthology? Precisely because of the ironic situations we have been describing. There are dozens or even hundreds of different "philosophies" of gender, yet on some level we are able to discuss and compare them all to one another. There is little that could explain the simultaneous difference and similarity of philosophers' views on gender, other than the plain existence of historical records. Time keeps moving and changing, and yet its little traces tie us all together, enabling college students in the twentieth century C.E. to connect themselves somehow with blind storytellers in the eighth century B.C.E. Yet at the same time historical records cause misunderstandings between readers and writers in different ages. The irony, then, is this: fundamental texts in Western intellectual history disagree with contemporary notions formed under their very influence. History makes it possible both to know and to misunderstand the very basis of our own ways of thinking, to be unclear in our understanding of our own conscious thoughts.

In this, too, we can make an analogy to color. It seems likely, on the face of it, that the sky was roughly the same color three thousand years ago that it is today. Certainly, our words for colors and our ways of thinking and talking about color, even our science of color, are derived in large part from the ancient Greeks. Yet do we know where the average Greek cut off what we would call the "blue" range of the spectrum from what we would call the "green" range? How? Was the sky even the same color then that it is now? Haven't atmospheric conditions changed drastically since then? Suppose the sky was brighter and the water warmer in ancient Greece; mightn't it be possible, then, that they would have tended to think of the color of the sky as electrifying, warm, or passionate, and not cool and placid as we tend to? Indeed, can we even usefully translate color terms from ancient Greek into contemporary English? The point is that, even in the case of something as plain and obvious as color, we can be surprised by what our ancestors thought in its regard, and we can be enlightened in our notions of color by bringing our own mysterious history of color into our present awareness. It seems likely as well that our understanding of our contemporary notion of blue might be enlarged and revised in the light of historical research; after studying the ancient Greeks' notion of blue, we might decide to change our own.

The case of gender is analogous again, but the "historicity" of our notions of gender is even more surprising, rich, and enlightening than that of our notions of color, because our emotions, our relationships, our physical appearance, our political organization, and other exceptionally changeable aspects of human life are tied up with it. For instance, we tend to believe today that the call for the complete equality of the sexes is very "radical," very "progressive," in comparison to the notions of our ancestors. But Plato, as we will see, advocated sexual equality—on the face of it, in far broader terms than it is normally put today—almost 2400 years ago. Views similar to Plato's, at least in this regard, have been offered by many thinkers since his time. By studying Plato, we get a clearer picture of our own philosophical view. Whether we ultimately agree or disagree with him, we get a better understanding of ourselves.

Thus, the goal of this historical anthology is to find the "family roots" of today's notions about gender, perhaps even of today's politics of gender, in order to reflect upon and enrich the vision of gender that we presuppose when we make political speeches or moral judgments. Just as Alex Haley's discovery of his African ancestors clarified his thoughts about contemporary American race relations, just as finding an old picture of your great-grandmother might inspire you to wear your hair a different way or to reinterpret your grandfather's old stories, discovering the history of Western thoughts about gender can be an oddly familiar surprise that helps you to think more clearly about yourself and your society.

Parts One and Two (especially the former), include readings from ancient and foundational texts in the Western, Judeo-Christian, tradition. They provide an opportunity to "clean out the noise" in that game of "telephone" that has founded our notions of gender, to go back to the original sources from which our current worldviews are derived and of which we are often, and perhaps often rightly, critical. Parts Three and Four offer readings from the tradition in which contemporary American academics and politics place themselves—what we might call " the modern liberal tradition" or "the enlightenment and post-enlightenment tradition." These thinkers have given us the notions of equality, work, family, nationhood, and a host of other notions that inform contemporary discussions of the gender issue. Parts Five and Six offer readings from the twentieth century, which are immediate influences on today's studies in politics, psychology, and literature. The goal of the collection is that you can revise your notions of our own tradition and give credit and censure where they are properly due, as well as to reflect upon our current assumptions about gender in light of some very thoughtful works from our tradition.

GENDER AS A CONTEMPORARY ISSUE

In this regard, it is well worth thinking about why gender has become the popular political concern it is today. Why are there classes in feminism or in gender studies today, and not one hundred or two hundred years ago, especially when, as we mentioned, there were advocates then of what we would now call "feminism"? One common answer is that public discussion of an issue does some sort of moral or political good, and that our era has learned from the mistakes of its predecessors not to "cover things up"; i.e., that bringing issues out into the open is part of what we call "progress." One bias that the good philosopher must put aside, however, is her or his bias in favor of her or his own time period, in favor of the sheer movement of time. Why should we think that talking about gender in a class or as a campaign issue or on a TV talk show has any moral or political effect at all? Why think that these discussions are anything more than our particular social habits, just the fashionable coffee-break topic of one or two generations? If we are to gain a really clear understanding of gender, one thing worth reflecting upon is our ulterior motive, the reason why we are interested in gender at all, and historical readings may provide some insight into this as well.

The contemporary historian Michel Foucault (he died in 1984) was influenced by the deconstructionists of whom we spoke above. In his last work, *The History of Sexuality,* some passages of which appear in Part Six, he proposed a thesis about the contemporary discussion of sex that may be applicable to that of gender. He stated in Volume I:

> *[T]he[re] exist[s] in our era a discourse in which sex, the revelation of truth, the overturning of global laws, the proclamation of a new day to come, and the promise of a certain felicity are linked together. Today it is sex that serves as a support for . . . preaching. A great sexual sermon has swept through our societies over the last decades; it has chastised the old order, denounced hypocrisy, and praised the rights of the immediate and real; it has made people dream of a New City.[4]*

Foucault's remarks should warn us that talking about gender, like talking about sex, may itself serve a certain political or psychological or religious purpose for us, satisfy a certain ulterior or unconscious or spiritual desire. After all, talking or writing about private things gives us a certain illicit kick, and we can increase the intensity of that pleasure, not only by talking more about gender, but also by making our talk seem more illicit, more secret, more politically explosive than it might seem otherwise. Similarly, something as intimately tied to our bodies, our physical weaknesses, our mortality, as gender is may make us uncomfortable, and we may ease that anxiety through idle chatter. Thus, it may be the case, just as Foucault claims is the case with sex, that our belief that political progress has been and is achieved through an intellectual or academic study of gender and its political and social consequences may just be the result of our contemporary love of spectacle, of voyeurism into the intimate details of people's lives—in other words, it may be the case that our academic interest in gender is not very different from our personal interest in talk shows.

---

[4] Michel Foucault, *The History of Sexuality, Volume I: An Introduction.* Translated by Robert Hurley. (New York: Vintage, 1978 [1980]) pp. 7–8.

Gender is a "hot" topic these days, and there is a lot of pressure from all sides to take a position with regard to it. In addition, sexuality can be an embarrassing issue; in a classroom surrounded by people who you may or may not know well, or to some of whom you may be attracted, or who may be attracted to you, it can be uncomfortable expressing and developing your opinions about such a personal topic. This book is intended to help you think independently and responsibly about the subject of gender, for just these reasons. Ultimately, even though there is a lot to learn from a class on the subject, gender is not just "academic." Our opinions about it influence the way we interact with others, and the way we comport ourselves, over the whole course of our lives.

Hence, one thing that an historical consideration of gender may contribute to our thinking about gender is simply to clear away the spectacle which the issue of gender has acquired for us; to cool the temperature of our arguments about gender issues and to help us reflect more calmly and practically about the whole thing. Thus, an historical approach to the study of gender can help us confront the social pressures which bear upon our thinking about it with both serenity and maturity. It is well worth remembering that no matter how far back we go in history, there has always been sex, and as long as there has been sex, there has been more or less distinction and confusion between the genders. There is little to fear from thinking the whole thing through one more time.

SUGGESTED READINGS—
INTRODUCTION

Abel, Elizabeth, and Emily K. Abel (eds.). *The Signs Reader: Women, Gender, and Scholarship.* Chicago: University of Chicago Press, 1983.

Ashton-Jones, Evelyn, and Gary A. Olson (eds.). *The Gender Reader.* New York: Simon and Schuster, 1991.

Baier, Annette. *Moral Prejudices.* Cambridge: Harvard University Press, 1993.

Bartky, Sandra Lee. *Femininity and Domination.* New York: Routledge, 1990.

Bock, Gisela (ed.). *Beyond Equality and Difference.* New York: Routledge, 1992.

Bordo, Susan. "Feminist Scepticism and the 'Maleness' of Philosophy." *Journal of Philosophy* 85: pp. 619–29, 1988.

Butler, Judith. *Gender Trouble: Feminism and the Subversion of Identity.* New York: Routledge, 1989.

Card, Claudia (ed.). *Feminist Ethics.* Lawrence: University Press of Kansas, 1991.

Clark, L. M. G., and Lynda Lange (eds.). *The Sexism of Social and Political Theory: Women and Reproduction from Plato to Nietzsche.* Toronto: University of Toronto Press, 1979.

Caltterbaugh, Kenneth. *Contemporary Perspectives on Masculinity: Men, Women, and Politics in Modern Society.* Boulder: Westview, 1990.

Cole, Eve B., and Susan Coultrap-McQuin (eds.). *Explorations in Feminist Ethics.* Bloomington: Indiana Unitersity Press, 1992.

Coole, Diana. *Women and Political Theory.* Boulder: Lynne Reiner Publishers, 1993.

Dinnerstein, Dorothy. *The Mermaid and the Minotaur.* New York: Harper and Row, 1977.

Elshtain, Jean Bethke (ed.). *The Family in Political Thought.* Amherst: University of Massachusetts Press, 1981.

Flax, Jane. *Thinking Fragments: Psychoanalysis, Feminism, and Postmodernism in the Contemporary West.* Berkeley: University of California Press, 1990.

Fraser, Nancy. *Unruly Practices: Gender, Discourse and Power in Social Theory.* Minneapolis: University of Minnesota Press, 1989.

Fuss, Diana. *Essentially Speaking: Feminism, Nature, and Difference.* New York: Routledge, 1990.

Gatens, Moira. *Feminism and Philosophy.* Bloomington: University of Indiana Press, 1991.

Grimshaw, Jean. *Philosophy and Feminist Thinking.* Minneapolis: University of Minnesota Press, 1986.

Hirsch, Marianne, and Evelyn Fox Keller (eds.). *Conflicts in Feminism.* New York: Routledge, 1990.

Gallop, Jane. *The Daughter's Seduction: Feminism and Psychoanalysis.* Ithaca: Cornell University Press, 1982.

Genova, Judith. (ed.). *Power, Gender, Values.* Alberta: Academic Press, 1987.

Griffiths, Morwenna, and Margaret Whitford (eds.). *Feminist Perspectives in Philosophy.* Bloomington: Indiana University Press, 1988.

Grosz, Elizabeth. *Volatile Bodies: Toward a Corporeal Feminism.* Bloomington: Indiana University Press, 1994.

Harding, Sandra, and Merrill B. Hintikka (eds.). *Discovering Reality: Feminist Perspectives on Epistemology, Metaphysics, Methodology, and Philosophy of Science.* Dordrecht: D. Reidel Publising Company, 1983.

Holstrom, Nancy. "Do Women Have a Distinct Nature?" *Philosophical Forum* 14: 25–42, 1982.

Jaggar, Alison M. *Feminist Politics and Human Nature.* Totowa, NJ: Rowman and Allanheld, 1983.

———— (ed.). *Living With Contradictions: Controversies in Feminist Social Ethics.* Boulder: Westview Press, 1994.

Jagger, Alison, and Susan Bordo (eds.). *Gender/Body/Knowledge: Feminist Reconstruction of Being and Knowing.* New Brunswick: Rutgers University Press, 1989.

Kennedy, Ellen, and Susan Mendus (eds.). *Women in Western Political Philosophy.* New York: St. Martin's Press, 1987.

Kournany, J. A., J. P. Sterba, and R. Tong (eds.). *Feminist Philosophies: Problems, Theories and Applications.* Englewood Cliffs: Prentice Hall.

May, Larry, and Robert A. Strickwerda, eds. *Rethinking Masculinity: Philosophical Explorations in Light of Feminism.* Totowa, NJ: Rowman and Littlefield, 1992.

Mitchell, Juliet and Ann Oakley. *The Rights and Wrongs of Women.* Harmandsworth: Penguin Press, 1976.

Mooney, Edward F. "Gender, Philosophy and the Novel." *Metaphilosophy* 18: 241–252, 1987.

Nelson, Julie A. "Thinking About Gender." *Hypatia* 7(3): 138–154, 1992.

Nicholson, Linda J. *Gender and History: The Limits of Social Theory in the Age of the Family.* New York: Columbia University Press, 1986.

Nussbaum, Martha, and Amartya Sen (eds.) *The Quality of Life.* Oxford: Oxford University Press, 1993.

Okin, Susan Moller. *Justice, Gender and the Family.* New York: Basic Books, 1989.

————. *Women in Western Political Thought.* Princeton: Princeton University Press, 1979.

Paglia, Camille. *Sexual Personae.* New Haven: Yale University Press, 1990.

Pollitt, Katha. *Reasonable Creatures: Essays on Women and Feminism.* New York: Knopf, 1994.

Pomeroy, Sarah B. *Goddesses, Whores, Wives, and Slaves.* New York: Schocken, 1975.

Reinisch, J. M., L. A. Rosenbloom, and S. A. Sanders (eds.). *Masculinity–Femininity: Basic Perspectives.* Oxford: Oxford University Press, 1987.

Rhode, Deborah L. (ed.). Theoretical Perspectives on Sexual Difference. New Haven: Yale University Press, 1992.

Sayers, Janet. Biological Politics. London: Tavistock, 1982.

Scheman, Naomi. "The Unavoidability of Gender." *Journal of Social Philosophy,* 21: 34–39, 1990.

Scott, Joan Wallace. *Gender and the Politics of History.* New York: Columbia University Press, 1988.

Silverman, Kaja. *Male Subjectivity at the Margins.* New York: Routledge, 1992.

Tong, Rosemarie. *Feminist Thought: A Comprehensive Introduction.* Boulder: Westview Press, 1989.

Tuana, Nancy. *The Less Noble Sex: Scientific, Religious, and Philosophical Conceptions of Woman's Nature.* Bloomington: Indiana University Press, 1993.

———. *Feminine and Feminist Ethics.* Belmont: Wadsworth, 1993.

Vetterling-Braggin, Mary (ed.). *'Femininity', 'Masculinity', and 'Androgyny': A Modern Philosophical Discussion.* Totowa, NJ: Littlefield and Adams, 1982.

Warren, Mary Anne (ed.). *The Nature of Woman: An Encyclopedia and Guide to the Literature.* Port Reyes: Edgepress, 1980.

PART 1

MYTHS AND ARCHETYPES:
BINARY OPPOSITIONS IN THE ORIGINAL

*Hesiod, Homer, Sappho, the Pythagoreans,
Parmenides, the Old Testament books of Genesis and
Ruth, and some laws regarding women and marriage*

INTRODUCTION

WHY MYTHS AND ARCHETYPES?

In his third great "critique," *The Critique of Judgement,* the eighteenth-century philosopher Immanuel Kant claimed that artistic genius can be recognized by its legacy of "inimitable examples." "For this reason," he wrote, "the models of fine art are the only means of handing down this art to posterity."[1] Kant's point here is that great works of art—works of true genius—cannot be copied, but must be continually reinvoked by other artists and audiences ever after. Such works of art inform the imagination of the cultures to which they contribute; they help shape the thinking of individuals within those cultures for generation after generation.

Kant claims that because of their influence over our imaginations, such works of art are informative about nature and God and humanity in a different way from math and science. They provide us with what he calls "aesthetic ideas"—ways to see, ideas through which to experience, our world. For instance, Michelangelo's representation of God's hand almost touching the hand of Adam (painted on the ceiling of the Sistine chapel) encapsulates in its way the vision of the relationship between God and Nature which afterwards informed the scientific revolution. It also serves, even today, as an icon for that relationship and as an inspiration to other artists to create their own variations on its theme.

---

[1] Immanuel Kant, *The Critique of Judgement.* Translated by James Creed Meredith. (Oxford: Oxford University Press, 1988 (1957)), p. 171.

Perhaps the most influential and profound of such works of genius are the literatures that we now call, "scripture" and "myth." Indeed, even Michelangelo, in creating his own masterpiece, relied upon the images provided in the Old Testament and upon ideals of the human form taken from ancient Greek statues. As Kant put it, ". . . only those models can become classical of which the ancient . . . languages . . . are the medium. . . . In this way, Jupiter's eagle, with the lightning in its claws, is an attribute of the mighty king of heaven, and the peacock of its stately queen." [2]

In the same way that Jupiter's eagle tells us something about how we think of divinity and power in general, the attributes that the authors of mythical and scriptural works give to their male and female characters can tell us something about how we think of gender in general. Without saying anything one way or another about the truth of the events or entities described in these works, we can nonetheless explore our own cultural imagination, explore our own traditions and presuppositions about gender, through a careful reading of them. For instance, though you may not believe that a snake really talked the woman into disobeying God and eating the fruit of the tree of the knowledge of good and evil (Genesis 3), this story does exemplify certain traditional notions about women being lured into sinfulness by crafty people, about women being easily deceived. It tells us something about our own beliefs about human nature and about gender.

We can call the male and female characters and their masculine and feminine characteristics, as they are represented in such culturally definitive works of art, *paradigms* or *archetypes* of gender—something like Kant's "aesthetic ideas." Indeed, as paradigms, they tell us mostly only about gender itself, the universal, and about what we might put on our lists of masculine and feminine characteristics. They cannot tell us much about real men and women or about the scientific criteria for sex typing. For example, the biblical description of God (the father) creating the universe (Genesis 1) tells us something about the connotations associated with our notion of masculinity—that we think of it as powerful, perhaps, or creative—but it tells us nothing about the power or creativity of men in general, or of any particular man. To study these more concrete, particular questions, we would have to look at a different sort of literature—sociology, history, biology, psychology, etc. Some of these less abstract concerns will be addressed in later sections.

A careful reading of the passages in this section, however—in which these paradigms appear—can reveal the sometimes surprising underpinnings of our own notions of gender, just as knowing the etymology of a word that you use every day can add a surprising element to a familiar thought. For example, knowing that the ancient Greek word, *sophia*—meaning "wisdom"—is the root of our English word "sophisticated" may add a new twist to your use of the English word—it may not seem as derogatory, or it may be more clearly distinguished from words like "blase" or "fancy." Similarly, knowing the source, the good and the bad effects, and the nature of Achilles' "rage" in Homer's *Iliad* may enlighten our own commonplace that "aggression is masculine"—perhaps coloring its potential violence with

---

[2] Ibid. pp. 171, 177.

the possibility of victory and heroism, or with protectiveness and loyalty, or distinguishing the term "aggressive" more clearly from words like "overbearing" or "violent" or "unjust."

In addition to the light these works may shed on our contemporary notions of culture, they enlighten our reading of later texts, just as Kant claimed. For instance, a familiarity with the Adam and Eve of the Bible is important to a good understanding of the Adam and Eve of Milton's *Paradise Lost,* excerpted in Part Four. Milton "reinterprets" the masculinity and femininity of these characters, and much of his rethinking is lost without the comparison. Thus, these works are crucial to both the philosophical enterprise of searching for the correct definition and attribution of gender terms, and to the literary-critical enterprise of judging the art of later ages.

Thus, in this section, we will devote our attention to passages on gender from the mythical and scriptural works that inform what we call "Western Civilization." The hope is that from these can be gleaned the paradigms of masculinity and femininity that inform both our own intuitions and our reading of the characterizations of gender in Western literature through the ages.

THE EARLY ANCIENT GREEK WORLDVIEW

We may divide Greek civilization before Socrates into three eras. There is that time which precedes Homer and Hesiod, to which these two authors refer—i.e., Greek civilization prior to the eighth century B.C.E.—we may call this "preHomeric" Greece. Then there would be the time during which Homer and Hesiod wrote—the eighth and early seventh centuries B.C.E. We will call this "archaic." Then, in the sixth and fifth centuries B.C.E., we find a number of writers (we will read only two) engaging in philosophical and scientific investigations, which we will call the "pre-Socratic" Greeks. In any case, we can say that the early ancient Greeks in all three eras understood the question of gender in a different way from how we might today.

PreHomeric Greek society was not politically unified as a nation. Rather, Greece consisted of a loose collection of cities, called "city-states," each with its own type of government and its own customs. The city-states were united with one another by their shared race and religion—although there were various liturgies in the different cities, they still shared a history and a belief in roughly the same pantheon of gods. Many cities were monarchies, hence the notion of the city-state tended to be associated with that of the (dynastic) family and of the king as a representative human individual. Nature, fate, time, and other forces beyond human control are explored in these early Greek works, as oppositions to all that is human. Their effect upon human beings and upon their families and cities, as reflections of our human nature, is ultimately the subject of study of the "archaic" Greeks.

The early Greek economy was based in agriculture; yet early Greek social mores comprised what we today call an "honor culture." The skills of a good warrior—including loyalty to one's home city-state and household—were considered uppermost among moral virtues; yet these ideals lived alongside the more homely virtues of the farmer. In the Greek's personal life, the household was the unifying theme and the ultimate value, just as the dynastic house was in the Greek city-state. The conflict and the unity between the farmer and the warrior are described by both Hesiod and Homer, each in his way. As we will see in the next chapter, the early Greek social and political systems were submitted to criticism by Socrates and the later Greek philosophers in the fifth through the third centuries B.C.E.; however, these would not have been as significant had not the earlier Greek honor-culture been so entrenched.

As you can imagine, life in the Greece described by Homer and Hesiod was often unstable and violent: there were frequent squabbles, and even wars, among the city-states themselves; governments sometimes seemed peevish; and all this in an economy dependent upon the seasons for safety and sustenance and relatively helpless in the face of the weather. Thus, the religion, the art, and the science of early Greece struggled to understand, accommodate, arrange, or defeat the host of mysterious and violent natural and divine forces that seemed to have power over the human will. For the early Greeks, gender was understood as part and parcel of these mysteries of nature.

The early Greek gods were *anthropomorphic* (i.e., "like humans"), with the primary distinction of being immortal; thus, the gods were thought to give human-yet-super-human qualities to the human and natural world. All the strengths of human nature—reason, inventiveness, fighting skill, loyalty, faith, etc.—were magnified in the gods and reflected in the overwhelming strength of the natural world to which the gods gave their rule and will. Similarly, however, the gods invested nature with magnified human weaknesses—emotions like jealousy, hate, rage, passion, etc. Believing themselves to be both similar and subject to beings like—yet greater than—themselves, the early Greeks sought, at least in part, to understand the natural world by understanding themselves.

Thus, the gender paradigms of the Homeric and Hesiodic gods and mythical creatures reveal, for each author in his different way, the Greek ideas of the origin, character, and effect of gender as a natural force upon human life, from within and especially from without. This essentially philosophical understanding of gender would allow one to take one's proper place in the city-state or household, just as a good warrior would perform to perfection the duties and skills proper to his or her rank. The information to be gleaned from these texts regarding the issue of gender, then, will be very abstract—the origin, character, and effect of femininity and masculinity as natural and divine—i.e., super-human—forces. Nonetheless, the vision of gender provided by these texts will have an ultimately practical, ethical implication: that we behave virtuously and achieve a good human life—by Greek standards—through an understanding of the abstract forces that play upon us.

THE OLD TESTAMENT WORLDVIEW

There are both similarities and differences between the social structures and moral outlooks of the archaic Greeks and the authors of the Old Testament. The writing of the Old Testament spans a much longer period of time—from the twelfth to the second centuries B.C.E.—than does that of the Greek texts included here. Thus, despite great differences among the Greek authors, the Old Testament texts provide a still less coherent medium for our investigation than do they.

It is important to note that scholars have discerned three separate and very different authors in the early books of the Bible, two of whom are named for their different appellations for God. The *Jawist* (or "J") author is the oldest, followed by the "E" (for *Elohist*) author. Likely much later, the "P" or *Priestly* authors edited, collected, and added material to the Old Testament. Each of these three different sets of authors brought a different perspective to the texts, sometimes even differing over their answers to doctrinal questions, and in general giving different characterizations of God. The *Jawist* and *Elohist* authors tend to paint God as *immanent* (i.e., as a participant here with us, in human affairs of this world, and hence, as rather anthropomorphic). The *Priestly* version presents a *transcendent* God (i.e., a God who is separate and categorically different from human beings and their concerns). Thus, there are inconsistencies, even contradictions, to be found in the text, sometimes even within the same book of the Old Testament. Though all the selections are in a sense from the same text, we will be looking at different authors here every bit as much as we will with the Greeks.

The chief unifying feature of the Old Testament texts—as well as their chief distinguishing feature from those of the Greeks—is the singular and all-powerful God they depict and describe. On this account, we call the Old Testament religion *monotheist,* vs. the *polytheism* of the Greeks. As we have mentioned, God is not unambiguously drawn in the Old Testament—sometimes this God has an ambiguous gender; sometimes God is a gentle, sometimes a cruel God; sometimes God is immanent, sometimes transcendent, etc. Thus, the texts themselves yield a myriad of interpretations; still the singularity of this God gives the biblical metaphysics and moral vision their primary distinction from the Greeks.

Like the early Greeks, the early tribes were not politically organized into a single nation. Although their civilization did contain great cities, they did not gather themselves into the political units of city-states, but rather into rural, sometimes nomadic, agricultural communities comprised of—not just ruled by—the descendants of particular families. Hence, the natural, or super-human, world is not the primary "other" to the protagonists of the Old Testament stories, as it is in the early Greek texts. The Old Testament does not depict the human world as a stationary and ordered place within the unpredictable super-human world, as did the Greeks. Rather, in the Old Testament, the human world itself is seen as internally divided and mobile, with only God "outside" it, overseeing, judging, and controlling both human and natural affairs as if they were of a piece, and subject to God. Since the singular God of the Bible creates and has authority over both nature and the human struggle against it, we see in the Old Testament the struggle to understand and obey God's will regardless of its effects on nature, human happiness, or civilization.

This is evident in the Jawist version of the creation story, the story of Adam and Eve. God puts the tree, with its tempting fruit, in the middle of the garden; He forbids Adam to eat it; Adam disobeys; God punishes him. There is no further explanation, the author implies, than God's will and our inherent human weakness. Perhaps we can know what God's will is, but we are not able here, as we might be in a Greek text, to understand God's reasoning and use His decisions to our advantage. All we can do is to try to put God on our side by demonstrating our faith in Him.

The primary human struggle depicted in the Old Testament, then, is the struggle "within"—the burden of our inherent sinfulness, the difficulties presented to us by life among other human beings, our closeness and nearness to God as His creatures—these are the obstacles to human good that are of main concern in the Old Testament texts. And the human good towards which we strive is depicted here, not—as it is for the Greeks—as an honorable and excellent human life that emulates and/or conquers the super-human life of the gods, but rather a life of utter submission to God and the protection from God that we hope will ensue upon it.

Thus, gender, in the Old Testament, is depicted not so much as an abstract natural force, as a concrete human characteristic, given by God, upon which follow certain kinds of obligations and certain kinds of obstacles to meeting these obligations. In other words, various human characteristics, including gender, are here to be understood as unique kinds of divine contributions to the human lot, with their own roles to play in our interior struggle. Knowledge of gender, as it is described in this text, gives us information not so much about the natural world or fate as it does about ourselves; knowledge of gender points us inward, towards our own obligations, our own sins, our own personal histories, and ultimately our own salvation. Thus, the practical import of gender is far more clear in the Old Testament than it is with the preSocratic Greeks—knowledge of our sex, given by God, is thought here simply to tell us what behavior God expects from us.

1. HESIOD
(Greek, Late Eighth–
Early Seventh Century, B.C.E.)

Hesiod, a lyric poet from central Greece, or Boiotia, is thought to have flourished a little after Homer. Championing the idyllic life of the farmer, Hesiod invests concrete, naturalistic imagery with transcendent significance. We find in Hesiod the first gesture towards an abstract philosophical vocabulary, achieved primarily by stretching to their maximum the meanings of simple, familiar, terms, and names of Greek divinities. Today, Hesiod's name is less commonly known than Homer's; however, Hesiod's two major poems, excerpted below, were well known among the ancient Greeks, and are crucially important to our understanding of Western philosophical origins. We begin with Hesiod, because the content of his poems depicts a still earlier pre-history than the events described by Homer.

THEOGONY

The *Theogony* or "birth of the gods" is a detailed creation story that provides a full catalogue of the Greek gods. While the mythology upon which the *Theogony* depends is the same mythology we find in Homer, and was surely very familiar to Hesiod's audience, the poem is far from unoriginal. Hesiod's is a unique proto-scientific mythology, in which the various divinities represent natural phenomena, and which is consequently almost as much a philosophical explanation of the origins of the universe (a *cosmogony*[3]) as it is a story of the gods. One of the natural phenomena whose character and origins are explored in the *Theogony* is gender. Indeed, the femininity and masculinity of the first-born gods is crucial to Hesiod's reasoning as to how and why the succeeding gods are born.

THE FIRST GODS

The substance of the poem begins with the birth of the first god, Chaos. "Chaos" can be understood as "the gap" or the "yawn," which is created by the separation of two or more things from each other. Thus, to be born, to come into existence, as Hesiod depicts it here, is to be distinguished as an entity from other entities, where the distinction itself—Chaos—must exist prior to the distinct entities. For example, without the knife-cuts in a cake, there can be no distinct pieces of cake. This creative act is here depicted as a male divinity. Here, we will follow the genealogy only as far as the birth of the Titans, the parents of the more familiar Olympian gods.

> First of all there came Chaos,
> and after him came
> Gaia of the broad breast,
> to be the unshakable foundation
> of all the immortals who keep the crests
> of snowy Olympos,
> and Tartaros the foggy in the pit
> of the wide-wayed earth,
> and Eros who is love, handsomest among all
> the immortals,
> who breaks the limbs' strength
> who in all gods, in all human beings
> overpowers the intelligence in the breast,
> and all their shrewd planning.
> From Chaos was born Erebos, the dark,
> and black Night,
> and from Night again Aither and Hemera,
> the day, were begotten,
> for she lay in love with Erebos
> and conceived and bore these two.
> But Gaia's first born was one
> who matched her every dimension,

---

[3] Both our words "cosmogony" and "cosmology" (as well as "cosmetics") are derived from the Greek word "Kosmos," meaning both "order" and "ornament." The implication is that for the Greeks, order is beautiful, and thus the study of the order of nature is also a study of the divine beauty of nature.

Ouranos, the starry sky,
to cover her all over,
to be an unshakable standing-place
for the blessed immortals.

ᕮ ᕮ ᕮ

and after this
she lay with Oranos, and bore him
deep swirling Okeanos
the ocean-stream; and Koios, Krios,
Hyperion, Iapetos,
and Theia too and Rheia, and Themis,
and Mnemosyne,
Phoibe of the wreath of gold,
and Tethys the lovely.
After these her youngest-born
was devious-devising Kronos,
most terrible of her children;
and he hated his strong father.

ᕮ ᕮ ᕮ

And still other children were born
to Gaia and Ouranos,
three sons, big and powerful, so great
they could never be told of,
Kottos, Briareos, and Gyes,
overmastering children.

ᕮ ᕮ ᕮ

[E]very time each one
was beginning
to come out, [Ouranos] would push them back again,
deep inside Gaia,
and would not let them into the light,
and Ouranos exulted
in his wicked work; but great Gaia
groaned within for pressure
of pain; and then she thought of an evil,
treacherous attack.
Presently creating the element of grey flint
she made of it a great sickle,
and explained it to her own children,
and spoke, in the disturbance of her heart,
to encourage them:

"My sons, born to me of a criminal father,
if you are willing
to obey me, we can punish your father
for the brutal treatment
he put upon you, for he was first to think
of shameful dealing."
So she spoke, but fear took hold of all,
nor did one of them
speak, but then great devious-devising Kronos
took courage
and spoke in return,
and gave his gracious mother an answer:
"My mother, I will promise to undertake
to accomplish
this act, and for our father,
him of the evil name, I care
nothing, for he was the first
to think of shameful dealing."
So he spoke, and giant Gaia
rejoiced greatly in her heart
and took and hid him in a secret ambush,
and put into his hands
the sickle, edged like teeth, and told him
all her treachery.
And huge Ouranos came on
bringing night with him, and desiring
love he embraced Gaia and lay over her stretched out
complete, and from his hiding place his son
reached with his left hand
and seized him, and holding in his right
the enormous sickle
with its long blade edged like teeth,
he swung it sharply,
and lopped the members of his own father,
and threw them behind him
to fall where they would,
but they were not lost away when they were flung
from his hand, but all the bloody drops
that went splashing from them
were taken in by Gaia, the earth,
and with the turning of the seasons
she brought forth the powerful Furies
and the tall Giants

⌒ ⌒ ⌒

But the members themselves, when Kronos
had lopped them with the flint,

⌒ ⌒ ⌒

[grew into] a girl, whose course first took her
to holy Kythera,

⌒ ⌒ ⌒

and the gods call her
Aphrodite and men do too,

⌒ ⌒ ⌒

and here is the privilege she was given
and holds from the beginning,
and which is the part she plays among men
and the gods immortal:
the whispering together of girls,
the smiles and deceptions,
the delight, and the sweetness of love,
and the flattery.
But their great father Ouranos,
who himself begot them,
bitterly gave to those others, his sons,
the names of Titans, . . .

Gaia (Earth), a female divinity, is the first god to be created (distinguished as an entity) after Chaos. Then comes Tartaros (the Underworld), a male divinity, and Eros (Love), another male divinity. Until the appearance of Eros, all the gods born are born otherwise than by sexual reproduction. A principle of distinction and separation (Chaos) had to exist, Hesiod implies, before a principle of reunification (Eros) could be meaningful; and sexual reproduction, birth as we know it, is impossible without Eros. Hesiod puts all this forward with only the simple imagery of familiar gods and natural entities.

Gaia's mate, Ouranos (Sky), is born only after these other divinities, and he is born from Gaia herself; i.e., there is parentage here, but not sexual reproduction. Night, also a female divinity in Gaia's "generation," through sexual reproduction with Erebos (Darkness), gives birth to Hemera (Day) and Aither. Thus, this first appearance of important binary distinctions (between Heaven and Earth, and Night and Day, etc.) is automatically associated with the distinction between male and female. However, these distinctions come only in the sixth and seventh, not the first two, gods. Earth and Night both give birth out of themselves to *their opposites* (Earth to Sky and Night to Day). This natural binary distinction, then (though, in the case of Night and Erebos, not the sexual one), is founded in the female divinity. Thus, opposition, or duality, itself seems to find its source in femininity. We will see in other passages that it is paradigmatic of Hesiodic females to produce both good and evil. Hesiod's use of these binary oppositions is a poetic representation of what will later become a scientific principle of *change:* nothing can change *from* it-self, but from what it is not—its opposite.

At any rate, these original gods, through both asexual and sexual means, fill the whole natural world, which is consequently endowed with a divine order. Thus, Hesiod gives us not just a notion of the origin of the universe, but also of its order. Gaia and Ouranos and Night and Erebos complete the creation of what is at once the physical universe and the divine pantheon. This infusing of the natural world with divine significance is a predecessor to the early Greek belief in *animism*—i.e., that all natural entities are alive and spiritual, indicating that gender here is not just a physical attribute of some animals, but a force at play in the natural world.

One might assume that Hesiod's male divinities would be more powerful than the female; but the discussion of Aphrodite, for instance, who "was given . . . privilege . . . among men and the gods immortal" quickly checks this assumption. The typically masculine power seems to be an active, directed, creative force, where the typically feminine power seems to be more stationary, but also less clear; it is that towards which the masculine divinities are drawn or directed, that from which springs both the good and the evil fate that awaits humans and gods, male and female. Thus, the feminine principles seem to be exterior, natural, amorphous, and multiple as compared to the masculine principles, which seem to be clearly drawn, singular, and driven from the interior outward.

ZEUS AND METIS

Another relevant story from the *Theogony* describes Zeus' treatment of his first wife, Metis. Metis was an Okeanid, a daughter of the male Okeanos (Ocean) and the female Tethys (Sea), and the mother of Athene, goddess of wisdom. Metis' power and wisdom, demonstrated in her production of Athene, is considered by Zeus and his "grandparents," Gaia and Ouranos, to be a threat to his rulership over the gods.

> Zeus, as King of the gods,
> took as his first wife Metis,
> and she knew more than all the gods
> or mortal people.
> But when she was about to be delivered
> of the goddess, gray-eyed
> Athene, then Zeus, deceiving her perception
> by treachery
> and by slippery speeches,
> put her away inside his own belly.
> This was by the advices of Gaia,
> and starry Ouranos,
> for so they counseled,
> in order that no other everlasting
> god, beside Zeus, should ever be given
> the kingly position.
> For it had been arranged that, from her,

children surpassing in wisdom
should be born, first the gray-eyed girl,
the Tritogeneia
Athene; and she is the equal of her father
in wise counsel
and strength; but then a son to be King
over gods and mortals
was to be born of her, and his heart
would be overmastering:
but before this, Zeus put her away
inside his own belly
so that this goddess should think for him,
for good and for evil.

This story is very telling of the relative powers of masculinity and femininity according to Hesiod. Metis is an exceptionally powerful force, hence the great threat that she poses to Zeus; but her power is as yet undirected, a potency yet unmanifest. Zeus controls her power by eating her; he does not destroy Metis, but rather puts her to use for his purposes. Despite Metis' power and intelligence, she is subsumed by him. Thus, here, we see a paradigmatically overwhelming but unknown feminine force countered by a paradigmatically decisive masculine victory. Again, in addition, we see that the consumed Metis thinks for Zeus "for good and evil"—i.e., again, the feminine character has a dual or multiple moral significance, which is put to use for the male.

PROMETHEUS AND PANDORA

The creation of the first woman, the Greek "Eve," if you will, is described in both of Hesiod's great poems. In the *Theogony,* Hesiod stresses the mythological significance of human sexuality, placing our lives into the context of the cosmology as a whole.

. . . [H]e would not
give the force of weariless fire
to the ash-tree people,
not to people who inhabit the earth
and are mortal,
no, but the strong son of Iapetos
outwitted him
and stole the far-seen glory
of weariless fire, hiding it
in the hollow fennel stalk;
this bit deep into the feeling
of Zeus who thunders on high,

and next, for the price of the fire,
he made an evil thing for mankind.
For the renowned smith of the strong arms
took earth, and molded it,
through Zeus's plans, into the likeness
of a modest young girl,
and the goddess gray-eyed Athene
dressed her and decked her
in silverish clothing, and over her head
she held, with her hands,
an intricately wrought veil in place,
a wonder to look at,
and over this on her head
she placed a wreath of gold

       ☞ ☞ ☞

But when, to replace good,
he had made this beautiful evil
thing, he led her out
where the rest of the gods and mortals
were, in the pride and glory
that the grey-eyed daughter of a great
father had given; wonder
seized both immortals and mortals
as they gazed on this sheer deception,
more than mortals can deal with.
For from her originates the breed
of female women,
and they live with mortal men,
and are a great sorrow to them,
and hateful poverty they will not share,
but only luxury.

       ☞ ☞ ☞

so Zeus of the high thunder established women,
for mortal
men an evil thing,
and they are accomplished in bringing hard labors.
   And Zeus made, in place
of the good, yet another evil.
For whoever, escaping marriage
and the sorrowful things women do,
is unwilling to marry, must come then
to a mournful old age

bereft of one to look after it,
and in need of livelihood
lives on, and when he dies
the widow-inheritors divide up
what he has. While if the way of marriage
befalls one
and he gets himself a good wife,
one with ways suited to him,
even so through his lifetime the evil remains,
balancing
the good, and he whose luck
is to have cantankerous children
lives keeping inside him discomfort
which will not leave him
in heart and mind; and for this evil
there is no healing.

This passage is certainly a very telling one regarding our own mythology of the relation and conflict between the sexes, and it raises a theme that will be much repeated in these ancient texts. Prometheus is depicted as the agent of the defiant deed, while Pandora is merely the punishment bestowed upon him for it. She, the first woman, is described in wholly glowing terms, as beautiful and wonderful, until all of sudden she is described as "sheer deception." She plays the dual role of punishment and object of adoration. That woman marks both good and bad achievements, and that she does so always with a double edge, is clarified in the next passage, essentially Zeus' insistence that men "can't live with 'em, can't live without 'em": the human woman makes the life of the human man always balanced by good and evil rewards.

WORKS AND DAYS

The Pandora story in Hesiod's other great poem, the *Works and Days,* has a different emphasis. Here, we get the entirety of the familiar story: Pandora is given the infamous jar in which are held all the evils that befall human beings. In this poem, Hesiod's focus is not on the grand metaphysical issues of the *Theogony,* but the more homespun ethical issues involved in understanding the human condition. That the Pandora story here is intended to motivate human virtue, instead of to place human beings in the order of nature, is evidenced by Hesiod's claim that the Pandora story and the story of the "five generations of men"—succeeding *de*generations from the gods—are just two different ways of putting the same point: trying to describe the proper life for a human being.

PANDORA

"... As the price of fire I will give them an evil,
and all men shall fondle

this, their evil, close to their hearts,
and take delight in it."

⌒ ⌒ ⌒

The goddess gray-eyed Athene dressed and arrayed her;
the Graces,
who are goddesses, and hallowed Persuasion
put necklaces
of gold upon her body, while the Seasons,
with glorious tresses,
put upon her head a coronal of spring flowers,
[and Pallas Athene put all decor upon her body].
But into her heart Hermes, the guide,
the slayer of Argos,
put lies, and wheedling words
of falsehood, and a treacherous nature,
made her as Zeus of the deep thunder wished,
and he, the gods' herald,
put a voice inside her, and gave her
the name of woman,
Pandora, because all the gods
who have their homes on Olympos
had given her each a gift, to be a sorrow to men
who eat bread. Now when he had done
with this sheer, impossible
deception, the Father sent the gods' fleet messenger,
Hermes,
to Epimetheus, bringing her, a gift,
nor did Epimetheus
remember to think how Prometheus had told him never
to accept a gift from Olympian Zeus,
but always to send it
back, for fear it might prove
to be an evil for mankind.
He took the evil, and only perceived it
when he possessed her.
Since before this time the races of men
had been living on earth
free from all evils, free from laborious work,
and free from
all wearing sicknesses that bring
their fates down on men
[for men grow old suddenly
in the midst of misfortune];
but the woman, with her hands lifting away the lid
from the great jar,

scattered its contents, and her design
was sad troubles for mankind.
Hope was the only spirit that stayed there
in the unbreakable
closure of the jar, under its rim,
and could not fly forth
abroad, for the lid of the great jar
closed down first and contained her.

Certain themes of the *Theogony* appear again here, but always under the auspices of the study of human nature. Pandora is again a "delightful evil"; again, her creation is Prometheus' punishment for his theft of fire. But where the *Theogony* focused on the motivation and character of Zeus, the *Works and Days* stresses human mortality—the hopeless, wearied, character of men's lives, of which mortal woman is only the hapless cause. Again, Pandora's agency is ambiguous. Zeus fills the jar and sends it to Pandora, who merely opens her gift. (We will see this theme reiterated in the biblical Adam and Eve story, in which Eve's unwitting susceptibility to the serpent parallels Pandora's to Zeus here.)

Humanity and its inherent weaknesses—and thus, the incessant laboring with which human life is fraught—can be said to be characteristically masculine, according to Hesiod. The vehicle by which these are brought into the world is feminine. The man works, the woman presses him on, crowns his work with hope and despair, and enjoys the fruits of his labor. Thus, the woman, represented as somehow other than, or beyond, the human worker, is associated with the outside natural forces within which, and yet also *for* which, he struggles. In this vein, it is worth noting that Hope—which is left inside the jar after it is opened—is also female. Thus, again, we see the double edge of the female reward for man's actions. The femininity of Hope—indeed the gender of many of the divinities—may be attributable to the Greek language itself, in which nouns are gendered (masculine, feminine, and neuter). Since Homer and Hesiod—the archaic influences on preSocratic thought—were poets, the influence of the Greek language on Western notions of gender may be stronger than we normally imagine.

2. HOMER
(Greek, Eighth Century B.C.E.)

The epic poems of Homer, the *Iliad* and the *Odyssey,* are the earliest surviving Greek literature. The ancient Greeks of the classical period (whose works are excerpted in the next section) considered Homer to be the first and greatest Greek poet, and this evaluation has remained to the present day. Homer provides students and scholars with their richest source for both Greek mythology and Greek prehistory. Thus, his epics are fundamental texts in the study of any Western paradigms, including those of gender. Indeed, Homer is an almost inexhaustible source of those "inimitable examples" which give shape to the Western imagination. It would be impossible, therefore, to excerpt all the passages from Homer relevant to our project; just a few of the most relevant ones follow.

THE *ILIAD*

The *Iliad,* like the *Works and Days,* is a study of human nature and—again, as in that work—therefore of masculinity, taking the man as the paradigmatically human being. The anthropomorphic gods reflect human nature on a more powerful scale; they too, contribute essentially to Homer's study of humanity.

The *Iliad* is primarily a study of the consequences of a man's anger—Achilleus', in this case—under various enabling and inhibiting external conditions. This story of "the rage of Peleus' son Achilleus"—the development of the war after Achilleus withdraws himself, and the ultimate Achaean victory against Troy after he returns to battle— is set within a divinely animated universe, in which feminine beauty and masculine passion provide the motivation for events both mortal and divine. These background assumptions, not so very different in this regard from those of Hesiod, draw a parallel between sexual relations and the relations among city-states, reiterating the Greek association of the city with the dynastic household. In the *Iliad* we see the tragic side of this parallel: the destroyed, violated society that at once represents the broken home. The origins of Greek civilization and of manhood, Homer seems to imply, are violent; they are founded in the destruction of a part of one's own country, oneself, presumably that barbaric part that commits injustice by taking that (feminine) reward to which it is not entitled.

The *Iliad* tells the story of the Achaean victory against Troy (an Eastern Greek city-state, on the coast of Asia Minor), thought to be a seminal event in the development of ancient Greek civilization. The destruction of Troy occurred in an age already long past by the time of Homer's writing, in the "heroic age" described above by Hesiod. The Trojan war was originally instigated when Paris, the son of Priam, King of Troy, judged Aphrodite the most beautiful deity. As a reward, Paris was allowed to take for himself the most beautiful of mortal women—Helen, wife of Menelaos, King of Sparta. In order to regain Helen by force, Menelaus united the Achaeans against Troy under the command of his brother, Agamemnon. For nine years the Achaeans held their own against Troy, but in the tenth year Agamemnon had a falling-out with his best fighter Achilleus, who, out of spite for Agamemnon, withdrew from the fighting with all of his men. Their argument is where the poem begins.

ACHILLEUS AND AGAMEMNON

Agamemnon had been in possession of a young girl, Chryseis, daughter of a Trojan priest of Apollo, taken as booty during the war. Kalchas, a prophet, instructs Agamemnon that he must return the girl to the Trojans in order to end the scourge with which Apollo has punished their armies, but Agamemnon will not do so unless he is recompensed out of the booty of his men. Achilleus objects. Nonetheless,

Agamemnon returns the girl and takes Achilleus' prize—a woman, Briseis—as re-
payment for his loss and revenge against Achilleus for their argument. Achilleus, in
his anger, refuses to fight for the Achaeans and threatens to return home.

FROM **BOOK I**

Sing, goddess, the anger of Peleus' son Achilleus
and its devastation, which put pains thousandfold upon the Achaians.

❧ ❧ ❧

[AGAMEMNON TO ACHILLEUS:] 'I wish greatly to have her
in my own house; since I like her better than Klytaimestra
my own wife, for in truth she is no way inferior,
neither in build nor stature nor wit, not in accomplishment.
Still I am willing to give her back, if such is the best way.
I myself desire that my people be safe, not perish.
Find me then some prize that shall be my own, lest I only
among the Argives go without, since that were unfitting;
you are all witnesses to this thing, that my prize goes elsewhere.'
    Then in answer again spoke brilliant swift-footed Achilleus:

❧ ❧ ❧

But what we took from the cities by storm has been distributed;
it is unbecoming for the people to call back things once given.

❧ ❧ ❧

    Then in answer again spoke powerful Agamemnon:
'Not that way, good fighter though you be, godlike Achilleus,
strive to cheat, for you will not deceive, you will not persuade me.
What do you want? To keep your own prize and have me sit here
lacking one? Are you ordering me to give this girl back?
Either the great-hearted Achaians shall give me a new prize
chosen according to my desire to atone for the girl lost,
or else if they will not give me one I myself shall take her,
your own prize, or that of Aias, or that of Odysseus.

❧ ❧ ❧

    Then looking darkly at him Achilleus of the swift feet spoke:
'O wrapped in shamelessness, with your mind forever on profit,
how shall any one of the Achaians readily obey you
either to go on a journey or to fight men strongly in battle?

❧ ❧ ❧

o great shamelessness, we followed, to do you favour,
you with the dog's eyes, to win your honour and Menelaos'
from the Trojans. You forget all this or else you care nothing.
And now my prize you threaten in person to strip from me,
for whom I laboured much, the gift of the sons of the Achaians.
Never, when the Achaians sack some well-founded citadel
of the Trojans, do I have a prize that is equal to your prize.
Always the greater part of the painful fighting is the work of
my hands; but when the time comes to distribute the booty
yours is far the greater reward, and I with some small thing
yet dear to me go back to my ships when I am weary with fighting.
Now I am returning to Phthia, since it is much better
to go home again with my curved ships, and I am minded no longer
to stay here dishonoured and pile up your wealth and your luxury.'

[AGAMEMNON TO ACHILLEUS:] 'Go home then with your own ships and your own
   companions,
be king over the Myrmidons. I care nothing about you.
I take no account of your anger. But here is my threat to you.
Even as Phoibos Apollo is taking away my Chryseis.
I shall convey her back in my own ship, with my own
followers; but I shall take the fair-cheeked Briseis,
your prize, I myself going to your shelter, that you may learn well
how much greater I am than you, and another man may shrink back
from likening himself to me and contending against me.'

The goddess standing behind Peleus' son caught him by the fair hair,
appearing to him only, for no man of the others saw her.
Achilleus in amazement turned about, and straightaway
knew Pallas Athene and the terrible eyes shining.
He uttered winged words and addressed her: 'Why have you come now,
o child of Zeus of the aegis, once more? Is it that you may see
the outrageousness of the son of Atreus Agamemnon?
Yet will I tell you this thing, and I think it shall be accomplished.
By such acts of arrogance he may even lose his own life.'
   Then in answer the goddess grey-eyed Athene spoke to him:
'I have come down to stay your anger—but will you obey me?—
from the sky; and the goddess of the white arms Hera sent me,
who loves both of you equally in her heart and cares for you.

   Then in answer again spoke Achilleus of the swift feet:
'Goddess, it is necessary that I obey the word of you two,

angry though I am in my heart. So it will be better.
If any man obeys the gods, they listen to him also.

So he spoke in tears and the lady his mother heard him
as she sat in the depths of the sea at the side of her aged father,

Thetis [Achilleus' mother] answered him then letting the tears fall: 'Ah me,
my child. Your birth was bitterness. Why did I raise you?
If only you could sit by your ships untroubled, not weeping,
since indeed your lifetime is to be short, of no length.
Now it has befallen that your life must be brief and bitter
beyond all men's. To a bad destiny I bore you in my chambers.
But I will go to cloud-dark Olympos and ask this
thing of Zeus who delights in the thunder. Perhaps he will do it.

'Father Zeus, if ever before in word or action
I did you favour among the immortals, now grant what I ask for.
Now give honour to my son short-lived beyond all other
mortals. Since even now the lord of men Agamemnon
dishonours him, who has taken away his prize and keeps it.
Zeus of the counsels, lord of Olympos, now do him honour.
So long put strength into the Trojans, until the Achaians
give my son his rights, and his honour is increased among them.'
    She spoke thus. But Zeus who gathers the clouds made no answer
but sat in silence a long time. And Thetis, as she had taken
his knees, clung fast to them and urged once more her question:
'Bend your head and promise me to accomplish this thing,
or else refuse it, you have nothing to fear, that I may know
by how much I am the most dishonoured of all gods.'
    Deeply disturbed Zeus who gathers the clouds answered her:
'This is a disastrous matter when you set me in conflict
with Hera, and she troubles me with recriminations.
Since even as things are, forever among the immortals
she is at me and speaks of how I help the Trojans in battle.
Even so, go back again now, go away, for fear she
see us. I will look to these things that they be accomplished.

Chryseis is first and foremost a mark of Agamemnon's power and station.
Agamemnon has, in a sense, forgotten what he is fighting for (the return of his
brother's wife, and the consequent restoration of the Greek household) and has become lost in the glory of the battle itself. Hence, Achilleus' argument against him
stresses a notion of "true" honor as a counter to Agamemnon's shallowness.

Achilleus, though he also values Briseis as a prize and a mark of honor, and so sees her theft by Agamemnon as a personal disgrace, will not do himself the greater dishonor of taking in revenge something that does not belong to him. This makes Achilleus the hero of the piece—despite his temper and the mistaken judgments he will make in the course of the story—because he upholds the Greek values of household, honor, and city over his personal reputation or power.

While Chryseis, Briseis and Thetis all represent certain entitlements that crown men's actions, the ground of the two captives' entitlement is quite different from that of divinities. The obligations imposed by the human women are marks of his high status, in the way that having employees marks a person's status, even though they impose obligations upon him or her. However, the male's obligation towards the divine females, as we will see, marks his humble, fallible status, and as such, he represents humankind in general as opposed to the immortal and divine. This latter point is best exemplified in Athene's control over Achilleus' temper, a stark contrast to Chryseis and Briseis, who are essentially pawns in the argument between Achilleus and Agamemnon.

PARIS AND HELEN

In Book III, there is a glimmer of hope for peace: Paris—also called Alexandros—offers to fight Menelaos one-on-one for Helen. This is prompted by a chiding Paris receives from his brother Hektor, the best of the Trojan warriors. Helen is alerted that her fate is being decided, prompting her to reflect upon her old life with Menelaos and her new one with Paris. Most of the observers believe that Menelaos will win the fight; however, Zeus' promise to Thetis, combined with Aphrodite's lingering favor for Paris, lead the goddess to intercede on Paris' behalf, whisking him away just as Menelaos is about to strike the fatal blow.

FROM **BOOK III**

But Hektor saw him and in words of shame rebuked him:
'Evil Paris, beautiful, woman-crazy, cajoling,
better had you never been born, or killed unwedded.
Truly I could have wished it so; it would be far better
than to have you with us to our shame, for others to sneer at.
Surely now the flowing-haired Achaians laugh at us,
thinking you are our bravest champion, only because your
looks are handsome, but there is no strength in your heart, no courage.
Were you like this that time when in sea-wandering vessels
assembling oarsmen to help you you sailed over the water,
and mixed with the outlanders, and carried away a fair woman
from a remote land, whose lord's kin were spearmen and fighters,
to your father a big sorrow, and your city, and all your people,
to yourself a thing shameful but bringing joy to the enemy?

And now you would not stand up against warlike Menelaos?
Thus you would learn of the man whose blossoming wife you have taken.

[PARIS TO HECTOR] Never to be cast away are the gifts of the gods, magnificent,
which they give of their own will, no man could have them for wanting them.
Now though, if you wish me to fight it out and do battle,
make the rest of the Trojans sit down, and all the Achaians,
to fight together for the sake of Helen and all her possessions.
That one of us who wins and is proved stronger, let him
take the possessions fairly and the woman, and lead her homeward.

Now to Helen of the white arms came a messenger, Iris,

She came on Helen in the chamber; she was weaving a great web,
a red folding robe, and working into it the numerous struggles
of Trojans, breakers of horses, and bronze-armoured Achaians,
struggles that they endured for her sake at the hands of the war god.
Iris of the swift feet stood beside her and spoke to her:

. . . Menelaos the warlike and Alexandros will fight
with long spears against each other for your possession.
You shall be called beloved wife of the man who wins you.'
Speaking so the goddess left in her heart sweet longing
after her husband of time before, and her city and parents.

Now when these two were armed on either side of the battle,
they strode into the space between the Achaians and Trojans,
looking terror at each other; and amazement seized the beholders,

First of the two Alexandros let go his spear far-shadowing
and struck the shield of Atreus' son on its perfect circle
nor did the bronze point break its way through, but the spearhead bent back
in the strong shield. And after him Atreus' son, Menalaos
was ready to let go the bronze spear, with a prayer to Zeus father:

So he spoke, and balanced the spear far-shadowed, and threw it
and struck the shield of Priam's son on its perfect circle.
All the way through the glittering shield went the heavy spearhead
and smashed its way through the intricately worked corselet;

straight ahead by the flank the spearhead shore through his tunic,
yet he bent away to one side and avoided the dark death.
Drawing his sword with the silver nails, the son of Atreus
heaving backward struck at the horn of his helmet; the sword-blade
three times broken and four times broken fell from his hand's grip.
Groaning, the son of Atreus lifted his eyes to the wide sky:
'Father Zeus, no God beside is more baleful than you are.
Here I thought to punish Alexandros for his wickedness;
and now my sword is broken in my hands, and the spear flew vainly
out of my hands on the throw before, and I have not hit him.'

He spoke, and flashing forward laid hold of the horse-haired helmet
and spun him about, and dragged him away toward the strong-greaved Achaians,
for the broidered strap under the softness of his throat strangled Paris,
fastened under his chin to hold on the horned helmet.
Now he would have dragged him away and won glory forever
had not Aphrodite daughter of Zeus watched sharply.
She broke the chinstrap, made from the hide of a slaughtered bullock,
and the helmet came away empty in the heavy hand of Atreides.
The hero whirled the helmet about and sent it flying
among the strong greaved Achaians, and his staunch companions retrieved it.
He turned and made again for his man, determined to kill him
with the bronze spear. But Aphrodite caught up Paris
easily, since she was divine, and wrapped him in a thick mist
and set him down again in his own perfumed bedchamber.
She then went away to summon Helen, and found her
on the high tower, with a cluster of Trojan women about her.

⌒ ⌒ ⌒

So she spoke, and troubled the spirit in Helen's bosom.

⌒ ⌒ ⌒

'Strange divinity! Why are you still so stubborn to beguile me?

⌒ ⌒ ⌒

'Is it because Menelaos has beaten great Alexandros
and wishes, hateful even as I am, to carry me homeward,
is it for this that you stand in your treachery now beside me?
Go yourself and sit beside him, abandon the gods' way,
turn your feet back never again to the path of Olympos
but stay with him forever, and suffer for him, and look after him
until he makes you his wedded wife, or makes you his slave girl.
Not I. I am not going to him. It would be too shameful.
I will not serve his bed, since the Trojan women hereafter
would laugh at me, all, and my heart even now is confused with sorrows.

⌒ ⌒ ⌒

Paris then in turn spoke to her thus and answered her:
'Lady, censure my heart no more in bitter reprovals.
This time Menelaos with Athene's help has beaten me;
another time I shall beat him. We have gods on our side also.
Come, then, rather let us go to bed and turn to love-making.
Never before as now has passion enmeshed my senses,
not when I took you the first time from Lakedaimon the lovely
and caught you up and carried you away in seafaring vessels,
and lay with you in the bed of love on the island Kranae,
not even then, as now, did I love you and sweet desire seize me.'
    Speaking, he led the way to the bed; and his wife went with him.

In these passages we see a nice study of preHomeric Greek paradigms of sexual roles. Paris is characterized as "a lover, not a fighter," a ladies' man whose good looks have caused a lot of trouble for everyone. Paris' character is here posed as an opposite, both to Hektor's courageous heroism and to the Achaean's great army, represented by Menelaos. This is represented by Homer as Paris' association with femininity.

A parallel to the conflict between Menelaos and Paris is Helen's internal conflict between her past and her present. Helen has sympathies for both Achaeans and Trojans, and she has resentment for both sides, too; and these mixed feelings towards others are at once mixed feelings about herself. In her sympathy for the Achaeans, she also feels a nostalgia for her old life and shame over her abandonment of it. In her sympathy for the Trojans, she feels flattered and freshly obligated. Thus, Helen encompasses within herself the entirety of the conflicts that compose the story and the war. Helen's complex representation of femininity in these passages of the *Iliad* is exemplified by Homer in two ways—her weaving and her fretting. Both of these symbols of femininity will reappear many times in Western literature.

ACHILLEUS AND HEKTOR

A transformation is effected in Achilleus by the death of his best friend, Patroklus. In book XVI, Patroklus, "crying like some poor little girl" had begged Achilleus, for the embattled Achaeans' sake, at least to give Patroklus his armor and a chance to be victorious, if Achilleus would not return to battle himself. Achilleus, while still stubbornly refusing to fight, yielded to his friend's request, and sent Patroklus, in Achilleus' own armor, to his death at the hands of Hektor. Achilleus sees this tragedy as the result of his own rage, with the consequences that the pettiness of his anger at Agamemnon and the irrationality of his decision not to fight for the Achaeans are both redirected against the Trojans and magnified to an almost super-human extent.

FROM **BOOKS XVIII, XIX, XX, XXI, XXII**

'. . . Patroklos has fallen, and now they are fighting over his body
which is naked. Hektor of the shining helm has taken his armour.'

He spoke, and the black cloud of sorrow closed on Achilleus.
In both hands he caught up the grimy dust, and poured it
over his head and face, and fouled his handsome countenance,
and the black ashes were scattered over his immortal tunic.
And he himself, mightily in his might, in the dust lay
at length, and took and tore at his hair with his hands, and defiled it.

⌒ ⌒ ⌒

He cried out terribly, aloud, and the lady his mother heard him.

⌒ ⌒ ⌒

Then sighing heavily Achilleus of the swift feet answered her:
'My mother, all these things the Olympian brought to accomplishment.
But what pleasure is this to me, since my dear companion has perished,
Patroklos, whom I loved beyond all other companions,
as well as my own life. I have lost him, and Hektor, who killed him,
has stripped away that gigantic armour, a wonder to look on
and splendid, which the gods gave Peleus, a glorious present,

⌒ ⌒ ⌒

you can never again receive him
won home again to his country; since the spirit within does not drive me
to go on living and be among men, except on condition
that Hektor first be beaten down under my spear, lose his life
and pay the price for stripping Patroklos, the son of Menoitios.'

⌒ ⌒ ⌒

'But seeing that it is I, Patroklos, who follow you underground,
I will not bury you till I bring to this place the armour
and the head of Hektor, since he was your great-hearted murderer.
Before your burning pyre I shall behead twelve glorious
children of the Trojans, for my anger over your slaying.
Until then, you shall lie where you are in front of my curved ships
and beside you women of Troy and deep-girdled Dardanian women
shall sorrow for you night and day and shed tears for you, those whom
you and I worked hard to capture by force and the long spear
in days when we were storming the rich cities of mortals.'
    So speaking brilliant Achilleus gave orders to his companions
to set a great cauldron across the fire, so that with all speed
they could wash away the clotted blood from Patroklos.

⌒ ⌒ ⌒

Thetis of the silver feet came to the house of Hephaistos,

⌒ ⌒ ⌒

now I come to your knees; so might you be willing
to give me for my short-lived son a shield and a helmet
and two beautiful greaves fitted with clasps for the ankles
and a corselet. What he had was lost with his steadfast companion
when the Trojans killed him. Now my son lies on the ground, heart sorrowing.'
    Hearing her the renowned smith of the strong arms answered her:
'Do not fear. Let not these things be a thought in your mind.

⌒ ⌒ ⌒

So he spoke, and left her there, and went to his bellows.

⌒ ⌒ ⌒

There were five folds composing the shield itself, and upon it
he elaborated many things in his skill and craftsmanship.

⌒ ⌒ ⌒

    On it he wrought in all their beauty two cities of mortal
men. And there were marriages in one, and festivals.
They were leading the brides along the city from their maiden chambers
under the flaring of torches, and the loud bride song was arising.

⌒ ⌒ ⌒

The people were assembled in the market place, where a quarrel
had arisen, and two men were disputing over the blood price
for a man who had been killed. One man promised full restitution
in a public statement, but the other refused and would accept nothing.
Both then made for an arbitratror, to have a decision:

⌒ ⌒ ⌒

    But around the other city were lying two forces of armed men
shining in their war gear. For one side counsel was divided
whether to storm and sack, or share between both sides the property
and all the possessions the lovely citadel held hard within it.
But the city's people were not giving way, and armed for an ambush.
Their beloved wives and their little children stood on the rampart

⌒ ⌒ ⌒

All closed together like living men and fought with each other
and dragged away from each other the corpses of those who had fallen.

⌒ ⌒ ⌒

                                        Thetis
came to the ships and carried with her the gifts of Hephaistos.
She found her beloved son lying in the arms of Patroklos
crying shrill, and his companions in their numbers about him

mourned. She, shining among divinities, stood there beside them.
She clung to her son's hand and called him by name and spoke to him:
'My child, now, though we grieve for him, we must let this man lie
dead, in the way he first was killed through the gods' designing.
Accept rather from me the glorious arms of Hephaistos,
so splendid, and such as no man has ever worn on his shoulders.'

≈ ≈ ≈

'Go then and summon into assembly the fighting Achaians,
and unsay your anger against Agamemnon, shepherd of the people,
and arm at once for the fighting, and put your war strength upon you.'

≈ ≈ ≈

But now, when all the Achaians were in one body together,
Achilleus of the swift feet stood up before them and spoke to them:

≈ ≈ ≈

'Now I am making an end of my anger. It does not become me
unrelentingly to rage on. Come, then! The more quickly
drive on the flowing-haired Achaians into the fighting,
so that I may go up against the Trojans, and find out
if they still wish to sleep out beside the ships. I think rather
they will be glad to rest where they are, whoever among them
gets away with his life from the fury of our spears' onset.'

≈ ≈ ≈

Now in the time when the gods were still distant from the mortals,
so long the Achaians were winning great glory, since now Achilleus
showed among them, who had stayed too long from the sorrowful fighting.
But the Trojans were taken every man in the knees with trembling
and terror, as they looked on the swift-footed son of Peleus
shining in all his armour, a man like the murderous war god.

≈ ≈ ≈

when Hektor saw Polydoros, his own brother,
going limp to the ground and catching his bowels into his hands,
the mist closed about his eyes also, he could stand no longer
to turn there at a distance, but went out to face Achilleus
hefting his sharp spear, like a flame. Seeing him Achilleus
balanced his spear in turn, and called out to him, and challenged him:
'Here is the man who beyond all others has troubled my anger,
who slaughtered my beloved companion. Let us no longer
shrink away from each other along the edgeworks of battle.'
He spoke, and looking darkly at brilliant Hektor spoke to him:
'Come nearer, so that sooner you may reach your appointed destruction.'

But with no fear Hektor of the shining helm answered him:
'Son of Peleus, never hope by words to frighten me
as if I were a baby. I myself understand well enough
how to speak in vituperation and how to make insults.
I know that you are great and that I am far weaker than you are.
Still all this lies on the knees of the gods; and it may be
that weaker as I am I might still strip the life from you
with a cast of the spear, since my weapon too has been sharp before this.'

The aged Priam had taken his place on the god-built bastion,
and looked out and saw gigantic Achilleus, where before him
the Trojans fled in the speed of their confusion, no war strength
left them. He groaned and descended to the ground from the bastion
and beside the wall set in motion the glorious guards of the gateway;
'Hold the gates wide open in your hands, so that our people
in their flight can get inside the city, for here is Achilleus
close by, stampeding them, and I think there will be disaster.
But once they are crowded inside the city and get wind again,
shut once more the door-leaves closely fitted together.
I am afraid this ruinous man may spring into our stronghold.'

The old man groaned aloud and with both hands high uplifted
beat his head, and groaned amain, and spoke supplicating
his beloved son, who there still in front of the gateway
stood fast in determined fury to fight with Achilleus.
The old man stretching his hands out called pitifully to him:
'Hektor, beloved child, do not wait the attack of this man
alone, away from the others. You might encounter your destiny
beaten down by Peleion, since he is far stronger than you are.
A hard man: I wish he were as beloved of the immortal
as loved by me. Soon he would lie dead, and the dogs and the vultures
would eat him, and bitter sorrow so be taken from my heart.
He has made me desolate of my sons, who were brave and many.
He killed them, or sold them away among the far-lying islands.
Even now there are two sons, Lykaon and Polydoros,
whom I cannot see among the Trojans pent up in the city,
sons Laothoë a princess among women bore to me.
But if these are alive somewhere in the army, then I can
set them free for bronze and gold; it is there inside, since
Altes the aged and renowned gave much with his daughter.
But if they are dead already and gone down to the house of Hades,
it is sorrow to our hearts, who bore them, myself and their mother,
but to the rest of the people a sorrow that will be fleeting

beside their sorrow for you, if you go down before Achilleus.
Come then inside the wall, my child, so that you can rescue
the Trojans and the women of Troy, neither win the high glory
for Peleus' son, and yourself be robbed of your very life. Oh, take
pity on me, the unfortunate still alive, still sentient
but ill-starred, whom the father, Kronos' son, on the threshold of old age
will blast with hard fate, after I have looked upon evils
and seen my sons destroyed and my daughters dragged away captive
and the chambers of marriage wrecked and the innocent children taken
and dashed to the ground in the hatefulness of war, and the wives
of my sons dragged off by the accursed hands of the Achaians.'

❧ ❧ ❧

So the old man spoke, and in his hands seizing the grey hairs
tore them from his head, but could not move the spirit in Hektor.

❧ ❧ ❧

[F]irst of the two to speak was tall helm-glittering Hektor:
'Son of Peleus, I will no longer run from you, as before this
I fled three times around the great city of Priam, and dared not
stand to your onfall. But now my spirit in turn has driven me
to stand and face you. I must take you now, or I must be taken.
Come then, shall we swear before the gods? For these are the highest
who shall be witnesses and watch over our agreements.
Brutal as you are I will not defile you, if Zeus grants
to me that I can wear you out, and take the life from you.
But after I have stripped your glorious armour, Achilleus,
I will give your corpse back to the Achaians. Do you do likewise.

❧ ❧ ❧

Let me at least not die without a struggle, inglorious,
but do some big thing first, that men to come shall know of it.'
So he spoke, and pulling out the sharp sword that was slung
at the hollow of his side, huge and heavy, and gathering
himself together, he made his swoop, like a high-flown eagle
who launches himself out of the murk of the clouds on the flat land
to catch away a tender lamb or a shivering hare; so
Hektor made his swoop, swinging his sharp sword, and Achilleus
charged, the heart within him loaded with savage fury.

❧ ❧ ❧

brilliant Achilleus drove the spear as he came on in fury,
and clean through the soft part of the neck the spearpoint was driven.
Yet the ash spear heavy with bronze did not sever the windpipe,
so that Hektor could still make exchange of words spoken.

But he dropped in the dust, and brilliant Achilleus vaunted above him:
'Hektor, surely you thought as you killed Patroklos you would be
safe, and since I was far away you thought nothing of me,
o fool, for an avenger was left, far greater than he was,
behind him and away by the hollow ships. And it was I;
and I have broken your strength; on you the dogs and the vultures
shall feed and foully rip you; the Achaians will bury Patroklos.'
　　In his weakness Hektor of the shining helm spoke to him:
'I entreat you, by your life, by your knees, by your parents,
do not let the dogs feed on me by the ships of the Achaians,
but take yourself the bronze and gold that are there in abundance,
those gifts that my father and the lady my mother will give you,
and give my body to be taken home again, so that the Trojans
and the wives of the Trojans may give me in death my rite of burning.'
　　But looking darkly at him swift-footed Achilleus answered:
'No more entreating of me, you dog, by knees or parents.'

He spoke, and now thought of shameful treatment for glorious Hektor.
In both of his feet at the back he made holes by the tendons
in the space between ankle and heel, and drew thongs of ox-hide through them,
and fastened them to the chariot so as to let the head drag,
and mounted the chariot, and lifted the glorious armour inside it,
then whipped the horses to a run, and they winged their way unreluctant.
A cloud of dust rose where Hektor was dragged, his dark hair was falling
about him, and all that head that was once so handsome was tumbled
in the dust; since by this time Zeus had given him over
to his enemies, to be defiled in the land of his fathers.
　　So all his head was dragged in the dust; and now his mother
tore out her hair, and threw the shining veil far from her
and raised a great wail as she looked upon her son; and his father
beloved groaned pitifully, and all his people about him
were taken with wailing and lamentation all through the city.
It was most like what would have happened, if all lowering
Ilion had been burning top to bottom in fire.

As Achilleus expands his capacities for both anger and heroism, he seems to
cross the boundary between the human and the non-human, to move beyond the
human strength and petty disputes, which mark his human state, to another realm of
existence. Note for instance that Achilleus, in his grief, covers his own body with
dirt, and tears out his hair. This foreshadows the treatment he will deliver to
Hektor's dead body, and it apes a burial ceremony. In one sense, then, this non-
human realm is represented metaphorically as Achilleus' own death. Through
this metaphor, Homer represents the enormity of the spiritual change that Achilleus
has undergone. The armor clearly represents at once both divine protection and

death—it is both armor and tomb. As long as we are alive, Homer seems to imply, we are never safe from death; only in death can mere human beings—still represented by the male—find any parcel of immortality, or of peace.

The description of the shield that Hephaistos makes for Achilleus to replace the armor (much edited, unfortunately, here) is among the most stirring images to be found in Western literature. On it, a city ruled by justice and unity is opposed to one wracked by war and destruction. The happiness of the first city is marked by the occupation of its people in marriages, festivals, and the fair arbitration of their conflicts. The unity of the city is once again, and perhaps here most clearly, associated with the unity of the household—marriage—and this unity of man and woman in the happy household is also associated with justice as an alternative to war. Similarly, the war-torn city tears its households apart. Note again, that youth and old age, both "ends" of the man's life, stand with the women, associating the limits of human life, and the duality of these limits, with femininity. Ultimately, Achilleus' actions—defiling Hektor's body—are impious; he has not only exceeded the limits of human strength and anger, he has also abandoned the religious rituals proper to the human state. It is important to note in this regard that Hektor, unlike Achilleus, is a married man. As with the imagery on Hephaistos' shield, marriage here represents all the rituals that are to be observed in the happy, just city. Thus, Hektor represents piety, hence his dying wish that his body receive the proper burial. In his married state is the unity, propriety, and piety of the whole city, a state in which masculinity and femininity, and whatever they represent, are combined. The just city is the harmoniously unified city, and the death of Hektor represents the destruction of this city that was the Trojan war itself. Thus, his wife Andromache weeps for both a broken city and a broken home; the ritual of grief, like the keeping of the home and hearth, falls to the women.

> the wife of Hektor had not yet
> heard: for no sure messenger had come to her and told her
> how her husband had held his ground there outside the gates;
> but she was weaving a web in the inner room of the high house,
> a red folding robe, and inworking elaborate figures.
> She called out through the house to her lovely-haired handmaidens
> to set a great cauldron over the fire, so that there would be
> hot water for Hektor's bath as he came back out of the fighting;
> poor innocent, nor knew how, far from waters for bathing,
> Pallas Athene had cut him down at the hands of Achilleus.

> ⌒ ⌒ ⌒

> The darkness of night misted over the eyes of Andromache.
> She fell backward, and gasped the life breath from her, and far off
> threw from her head the shining gear that ordered her headdress,
> the diadem and the cap, and the holding-band woven together,
> and the circlet, which Aphrodite the golden once had given her
> on that day when Hektor of the shining helmet led her forth

from the house of Eëtion, and gave numberless gifts to win her.
And about her stood thronging her husband's sisters and the wives of his
        brothers
and these, in her despair for death, held her up among them.
But she, when she breathed again and the life was gathered back into her,
lifted her voice among the women of Troy in mourning:
'Hektor, I grieve for you. You and I were born to a single
destiny, you in Troy in the house of Priam, and I
in Thebe, underneath the timbered mountain of Plakos
in the house of Eëtion.

ᘓ ᘓ ᘓ

But now, beside the curving ships, far away from your parents,
the writhing worms will feed, when the dogs have had enough of you,
on your naked corpse, though in your house there is clothing laid up
that is fine-textured and pleasant, wrought by the hands of women.
But all of these I will burn up in the fire's blazing,
no use to you, since you will never be laid away in them;
but in your honour, from the men of Troy and the Trojan women.'
        So she spoke, in tears; and the women joined in her mourning.

At the end of the *Iliad,* Achilleus ultimately recognizes his impiety through sympathy for the noble Priam, king of Troy, and returns Hektor's body. Thus, Achilleus' story is a microcosm of the story of the birth of Greek civilization out of the ravages of the Trojan war.

from **BOOK XXIV**

[PRIAM TO ACHILLEUS:] 'Honor then the gods, Achilleus, and take pity upon me
remembering your father, yet I am still more pitiful;
I have gone through what no other mortal on earth has gone through;
I put my lips to the hands of the man who has killed my children.'
        So he spoke, and stirred in the other a passion of grieving
for his own father. He took the old man's hand and pushed him
gently away, and the two remembered, as Priam sat huddled
at the feet of Achilleus and wept close for manslaughtering Hektor
and Achilleus wept now for his own father, now again
for Patroklos. The sound of their mourning moved in the house. Then
when great Achilleus had taken full satisfaction in sorrow
and the passion for it had gone from his mind and body, thereafter
he rose from his chair, and took the old man by the hand, and set him
on his feet again, in pity for the grey head and the grey beard,
and spoke to him and addressed him in winged words: 'Ah, unlucky,
surely you have had much evil to endure in your spirit.
How could you dare to come alone to the ships of the Achaians

and before my eyes, when I am one who have killed in such numbers
such brave sons of yours? The heart in you is iron. Come, then,
and sit down upon this chair, and you and I will even let
our sorrows lie still in the heart for all our grieving. There is not
any advantage to be won from grim lamentation.
Such is the way the gods spun life for unfortunate mortals,
that we live in unhappiness, but the gods themselves have no sorrows.

The Achaean victory parallels Achilleus' triumph and shame regarding Hektor; the destruction of Troy and the defilement of Hektor's body are represented by Homer as the ultimate impieties that give birth to the Greek civilization of the Homeric age. Civilization, Homer implies, provides the means through which human beings, constantly threatened by their own impiety and savagery, may achieve the best of which their species is capable. Civilization, therefore, is like the reconciliation of man and wife after a separation (such as is depicted in the *Odyssey,* excerpted next) or like the reconciliation of enemies after a war. Through war, the "barbarian" Troy is defeated, but also acknowledged, lastingly incorporated into the history of Greek civilization. Similarly, after rage and impiety, the individual man is represented by Homer as capable of achieving a peaceful maturity which is nonetheless mindful of its capacity for violence.

THE *ODYSSEY*

The *Odyssey,* despite its Homeric authorship and epic form, is a very different sort of poem from the *Iliad.* In it, the "resourceful" Odysseus (who appeared in the *Iliad* as a secondary character) encounters and overcomes many great difficulties returning home to Ithaka after the Trojan war. Once home, Odysseus defeats the many rivals who have been courting his wife, Penelope, and restores the great household and city, which had been rent apart by the war. The poem is essentially an adventure story, far more fanciful and simple than the *Iliad.* This is appropriate to its ultimately happy theme: it is a story above all of victory, reconciliation, balance—all represented by the reunion of husband and wife. Thus, the *Odyssey,* in a sense, completes the story told on the shield Hephaestos made for Achilleus in the *Iliad:* it is a return to the happy city from the city torn apart by war.

As a story whose central themes are those of home and marriage, the *Odyssey* is filled with reflections on the nature of gender. We cannot hope to discuss everything relevant to the issue in a few pages, but we can point the way to the more thorough reading of the treatment of gender in the *Odyssey* to which the reader may turn his or her energies later. Of primary importance to this project is the simple fact that Odysseus—a kind of paradigmatic or heroic husband—is away from home for many years, while Penelope—the ideal or paradigmatic wife—waits at home for him the whole time. Thus, the metaphorical associations of women with the city-state and the home, with civility and tradition, and with the end or goal of men's actions, which merely formed a background of femininity in the *Iliad,* is brought to the fore in the *Odyssey.*

Odysseus, however, unlike Achilleus, has long since cast his lot with Penelope, with the city, and with the traditions of a great household, and thus is in an important sense no longer a mere individual but a member of a city-state and family. Odysseus is able to still his passion and agency for the sake of a higher goal, where the raging Achilleus, during most of the *Iliad,* is not. Thus, while the two books paint a similar picture of femininity, the *Odyssey* gives the feminine realm—home and city—some pride of place, where the *Iliad* places it in the background of the masculine storyline. In the *Odyssey,* men achieve their best, not individually but as a society; not as warriors, but as husbands, fathers, and sons. Truly, marriage and the city-state seem to represent for the early Greeks and for Homer what is most divine in us. Thus, while the *Iliad* was, literally, "about Achilleus' rage," the *Odyssey* is about Odysseus himself, most divine among men, beginning: "Tell me, Muse, of the man of many ways, who was driven/ far journeys, after he had sacked Troy's sacred citadel. . . . struggling for his own life and the homecoming of his companions."

PENELOPE AND THE SUITORS

The story opens shortly before the gods' chosen time for Odysseus' return home. He has been away from Ithaka, his city, for many, many years, and the situation there has become almost unmanageable. Penelope and Telemachos, Odysseus' wife and son, have been besieged, and Odysseus' house overrun, by a band of men wanting to marry Penelope and take possession of Odysseus' great household. These "haughty suitors" have taken advantage of Odysseus' absence and of the strongly compelling moral obligations incumbent upon Greek hosts to entertain their guests, threatening the stability of the household itself. Telemachos, who is still young and has grown up without his father, has resisted taking any action against the suitors, and Penelope, resolute in her commitment to Odysseus, has tried to stall them as best she can but cannot hold out much longer. Antinoös, one of the suitors, complains to Telemachos:

FROM **BOOK II**

'High-spoken intemperate Telemachos, what accusations
you have made to our shame, trying to turn opinion against us!
And yet you have no cause to blame the Achaian suitors,
but it is your own dear mother, and she is greatly resourceful.
And now it is the third year, and will be the fourth year presently,
since she has been denying the desires of the Achaians.
For she holds out hope to all, and makes promises to each man,
sending us messages, but her mind has other intentions.
And here is another strategem of her heart's devising.
She set up a great loom in her palace, and set to weaving
a web of threads long and fine. Then she said to us:
"Young men, my suitors now that the great Odysseus has perished,

wait, though you are eager to marry me, until I finish
this web, so that my weaving will not be useless and wasted.
This is a shroud for the hero Laertes, for when the destructive
death which lays men low shall take him, lest any
Achaian woman in this neighborhood hold it against me
that a man of many conquests lies with no sheet to wind him."
So she spoke, and the proud heart in us was persuaded.
Thereafter in the daytime she would weave at her great loom,
but in the night she would have torches set by, and undo it.
So for three years she was secret in her design, convincing
the Achaians, but when the fourth year came with the seasons returning,
one of her women, who knew the whole of the story, told us,
and we found her in the act of undoing her glorious weaving.
So, against her will and by force, she had to finish it.
Now the suitors answer you thus, so that you yourself
may know it in your mind, and all the Achaians may know it:
send your mother back, and instruct her to be married
to any man her father desires and who pleases her also.
But if she continues to torment the sons of the Achaians,
since she is so dowered with the wisdom bestowed by Athene,
to be expert in beautiful work, to have good character
and cleverness, such as we are not told of, even of the ancient
queens, the fair-tressed Achaian women of times before us,
Tyro and Alkmene and Mykene, wearer of garlands;
for none of these knew thoughts so wise as those Penelope
knew; yet in this single matter she did not think rightly;
so long, I say, will your livelihood and possessions be eaten
away, as long as she keeps this purpose, one which the very
gods, I think, put into her heart. She is winning a great name
for herself, but for you she is causing much loss of substance.
We will not go back to our own estates, nor will we go elsewhere
until she marries whichever Achaian man she fancies.'

Penelope, like Helen, is a weaver. Again the "web" is used by Homer as a feminine image. Penelope, again like Helen, is no stranger to fretting; she has been sitting for long hours, threading together formerly disparate strands of the story at
hand. Penelope's weaving is similar to Helen's in all these respects. Penelope, however, has cleverly connived never to finish her robe. Where Helen accepted and
came to love her new husband and city, Penelope will not desert Odysseus, and thus
she will not finish her work. Penelope tells the suitors that the robe was to be a
shroud for her father-in-law, Laertes, of whose household she is now the primary
representative. By not completing the shroud, Penelope has, in a sense, tied the
honor of her parents' generation to the maintenance of her marriage. Now that
the suitors have found out her scheme, however, she has to finish the shroud; and
the destruction of her home, family, and city seems immanent.

ODYSSEUS' ADVENTURES: CIRCE, THE SIRENS, SKYLLA AND CHARYBDIS

These events in Ithaka take place just as Odysseus, for his part, is about to begin the last leg of his journey home. He has been saved from a shipwreck and detained on an island by the nymph, Kalypso, who desires Odysseus for her husband. The gods send word, however, of the threat posed to his wife and son by the suitors, and Odysseus leaves Kalypso's island for home.

FROM **BOOK V**

'Son of Laertes and seed of Zeus, resourceful Odysseus,
are you still all so eager to go on back to your own house
and the land of your fathers? I wish you well, however you do it,
but if you only knew in your own heart how many hardships
you were fated to undergo before getting back to your country,
you would stay here with me and be the lord of this household
and be an immortal, for all your longing once more to look on
that wife for whom you are pining all your days here. And yet
I think that I can claim that I am not her inferior
either in build or stature, since it is not likely that mortal
women can challenge the goddesses for build and beauty.'
Then resourceful Odysseus spoke in turn and answered her:
'Goddess and queen, do not be angry with me. I myself know
that all you say is true and that circumspect Penelope
can never match the impression you make for beauty and stature.
She is mortal after all, and you are immortal and ageless.
But even so, what I want and all my days I pine for
is to go back to my house and see my day of homecoming.
And if some god batters me far out on the wine-blue water,
I will endure it, keeping a stubborn spirit inside me,
for already I have suffered much and done much hard work
on the waves and in the fighting. So let this adventure follow.'

In Odysseus' response to Kalypso, we see perhaps the clearest expression of Odysseus' virtue—he actually chooses his own human life over the divine one offered by Kalypso. Odysseus' decision to return home—i.e., his faithfulness to Penelope—provides the setting for all the adventures which comprise the story of Odysseus, and which are told in the manner of a "flashback" to his hosts, the Phaiakians, on his return from Kalypso's island. Everything he did, we may infer, he did in order to get home to his wife, family, and city.

After losing all the other ships in his fleet, Odysseus and a small complement of men sail on for home.

FROM **BOOK X**

'From there we sailed on further along, glad to have escaped death,
but grieving still at heart for the loss of our dear companions.

We came to Aiaia, which is an island. There lived Circe
of the lovely hair, the dread goddess who talks with mortals.

⌐ ⌐ ⌐

In the forest glen they came on the house of Circe. It was
in an open place, and put together from stones; well polished,
and all about it there were lions, and wolves of the mountains,
whom the goddess had given evil drugs and enchanted,
and these made no attack on the men, but came up thronging
about them, waving their long tails and fawning, in the way
that dogs go fawning about their master, when he comes home
from dining out, for he always brings back something to please them;
so these wolves with great strong claws and lions came fawning
on my men, but they were afraid when they saw the terrible big beasts.
They stood there in the forecourt of the goddess with the glorious
hair, and heard Circe inside singing in a sweet voice
as she went up and down a great design on a loom, immortal
such as goddesses have, delicate and lovely and glorious
their work. Now Polites leader of men, who was
the best and dearest to me of my friends, began the discussion:
"Friends, someone inside going up and down a great piece
of weaving is singing sweetly, and the whole place murmurs to the echo
of it, whether she is woman or goddess. Come let us call her."
    'So he spoke to them, and the rest gave voice, and called her,
and at once she opened the shining doors, and came out, and invited
them in, and all in their innocence entered only
Eurylochos waited outside, for he suspected treachery.
She brought them inside and seated them on chairs and benches,
and mixed them a potion with barley and cheese and pale honey
added to Pramneian wine, but put into the mixture
malignant drugs, to make them forgetful of their own country.
When she had given them this and they had drunk it down, next thing
she struck them with her wand and drove them into her pig pens
and they took on the look of pigs, with the heads and voices
and bristles of pigs, but the minds within them stayed as they had been
before. So crying they went in, and before them Circe
threw down acorns for them to eat, and ilex and cornel
buds, such food as pigs who sleep on the gound always feed on.

⌐ ⌐ ⌐

But as I went up through the lonely glens, and was coming
near to the great house of Circe, skilled in medicines,
there as I came up to the house, Hermes, of the golden
staff, met me on my way, in the likeness of a young man
with beard new grown, which is the most graceful time of young manhood.
He took me by the hand and spoke to me and named me saying:

☞ ☞ ☞

'I will find you a way out of your troubles, and save you.
Here, this is a good medicine, take it, and go into Circe's
house; it will give you power against the day of trouble.
And I will tell you all the malevolent guiles of Circe.
She will make you a potion, and put drugs in the food, but she will not
even so be able to enchant you, for this good medicine
which I give you now will prevent her. I will tell you the details
of what to do. As soon as Circe with her long wand strikes you,
then drawing from beside your thigh your sharp sword, rush
forward against Circe, as if you were raging to kill her,
and she will be afraid, and invite you to go to bed with her.
Do not then resist and refuse the bed of the goddess,
for she will set free your companions, and care for you also;
but bid her swear the great oath of the blessed gods, that she
has no other evil hurt that she is devising against you,
so she will not make you weak and unmanned, once you are naked.'

☞ ☞ ☞

I stood outside at the doors of the goddess with the glorious
hair, and standing I shouted aloud; and the goddess heard me,
and at once she opened the shining doors and came out and invited
me in; and I, deeply troubled in my heart, went in with her.
She made me sit down in a chair that was wrought elaborately
and splendid with silver nails, and under my feet was a footstool.
She made a potion for me to drink and gave it in a golden
cup, and with evil thoughts in her heart added the drug to it.
Then when she had given it and I drank it off, without being
enchanted, she struck me with her wand and spoke and named me:
"Go to your sty now and lie down with your other friends there."
'So she spoke, but I, drawing from beside my thigh the sharp sword,
rushed forward against Circe as if I were raging to kill her,
but she screamed aloud and ran under my guard, and clasping both knees
in loud lamentation spoke to me and addressed me in winged words:
"What man are you and whence? Where are your city and parents?
The wonder is on me that you drank my drugs and have not been
enchanted, for no other man beside could have stood up
under my drugs, once he drank and they passed the barrier
of his teeth. There is a mind in you no magic will work on.
You are then resourceful Odysseus. Argeiphontes
of the golden staff was forever telling me you would come
to me, on your way back from Troy with your fast black ship.
Come then, put away your sword in its sheath, and let us
two go up into my bed so that, lying together
in the bed of love, we may then have faith and trust in each other."

'So she spoke, and I answered her again and said to her:
"Circe, how can you ask me to be gentle with you, when it
is you who turned my companions into pigs in your palace?
And now you have me here myself, you treacherously
ask me to go into your chamber, and go to bed with you,
so that when I am naked you can make me a weakling, unmanned.
I would not be willing to go to bed with you unless
you can bring yourself, O goddess, to swear me a great oath
that there is no other evil hurt you devise against me."
    'So I spoke, and she at once swore me the oath, as I asked her,
But after she had sworn me the oath, and made an end of it,
I mounted the surpassingly beautiful bed of Circe.

⤢ ⤢ ⤢

'When Circe noticed how I sat there without ever putting
my hands out to the food, and with the strong sorrow upon me,
she came close, and stood beside me and addressed me in winged words:
"Why Odysseus, do you sit so, like a man who has lost his
voice, eating your heart out, but touch neither food nor drink, Is it
that you suspect me of more treachery? But you have nothing
to fear, since I have already sworn my strong oath to you."
    'So she spoke, but I answered her again and said to her:
"Oh, Circe, how could any man right in his mind ever
endure to taste of the food and drink that are set before him,
until with his eyes he saw his companions set free? So then,
if you are sincerely telling me to eat and drink, set them
free, so my eyes can again behold my eager companions."
    'So I spoke, and Circe walked on out through the palace,
holding her wand in her hand, and opened the doors of the pigsty,
and drove them out. They looked like nine-year-old porkers. They stood
ranged and facing her, and she, making her way through their
ranks, anointed each of them with some other medicine,
and the bristles, grown upon them by the evil medicine Circe
had bestowed upon them before, now fell away from them,
and they turned back once more into men, younger than they had been
and taller for the eye to behold and handsomer by far.

⤢ ⤢ ⤢

There for all our days until a year was completed
we sat there feasting on unlimited meat and sweet wine.
But when it was the end of a year, and the months wasted
away, and the seasons changed, and the long days were accomplished,
then my eager companions called me aside and said to me:
"What ails you now? It is time to think about our own country,
if truly it is ordained that you shall survive and come back
to your strong-founded house and to the land of your fathers."

'So they spoke, and the proud heart in me was persuaded.
So for the whole length of the day until the sun's setting
we sat there feasting on unlimited meat and sweet wine.
But when the sun went down and the sacred darkness came over,
they lay down to sleep all about the shadowy chambers,
but I, mounting the surpassingly beautiful bed of Circe,
clasped her by the knees and entreated her, and the goddess
listened to me, and I spoke to her and addressed her in winged words:
"O Circe, accomplish now the promise you gave, that you
would see me on my way home. The spirit within me is urgent
now, as also in the rest of my friends, who are wasting
my heart away, lamenting around me, when you are elsewhere."
    'So I spoke, and she, shining among goddesses, answered:
"Son of Laertes and seed of Zeus, resourceful Odysseus,
you shall no longer stay in my house when none of you wish to;
but first there is another journey you must accomplish
and reach the house of Hades and of revered Persephone,
there to consult with the soul of Teiresias the Theban
the blind prophet, whose senses stay unshaken within him,
to whom alone Persephone has granted intelligence
even after death, but the rest of them are flittering shadows."

Yet I did not lead away my companions without some
loss. There was one, Elpenor, the youngest man, not terribly
powerful in fighting nor sound in his thoughts. This man,
apart from the rest of his friends, in search of cool air, had lain
down drunkenly to sleep on the roof of Circe's palace,
and when his companions stirred to go he, hearing their tumult
and noise of talking, started suddenly up, and never thought,
when he went down, to go by way of the long ladder,
but blundered staight off the edge of the roof, so that his neck bone
was broken out of its sockets, and his soul went down to Hades.

Circe entrances and enslaves the men (turning them into pigs), but when she
feels she has met her match (when Odysseus proves impervious to her magic), she
becomes a trustworthy servant and friend. Circe is a temptress, powerful and mysterious, until Odysseus "masters" her. After that point, Circe serves Odysseus' ends,
just as the powerful Metis, in the passage of the *Theogony* above, serves Zeus' ends
after Zeus eats her. Interestingly, the primary purpose towards which Odysseus puts
Circe's powers is his reunion with his real, human wife Penelope. Also of note,
then, is that Circe, like Penelope, is weaving when the men arrive.

Odysseus proceeds from Circe's island to the underworld, where Circe has instructed him to go before returning home. There, Elpinor, the crewman who had died
leaving Circe, pleads with Odysseus to return to Circe's island and bury his body.

Odysseus keeps his promise to do so, showing not only due respect for the gods and loyalty to his crew, but also good judgment. Odysseus would rather lengthen his trip by doubling back to Circe than risk not completing it, demonstrating again his ability to defer the satisfaction of his desires for the sake of a higher good.

FROM **BOOK XII**

Then the queenly Circe spoke in words and addressed me:
"So all that has been duly done. Listen now, I will tell you
all, but the very god himself will make you remember.
You will come first of all to the Sirens, who are enchanters
of all mankind and whoever comes their way and that man
who unsuspecting approaches them, and listens to the Sirens
singing, has no prospect of coming home and delighting
his wife and little children as they stand about him in greeting,
but the Sirens by the melody of their singing enchant him.
They sit in their meadow, but the beach before it is piled with boneheaps
of men now rotted away, and the skins shrivel upon them.
You must drive straight on past, but melt down sweet wax of honey
and with it stop your companions' ears, so none can listen;
the rest, that is, but if you yourself are wanting to hear them,
then have them tie you hand and foot on the fast ship, standing
upright against the mast with the ropes' ends lashed around it,
so that you can have joy in hearing the song of the Sirens;
but if you supplicate your men and implore them to set you
free, then they must tie you fast with even more lashings.
    "Then, for the time when your companions have driven you past them,
for that time I will no longer tell you in detail which way
of the two your course must lie, but you yourself must consider
this in your own mind. I will tell you the two ways of it.

Halfway up the cliff there is a cave, misty-looking
and turned toward Erebos and the dark, the very direction
from which, O shining Odysseus, you and your men will be steering
your hollow ship; and from the hollow ship no vigorous
young man with a bow could shoot to the hole in the cliffside.
In that cavern Skylla lives, whose howling is terror.
Her voice indeed is only as loud as a new-born puppy
could make, but she herself is an evil monster. No one,
not even a god encountering her, could be glad at that sight.
She has twelve feet, and all of them wave in the air. She has six
necks upon her, grown to great length, and upon each neck
there is a horrible head, with teeth in it, set in three rows

close together and stiff, full of black death. Her body
from the waist down is holed up inside the hollow cavern,
but she holds her heads poked out and away from the terrible hollow,
and there she fishes, peering all over the cliffside, looking
for dolphins or dogfish to catch or anything bigger,
some sea monster, of whom Amphitrite keeps so many;
never can sailors boast aloud that their ship has passed her
without any loss of men, for with each of her heads she snatches
one man away and carries him off from the dark-prowed vessel.
    "The other cliff is lower; you will see it, Odysseus,
for they lie close together, you could even cast with an arrow
across. There is a great fig tree grows there, dense with foliage,
and under this shining Charybdis sucks down the black water.
For three time a day she flows it up and three time she sucks it
terribly down; may you not be there when she sucks down water,
for not even the Earthshaker could rescue you out of that evil.
But sailing your ship swiftly drive her past and avoid her,
and make for Skylla's rock instead, since it is far better
to mourn six friends lost out of your ship than the whole company."
    'So she spoke, but I in turn said to her in answer:
"Come then, goddess, answer me truthfully this: is there
some way for me to escape away from deadly Charybdis,
but yet fight the other one off, when she attacks my companions?"
    'So I spoke, and she, shining among goddesses, answered:
"Hardy man, your mind is full forever of fighting
and battle work. Will you not give way even to the immortals?
She is no mortal thing but a mischief immortal, dangerous
difficult and bloodthirsty, and there is no fighting against her,
not any force of defense. It is best to run away from her.

                                                      ☞   ☞   ☞

    'So she spoke, and Dawn of the golden throne came on us.
She, shining among goddesses, went away, up the island.
Then, going back on board my ship, I told my companions
also to go aboard, and to cast off the stern cables,

                                                      ☞   ☞   ☞

    'So as I was telling all the details to my companions,
meanwhile the well-made ship was coming rapidly closer
to the Sirens' isle, for the harmless wind was driving her onward;
but immediately then the breeze dropped, and a windless
calm fell there, and some divinity stilled the tossing
waters. My companions stood up, and took the sails down,
and stowed them away in the hollow hull, and took their places
for rowing, and with their planed oarblades whitened the water.

Then I, taking a great wheel of wax, with the sharp bronze
cut a little piece off, and rubbed it together in my heavy
hands, and soon the way grew softer, under the powerful
stress of the sun, and the heat and light of Hyperion's lordling.
One after another, I stopped the ears of all my companions,
and they then bound me hand and foot in the fast ship, standing
upright against the mast with the ropes' ends lashed around it,
and sitting then to row they dashed their oars in the gray sea.
But when we were as far from the land as a voice shouting
carries, lightly plying, the swift ship as it drew nearer
was seen by the Sirens, and they directed their sweet song toward us:
"Come this way, honored Odysseus, great glory of the Achaians,
and stay your ship, so that you can listen here to our singing;
for no one else has ever sailed past this place in his black ship
until he has listened to the honey-sweet voice that issues
from our lips; then goes on, well pleased, knowing more than ever
he did; for we know everything that the Argives and Trojans
did and suffered in wide Troy through the gods' despite.
Over all the generous earth we know everything that happens.
    'So they sang, in sweet utterance, and the heart within me
desired to listen, and I signaled my companions to set me
free, nodding with my brows, but they leaned on and rowed hard,
and Perimedes and Eurylochos, rising up, staightway
fastened me with even more lashings and squeezed me tighter.
But when they had rowed on past the Sirens, and we could no longer
hear their voices and lost the sound of their singing, presently
my eager companions took away from their ears the beeswax
with which I had stopped them. Then they set me free from my lashings.

    'So we sailed up the narrow strait lamenting. On one side
was Skylla and on the other side was shining Charybdis,
who made her terrible ebb and flow of the sea's water.
When she vomited it up, like a caldron over a strong fire,
the whole sea would boil up in turbulance, and the foam flying
spattered the pinnacles of the rocks in either direction;
but when in turn again she sucked down the sea's salt water,
the turbulence showed all the inner sea, and the rock around it
groaned terribly, and the ground showed at the sea's bottom,
black with sand; and green fear seized upon my companions.
We in fear of destruction kept our eyes on Charybdis;
but meanwhile Skylla out of the hollow vessel snatched six
of my companions, the best of them for strength and hands' work
and when I turned to look at the ship, with my other companions,
I saw their feet and hands from below, already lifted

high above me, and they cried out to me and called me
by name, the last time they ever did it, in heart's sorrow.
And as a fisherman with a very long rod, on a jutting
rock, will cast his treacherous bait for the little fishes,
and sinks the horn of a field-ranging ox into the water,
then hauls them up and throws them on the dry land, gasping
and stuggling, so they gasped and struggled as they were hoisted
up the cliff. Right in her doorway she ate them up. They were screaming
and reaching out their hands to me in this horrid encounter.
That was the most pitiful scene that these eyes have looked on
in my sufferings as I explored the routes over the water.

In this string of adventures is a phenomenally rich source of Western paradigms of femininity and its relations to masculinity. Indeed, the fact that all of the harrowing obstacles Odysseus overcomes during this, the most action-packed section of the poem, are female or feminine, is by itself a stunning comment on Greek notions of femininity. Overall, we get a sense of the hero here—perhaps the clearest such sense in any of these early Greek texts—struggling for his humanity amidst a myriad of powerful feminine forces.

After returning to Circe's island and burying Elpinor, Odysseus faces two more female dangers: the Sirens, and Skylla and Charybdis. The qualities of feminine evil, as Homer understands them, are vividly drawn in these two sets of monsters. The Sirens are temptresses, whose song no man who hears can resist. Like the webs woven by other female characters, the Sirens' song is morally ambiguous. They keep mortal men from returning home to their wives and families, but they do not kill or torture these men—on the contrary, their song is irresistibly pleasant. The Sirens claim that they know everything that happens on earth—implying that knowledge is precisely what makes their song so delightful. Certainly their knowledge allies them with other prophetic women depicted in the selections above: it would seem that Homer includes in the feminine a knowledge or vision beyond the capacities of men. Odysseus resists the Sirens, but finagles, nonetheless, to hear their knowing song. Thus, Odysseus once again outwits a feminine power greater than himself and puts it to work for his own human ends.

After the Sirens, Odysseus faces Skylla and Charybdis, a pair of evils through which Odysseus must go if he is to return home. These are feminine powers that Odysseus cannot turn to human ends; he will have to avoid them because he will not be able to master them. These wholly inhuman, wholly foreign, female figures are imaged first and foremost as open mouths; like that of the sirens, Skylla and Charybdis' power is somehow oral. While Odysseus is unable to turn these feminine forces to his advantage as he has others, he is nonetheless able to avoid them, steering safely through this pair of yawning mouths; but not without the loss of six crewmen. Odysseus seems here to be depicted as having the ability to harness both good and evil feminine forces for the sake of a stable city and household, implying that lesser men, cowards and villains, would be overwhelmed by these forces and let their cities crumble, presumably into a feminine abyss.

ODYSSEUS AND PENELOPE

Meanwhile, things have come to a head at home. Telemachos' search has brought
him back to Ithaka, where Penelope is barely able any longer to keep the suitors at
bay. Odysseus returns to the city and, in order to gain intelligence of the situation,
goes "undercover," disguised as an old beggar. He reveals his identity only to
Telemachos, with whom he devises a plan against the suitors. Penelope, inspired by
Athene, has challenged the suitors to an archery contest for her hand. Odysseus, in
the guise of the old beggar, puts up at the house and asks to participate in the
archery contest. Of course Odysseus wins the contest, and when he does, the suitors
revolt. At this point, Penelope is sent away, and Odysseus reveals his identity to the
suitors. A full-scale battle ensues, Odysseus and Telemachos are supremely victorious, and Odysseus finally reclaims his household. The few closing scenes (from
book XXIII) excerpted below depict Odysseus' ultimate reunion with Penelope.

FROM **BOOK XXIII**

She spoke and came down from the chamber, her heart pondering
much, whether to keep away and question her dear husband
or to go up to him and kiss his head, taking his hands.
But then, when she came in and stepped over the stone threshold,
she sat across from him in the firelight, facing Odysseus,
by the opposite wall, while he was seated by the tall pillar,
looking downward, and waiting to find out if his majestic
wife would have anything to say to him, now that she saw him.
She sat a long time in silence, and her heart was wondering.
Sometimes she would look at him, with her eyes full upon him,
and again would fail to know him in the foul clothing he wore.
Telemachos spoke to her and called her by name and scolded her:
'My mother, my harsh mother with the hard heart inside you,
why do you withdraw so from my father, and do not
sit beside him and ask him questions and find out about him?
No other woman, with spirit as stubborn as yours, would keep back
as you are doing from her husband who, after much suffering,
came at last in the twentieth year back to his own country.
But always you have a heart that is harder than stone within you.
     Circumspect Penelope said to him in answer:
'My child, the spirit that is in me is full of wonderment,
and I cannot find anything to say to him, nor question him,
nor look him straight in the face. But if he is truly Odysseus,
and he has come home, then we shall find other ways, and better,
to recognize each other, for we have signs that we know of
between the two of us only, but they are secret from others.
     So she spoke, and much enduring noble Odysseus
smiled, and presently spoke in winged words to Telemachos:

'Telemachos, leave your mother to examine me in the palace
as she will, and presently she will understand better;
but now that I am dirty and wear foul clothing upon me,
she dislikes me for that, and says I am not her husband.
But let us make our plans how all will come out best for us.

⌐ ⌐ ⌐

Now the housekeeper Eurynome bathed great-hearted
Odysseus in his own house, and anointed him with olive oil,
and threw a beautiful mantle and a tunic about him;
and over his head Athene suffused great beauty, to make him
taller to behold and thicker, and on his head she arranged
the curling locks that hung down like hyacinthine petals.
And as when a master craftsman overlay gold on silver,
and he is one who was taught by Hephaistos and Pallas Athene
in art complete, and grace is on every work he finishes;
so Athene gilded with grace his head and his shoulders.
Then, looking like an immortal, he strode forth from the bath,
and came back then and sat on the chair from which he had risen,
opposite his wife and now he spoke to her, saying:
'You are so strange. The gods, who have their homes on Olympos,
have made your heart more stubborn than for the rest of womankind.
No other woman, with spirit as stubborn as yours, would keep back
as you are doing from her husband who, after much suffering,
came at last in the twentieth year back to his own country.
Come then, nurse, make me up a bed, so that I can use it
here; for this woman has a heart of iron within her.
    Circumspect Penelope said to him in answer:
'You are so strange, I am not being proud, nor indifferent,
nor puzzled beyond need, but I know very well what you looked like
when you went in the ship with the sweeping oars, from Ithaka.
Come then, Eurykleia, and make up a firm bed for him
outside the well-fashioned chamber: that very bed that he himself
built. Put the firm bed here outside for him, and cover it
over with fleeces and blankets, and with shining coverlets.'
    So she spoke to her husband, trying him out, but Odysseus
spoke in anger to his virtuous-minded lady:
'What you have said, dear lady, has hurt my heart deeply. What man
has put my bed in another place? But it would be difficult
for even a very expert one, unless a god, coming
to help in person, were easily to change its position.
But there is no mortal man alive, no strong man, who lightly
could move the weight elsewhere. There is one particular feature
in the bed's construction. I myself, no other man, made it.
There was the bole of an olive tree with long leaves growing
strongly in the courtyard, and it was thick, like a column.

I laid down my chamber around this, and built it, until I
finished it, with close-set stones, and roofed it well over,
and added the compacted doors, fitting closely together.
Then I cut away the foliage of the long-leaved olive,
and trimmed the trunk from the roots up, planing it with a brazen
adze, well and expertly, and trued it straight to a chalkline,
making a bed post of it, and bored all holes with an auger.
I began with this and built my bed, until it was finished,
and decorated it with gold and silver and ivory.
Then I lashed it with thongs of oxhide, dyed bright with purple.
There is its character, as I tell you; but I do not know now,
dear lady, whether my bed is still in place, or if some man
has cut underneath the stump of the olive, and moved it elsewhere.'
    So he spoke, and her knees and the heart within her went slack
as she recognized the clear proofs that Odysseus had given,
but then she burst into tears and ran straight to him, throwing
her arms around the neck of Odysseus, and kissed his head, saying:
'Do not be angry with me, Odysseus, since, beyond other men,
you have the most understanding. The gods granted us misery,
in jealousy over the thought that we two, always together,
should enjoy our youth, and then come to the threshold of old age.
Then do not now be angry with me nor blame me, because
I did not greet you, as I do now, at first when I saw you.
For always the spirit deep in my very heart was fearful
that some one of mortal men would come my way and deceive me
with words. For there are many who scheme for wicked advantage.
For neither would the daughter born to Zeus, Helen of Argos,
have lain in love with an outlander from another country,
if she had known that the warlike sons of the Achaians would bring her
home again to the beloved land of her fathers.
It was a god who stirred her to do the shameful thing she
did, and never before had she had in her heart this terrible
wildness, out of which came suffering to us also.
But now, since you have given me accurate proof describing
our bed, which no other mortal man beside has ever seen,
but only you and I, and there is one serving woman,
Aktor's daughter, whom my father gave me when I came here,
who used to guard the doors for us in our well-built chamber;
so you persuade my heart, though it has been very stubborn.'
    She spoke, and still more roused in him the passion for weeping.
He wept as he held his lovely wife, whose thoughts were virtuous.
And as when the land appears welcome to men who are swimming,
after Poseidon has smashed their strong-built ship on the open
water, pounding it with the weight of wind and the heavy
seas, and only a few escape the gray water landward
by swimming, with a thick scurf of salt coated upon them,

and gladly set foot on the shore, escaping the evil;
so welcome was her husband to her as she looked upon him,
and she could not let him go from the embrace of her white arms.
Now Dawn of the rosy fingers would have dawned on their weeping,
had not the gray-eyed goddess Athene planned it otherwise.
She held the long night back at the outward edge, she detained
Dawn of the golden throne by the Ocean, and would not let her
harness her fast-footed horses who bring the daylight to people:
Lampos and Phaethon, the Dawn's horses, who carry her.
Then resourceful Odysseus spoke to his wife, saying:
'Dear wife, we have not yet come to the limit of all our
trials. There is unmeasured labor left for the future,
both difficult and great, and all of it I must accomplish.
So the soul of Teiresias prophesied to me, on that day
when I went down inside the house of Hades, seeking
to learn about homecoming, for myself and for my companions.
But come, my wife, let us go to bed, so that at long last
we can enjoy the sweetness of slumber, sleeping together.'

3. SAPPHO
(Greek, Late Seventh–
Early Sixth Century B.C.E.)

Sappho was born in Lesbos, a Greek island in the Aegean Sea, in about 630 B.C.E. She was likely born into an influential family and married to a wealthy merchant, from which privileged position she was able to write quite prolifically. Her stunning lyric poetry was provocative and stylistically innovative. She is mentioned by several later Greek writers, including Plato and Aristotle. Plato depicts Socrates calling her "the fair Sappho,"[4] and was reputed to have himself called her "the tenth muse." Certainly hers is, among the ancient Greek lyricists, the most vivid and compelling philosophical exploration of the complex subjective themes of self, the creative inspiration of the poet, and the vicissitudes of love.

Sappho's emotional world, as depicted in her poems, is a world of women. Her female lovers (there are three major figures whom she mentions), her female friends, her female rivals, and a few important goddesses, in addition to the seemingly many voices interior to herself, are her interlocutors in the poems, which often take a dialogic form. Her two most famous poems, "To Me He Seems Like a God" and the poem to Anactoria, which appear in full here, bring to articulation two different faces of the raw ardor of a woman in love with a woman she cannot have. In the first, Sappho's rival is a man who, because he is a man, enjoys free reign over the woman Sappho desires. In the second, Sappho compares being in the

---

[4] Plato, *Phaedrus*, 235c

presence of her beloved to a noble victory in war. Through these images, Sappho gives the reader surprising and profoundly romantic treatments of many of the themes that had concerned Homer and Hesiod: the contrast between human frailty and divine immortality, the character of the heroes and the good life for human beings, the analogy between the happy household and the strong city-state, etc.

20

It seems to me that man is equal to the gods,
that is, whoever sits opposite you
and, drawing nearer, savours, as you speak,
the sweetness of your voice

and the thrill of your laugh, which have so stirred the heart
in my own breast, that whenever I catch
sight of you, even if for a moment,
then my voice deserts me

and my tongue is struck silent, a delicate fire
suddenly races underneath my skin,
my eyes see nothing, my ears whistle like
the whirling of a top

and sweat pours down me and a trembling creeps over
my whole body, I am greener than grass,
at such time, I seem to be no more than
a step away from death;

but all can be endured since even a pauper . . .

21

Some an army of horsemen, some an army on foot
and some say a fleet of ships is the loveliest sight
on this dark earth; but I say it is whatever you desire:

and it is possible to make this perfectly clear
to all; for the woman who far surpassed all others
in her beauty, Helen, left her husband —
the best of all men —

behind and sailed far away to Troy; she did not spare
a single thought for her child nor for her dear parents
but [the goddess of love] led her astray
[to desire . . .]

        [. . . which]
reminds me now of Anactoria
although far away,

whose long-desired footstep, whose radiant, sparkling face
I would rather see before me than the chariots
of Lydia or the armour of men
who fight wars on foot . . .

These poems offer occasions for reflection on many subtle questions of gender difference and similarity, including with regard to authorship. Sappho, for instance, continues to depict the beloved as feminine, and so refocuses our attention to gender differences in the character of *lovers*. The quality of Sappho's love, the position in which she places the lover, seems quite different from that of male lovers depicted elsewhere in ancient texts. Do women love differently from men? Sappho offers occasions for speculation on this and other themes about humanity and divinity—such as the fear of growing old, the longing for a lost virginity, the nature of Hera's and Aphrodite's powers, and the concrete pleasures and pains of sexual ecstasy. All of these issues, beautifully considered by Sappho, tell us about our mortality and our longing for immortality—themes that were central to Homer and Hesiod, but treated in a very different way.

Interestingly, Sappho's poems are written in the first person and read as if they were autobiographical. But the fact is, we know little about Sappho's life from sources other than her poems; thus, the intimate and richly erotic tone of her work may be attributable more to her own feminine imagination as a poet than to her personal feelings as a woman. We can see from Homer's texts that Greek women of Sappho's time period were restricted to the home and city. Within this confined space, however, women's activities were less restricted in preSocratic times than they would be in later Classical Greece. Sappho's work, both in its erotic content and in its lyricism, is innovative for its time: her creative genius raises questions about the social conditions that permitted it to blossom—or that may have restricted it from an even more prolific and renowned yield.

40

Mother dear, I simply cannot weave my cloth;
                  I'm overpowered
by desire for a slender young man — and it's
                  Aphrodite's fault

69

[Why am I unhappy?]
Am I still longing
            for my lost virginity?

71

BRIDE: Virginity, virginity,
            have you deserted me, where have you gone?
VIRGINITY: I will never return to you again,
                never return to you again

72

The Marriage of Hector and Andromache

A herald came . . . Idaeus . . . swift messenger . . .

'Hector and his companions are bringing a woman
with sparkling eyes, graceful Andromache, from sacred
Thebe,
from the ever-flowing streams of Placia, in their ships
across the salt-filled sea;
and with her they also carry
many golden bracelets, purple clothing, engraved trinkets,
ivory and silver goblets too numerous to count.'
This was Idaeus' speech.
And Hector's beloved father
quickly leapt up and the story spread through the wide city
to those who held Hector dear.
At once the sons of Ilus
yoked mules to broad-wheeled carts and a crowd of women
and girls
whose ankles were slim, climbed on, while the daughters of
Priam . . .

. . . and the sweet music of the flute was mingled with the
clash
of castanets and the young women sang a sacred song
so clearly that their wondrous echo reached the sky . . .

. . . and in the streets, the mingled scents of myrrh and cassia
and frankincense;
with one voice the elder women shouted
for joy and with a clear cry all the men called on Paean,
the noble archer, the skilled lyre player and they all sang
in praise of Hector and Andromache who were like gods

4. PYTHAGORAS AND PYTHAGOREANS
(Greek, Sixth–Fifth Century B.C.E.)

Pythagoras, probably familiar to readers as the discoverer of the Pythagorean theorem in geometry, was also a pivotal figure in preSocratic Greek philosophy and in Greek politics prior to the rise of Athens. Born in Samos, to the East of the Greek peninsula, he moved to Croton, in present-day southern Italy, when he was about forty years old. There he founded a city and ruled it according to his own philosophical principles. Since Pythagoreanism was based in a notion of divinity, Pythagoreans ruled in Croton as members of a kind of sacred sect, to which few were initiated. The influence of Pythagoreanism extended well beyond even its long-lived rule in Croton; there are many claims from the Pythagoreans preserved in later authors, but—apparently out of religious belief—all such claims are attributed to Pythagoras himself.

PreSocratic philosophy in general centered on two philosophical concerns: 1) establishing the origin (called the *arche*) of all existing things, and 2) establishing an explanation for the change that occurs among things existing in the natural world. Many early preSocratics attempted to understand creation and change in a basically scientific way, by looking for the fundamental natural elements of things, and by investigating the qualities of those elements from which change might occur. For instance, Thales—credited with being the very first philosopher—claimed that of the four elements that the Greek thinkers believed to comprise the world (Earth, Air, Fire, and Water), *Water* was the first element from which everything that exists had sprung. Thus, he claimed that the *arche,* on which the whole world rested, was water, whose properties were such that, through freezing and heating, it could change into solid and gaseous objects—i.e., it could change into the other three elements from which nature was constructed.

These early thinkers, though naive to our sensibility, made a stunning breakthrough in the history of thought. They recognized, as had Homer and Hesiod before them, that things may not be as they seem; but rather than attributing the "reality" of the world to the gods, they claimed that through study, human beings could *know* the reality that lay behind the appearance of things. The Pythagoreans believed that the reality behind the appearances of things in the world, which explained both their origin and change, was number. Everything that exists, they claimed, displays the properties of number. Thus, Pythagorean philosophy was based in something like what we today call "number theory"—an investigation and explication of the various properties of number. Number, for them however, was a divine principle, immortally alive, as the Homeric gods had been thought to be. Thus, the study of number was thought to be a religious obligation, and the knowledge in which this study resulted, a revelation of divine mysteries. Importantly, the Pythagoreans also believed that the *human* soul was *immortal,* reincarnated through eternity in the bodies of different humans and non-human animals.

As mentioned above, preSocratic philosophers sought to explain change as well as origins, and had already by Pythagoras' time established a habit of doing so through a notion of *binary opposition.* Day changes to Night, Life changes to Death, what is wet dries out, what is hot cools off: that changes occur from something to what it is not, or its opposite, seemed a sensible, observable way to understand how nature evolved over time. The Pythagoreans were the first to make a list of the fundamental oppositions through which all other change occurred, and one of these fundamental duos was that between male and female. The Pythagorean table of opposites lines up the ten basic oppositions in a seeming association with each other, so that we can glean a sense of the Pythagorean definitions of male and female from their association with the other nine oppositions. It is striking how similar some of these associations are to the notions of gender we have seen in Hesiod and Homer. In the oppositions of good and bad, light and darkness, right and left, we may see the beginnings of the more sternly derogatory view of femininity that we have come to believe is our Western inheritance.

The idea of order is intimately connected with Limit (*peras*), the opposite of which is the unlimited (*apeiron*), and these are the two most basic, and hence most universal, principles of Pythagorean cosmology. According to the Pythagoreans, the world or cosmos is compounded of these elements, summarized in the famous "Table of Opposites" which has been preserved by Aristotle.

THE PYTHAGOREAN TABLE OF OPPOSITES

Limit	Unlimited
Odd	Even
One	Plurality
Right	Left
Male	Female
At rest	Moving
Straight	Crooked
Light	Darkness
Good	Bad
Square	Oblong

That the oppositions are to be associated with each other is demonstrated in the following passage from Aristotle about the Pythagoreans, in which Unlimited is associated with Even, with Plurality, and with Oblong; Limit with Odd, One, and Square.

The Pythagoreans identify the Unlimited with the Even. For this, they say, when it is enclosed and limited by the Odd provides things with the element of unlimitedness. An indication of this is what happens in numbers: if gnomons are placed around the unit and apart from the unit, in the latter case the resulting figure is always *other*, in the former it is always *one*.

Aristotle is referring to the following figures:

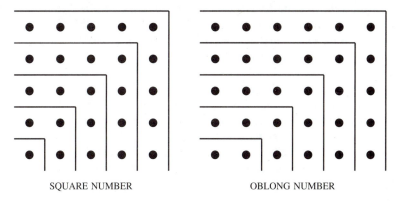

SQUARE NUMBER   OBLONG NUMBER

Moral connotations of the oppositions are clearly intended, but not easily inter-pretable. Although the female body is curvaceous, it is not clear how the female should be thought crooked, and although the Earth is depicted as female and the Sky as male in Hesiod, it is arguable, but not obvious, why they should be associated with dark and light. Still, the Pythagorean table of opposites offers a surprisingly early and fascinating overview of thinking in terms of binary oppositions.

5. PARMENIDES
(Greek, Early Fifth Century B.C.E.)

The preSocratic philosopher Parmenides came from Elea, on the western coast of Italy; thus, he and his followers (of which Zeno, the author of several famous paradoxes, was noteworthy) were called the "Eleatic" school. Profoundly influential on Plato and other later Greek thinkers, Parmenides provides us with the first documented case in philosophy of a deductive argument. In "The Way of Truth," the central section of his famous and beautiful poem, Parmenides argues that what really exists is One—the *arche*—unchanging and eternal. Thus, Parmenides set himself apart from the Pythagoreans and from the earlier Greek writers, who believed in inherent natural oppositions and/or a host of different gods.

Obviously, if what really exists is One, there can be no real distinctions among existent things—including the distinction between male and female. Indeed, Parmenides claimed that there is no such distinction in reality, and that all binary oppositions were mere "opinions," i.e., mere appearances to us of the One true existence. Parmenides is the first thinker to imply that masculinity and femininity are just words, with no referent in reality.

"THE WAY OF TRUTH"

In the central portion of the poem, Parmenides offers the first philosophical argument—for the claim that what exists is one, eternal, unchanging, and indivisible. It is of interest to us in a mostly negative way; i.e., Parmenides is arguing that there really is no such thing as gender—or anything else particular, for that matter. Everything but the One, which really exists, is a mere illusion. We will look at just a few of the arguments Parmenides offers for this claim.

> 6. One should both say and think that Being Is; for To Be is possible, and Nothingness is not possible. This I command you to consider; for from the latter way of search first of all I debar you. But next I debar you from that way along which wander mortals knowing nothing, two-headed, for perplexity in their bosoms steers their intelligence astray, and they are carried along as deaf as they are blind, amazed, uncritical hordes, by who To Be and Not To Be are regarded as the same and not the same, and (*for whom*) in everything there is a way of opposing stress.

7, 8. For this (*view*) can never predominate, that That Which Is Not exists. You must debar your thought from this way of search, nor let ordinary experience in its variety force you along this way, (*namely, that of allowing*) the eye, sightless as it is, and the ear, full of sound, and the tongue, to rule; but (*you must*) judge by means of the Reason (*Logos*) the much-contested proof which is expounded by me.

There is only one other description of the way remaining, (*namely*), that (*What Is*) Is. To this way there are very many sign-posts: that Being has no coming-into-being and no destruction, for it is whole of limb, without motion, and without end. And it never Was, nor Will Be, because it Is now, a Whole all together, One, continuous; for what creation of it will you look for? How, whence (*could it have*) sprung? Nor shall I allow you to speak or think of it as springing from Not-Being; for it is neither expressible nor thinkable that What-Is-Not Is.

⌒ ⌒ ⌒

Nor is being divisible, since it is all alike. Nor is there anything (*here or*) there which could prevent it from holding together, nor any lesser thing, but all is full of Being. Therefore it is altogether continuous; for Being is close to Being.

"THE WAY OF OPINION"

After arguing that what exists is One, Parmenides attempts to explain why it *seems* (i.e., appears) as if more than one thing exists. In the "Way of Opinion," he claims that the sets of oppositions through which the ancients Greeks understood the natural world are a function of language use, or "naming," which, according to Parmenides, is always somewhat short of the truth being named. In other words, a name is always partly fictional: people *say* "there *is* night and day," but that can only *mean*, according to Parmenides, that *we have marked time* by these two distinct names. Thus, existence itself, claims Parmenides, is one attribute, one entity, and all distinctions within it are done by naming. This is a little like the problem discussed in the Introduction, in which we considered the possibility that gender is "nothing but words."

At this point I cease my reliable theory (*Logos*) and thought, concerning Truth; from here onwards you must learn the opinions of mortals, listening to the deceptive order of my words.

They have established (*the custom of*) naming two forms, one of which ought not to be (*mentioned*): that is where they have gone astray. They have distinguished them as opposite in form, and have marked them off from another by giving them different signs: on one side the flaming fire in the heavens, mild, very light (*in weight*), the same as itself in every direction, and not the same as the other. This (*other*) also is by itself and opposite: dark Night, a dense and heavy body. This world-order I describe to you throughout as it appears with all its phenomena, in order that no intellect of mortal men may outstrip you.

9. But since all things are named Light and Night, and names have been given
to each class of things according to the power of one or the other (*Light or
Night*), everything is full equally of Light and invisible Night, as both are equal,
because to neither of them belongs any share (of the other).

6. THE OLD TESTAMENT
(Hebrew and Aramaic, Oral Tradition
Twelfth–Second Centuries B.C.E.,
Probably Written Down for the First Time
During the Last Two Centuries B.C.E.)

The first five books of the Old Testament (called the Pentateuch) tell the story of the
origin of the Israelites, their covenant with God, their enslavement in Egypt, and
their escape from slavery and eventual unification in Jerusalem under God and
God's law. In the succeeding books (Joshua and following) we find historical stories
of the Israelite kingdoms (of their eventual conquest, of the exile and enslavement
of the Jews by the Babylonians, and of the more beneficent rule they received after
the conquest of Jerusalem by the Persians), mixed with prophecies and fictional stories with moral and theological goals. Thus, the Old Testament is a large collection
of different works, each with different levels of significance and a monumental importance in Western thought and culture. Even though we focus on particular sections of the Old Testament, then, we will not be able to give univocal interpretations.

Here, we will look at just a few important Old Testament treatments of the question of gender: the stories of Adam and Eve from Genesis, plus the story of Ruth,
conspicuous among the books of the Old Testament for having a female protagonist.
In addition, we will look at just a few of the religious laws from Exodus, Leviticus,
and Deuteronomy, having to do with sex, sexuality, and women. Thus, while we cannot begin to offer a thorough investigation of Old Testament views on gender, we will
get a smattering of opinions from which we can begin to formulate a general view.

GENESIS

As was mentioned in the introduction to this section, there are several different sets
of authors thought to be responsible for the book of Genesis (and the other books of
the Pentateuch). There are two distinct creation myths offered up in chapters 1–4 of
Genesis; the two stories have very different themes and styles and order the creation in wholly different ways. They are clearly the work of two different authors.

THE FIRST CREATION STORY

The creation story that appears first in the Bible, as we find it ordered today,
is thought to be of a later origin, historically, than the second. It is the "priestly"

version, probably written in the late sixth century B.C.E. It is a far more abstract, metaphysical working of God's creation of the world than the second version. In it, God creates *ex nihilo* ("from nothing") and by His word alone.

> In the beginning of creation, when God made heaven and earth, the earth was without form and void with darkness over the face of the abyss and a mighty wind that swept over the surface of the waters. God said, 'Let there be light,' and there was light; and God saw that the light was good, and he separated light from darkness. He called the light day, and the darkness night. So evening came, and morning came, the first day.
>
> God said, 'Let there be a vault between the waters, to separate water from water.' So God made the vault, and separated the water under the vault from the water above it, and so it was; and God called the vault heaven. Evening came, and morning came, a second day.
>
> God said, 'Let the waters under heaven be gathered into one place, so that dry land may appear'; and so it was. God called the dry land earth, and the gathering of the waters he called seas; and God saw that it was good. Then God said, 'Let the earth produce fresh growth, let there be on the earth plants bearing seed, fruit-trees bearing fruit each with seed according to its kind.' So it was; the earth yielded fresh growth, plants bearing seed according to their kind and trees bearing fruit each with seed according to its kind and God saw that it was good. Evening came, and morning came, a third day.
>
> God said, 'Let there be lights in the vault of heaven to separate day from night, and let them serve as signs both for festivals and for seasons and years. Let them also shine in the vault of heaven to give light on earth.' So it was God made the two great lights, the greater to govern the day and the lesser to govern the night; and with them he made the stars. God put these lights in the vault of heaven to give light on earth, to govern day and night, and to separate light from darkness; and God saw that it was good. Evening came and morning came, a fourth day.
>
> God said, 'Let the waters teem with countless living creatures, and let birds fly above the earth across the vault of heaven.' God then created the great sea-monsters and all living creatures that move and swarm in the water according to their kind, and every kind of bird; and God saw that it was good. So he blessed them and said, 'Be fruitful and increase, fill the waters of the seas; and let the birds increase on land.' Evening came, and morning came, a fifth day.
>
> God said, 'Let the earth bring forth living creatures, according to their kind: cattle, reptiles, and wild animals, all according to their kind.' So it was; God made wild animals, cattle, and all reptiles, each according to its kind; and he saw that it was good. Then God said, 'Let us make man in our image and likeness to rule the fish in the sea, the birds of heaven, the cattle, all wild animals on earth, and all reptiles that crawl upon the earth.' So God created man in his own image; in the image of God he created him; male and female he created them. God blessed them and said to them, 'Be fruitful and increase, till the earth and subdue it, rule over the fish in the sea, the birds of heaven, and every living thing that

moves upon the earth.' God also said, 'I give you all plants that bear seed everywhere on earth, and every tree bearing fruit which yields seed; they shall be yours for food. All green plants I give for food to the wild animals, to all the birds of heaven, and to all reptiles on earth, every living creature.' So it was; and God saw all that he had made, and it was very good. Evening came, and morning came, a sixth day.

   Thus heaven and earth were completed with all their mighty throng. On the sixth day God completed all the work he had been doing, and on the seventh day he ceased from all his work. God blessed the seventh day and made it holy, because on that day he ceased from all the work he had set himself to do.

   This is the story of the making of heaven and earth when they were created.

   In this version of the creation, God makes the universe in six days, resting on the seventh. Creation is accomplished by God's word; He *says* "let there be ____" and there it is. God makes things comes to be by just saying so, where human beings must work—reddening their hands, breaking their backs, etc.—to bring something into existence (like a field of vegetables, or a house, or a baby).

   The land animals, including human beings, are not created until the last "working day," and human beings last of all. In this version, male and female human beings are created together, and presumably are to share the rule over other living things that God commands them to accept. Scholars and moral and political philosophers have debated for centuries the nature of this "rule" over the Earth, as well as the exact meaning of our being created "in God's image." If we are male and female, and are created in the image of God, then perhaps God is male and female. Perhaps, on the other hand, we are a mere image of God (and not gods ourselves) because we are divided into two sexes. Certainly, our "rulership" of the Earth is associated with our "being fruitful and multiplying"; perhaps the union of male and female in sex, and the pro-"creation" that it accomplishes, is a part of our likeness to God and our power over other creatures. However we interpret the passage, we are prompted to do so by its powerful yet puzzling image of the Earth's beginnings. Why does God create the universe at all? Its existence, and ours within it, is explained in the passage and yet remains a mystery.

THE SECOND CREATION STORY

It is not until the second version of creation that we find the familiar story of Adam and Eve, without doubt the most fundamental exploration of gender in Judeo-Christian tradition. This version was written by the earliest, or "Jawist," author, probably in the tenth century B.C.E. In this version, God is an immanent God, who walks and talks with Adam and Eve and takes a personal interest in their welfare. The imagery here is not at all abstract; in fact, it is not even scientific in its interest with regard to creation. The creation of the sun and moon, heaven and earth, is incidental to the action, hurriedly summarized in the first two verses. This is first and foremost a story of the origin of human beings, an explanation of human nature, a guide to human action.

When the LORD God made earth and heaven, there was neither shrub nor plant growing wild upon the earth, because the LORD God had sent no rain on the earth; nor was there any man to till the ground. A flood used to rise out of the earth and water all the surface of the ground. Then the LORD God formed a man from the dust of the ground and breathed into his nostrils the breath of life. Thus the man became a living creature. Then the LORD God planted a garden in Eden away to the east, and there he put the man whom he had formed. The LORD God made trees spring from the ground, all trees pleasant to look at and good for food; and in the middle of the garden he set the tree of life and the tree of the knowledge of good and evil.

There was a river flowing from Eden to water the garden, and when it left the garden it branched into four streams. The name of the first is Pishon, that is the river which encircles all the land of Havilah, where the gold is. The gold of that land is good; bdellium and cornelians are also to be found there. The name of the second river is Gihon; this is the one which encircles all the land of Cush. The name of the third is Tigris; this is the river which runs east of Asshur. The fourth river is the Euphrates.

The LORD God took the man and put him in the garden of Eden to till it and care for it. He told the man, 'You may eat from every tree in the garden, but not from the tree of the knowledge of good and evil; for on the day that you eat from it, you will certainly die.' Then the LORD God said, 'It is not good for the man to be alone. I will provide a partner for him.' So God formed out of the ground all the wild animals and all the birds of heaven. He brought them to the man to see what he would call them, and whatever the man called each living creature, that was its name. Thus the man gave the names to all cattle, to the birds of heaven, and to every wild animal; but for the man himself no partner had yet been found. And so the LORD God put the man into a trance, and while he slept, he took one of his ribs and closed the flesh over the place. The LORD God then built up the rib, which he had taken out of the man, into a woman. He brought her to the man, and the man said:

'Now this, at last—
bone from my bones,
flesh from my flesh!—
this shall be called woman,
for from man was this taken.'

That is why a man leaves his father and mother and is united to his wife, and the two become one flesh. Now they were both naked, the man and his wife, but they had no feeling of shame towards one another.

The serpent was more crafty than any wild creature that the LORD God had made. He said to the woman, 'Is it true that God has forbidden you to eat from any tree in the garden?' The woman answered the serpent, 'We may eat the fruit of any tree in the garden, except for the tree in the middle of the garden; God has forbidden us either to eat or to touch the fruit of that; if we do, we shall die.' The serpent said, 'Of course you will not die. God knows that as soon as you eat it, your eyes will be opened and you will be like gods knowing both good and evil.' When the woman saw that the fruit of the tree was good to eat, and that it was pleasing to the eye and tempting to contemplate, she took some and ate it. She also gave her husband some and he ate it. Then the eyes of both of them were opened and they discovered that they were naked; so they stitched fig-leaves together and made themselves loincloths.

The man and his wife heard the sound of the LORD God walking in the garden at the time of the evening breeze and hid from the LORD God among the trees of the garden. But the LORD God called to the man and said to him, 'Where are you?' He replied, 'I heard the sound as you were walking in the garden, and I was afraid because I was naked, and I hid myself.' God answered, 'Who told you that you were naked? Have you eaten from the tree which I forbade you?' The man said, 'The woman you gave me for a companion, she gave me fruit from the tree and I ate it.' Then the LORD God said to the woman, 'What is this that you have done?' The woman said, 'The serpent tricked me, and I ate.' Then the LORD God said to the serpent:

'Because you have done this you are accursed
more than all cattle and all wild creatures.
On your belly you shall crawl, and dust you shall eat
all the days of your life.
I will put enmity between you and the woman,
between your brood and hers.
They shall strike at your head,
and you shall strike at their heel.'

To the woman he said:

'I will increase your labour and your groaning,
and in labour you shall bear children.
You shall be eager for your husband,
and he shall be your master.'

And to the man he said:

'Because you have listened to your wife
and have eaten from the tree which I forbade you,
accursed shall be the ground on your account.
With labour you shall win your food from it
all the days of your life.
It will grow thorns and thistles for you,
none but wild plants for you to eat.
You shall gain your bread by the sweat of your brow
until you return to the ground;
for from it you were taken.
Dust you are, to dust you shall return.'

The man called his wife Eve because she was the mother of all who live. The LORD God made tunics of skins for Adam and his wife and clothed them. He said, 'The man has become like one of us, knowing good and evil; what if he now reaches out his hand and takes fruit from the tree of life also, eats it and lives for ever?' So the LORD God drove him out of the garden of Eden to till the ground from which he had been taken. He cast him out, and to the east of the garden of Eden he stationed the cherubim and a sword whirling and flashing to guard the way to the tree of life.

There are many insightful implications—and a vast number of different, sometimes conflicting, implications—about sex and gender to be drawn from this remarkable story. To start, God places the first human being in a lush garden, abundantly furnished with good things. Originally, we may infer, people in God's good graces did not want for anything; their lives were easy, effortless, more like that of God Himself. Beneficently, God decides that it is not good for Adam to be alone, presumably giving legitimacy to our sense that loneliness is a fundamental human tragedy. God's first attempt, however, to provide companionship for Adam is to create the animals, not the woman, and Adam's first way of availing himself of companionship is to name the animals. Thus, language is marked as a basic human capacity, distinguishing us from the animals, and basing our social relations; it is powerful in a way that corresponds to God's creation by word in the first version of the story. But this is not good enough for us; Adam needs someone who befits him better than do the animals, a helper in his work of naming rather than an object to be named by him. Thus God creates Eve from Adam's rib. Adam and Eve before their Fall would seem to be not just innocent, but in a sense pre-moral, or perfect beings, sharing fully each other's interests, pleasures, and pain, as if these were their own.

The serpent is a powerful image; "more crafty than the other animals," he tells Eve that God has lied to Adam, and that human beings will not die if they eat the fruit of the tree of the knowledge of good and evil, which God has forbidden them. Because of the serpent's words, Eve comes to doubt God (she wonders if God has told Adam the truth about dying as they eat the apple) and Adam (she wonders if Adam has been duped by God). Further, however, she comes to doubt the serpent himself; she *tests* the fruit after he speaks to her. Thus, Eve, and by implication women, are introduced to the notion of lying and therefore are suspicious of all they hear.

After eating the fruit, Adam and Eve recognize their nakedness and cover it up. Since the fruit is of the tree of the knowledge of good and evil, we may assume that by clothing themselves, they are covering up their moral knowledge, trying to put forward a certain new kind of lie. Their eating of the apple and covering up afterwards represent the first *free* human actions; Adam and Eve disobey God and by doing so, they assert their will free of divine constraints. With the ability to act freely, however, comes a responsibility for their own actions, and Adam and Eve deny that responsibility by blaming others (Adam blames Eve, Eve blames the serpent). Thus, another lie follows their earlier lies, and God, seeing through their lies, punishes them.

There are many different avenues along which one may interpret this story of the "fall." Our interest is its sexual significance: what is the sexuality of freedom here, and of responsibility? One common interpretation is that "eating the fruit" represents Adam and Eve engaging in the sexual act, coming to know each other's bodies and their differences through sexual activity. On this reading, we might say that Adam and Eve have come to an age of responsibility for themselves, their bodies, and their sexuality, an age that is recognized as such in almost all cultures—puberty. In their innocence, before they were able to exercise their freedom and before they were saddled with the responsibility for their actions, Adam and Eve could hardly have *evaded* their responsibilities—they could not, in an important sense, lie. Thus, we can take from the passage that human beings are not capable of the fundamental moral wrong until they have reached the age of sexual maturity.

Of particular note are the punishments that God doles out to Adam, Eve, and the serpent on account of their fall from grace. The serpent will have to crawl, eat dirt, and be an enemy of women ever after. Does the serpent represent all animals? Does he represent nature, now set off from human culture? Is he a masculine symbol? Is he representative of all those who lie to women? Is he, as a speaker, representative of divinity or wisdom? All these interpretations seem reasonable; whichever one one chooses, the upshot is an ongoing conflict with women. Adam is punished with perpetual difficult labor, struggling against the elements for his survival; this is not unlike the image of human nature in, say, Hesiod. Eve will have to work, to have painful labor in the bearing of children, to be desirous of her husband, and so to be his servant. This is without doubt a strong biblical statement that women should be perpetually subservient to men and that women, unlike men, are to be associated with sexual desire. Both Adam and Eve are exiled from the lush garden, forced to survive and make a community by themselves and with great difficulties. While God's creation is effortless, then, we see that human creation comes always at a cost.

These punishments give us a vision of human nature and human life that is uniquely biblical. Here is a rather internalized, lonely view of human existence and a rather personal, inherently sexual, view of morality and responsibility. Where the Greeks' notion of the human state was one of natural strengths and weaknesses with which each human did his or her best, the biblical version is of a blissful state sullied by a free and wrongful moral action on the part of human beings. Thus, human beings are here seen as bearing a great deal of responsibility for themselves and for the world—the biblical view really centers on humanity.

EXODUS AND LEVITICUS: SOME LAWS REGARDING MARRIAGE AND SEXUALITY

The subservience of women to men is codified in later books of the Pentateuch, as are the rights of women and men in and out of marriage. In these laws, women's subservience amounts to their being the property of men. It is only as property, for instance, that women in the Old Testament have many of their rights.

[EXODUS]

[21] These are the laws you shall set before them:

When you buy a Hebrew slave, he shall be your slave for six years, but in the seventh year he shall go free and pay nothing.

If he comes to you alone, he shall go away alone; but if he is married, his wife shall go away with him.

If his master gives him a wife, and she bears him sons or daughters, the woman and her children shall belong to her master, and the man shall go away alone. But if the slave should say, 'I love my master, my wife, and my children; I will not go free', then his master shall bring him to God: he shall bring him to the door or the door-post, and his master shall pierce his ear with an awl, and the man shall be his slave for life.

When a man sells his daughter into slavery, she shall not go free as a male slave may. If her master has not had intercourse with her and she does not please him, he shall let her be ransomed. He has treated her unfairly and therefore has no right to sell her to strangers. If he assigns her to his son, he shall allow her the rights of a daughter. If he takes another woman, he shall not deprive the first of meat, clothes, and conjugal rights. If he does not provide her with these three things, she shall go free without any payment.

When a man strikes his slave or slave-girl in the eye and destroys it, he shall let the slave go free in compensation for the eye. When he knocks out the tooth of a slave or a slave-girl, he shall let the slave go free in compensation for the tooth.

[22] When a man seduces a virgin who is not yet betrothed, he shall pay the bride-price for her to be his wife. If her father refuses to give her to him, the seducer shall pay in silver a sum equal to the bride-price for virgins.

You shall not allow a witch to live.

Whoever has unnatural connection with a beast shall be put to death.

[LEVITICUS]

18 The LORD spoke to Moses and said, Speak to the Israelites in these words: I am the LORD your God. You shall not do as they do in Egypt where you once dwelt, nor shall you do as they do in the land of Canaan to which I am bringing you; you shall not conform to their institutions. You must keep my laws and conform to my institutions without fail: I am the LORD your God. You shall observe my institutions and my laws; the man who keeps them shall have life through them. I am the LORD.

No man shall approach a blood-relation for intercourse. I am the LORD. You shall not bring shame on your father by intercourse with your mother: she is your mother; you shall not bring shame upon her. You shall not have intercourse with your father's wife: that is to bring shame upon your father. You shall not have intercourse with your sister, your father's daughter, or your mother's daughter, whether brought up in the family or in another home; you shall not bring shame upon them. You shall not have intercourse with your son's daughter or your daughter's daughter: that is to bring shame upon yourself. You shall not have intercourse with a daughter of your father's wife; begotten by your father; she is your sister, and you shall not bring shame upon her. You shall not have intercourse with your father's sister: she is a blood-relation of your father. You shall not have intercourse with your mother's sister: she is a blood-relation of your mother. You shall not bring shame upon your father's brother by approaching his wife: she is your aunt. You shall not have intercourse with your daughter-in-law: she is your son's wife; you shall not bring shame upon her. You shall not have intercourse with your brother's wife: that is to bring shame upon him. You shall not have intercourse with both a woman and her daughter, nor shall you take her son's daughter or her daughter's daughter to have intercourse with them: they are her blood-relations, and such conduct is lewdness. You shall not take a woman who is your wife's sister to make her a rival-wife, and to have intercourse with her during her sister's lifetime.

You shall not approach a woman to have intercourse with her during her period of menstruation. You shall not have sexual intercourse with the wife of your fellow-countymen and so make yourself unclean with her. You shall not surrender any of your children to Moloch and thus profane the name of your God: I am the LORD. You shall not lie with a man as with a woman: that is an abomination. You shall not have sexual intercourse with any beast to make yourself unclean with it, nor shall a woman submit herself to intercourse with a beast: that is a violation of nature. You shall not make yourselves unclean in any of these ways; for in these ways the heathen, whom I am driving out before you, made themselves unclean. This is how the land became unclean, and I punished it for its iniquity so that it spewed out its inhabitants. You, unlike them, shall keep my laws and my rules: none of you, whether natives or aliens, settled among you, shall do any of these abominable things. The people who were there before you did these abominable things and the land became unclean. So the land will not spew you out for making it unclean as it spewed them out; for anyone who does any of these abominable things shall be cut off from his people. Observe my charge, therefore, and follow none of the abominable institutions customary before your time; do not make yourselves unclean with them. I am the LORD your God.

☞ ☞ ☞

19 When a man has intercourse with a slave-girl who has been assigned to another man and neither ransomed nor given her freedom, inquiry shall be made. They shall not be put to death, because she has not been freed. The man shall bring his guilt-offering, a ram, to the LORD to the entrance of the Tent of the Presence, and with it the priest shall make expiation for him before the LORD for his sin, and he shall be forgiven the sin he has committed.

When you enter the land, and plant any kind of tree for food, you shall treat it as bearing forbidden fruit. For three years it shall be forbidden and may not eaten. In the fourth year all its fruit shall be a holy-gift to the LORD, and this releases it for use. In the fifth year you may eat its fruit, and thus the yield it gives you shall be increased. I am the LORD your God.

You shall not eat meat with the blood in it. You shall not practise divination or soothsaying. You shall not round off your hair from side to side, and you shall not shave the edge of your beards. You shall not gash yourselves in mourning for the dead; you shall not tattoo yourselves. I am the LORD.

Do not prostitute your daughter and so make her a whore; thus the land shall not play the prostitute and be full of lewdness. You shall keep my sabbaths, and revere my sanctuary. I am the LORD.

20 If a man commits adultery with his neighbours's wife, both adulterer and aldulteress shall be put to death. The man who has intercourse with his father's wife has brought shame on his father. They shall both be put to death; their blood shall be on their own heads. If a man has intercourse with his daughter-in-law, they shall both be put to death. Their deed is a violation of nature; their blood shall be on their own heads. If a man has intercourse with a man as with a woman, they both commit an abomination. They shall be put to death; their blood shall be on their own heads. If a man takes both a woman and her mother, that is lewdness. Both he and they shall be burned, thus there shall be no lewdness in your midst. A man who has sexual intercourse with any beast shall be put to death, and you shall kill the beast. If a woman approaches any animal to have intercourse with it, you shall kill both woman and beast. They shall be put to death; their blood shall be on their own heads. If a man takes his sister, his father's daughter, and they see one another naked, it is a scandalous disgrace. They shall be cut off in the presence of their people. The man has had intercourse with his sister and he shall accept responsibility. If a man lies with a woman during her monthly period and brings shame upon her, he has exposed her discharge and she has uncovered the source of her discharge; they shall both be cut off from their people. You shall not have intercourse with your mother's sister or your father's sister: it is the exposure of a blood-relation. They shall accept responsibility. A man who has intercourse with his uncle's wife has brought shame upon his uncle. They shall accept responsibility for their sin and shall be proscribed and put to death. If a man takes his brother's wife, it is impurity. He has brought shame upon his brother; they shall be proscribed.

27 The LORD spoke to Moses and said, Speak to the Israelites in these words: When a man makes a special vow to the LORD which requires your valuation of living persons, a male between twenty and sixty years old shall be valued at fifty silver shekels, that is shekels by the sacred standard. If it is a female, she shall be valued at thirty shekels. If the person is between five years old and twenty, the valuation shall be twenty shekels for a male and ten for a female. If the person is between a month and five years old, the valuation shall be five shekels for a male and three for a female. If the person is over sixty and a male, the valuation shall be fifteen shekels, but if a female, ten shekels. If the man is too poor to pay the amount of your valuation, the person shall be set before the priest, and the priest shall value him according to the sum which the man who makes the vow can afford: the priest shall make the valuation.

RUTH

The book of Ruth, which follows and is set in the same time period as the book of Judges, is a short but fascinating study of feminine devotion and of relationships between women. The book of Ruth is a happy story, filled with heroism and without any villainy, depicting the good consequences of fulfilling one's family obligations and obeying the law. Ruth is depicted as a great and unique female heroine, and her heroism legitimates her place in the ancestry of David.

Long ago, in the time of the judges, there was a famine in the land, and a man from Bethlehem in Judah went to live in the Moabite country with his wife and his two sons. The man's name was Elimelech, his wife's name was Naomi, and the names of his two sons Mahlon and Chilion. They were Ephrathites from Bethlehem in Judah. They arrived in the Moabite country and there they stayed.
    Elimelech Naomi's husband died, so that she was left with her two sons. These sons married Moabite women, one of whom was called Orpah and the other Ruth. They had lived there about ten years, when both Mahlon and Chilion died, so that the woman was bereaved of her two sons as well as of her husband. Thereupon she set out with her two daughters-in-law to return home, because she had heard while still in the Moabite country that the LORD had cared for his people and given them food. So with her two daughters-in-law she left the place where she had been living, and took the road home to Judah. Then Naomi said to her two daughters-in-law, 'Go back, both of you, to your mothers' homes. May the LORD keep faith with you, as you have kept faith with the dead and with me; and may he grant each of you security in the home of a new husband.' She kissed them and they wept aloud. Then they said to her, 'We will return with you to your own poeple.' But Naomi said, 'Go back, my daughters. Why should you go with me? Am I likely to bear any more sons to be husbands for you? Go back, my daughters, go. I am too old to marry again. But even if I could say that I had hope for a child, if I were to marry this night and if I were to bear sons, would you then wait until they grew up? Would you then refrain from marrying? No, no, my daughters, my lot is more bitter than yours, because the LORD has been against me.' At this they wept again. Then Orpah kissed her mother-in-law and returned to her people, but Ruth clung to her.

'You see,' said Naomi, 'your sister-in-law has gone back to her people and her gods; go back with her.' 'Do not urge me to go back and desert you', Ruth answered. 'Where you go, I will go, and where you stay, I will stay.

Your people shall be my people, and your God my God. Where you die, I will die, and there I will be buried. I swear a solemn oath before the LORD your God: nothing but death shall divide us.' When Naomi saw that Ruth was determined to go with her, she said no more, and the two of them went on until they came to Bethlehem. When they arrived in Bethlehem, the whole town was in great excitement about them, and the women said, 'Can this be Naomi?' 'Do not call me Naomi,' she said, 'call me Mara, for it is a bitter lot that the Almighty has sent me. I went away full, and the LORD has brought me back empty. Why do you call me Naomi? The LORD has pronounced against me; the Almighty has brought disaster on me.' This is how Naomi's daughter-in-law, Ruth the Moabitess, returned with her from the Moabite country. The barley harvest was beginning when they arrived in Bethlehem.

Now Naomi had a kinsman on her husband's side, a well-to-do man of the family of Elimelech; his name was Boaz. Ruth the Moabitess said to Naomi, 'May I go out to the cornfields and glean behind anyone who will grant me that favour?' 'Yes, go, my daughter', she replied. So Ruth went gleaning in the fields behind the reapers. As it happened, she was in that strip of the fields which belonged to Boaz of Elimelech's family, and there was Boaz coming out from Bethlehem. He greeted the reapers, saying, 'The LORD be with you'; and they replied, 'The LORD bless you.' Then he asked his servant in charge of the reapers, 'Whose girl is this?' 'She is a Moabite girl', the servant answered, 'who has just come back with Naomi from the Moabites country. She asked if she might glean and gather among the swathes behind the reapers. She came and has been on her feet with hardly a moment's rest from daybreak till now.' Then Boaz said to Ruth, 'Listen to me, my daughter: do not go and glean in any other field, and do not look any further, but keep close to my girls. Watch where the men reap, and follow the gleaners; I have given them orders not to molest you. If you are thirsty, go and drink from the jars the men have filled.' She fell prostrate before him and said, 'Why are you so kind as to take notice of me when I am only a foreigner?' Boaz answered, 'They have told me all that you have done for your mother-in-law since your husband's death, how you left your father and mother and the land of your birth, and came to a people you did not know before. The LORD reward your deed; may the LORD the God of Israel, under whose wings you have come to take refuge, give you all that you deserve.' 'Indeed, sir,' she said, 'you have eased my mind and spoken kindly to me; may I ask you as a favour not to treat me only as one of your slave-girls?' When meal-time came round, Boaz said to her, 'Come here and have something to eat, and dip your bread into the sour wine.' So she sat beside the reapers, and he passed her some roasted grain. She ate all she wanted and still had some left over. When she got up to glean, Boaz gave the men orders. 'She', he said, ' may glean even among the sheaves; do not scold her. Or you may even pull out some corn from the bundles and leave it for her to glean, without reproving her.'

So Ruth gleaned in the field till evening, and when she beat out what she had gleaned, it came to about a bushel of barley. She took it up and went into the town, and her mother-in-law saw how much she had gleaned. Then Ruth brought out what she had saved from her meal and gave it to her. Her mother-in-law asked her, 'Where did you glean today? Which way did you go? Blessings on the man who kindly took notice of you.' So she told her mother-in-law whom she had been working with. 'The man with whom I worked today', she said, 'is called Boaz.' 'Blessings on him from the LORD', said Naomi. 'The LORD has kept faith with the living and the dead. For this man is related to us and is our next-of-kin.' 'And what is more,' said Ruth the Moabitess, 'he told me to stay close to his men until they had finished all his harvest.' 'It is best for you, my daughter,' Naomi answered, 'to go out with his girls; let no one catch you in another field.' So she kept close to his girls, gleaning with them till the end of both barley and wheat harvests; but she lived with her mother-in-law.

One day Ruth's mother-in-law Naomi said to her, ' My daughter, I want to see you happily settled. Now there is our kinsman Boaz; you were with his girls. Tonight he is winnowing barley at his threshing-floor, but do not make yourself known to the man until he has finished eating and drinking. But when he lies down, take note of the place where he lies. Then go in, turn back the covering at his feet and lie down. He will tell you what to do.' ' I will do whatever you tell me', Ruth answered. So she went down to the threshing-floor and did exactly as her mother-in-law had told her. When Boaz had eaten and drunk, he felt at peace with the world and went to lie down at the far end of the heap of grain. She came in quietly, turned back the covering at his feet and lay down. About midnight something disturbed the man as he slept; he turned over and, lo and behold, there was a woman lying at his feet. 'Who are you?' he asked. 'I am your servant, Ruth', she replied. 'Now spread your skirt over your servant, because you are my next-of-kin.' He said, 'The LORD has blessed you, my daughter. This last proof of your loyalty is greater than the first; you have not sought after any young man, rich or poor. Set your mind at rest, my daughter. I will do whatever you ask; for, as the whole neighbourhood knows, you are a capable woman. Are you sure that I am the next-of-kin? There is a kinsman even closer than I. Spend the night here and then in the morning, if he is willing to act as your next-of-kin, well and good; but if he is not willing, I will do so; I swear it by the LORD. Now lie down till morning.' So she lay at his feet till morning, but rose before one man could recognize another; and he said, 'It must not be known that a woman has been to the threshing-floor.' Then he said, 'Bring me the cloak you have on, and hold it out.' So she held it out, and he put in six measures of barley and lifted it on her back, and she went to the town. When she came to her mother-in-law, Naomi asked, 'How did things go with you, my daughter?' Ruth told her all that the man had done for her. ' He gave me these six measures of barley,' she said; 'he would not let me come home to my mother-in-law empty handed.' Naomi answered, 'Wait, my daughter, until you see what will come of it. He will not rest until he has settled the matter today.'

Now Boaz had gone up to the city gate, and was sitting there; and, after a time, the next-of-kin of whom he had spoken passed by. 'Here,' he cried, calling him by name, 'come and sit down.' He came and sat down. Then Boaz stopped ten elders of the town, and asked them to sit there, and they did so. Then he said to the next-of-kin, 'You will remember the strip of field that belonged to our brother Elimelech. Naomi has returned from the Moabite country and is selling it. I promised to open the matter with you, to ask you to acquire it in the presence of those who sit here, in the presence of the elders of my people. If you are going to do your duty as next-of-kin, then do so, but if not, someone must do it. So tell me, and then I shall know; for I come after you as next-of-kin.' Then Boaz said, 'On the day when you acquire the field from Naomi, you also acquire Ruth the Moabitess, the dead man's wife, so as to perpetuate the name of the dead man with his patrimony.' Thereupon the next-of-kin said, 'I cannot act myself, for I should risk losing my own patrimony. You must therefore do my duty as next-of-kin. I cannot act.'

Now in those old days, when property was redeemed or exchanged, it was the custom for a man to pull off his sandal and give it to the other party. This was the form of attestation in Israel. So the next-of-kin said to Boaz, 'Acquire it for yourself', and pulled off his sandal. Then Boaz declared to the elders and all the people, 'You are witnesses today that I have acquired from Naomi all that belonged to Elimelech and all that belonged to Mahlon and Chilion; and, further, that I have myself acquired Ruth the Moabitess, wife of Mahlon, to be my wife, to perpetuate the name of the deceased with his patrimony, so that his name may not be missing among his kindred and at the gate of his native place. You are witnesses this day.' Then the elders and all who were at the gate said, 'We are witnesses. May the LORD make this woman, who has come to your home, like Rachel and Leah, the two who built up the house of Israel. May you do great things in Ephrathah and keep a name alive in Bethlehem. May your house be like the house of Perez, whom Tamar bore to Judah, through the offspring the LORD will give you by this girl.'

So Boaz took Ruth and made her his wife. When they came together, the LORD caused her to conceive and she bore Boaz a son. Then the women said to Naomi, 'Blessed be the LORD today, for he has not left you without a next-of-kin. May the dead man's name be kept alive in Israel. The child will give you new life and cherish you in your old age; for your daughter-in-law who loves you, who has proved better to you than seven sons, has borne him.' Naomi took the child and laid him in her lap and became his nurse. Her neighbours gave him a name: 'Naomi has a son,' they said; 'we will call him Obed.' He was the father of Jesse, the father of David.

This is the geneology of Perez: Perez was the father of Hezron, Hezron of Ram, Ram of Amminadab, Amminadab of Nahshon, Nahshon of Salmon, Salmon of Boaz, Boaz of Obed, Obed of Jesse, and Jesse of David.

Ruth is the very picture of a strong woman. She gleans barley, working among the men, for what are stated to be very long days. She is devoted more to her mother-in-law than to any man in the story, including her husband; in fact, she takes over the job of providing for Naomi after the death of Naomi's husband. Note that Ruth's willingness to marry Boaz is not based upon any sexual attraction to him, but rather on Ruth's obedience to Naomi. What both Naomi and Ruth seem to like about Boaz are his kindness and integrity. He is observant of the law and respectful of Ruth even though Ruth is in a vulnerable position—both when he finds her in the fields, and when he finds her at his feet in bed. It would seem that Boaz meets Naomi's and Ruth's standards for a good husband—a kind man and a good provider. Boaz may be, like Adam, lonely and in need of companionship, and so this may all be as he would like; but the reader is not told anything about Boaz's wishes. His will is simply not of interest.

Thus, we see here, in a sense, a woman's book, filled with women's choices and women's love for each other. Naomi and Ruth live together in the absence of men, looking out for each other and making decisions that are in their own and each other's best interests. The story tells us about the biblical vision of the "good woman"—one who is strong and obedient—but it also tells us about the biblical vision of a world arranged as women would have it, and it is apparently a happy, well-functioning community.

SUGGESTED READINGS—PART ONE

Allen, Reginald. *Greek Philosophy from Thales to Aristotle.* New York: Free Press, 1966.

Arthur, Marylin B. "Early Greece: The Origins of the Western Attitude Toward Women," in *Women in the Ancient World,* J. Peradotto and J.P. Sullivan (eds). Albany: State University of New York Press, 1984.

———— "The Divided World of *Iliad* VI,"in *Reflections of Women in Antiquity,* Helen P. Foley (ed). New York: Gordon and Breach Science Publishers, 1981.

Barnstone, Willis (ed.) *Sappho and the Greek Lyric Poets.* New York: Schocken, 1988.

Bloom, Harold. *The Book of J.* New York: Grove Weidenfeld, 1990.

Burkert, W. *Greek Religion, Archaic and Classical.* Oxford: Oxford University Press, 1985.

Cairus, Douglas L. *Aidos: The Psychology and Ethics of Honor and Shame in Ancient Greek Literature.* Oxford: Clarendon Press, 1993.

Claus, D.B. "Defining Moral Terms in *Works and Days.*" *Transactions and Proceedings of the American Philological Association.* 107: 73–84, 1977.

Cottrell, Jack. *Gender Roles in the Bible: Creation, the Fall and Redemption: A Critique of Feminist Biblical Interpretation.* Joplin: College Press, 1994.

Deen, Edith. *All of the Women of the Bible.* New York: Harper & Brothers, 1955.

DuBois, Page. "Sappho and Helen," in *Women in the Ancient World,* J. Peradotto and J.P. Sullivan (eds). Albany: State University of New York Press, 1984.

Farron, S. "The Portrayal of Women in *The Iliad.*"*Acta Classica* 22: 15–31, 1979.

Foley, Helen P. "'Reverse Similes' and Sex Roles in the *Odyssey.*" *Women in the Ancient World,* J. Peradotto and J.P. Sullivan (eds). Albany: State University of New York Press, 1984.

Gaster, Theodor H. *Myth, Legend and Custom in the Old Testament.* New York: Harper & Row, 1969.

Guthrie, K.S. *The Pythagorean Sourcebook and Library.* Grand Rapids: Phanes Press, 1987.

Guthrie, W.K.C. *The Greek Philosophers From Thales to Aristotle.* New York: Harper & Row, 1960.

Harding, Sandra. "Is Gender a Variable in Conceptions of Rationality: A Survey of Issues." *Dialectica* 36: 225–242, 1982.

Harris, Kevin. *Sex, Ideology and Religion: The Representation of Women in the Bible.* Tottowa: Barnes and Noble, 1984.

Hesiod. *Hesiod.* R. Lattimore (trans). Ann Arbor: University of Michigan Press, 1978.

Homer. *The Iliad.* R. Fagles (trans). New York: Penguin Books, 1990.

———. *The Iliad of Homer.* R. Lattimore (trans). Chicago: University of Chicago Press, 1967.

———. *The Odyssey of Homer.* R. Lattimore (trans). New York: Harper & Row, 1975.

Howatson, M.C., and Ian Chilvers. *The Concise Oxford Companion to Classical Literature.* Oxford: Oxford University Press, 1993.

Irwin, Terence (ed). *Classical Philosophy: Collected Papers Vol. I: Philosophy Before Socrates.* New York: Garland, 1995.

Jenkyns, Richard. *Three Classical Poets: Sappho, Catullus, and Juvenal.* Cambridge: Harvard University Press, 1982.

Kam, Rose. *Their Stories, Our Stories: Women of the Bible.* New York: Continuum, 1995.

Kirk, G.S., J.E. Raven and M. Schofield (eds). *The Presocratic Philosophers.* Cambridge: Cambridge University Press, 1983.

Kirk, G.S. (ed). *The Iliad: A Commentary.* Cambridge: Cambridge University Press, 1985.

Lamberton, Robert. *Hesiod.* New Haven: Yale University Press, 1988.

Lefkowitz, M.R. *Women in Greek Myth.* London: Duckworth, 1986.

McKirahan, Richard D., Jr. *Philosophy Before Socrates: an Introduction with Texts and Commentaries.* Indianapolis: Hackett, 1994.

Mickelsen, Alvera (ed). *Women, Authority and the Bible.* Downers Grove: InterVarsity Press, 1986.

Mourelatos, Alexander P.D. (ed). *The Pre-Socratics: A Collection of Critical Essays.* Garden City: Anchor Books, 1974.

Murray, Oswyn. *Early Greece.* Cambridge: Harvard University Press, 1993.

———. *The Route of Parmenides.* New Haven: Yale University Press, 1970.

Nye, Andrea. "Rethinking Male and Female: The Pre-Hellenic Philosophy of Mortal Opinion." *History of European Ideas* 9: 261–280, 1988.

Ostriker, Alicia. *Feminist Revision and the Bible.* Oxford: Blackwell, 1993.

———. *The Nakedness of the Fathers: Biblical Visions and Revisions.* New Brunswick: Rutgers University Press, 1994.

Page, Sir Denys Lionel. *Sappho and Alcaeus.* Oxford: Clarendon Press, 1979.

Pantel, Pauline Schmitt, (ed). *A History of Women In the West I: From Ancient Goddesses to Christian Saints.* Cambridge: Harvard University Press, 1993.

Pardes, Ilana. *Countertraditions in the Bible: A Feminist Approach.* Cambridge: Harvard University Press, 1992.

Phillips, J.A. *Eve: The History of an Idea.* San Francisco: Harper & Row, 1984.

Redfield, J.M. *Nature and Culture in the Iliad: The Tragedy of Hector.* Chicago: University of Chicago Press, 1975.

Rissman, Leah. *Love as War: Homeric Allusion in the Poetry of Sappho.* Konigstein: Hain, 1983.

Sappho. *Poems and Fragments.* Josephine Balmer (ed.) Secaucus: Meadowland Books, 1984.

Sihvola, Juha. *Decay, Progress, The Good Life?: Hesiod and Protogoras on the Development of Culture.* Helsinki: Societus Scientiarum Fennica, 1989.

Snell, Bruno. *The Discovery of the Mind: The Greek Origins of European Thought.* Oxford: Blackwell, 1953.

Stigers, Eva S. "Sappho's Private World," in *Reflections of Women in Antiquity*. Helen P. Foley (ed). New York: Gordon and Breach, 1981.

Sussman, Linda S. "Workers and Drones: Labor, Idleness and Gender Definition in Hesiod's Beehive," in *Women in the Ancient World*. J. Peradotto and J.P. Sullivan (eds). Albany: State University of New York Press, 1984.

Thalmann, William G. *Conventions of Form and Thought in Early Greek Epic Poetry*. Baltimore: Johns Hopkins University Press, 1984.

Vlastos, Gregory. *Studies in Greek Philosophy (V. I)— The Presocratics*. Princeton: Princeton University Press, 1995.

Weil, Simone. *"The Iliad,* Poem of Might" in *Simone Weil: An Anthology,* S. Miles (ed). New York: Weidenfeld and Nicolson, 1986.

West, M.L. *The Hesiodic Catalogue of Women*. Oxford: Oxford University Press, 1985.

Winkler, Jack. "Gardens of Nymphs: Public and Private in Sappho's Lyrics." in *Reflections of Women in Antiquity*. Helen P. Foley (ed). New York: Gordon and Breach, 1981.

PART TWO

THE CLASSICAL PERIOD:
GENDER AS A QUESTION
OF VIRTUE AND POLITY

Aeschylus, Sophocles, Plato, Aristotle and St. Paul

INTRODUCTION

THE SIGNIFICANCE OF THE GOLDEN AGE

The twentieth-century philosopher, Alfred North Whitehead, is famous for saying, (among other things) that the history of Western philosophy is a series of footnotes to Plato. Without going so far as that, we can certainly say that Plato and Aristotle, along with the dramatists and orators of the "golden age" of ancient Greece, are the cornerstones of Western philosophy and, it could be argued, Western culture. It is within these thinkers that we find the first sustained reflections on existence, logic, knowledge, moral goodness, beauty, and the human condition; and in many ways their views on these issues remain the definitive statements to which all other Western thinkers compare themselves. Therefore, if we are to understand the development of thought about gender within Western culture, it is imperative that we consider how these ancient Greeks of the fifth through the fourth centuries B.C.E. treated the issue.

Today there is a commonly held, but quite wrong, impression of these fundamental figures: that they overlooked the role and nature of women entirely, except as an afterthought and an unflattering comparison to men. But both Plato and Aristotle, as well as the Greek dramatists who were their literary counterparts, devoted considerable attention to the questions of gender and sex, in a variety of texts and contexts. Contemporary scholars disagree about whether the Greek conceptions of femininity were right or wrong, good or bad—but few can deny that the great Greek thinkers treated the question in what were, for their time, new and thoughtful ways. Plato, in particular, advocated a radical equality of the sexes in the *Republic,* probably his most famous work. His defense of women's status has led some scholars to call him "the first feminist." Plato was, at any rate, a far more radical proponent of women's equality with men than his own student, Aristotle, who is generally taken to be quite representative of the attitudes of his day towards women. Yet others claim that, however stunning Plato's views of women might have been for his time, they remain, by our standards, irreparably sexist. As we will see below, Aristotle's view is on the face of it patently sexist, yet some philosophers have found the underlying themes of Aristotle's ethics to be similar to some recent feminist ethics (for instance, Carol Gilligan, whose work is excerpted in Part Six), and the Greek tragic heroines also promote debate along these lines among literary critics and modern playwrights. The passages that follow offer you an opportunity to judge for yourself how fair-minded and accurate are these foundational reflections on femininity and masculinity.

One important historical occurrence ties all these important thinkers together: the rise of Athens to political prominence among the Greek city-states in the first quarter of the fifth century B.C.E. After its success in the Persian War, Athens became the foremost military power among the Greeks, and consequently set the cultural standards for the entire area as well. The political system of Athens at the time was a quite radical participatory democracy (at least in the sense that all citizens served in the government; citizenship in Athens was restricted to free men). Thus, public speaking—the ability to sway the sympathies of a large crowd—was a skill held in very high regard indeed. In addition, Athens was the principal city for theatrical productions, where the contests for excellence in playwriting were held. Thus Athens was a phenomenally wealthy, diverse, intellectually and culturally stimulating city, in which the military and political virtues held in high regard across Greece were particularly prominent. It is no surprise that such a city—the city of the goddess of wisdom, Athena—mothered the playwrights and philosophers who themselves fathered Western political criticism, literary style, literary criticism, moral theory, and metaphysics.

GENDER AND CHARACTER IN ANCIENT GREECE

The ancient Greeks understood the question of gender in a very different way from how we might today. For them, gender was understood as a part of a general inquiry into the order and foundations of nature, morality, and the state, and through the particular character of individual people and cities. Sharing a common tradition in Homer and Hesiod, these thinkers understood universal qualities like masculinity and femininity as rationally explainable, on par with any other natural or human phenomena, and manifested in a unique way in each particular person or city. A person who understood the order and origin of nature would thereby, these thinkers imply, be able to take his or her proper place in that order, by behaving in accordance with his or her role in the state, whose rational order was itself a part and a reflection of the divine order to be found in the natural world. Then and only then would an individual be able to flourish and be happy, which for the Greeks of this time was the ultimate goal of moral action. In this way, human happiness, political and social obligation, and the physical conditions of people and their environment were of a piece, the particulars through which the natural forces at work in the universe expressed themselves. Thus, for these thinkers, the question of gender was ultimately answered through an investigation of nature, virtue (or "excellence" of character), and the state (or its laws). For the Greeks, the proper treatment or behavior of women was simply one among many considerations with which the moral or political thinker naturally concerned himself.

We could say that the thinkers of this era treated the question of gender primarily through their investigations of the notion of nature and moral character. The dramatists Aeschylus and Sophocles treat the question of gender through the consequences of the actions of their tragic characters; Plato and Aristotle look at gender through the philosophical analysis of good and bad human characteristics. Each of these thinkers adopts, in different ways, the Homeric and Hesiodic notion that the dynastic household, its ancestry, and its head are *microcosms* of the constitution, tradition, and leader of a city. Thus, the personal motivations and personality traits of household members and individuals at once also signify the political motivations and cultural traits of a Greek city-state. These personal and political histories of the individual characters and their cities have their virtuous and vicious strains by nature, as well their moral ideals, the combination and conflict between which is the stuff of tragedy and political theory.

Because of the analogy that holds between the city and the household and individual, the "good woman" or "good man" tends to be associated with the "really Greek woman or man," and the "bad woman" tends to be associated with treason, foreign alliances, or unjust law, and the same for men, in the Greek dramas. The tragic character, then, is one who has divided loyalties and a divided nature—a "true" Greek in a foreign or unjust state or situation, or a "true" foreigner in a Greek territory, family, or tradition. Thus, the tragedy always expresses itself in the form of an injustice or treason, and its resolution is always in some sense the rectification of this injustice. In terms of gender, then, these Greek authors offer us their insights into the kinds of tragic conflict that women and men by their natures call upon themselves, the kinds of inner conflicts and political schisms typical of men and women, and the kinds of resolutions available to members of each sex according to nature and by virtue of Greek cultural and moral traditions.

Plato and Aristotle also consider the question of gender in terms of human nature and political goods. As philosophers rather than dramatists, however, they do not explore these issues through tragic characters, but rather through rational discourse about humanity and the state. The primary purpose for them is to understand justice and moral good themselves, and the roles of men and women in the state and the household, and the goodness of their characters, are treated as derivable from these principles. Of course, in neither case are the definitions of justice or goodness unarguable; in fact, Plato and Aristotle disagree quite strongly with each other about them. Nevertheless, their claims about the just treatment and behavior of men and women are for them arguable primarily in terms of these more fundamental goods. Plato and Aristotle will share with their contemporaries, the playwrights, a sense for the interdependence of the notions of "justice" and "Greekness," and hence for the relation between injustice and divided loyalties. But the philosophers' perspective is in this matter a wider one, in which critical reflection on Greek culture and the search for more universal notions of "law" and "good" are welcome. Thus they offer, as a part of their moral and political thought, rigorous and systematic treatments of human nature, and consequently of the natures of women and men.

CHARACTER, NATURE, AND LAW

Both the tragedy and philosophy of this period can be seen as a development from the various natural-scientific, religious, and political strains of preSocratic thought, such as those presented in the last section. We might summarize this development as the ancient Greeks themselves seem to have understood it—as the development of the belief that the character of individuals and cities, and the human moral and political good towards which they strove, is hidden in the similarities and differences, the harmony and dissonance, between nature and law—or in Greek, *physis* and *nomos*. Where a person is by nature wildly out of harmony with the laws of her or his city, or where the laws of a city are wildly out of harmony with the order of nature, the resulting situation is tragic or unjust. When, on the other hand, one's nature—one's passions and inclinations—are well harmonized with his or her ideals, or with the conventions and traditions of his or her city, such a person is called *virtuous,* i.e., he or she achieves what human beings at their best are supposed to achieve.

A continuing debate at the time, and one which the characters in the dramas as well as in the Platonic dialogues play out, concerns whether the foundation of virtue lies in nature or convention (in *physis* or *nomos*).[1] A typical claim for someone holding that nature is the basis of virtue would be that the good person or city is one that acts or enacts laws as much like the natural good—we might call it "justice"—as possible. Thus, natural justice is thought to stand in a position of authority over human actions and human conventions. A typical claim for someone holding that convention or law is the basis of virtue is that the good person or city is one that satisfies the passions and inclinations of citizens within the conventional bounds of the written law. According to such a view, law is in a position of authority over human actions and passions, and nature is imagined as a low thing, outshone by the human achievements of culture and law. This debate is often represented in the dramas as a conflict between a character's *rights* (the position to which he or she is entitled according to law) and his or her *fate* (his or her ultimate

---

[1] This debate is not unlike the modern debates over the origins of gender roles in "nature" or "nurture," or the preSocratic debates about the divine or human origin of sexual difference. You may want to revisit this "*nomos/physis*" distinction when reading later chapters.

just disposition). In the Platonic dialogues, it is often represented as an argument between Socrates, the main character in the dialogues and a believer in the authority of natural law or justice, and a *sophist,* a teacher of public speaking. The sophists, on account of the democratic legislative and judicial systems in Athens, were very powerful people. Most of the sophists who appear in Plato's dialogues believed in the authority of conventional law; in other words, they claimed that the "right" law was whatever law was instituted by the government. Aristotle tends to engage in the debate more openly and explicitly, working out for himself the proper authority in any particular matter.

The distinction between the nature and the conventions of justice is one aspect of a deeper philosophical question that is brought into its full light by the thinkers of the "golden age": the distinction and relation between *reality* and *appearance,* or between what is the case and what seems to be the case. An unjust law is one sign of this. The law is supposed to be just; i.e., it is supposed to be the appearance or manifestation of justice. The occasion of an unjust law, however, shows us that the law may not really be as it appears to be. Thus, we see in the unjust law both the discrepancy between appearances and reality and the relation between them, revealed in our unearthed expectation that the law be just. Similarly, a tragedy reveals that a character who has lived a good life by all appearances may not really be good or happy. The "appearance/reality" distinction may be considered the overriding concern of all philosophy, maybe even the motivation behind all science and literature. In terms of gender, the "feminine man" or the "masculine woman" would be the sign of this distinction, and it is precisely how to understand such cases that concerns the thinkers in this chapter, whether they approach it in a philosophical, scientific, or literary way.

Despite the tradition and outlook that they share, then, the four Greek thinkers in this section differ widely in their specific claims and methods regarding how women and men ought to behave, how they should be treated under law, and of what the reality of femininity and masculinity consists, at least partly because they have differing presuppositions about human nature and the natures of justice, truth, beauty, and good. They also differ greatly in their literary styles and in the notions of education and entertainment that these differing styles imply. In particular, the Greek dramatists tended to tell stories that were already familiar to everyone in their audiences, stories from Homer and Hesiod and other early poets and religious doctrines. By retelling these familiar stories, the dramatists are far more subtle and seductive in putting across interpretations and ethical views that differ from the pre-Homeric and Homeric Greek ideals. On many occasions, they seem not to differ from, but only to explore and expand earlier Greek notions. The sophists also presented opinions that shared the worldview, and often retold the same stories, as in earlier times. Plato and Aristotle differ in style and method from the dramatists and sophists, each using in his own way a purely "philosophical" method—making new myths, telling new stories, rationally examining differing opinions. In what follows, we will hope to flesh out these presuppositions in order to interpret their notions of masculinity and femininity in as thorough and rich a manner as possible, thereby availing ourselves fully of this magnificent era in the history of Western literature.

THE NEW TESTAMENT

The New Testament consists of the four Gospels, which tell the story of the life of Christ; the Acts of the Apostles, written by Luke, the author of the third Gospel, and recording the history of the development of the Christian Church after Christ's death; a series of letters, mostly written by St. Paul, who after his conversion to Christianity was primarily responsible for spreading the religion; and the apocalyptic Revelation of John. Christianity begins, historically, with Judaism. Indeed, much of the New Testament, written during the last half of the first century C.E., is taken up with the story of the development of the Christian Church out of—and also away from—Judaism.

While the God of the New Testament is the same God worshipped in the Old Testament texts—singular and all-powerful—the New Testament accepts that Jesus of Nazareth, who was an itinerant Jewish teacher, is the son of God and the messiah. While later Christian thinkers were taken up with theological questions regarding the seeming philosophical paradoxes implicit in Christ's divinity, the authors of the New Testament simply accepted Jesus as their savior and messiah on the basis of faith and personal revelations. Thus, they took it as their goal to persuade others of their belief and to strengthen and organize the new Church.

This is particularly the case, as we will see, with St. Paul, whose letters are often responses to the concerns of new converts in the various cities he visited. The Gospels present the life of Christ, focusing on his teachings and on the lessons to be learned from and about his death and resurrection. The Acts and Letters attempt to delineate Christian doctrine and the extent of the influence of the Church, according to the authors' best interpretations of Christ's teachings.

1. AESCHYLUS
(Greek, 513/12–456/5 B.C.E.)

Aeschylus was the first of the great tragic playwrights of the golden age. He won his first first prize for tragedy in 484 B.C.E. and is thought to have won twelve more first prizes during his lifetime; posthumous productions of his work continued to take first prize. Scholars believe that Aeschylus wrote over seventy plays in all, though only seven have survived. We will concern ourselves with three of these seven, known today as the "*Oresteia Trilogy.*"

THE *ORESTEIA* TRILOGY

Aeschylus' great trilogy, the *Oresteia* (named for Orestes, the hero of the second and central play) takes its inspiration from one of the same stories that Homer described in the *Iliad* and the *Odyssey*. Here we see the trials of the descendants of Atreus, father of Agamemnon and Menelaus and ruler of Argos, living out the curse set upon them by Atreus' brother, Thyestes. Atreus, in retribution against Thyestes for seducing his wife, and in order to claim the throne of Argos, had killed

Thyestes' children and fed them to their father. It was Agamemnon and Menelaus, the sons of Atreus, who together had waged the war against Troy. The three plays of the *Oresteia—Agamemnon, The Libation Bearers,* and *The Eumenides*—follow the trials of Agamemnon's family after his return to Argos from Troy.

The actions of Clytaemnestra, Agamemnon's wife, fuel the entire trilogy. In retribution against Agamemnon for sacrificing their eldest daughter Iphigeneia and for taking a lover (Cassandra) during the war, and having her own ambitions on the throne of Argos, she murders Agamemnon. Clytemnestra had previously taken Thyestes' son Aegisthus as her lover and had exiled her son Orestes so that she and Aegisthus could rule Argos unimpeded. Her daughter Electra remains in Argos, building resentment against her mother and Aegisthus but helpless towards the situation without Orestes' help. In the second play, *The Libation Bearers,* Orestes returns and kills his mother and Aegisthus. The third play, *The Eumenides,* is far more universal in its theme. Orestes, pursued by the Furies—the avenging spirits of Clytaemnestra—makes his appeal to Apollo and Athene. To resolve the tragic conflicts of the house of Atreus, Athene and Apollo must ultimately resolve their own conflicts with the Furies themselves. Thus, Greek culture develops from a barbaric and tragic encounter with fate into one in which reasoned discourse and law (represented by Apollo) give a meaningful place to the passions (represented by the Furies), over which they nonetheless rule. This resolution is presided over by Athene and is the ultimate completion of the domestic tragedy.

The sexuality of the characters here is an integral motivator for the action of the plays—they cannot be understood without attending to it. Clytaemnestra is a complex working of a paradigmatic feminine character. She has a strength both virtuous and vicious in its expression. Orestes is the pivotal character of the trilogy, since he both inherits the curse and occasions its ultimate rectification. He exemplifies both strength and weakness, both the Greek greatness and its failures, and thus is the hero of the central play. Orestes, not unlike the images of masculine struggle in Homer and Hesiod, must acknowledge and master various feminine and domestic forces in order to ascertain and do his duty. Apollo and the Furies (who are female and avenge the female) play out the battle between the sexes on the universal, or at least pan-Hellenic, plane. Athene, in whom masculinity and femininity are harmonized (it is of note that this harmony occurs in a female divinity) brings the possibility for harmony between the emotional (female) Furies and the rational (male) Apollo, and ultimately, between the gods and human beings.

AGAMEMNON

In this first play of the trilogy, Agamemnon returns to Argos after ten years of fighting at Troy, bringing with him his Trojan captive and concubine, Cassandra. Clytaemnestra, Agamemnon's wife and the sister of Helen of Troy, has had something near to a premonition that Agamemnon has taken this concubine, and that he has sacrificed his and Clytaemnestra's daughter, Iphigeneia, in an effort to sway the gods to the Achaeans' side in the war. In a spirit of vengeance and desperation, Clytaemnestra has taken her own lover, Aegisthus, and has plotted with him to murder Agamemnon and Cassandra. The climax of the play is this murder, and it is represented as the natural, or fated, culmination of both Agamemnon's and Clytaemnestra's characters. They are both strong, decisive, vengeful and somewhat ego-maniacal. The extension of the war had been depicted as the natural outcome of these strains in Agamemnon's character, and they resulted in the rending apart of the community of Greeks. The extension of this civil discord is depicted as the natural outcome of these same strains in Clytaemnestra's character, resulting in the rending apart of the house of Atreus. Both these destructive acts are depicted as unavoidable, because they play out the miserable fate attendant upon Atreus' original action.

AGAMEMNON'S HOMECOMING AND THE BACKDROP OF THE TROJAN WAR

In the early scenes of the play, the chorus set the story into the context of the Trojan war, prepared to greet the returning Agamemnon as a great king and war hero. Clytaemnestra has represented herself to them as the loving wife, and they expect her to welcome Agamemnon home with all the glory they think is due him.

CHORUS: Cry, cry for death, but good win out in glory in the end.

⌐ ⌐ ⌐

Zeus has led us on to know,
the Helmsman lays it down as law
that we must suffer, suffer into truth.
We cannot sleep, and drop by drop at the heart
the pain of pain remembered comes again,
and we resist, but ripeness comes as well.
From the gods enthroned on the awesome rowing-bench
there comes a violent love.

⌐ ⌐ ⌐

CLYTAEMNESTRA: The city's ours—in our hands this very day!
I can hear the cries in crossfire rock the walls.
Pour oil and wine in the same bowl,
what have you, friendship? A struggle to the end.
So with the victors and the victims—outcries,
you can hear them clashing like their fates.

⌐ ⌐ ⌐

And even if the men come back with no offence
to the gods, the avenging dead may never rest—
Oh let no new disaster strike! And here
you have it, what a woman has to say.
Let the best win out, clear to see.
A small desire but all that I could want.

LEADER: Spoken like a man, my lady, loyal,
full of self-command, I've heard your sign
and now your vision.

⌒ ⌒ ⌒

CLYTAEMNESTRA: I cried out long ago!—
for joy, when the first herald came burning
through the night and told the city's fall.
And there were some who smiled and said,
'A few fires persuade you Troy's in ashes.
Women, women, elated over nothing.'

You made me seem deranged.
For all that I sacrificed—a woman's way,
you'll say—station to station on the walls
we lifted cries of triumph that resounded
in the temples of the gods. We lulled and blessed
the fires with myrrh and they consumed our victims.

Turning to the HERALD.

But enough. Why prolong the story?
From the king himself I'll gather all I need.
Now for the best way to welcome home
my lord, my good lord. . .
                                    No time to lose!
What dawn can feast a woman's eyes like this?
I can see the light, the husband plucked from war
by the Saving God and open wide the gates.

Tell him that, and have him come with speed,
the people's darling—how they long for him.
And for his wife,
may he return and find her true at hall,
just as the day he left her, faithful to the last.
A watchdog gentle to him alone,

Glancing towards the palace.

                        savage
to those who cross his path. I have not changed.
The strains of time can never break our seal.
In love with a new lord, in ill repute I am
as practised as I am in dyeing bronze.

That is my boast, teeming with the truth.
I am proud, a woman of my nobility—
I'd hurl it from the roofs!

She turns sharply, enters the palace.

⌒ ⌒ ⌒

AGAMEMNON *enters in his chariot, his*
plunder borne before him by his
entourage; behind him, half hidden,
stands CASSANDRA. *The old men press*
towards him.

CHORUS: Come, my king, the scourge of Troy,
    the true son of Atreus—
How to salute you, how to praise you
neither too high nor low, but hit
the note of praise that suits the hour?
So many prize some brave display,
they prefer some flaunt of honour
    once they break the bounds.

ᕱ ᕱ ᕱ

I say Well fought, well won—
    the end is worth the labour!
Search, my king, and learn at last
who stayed at home and kept their faith
    and who betrayed the city.

AGAMEMNON: First,
    with justice I salute my Argos and my gods,
my accomplices who brought me home and won
my rights from Priam's Troy—the just gods.
No need to hear our pleas. Once for all
they consigned their lots to the urn of blood,
they pitched on death for men, annihilation
for the city. Hope's hand, hovering
over the urn of mercy, left it empty.
Look for the smoke—it is the city's seamark,
building even now.
                The storms of ruin live!
Her last dying breath, rising up from the ashes
sends us gales of incense rich in gold.

For that we must thank the gods with a sacrifice
our sons will long remember. For their mad outrage
of a queen we raped their city—we were right.
The beast of Argos, foals of the wild mare,
thousands massed in armour rose on the night
the Pleiades went down, and crashing through
their walls our bloody lion lapped its fill,
gorging on the blood of kings.
             Our thanks to the gods,
long drawn out, but it is just the prelude.

> CLYTAEMNESTRA *approaches with her*
> *women; they are carrying dark red*
> *tapestries.* AGAMEMNON *turns to the*
> *leader.*

Now I go to my father's house—
I give the gods my right hand, my first salute.
The ones who sent me forth have brought me home.

> *He starts down from the chariot, looks at*
> CLYTAEMNESTRA, *stops, and offers up a*
> *prayer.*

Victory, you have sped my way before,
now speed me to the last.

> CLYTAEMNESTRA *turns from the king to the*
> CHORUS.

CLYTAEMNESTRA: Old nobility of Argos
gathered here, I am not ashamed to tell you
how I love the man. I am older,
and the fear dies away . . . I am human.
Nothing I say was learned from others.
This is my life, my ordeal, long as the siege
he laid at Troy and more demanding.
                                                First,
when a woman sits at home and the man is gone,
the loneliness is terrible,
unconscionable . . .
and the rumours spread and fester,
a runner comes with something dreadful,
close on his heels the next and his news worse,
and they shout it out and the whole house can hear;
and wounds—if he took one wound for each report
to penetrate these walls, he's gashed like a dragnet,
more, if he had only died . . .
for each death that swelled his record, he could boast
like a triple-bodied Geryon risen from the grave,
'Three shrouds I dug from the earth, one for every body
that went down!'
                        The rumours broke like fever,
broke and then rose higher. There were times
they cut me down and eased my throat from the noose.
I wavered between the living and the dead.

> *Turning to* AGAMEMNON.

And so
our child is gone, not standing by our side, ,
the bond of our dearest pledges, mine and yours;
by all rights our child should be here . . .
Orestes. You seem startled.
You needn't be. Our loyal brother-in-arms
will take good care of him, Strophios the Phocian.
He warned from the start we court two griefs in one.
You risk all on the wars—and what if the people
rise up howling for the king, and anarchy
should dash our plans?
                        Men, it is their nature,
trampling on the fighter once he's down.
Our child is gone. That is my self-defence
and it is true.
                    For me, the tears that welled
like springs are dry. I have no tears to spare.
I'd watch till late night, my eyes still burn,
I sobbed by the torch I lit for you alone.

Glancing towards the palace.

I never let it die . . . but in my dreams
the high thin wail of a gnat would rouse me,
piercing like a trumpet—I could see you
suffer more than all
the hours that slept with me could ever bear.

I endured it all. And now, free of grief,
I would salute that man the watchdog of the fold,
the mainroyal, saving stay of the vessel,
rooted oak that thrusts the roof sky-high,
the father's one true heir.
Land at dawn to the shipwrecked past all hope,
light of the morning burning off the night of storm,
the cold clear spring to the parched horseman—
    the ecstasy, to flee the yoke of Fate!

☙ ☙ ☙

It is right to use the titles he deserves.
Let envy keep her distance. We have suffered
long enough.

Reaching towards AGAMEMNON.

        Come to me now, my dearest,
down from the car of war, but never set the foot
that stamped out Troy on earth again, my great one.

Women, why delay? You have your orders.
Pave his way with tapestries.

> *They begin to spread the crimson*
> *tapestries between the king and the*
> *palace doors.*

Quickly.
Let the red stream flow and bear him home
to the home he never hoped to see—Justice,
lead him in!
                    Leave all the rest to me.
The spirit within me never yields to sleep.
We will set things right, with the god's help.
We will do whatever Fate requires.

"Cry, cry for death, but good win out in glory in the end" and "we must suffer, suffer into truth" are repeated by the chorus[2] several times, giving the play—and indeed, tragedy in general—its theme. The various misfortunes fated to this family and city must play themselves out, but through the characters' willingness to accept this fate nobly, it is hoped that the curse of the house of Atreus will eventually be exhausted, and good will be restored. The chorus believes that with Agamemnon's return, the city's suffering will be over. As they see it, the war and its consumption of their wealth and populace have been the only suffering they have had to face. Clytaemnestra has encouraged them in this mistaken belief, playing all the while the loyal loving wife. Agamemnon, too, has enabled the chorus in their folly, presenting himself to them as a righteous king and a moral leader. In this way, the audience is set up for the tragic climax, in which they will discover how false is the facade of the king and queen.

Gender imagery plays an important part in setting up these false expectations. In particular, the entitlements of women are contrasted to the actions of women throughout these opening speeches. Helen had abandoned her Atrean city, to which she owes the rights and responsibilities of rulership; her actions went against the woman's right—as these rights are understood by the chorus—and so led to misery in the city. Clytaemnestra is represented in these early speeches as upholding the woman's right to rule—again, as understood by the chorus—ruling in her husband's stead while he fought nobly away from home. Agamemnon too, is represented as having manly virtues—bravery in battle, decisiveness about the sacrifice of Iphigeneia, lusty and masterful possession of Cassandra.

---

[2] The Greek chorus is a literary device about which there has been much literary-critical debate. In general, the chorus is a group of characters who are situated as would be "ordinary" citizens of the city at the time of the action of the play (although there are exceptions to this — for instance, the chorus of "furies" in the third play of Aeschylus' *Oresteia*). In other words, the chorus is reflective upon the events of the tragedy, which are not, after all happening to them; but they do so *as if* the events were *really* happening in front of them. They do not already know, as the audience may, the myth that is being retold in the tragedy or the interior motivations of the characters.

The chorus is thinking of gender roles—actions in accordance with rights—in terms of conventional law, or *nomos.* Their mistake comes in not recognizing that Atreus' original action, and the curse he put on his descendants, violently tore the *nomos,* the conventional law founded in the king's actions, from *physis,* the natural justice, or "fate," which is founded in the gods' actions. Agamemnon retains his rights to rule, but not his ability to rule well. Clytaemnestra, on the other hand, will avenge Agamemnon's actions and demand her legal right to rule in his stead. The conventional woman's role that the chorus expects Clytaemnestra to play, therefore, is not her just fate. She is destined to exercise her *natural* right, to exact vengeance upon a husband who has violated his *natural* duty by killing his daughter and betraying his wife.

THE MURDER AND THE JUDGMENT

When Agamemnon and Clytaemnestra met each other once again, their two strong wills immediately clashed. Clytaemnestra wanted Agamemnon to come inside the house where Aegisthus was waiting to kill him, while Agamemnon wanted to stay outside with the crowd. Clytaemnestra, however, unlike Agamemnon, was willing to appear to yield, in order to connive to get her way. Hence, Clytaemnestra won; in the following passages, Agamemnon and his concubine Cassandra go inside the palace and are killed.

> CLYTAEMNESTRA *emerges from the palace and goes to* CASSANDRA, *impassive in the chariot.*

CLYTAEMNESTRA: Won't you come inside? I mean you, Cassandra.
   Zeus in all his mercy wants you to share
   some victory libations with the house.
   The slaves are flocking. Come, lead them
   up to the altar of the god who guards
   our dearest treasures.
            Down from the chariot,
   this is no time for pride.

              ☙ ☙ ☙

LEADER: I think
   the stranger needs an interpreter, someone clear.
   She's like a wild creature, fresh caught.

CLYTAEMNESTRA: She's mad,
   her evil genius murmuring in her ears.
   She comes from a *city* fresh caught.
   She must learn to take the cutting bridle
   before she foams her spirit off in blood—
   and that's the last I waste on her contempt!

> *Wheeling, re-entering the palace. The*
> LEADER *turns to* CASSANDRA, *who remains*
> *transfixed.*

CASSANDRA: His *fire!*—

    sears me, sweeps me again—the torture!
    Apollo Lord of the Light, you burn,
    you blind me—
               Agony!
                       She is the lioness,
    she rears on her hind legs, she beds with the wolf
    when her lion king goes ranging—
                           she will kill me—
    Ai, the torture!

                       ☙ ☙ ☙

> *Regaining her composure and moving to*
> *the altar.*

               We will die,
    but not without some honour from the gods.
    There will come another to avenge us,
    born to kill his mother, born
    his father's champion. A wanderer, a fugitive
    driven off his native land, he will come home
    to cope the stones of hate that menace all he loves.
    The gods have sworn a monumental oath: as his father lies
    upon the ground he draws him home with power like a prayer.

    Then why so pitiful, why so many tears?
    I have seen my city faring as she fared,
    and those who took her, judged by the gods,
    faring as they fare. I must be brave.
    It is my turn to die.

                       ☙ ☙ ☙

> *Cries break out within the palace.*

AGAMEMNON: Aagh!
    Struck deep—the death-blow, deep—

LEADER: Quiet. Cries,
    but who? Someone's stabbed—

AGAMEMNON: Aaagh, again . . .
    second blow—struck home.

LEADER: The work is done,
    you can feel it. The king, and the great cries—

Close ranks now, find the right way out.

> *But the old men scatter.*

⌒ ⌒ ⌒

> *He rushes at the doors. They open and*
> *reveal a silver cauldron that holds the*
> *body of* AGAMEMNON *shrouded in bloody*
> *robes, with the body of* CASSANDRA *to his*
> *left and* CLYTAEMNESTRA *standing to his*
> *right, sword in hand. She strides towards*
> *the chorus.*

CLYTAEMNESTRA: Words, endless words I've said to serve the moment—
now it makes me proud to tell the truth.
How else to prepare a death for deadly men
who seem to love you? How to rig the nets
of pain so high no man can overleap them?
I brooded on this trial, this ancient blood feud
year by year. At last my hour came.
Here I stand and here I struck
and here my work is done.
I did it all. I don't deny it, no.
He had no way to flee or fight his destiny—

> *Unwinding the robes from* AGAMEMNON'S
> *body, spreading them before the altar*
> *where the old men cluster around them,*
> *unified as a chorus once again.*

It is right and more than right. He flooded
the vessel of our proud house with misery,
with the vintage of the curse and now
he drains the dregs. My lord is home at last.

LEADER: You appal me, you, your brazen words—
exulting over your fallen king.

CLYTAEMNESTRA: And you,
you try me like some desperate woman.
My heart is steel, well you know. Praise me,
blame me as you choose. It's all one.
Here is Agamemnon, my husband made a corpse
by this right hand—a masterpiece of Justice.
Done is done.

⌒ ⌒ ⌒

And now you sentence me?—
you banish *me* from the city, curses breathing
down my neck? But *he*—
name one charge you brought against him then.
He thought no more of it than killing a beast,
and his flocks were rich, teeming in their fleece,
but he sacrificed his own child, our daughter,
the agony I laboured into love
to charm away the savage winds of Thrace.
Didn't the law demand you banish him?—
hunt him from the land for all his guilt?
But now you witness what I've done
and you are ruthless judges.

Threaten away!

⤚ ⤚ ⤚

This is no concern of yours.
The hand that bore and cut him down
will hand him down to Mother Earth.
This house will never mourn for him.
    Only our daughter Iphigeneia,
by all rights, will rush to meet him
first at the churning straits,
the ferry over tears—
she'll fling her arms around her father,
pierce him with her love.

CHORUS: Each charge meets counter-charge.
    None can judge between them. Justice. . . .

CLYTAEMNESTRA: . . . Fathers of Argos, turn for home before you act
    and suffer for it. What we did was destiny.
    If we could end the suffering, how we would rejoice.
    The spirit's brutal hoof has struck our heart.
    And that is what a woman has to say.
    Can you accept the truth?

Cassandra provides a parallel to Clytaemnestra's higher understanding of justice, in her prophesying. Cassandra, however, since she has no conventional rights or role at all (she is a foreigner and a concubine), cannot manifest her prophetic gift in action, nor even in coherent speech, whereas Clytaemnestra is in full control of her actions and speech because of her rightful position as queen. Both women, however, are able to understand their natural obligations and to accept their fate; in this play, the women are never surprised. The women's characters have a seemingly super-human, natural insight, which allies them with fate and natural justice, despite their mortality and human weakness. Notably, Clytaemnestra's strength and will and her desire to rule appear manly to the chorus.

That Clytaemnestra is indeed behaving justly despite the violence of her act is evidenced in her closing speeches, in which she points to the real, natural good which will come of this "sorrow, sorrow: " Iphigeneia will kiss her father in the underworld, and the house of Atreus will be restored to legitimate and just rulership. Thus, we get a picture from the play as a whole that the woman's natural right has not been manifested in law, and that therefore the apparently good law—represented in the person of the apparently good king—is unjust. The city, unbeknownst to the chorus, audience, and Agamemnon himself, had been rent apart long ago by Atreus' act, and Agamemnon's behavior merely demonstrated this fissure. Clytaemnestra's decisive action, though violent, is a step towards the reunion of the city; it is an action which has its natural consequences, however, and they must be played out before the city can be restored to justice.

THE LIBATION BEARERS

The second and central play of the Oresteia trilogy begins with what should be by now a familiar scene—a man returning home to his family and city to restore himself to the throne. This time, however, the returning hero has not honored himself in battle. He is Orestes, son of Clytaemnestra and Agamemnon, who has been sequestered in another city while his mother and her lover rule his city illegitimately—at least from his point of view. Orestes is coming home to kill his mother and Aegisthus. As when his father returned to their city, the citizens hope for Orestes, as the legitimate ruler, to restore order and justice and reunite the city under a just law.

The action of *The Libation Bearers,* unlike that of the two plays that bracket it in the trilogy, is entirely earthbound and human, completely ensnared in the ambiguities and illusions of the civil law or *nomos.* Aeschylus positions this play in a masculine role in the trilogy, allying masculinity with the law, the human world, the civil society. We can see this in various different ways, not least of which is the fact that the protagonist of this play is male where the protagonists of the other two plays are female—Clytaemnestra in the first play and the Furies in the last. Orestes, though willing and eager to act, does not inspire the audience to copy his noble deed. Rather, he is all swept up in the human world of action and law, myopically pursuing the throne, without a sense for the higher justice of Clytaemnestra's actions, nor for the natural obligations of a son to his mother. For Aeschylus, this human-male condition of discomfort and lack of clarity is an object of scrutiny, and his genius as a playwright is perhaps best demonstrated in his analysis of the interplay of strength and weakness, nature and convention, legitimacy and illegitimacy, justice and injustice, knowledge and ignorance, that results in what is known as the human character.

The play opens with Electra, at her mother's bidding, arriving at her father's gravesite to pour a libation as a gesture of mourning—hence, the title. This act sets the theme of the play, whose whole action is, in a sense, a gesture of mourning. Like Electra's libation, her brother Orestes' murder of his mother and Aegisthus is figured by the title as a kind of ritual, a gesture of honor for his dead father.

ORESTES AND CLYTAEMNESTRA

Orestes plans to enter the house masquerading as a stranger and to kill Aegisthus when, according to custom, he takes Orestes in as guest. Thus, Orestes will abuse the conventional obligations of a host to his guest, and this abuse is represented as a pretense of being foreign. Orestes, rather than judging the actions of his stepfather and king by the standard of justice, merely plays conventions against themselves in order to get his own way. He exacts Electra's promise to keep his identity a secret and enters the house to kill first Aegisthus and then his own mother.

To establish his plan, Orestes inquires of the chorus about Clytaemnestra's libation. This is a moment of conscience for Orestes, a chance to reflect upon the justice of his actions, but he misses the opportunity it provides. The chorus explains that Clytaemnestra has ordered the libation because of a dream she recently had. Orestes interprets the dream as a justification of the murder he is about to do. We see, however, as he is about to kill Clytaemnestra, that the dream is an image of her son's character and of the tragic nature of her relationship to him. Had Orestes interpreted it the same way, as we see, he might have stayed his hand.

LEADER: I know, my boy,
   I was there. She had bad dreams. Some terror
   came groping through the night, it shook her,
   and she sent these cups, unholy woman.

ORESTES: And you know the dream, you can tell it clearly?

LEADER: She dreamed she bore a snake, said so herself and . . .

ORESTES: Come to the point—where does the story end?

LEADER: . . . she swaddled it like a baby, laid it to rest.

ORESTES: And food, what did the little monster want?

LEADER: She gave it her breast to suck—she was dreaming.

ORESTES: And didn't it tear her nipple, the brute inhuman—

LEADER: Blood curdled the milk with each sharp tug . . .

ORESTES: No empty dream. The vision of a man.

LEADER: . . . and she woke with a scream, appalled,

        ☞ ☞ ☞

ORESTES:

        ☞ ☞ ☞

   If the serpent came from the same place as I,
   and slept in the bands that swaddled me, and its jaws
   spread wide for the breast that nursed me into life

and clots stained the milk, mother's milk,
and she cried in fear and agony—so be it.
As she bred this sign, this violent prodigy
so she dies by violence. I turn serpent,
I kill her. So the vision says.

☙ ☙ ☙

CHORUS:

A scream inside the palace.

☙ ☙ ☙

—Listen!
          —What's happening?
                    —The house,
what have they done to the house?

LEADER: Back,
     till the work is over! Stand back—
     they'll count us clean of the dreadful business.

> *The women scatter; a wounded* SERVANT
> *OF* AEGISTHUS *enters.*

Look, the die is cast, the battle's done.

SERVANT: Ai,
     Ai, all over, master's dead—Aie,
     a third, last salute. Aegisthus is no more.

☙ ☙ ☙

> *The door opens, and* CLYTAEMNESTRA
> *comes forth.*

CLYTAEMNESTRA: What now?
     Why this shouting up and down the halls?

SERVANT: The dead are cutting down the quick, I tell you!

CLYTAEMNESTRA: Ah, a riddle. I do well at riddles.
     By cunning we die, precisely as we killed.
     Hand me the man-axe, someone, hurry!

> *The* SERVANT *dashes out.*

Now we will see. Win all or lose all,
we have come to this—the crisis of our lives.

> *The main doors open;* ORESTES, *sword*
> *in hand, is standing over the body of*
> AEGISTHUS, *with* PYLADES *close behind*
> *him.*

ORESTES: It's you I want. This one's had enough.

CLYTAEMNESTRA: Gone, my violent one—Aegisthus, very dear.

ORESTES: You love your man? Then lie in the same grave.
You can never be unfaithful to the dead.

> *Pulling her towards* AEGISTHUS' *body.*

CLYTAEMNESTRA: Wait, my son—no respect for this, my child?
The breast you held, drowsing away the hours,
soft gums tugging the milk that made you grow? . . .

> ORESTES *turns to* PYLADES.

ORESTES:

> *Wheeling on* CLYTAEMNESTRA, *thrusting
> her towards* AEGISTHUS.

⌒ ⌒ ⌒

I want to butcher you—right across his body!
In life you thought he dwarfed my father—*Die!*—
go down with him forever!
You love this man,
the man you should have loved you hated.

CLYTAEMNESTRA: I gave you life. Let me grow old with you.

ORESTES: What—kill my father, then you'd live with me?

CLYTAEMNESTRA: Destiny had a hand in that, my child.

ORESTES: This too: destiny is handing you your death.

CLYTAEMNESTRA: You have no fear of a mother's curse, my son?

ORESTES: Mother? You flung me to a life of pain.

CLYTAEMNESTRA: Never flung you, placed you in a comrade's house.

ORESTES: —Disgraced me, sold me, a freeborn father's son.

CLYTAEMNESTRA: Oh? then name the price I took for you.

ORESTES: I am ashamed to mention it in public.

CLYTAEMNESTRA: Please, and tell your father's failings, too.

ORESTES: Never judge him—he suffered, you sat here at home.

CLYTAEMNESTRA: It hurts women, being kept from men, my son.

ORESTES: Perhaps . . . but the man slaves to keep them safe at home.

CLYTAEMNESTRA: —I see murder in your eyes, my child—mother's murder!

ORESTES: You are the murderer, not I—and you will kill yourself.

CLYTAEMNESTRA: Watch out—the hounds of a mother's curse will hunt you
down.

ORESTES: But how to escape a father's if I fail?

CLYTAEMNESTRA: I must be spilling live tears on a tomb of stone.

ORESTES: Yes, my father's destiny—it decrees your death.

CLYTAEMNESTRA: Ai—you are the snake I bore—I gave you life!

ORESTES: *Yes*!
That was the great seer, that terror in your dreams.
You killed and it was outrage—suffer outrage now.

> *He draws her over the threshold; the*
> *doors close behind them, and the chorus*
> *gathers at the altar.*

The conversation between Orestes and Clytaemnestra is a beautiful example of a tragic misunderstanding, with Orestes grabbing at straws to justify his upcoming act and Clytaemnestra arguing incisively for her life and for the respect due a mother from her son. Finally, seeing that Orestes is unable to understand or even consider the wrong done her by his father—that he is unable even to imagine a wife's rights from a husband—she resigns herself to her death. Orestes remains unable to take responsibility for his actions or to reflect upon Clytaemnestra's words, insisting that she is to blame for what he is about to do.

Clytaemnestra's dream, of course, is worthy of a moment's reflection. The son as snake: nurtured by its mother, it draws blood instead of milk. On the most fundamental level, this represents the character of the bad son, turning on the mother who has raised, fed, and loved him—whatever else she may have done. On a deeper level, Orestes is imaged in the dream as a kind of cannibal—he drinks her blood— or barbarian—he seems to be a "foreigner," an animal, not a part of the human society represented by his mother. She, like the good host, offers him food and comfort, the ties of family and home—and he not only refuses these kindnesses, but he robs his host. In the dream, we see the most fundamental difference between Orestes' and Clytaemnestra's seemingly similar acts of murder. Clytaemnestra, Aeschylus implies, sought vengeance for an injustice; Orestes merely seeks his legal right. Thus, the tragedy of the play is the moral emptiness of law divorced from justice, and this political tragedy is represented in terms of the dynastic family, as a son killing his mother.

After the act, Orestes ties the couple up in the same robe with which Clytaemnestra covered Agamemnon. The web, or robe, by now a well-worn feminine symbol from Homeric epics and other early Greek poetry (and shown here to be feminine in that it belonged to Clytaemnestra) is turned against the female. Orestes misunderstands the robe's significance, just as he did the dream's, taking it to be a trap such as a hunter or robber would use. Orestes' repeated misreadings of the signs that portend his fate at this point exact their price. Almost immediately after the murder, Orestes doubts the justice of his actions and is plagued by fear and conscience, personified in his mind, as a vision of a host of women chasing him. Orestes, beginning now through conscience to understand his act, sees the "snakes" as the wreaths of the furious spirits that now harry him.

ORESTES:

⌒ ⌒ ⌒

Clutching AGAMEMNON'S *robes, burying his face in them and weeping.*

Now I can praise you, now I am here to mourn.
You were my father's death, great robe, I hail you!
Even if I must suffer the work and the agony
and all the race of man—
                    I embrace you . . . you,
my victory, are my guilt, my curse, and still—

⌒ ⌒ ⌒

Staring at the women and beyond,
ORESTES *screams in terror.*

No, no! Women—look—like Gorgons,
shrouded in black, their heads wreathed,
swarming serpents!
                    —Cannot stay, I must move on.

LEADER: What dreams can whirl you so? You of all men,
you have your father's love. Steady, nothing
to fear with all you've won.

ORESTES: No dreams, these torments,
not to me, they're clear, real—the hounds
of mother's hate.

THE EUMENIDES

The third and final play of the trilogy is the "*Eumenides*" or "Furies." These are the spirits that haunted Orestes at the end of the second play, the divine spirits of retribution who have taken up Clytaemnestra's cause, torturing Orestes' conscience. In this play, he takes his cause against the Furies to Apollo, asking for the god's help in vanquishing them. After trying unsuccessfully to argue against the Furies himself, Apollo stands by Orestes as he takes the case to Athene. Athene, the goddess of wisdom, turns the question over to an Athenian jury, casting the deciding vote herself. Through Athene, the Furies are satisfied: though they lose their case against Orestes, they win a respected place in Greek civilization.

THE ARGUMENT

In the following passages, the case is presented to Athene and adjudicated by her.

ATHENA: The trial begins! Yours is the first word—
the prosecution opens. Start to finish,
set the facts before us, make them clear.

LEADER: Numerous as we are, we will be brief.

To ORESTES.

Answer count for count, charge for charge.
First, tell us, did you kill your mother?

ORESTES: I killed her. There's no denying that.

LEADER: Three falls in the match. One is ours already.

ORESTES: You exult before your man is on his back.

LEADER: But *how* did you kill her? You must tell us that.

ORESTES: I will. I drew my sword—more, I cut her throat.

LEADER: And who persuaded you? who led you on?

ORESTES: This god and his command.

Indicating APOLLO.

He bears me witness.

LEADER: The Seer? He drove you on to matricide?

ORESTES: Yes,
and to this hour I have no regrets.

LEADER: If the verdict
brings you down, you'll change your story quickly.

ORESTES: I have my trust; my father will help me from the grave.

LEADER: Trust to corpses now! You made your mother one.

ORESTES: I do. She had two counts against her, deadly crimes.

LEADER: How? Explain that to your judges.

ORESTES: She killed her husband—killed my father too.

LEADER: But murder set her free, and you live on for trial.

ORESTES: She lived on. You never drove *her* into exile—why?

LEADER: The blood of the man she killed was not her own.

ORESTES: And I? Does mother's blood run in my veins?

LEADER: How could she breed you in her body, murderer?
  Disclaim your mother's blood? She gave you life.

ORESTES:

ORESTES turns to APOLLO.

Bear me witness—show me the way, Apollo!
Did I strike her down with justice?
Strike I did, I don't deny it, no.
But how does our bloody work impress you now?—
Just or not? Decide.
I must make my case to them.

Looking to the judges.

APOLLO: *Just,*
  I say, to you and your high court, Athena. . . .

꒰ ꒰ ꒰

—Not the same

for a noble man to die, covered with praise,
his sceptre the gift of god—murdered, at that,
by a woman's hand, no arrows whipping in
from a distance as an Amazon would fight.
But as you will hear, Athena, and your people
poised to cast their lots and judge the case.

꒰ ꒰ ꒰

LEADER: So
  you'd force this man's acquittal? Behold, Justice!

Exhibiting APOLLO *and* ORESTES.

Can a son spill his mother's blood on the ground,
then settle into his father's halls in Argos?
Where are the public altars he can use?
Can the kinsmen's holy water touch his hands?

APOLLO: Here is the truth, I tell you—see how right I am.
  The woman you call the mother of the child
  is not the parent, just a nurse to the seed,
  the new-sown seed that grows and swells inside her.
  The *man* is the source of life—the one who mounts.
  She, like a stranger for a stranger, keeps
  the shoot alive unless god hurts the roots.
  I give you proof that all I say is true.
  The father can father forth without a mother.
  Here she stands, our living witness. Look—

Exhibiting ATHENA.

Child sprung full-blown from Olympian Zeus,
never bred in the darkness of the womb
but such a stock no goddess could conceive!

And I, Pallas, with all my strong techniques
will rear your host and battlements to glory.
So I dispatched this suppliant to your hearth
that he might be your trusted friend for ever,
that you might win a new ally, dear goddess.
He and his generations arm-in-arm with yours,
your bonds stand firm for all posterity—

ATHENA: Now
have we heard enough? May I have them cast
their honest lots as conscience may decide?

ḙ ḙ ḙ

ATHENA: My work is here, to render the final judgement.
Orestes,

> *Raising her arm, her hand clenched as if
> holding a ballot-stone.*

I will cast my lot for you.
No mother gave me birth.
I honour the male, in all things but marriage.
Yes, with all my heart I am my Father's child.
I cannot set more store by the woman's death—
she killed her husband, guardian of their house.
Even if the vote is equal, Orestes wins.

Shake the lots from the urns. Quickly,
you of the jury charged to make the count.

> *Judges come forward, empty the urns,
> and count the ballot-stones.*

ḙ ḙ ḙ

> *Receiving the judges' count, Athena lifts
> her arm once more.*

ATHENA: The man goes free,
cleared of the charge of blood. The lots are equal. . . .

The question to be decided is which of the two murders was more just,
Clytaemnestra's of Agamemnon and Cassandra, or Orestes' of Clytaemnestra and
Aegisthus. Orestes claims that he was within his rights to kill his mother, because

she had killed her husband and her king. Apollo argues that Clytaemnestra's action was not honorable, since she trapped her victim instead of facing him, and that anyway, Orestes' familial obligations are stronger to his father than to his mother. Essentially, Apollo argues against the rights of mothers. The Furies argue, on the contrary, that Orestes' act was the less honorable, since mothers and sons are blood relatives, but husbands and wives are not. According to them, the rights of women, and of mothers in particular, are the foundation of the community, and Orestes' act makes him unfit for human society. Thus the argument represents on the larger scale a contest of the rights of mothers against those of fathers, and the role of women in civilized society versus that of men.

ATHENE AND THE FURIES

Athene is quick to side with the men in this and any dispute, perhaps too quick. For after she settles the case in favor of Orestes, she listens sympathetically to the Furies' appeal. Here, Aeschylus makes his final statement on the respective roles and rights of men and women in Greek society. Athene is able to reason with the Furies and to grant them a satisfactory place in civilization, while not overturning her acquittal of Orestes. Thus, while the seemingly masculine world of conventional law, or *nomos*—on which rests Orestes' right to the throne—ultimately takes pride of place in civil society, it can only stand upon the foundation of the older, natural, apparently feminine sense of retribution—on which rests Clytaemnestra's right to vengeance. The son rules, but he remains his mother's son, carrying within him the female source of his life and power.

> *The* FURIES *reel in wild confusion around*
> ATHENA.

FURIES: You, you younger gods!—you have ridden down
the ancient laws, wrenched them from my grasp—
and I, robbed of my birthright, suffering, great with wrath,
I loose my poison over the soil, aieee!—
poison to match my grief comes pouring out my heart,
cursing the land to burn it sterile and now
rising up from its roots a cancer blasting leaf and child,
now for Justice, Justice!—cross the face of the earth
the bloody tide comes hurling, all mankind destroyed.
. . . Moaning, only moaning? What will I do?
    The mockery of it, Oh unbearable,
mortified by Athens,
we the daughters of Night,
our power stripped, cast down.

ATHENA: Yield to me.
No more heavy spirits. You were not defeated—
the vote was tied, a verdict fairly reached

with no disgrace to you, no Zeus brought
luminous proof before us. He who spoke
god's oracle, he bore witness that Orestes
did the work but should not suffer harm.

And now you'd vent your anger, hurt the land?
Consider a moment. Calm yourself. Never
render us barren, raining your potent showers
down like spears, consuming every seed.
By all my rights I promise you your seat
in the depths of earth, yours by all rights—
stationed at hearths equipped with glistening thrones,
covered with praise! My people will revere you.

⤳ ⤳ ⤳

ATHENA: No, I will never tire
of telling you your gifts. So that you,
the older gods, can never say that I,
a young god and the mortals of my city
drove you outcast, outlawed from the land.

But if you have any reverence for Persuasion,
the majesty of Persuasion,
the spell of my voice that would appease your fury—
Oh please stay . . .
                          and if you refuse to stay,
it would be wrong, unjust to afflict this city
with wrath, hatred, populations routed. Look,
it is all yours, a royal share of our land—
justly entiled, glorified for ever.

LEADER: Queen Athena,
where is the home you say is mine to hold?

ATHENA: Where all the pain and anguish end. Accept it.

LEADER: And if I do, what honour waits for me?

ATHENA: No house can thrive without you.

LEADER: You would do that,
grant me that much power?

ATHENA: Whoever reveres us—
we will raise the fortunes of their lives.

LEADER: And you will pledge me that, for all time to come?

ATHENA: *Yes*—I must never promise things I cannot do.

LEADER: Your magic is working ... I can feel the hate,
the fury slip away.

☞ ☞ ☞

FURIES: Rejoice!—
rejoice—the joy resounds—
all those who dwell in Athens,
spirits and mortals, come,
govern Athena's city well.
revere us well, we are your guests;
you will learn to praise your Furies,
you will praise the fortunes of your lives.

ATHENA:

☞ ☞ ☞

> ATHENA'S *entourage comes forward,*
> *bearing crimson robes.*

Bright eye of the land of Theseus,
come forth, my splendid troupe. Girls and mothers,
trains of aged women grave in movement,
dress our Furies now in blood-red robes.
Praise them—let the torch move on!
So the love this family bears towards our land
will bloom in human strength from age to age.

> *The women invest the* FURIES *and sing the*
> *final chorus. Torches blaze; a procession*
> *forms, including the actors and the*
> *judges and the audience.* ATHENA *leads*
> *them from the theatre and escorts them*
> *through the city.*

THE WOMEN OF THE CITY: This peace between Athena's people and their guests
must never end. All-seeing Zeus and Fate embrace,
down they come to urge our union on—
Cry, cry, in triumph, carry on the dancing on and on!

Here is a very sophisticated working of the rights of the male and female and of all they represent. Athene, goddess of wisdom, is the supreme and most just judge, and she is a female divinity. It seems that only she is able to think fairly about both the masculine and the feminine claims; thus as in some earlier works, we see a female figure representing a moral and a gender duality, as well as the end, or final judge, of men's actions. Indeed, Athene and the Furies have the last words in this matter, negotiating the final arrangements for the Furies long after Orestes and Apollo have gone.

Note that the Furies state over and over that they represent the *older* generation. They are the spirits of a pre-civilized Greece, the Greece whose accommodation by the forces of civilization was the theme of the *Iliad.* The Furies are, then, a kind of foreign element, but one which must be acknowledged as the foundation and ground of civil community. All the disordered emotions that give birth to human actions, Aeschylus seems to say, are feminine. While they must ultimately be submitted to law, they are that which the law is meant to protect.

2. SOPHOCLES
(*Greek, 495–405 B.C.E.*)

Sophocles represents the middle, and perhaps the paradigmatic, era of Greek tragedy. His creative reworking of familiar myths—sometimes even of his own earlier versions of them—gives readers a unique insight into the artist's work. Winning his first first prize for tragedy in 468, defeating Aeschylus for the prize, Sophocles is reputed to have won twenty-three more times. Only seven of his plays still survive. His "Theban Plays" tell the story of the house of Oedipus, king of Thebes, the mythological character upon whom psychoanalysts base the "Oedipus complex" of childhood development. Although many dramatists took their inspiration from this story, Sophocles' has come down to us as the classic version.

THE "THEBAN PLAYS"

The three plays, which treated chronologically form a trilogy, were actually written over a long period of time and demonstrate considerable changes of artistic perspective on Sophocles' part. They were also written out of their historical order: *Antigone* was written first, although the events it describes occur after those of the other plays. Here, we will look only at the first and last plays in the chronological order of the story—*Oedipus the King* and *Antigone.* Like those in the *Oresteia* trilogy, they trace the consequences of a family curse through two generations. Here, as in Aeschylus, the process of the family members coming to terms with their fate parallels the process of their city coming to justice. For Oedipus, however, the crime whose consequences he must face is a crime locked in his own past, in his own nature—hence, the fascinating character study he provides both for Sophocles and for his audiences.

OEDIPUS THE KING

Oedipus was fated to kill his father and marry his mother. In *Oedipus the King,* the entire movement of the tragedy is Oedipus' slow realization that he has not escaped this fate and has indeed killed his father and married (and fathered children with) his mother—all without knowing it at the time. While the play is a commentary upon the fragility and irony of our belief in human self-determination and freedom, it is also an examination of human strength and weakness, particularly with regard to the trials of sexual maturity. For fate, while on the one hand the vehicle of the gods' wills that determines human actions, is on the other hand a representation of those various forces of nature over which human beings have little or no rational control—including our sexual and other passions.

The play opens with a tragedy: the city of Thebes, ruled well by Oedipus for many years—ever since he arrived from Corinth, solved the riddle of the Sphinx, and married the widowed queen of Thebes—is plagued. Oedipus states that the city's sorrows are his own and vows to do whatever he can to cure this blight. Creon, Oedipus' brother-in-law (and, unbeknownst to Oedipus, his uncle) has heard from a seer that the plague will continue until the murderer of Laius is brought to justice. Laius was Jocasta's first husband and Oedipus' predecessor as king of Thebes (and, of course, his father). Unbeknownst to Oedipus or to his virtuous counsellor Creon, then, the plague upon the city is the result of Oedipus' own actions. The plague ravaging the city is, in a sense, its own hideous ancestry, its own parent, appearing like a foreign element in its midst. A barbarous or pre-civilized justice, associated with family, breaks through the conventions of the city and gives testimony to the underlying, or natural, state of affairs just as a disease breaks through one's ordinary outward demeanor and gives rise to symptoms. The whole play will consist of a deduction on Oedipus' part, from the evidence before him (the misery of his city) to its cause—his own crime many years before. The evidence he faces is a civic crisis, while its cause is a family curse. Thus, his investigation uncovers the family relations that are hidden behind civic relations. Similarly, curing the city of the plague will require cleansing the family of its curse—Oedipus bringing himself to justice.

Oedipus and his wife/mother Jocasta, the hero and heroine of the play, have each contributed to their plight in different ways, and so face the recognition of their acts very differently. The differences in their relations to their own destiny represent, at least in part, the differences in male and female sexual development. Their ultimate response to the knowledge of their acts, while tragic in both cases, evinces a difference between the sexes with regard to the achievement of virtue—where virtue consists in a good comportment of oneself towards one's fate and therefore, in a sense, in facing one's death nobly. Oedipus was entirely ignorant of his crimes at the time he committed them, and so, despite them, in a sense remains "innocent." He closes the play with a tragic dignity. Jocasta, while also ignorant of her crimes at the time of their commission, has tried throughout her life to thwart her fate. Thus, in the final analysis, Oedipus is a virtuous man in spite of his crimes, and Jocasta is a vicious woman, despite her innocence. Yet Sophocles' breadth of vision is such that both characters remain sympathetic.

OEDIPUS AND THE REDISCOVERY OF HIMSELF

Oedipus' ignorance of his crimes does not consist in his ignorance of his actions, but in his misunderstanding their significance. Thus, the suspense built by Oedipus'

slow deduction is very subtle, effected wholly through Oedipus' deepening interpretation of himself. While only some of the evidence presented in the case is actually in the form of prophecy, the whole action of the play is a sort of reading of
clues or signs; Oedipus, the chorus, and the audience are all involved in a search for
the hidden meaning behind the words of the characters in the play. Here in the
realm of sexual desire, hidden wishes are not so clearly distinct from overt acts as
we might like. We are able when reading *Oedipus* to face the sheer repugnance and
secret attractiveness of Oedipus' act.

The movement of the play echoes a repeating philosophical theme in Greek
thought. Through this basically legal procedure, Oedipus will grasp a truth beyond
reason and method. Thus as readers, we are given evidence that nature and truth,
though possibly beyond reason in themselves, are accessible to reason; reality can
be known through appearances, if we rightly interpret them. With regard to gender,
we may conclude that though femininity and masculinity are expressed by every
character in a different way, and mixed in a different proportion, there is an underlying and knowable truth to sexuality that binds all the characters to their fates.

The first clue to Oedipus' fate comes through Creon from the oracle of Apollo.
The oracle instructs that the plague can be lifted only if the murderer of the former
king (Jocasta's first husband) Laius, is brought to justice. Laius and his entourage
had been killed on their way home from a journey, and only one person escaped to
tell what happened. The blind seer Tiresias is loath to speak at first, but eventually
he answers Oedipus' question.

TIRESIAS:

⌒ ⌒ ⌒

I charge you, then, submit to that decree
you just laid down: from this day onward
speak to no one, not these citizens, not myself.
You are the curse, the corruption of the land!

OEDIPUS: You, shameless—
aren't you appalled to start up such a story?
You think you can get away with this?

TIRESIAS: I have already.
The truth with all its power lives inside me.

OEDIPUS: Who primed you for this? Not your prophet's trade.

TIRESIAS: You did, you forced me, twisted it out of me.

OEDIPUS: What? Say it again—I'll understand it better.

TIRESIAS: Didn't you understand, just now?
Or are you tempting me to talk?

OEDIPUS: No, I can't say I grasped your meaning.
Out with it, again!

TIRESIAS: I say you are the murderer you hunt.

OEDIPUS: That obscenity, twice—by god, you'll pay.

⌒ ⌒ ⌒

TIRESIAS: . . . So,
   you mock my blindness? Let me tell you this.
   You with your precious eyes,
   you're blind to the corruption of your life,
   to the house you live in, those you live with—
   who *are* your parents? Do you know? All unknowing
   you are the scourge of your own flesh and blood,
   the dead below the earth and the living here above,
   and the double lash of your mother and your father's curse
   will whip you from this land one day, their footfall
   treading you down in terror, darkness shrouding
   your eyes that now can see the light!
                                          Soon, soon
   you'll scream aloud—what haven won't reverberate?
   What rock of Cithaeron won't scream back in echo?
   That day you learn the truth about your marriage,
   the wedding-march that sang you into your halls,
   the lusty voyage home to the fatal harbor!
   And a crowd of other horrors you'd never dream
   will level you with yourself and all your children.

⌒ ⌒ ⌒

OEDIPUS: Enough! Such filth from him? Insufferable—
   what, still alive? Get out—
   faster, back where you came from—vanish!

⌒ ⌒ ⌒

> *Turning his back on* TIRESIAS, *moving
> toward the palace.*

TIRESIAS: I will go,
   once I have said what I came here to say.
   I will never shrink from the anger in your eyes—
   you can't destroy me. Listen to me closely:
   the man you've sought so long, proclaiming,
   cursing up and down, the murderer of Laius—
   he is here. A stranger,
   you may think, who lives among you,
   he soon will be revealed a native Theban
   but he will take no joy in the revelation.
   Blind who now has eyes, beggar who now is rich,

he will grope his way toward a foreign soil,
a stick tapping before him step by step.

                                        OEDIPUS *enters the palace.*

Revealed at last, brother and father both
to the children he embraces, to his mother
son and husband both—he sowed the loins
his father sowed, he spilled his father's blood!

Go in and reflect on that, solve that.
And if you find I've lied
from this day onward call the prophet blind.

                                        TIRESIAS *and the boy exit to the side.*

Tiresias' message to Oedipus is that Oedipus is not the foreigner he imagines himself to be. Indeed, Oedipus is a native Theban masquerading as a foreigner (he thinks he is from Corinth) whose intelligence and love for his city has earned him the throne. In a sense, therefore, Oedipus is like other earlier heroes, coming home from a foreign land, reclaiming his parentage and history. Thus Oedipus, like Greece herself in the Trojan war, recovers his identity as a Theban by reappropriating a part of its own denied and forgotten history, a part of himself to which he had made himself a stranger. However, Oedipus' "forgotten parentage" is also the pre-human, pre-rational, sexual instinct that we all tend to think of as "animalistic" and therefore foreign to civil, or Greek, conduct.

Oedipus, in his distress, suspects Creon of inventing the story in order to weaken Oedipus and make a play for the throne. He reveals his suspicions to his wife, Jocasta.

                              The CHORUS *draws away, leaving* OEDIPUS
                              and JOCASTA *side by side.*

JOCASTA: For the love of god,
    Oedipus, tell me too, what is it?
    Why this rage? You're so unbending.

OEDIPUS: I will tell you. I respect you, Jocasta,
    much more than these men here. . .

                              Glancing at the CHORUS.

    Creon's to blame, Creon schemes against me.

JOCASTA: Tell me clearly, how did the quarrel start?

OEDIPUS: He says *I* murdered Láius—I am guilty.

JOCASTA: How does he know? Some secret knowledge
    or simple hearsay?

OEDIPUS: Oh, he sent his prophet in
    to do his dirty work. You know Creon,
    Creon keeps his own lips clean.

JOCASTA: A prophet?
Well then, free yourself of every charge!
Listen to me and learn some peace of mind:
no skill in the world,
nothing human can penetrate the future.
Here is proof, quick and to the point.

An oracle came to Laius one fine day
(I won't say from Apollo himself
but his underlings his priests) and it declared
that doom would strike him down at the hands of a son,
our son, to be born of our own flesh and blood. But Laius,
so the report goes at least, was killed by strangers,
thieves, at a place where three roads meet ... my son—
he wasn't three days old and the boy's father
fastened his ankles, had a henchman fling him away
on a barren, trackless mountain.
                                              There, you see?
Apollo brought neither thing to pass. My baby
no more murdered his father than Laius suffered—
his wildest fear—death at his own son's hands.
That's how the seers and all their revelations
mapped out the future. Brush them from your mind.
Whatever the god needs and seeks
he'll bring to light himself, with ease.

☞ ☞ ☞

OEDIPUS: Where did this thing [Laius' murder] happen? Be precise.

JOCASTA: A place called Phocis, where two branching roads,
one from Daulia, one from Delphi,
come together—a crossroads.

OEDIPUS: When? How long ago?

JOCASTA: The heralds no sooner reported Laius dead
than you appeared and they hailed you king of Thebes.

☞ ☞ ☞

OEDIPUS: I have a terrible fear the blind seer can see.
I'll know in a moment. One thing more—

JOCASTA: Anything,
afraid as I am—ask, I'll answer, all I can.

OEDIPUS: Did he go with a light or heavy escort,
several men-at-arms, like a lord, a king?

JOCASTA: There were five in the party, a herald among them,
and a single wagon carrying Laius.

OEDIPUS: Ai—
now I can see it all, clear as day.
Who told you all this at the time, Jocasta?

JOCASTA: A servant who reached home, the lone survivor.

☙ ☙ ☙

. . . he'll come.
But even I have a right, I'd like to think,
to know what's torturing you, my lord.

OEDIPUS: And so you shall—I can hold nothing back from you,
now I've reached this pitch of dark foreboding.

☙ ☙ ☙

My father was Polybus, king of Corinth.
My mother, a Dorian, Merope. And I was held
the prince of the realm among the people there,
till something struck me out of nowhere,
something strange . . . worth remarking perhaps,
hardly worth the anxiety I gave it.
Some man at a banquet who had drunk too much
shouted out—he was far gone, mind you—
that I am not my father's son. Fighting words!

☙ ☙ ☙

And so,
unknown to mother and father I set out for Delphi,
and the god Apollo spurned me, sent me away
denied the facts I came for,
but first he flashed before my eyes a future
great with pain, terror, disaster—I can hear him cry,
"You are fated to couple with your mother, you will bring
a breed of children into the light no man can bear to see—
you will kill your father, the one who gave you life!"
I heard all that and ran. I abandoned Corinth,
from that day on I gauged its landfall only
by the stars, running, always running
toward some place where I would never see
the shame of all those oracles come true.
And as I fled I reached that very spot
where the great king, you say, met his death.
Now, Jocasta, I will tell you all.

Making my way toward this triple crossroad
I began to see a herald, then a brace of colts
drawing a wagon, and mounted on the bench ... a man,
just as you've described him, coming face-to-face,
and the one in the lead and the old man himself
were about to thrust me off the road—brute force—
and the one shouldering me aside, the driver,
I strike him in anger!—and the old man, watching me
coming up along his wheels—he brings down
his prod, two prongs straight at my head!
I paid him back with interest!
Short work, by god—with one blow of the staff
in this right hand I knock him out of his high seat,
roll him out of the wagon, sprawling headlong—
I killed them all—every mother's son!

Oh, but if there is any blood-tie
between Laius and this stranger . . .
what man alive more miserable than I?
More hated by the gods?

⌐ ⌐ ⌐

Wasn't I born for torment? Look me in the eyes!
I am abomination—heart and soul!
I must be exiled, and even in exile
never see my parents, never set foot
on native ground again. Else I am doomed
to couple with my mother and cut my father down . . .
Polybus who reared me, gave me life.

⌐ ⌐ ⌐

JOCASTA: What did I say? What struck you so?

OEDIPUS: You said *thieves*—
he told you a whole band of them murdered Laius.
So, if he still holds to the same number,
I cannot be the killer. One can't equal many.
But if he refers to one man, one alone,
clearly the scales come down on me:
I am guilty.

JOCASTA: Impossible. Trust me,
I told you precisely what he said,
and he can't retract it now;
the whole city heard it, not just I.

⌐ ⌐ ⌐

> So much for prophecy. It's neither here nor there.
> From this day on, I wouldn't look right or left.

OEDIPUS: True, true. Still, that shepherd,
someone fetch him—now!

OEDIPUS and JOCASTA *enter the palace.*

While they await the arrival of the servant, a messenger arrives from Corinth to inform Oedipus that Polybus, the king of that city, is dead and that Oedipus is his successor. It would seem, then, that Oedipus' fears are quashed. However, during the conversation, the messenger tells Oedipus that he is not really Polybus' son—that he was adopted. The messenger states that a shepherd from Thebes gave him a baby—Oedipus—many years ago, and that he gave the baby to his master, the king, to raise. This news is, of course, frightening to Oedipus, who awaits the full story from the shepherd.

[SHEPHERD,] *confused,* [glances] *from the*
MESSENGER *to the King.*

☞ ☞ ☞

OEDIPUS:

Pointing to the MESSENGER.

This one here—ever have dealings with him?

SHEPHERD: Yes, I suppose . . .
it's all so long ago.

MESSENGER: Come, tell me,
you gave me a child back then, a boy, remember?
A little fellow to rear, my every own.

SHEPHERD: What? Why rake up that again?

MESSENGER: Look, here he is, my fine old friend—
the same man who was just a baby then.

SHEPHERD: Damn you, shut your mouth—quiet!

☞ ☞ ☞

OEDIPUS: Did you give him that child? He's asking.

SHEPHERD: I did . . . I wish to god I'd died that day.

OEDIPUS: You've got your wish if you don't tell the truth.

☞ ☞ ☞

SHEPHERD: Oh no,
I'm right at the edge, the horrible truth—I've got to say it!

OEDIPUS: And I'm at the edge of hearing horrors, yes, but I must hear!

SHEPHERD: All right! His son, they said it was—his son!
   But the one inside, your wife,
   she'd tell it best.

OEDIPUS: My wife—
   she gave it to you?

SHEPHERD: Yes, yes, my king.

OEDIPUS: Why, what for?

SHEPHERD: To kill it.

OEDIPUS: Her own child,
   how could she?

SHEPHERD: She was afraid—
   frightening prophecies.

OEDIPUS: What?

SHEPHERD: They said—
   he'd kill his parents.

OEDIPUS: But you gave him to this old man—why?

SHEPHERD: I pitied the little baby, master,
   hoped he'd take him off to his own country,
   far away, but he saved him for this, this fate.
   If you are the man he says you are, believe me,
   you were born for pain.

OEDIPUS: O god—
   all come true, all burst to light!
   O light—now let me look my last on you!
   I stand revealed at last—
   cursed in my birth, cursed in marriage,
   cursed in the lives I cut down with these hands!

> *Rushing through the doors with a great
> cry. The Corinthian* MESSENGER, *the*
> SHEPHERD *and attendants exit slowly to
> the side.*

Thus Oedipus learns that he has not escaped his fate. To the extent that fate, in this play as well as in the last, represents the natural or divine law that is beyond the jurisdiction of human conventions, we may say that Oedipus' and Jocasta's fates represent the natural drives that lie beyond the "jurisdiction" of the best-laid plans of men and women. The passions and longing that we try to deny and therefore call "perversion" and "fantasy" include the ambiguous sexual attractions we feel towards our own parents. If one never learned one's parents, in the sense that one never learned how one's parents got to be one's parents—one would never realize why one ought to curb one's sexual attractions to them. In this sense, "coming to know one's parents" represents learning the "facts of life." Oedipus is coming of age, beginning to be responsible for his own "foreign" sexual instincts.

The tragedy here, then, is not the divisions in the city or in the character of its leader, but precisely the secret coherence of what only seem to be separate elements. It is not the distance between law and nature that makes for conflict here, but the eerie closeness of the two to each other. This is particularly the case, of course, with the laws regarding marriage, which, as we have seen, are paradigmatic in ancient Greece, representing at once the institution of the household and of the city itself.

OEDIPUS AND JOCASTA CONFRONT THEIR ACT

When the "riddle" of their act finally has been solved, Oedipus and Jocasta each take action in a different way. The consequences of their acts, however, have not played themselves out entirely, and thus we may assume that justice is not entirely restored at the end of this first play of the trilogy.

> *Enter a* MESSENGER *from the palace.*

MESSENGER: The queen is dead.

LEADER: Poor lady—how?

MESSENGER: By her own hand. But you are spared the worst,
  you never had to watch . . . I saw it all,
  and with all the memory that's in me
  you will learn what that poor woman suffered.

  Once she'd broken in through the gates,
  dashing past us, frantic, whipped to fury,
  ripping her hair out with both hands—
  straight to her rooms she rushed, flinging herself
  across the bridal-bed, doors slamming behind her—

  ⌒ ⌒ ⌒

  Oh how she wept, mourning the marriage-bed
  where she let loose that double brood—monsters—
  husband by her husband, children by her child.
                                        And then—
  but how she died is more than I can say. Suddenly
  Oedipus burst in, screaming, he stunned us so
  we couldn't watch her agony to the end,
  our eyes were fixed on him. Circling
  like a maddened beast, stalking, here, there,
  crying out to us—

⌒ ⌒ ⌒

And there we saw the woman hanging by the neck,
cradled high in a woven noose, spinning,
swinging back and forth. And when he saw her,
giving a low, wrenching sob that broke our hearts,
slipping the halter from her throat, he eased her down,
in a slow embrace he laid her down, poor thing ...
then, what came next, what horror we beheld!

He rips off her brooches, the long gold pins
holding her robes—and lifting them high,
looking straight up into the points,
he digs them down the sockets of his eyes, crying, "You,
you'll see no more the pain I suffered, all the pain I caused!
Too long you looked on the ones you never should have seen,
blind to the ones you longed to see, to know! Blind
from this hour on! Blind in the darkness—blind!"
His voice like a dirge, rising, over and over
raising the pins, raking them down his eyes.
And at each stroke blood spurts from the roots,
splashing his beard, a swirl of it, nerves and clots—
black hail of blood pulsing, gushing down.

These are the griefs that burst upon them both,
coupling man and woman. The joy they had so lately,
the fortune of their old ancestral house
was deep joy indeed. Now, in this one day,
wailing, madness and doom, death, disgrace,
all the griefs in the world that you can name,
all are theirs forever.

⌒ ⌒ ⌒

OEDIPUS: What I did was best—don't lecture me,
   no more advice. I, with *my* eyes,
   how could I look my father in the eyes
   when I go down to death? Or mother, so abused . . .
   I have done such things to the two of them,
   crimes too huge for hanging.
                              Worse yet,
   the sight of my children, born as they were born,
   how could I long to look into their eyes?
   No, not with these eyes of mine, never.
   Not this city either, her high towers,
   the sacred glittering images of her gods—
   I am misery! I, her best son, reared

as no other son of Thebes was ever reared,
I've stripped myself, I gave the command myself.

⤚ ⤚ ⤚

             Marriages! O marriage,
you gave me birth, and once you brought me into the world
you brought my sperm rising back, springing to light
fathers, brothers, sons—one murderous breed—
brides, wives, mothers. The blackest things
a man can do, I have done them all!
                    No more—
it's wrong to name what's wrong to do. Quickly,
for the love of god, hide me somewhere,
kill me, hurl me into the sea
where you can never look on me again.

    The play ends with the succession of Creon to the throne. In a final act of friendship, he forgives Oedipus for his suspiciousness and allows Oedipus to see his children before he must be exiled from the city, in accordance with his own decree.

                           Enter CREON *from the palace, attended by*
                           palace guards.

CREON: I haven't come to mock you, Oedipus,
    or to criticize your former failings.

                       Turning to the guards.

⤚ ⤚ ⤚

OEDIPUS: Please, in god's name . . . you wipe my fears away,
    come so generously to me, the worst of men
    Do one thing more, for your sake, not mine.

⤚ ⤚ ⤚

OEDIPUS:

⤚ ⤚ ⤚

I command you—I beg you . . .
the woman inside, bury her as you see fit.
It's the only decent thing,
to give your own the last rites. As for me,
never condemn the city of my fathers
to house my body, not while I'm alive, no,

⤚ ⤚ ⤚

About my children, Creon, the boys at least,
don't burden yourself. They're men,

wherever they go, they'll find the means to live.
But my two daughters, my poor helpless girls,
clustering at our table, never without me
hovering near them ... whatever I touched,
they always had their share. Take care of them,
I beg you.

☙ ☙ ☙

> *Clutching his daughters as the guards*
> *wrench them loose and take them through*
> *the palace doors.*

CREON: Still the king, the master of all things?
No more: here your power ends.
None of your power follows you through life.

> *Exit* OEDIPUS *and* CREON *to the palace.*
> *The* CHORUS *comes forward to address the*
> *audience directly.*

CHORUS: People of Thebes, my countrymen, look on Oedipus.
He solved the famous riddle with his brilliance,
he rose to power, a man beyond all power.
Who could behold his greatness without envy?
Now what a black sea of terror has overwhelmed him.
Now as we keep our watch and wait the final day,
count no man happy till he dies, free of pain at last.

Jocasta is no prophet like Cassandra, she does not exercise her mother's right like Clytaemnestra, and she does not avoid action like Electra. She kills herself rather than live with her fate. It is clear, however, that Jocasta suspects the truth all along—else why would she know to avoid investigating the allegations? Thus, Jocasta seems to have a vision of the truth that earlier feminine characters evinced, but she willingly ignores it. Oedipus, however, chooses to blind himself, thus imitating Tiresias and symbolically accepting the hidden truth that is not visible to the eyes, accepting the prophetic vision of the blind seer over the power of the king. In addition, Oedipus admits his injustice to Creon. Hence, Oedipus ends the plague by exiling Laius' murderer—himself—from the city. Thus, Oedipus is morally ambiguous—the complexity of the play is consistent to the end. Creon warns Oedipus that he is not really in position to heal the city. He has done all he can, but he must let fate run its course.

ANTIGONE

Antigone is perhaps the most stunning of all tragic heroines. She does indeed restore Thebes to virtue and community and end the curse on her father's house. The nineteenth-century philosopher Hegel (excerpted in Part Four) used Antigone's heroic figure to represent the very essence of ethical life of family. As in the *Eumenides,* only more clearly here, Antigone achieves the restoration of the city and family through a kind of marriage—a union of the feminine and masculine in an eternal life together, the making of a place for feminine passion within the conventional and apparently masculine rational order.

Creon, Oedipus' brother-in-law/uncle, has taken over the throne of Thebes since Oedipus' exile (and later, death), and he has grown into quite a tyrant. In an attempt on the throne, Oedipus' two sons had quarrelled, and the younger son, Eteocles, succeeded in banishing the elder, Polyneices. Polyneices waged war on Thebes with his adopted countrymen from Argos, trying to reclaim his right, and the two brothers killed each other in the battle. Creon has forbidden the Thebans to bury Polyneices because of his treachery, but while Creon's edict may be the law of the land, it flouts the law of the gods, which directs human beings to honor the dead with decent funerary rituals and burials. Interestingly, Creon's decision also ignores Polyneices' legal right to the throne. Thus, by baldly exercising his sheer power of office, Creon raises questions for the audience and the other characters about the internal consistency of the conventional law itself; both Creon and Polyneices have some legal claim to the throne of Thebes, which is why the rulership of the city had to be decided by violence. In this play, it is Creon, the man, who attempts to escape his fate and to thwart the natural order that comes to us from the gods (i.e., he acts as Jocasta did in the first play), and Antigone, the woman, who faces her fate.

Antigone, Oedipus' loyal daughter, decides to bury her brother, thus breaking the law, but obeying the gods. Antigone, like so many of the female characters in early Greek works, has a vision that exceeds both human law and human life. Sophocles associates her with nature, in the sense of *physis,* with the earth (she, unlike all the other characters, touches the dust to bury Polyneices), with motherhood, with death, and with justice. On account of all this, plus being the oldest living member of Laius' family, Antigone represents the woman's natural right, similarly to Clytaemnestra or the Furies.

Sophocles characterizes Creon, on the other hand, as almost a farce of the "manly" position. Because Eteocles had banished Polyneices, (and it therefore so happened that Eteocles stayed in Thebes and fought with the Thebans where Polyneices fought for Thebes from outside and with the Argives), Creon has judged Eteocles a hero and Polyneices a traitor. In other words, Creon has no concept whatsoever of real family loyalties, real patriotism, or real entitlement to the rulership of Thebes; any man who happens to be outside the city wall is a foreigner, and any man who happens to be inside it is a citizen. He is also forgetful of the rights of women. To Creon, women are utterly foreign.

THE JUDGEMENT

Antigone is engaged to Creon's son, Haemon. In order to uphold his own authority, and to follow through on his pronouncement, Creon will have to abandon his own family loyalties by dismissing his son's will, breaking his son's heart, killing the woman who might otherwise someday give birth to his heirs and establish his own true Theban dynasty. Creon's vicious action also breaks the heart of Antigone's sister, Ismene, who in deference to Creon's edict had refused to help Antigone bury their brother. Willing to die for her family, but not to break the law for it, Ismene lies and claims she has participated, but Antigone is a harsh heroine, as devoted to truth as to divine law.

ANTIGONE: I did it. I don't deny a thing.

CREON:

You, tell me briefly, no long speeches—
were you aware a decree had forbidden this?

ANTIGONE: Well aware. How could I avoid it? It was public.

CREON: And still you had the gall to break this law?

ANTIGONE: Of course I did. It wasn't Zeus, not in the least,
who made this proclamation—not to me.
Nor did that Justice, dwelling with the gods
beneath the earth, ordain such laws for men.
Nor did I think your edict had such force
that you, a mere mortal, could override the gods,
the great unwritten, unshakable traditions.
They are alive, not just today or yesterday:
they live forever, from the first of time,
and no one knows when they first saw the light.

These laws—I was not about to break them,
not out of fear of some man's wounded pride,
and face the retribution of the gods.
Die I must, I've known it all my life—
how could I keep from knowing?—even without
your death-sentence ringing in my ears.
And if I am to die before my time
I consider that a gain. Who on earth,
alive in the midst of so much grief as I,
could fail to find his death a rich reward?
So for me, at least, to meet this doom of yours
is precious little pain. But if I had allowed
my own mother's son to rot, an unburied corpse—
that would have been an agony! This is nothing.
And if my present actions strike you as foolish,
let's just say I've been accused of folly
by a fool.

CREON:

⟱ ⟱ ⟱

This girl was an old hand at insolence
when she overrode the edicts we made public.
But once she had done it—the insolence,
twice over—to glory in it, laughing,
mocking us to our face with what she'd done.
I am not the man, not now: she is the man
if this victory goes to her and she goes free.

Never! Sister's child or closer in blood
than all my family clustered at my altar
worshiping Guardian Zeus—she'll never escape,
she and her blood sister, the most barbaric death.
Yes, I accuse her sister of an equal part
in scheming this, this burial.

To his attendants.

Bring her here!
I just saw her inside, hysterical, gone to pieces.
It never fails: the mind convicts itself
in advance, when scoundrels are up to no good,
plotting in the dark. Oh but I hate it more
when a traitor, caught red-handed,
tries to glorify his crimes.

ANTIGONE: Creon, what more do you want
than my arrest and execution?

CREON: Nothing. Then I have it all.

ANTIGONE: Then why delay? Your moralizing repels me,
every word you say—pray god it always will.
So naturally all I say repels you too.
Enough.
Give me glory! What greater glory could I win
than to give my own brother decent burial?

⟱ ⟱ ⟱

CREON: Wasn't Eteocles a brother too—cut down, facing him?

ANTIGONE: Brother, yes, by the same mother, the same father.

CREON: Then how can you render his enemy such honors,
such impieties in his eyes?

ANTIGONE: He will never testify to that,
Eteocles dead and buried.

CREON: He will—
  if you honor the traitor just as much as him.

ANTIGONE: But it was his brother, not some slave that died—

CREON: Ravaging our country!—
  but Eteocles died fighting in our behalf.

ANTIGONE: No matter—Death longs for the same rites for all.

CREON: Never the same for the patriot and the traitor.

ANTIGONE: Who, Creon, who on earth can say the ones below
  don't find this pure and uncorrupt?

CREON: Never. Once an enemy, never a friend,
  not even after death.

ANTIGONE: I was born to join in love, not hate—
  that is my nature.

CREON: Go down below and love,
  if love you must—love the dead! While I'm alive,
  no woman is going to lord it over me. . . .

> *Enter* ISMENE *from the palace, under guard.*

≈ ≈ ≈

ISMENE: I did it, yes—
  if only she consents—I share the guilt,
  the consequences too.

ANTIGONE: No,
  Justice will never suffer that—not you,
  you were unwilling. I never brought you in.

ISMENE: But now you face such dangers ... I'm not ashamed
  to sail through trouble with you,
  make your troubles mine.

ANTIGONE: Who did the work?
  Let the dead and the god of death bear witness!
  I have no love for a friend who loves in words alone.

ISMENE: Oh no, my sister, don't reject me, please,
  let me die beside you, consecrating
  the dead together.

ANTIGONE: Never share my dying,
  don't lay claim to what you never touched.
  My death will be enough.

ISMENE: What do I care for life, cut off from you?

ANTIGONE: Ask Creon. Your concern is all for him.

~ ~ ~

ISMENE: How can I live alone, without her?

CREON: Her?
Don't even mention her—she no longer exists.

ISMENE: What? You'd kill your own son's bride?

CREON: Absolutely:
there are other fields for him to plow.

ISMENE: Perhaps,
but never as true, as close a bond as theirs.

CREON: A worthless woman for my son? It repels me.

ISMENE: Dearest Haemon, your father wrongs you so!

~ ~ ~

LEADER: So, it's settled then? Antigone must die?

CREON: Settled, yes—we both know that.

To the guards.

Stop wasting time. Take them in.
From now on they'll act like women.
Tie them up, no more running loose;
even the bravest will cut and run,
once they see Death coming for their lives.

The guards escort ANTIGONE *and* ISMENE
into the palace. CREON *remains while the*
old citizens form their CHORUS.

~ ~ ~

Enter HAEMON *from the palace.*

CREON:

Turning to HAEMON.

Son, you've heard the final verdict on your bride?
Are you coming now, raving against your father?
Or do you love me, no matter what I do?

HAEMON: Father, I'm your *son* ... you in your wisdom
set my bearings for me—I obey you.

No marriage could ever mean more to me than you,
whatever good direction you may offer.

CREON: Fine, Haemon.
That's how you ought to feel within your heart,
subordinate to your father's will in every way.
That's what a man prays for: to produce good sons—

      ☙ ☙ ☙

         Oh Haemon,
never lose your sense of judgment over a woman.
The warmth, the rush of pleasure, it all goes cold
in your arms, I warn you . . . a worthless woman
in your house, a misery in your bed.
What wound cuts deeper than a loved one
turned against you? Spit her out,
like a mortal enemy—let the girl go.
Let her find a husband down among the dead.
Imagine it: I caught her in naked rebellion,
the traitor, the only one in the whole city.
I'm not about to prove myself a liar,
not to my people, no, I'm going to kill her!
That's right—so let her cry for mercy, sing her hymns
to Zeus who defends all bonds of kindred blood.
Why, if I bring up my own kin to be rebels,
think what I'd suffer from the world at large.
Show me the man who rules his household well:
I'll show you someone fit to rule the state.

      ☙ ☙ ☙

We must defend the men who live by law,
never let some woman triumph over us.
Better to fall from power, if fall we must,
at the hands of a man—never be rated
inferior to a woman, never.

LEADER: To us,
unless old age has robbed us of our wits,
you seem to say what you have to say with sense.

HAEMON: Father, only the gods endow a man with reason,
the finest of all their gifts, a treasure.

      ☙ ☙ ☙

Of course it's not for you,
in the normal run of things, to watch

whatever men say or do, or find to criticize.
The man in the street, you know, dreads your glance,
he'd never say anything displeasing to your face.
But it's for me to catch the murmurs in the dark,
the way the city mourns for this young girl.
"No woman," they say, "ever deserved death less,
and such a brutal death for such a glorious action.
She, with her own dear brother lying in his blood—
she couldn't bear to leave him dead, unburied,
food for the wild dogs or wheeling vultures.
Death? She deserves a glowing crown of gold!"
So they say, and the rumor spreads in secret,
darkly. . .
                    I rejoice in your success, father—
nothing more precious to me in the world.

⌒ ⌒ ⌒

                                        No,
it's no disgrace for a man, even a wise man,
to learn many things and not to be too rigid.
You've seen trees by a raging winter torrent,
how many sway with the flood and salvage every twig,
but not the stubborn—they're ripped out, roots and all.
Bend or break. The same when a man is sailing:
haul your sheets too taut, never give an inch,
you'll capsize, and go the rest of the voyage
keel up and the rowing-benches under.

Oh give way. Relax your anger—change!

⌒ ⌒ ⌒

LEADER: You'd do well, my lord, if he's speaking to the point,
to learn from him,

Turning to HAEMON.

                    and you, my boy, from him.
You both are talking sense.

CREON: So,
men our age, we're to be lectured, are we?—
schooled by a boy his age?

HAEMON: Only in what is right. But if I seem young,
look less to my years and more to what I do

CREON: Do? Is admiring rebels an achievement?

HAEMON: I'd never suggest that you admire treason.

⤳ ⤳ ⤳

CREON: Am I to rule this land for others—or myself?

HAEMON: It's no city at all, owned by one man alone.

CREON: What? The city *is* the king's—that's the law!

HAEMON: What a splendid king you'd make of a desert island—
you and you alone.

CREON:

To the CHORUS.

This boy, I do believe,
is fighting on her side, the woman's side.

HAEMON: If you are a woman, yes—
my concern is all for you.

CREON: Why, you degenerate—bandying accusations,
threatening me with justice, your own father!

HAEMON: I see my father offending justice—wrong.

CREON: Wrong?
To protect my royal rights?

HAEMON: Protect your rights?
When you trample down the honors of the gods?

CREON: You, you soul of corruption, rotten through—
woman's accomplice!

HAEMON: That may be,
but you will never find me accomplice to a criminal.

CREON: That's what *she* is,
and every word you say is a blatant appeal for her—

HAEMON: And you, and me, and the gods beneath the earth.

CREON: You will never marry her, not while she's alive.

Creon's near-mania for power comes out during his interchanges with Antigone
and Haemon. As both Haemon and Antigone argue, however, Creon's political fall
may be the first step to his moral salvation. Antigone argues that piety and justice
demanded that she bury her brother even if she would be executed for doing so. She
appeals primarily to the higher law of the gods and to the religious necessity of her
own action, rather than on Creon's impiety or on his right to the throne. She concerns herself with human life and religious society, casting aside concerns for one's
legal position. Indeed, her act of burial metaphorically heals the wounds inflicted
on the earth by the blades of men's plows. This metaphor is furthered by Creon's
claim that there are "other furrows for [Haemon's] plow."

Haemon, like Odysseus, understands the notion of the higher law and is able to accommodate it into an argument about civil authority and rights that appeals to his father's sensibilities. For Creon, the conventional law is everything. Women, for him, represent disorder, lack of discipline, and passion, attributes that to him appear cowardly and unlawful. For Haemon, on the other hand, the law, the city, and the ruler all exist within a larger context, which affects them in ways they may not predict or understand. Haemon ultimately gives up the argument and joins Antigone, leaving Creon utterly alone in the world. The story, then, develops into a story about marriage—once again the symbol for the reunification of the city and the end of the family curse.

The content and outcome of Antigone's virtue differs from that of Oedipus, as does Creon's vice from that of Jocasta. This is apparently because the virtues of men and women, like their vices, differ while remaining virtue and vice. Virtue for Antigone, as well as for Oedipus, consists in recognizing and facing fate and the law of the gods—but where for Oedipus, this means good rulership of Thebes before his realization, and self-mutilation and self-imposed exile afterward, for Antigone it means defying the law of the kingdom and facing the possibility of execution at someone else's hands. For Creon, viciousness means tyranny over others, while for Jocasta, it means tyranny over herself. Thus, self-mastery and autonomy seem to be the virtue of a man and the vice of a woman. Abandonment to others, to passion, and to fate seem to be the virtue of a woman and the vice of a man.

THE EXECUTION

Antigone is put to death at Creon's order right before he discovers from the seer Tiresias the injustice of his condemnation of her.

> ANTIGONE: O tomb, my bridal-bed—my house, my prison
> cut in the hollow rock, my everlasting watch!
> I'll soon be there, soon embrace my own,
> the great growing family of our dead
> Persephone has received among her ghosts.
>
>   I,
>
> the last of them all, the most reviled by far,
> go down before my destined time's run out.
> But still I go, cherishing one good hope:
> my arrival may be dear to father,
> dear to you, my mother,
> dear to you, my loving brother, Eteocles—
> When you died I washed you with my hands,
> I dressed you all, I poured the sacred cups
> across your tombs. But now, Polynices,
> because I laid your body out as well,
> this, this is my reward. Nevertheless
> I honored you—the decent will admit it—
> well and wisely too.

Never, I tell you.
if I had been the mother of children
or if my husband died, exposed and rotting—
I'd never have taken this ordeal upon myself,
never defied our people's will. What law,
you ask, do I satisfy with what I say?
A husband dead, there might have been another.
A child by another too, if I had lost the first.
But mother and father both lost in the halls of Death,
no brother could ever spring to light again.
For this law alone I held you first in honor.
For this, Creon, the king, judges me a criminal
guilty of dreadful outrage, my dear brother!
And now he leads me off, a captive in his hands,
with no part in the bridal-song, the bridal-bed,
denied all joy of marriage, raising children—
deserted so by loved ones, struck by fate,
I descend alive to the caverns of the dead.

What law of the mighty gods have I transgressed?
Why look to the heavens any more, tormented as I am?
Whom to call, what comrades now? Just think,
my reverence only brands me for irreverence!
Very well: if this is the pleasure of the gods,
once I suffer I will know that I was wrong.
But if these men are wrong, let them suffer
nothing worse than they mete out to me—
these masters of injustice!

LEADER: Still the same rough winds, the wild passion
   raging through the girl.

CREON:

To the guards.

Take her away.
   You're wasting time—you'll pay for it too.

ANTIGONE: Oh god, the voice of death. It's come, it's here.

CREON: True. Not a word of hope—your doom is sealed.

ANTIGONE: Land of Thebes, city of all my fathers—
   O you gods, the first gods of the race!
   They drag me away, now no more delay.
   Look on me, you noble sons of Thebes—
   the last of a great line of kings,
   I alone, see what I suffer now

at the hands of what breed of men—
all for reverence, my reverence for the gods!

She leaves under guard: the CHORUS
gathers.

Convinced by Tiresias that his actions have been unjust and will be punished by
the gods, Creon rushes to stop the execution. A messenger returns to tell Creon's
wife, Eurydice, that he was too late. Not only is Antigone dead, her son Haemon is
dead as well.

MESSENGER: I—dear lady,
I'll speak as an eye-witness. I was there.

e e e

I escorted your lord, I guided him
to the edge of the plain where the body lay,
Polynices, torn by the dogs and still unmourned.
And saying a prayer to Hecate of the Crossroads,
Pluto too, to hold their anger and be kind,
we washed the dead in a bath of holy water
and plucking some fresh branches, gathering ...
what was left of him, we burned them all together
and raised a high mound of native earth, and then
we turned and made for that rocky vault of hers,
the hollow, empty bed of the bride of Death.
And far off, one of us heard a voice,
a long wail rising, echoing
out of that unhallowed wedding-chamber,
he ran to alert the master and Creon pressed on,
closer—the strange, inscrutable cry came sharper,
throbbing around him now, and he let loose
a cry of his own, enough to wrench the heart,
"Oh god, am I the prophet now? going down
the darkest road I've ever gone? My son—
it's *his* dear voice, he greets me! Go, men,
closer, quickly! Go through the gap,
the rocks are dragged back—
right to the tomb's very mouth—and look,
see if it's Haemon's voice I think I hear,
or the gods have robbed me of my senses."

The king was shattered. We took his orders,
went and searched, and there in the deepest,
dark recesses of the tomb we found her ...
hanged by the neck in a fine linen noose,
strangled in her veils—and the boy,
his arms flung around her waist,

clinging to her, wailing for his bride,
dead and down below, for his father's crimes
and the bed of his marriage blighted by misfortune.
When Creon saw him, he gave a deep sob,
he ran in, shouting, crying out to him,
"Oh my child—what have you done? what seized you,
what insanity? what disaster drove you mad?
Come out, my son! I beg you on my knees!"
But the boy gave him a wild burning glance,
spat in his face, not a word in reply,
he drew his sword—his father rushed out,
running as Haemon lunged and missed!—
and then, doomed, desperate with himself,
suddenly leaning his full weight on the blade,
he buried it in his body, halfway to the hilt.
And still in his senses, pouring his arms around her,
he embraced the girl and breathing hard,
released a quick rush of blood,
bright red on her cheek glistening white.
And there he lies, body enfolding body . . .
he has won his bride at last, poor boy,
not here but in the houses of the dead.

Creon shows the world that of all the ills
afflicting men the worst is lack of judgment.

Thus, in death, Antigone and Haemon are married, and Antigone is saved from the everlasting maidenhood that she had bemoaned. This marriage in death, unlike the marriage of divinities at the end of the *Eumenides,* ends the family curse only by ending the family line. Oedipus' sexuality is ultimately legitimated, as all sexuality is, for the ancients legitimated in marriage. But by consummating this marriage only in death, Sophocles brings us to a far deeper, far sadder, vision of our human "coming of age." Underlying even our sexuality is a truth we cannot escape, a truth that, perhaps unlike sexuality, has an equal and absolute authority over men and women. The final outcome of our lives is our deaths; death alone will bring our lives—our sex acts and our sexual passions—to their culmination. His or her own death is the hidden truth about him or herself which the king, the hero, the individual, must eventually face.

3. PLATO
(Greek, 427–347 B.C.E.)

As the famous remark of Alfred North Whitehead's, with which this chapter begins implies, Plato is, in a sense at least, the fundamental thinker in Western philosophy. Certainly we need not accept Plato's answers to any of the important philosophical problems on which he wrote, but if we are to attempt responsible answers to any of these questions ourselves, we must acknowledge that there are very few philosophical questions that Plato did not raise, and that most were asked by Plato for the very first time. Plato gives a fairly subtle working of the definitions of masculinity and femininity and of the status of men and women, hidden within his philosophical dialogues on Love, Knowledge, Political Good, and Truth. In order to gather from these dialogues his theories on gender, it would be good to know a little bit about Platonic theory in general.

METHOD

Perhaps the first thing to realize about Plato's work is that he wrote *dialogues.* A philosophical dialogue presents various opinions and arguments through characters, much like a play. Unlike a play, however, the first priority of a dialogue is to engage its audience intellectually, not to move them emotionally (although you may find yourself also quite stirred by certain passages in a dialogue).

In all but one—probably the last—of the Platonic dialogues that have come down to us, the (or a) main character is Socrates, Plato's real-life teacher. Socrates is sometimes thought to be the representative of Plato's own view, although this claim is more obvious and easily supported for some dialogues than for others. Socrates, most likely on account of his strict commitment to his own philosophical method—the method of *questioning,* challenging the claims made by important people in Athens—made serious political enemies in that city, and at age seventy was brought up on charges before the Athenian court. He was convicted of worshipping other than the state gods and of corrupting the youth, and was sentenced to death. As was the custom in Athens, Socrates chose his own method of execution— drinking poison—which he carried out in his prison cell in 399 B.C.E.

Plato himself does not appear as a character in any of the dialogues, although Socrates mentions in the first dialogue (the *Apology,* which depicts Socrates defending himself at his trial) that Plato is present in court. Therefore, when reading a Platonic dialogue, we are forced to work our own way through the arguments and stories presented, deciding what Plato himself is actually advocating by deciding whose opinion is the better one, improving weak arguments with which we agree, and criticizing arguments with which we do not agree. The dialogues contain within them a variety of styles: long speeches by a single character, Socratic questioning, quick arguments back and forth between two characters, complex philosophical arguments, flowery orations, bitter personal debates, tall tales, and myths. What unifies each dialogue is its pursuit of a single important philosophical question, such as (in the *Republic*) "what is justice?" as well as, in most dialogues, the figure of Socrates.

Socrates' philosophical method of questioning, then, is one among several methods used by Plato in his dialogues; it is, however, a particularly important one. Socrates almost never puts forward direct claims of his own; rather, he develops and refines the claims of other characters (called the *interlocutors*) by asking them questions. Socrates claims in several of the dialogues that he derived his method as a matter of religious conviction, and associates his method with his oft-repeated claim that he was in fact ignorant and could not teach. In the *Apology,* Socrates tells the story of how he derived his method:

> *"[O]ne day [my friend Chaerephon] actually went to Delphi [an oracular temple of Apollo] and asked . . . whether there was anyone wiser than myself. The priestess replied that there was no one. . . .*
>
> *When I heard about the oracle's answer, I said to myself, What does the god mean? . . . I am only too conscious that I have no claim to wisdom, great or small.*
>
> *After puzzling about it for some time, I set myself . . . to check the truth of it in the following way. I went to interview a man with a high reputation for wisdom because I felt that here if anywhere I should succeed in disproving the oracle. . . . Well, I gave a thorough examination to this person . . . and in conversation with him I formed the impression that although in many people's opinion, and especially his own, he appeared to be wise, in fact he was not. . . .*
>
> *. . . It seems to me that . . . [t]he wisest of you men is he who has realized, like Socrates, that in respect of wisdom he is really worthless.*[3]

Socrates is the wisest man, because he is the only person who knows that he doesn't know anything—this is called his *learned ignorance.* The various experts with whom he spoke, many of them Sophists, believed themselves to know something when they actually didn't know what they were talking about, and hence, their beliefs contained a positive falsehood. This meant that they knew even less than if they knew they were ignorant. Of all the "experts" with whom Socrates claimed to have spoken, he described the Sophists as knowing the very least of anybody. Artists and poets, like the rhapsodists who recited Homer's poetry in Athens, were only slightly less ignorant than the Sophists, according to Socrates, because although their art often contained some elements of truth, the artists themselves didn't understand anything about their own work. The "experts" who came off the best, according to Socrates in the *Apology,* were the craftspeople—carpenters and such—because at least they really knew how to make the things they made, and were able tell others how to make them; however, even the craftspeople, Socrates claimed, tended to overestimate their knowledge, and so they too were more ignorant than himself. Socrates tends, then, to champion craftsmanship over art, for just the kind of reasons given here. Crafts can be clearly described, their goal—the product—is never obscure, and they can be taught.

Socrates tends, then, to model philosophical knowledge on craftsmanship. He believes that if someone has full knowledge of something, he or she should be able to articulate and teach it. Since the more humble work of craftsmanship tends to be domestic and to involve women more than does that of art, particularly in the ancient world, the "*art/craft distinction*" may provide some insight into Plato's notions of gender. For instance, in the *Theaetetus,* excerpted later, Socrates will

---

[3] Plato, *Apology* . Translated by Hugh Tredennick, in *The Collected Dialogues of Plato.* Edited by Edith Hamilton and Huntington Cairnes. (New Jersey: Princeton University Press, 1961 (1980)), pp. 7-9.

compare philosophy to the craft of midwifery; this is certainly a craft and not a fine art, and it is typically a woman's job.

METAPHYSICS

The fundamental claim uniting all the dialogues and all the areas of Platonic thought is that what really exists are the *Forms,* which are purely intelligible objects (i.e., they are not material or physical) that are the templates of everything that appears in the material world. For instance, in the *Republic,* it becomes clear that Plato believes Justice is a form, of which people's just actions are appearances or parts. The Platonic Forms are absolute universals as opposed to the particulars, which are the various appearances of the forms in the perceivable world, and they exist on a whole other plane of reality—a more real plane—than do the material objects or physical actions of which they are the forms. The Forms are the universal principles that make every case of anything a case of that thing. For instance, to keep with our example from the *Republic,* the form of Justice is whatever all just actions share that makes them just actions. Similarly, the form of Beauty itself is what makes, say, a particular beautiful woman, or even a beautiful passage in a poem, beautiful. Perhaps the clearest discussion of the Forms appears in the dialogue *Phaedo:* there, Socrates describes the Form as "the real nature of any given thing—what it actually is," and as the object "in itself."[4] Thus, we can think of the Forms as "Tallness-in-itself," "Justice-in-itself," "Beauty-in-itself," "Equality-in-itself," etc., a wealth of objects as they exist in themselves, wholly divorced from the material world in which we find them all mixed together.

The things of the material world, for Plato, were mere images, appearances of the Forms, and they derived their characteristics from the Forms, through what is called *participation,* which is Plato's answer to the "appearance/reality distinction." For Plato, each material thing is a confused set of various participations in various different forms; for instance, an orange participates in the form of orange-color, in the form of roundness, sweetness, wetness, etc. Further, the things in this world participate in the forms to different degrees—a still-life painting of a bowl of oranges participates in many of the same forms as the orange (the orange we eat) but to a lesser degree; similarly, a circle drawn with a compass participates in the form of roundness to a higher degree than does the orange. Thus, for Plato, existence can be described as a hierarchy of more and less real things, the most real being the Forms, and the least real, according to Socrates in the *Republic,* being shadows and reflections of things.

ETHICS

According to Socrates, all the above claims, however important or true, take a second place to the way we live our lives. Socrates claimed that the unexamined life is

---

[4] *Phaedo,* 65d-e

not worth living. For Socrates, all knowledge ultimately has a moral component: for instance, wisdom was a moral virtue for the Greeks. This moral component is associated with Socrates' stated belief in reincarnation. According to Socrates, each person is reincarnated according to how good a life he or she has led, and so, in order to continue into eternity to live good lives, it is vital that we live this one rightly.

The Socratic claims about reincarnation (about whose seriousness to Plato scholars often dispute) are tied up with his *theory of recollection.* According to Socrates, as he is represented by Plato, the learning that a person does during his or her life is a process of remembering what his or her soul, living immortally throughout infinite lifetimes, always already has known (and has forgotten before being born into this life). Thus, learning can be understood here as something similar to Oedipus' deduction, in *Oedipus the King,* as bringing to consciousness what on some level one already knows.

Recollection and reincarnation, then, are important to our inquiry into the nature of gender. Not only is it perfectly possible, according to Socrates, that a man should be reincarnated as a woman, it is possible that he should be reincarnated as, say, a female duck or pig. This reincarnation will depend on the kind of life he has lived "this time around," and so we can find in Plato an investigation of the comparative virtue of living as a man or as a woman. Our knowledge about gender seems to play, according to Plato, a role in our decisions about who we ought to love and why, about what we ought to do and why, about what kind of a person we really are and why.

REPUBLIC V

Perhaps the most famous and important discussion of gender among ancient Greek texts appears in the fifth book of Plato's *Republic.* Socrates has been trying during the first four books to establish with his friends a definition of Justice. As a part of their investigation, Socrates and his two main companions, Glaucon and Adeimantus, built and explored a hypothetical or ideal city. Their goal was to make the city the best possible one in which human beings could live; since a good city must of course be just, they proposed to find justice there. If the city is to be just, Socrates suggests, then it will have to be protected from both external and internal unrest. This job falls to a class called the "guards," or "auxiliaries"—roughly a combination of soldiers and police who, like our own military, must be trained very strictly and carefully in order to do their jobs loyally and reliably.

In the earlier books, Socrates and his companions investigated the character and education that would be necessary to ensure good guards— e.g., they would need obedience and courage, the particular virtues proper to guards. Socrates there mentioned in passing that anyone, man or woman, with this loyal, yet aggressive, character should be educated for guardianship and given moral and literary education and rigorous physical training. Arguing that private marriages would destroy the camaraderie and trust of the guards, he suggested that wives be shared in common.

These statements on Socrates' part did not go unnoticed by his interlocutors. In the fourth book, right before our excerpt begins, Socrates and the others have finished building the city and have found justice within it. They should be ready to look for the form of justice itself. Nonetheless, at the beginning of book five, Adeimantus and another interlocutor, Polemarchus, want to go back and discuss the status of women in the good city. What follows are Socrates' arguments that the best city should have arranged marriages, communal wives and children, and identical education for men and women.

SOCRATES: We must now, said I, go back to what should have been said earlier in sequence. However, this may well be the right way: after we have completed the parts that men must play, we turn to those of women, especially as you call on me to do so.

For men of such a nature and education as we have described there is, in my opinion, no other right way to deal with wives and children than following the road upon which we started them. We attempted, in our argument, to establish the men as guardians of the flock.—Yes.

Let us then give them for the birth and upbringing of children a system appropriate to that function and see whether it suits us or not.—How?

Like this: do we think that the wives of our guardian watchdogs should join in whatever guardian duties the men fulfill, join them in the hunt, and do everything else in common, or should we keep the women at home as unable to do so because they must bear and rear their young, and leave to the men the labour and the whole care of the flock?

All things, he said, should be done in common, except that the women are physically weaker and the men stronger.

And is it possible, I asked, to make use of living creatures for the same purposes unless you give them the same upbringing and education?—It is not possible.

So if we use the women for the same tasks as the men, they must be taught the same things.—Yes.

Now we gave the men artistic and physical culture.—Yes.

So we must give both also to the women, as well as training in war, and use them for the same tasks.—That seems to follow from what you say.

Perhaps, I said, many of the things we are saying, being contrary to custom, would stir up ridicule, if carried out in practice in the way we are telling them.—They certainly would, he said.

What, I asked, is the most ridiculous feature you see in this? Or is it obviously that women should exercise naked in the palaestra along with the men, not only the young women but the older women too, as the old men do in the gymnasia when their bodies are wrinkled and not pleasant to look at and yet they are fond of physical exercise?—Yes, by Zeus, he said, it would appear ridiculous as things stand now.

Surely, I said, now that we have started on this argument, we must not be afraid of all the jokes of the kind that the wits will make about such a change in physical and artistic culture, and not least about the women carrying arms and riding horses.—You are right, he said.

As we have begun this discussion we must go on to the tougher part of the law and beg these people not to practise their own trade of comedy at our expense but to be serious and to remember that it is not very long since the Greeks thought it ugly and ridiculous, as the majority of barbarians still do, for men to be seen naked. When first the Cretans and then the Lacedaemonians started their physical training, the wits of those days could have ridiculed it all, or do you not think so?—I do.

But I think that after it was found in practice to be better to strip than to cover up all those parts, then the spectacle ceased to be looked on as ridiculous because reasonable argument had shown that it was best. This showed that it is foolish to think anything ridiculous except what is bad, or to try to raise a laugh at any other spectacle than that of ignorance and evil as being ridiculous, as it is foolish to be in earnest about any other standard of beauty than that of the good.—Most certainly.

Must we not first agree whether our proposals are possible or not? And we must grant an opportunity for discussion to anyone who, in jest or seriously, wishes to argue the point whether female human nature can share all the tasks of the male sex, or none at all, or some but not others, and to which of the two waging war belongs. Would this not be the best beginning and likely to lead to the best conclusion?—Certainly.

Do you then want us to dispute among ourselves on behalf of those others, lest the other side of the argument fall by default?—There is nothing to stop us.

Let us then speak on their behalf: "Socrates and Glaucon, there is no need for others to argue with you. You yourselves, when you began to found your city, agreed that each person must pursue the one task for which he is fitted by nature." I think we did agree to this, of course.—"Can you deny that a woman is by nature very different from a man?—Of course not. "And is it not proper to assign a different task to each according to their nature?"—Certainly. "How then are you not wrong and contradicting yourselves when you say that men and women must do the same things, when they have quite separate natures?" Do you have any defence against that argument, my good friend?

That is not very easy offhand, he said, but I ask and beg you to explain the argument on our side, whatever it is.

It is these and many other difficulties that I foresaw, Glaucon, I said, when I was afraid and hesitated to tackle the law concerning the acquiring of wives and the upbringing of children.—By Zeus, he said, it does not seem at all easy.

It is not, said I, but the fact is that whether a man falls into a small swimming pool or in the middle of the ocean, he must swim all the same.—Certainly.

So then we must swim too and try to save ourselves from the sea of our argument, hoping that a dolphin will pick us up or we may find some other miraculous deliverance.—It seems so.

Come now, said I, let us see if we can find a way out. We have agreed that a different nature must follow a different occupation and that the nature of man and woman is different, and we now say that different natures must follow the same pursuits. This is the accusation brought against us.—Surely.

How grand is the power of disputation, Glaucon.—Why?

Because, I said, many people fall into it unwittingly and think they are not disputing but conversing because they cannot analyze their subject into its parts, but they pursue mere verbal contradictions of what has been said, thus engaging in a dispute rather than in a conversation.

Many people, he said, have that experience, but does this also apply to us at the present moment?

It most certainly does, I said. I am afraid we have indeed unwittingly fallen into disputation.—How?

We are bravely, but in a disputatious and verbal fashion, pursuing the principle that a nature which is not the same must not engage in the same pursuits, but when we assigned different tasks to a different nature and the same to the same nature, we did not examine at all what kind of difference and sameness of nature we had in mind and in what regard we were distinguishing them.—No, we did not look into that.

We might therefore just as well, it seems, ask ourselves whether the nature of bald men and long-haired men is the same and not opposite, and then, agreeing that they are opposite, if we allow bald men to be cobblers, not allow long-haired men to be, or again if long-haired men are cobblers, not allow the others to be.—That would indeed be ridiculous.

Is it ridiculous for any other reason than because we did not fully consider their same or different natures in every respect but we were only watching the kind of difference and sameness which applied to those particular pursuits? For example, a male and a female physician, we said, have the same nature of soul, or do you not think so?—I do.

But a physician and a carpenter have a different nature?—Surely.

Therefore, I said, if the male and the female are seen to be different as regards a particular craft or other pursuit we shall say this must be assigned to one or the other. But if they seem to differ in this particular only, that the female bears children while the male begets them, we shall say that there has been no kind of proof that a woman is different from a man as regards the duties we are talking about, and we shall still believe that our guardians and their wives should follow the same pursuits.—And rightly so.

Next we shall bid anyone who holds the contrary view to instruct us in this: with regard to what craft or pursuit concerned with the establishment of the city is the nature of man and woman not the same but different?—That is right.

Someone else might very well say what you said a short time ago, that it is not easy to give an immediate reply, but that it would not be at all difficult after considering the question.—He might say that.

Do you then want us to beg the one who raises these objections to follow us to see whether we can show him that no pursuit connected with the management of the city belongs in particular to a woman?—Certainly.

Come now, we shall say to him, give us an answer: did you mean that one person had a natural ability for a certain pursuit, while another had not, when the first learned it easily, the latter with difficulty? The one, after a brief period of instruction, was able to find things out for himself from what he had learned, while the other, after much instruction, could not even remember what he had learned; the former's body adequately served his mind, while the other's physical reactions opposed his. Are there any other ways in which you distinguished the naturally gifted in each case from those who were not?—No one will say anything else.

Do you know of any occupation practised by mankind in which the male sex is not superior to the female in all these respects? Or shall we pursue the argument at length by mentioning weaving, baking cakes, cooking vegetables, tasks in which the female sex certainly seems to distinguish itself, and in which it is most laughable of all for women to be inferior to men?

What you say is true, he said, namely that one sex is much superior to the other in almost everything, yet many women are better than many men in many things, but on the whole it is as you say.

There is therefore no pursuit connected with city management which belongs to woman because she is a woman, or to a man because he is a man, but various natures are scattered in the same way among both kinds of persons. Woman by nature shares all pursuits, and so does man, but in all of them woman is a physically weaker creature than man.—Certainly.

Shall we then assign them all to men, and none to a woman?—How can we?

One woman, we shall say, is a physician, another is not, one is by nature artistic, another is not.—Quite so.

One may be athletic or warlike, while another is not warlike and has no love of athletics.—I think so.

Further, may not one woman love wisdom, another hate it, or one may be high-spirited, another be without spirit?—That too.

So one woman may have a guardian nature, the other not. Was it not a nature with these qualities which we selected among men for our male guardians too?—We did.

Therefore the nature of man and woman is the same as regards guarding the city, except in so far as she is physically weaker, and the man's nature stronger.—So it seems.

Such women must then be chosen along with such men to live with them and share their guardianship, since they are qualified and akin to them by nature.—Certainly.

Must we not assign the same pursuits to the same natures?—The same.

We have come round then to what we said before, and we agree that it is not against nature to give to the wives of the guardians an education in the arts and physical culture.—Definitely not.

We are not legislating against nature or indulging in mere wishful thinking since the law we established is in accord with nature. It is rather the contrary present practice which is against nature as it seems.—It appears so.

Now we were to examine whether our proposals were possible and the best.—We were.

That they are possible is now agreed?—Yes.

After this we must seek agreement whether they are the best.—Clearly.

With a view to having women guardians, we should not have one kind of education to fashion the men, and another for the women, especially as they have the same nature to begin with.—No, not another.

What is your opinion of this kind of thing?—Of what?

About thinking to yourself that one man is better and another worse, or do you think that they are all alike?—Certainly not.

In the city we were establishing, do you think the guardians are made better men by the education they have received, or the cobblers who were educated for their craft?—Your question is ridiculous.

I know, said I. Well, are these guardians not the best of all the citizens?—By far.

Will then these women guardians not be the best of women?—That too by far.

Is there anything better for a city than to have the best possible men and women?—Nothing.

And it is the arts and physical culture, as we have described them, which will achieve this?—Of course.

So the institution we have established is not only possible but also the best.—That is so.

The women then must strip for their physical training, since they will be clothed in excellence. They must share in war and the other duties of the guardians about the city, and have no other occupation; the lighter duties will be assigned to them because of the weakness of their sex. The man who laughs at the sight of naked women exercising for the best of reasons is "plucking the unripe fruit of laughter", he understands nothing of what he is laughing at, it seems, nor what he is doing. For it is and always will be a fine saying that what is beneficial is beautiful, what is harmful is ugly.—Very definitely.

Let us say then that we have escaped from one wave of criticism in our discussion of the law about women, and we have not been altogether swamped when we laid it down that male and female guardians must share all their duties in common, and our argument is consistent when it states that this is both possible and beneficial.—It is, he said, certainly no small wave from which you are escaping.

You will not say this was a big one when you see the one that follows, I said.—Speak up, then, he said, and let me see it.

I think, I said, that the law follows from the last and those that have gone before.—What law?

All these women shall be wives in common to all the men, and not one of them shall live privately with any man; the children too should be held in common so that no parent shall know which is his own offspring, and no child shall know his parent.

This proposal raises far more doubts than the last, both as to its possibility and its usefulness, he said.

I do not think its usefulness will be disputed, I said, namely that it is not a great blessing to hold wives in common, and children too, provided it is possible. I think that most controversy will arise on the question of its possibility.—Both points, he said, will certainly be disputed.

You mean that I will have to fight a combination of arguments. I thought I could escape by running away from one of them, if you thought the proposal beneficial, and that it would only remain for me to argue its possibility.—I saw you running away, he said, but you must explain both.

Well, I said, I must take my punishment. Allow me, however, to indulge myself as if on holiday, as lazy-minded people feast on their own thoughts whenever they take a walk alone. Instead of finding out how something they desire may become a reality, such people pass over that question to avoid wearying themselves by deliberating on what is possible and what is not; they assume that what they desire is available; they arrange the details and enjoy themselves thinking about all they will do when it has come to pass, thus making a lazy mind even lazier. I am myself at this moment getting soft, and I want to delay consideration of the feasibility of our proposal until later. I will assume that it is feasible and examine, if you will allow me, how the rulers will arrange these things when they happen and I will argue that this will be most beneficial to the city and to the guardians. This I will try to examine along with you, and deal with the other question later, if you permit.—I permit it, he said, carry on with your examination.

I think that surely our rulers, if indeed they are worthy of the name, and their auxiliaries as well, will be willing, the latter to do what they are told, the former to give the orders, in part by obeying the laws themselves, and in part, in such matters as we have entrusted to them, by imitating these laws.—That is likely.

You then, as their lawgiver, just as you chose the men, will in the same manner choose the women and provide as far as possible those of the same nature. Since they have their dwellings and meals together and none of them possess anything of the kind as private property, they will be together and mix together both in the gymnasia and in the rest of their education and they will, I think, be driven by inborn necessity to have intercourse with one another. Or do you not think that what I say will of necessity happen?

The necessity is not of a mathematical but of an erotic kind, he said, and this is probably stronger in persuading and compelling the mass of the people.

Yes indeed, I said. The next point is, Glaucon, that promiscuity is impious in a city of fortunate people, nor will the rulers allow it.—It is not right.

After this we must obviously make marriage as sacred as possible, and sacred marriages will be those which are the most beneficial.—Most certainly.

How then will they be most beneficial? Tell me, Glaucon: I see that at home you have hunting dogs and quite a number of pedigree birds. Did you then, by Zeus, pay any attention to their unions and breeding?—In what way? he asked.

In the first place, though they are all of good stock, are there not some who are and prove themselves to be best?—There are.

Do you breed equally from them all, or are you anxious to breed most from the best?—From the best.

Further, do you breed from the youngest, or from the oldest, or from those in their prime?—From those in their prime.

And do you think that if they were not bred in this way, your stock of birds and dogs would deteriorate considerably?—I do.

Do you think things are any different in the case of horses and the other animals?—That would indeed be absurd.

Good gracious, my friend, I said, how great is our need for extremely able rulers if the same is true for the human race.—It is, but what about it?

Because they will need to use a good many drugs. For people who do not need drugs but are willing to follow a diet even an inferior physician will be sufficient, but when drugs are needed, we know that a bolder physician is required.—True, but what do you have in mind?

This, I said: our rulers will probably have to make considerable use of lies and deceit for the good of their subjects. We said that all such things are useful as a kind of drug.—And rightly so.

This "rightly" will occur frequently in matters of marriage and the bearing of children.—How so?

It follows from our previous agreement that the best men must have intercourse with the best women as frequently as possible, and the opposite is true of the very inferior men and women; the offspring of the former must be reared, but not the offspring of the latter, if our herd is to be of the highest possible quality. Only the rulers should know of these arrangements, if our herd of guardians is to avoid all dissension as far as possible.—Quite right.

Therefore certain festivals will be established by law at which we shall bring the brides and grooms together; there will also be sacrifices, and our poets must compose hymns to celebrate the marriages. The number of marriages we shall leave to the rulers to decide, in such a way as to keep the number of males as stable as possible, taking into account war, disease, and similar factors so that our city shall, as far as possible, become neither too big nor too small.—Right.

There will have to be some clever lots introduced, so that at each marriage celebration the inferior man we mentioned will blame chance but not the rulers.—Quite so.

The young men who have distinguished themselves in war or in other ways must be given awards consisting of other prizes and also more abundant permission to sleep with women, so that we may have a good excuse to have as many children as possible begotten by them.—Right.

As the children are born, officials appointed for the purpose—be they men or women or both, since our offices are open to both women and men—will take them.—Yes.

The children of good parents they will take to a rearing pen in the care of nurses living apart in a certain section of the city; the children of inferior parents, or any child of the others born defective, they will hide, as is fitting, in a secret and unknown place.—Yes, he said, if the breed of the guardians is to remain pure.

The nurses will also see to it that the mothers are brought to the rearing pen when their breasts have milk, but take every precaution that no mother shall know her own child; they will provide wet nurses if the number of mothers is insufficient; they will take care that the mothers suckle the children for only a reasonable time; the care of sleepless children and all other troublesome duties will belong to the wet nurses and other attendants.

You are making it very easy, he said, for the wives of the guardians to have children.

And that is fitting, I said. Let us take up the next point of our proposal: We said that the children's parents should be in their prime.—True.

Do you agree that a reasonable interpretation of this is twenty years for a woman and thirty years for a man?—Which years?

A woman, I said, is to bear children for the state from the age of twenty to the age of forty, a man after he has passed "his peak as a racer" begets children for the state till he reaches fifty.—This, he said, is the physical and mental peak for both.

If a man either younger or older than this meddles with procreation for the state, we shall declare his offence to be neither pious nor right as he begets for the city a child which, if it remains secret, will be born without benefit of the sacrifices and prayers which priests and priestesses and the whole city utter at every marriage festival, that the children of good and useful parents may always prove themselves better and more useful; but this child is born in darkness, the result of dangerous incontinence.—Right.

The same law will apply, I said, if a man still of begetting years unites with a woman of child-bearing age without the sanction of the rulers; we shall say that he brings to the city an unauthorized and unhallowed bastard.—Quite right.

However, I think that when women and men have passed the age of having children, we shall leave them free to have intercourse with anyone they wish, with these exceptions: for a man, his daughter or mother, or the daughter's daughters, or his mother's female progenitors; for a woman, a son or father, their male issue or progenitors. Having received these instructions they should be very careful not to bring a single child into the light, but if one should be conceived, and, forces its way to the light, they must deal with it knowing that no nurture is available for it.

This too, he said, is sensibly spoken, but how shall they know their fathers and daughters and those other relationships you mentioned?

They have no means of knowing, I said, but all the children who are born in the tenth and seventh month after a man became a bridegroom he will call sons if they are male, daughters if they are female, and they will call him father, and so too he will call their offspring his grandchildren who in turn will call the first group their grandfathers and grandmothers. Those born during the time when their fathers and mothers were having children they will call their brothers and sisters, so that, as I said, these groups will have no sexual relations with each other. But the law will allow brothers and sisters to live together if the lot so falls and the Pythian approves.—Quite right.

This then is the holding in common of wives and children for the guardians of your city. We must now confirm in our argument that it conforms with the rest of our constitution and is by far the best. Or how are we to proceed?—In that way, by Zeus.

Is not the first step towards agreement to ask ourselves what we say is the greatest good in the management of the city? At this the lawgiver must aim in making his laws. Also what is the greatest evil. Then we should examine whether the system we have just described follows the tracks of the good and not those of evil.—By all means.

Is there any greater evil we can mention for a city than whatever tears it apart into many communities instead of one?—There is not.

Do not common feelings of pleasure and pain bind the city together, when as nearly as possible all the citizens equally rejoice or feel pain at the same successes and failures?—Most certainly.

For such feelings to be isolated and private dissolves the city's unity, when some suffer greatly while others greatly rejoice at the same public or private events.—Of course.

And that sort of thing happens whenever such words as "mine" and "not mine"—and so with "another's"—are not used in unison.—Most certainly.

And the city which most closely resembles the individual? When one of us hurts his finger, the whole organism which binds body and soul together into the unitary system managed by the ruling part of it shares the pain at once throughout when one part suffers. This is why we say that the man has a pain in his finger, and the same can be said of any part of the man, both about the pain which any part suffers, and its pleasure when it finds relief.

Certainly, he said. As for your question, the best managed city certainly closely resembles such an organism.

And whenever anything good or bad happens to a single one of its citizens, such a city will certainly say that this citizen is a part of itself, and the whole city will rejoice or suffer with him.—That must be so, if it has good laws.

It is time now, I said, for us to return to our own city and to look there for the features we have agreed on, whether it. or any other city, possesses them to the greatest degree.—We must do so.

Well then. There are rulers and people in the other cities as well as in this one?—There are.

And they all call each other fellow-citizens.—Of course.

Besides the word fellow-citizens, what do the people call the rulers in the other cities?

In many they call them masters, but in democracies they call them by this very name, rulers.

What do the people call them in our city? Besides fellow citizens, what do they call the rulers?—Saviours and helpers.

And what do the rulers call the people?—Providers of food and wages.

What do the rulers call the people in the other cities?—Slaves.

And what do the rulers call each other?—Fellow rulers.

And ours?—Fellow guardians.

Can you tell me whether a ruler in the other cities might address one of his fellow rulers as his kinsman and another as an outsider?—Certainly, many could.

He then considers his kinsman, and addresses him, as his own, but not the outsider?—That is so.

What about your guardians? Can any of them consider any other of his fellow guardians an outsider and address him as such?

Not in any way, he said, for when he meets any one of them he will think he is meeting a brother or a sister, a father or a mother, a son or a daughter, their offspring or progenitors.

You put that very well, I said, but, further, tell me this: will you legislate these family relationships as names only, or must they act accordingly in all they do? Must a man show to his fathers the respect, solicitude, and obedience to parents required by law? Otherwise, if he acts differently, he will fare worse at the hands of gods and men as one whose actions are neither pious nor just. Will these be the sayings that ring in his ears on the part of all citizens from childhood both about their fathers, those pointed out to them as such, and about their other kindred—or will there be other voices?

It will be those, he said; it would be absurd if their lips spoke these names of kindred without appropriate action following.

So in our city more than any other, when any individual fares well or badly, they would all speak in unison the words we mentioned just now, namely that "mine" is doing well, or "mine" is doing badly.—That also is very true.

And we said that such a belief and its expression are followed by common feelings of pleasure and pain.—And we were right.

So our citizens will to the greatest extent share the same thing which they call "mine," with the result that they in the highest degree share common feelings of pleasure and pain.—Surely.

And besides other arrangements, the reason for this is the holding of wives and children in common among the guardians.—More than anything else.

This we agreed was the greatest blessing for a city, and we compared a well run city to the body's reactions to pain or pleasure in any part of it.—And we were right to agree on that.

So then the cause of the greatest good for our city has been shown to be the common ownership of wives and children among the auxiliaries.—Certainly.

Socrates' is a radical set of arguments for other reasons besides just the positing of sex equality. He also suggests that modesty about our bodies is immature and keeps the city from functioning justly (hence, both men and women, young and old, should exercise together in the nude) and that the rulers of the good city should deceive the citizens by masquerading what really are arranged marriages as the results of a lottery. The implications of all the various radical suggestions in this book boil down to this: that physical similarities and differences between us—such as the differences between the sexes—are not real or important. Only the state of one's character should be important to the virtuous life.

This is most clearly argued in the passage about "bald-headedness" and cobblery. Socrates' point here is that certain personal qualities are relevant to the jobs we do and others are not. While it may be possible that some physical qualities are relevant for some jobs (for instance, physical strength may be relevant to boxing or working on a loading dock), it seems that for Socrates, this is only rarely the case. Most of the time, only one's personality or character is relevant to one's job, and so women and men with similar personalities ought to do similar jobs. Thus, in distinction from Aeschylus and Sophocles, Socrates here claims that there are not really distinct virtues for men and women, but that virtues are generically human. This plea implies that we should ignore the sexuality that comes inevitably with our bodily existence and attend instead to that part of us that, he seems to claim, has no sex: our soul.

Like the Greek dramatists, Socrates claims that the achievement of virtue, both for the individual and for the city, may conflict with freedom or happiness and with the passions that human beings would like to be free to express. Thus, he recommends that the rulers of the best city propound a *"noble lie"* to the guards, arranging their marriages as breeders do the couplings of dogs or horses, while pretending everything is a religious festival with randomly arranged couplings. This is a disturbing set of claims for many readers, especially those who live in a liberal democracy such as the United States and who value freedom of choice very highly. Socrates seems, however, to envision the good city as that city in which everyone links up with the best person for her or him. In this sense, the good rulers are "matchmakers," an image of the good philosopher of which Socrates avails himself in other dialogues. Socrates' commitment is to the happiness of the city, and although he implies that citizens will be happier in his ideal city, the designers of the city cannot make this their priority.

The good ruler is the one who produces virtuous citizens, and the good personal match is the one who will produce virtuous children. Socrates, like Aeschylus and Sophocles before him, suggests that virtue is the result of knowing and following the rational order of nature. Thus, the good ruler, as well as the good mate, must above all be rational. Hence, for Socrates, both our mates and our rulers should, ideally, be philosophers.

THEAETETUS

In this dialogue, Socrates is working with a young man, Theaetetus, who is studying math and shows promise in philosophy. They take up the question of knowledge, and Socrates elicits from Theaetetus a list of different disciplines and crafts that he considers to be based on knowledge. Socrates criticizes him, stating that "we are going an interminable way round, when our answer might be quite short and simple."[5] In other words, Socrates would like Theaetetus to give a single definition of knowledge instead of trying to give a list of things people know—which would take them forever to complete. This definition would be the single nature or principle that all known things share—i.e., the Form of Knowledge. But Theaetetus grows disheartened by the criticism, and begs off the discussion. At this point, Socrates musters his new student's courage through an interesting analogy.

> THEAET: But I assure you, Socrates, I have often tried to think this out, when I have heard reports of the questions you ask. But I can never persuade myself that anything I say will really do; and I never hear anyone else state the matter in the way that you require. And yet, again, you know, I can't even stop worrying about it.

---

[5] Plato, *Theaetetus 147c.*

SOC: Yes; those are the pains of labour, dear Theaetetus. It is because you are not barren but pregnant.

THEAET: I don't know about that, Socrates. I'm only telling you what's happened to me.

SOC: Then do you mean to say you've never heard about my being the son of a good hefty midwife, Phaenarete?

THEAET: Oh, yes, I've heard that before.

SOC: And haven't you ever been told that I practise the same art myself?

THEAET: No, I certainly haven't.

SOC: But I do, believe me. Only don't give me away to the rest of the world, will you? You see, my friend, it is a secret that I have this art. That is not one of the things you hear people saying about me, because they don't know; but they do say that I am a very odd sort of person, always causing people to get into difficulties. You must have heard that, surely?

THEAET: Yes, I have.

SOC: And shall I tell you what is the explanation of that?

THEAET: Yes, please do.

SOC: Well, if you will just think of the general facts about the business of midwifery, you will see more easily what I mean. You know, I suppose, that women never practise as midwives while they are still conceiving and bearing children themselves. It is only those who are past child-bearing who take this up.

THEAET: Oh, yes.

SOC: They say it was Artemis who was responsible for this custom; it was because she, who undertook the patronage of child-birth, was herself childless. She didn't, it's true, entrust the duties of midwifery to barren women, because human nature is too weak to acquire skill where it has no experience. But she assigned the task to those who have become incapable of child-bearing through age—honouring their likeness to herself.

THEAET: Yes, naturally.

SOC: And this too is very natural, isn't it?—or perhaps necessary? I mean that it is the midwives who can tell better than anyone else whether women are pregnant or not.

THEAET: Yes, of course.

SOC: And then it is the midwives who have the power to bring on the pains, and also, if they think fit, to relieve them; they do it by the use of simple drugs, and by singing incantations. In difficult cases, too, they can bring about the birth; or, if they consider it advisable, they can promote a miscarriage.

THEAET: Yes, that is so.

SOC: There's another thing too. Have you noticed this about them, that they are the cleverest of match-makers, because they are marvellously knowing about the kind of couples whose marriage will produce the best children?

THEAET: No, that is not at all familiar to me.

SOC: But they are far prouder of this, believe me, than of cutting the umbilical cord. Think now. There's an art which is concerned with the cultivation and harvesting of the crops. Now is it the same art which prescribes the best soil for planting or sowing a given crop? Or is it a different one?

THEAET: No, it is all the same art.

SOC: Then applying this to midwifery, will there be one art of the sowing and another of the harvesting?

THEAET: That doesn't seem likely, certainly.

SOC: No, it doesn't. But there is also an unlawful and unscientific practice of bringing men and women together, which we call procuring; and because of that the midwives—a most august body of women—are very reluctant to undertake even lawful matchmaking. They are afraid that if they practise this, they may be suspected of the other. And yet, I suppose, reliable matchmaking is a matter for no one but the true midwife.

THEAET: Apparently.

SOC: So the work of the midwives is a highly important one; but it is not so important as my own performance. And for this reason, that there is not in midwifery the further complication, that the patients are sometimes delivered of phantoms and sometimes of realities, and that the two are hard to distinguish. If there were, then the midwife's greatest and noblest function would be to distinguish the true from the false offspring—don't you agree?

THEAET: Yes, I do.

SOC: Now my art of midwifery is just like theirs in most respects. The difference is that I attend men and not women, and that I watch over the labour of their souls, not of their bodies. And the most important thing about my art is the ability to apply all possible tests to the offspring, to determine whether the young mind is being delivered of a phantom, that is, an error, or a fertile truth. For one thing which I have in common with the ordinary midwives is that I myself am barren of wisdom. The common reproach against me is that I am always asking questions of other people but never express my own views about anything, because there is no wisdom in me; and that is true enough. And the reason of it is this, that God compels me to attend the travail of others, but has forbidden me to procreate. So that I am not in any sense a wise man; I cannot claim as the child of my own soul any discovery worth the name of wisdom. But with those who associate with me it is different. At first some of them may give the impression of being ignorant and stupid; but as time goes on and our association continues, all whom God permits are seen to make progress—a progress which is amazing both to other people and to themselves. And yet it is clear that this is not due to anything they have learnt from me; it is that they discover within themselves a multitude of beautiful things, which they bring forth into the light. But it is I, with God's help, who deliver them of this offspring. And a proof of this may be seen in the many cases where people who did not realise this fact took all the credit to themselves and thought that I was no good. They have then proceeded to leave me sooner than they should, either of their own accord or through the influence of others. And after they have gone away from me they have resorted to harmful company, with the result that what remained within them

has miscarried; while they have neglected the children I helped them to bring
forth, and lost them, because they set more value upon lies and phantoms
than upon the truth; finally they have been set down for ignorant fools, both
by themselves and by everybody else. One of these people was Aristeides the
son of Lysimachus; and there have been very many others. Sometimes they
come back, wanting my company again, and ready to move heaven and earth
to get it. When that happens, in some cases the divine sign that visits me
forbids me to associate with them; in others, it permits me, and then they
begin again to make progress.

There is another point also in which those who associate with me are like
women in child-birth. They suffer the pains of labour, and are filled day and
night with distress; indeed they suffer far more than women. And this pain
my art is able to bring on, and also to allay. Well, that's what happens to
them; but at times, Theaetetus, I come across people who do not seem to me
somehow to be pregnant. Then I realise that they have no need of me, and
with the best will in the world I undertake the business of match-making; and
I think I am good enough—God willing—at guessing with whom they might
profitably keep company. Many of them I have given away to Prodicus; and a
great number also to other wise and inspired persons.

Well, my dear lad, this has been a long yarn; but the reason was that I have
a suspicion that you (as you think yourself) are pregnant and in labour. So I
want you to come to me as to one who is both the son of a midwife and
himself skilled in the art; and try to answer the questions I shall ask you as
well as you can.

Here, Socrates draws out the analogy of the good ruler, or the philosopher, to the
"matchmaker," but with new implications. The best matchmaker, Socrates claims,
is also the best midwife—delivering the children who are the "product" of the
match. Socrates draws the distinction, in the analogy, between the midwife of the
body—who delivers children of women—and the midwife of the soul—who delivers ideas and opinions of men. Through this double analogy, women are associated
with the body, and men with the soul or mind. This would seem in line with a lot of
the binary oppositions we have seen in the last section, as well as with modern and
contemporary scholars' intuitions (see for instance, the discussion of Descartes in
Part Three) about the representations of women in our society. In this analogy, however, the distinctions may become perplexing. Socrates, by comparing himself to
the midwife, associates his own craft with "women's work," characterizing his
teaching method as at least partly feminine. On this analogy, in addition, there is
something inherently feminine about bringing an idea into the world.

SYMPOSIUM

In the *Symposium*, the question is love. Several friends have assembled at the home
of Agathon, a bright and attractive young Athenian who has just won his first prize
for Tragedy. This is the second night of celebration: the big celebration the day

before has left most of the participants with bad hangovers (all but Socrates, who missed the party). They decide, instead of another night of revelry, to play a kind of party game, in which everyone gives speeches in praise of love. The first three speakers are Phaedrus, an admirer of the Sophists; Pausanius, a politician; and Eryximachus, a doctor, who all develop some useful points about love, but who ultimately present no coherent explanation of this deeply important phenomenon. One reason (among many) that these early speakers seem unable to make a clear theory of love is that they cannot seem to divorce their thinking about love from the various Greek conventions for its practice.

As in modern European and American society, and as we know from so many of the Greek sources excerpted above, marriage was a crucial political convention in ancient Greece. There was, however, an accepted relation of lovers outside of marriage, something similar to the practice, in modern Europe of recent centuries, of a married man keeping a mistress. It was acceptable in the Athens of Plato's time for older men—even married ones—to have a young male lover. These relationships were, then, in a sense illicit, and all the more titillating on that account, but they were nonetheless publicly recognized and without negative sanction. They also followed a certain traditional pattern, in which the young man was thought naturally to be unattracted to the older fellow, and to yield to his elder's entreaties purely for the sake of learning from his experience and knowledge. Thus, built into the Greek tradition of love was a relationship between what were essentially teachers and students, as well as the idea that young and ignorant people are more lovable than older wiser ones.

These conventions, as we see early in the dialogue, are in disagreement with the "facts" presented in the dialogue itself. For we learn early on that Agathon, who is young and attractive, is in love with Socrates, who is old and "snub-nosed" but the "wisest man in Athens." The two speeches excerpted below attempt to break through the appearances of Greek conventions and to explore philosophically this true nature of love. They do not agree with each other in very many respects at all, although there are similarities we can draw between them. It will be for you to decide whether they can be made coherent with each other, and whether either is adequate.

ARISTOPHANES' SPEECH

One party guest is Aristophanes, the comic playwright. At the time of the party, he is an old man, close to Socrates' age or even older, and he is a master of his craft. This historical character's work survives, is still produced and read, and still ranks with the best of comic theater. Thus, we can expect his speech to be funny, and it does not disappoint.

> First you must learn what Human Nature was in the beginning and what has happened to it since, because long ago our nature was not what it is now, but very different. There were three kinds of human beings, that's my first point— not two as there are now, male and female. In addition to these, there was a third, a combination of those two; its name survives, though the kind itself has

vanished. At that time, you see, the word "androgynous" really meant something: a form made up of male and female elements, though now there's nothing but the word, and that's used as an insult. My second point is that the shape of each human being was completely round, with back and sides in a circle; they had four hands each, as many legs as hands, and two faces, exactly alike, on a rounded neck. Between the two faces, which were on opposite sides, was one head with four ears. There were two sets of sexual organs, and everything else was the way you'd imagine it from what I've told you. They walked upright, as we do now, whatever direction they wanted. And whenever they set out to run fast, they thrust out all their eight limbs, the ones they had then, and spun rapidly, the way gymnasts do cartwheels, by bringing their legs around straight.

Now here is why there were three kinds, and why they were as I described them: The male kind was originally an offspring of the sun, the female of the earth, and the one that combined both genders was an offspring of the moon, because the moon shares in both. They were spherical and so was their motion, because they were like their parents in the sky.

In strength and power, therefore, they were terrible, and they had great ambitions. They made an attempt on the gods, and Homer's story about Ephialtes and Otos was originally about them: how they tried to make an ascent to heaven so as to attack the gods. Then Zeus and the other gods met in council to discuss what to do, and they were sore perplexed. They couldn't wipe out the human race with thunderbolts and kill them all off, as they had the giants, because that would wipe out the worship they receive, along with the sacrifices we humans give them. On the other hand, they couldn't let them run riot. At last, after great effort, Zeus had an idea.

"I think I have a plan," he said, "that would allow human beings to exist and stop their misbehaving: they will give up being wicked when they lose their strength. So I shall now cut each of them in two. At one stroke they will lose their strength and also become more profitable to us, owing to the increase in their number. They shall walk upright on two legs. But if I find they still run riot and do not keep the peace," he said, "I will cut them in two again, and they'll have to make their way on one leg, hopping."

So saying, he cut those human beings in two, the way people cut sorb-apples before they dry them or the way they cut eggs with hairs. As he cut each one, he commanded Apollo to turn its face and half its neck towards the wound, so that each person would see that he'd been cut and keep better order. Then Zeus commanded Apollo to heal the rest of the wound, and Apollo did turn the face around, and he drew skin from all sides over what is now called the stomach, and there he made one mouth, as in a pouch with a drawstring, and fastened it at the center of the stomach. This is now called the navel. Then he smoothed out the other wrinkles, of which there were many, and he shaped the breasts, using some such tool as shoemakers have for smoothing wrinkles out of leather on the form. But he left a few wrinkles around the stomach and the navel, to be a reminder of what happened long ago.

Now, since their natural form had been cut in two, each one longed for its own other half, and so they would throw their arms about each other, weaving themselves together, wanting to grow together. In that condition they would die from hunger and general idleness, because they would not do anything apart from each other. Whenever one of the halves died and one was left, the one that was left still sought another and wove itself together with that. Sometimes the half he met came from a woman, as we'd call her now, sometimes it came from a man; either way, they kept on dying.

Then, however, Zeus took pity on them, and came up with another plan: he moved their genitals around to the front! Before then, you see, they used to have their genitals outside, like their faces, and they cast seed and made children, not in one another, but in the ground, like cicadas. So Zeus brought about this relocation of genitals, and in doing so he invented interior reproduction, *by* the man *in* the woman. The purpose of this was so that, when a man embraced a woman, he would cast his seed and they would have children; but when male embraced male, they would at least have the satisfaction of intercourse, after which they could stop embracing, return to their jobs, and look after their other needs in life. This, then, is the source of our desire to love each other. Love is born into every human being; it calls back the halves of our original nature together; it tries to make one out of two and heal the wound of human nature.

Each of us, then, is a "matching half" of a human whole, because each was sliced like a flatfish, two out of one, and each of us is always seeking the half that matches him. That's why a man who is split from the double sort (which used to be called "androgynous") runs after women. Many lecherous men have come from this class, and so do the lecherous women who run after men. Women who are split from a woman, however, pay no attention at all to men; they are oriented more towards women, and lesbians come from this class. People who are split from a male are male-oriented. While they are boys, because they are chips off the male block, they love men and enjoy lying with men and being embraced by men; those are the best of boys and lads, because they are the most manly in their nature. Of course, some say such boys are shameless, but they're lying. It's not because they have no shame that such boys do this, you see, but because they are bold and brave and masculine, and they tend to cherish what is like themselves. Do you want me to prove it? Look, these are the only kind of boys who grow up to be politicians. When they're grown men, they are lovers of young men, and they naturally pay no attention to marriage or to making babies, except insofar as they are required by local custom. They, however, are quite satisfied to live their lives with one another unmarried. In every way, then, this sort of man grows up as a lover of young men and a lover of Love, always rejoicing in his own kind.

And so, when a person meets the half that is his very own, whatever his orientation, whether it's to young men or not, then something wonderful happens: the two are struck from their senses by love, by a sense of belonging to one another, and by desire, and they don't want to be separated from one another, not even for a moment.

These are the people who finish out their lives together and still cannot say what it is they want from one another. No one would think it is the intimacy of sex—that mere sex is the reason each lover takes so great and deep a joy in being with the other. It's obvious that the soul of every lover longs for something else; his soul cannot say what it is, but like an oracle it has a sense of what it wants, and like an oracle it hides behind a riddle. Suppose two lovers are lying together and Hephaestus stands over them with his mending tools, asking, "What is it you human beings really want from each other?" And suppose they're perplexed, and he asks them again: "Is this your heart's desire, then—for the two of you to become parts of the same whole, as near as can be, and never to separate, day or night? Because if that's your desire, I'd like to weld you together and join you into something that is naturally whole, so that the two of you are made into one. Then the two of you would share one life, as long as you lived, because you would be one being, and by the same token, when you died, you would be one and not two in Hades, having died a single death. Look at your love, and see if this is what you desire: wouldn't this be all the good fortune you could want?"

Surely you can see that no one who received such an offer would turn it down; no one would find anything else that he wanted. Instead, everyone would think he'd found out at last what he had always wanted: to come together and melt together with the one he loves, so that one person emerged from two. Why should this be so? It's because, as I said, we used to be complete wholes in our original nature, and now "Love" is the name for our pursuit of wholeness, for our desire to be complete.

Long ago we were united, as I said; but now the god has divided us as punishment for the wrong we did him, just as the Spartans divided the Arcadians. So there's a danger that if we don't keep order before the gods, we'll be split in two again, and then we'll be walking around in the condition of people carved on gravestones in bas-relief, sawn apart between the nostrils, like half dice. We should encourage all men, therefore, to treat the gods with all due reverence, so that we may escape this fate and find wholeness instead. And we will, if Love is our guide and our commander. Let no one work against him. Whoever opposes Love is hateful to the gods, but if we become friends of the god and cease to quarrel with him, then we shall find the young men that are meant for us and win their love, as very few men do nowadays.

Aristophanes offers us essentially a new myth. Through this myth, as through the stories of Hesiod and Homer, Aristophanes means to *explain* love, not just make a pretty speech about it. His claim, basically, is that people seek a sense of "whole-ness" through the love of our "other halves." One's proper beloved, then, is suited for him or her by nature, and, because of this, completes the life of the lover. Aristophanes' vision of the pre-human "hermaphrodites" covers the cases of both heterosexual and homosexual love. If one's original "other half" was of the same sex as her or himself, then she or he will be attracted to members of her or his own sex, and the opposite if one's original "other half" was of the opposite sex. In addition, the two "halves" in the story feel love equally for each other, implying that in the ideal love—contrary to Greek tradition on the matter—both parties love and are loved equally. Finally, Aristophanes' myth seems to get at the nature, rather than the conventions and games of love, because it begins from the human experience of love, the feeling that we have of needing this other person in order to be fully ourselves. Aristophanes captures some of the sadness of love, the loss we feel when we are not with our beloveds, the weaknesses we have for those we love. This is in contrast to the flowery praises of love that preceded his speech, and a surprising gesture from a comedian.

Several questions arise here, however, that Aristophanes does not answer. It is not clear, for instance, whether one's "other half" is like oneself or unlike oneself or a little of both. For instance, we often say that "opposites attract," yet we also often remark that a good couple is like "two peas in a pod," or something similar. Similarly, we might ask about other objects of people's affections: people love all kinds of things—money, family heirlooms, their plants and pets, even favorite clothes. Notably, in addition, bright young students often seem to love knowledge, which might explain Agathon's affection for Socrates and perhaps offer a criticism of the Athenian customs of love, but is not explained by Aristophanes' theory. Despite its failures in regard to these questions, Aristophanes' speech is one of the high points in the Platonic dialogues; perhaps one of the high points in all philosophy.

SOCRATES' SPEECH

Socrates' speech on love is a rich, complicated and beautiful discussion of the phenomenon, which can be understood on many different levels at once. He begins his talk in his usual method, by asking questions of Agathon, who spoke right before him. He ends it, however, with a myth of his own: the speech supposedly delivered by his teacher to Socrates himself, in his youth. His teacher, Diotima, is a woman who, unlike the other interlocutors, is most likely a fictional character and not a historical one. Plato, then, has gone to some lengths to bring a woman into this discussion of love.

> Now I'll let you go. I shall try to go through for you the speech about Love I once heard from a woman of Mantinea, Diotima—a woman who was wise about many things besides this: once she even put off the plague for ten years by telling the Athenians what sacrifices to make. She is the one who taught me the art of love, and I shall go through her speech as best I can on my own, using what Agathon and I have agreed to as a basis.
>
> Following your lead, Agathon, one should first describe who Love is and what he is like, and afterwards describe his works. . . .
>
> I think it will be easiest for me to proceed the way Diotima did and tell you how she questioned me. You see, I had told her almost the same things Agathon told me just now: that Love is a great god and that he belongs to beautiful things. And she used the very same arguments against me that I used against Agathon; she showed how, according to my very own speech, Love is neither beautiful nor good.

So I said, "What do you mean, Diotima? Is Love ugly, then, and bad?"

But she said, "Watch your tongue! Do you really think that, if a thing is not beautiful, it has to be ugly?"

⌒ ⌒ ⌒

It's the same with Love: when you agree he is neither good nor beautiful, you need not think he is ugly and bad; he could be something in between," she said.

"Yet everyone agrees he's a great god," I said.

"Only those who don't know?" she said. "Is that how you mean 'everyone?' Or do you include those who do know?"

"Oh, everyone together."

And she laughed. "Socrates, how could those who say that he's not a god at all agree that he's a great god?"

"Who says that?" I asked.

"You, for one," she said, "and I for another."

"How can you say this!" I exclaimed.

"That's easy," said she. "Tell me, wouldn't you say that all gods are beautiful and happy? Surely you'd never say a god is not beautiful or happy?"

"Zeus! Not I," I said.

"Well, by calling anyone 'happy,' don't you mean they possess good and beautiful things?"

"Certainly."

"What about Love? You agreed he needs good and beautiful things, and that's why he desires them—because he needs them."

"I certainly did."

"Then how could he be a god if he has no share in good and beautiful things."

"There's no way he could, apparently."

"Now do you see? You don't believe Love is a god either!"

"Then, what could Love be?" I asked. "A mortal?"

"Certainly not."

"Then, what is he?"

"He's like what we mentioned before," she said. "He is in between mortal and immortal."

"What do you mean, Diotima?"

"He's a great spirit, Socrates. Everything spiritual, you see, is in between god and mortal."

⌒ ⌒ ⌒

When Aphrodite was born, the gods held a celebration. Poros, the son of Metis, was there among them. When they had feasted, Penia came begging, as poverty does when there's a party, and stayed by the gates. Now Poros got drunk on nectar (there was no wine yet, you see) and, feeling drowsy, went into the garden of Zeus, where he fell asleep. Then Penia schemed up a plan to relieve her lack of resources: she would get a child from Poros. So she lay beside him and got pregnant with Love. That is why Love was born to follow Aphrodite and serve her: because he was conceived on the day of her birth. And that's why he is also by nature a lover of beauty, because Aphrodite herself is especially beautiful.

"As the son of Poros and Penia, his lot in life is set to be like theirs. In the first place, he is always poor and he's far from being delicate and beautiful (as ordinary people think he is); instead, he is tough and shriveled and shoeless and homeless, always lying on the dirt without a bed, sleeping at gates and in roadsides under the sky, having his mother's nature, always living with Need. But on his father's side he is a schemer after the beautiful and the good, he is brave, impetuous, and intense, an awesome hunter, always weaving snares, resourceful in his pursuit of intelligence, a lover of wisdom through all his life, a genius with enchantments, potions, and clever pleadings.

"He is by nature neither immortal nor mortal. But now he springs to life when he gets his way; now he dies—all in the very same day. Because he is his father's son, however, he keeps coming back to life, but then anything he finds his way to always slips away, and for this reason Love is never completely without resources, nor is he ever rich.

"He is in between wisdom and ignorance as well. In fact, you see, none of the gods loves wisdom or wants to become wise—for they are wise—and no one else who is wise already loves wisdom; on the other hand, no one who is ignorant will love wisdom either or want to become wise. For what's especially difficult about being ignorant is that you are content with yourself, even though you're neither beautiful and good nor intelligent. If you don't think you need anything, of course you won't want what you don't think you need."

"In that case, Diotima, who *are* the people who love wisdom, if they are neither wise nor ignorant?"

"That's obvious," she said. "A child could tell you. Those who love wisdom fall in between those two extremes. And Love is one of them, because he is in love with what is beautiful, and wisdom is extremely beautiful. It follows that Love *must* be a lover of wisdom and, as such, is in between being wise and being ignorant. This, too, comes to him from his parentage, from a father who is wise and resourceful and a mother who is not wise and lacks resource.

"My dear Socrates, that, then, is the nature of the Spirit called Love. Considering what you thought about Love, it's no surprise that you were led into thinking of Love as you did. On the basis of what you say, I conclude that you thought Love was *being loved*, rather than *being a lover.* I think that's why Love struck you as beautiful in every way: because it is what is really beautiful and graceful that deserves to be loved, and this is perfect and highly blessed; but being a lover takes a different form, which I have just described."

So I said, "All right then, my friend. What you say about Love is beautiful, but if you're right, what use is Love to human beings?"

"I'll try to teach you that, Socrates, after I finish this. So far I've been explaining the character and the parentage of Love. Now, according to you, he is love for beautiful things. But suppose someone asks us, 'Socrates and Diotima, what is the point of loving beautiful things?'

"It's clearer this way: 'The lover of beautiful things has a desire; what does he desire?'"

"That they become his own," I said.

"But that answer calls for still another question, this is, 'What will this man have, when the beautiful things he wants have become his own?'"

I said there was no way I could give a ready answer to that question.

Then she said, "Suppose someone changes the question, putting 'good' in place of 'beautiful,' and asks you this: 'Tell me, Socrates, a lover of good things has a desire; what does he desire?'"

"That they become his own," I said.

"And what will he have, when the good things he wants have become his own?"

"This time it's easier to come up with the answer," I said. "He'll have happiness."

"That's what makes happy people happy, isn't it—possessing good things. There's no need to ask further, 'What's the point of wanting happiness?' The answer you gave seems to be final."

"True," I said.

"Now this desire for happiness, this kind of love—do you think it is common to all human beings and that everyone wants to have good things forever and ever? What would you say?"

"Just that," I said. "It is common to all."

"Then, Socrates, why don't we say that everyone is in love," she asked, "since everyone always loves the same things? Instead, we say some people are in love and others not; why is that?"

"I wonder about that myself," I said.

"It's nothing to wonder about," she said. "It's because we divide out a special kind of love, and we refer to it by the word that means the whole—'love'; and for the other kinds of love we use other words."

"What do you mean?" I asked.

"Well, you know, for example, that 'poetry' has a very wide range, when it is used to mean 'creativity.' After all, everything that is responsible for creating something out of nothing is a kind of poetry; and so all the creations of every craft and profession are themselves a kind of poetry, and everyone who practices a craft is a poet."

"True."

"Nevertheless," she said, "as you also know, these craftsmen are not called poets. We have other words for them, and out of the whole of poetry we have marked off one part, the part the Muses give us with melody and rhythm, and we refer to this by the word that means the whole. For this alone is called 'poetry,' and those who practice this part of poetry are called poets."

"True."

"That's also how it is with love. The main point is this: every desire for good things or for happiness is 'the supreme and treacherous love' in everyone. But those who pursue this along any of its many other ways—through making money, or through the love of sports, or through philosophy—we don't say that *these* people are in love, and we don't call them lovers. It's only when people are devoted exclusively to one special kind of love that we use these words that really belong to the whole of it: 'love' and 'in love' and 'lovers.'"

"I am beginning to see your point," I said.

"Now there is a certain story," she said, "according to which lovers are those people who seek their other halves. But according to my story, a lover does not seek the half or the whole, unless, my friend, it turns out to be good as well. I say this because people are even willing to cut off their own arms and legs if they think they are diseased. I don't think an individual takes joy in what belongs to him personally unless by 'belonging to me' he means 'good' and by 'belonging to another' he means 'bad.' That's because what everyone loves is really nothing other than the good. Do you disagree?"

"Zeus! Not I," I said.

"Now, then," she said. "Can we simply say that people love the good?"

"Yes," I said.

"But shouldn't we add that, in loving it, they want the good to be theirs?"

"We should."

"And not only that," she said. "They want the good to be theirs forever, don't they?"

"We should add that too."

"In a word, then, love is wanting to possess the good forever."

"That's very true," I said.

"This, then, is the object of love," she said. "In view of that, how do people pursue it if they are truly in love? What do they do with the eagerness and zeal we call love? What is the real purpose of love? Can you say?"

"If I could," I said, "I wouldn't be your student, filled with admiration for your wisdom, and trying to learn these very things."

"Well, I'll tell you," she said. "It is giving birth in beauty, whether in body or in soul."

"It would take divination to figure out what you mean. I can't."

"Well, I'll tell you more clearly," she said. "All of us are pregnant, Socrates, both in body and in soul, and, as soon as we come to a certain age, we naturally desire to give birth. Now no one can possibly give birth in anything ugly; only in something beautiful. That's because when a man and a woman come together in order to give birth, this is a godly affair. Pregnancy, reproduction—this is an immortal thing for a mortal animal to do, and it cannot occur in anything that is out of harmony, but ugliness is out of harmony with all that is godly. Beauty, however, is in harmony with the divine. Therefore the goddess who presides at childbirth—she's called Moira or Eileithuia—is really Beauty. That's why, whenever pregnant animals or persons draw near to beauty, they become gentle and joyfully disposed and give birth and reproduce; but near ugliness they are foulfaced and draw back in pain; they turn away and shrink back and do not reproduce, and because they hold on to what they carry inside them, the labor is painful. This is the source of the great excitement about beauty that comes to anyone who is pregnant and already teeming with life: beauty releases them from their great pain. You see, Socrates," she said, "what Love wants is not beauty, as you think it is."

"Well, what is it, then?"

"Reproduction and birth in beauty."

"Maybe," I said.

"Certainly," she said. "Now, why reproduction? It's because reproduction goes on forever, it is what mortals have in place of immortality. A lover must desire immortality along with the good, if what we agreed earlier was right, that Love wants to possess the good forever. It follows from our argument that Love must desire immortality."

⌐ ⌐ ⌐

"But that's why I came to you, Diotima, as I just said. I knew I needed a teacher. So tell me what causes this, and everything else that belongs to the art of love."

"If you really believe that Love by its nature aims at what we have often agreed it does, then don't be surprised at the answer," she said. "For among animals the principle is the same as with us, and mortal nature seeks so far as possible to live forever and be immortal. And this is possible in one way only: by reproduction, because it always leaves behind a new young one in place of the old. Even while each living thing is said to be alive and to be the same—as a person is said to be the same from childhood till he turns into an old man—even then he never consists of the same things, though he is called the same, but he is always being renewed and in other respects passing away, in his hair and flesh and bones and blood and his entire body. And it's not just in his body, but in his soul too, for none of his manners, customs, opinions, desires, pleasures, pains, or fears ever remains the same, but some are coming to be in him while others are passing away. And what is still far stranger than that is that not only does one branch of knowledge come to be in us while another passes away and that we are never the same even in respect of our knowledge, but that each single piece of knowledge has the same fate. For what we call *studying* exists because knowledge is leaving us, because forgetting is the departure of knowledge while studying puts back a fresh memory in place of what went away, thereby preserving a piece of knowledge, so that it seems to be the same. And in that way everything mortal is preserved, not, like the divine, by always being the same in every way, but because what is departing and aging leaves behind something new, something such as it had been. By this device, Socrates," she said, "what is mortal shares in immortality, whether it is a body or anything else, while the immortal has another way. So don't be surprised if everything naturally values its own offspring, because it is for the sake of immortality that everything shows this zeal, which is Love."

Yet when I heard her speech I was amazed, and spoke: "Well," said I, "Most wise Diotima, is this really the way it is?"

And in the manner of a perfect sophist she said, "Be sure of it, Socrates. Look, if you will, at how human beings seek honor. You'd be amazed at their irrationality, if you didn't have in mind what I spoke about and if you hadn't pondered the awful state of love they're in, wanting to become famous and 'to lay up glory immortal forever,' and how they're ready to brave any danger for the sake of this, much more than they are for their children; and they are prepared to spend money, suffer through all sorts of ordeals, and even die for the sake of glory. Do you really think that Alcestis would have died for Admetus," she asked, "or that Achilles would have died after Patroclus, or that your Kodros would have died so as to preserve the throne for his sons, if they hadn't expected the memory of their virtue—which we still hold in honor—to be immortal? Far from it," she said. "I believe that anyone will do anything for the sake of immortal virtue and the glorious fame that follows; and the better the people, the more they will do, for they are all in love with immortality.

Now, some people are pregnant in body, and for this reason turn more to women and pursue love in that way, providing themselves through childbirth with immortality and remembrance and happiness, as they think, for all time to come; while others are pregnant in soul—because there surely *are* those who are even more pregnant in their souls than in their bodies, and these are pregnant with what is fitting for a soul to bear and bring to birth. And what is fitting? Wisdom and the rest of virtue, which all poets beget, as well as all the craftsmen who are said to be creative. But by far the greatest and most beautiful part of wisdom deals with the proper ordering of cities and households, and that is called moderation and justice. When someone has been pregnant with these in his soul from early youth, while he is still a virgin, and, having arrived at the proper age, desires to beget and give birth, he too will certainly go about seeking the beauty in which he would beget; for he will never beget in anything ugly. Since he is pregnant, then, he is much more drawn to bodies that are beautiful than to those that are ugly; and if he also has the luck to find a soul that is beautiful and noble and well-formed, he is even more drawn to this combination; such a man makes him instantly teem with ideas and arguments about virtue—the qualities a virtuous man should have and the customary activities in which he should engage; and so he tries to educate him. In my view, you see, when he makes contact with someone beautiful and keeps company with him, he conceives and gives birth to what he has been carrying inside him for ages. And whether they are together or apart, he remembers that beauty. And in common with him he nurtures the newborn; such people, therefore, have much more to share than do the parents of human children, and have a firmer bond of friendship, because the children in whom they have a share are more beautiful and more immortal. Everyone would rather have such children than human ones, and would look up to Homer, Hesiod, and the other good poets with envy and admiration for the offspring they have left behind—offspring, which, because they are immortal themselves, provide their parents with immortal glory and remembrance. For example," she said, "those are the sort of children Lycourgos left behind in Sparta as the saviors of Sparta and virtually all of Greece. Among you the honor goes to Solon for his creation of your laws. Other men in other places everywhere, Greek or barbarian, have brought a host of beautiful deeds into the light and begotten every kind of virtue. Already many shrines have sprung up to honor them for their immortal children, which hasn't happened yet to anyone for human offspring.

"Even you, Socrates, could probably come to be initiated into these rites of love. But as for the purpose of these rites when they are done correctly—that is the final and highest mystery, and I don't know if you are capable of it. I myself will tell you," she said, "and I won't stint any effort. And you must try to follow if you can.

"A lover who goes about this matter correctly must begin in his youth to devote himself to beautiful bodies. First, if the leader leads aright, he should love one body and beget beautiful ideas there; then he should realize that the beauty of any one body is brother to the beauty of any other and that if he is to pursue beauty of form he'd be very foolish not to think that the beauty of all bodies is one and the same. When he grasps this, he must become a lover of all beautiful bodies, and he must think that this wild gaping after just one body is a small thing and despise it.

"After this he must think that the beauty of people's souls is more valuable than the beauty of their bodies, so that if someone is decent in his soul, even though he is scarcely blooming in his body, our lover must be content to love and care for him and to seek to give birth to such ideas as will make young men better. The result is that our lover will be forced to gaze at the beauty of activities and laws and to see that all this is akin to itself, with the result the he will think that the beauty of bodies is a thing of no importance. After customs he must move on to various kinds of knowledge. The result is that he will see the beauty of knowledge and be looking mainly not at beauty in a single example— as a servant would who favored the beauty of a little boy or a man or a single custom (being a slave, of course, he's low and small-minded)—but the lover is turned to the great sea of beauty, and, gazing upon this, he gives birth to many gloriously beautiful ideas and theories, in unstinting love of wisdom, until, having grown and been strengthened there, he catches sight of such knowledge, and it is the knowledge of such beauty. . .

"Try to pay attention to me," she said, "as best you can. You see, the man who has been thus far educated in matters of Love, who has beheld beautiful things in the right order and correctly, is coming now to the goal of Loving: all of a sudden he will catch sight of something wonderfully beautiful in its nature; that, Socrates, is the reason for all his earlier labors:

"First, it always *is* and neither comes to be nor passes away, neither waxes nor wanes. Second, it is not beautiful this way and ugly that way, nor beautiful at one time and ugly at another, nor beautiful in relation to one thing and ugly in relation to another; nor is it beautiful here but ugly there, as it would be if it were beautiful for some people and ugly for others. Nor will the beautiful appear to him in the guise of a face or hands or anything else that belongs to the body. It will not appear to him as one idea or one kind of knowledge. It is not anywhere in another thing, as in an animal, or in earth, or in heaven, or in anything else, but itself by itself with itself, it is always one in form; and all the other beautiful things share in that, in such a way that when those others come to be or pass away, this does not become the least bit smaller or greater nor suffer any change. So when someone rises by these stages, through loving boys correctly, and begins to see this beauty, he has almost grasped his goal. This is what it is to go aright, or be lead by another, into the mystery of Love: one goes always upwards for the sake of this Beauty, starting out from beautiful things and using them like rising stairs: from one body to two and from two to all beautiful bodies, then from beautiful bodies to beautiful customs, and from customs to learning beautiful things, and from these lessons he arrives in the end at this lesson, which is learning of this very Beauty, so that in the end he comes to know just what it is to be beautiful.

"And there in life, Socrates, my friend," said the woman from Mantinea, "there if anywhere should a person live his life, beholding that Beauty. If you once see that, it won't occur to you to measure beauty by gold or clothing or beautiful boys and youths—who, if you see them now, strike you out of your senses, and make you, you and many others, eager to be with the boys you love and look at them forever, if there were any way to do that, forgetting food and drink, everything but looking at them and being with them. But how would it be, in our view," she said, "if someone got to see the Beautiful itself, absolute, pure, unmixed, not polluted by human flesh or colors or any other great nonsense of mortality, but if he could see the divine Beauty itself in its one form? Do you think it would be a poor life for a human being to look there and to behold it by that which he ought, and to be with it? Or haven't you remembered," she said, "that in that life alone, when he looks at Beauty in the only way that Beauty can be seen—only then will it become possible for him to give birth not to images of virtue (because he's in touch with no images), but to true virtue (because he is in touch with the true Beauty). The love of the gods belongs to anyone who has given birth to true virtue and nourished it, and if any human being could become immortal, it would be he."

Through the questioning method, Socrates establishes (first with Agathon, and then, in flashback, with Diotima) that love is neither beautiful nor ugly "in itself," but rather, between the two, running as a messenger between less beautiful lovers and their more beautiful beloveds. This, she implies, is the case with everything "spiritual," which finds itself between gods and human beings. Here, then, we see that love is a lack, and that we therefore love whatever we lack, whether it is another person, an inanimate object, or a god. Whatever it loves is beautiful, more beautiful than the lover, anyway. Diotima tells the young Socrates that love is born of resource and need, needing and loving beautiful things and cunningly plotting to get them. Thus, love is also a way that we seek immortality, plotting to satisfy our needs fully and eternally, like the gods.

Further, however, Diotima claims that love's true desire is not so much to possess beautiful things, but to express itself in beautiful things—"bring[ing] forth upon the beautiful"or "giv[ing] birth in beauty." This extends the image we saw in the *Theaetetus:* Diotima here claims that those who want to produce beautiful children will turn to women, and those who want to produce beautiful ideas will turn to men. Again, the production of children, and thus the love of women, takes second place here. However, the speech takes a male lover as its example, in accordance with the Greek custom. Perhaps we should interpret this to mean that if Diotima herself wanted to produce children, she would love a man, and if she wanted to produce ideas, she should love a woman.

According to Diotima, in this very famous passage, love itself develops in the soul, directing the lover towards higher and higher beloved objects. Each stage of love produces an idea that makes the beloved through which it was produced seem somehow incomplete. Thus for Diotima, as for Aristophanes, love is kind of search for wholeness—but not just for the completion that we feel in the presence of our human "other halves." The highest stage of love is the love of knowledge itself, the love of the forms, and this love becomes the passion for the philosophical life. Thus, we may assume, as in the *Republic,* that for Plato one's gender is ultimately irrelevant to the job of living a good life.

There is every reason to believe Socrates is making up this conversation off the top of his head. Diotima refers to Aristophanes' and Agathon's speeches; it seems unlikely that Socrates' parents would have arranged a female tutor for him—these and other hints point to Socrates' artistic license here. It is reasonable, then, to ask his rhetorical rationale for characterizing his teacher as a woman. Here is Socrates as a young man, having a purely intellectual conversation with a woman, where she—not Socrates—plays the "midwife" role and he "gives birth" to ideas through her. It appears obvious, despite what Socrates sometimes implies, that women are well capable of producing ideas and that they can produce them, even when matched up with a member of the opposite sex. This would of course be consistent with Socrates' claims in the *Republic* and would provide support for an argument for women's complete equality in the good city.

4. ARISTOTLE
(*Greek, 384–322 B.C.E.*)

Aristotle, who studied with Plato for twenty years, has wielded a mighty influence over Western intellectual history, perhaps even more all-encompassing than that of his teacher Plato, ending his career as tutor of Alexander the Great. Aristotle had exceptionally broad interests, producing greatly influential works in logic, physics, psychology, art criticism, politics, ethics, metaphysics, and—perhaps most useful in understanding Aristotle's style—biology. His father (Nicomachus, after whom Aristotle named one of his works in ethics) was the court physician at Macedonia, and Aristotle studied medicine early in his life. Although Aristotelian philosophy has little to do with modern medicine or biological science, some of the flavor of those pursuits comes across in even the most lofty of Aristotelian theories. The painter

Raphael, in his famous work, *The School of Athens,* represents Plato and Aristotle exiting a building together, with Plato pointing up and Aristotle pointing down. While this definitely oversimplifies the case, it captures Aristotle's predilection for concrete, methodical observation and analysis, in contrast to Plato's "otherworldly" theory of Forms. It would probably be useful to review some general Aristotelian theories before embarking on an investigation of his theory of gender.

THEORY OF ORGANIC WHOLES

For Aristotle, most objects of study could be understood on the model of a living organism. As any modern biologist could tell you, what distinguishes living organisms from inanimate things is a certain kind of organization, hence the shared root of the two words. Living things, according to Aristotle—and in this modern biologists would agree as well—are organized around their functions. A thing's *specific function,* according to Aristotle, is that which it is supposed to do, on account of the kind of thing it is. For instance, we could say that the specific function of a pen is to emit ink, or that the specific function of a cheetah is to run very fast. Whenever something seems designed for a particular purpose, according to Aristotle, the unique feature through which it achieves that purpose is its specific function. As Aristotle conceived it, everything exists for a purpose, and therefore everything has a specific function, including the universe, or existence, as a whole.

The organizational principle that enables organisms to pursue their functions is a part/whole relationship. Organisms are wholes, made up of parts, which can only be understood in relation to the whole of which they are parts. For instance, although we may study feet by themselves, it doesn't make sense, according to Aristotle, for a foot to *exist* by itself. If walking were not necessary to certain animals' specific functions, reasons Aristotle, there would be no feet in the universe at all. The parts of the universe as a whole, then, are also ordered in relation to each other as parts of a whole, and to understand each thing one must understand this order and that particular thing's role within it. For instance, if one wants to know about the human eye, the first thing one needs to know is that it exists in order for the human being to see, and in order to study human sight, the first thing one needs to know is that it exists in order for human beings to interact with the world while they go about their business. If one wanted to understand human interaction with the world while human beings go about their business, the first thing one needs to know is what the human business consists of—which inquiry involved Aristotle in psychology, ethics, and politics—and so on.

THE FOUR CAUSES

The hierarchical order of existence, for Aristotle, is a causal order. The purpose of each thing is a cause, or reason, why it has the function, and therefore the parts, that it has. For instance, in the example above, we can say that a pen emits ink *because* its purpose is to write. The cause of any particular thing is the answer to the question *Why* that thing is the way it is. As Aristotle understood it, there are four ways we can answer this question about any particular thing.

1. We can say that *x* is the way it is *because* it is composed of a particular material; for instance, we can say the pen is the way it is because it has a plastic sheath and a metal point wrapped around a flow of ink. This is called the pen's *material cause,* and it is, for Aristotle, the lowest cause, because it does not explain the pen very well at all—lots of things could be made up of plastic and metal and ink that are not pens, for instance, a telephone.

2. We can say that *x* is the way it is *because* it was made in a particular way, or by a particular thing or person; for instance, we can say the pen is the way it is because it was produced in the Bic Pen factory on an assembly line with lots of other pens. This is called the pen's *efficient cause,* and it is a slightly higher cause than the material cause, because it explains more about the pen—there are very few telephones coming off the assembly lines at pen factories. Aristotle's notion of efficient cause is probably the closest to our own most common use of the term "cause"—whatever brought about the thing in question as its effect.

3. We can say that *x* is the way it is *because* it is a specific kind of thing, i.e., it has the same shape and/or definition as other things of its kind; for instance, we can say that the pen is the way it is because it is a tube of ink, with a point that distributes the ink in a precise manner, that fits in a human hand. This is called the pen's *formal cause,* and it is a still higher cause, because it tells us quite a bit about the pen—it picks out everything that we would call a pen, and nothing that we wouldn't. The formal cause is something like what Plato would call the Form of the object—hence the similarity of the name—but for Aristotle, as we will discuss further, the formal cause cannot exist by itself, without the object of which it is the formal cause.

4. We can say that *x* is the way it is *because* it exists for a specific purpose; for instance, the pen is the way it is because its purpose is to write. This is called the pen's *final cause,* and it is the highest cause, according to Aristotle, because it thoroughly explains the pen. In other words, all the other causes of the pen are the way they are *because* pens are to write.

We have been using a pen—a man-made object—as our example of causation. For Aristotle, however— and this is probably where Aristotle will seem most controversial when we begin discussing gender—natural objects also have final causes, or purposes, which explain why they are the way they are. For instance, according to Aristotle—to use our other example—cheetahs have a purpose—to hunt successfully, say—in order to achieve which they have the shape and parents and flesh and bone that they have (their formal, efficient, and material causes, respectively). Thus, the whole natural world fits into a hierarchical ordering with respect to purposes, ordered in relation to the purpose of existence as a whole, which was Aristotle's notion of God.

SUBSTANCE

For Aristotle, each independent thing, i.e., each whole of interdependent parts, is called a *substance,* which he considered the primary "unit" of existence. Each substance in the material world he thought to be a union of form and matter (or formal cause and material cause). For him, there is no "other world," as there was for Plato, no abstract realm of purely intelligible existences. Rather, the "forms," insofar as they existed, were merely the forms *of* substances in this world. We can *think* about forms separately from the substances they inform, thought Aristotle, but the fact that we can do so shouldn't mislead us into thinking that these forms can *exist* separately from substances. Thus, Aristotle lays the groundwork for an empirical science of nature by claiming against Plato that we can know about something *real* when we study the material world. This will of course be relevant to Aristotle's distinction from Plato on the question of gender. Male and female are, for Aristotle, not simply the way certain things appear, but really the way they are.

ETHICS

Human beings, too, for Aristotle, have a natural final cause, as well (called our "end" or in Greek, *telos*). According to Aristotle, human beings exist in order to achieve a specific kind of happiness, or fulfillment, called in Greek *eudaimonia*. Happiness, our telos, is for Aristotle an objective state of human good in which there is lifelong intellectual, political, and emotional involvement and fulfillment; it has little to do with the passing feeling of pleasure that we call happiness today. A happy person, for Aristotle, had to have a certain role in his or her community and a certain standard of living; being a good citizen, for instance, was considered by Aristotle to be a crucial part of human happiness. Aristotle's stringent objective requirements for happiness and the various prerequisites they call for will, as we will see, differ for men and women; for instance, women could not be citizens in ancient Greek city-states, and thus,whatever happiness they could achieve would lack something vital from which men's happiness could benefit.

Our human specific function, through which we achieve happiness, according to Aristotle, is our rationality. Reason, he claimed, is a specific part of the human soul, not shared by other animals. Because we are rational creatures, Aristotle claimed, we are able to practice a set of particular human virtues, in which our appetites and emotions are guided or moderated by reason. Aristotle claimed that our happiness requires the practice of certain intellectual virtues as well—such as science, art, statesmanship and philosophy—which sharpen or enlarge our reason. As Aristotle understood virtue, it consisted of maintaining—almost habitually—a reasonable mean between extreme expressions of certain important appetites and emotions. For instance, he considered it virtuous to be disinclined towards both overeating and starving oneself, and he called this disposition the virtue of temperance.

One important psychological gender difference for Aristotle, as we will see, relates to men's and women's abilities to act virtuously. He did not believe that women could achieve the kind of virtue necessary to be really happy. It may be useful to discuss quickly the Aristotelian moral virtues, the possession of all of which he believed is necessary for happiness. *Courage* and *temperance* were for Aristotle, as for Plato, very important virtues. Aristotle claimed that courage was rational fear, and that the courageous individual avoided the extremes of fear, cowardliness (in which we fear too easily) and rashness (in which we don't fear easily enough). Temperance is a rational appetite for physical pleasures, like eating and sex. The temperate individual is able to avoid the extremes of self-indulgence (in which we indulge our appetites too easily) and what Aristotle called "insensibility" (we would probably call it something like "self-denial"). Interestingly, Aristotle adds to Plato's catalogue a number of more social, economic virtues, such as *liberality* and *magnificence, good temper* and *wit.* Liberality is rational giving of wealth or property— being charitable—and it avoids the extremes of prodigality and "meanness" (i.e., being penny-pinching and alienating others). Magnificence is something like liberality, only on a grander scale. According to Aristotle, is it a sort of rational showmanship, like being a good host. Good temper is rationally directed anger; for instance, thought Aristotle, it is important to be indignant when someone does something unfair, but not to get angry over silly unimportant things. The witty individual avoids the extremes of buffoonery and boorishness, of making a fool of oneself or having no sense of humor. *Justice* is a sort of cardinal virtue for Aristotle, the virtue that underlies the possibility of being virtuous in any other way. Justice is to be reasonable in one's overall treatment of other people, and the extremes it avoids are the many kinds of injustice. We might—rather superficially—group these injustices into being overly kind and being overly strict.

Aristotle's moral virtues offer a nice overview of the values of Greek society as we have read about them in earlier selections. Indeed, Aristotle is very much the methodical scientist even in his ethical theory—observing, analyzing, and summarizing the morality of his society. Not surprisingly, Aristotle believed that the moral virtues were to be understood as parts of a whole—the whole of a happy, good life as he understood it. Thus, like Plato, Aristotle believed in the "unity of the virtues"; in other words, practicing any one of the moral virtues depended on and enabled the practice of all the others.

VIRTUE AND GENDER

Aristotle is a far more controversial figure than Plato in feminist debate. As we will see, Aristotle clearly states in several places that females are less able to achieve virtue, and therefore happiness, than are males. He favors very strict domestic roles for women in the city and claims that women are constitutionally inferior to men. While Aristotle claims—somewhat in distinction from the Greek customs of the time—that wives should have recourse against bad husbands and that marriage is the first instinct and obligation of men, he believes that wives are and should be ruled by their husbands. It is believed, however, that Aristotle's theory of virtue is in some ways akin to a feminine view of how people ought to behave towards each other; for instance, you may find Aristotle's view similar to the feminine "ethics of responsibility" described by Carol Gilligan in Part Six. Still, these claims must be argued around or against Aristotle's own clear derogation of women. This, and the fact that Aristotle seems to typify the Greek worldview, also makes him an apt choice for our study of gender in ancient Greece.

THE GENERATION OF ANIMALS

Just as its title implies, *The Generation of Animals* is a biological study of reproduction. In it, Aristotle considers the significance of sexual reproduction and the precise contribution of each sex to the new life. In other words, this is Aristotle's answer to Orestes' and Apollo's question in the *Eumenides:* "Who is the true parent, the father or the mother?"

Some animals discharge semen plainly, for instance those which are by nature blooded animals; but it is not clear in which way Insects and Cephalopods do so. Here then is a point we must consider: Do all male animals discharge semen, or not all of them? and if not all, why is it that some do and some do not? and further, Do females contribute any semen, or not? and if they contribute no semen, is there no other substance at all which they contribute, or is there something else which is not semen? And there is a further question which we must consider: What is it which those animals that discharge semen contribute towards generation by means of it? and generally, what is the nature of semen, and (in the case of those animals which discharge this fluid) what is the nature of the menstrual discharge?

It is generally held that all things are formed and come to be out of semen, and semen comes from the parents. And so one and the same inquiry will include the two questions: (1) Do both the male and the female discharge semen, or only one of them? and (2) Is the semen drawn from the whole of the parent's body or not?—since it is reasonable to hold that if it is not drawn from the whole of the body it is not drawn from both the parents either. There are some who assert that the semen is drawn from the whole of the body, and so we must consider the facts about this first of all. There are really four lines of argument which may be used to prove that the semen is drawn from each of the parts of the body. The first is, the intensity of the pleasure involved; it is argued that any emotion, when its scope is widened, is more pleasant than the same emotion when its scope is less wide; and obviously an emotion which affects all the parts of the body has a wider scope than one which affects a single part of a few parts only. The second argument is that mutilated parents produce mutilated offspring, and it is alleged that because the parent is deficient in some one part no semen comes from that part, and that the part from which no semen comes does not get formed in the offspring. The third argument is the resemblances shown by the young to their parents: the offspring which are produced are like their parents not only in respect of their body as a whole, but part for part too; hence, if the reason for the resemblance of the whole is that the semen is drawn from the whole, then the reason for the resemblance of the parts is surely that something is drawn from each of the parts. Fourthly, it would seem reasonable to hold that just as there is some original thing out of which the whole creature is formed, so also it is with each of the parts; and hence if there is a semen which gives rise to the whole, there must be a special semen which gives rise to each of the parts. And these opinions derive plausibility from such evidence as the following: Children are born which resemble their parents in respect not only of congenital characteristics but also of acquired ones; for instance, there have been cases of children which have had the outline of a scar in the same places where their parents had scars, and there was a case at Chalcedon of a man who was branded on his arm, and the same letter, though somewhat confused and indistinct, appeared marked on his child. These are the main pieces of evidence which give some people ground for believing that the semen is drawn from the whole of the body.

Upon examination of the subject, however, the opposite seems more likely to be true; indeed, it is not difficult to refute these arguments, and besides that, they involve making further assertions which are impossible. First of all, then, resemblance is no proof that the semen is drawn from the whole of the body, because children resemble their parents in voice, nails, and hair and even in the way they move; but nothing whatever is drawn from these things; and there are some characteristics which a parent does not yet possess at the time when the child is generated, such as grey hair or beard. Further, children resemble their remoter ancestors, from whom nothing has been drawn for the semen. Resemblances of this sort recur after many generations.

The foregoing discussion will have made it clear that the female, though it does not contribute any semen to generation, yet contributes something, viz., the substance constituting the menstrual fluid (or the corresponding substance in bloodless animals). But the same is apparent if we consider the matter generally, from the theoretical standpoint. Thus: there must be that which generates, and that out of which it generates; and even if these two be united in one, at any rate they must differ in kind, and in that the *logos* of each of them is distinct. In those animals in which these two faculties are separate, the body—that is to say the physical nature—of the active partner and of the passive must the different. Thus, if the male is the active partner, the one which originates the movement, and the female *qua* female is the passive one, surely what the female contributes to the semen of the male will be not semen but material. And this is in fact what we find happening; for the natural substance of the menstrual fluid is to be classed as "prime matter."

These then are the lines upon which that subject should be treated. And what we have said indicates plainly at the same time how we are to answer the questions which we next have to consider, viz., how it is that the male makes its contribution to generation, and how the semen produced by the male is the cause of the offspring; that is to say, Is the semen inside the offspring to start with, from the outset a part of the body which is formed, and mingling with the material provided by the female; or does the physical part of the semen have no share nor lot in the business, only the *dynamis* and movement contained in it? This, anyway, is the active and efficient ingredient; whereas the ingredient which gets set and given shape is the remnant of the residue in the female animal. The second suggestion is clearly the right one, as is shown both by reasoning and by observed fact. (*a*) If we consider the matter on general grounds, we see that when some one thing is formed from the conjunction of an active partner with a passive one, the active partner is not situated within the thing which is being formed; and we may generalize this still further by substituting "moving" and "moved" for "active" and "passive." Now of course the female, *qua* female, is passive, and the male, *qua* male, is active—it is that whence the principle of movement comes. Taking, then, the widest formulation of each of these two opposites, viz., regarding the male *qua* active and causing movement, and the female *qua* passive and being set in movement, we see that the one thing which is formed is formed *from them* only in the sense in which a bedstead is formed from the carpenter and the wood, or a ball from the wax and the form. It is plain, then, that there is no necessity for any substance to pass from the male; and if any does pass, this does not mean that the offspring is formed from it as from something situated within itself during the process, but as from that which has imparted movement to it, or that which is its "form." The relationship is the same as that of the patient who has been healed to the medical art. (*b*) This piece of reasoning is entirely borne out by the facts. It explains why certain of those males which copulate with the females are observed to introduce no part at all into the female, but on the contrary the female introduces a part into the male. This occurs in certain insects. In those cases where the male introduces some part, it is the semen which produces the effect inside the female; but in the case of these insects, the same effect is produced by the heat and *dynamis* inside the (male) animal itself when the female inserts the part which receives the residue. And that is why animals of this sort take a long time over copulation, and once they have separated the young are soon produced.

on the other hand, the formation of the young does in fact take place in the female, whereas neither the male himself nor the female emits semen into the male, but they both deposit together what they have to contribute in the female—it is because that is where the material is out of which the creature that is being fashioned is made. And as regards this material, a good quantity of it must of necessity be available immediately, out of which the fetation is "set" and constituted in the first place, and after that fresh supplies of it must be continually arriving to make its growth possible. Hence, of necessity, it is in the female that parturition takes place. After all, the carpenter is close by his timber, and the potter close by his clay; and to put it in general terms, the working or treatment of any material, and the ultimate movement which acts upon it, is in all cases close by the material, *e.g.,* the location of the activity of house-building is in the houses which are being built. These instances may help us to understand how the male makes its contribution to generation; for not every male emits semen, and in the case of those which do, this semen is not a part of the fetation as it develops. In the same way, nothing passes from the carpenter into the pieces of timber, which are *his* material, and there is no part of the art of carpentry present in the object which is being fashioned: it is the shape and the form which pass from the carpenter, and they come into being by means of the movement in the material. It is his soul, wherein is the "form," and his knowledge, which cause his hands (or some other part of his body) to move in a particular way (different ways for different products, and always the same way for any one product); his hands move his tools and his tools move the material. In a similar way to this, Nature acting in the male of semen-emitting animals uses the semen as a tool, as something that has movement in actuality; just as when objects are being produced by any art the tools are in movement, because the movement which belongs to the art is, in a way, situated in them. Males, then, that emit semen contribute to generation in the manner described. Those which emit no semen, males into which the female inserts one of its parts, may be compared to a craftsman who has his material brought to him. Males of this sort are so weak that Nature is unable to accomplish anything at all through intermediaries: indeed, their movements are only just strong enough when Nature herself sits watching over the business; the result is that here Nature resembles a modeller in clay rather than a carpenter; she does not rely upon contact exerted at second hand when fashioning the object which is being given shape, but uses the parts of her own very self to handle it.

In all animals which can move about, male and female are separate; one animal is male and another female, though they are identical in species, just as men and women are both human beings, and stallion and mare are both horses. In plants, however, these faculties are mingled together; the female is not separate from the male; and that is why they generate out of themselves, and produce not semen but a fetation—what we call their "seeds." Empedocles puts this well in his poem, when he says:

So the great trees lay eggs; the olives first. . . ,

because just as the egg is a fetation from part of which the creature is formed while the remainder is nourishment, so from part of the seed is formed the growing plant, while the remainder is nourishment for the shoot and the first root. And in a sort of way the same happens even in those animals where male and female are separate; for when they have need to generate they cease to be separate and are united as they are in plants: their nature desires that they should become one. And this is plain to see when they are uniting and copulating [that one animal is produced out of the two of them].

The natural practice of those animals which emit no semen is to remain united for a long time, until (the male) has "set" the fetation: those Insects which copulate are an example of this. Other animals, however, remain united until the male has introduced from those "parts" of himself which he inserts one which will "set" the fetation but will take a longer time to do so: the blooded animals illustrate this. The former sort remain in copulation for a fair part of a day; whereas semen takes several days to "set" fetations, and when the creatures have emitted this they free themselves. Indeed, animals seem to be just like divided plants: as though you were to pull a plant to pieces when it was bearing its seed and separate it into the male and female present in it.

In all her workmanship herein Nature acts in every particular as reason would expect.

Aristotle agrees with Apollo: the male is the true parent. This is because the male, according to Aristotle, provides the *form* to the child, which is what gives the child its family resemblance, or identity. The female provides only material and a place for the fetus to develop. Aristotle claims that this is because masculinity is an active principle and femininity a passive one—probably the first important statement of this common belief in Western philosophy to appear.

It is notable that Aristotle has some difficulty in making his case. He seems to be so committed to the systematic applicability of his theory of causation that he does not consider very carefully any evidence that seems to oppose it, at least in this work. For if the form of the child comes from both parents, the hierarchical ordering of causation on which Aristotle insists—that one substance can have only one formal cause—would be challenged. Aristotle's presuppositions may be influenced primarily by his desire for a systematic theory, or he may have had a genuine and blinding prejudice against the female of the species.

THE HISTORY OF ANIMALS

The question of Aristotle's scientific prejudices may be more easily answered by an investigation of a perplexing passage from his *History of Animals*. This work, also essentially a work in biological science, is more akin to what we would today call the study of "evolution." Here, Aristotle is interested in the developments that distinguish higher species of animals from lower ones, including the development of sex differences.

> In all kinds in which there are the female and the male, nature has established much the same difference in the character of the females as compared with that of the males. But it is most evident in the case of humans and of the animals that have some size and of the viviparous quadrupeds. For the character of the females is softer, and quicker to be tamed, and more receptive of handling, and readier to learn, for example the female Laconian hounds are in fact cleverer than the males. The kind of hounds in Molossia is no different from those elsewhere in respect of hunting, but in shepherding it is superior by reason of size and of courage in facing wild animals. And those cross-bred from both, that is from the hounds produced in Molossia and from the Laconians, are superior in courage and love of work.
>
> All females are less spirited than the males, except the bear and leopard: in these the female is held to be braver. But in the other kinds the females are softer, more vicious, less simple, more impetuous, more attentive to the feeding of the young, while the males on the contrary are more spirited, wilder, simpler, less cunning. There are traces of these characters in virtually all animals, but they are all the more evident in those that are more possessed of character and especially in man. For man's nature is the most complete, so that these dispositions too are more evident in humans. Hence a wife is more compassionate than a husband and more given to tears, but also more jealous and complaining and more apt to scold and fight. The female is also more

dispirited and despondent than the male, more shameless and lying, is readier to deceive and has a longer memory; furthermore she is more wakeful, more afraid of action, and in general is less inclined to move than the male, and takes less nourishment. The male on the other hand, as we have said, is a readier ally and is braver than the female, since even among the cephalopods when the cuttlefish has been struck by the trident the male comes to the female's help, whereas the female runs away when the male has been struck.

The passage does indeed claim that Aristotle believes women less capable of achieving virtue than men. However, the aim of the passage is not so much to define the characteristics of females as to order the species, the claim being that sexual difference is more pronounced in higher animals than in lower ones. Thus, he is making not so much a moral claim as an "anthropological" one. Aristotle is here contributing to the *nomos/physis* debate by offering a complex theory of how cultural elaboration adds to natural sexual differences.

Note that Aristotle gives much more information about the females than about the males of the species. We may take it that this is because he assumes, as he seems to in the passage from the *Generation of Animals,* above, that the male standard is obvious and that delineating sex differences therefore involves mostly specifying how females differ from the norm. It is noteworthy, however, that the characteristics, male and female, are expressed in *comparatives;* i.e., "the female is *more* x than the male," and "the male *more* y than the female." This would imply that neither male nor female expresses the norm or the mean by itself. This foreshadows somewhat the complicated picture of gender roles that Aristotle will provide in the *Politics,* excerpted next. Aristotle's point overall is that as species become more intelligent and socially complex, the differences between their sexes become more elaborate and complicated, and that therefore the self-knowledge required for the achievement of virtue becomes both more difficult and more necessary to obtain for members of the higher species, both male and female. Each has its specific role in the human specific function—integrally tied to the city—and each therefore has a particular set of virtues proper to good functioning in its respective role.

THE *POLITICS*

For Aristotle, again unsurprisingly, given what we know of ancient Greek values, the happiness of an individual was only a part of the happiness of a community. Further, happiness was thought by him to be such an integral part of the happy society that he did not believe a person could be happy unless he or she lived in a good city. Thus, for Aristotle, the "final cause" of ethics is politics. This interdependence of citizens and city-states is based in the government's obligation to lead citizens towards virtue. The best possible government, Aristotle claimed, was actually responsible for its citizens' behavior, and so took education and inspiring leadership to be its first obligation.

As might be expected, Aristotle's vision of the social relationships of which human life is composed is described throughout the *Politics* along the lines of the theory of organic wholes. Each person and each relationship in which he or she engages is a part of the state, which therefore defines them as its parts. In Books I–III of the *Politics,* Aristotle describes the basic relationships that occur in the state. The first and most intimate such relation, according to Aristotle, and again unsurprisingly, is the relation between husband and wife in the household.

BOOK I, CHAPTER 2

In this, as in other fields, we shall be able to study our subject best if we begin at the beginning and consider things in the process of their growth. First of all, there must necessarily be a union or pairing of those who cannot exist without one another. Male and female must unite for the reproduction of the species—not from deliberate intention, but from the natural impulse, which exists in animals generally as it also exists in plants, to leave behind them something of the same nature as themselves. Next, there must necessarily be a union of the naturally ruling element with the element which is naturally ruled, for the preservation of both. The element which is able, by virtue of its intelligence, to exercise forethought, is naturally a ruling and master element; the element which is able, by virtue of its bodily power, to do the physical work, is a ruled element, which is naturally in a state of slavery; and master and slave have accordingly a common interest.

The female and the slave are naturally distinguished from one another. Nature makes nothing in a miserly spirit, as smiths do when they make the Delphic knife to serve a number of purposes: she makes each separate thing for a separate end; and she does so because the instrument is most perfectly made when it serves a single purpose and not a variety of purposes. Among barbarians, however, the female and the slave occupy the same position—the reason being that no naturally ruling element exists among them, and conjugal union thus comes to be a union of a female who is a slave with a male who is also a slave. This is why our poets have said,

> *Meet it is that barbarous peoples should be governed by the Greeks*

the assumption being that barbarian and slave are by nature one and the same.

The first result of these two elementary associations is the household or family. Hesiod spoke truly in the verse,

> *First house, and wife, and ox to draw the plough*

for oxen serve the poor in lieu of household slaves. The first form of association naturally instituted for the satisfaction of daily recurrent needs is thus the family; and the members of the family are accordingly termed by Charondas 'associates of the breadchest', as they are also termed by Epimenides the Cretan 'associates of the manager'.

The next form of association—which is also the first to be formed from more households than one, and for the satisfaction of something more than daily recurrent needs—is the village. The most natural form of the village appears to be that of a colony [or offshoot] from a family; and some have thus called the members of the village by the name of 'sucklings of the same milk', or, again, of 'sons and the sons of sons'. This, it may be noted, is the reason why cities were originally ruled, as the peoples of the barbarian world still are, by kings. They were formed of people who were already monarchically governed, for every household is monarchically governed by the eldest of the kin, just as villages, when they are offshoots from the household, are similarly governed in virtue of the kinship between their members. This is what Homer describes:

> *Each of them ruleth*
> *Over his children and wives,*

a passage which shows that they lived in scattered groups, as indeed men generally did in ancient times. The fact that men generally were governed by kings in ancient times, and that some still continue to be governed in that way, is the reason that leads everyone to say that the gods are also governed by a king. People make the lives of the gods in the likeness of their own—as they also make their shapes.

When we come to the final and perfect association, formed from a number of villages, we have already reached the city [or *polis*]. This may be said to have reached the height of full self-sufficiency; or rather we may say that while it comes into existence for the sake of mere life, it exists for the sake of a good life. For this reason every city exists by nature, just as did the earlier associations [from which it grew]. It is the end or consummation to which those associations move, and the 'nature' of things consists in their end or consummation; for what each thing is when its growth is completed we call the nature of that thing, whether it be a man or a horse or a family. Again the end, or final cause, is the best and self-sufficiency is both the end, and the best.

From these considerations it is evident that the city belongs to the class of things that exist by nature, and that man is by nature a political animal. He who is without a city, by reason of his own nature and not of some accident, is either a poor sort of being, or a being higher than man.

© © ©

We may now proceed to add that the city is prior in the order of nature to the family and the individual. The reason for this is that the whole is necessarily prior to the part. If the whole body is destroyed, there will not be a foot or a hand, except in that ambiguous sense in which one uses the same word to indicate a different thing, as when one speaks of a 'hand' made of stone; for a hand, when destroyed [by the destruction of the whole body], will be no better than a stone 'hand'. All things derive their essential character from their function and their capacity; and it follows that if they are no longer fit to discharge their function, we ought not to say that they are still the same things, but only that, by an ambiguity, they still have the same names.

We thus see that the city exists by nature and that it is prior to the individual. For if the individual is not self-sufficient when he is isolated he will stand in the same relation to the whole as other parts do to their wholes. The man who is isolated, who is unable to share in the benefits of political association, or has no need to share because he is already self-sufficient, is no part of the city, and must therefore be either a beast or a god. There is therefore a natural impulse in all men towards an association of this sort. But the man who first constructed such an association was none the less the greatest of benefactors. Man, when perfected, is the best of animals; but if he be isolated from law and justice he is the worst of all.

⌐ ⌐ ⌐

CHAPTER 3

Having ascertained, from the previous analysis, what are the elements of which the city is constituted, we must first consider the management of the household; for every city is composed of households. The parts of household management will correspond to the parts of which the household itself is constituted. A complete household consists of slaves and freemen. But every subject of inquiry should first be examined in its simplest elements; and the primary and simplest elements of the household are the connection of master and slave, that of the husband and wife, and that of parents and children. We must accordingly consider each of these connections, examining the nature of each and the qualities it ought to possess. The factors to be examined are therefore three: first, the relationship of master and slave; next, what may be called the marital relationship (for there is no word in our language which exactly describes the union of husband and wife); and lastly, what may be called the parental relationship, which again has no single word in our language peculiar to itself. But besides the three factors which thus present themselves for examination there is also a fourth, which some regard as identical with the whole of household management, and others as its principal part. This is the element called 'the art of acquisition', and we shall have to consider its nature.

⌐ ⌐ ⌐

CHAPTER 12

We said, in a previous passage, that there were three parts of the art of household management—the first, of which we have already spoken, being the art of controlling slaves: the second, the art of exercising paternal authority; and the third, that of exercising marital authority. While the head of the household rules over both wife and children, and rules over both as free members of the household, he exercises a different sort of rule in each case. His rule over his wife is like that of a statesman over fellow citizens; his rule over his children is like that of a monarch over subjects. The male is naturally fitter to command than the female, except where there is some departure from nature; and age and maturity are similarly fitter to command than youth and immaturity. In most cases where rule of the statesman's sort is exercised there is an interchange of ruling and being ruled: the members of a political association aim by their very nature at being equal and differing in nothing. It is none the less true that when one rules and the other is ruled, [the former] desires to establish a difference, in outward forms, in modes of address, and in titles of respect. This may remind us of the saying of Amasis about his foot-pan. The relation of the male to the female is permanently that in which the statesman stands to his fellow citizens. Paternal rule over children, on the other hand, is like that of a king over his subjects. The male parent is in a position of authority both in virtue of the affection to which he is entitled and by right of his seniority; and his position is thus in the nature of royal authority. Homer was right, therefore, to use the invocation

Father of Gods and of men

to address Zeus, who is king of them all. A king ought to be naturally superior to his subjects, and yet of the same stock as they are; and this is the case with the relation of age to youth, and of parent to child.

‿ ‿ ‿

CHAPTER 13

. . . What is true of the soul is evidently also true of the other cases; and we may thus conclude that it is natural in most cases for there to be both a ruling element and one that is ruled. The rule of the freeman over the slave is one kind of rule; that of the male over the female another; that of the grown man over the child another still. It is true that all these people possess in common the different parts of the soul; but they possess them in different ways. The slave is entirely without the faculty of deliberation; the female indeed possesses it, but in a form which lacks authority; and children also possess it, but only in an immature form. We must assume that the same holds with regard to moral goodness: they must all share in it, but not in the same way—each sharing only to the extent required for the discharge of his or her function. The ruler, accordingly, must possess moral goodness in its full and perfect form, because his function is essentially that of a master-craftsman, and reason is such a master-craftsman; but other people need only to possess moral goodness to the extent required of them. It is thus clear that while moral goodness is a quality of all those mentioned, the fact still remains that temperance—and similarly courage and justice—are not, as Socrates held, the same in a woman as they are in a man. One kind of courage is concerned with ruling, the other with serving; and the same is true of the other forms of goodness.

This conclusion also emerges clearly when we examine the subject in more detail. To speak in general terms, and to maintain that goodness consists in 'a good condition of the soul', or in 'right action', or in anything of the kind, is to be guilty of self-deception. Far better than such general definitions is the method

of simple enumeration of the different forms of goodness, as followed by
Gorgias. We must therefore hold that what the poet said of women

A modest silence is a woman's crown

contains a general truth—but a truth which does not apply to men.

◌   ◌   ◌

BOOK II, CHAPTER 2

A system in which women are common to all involves, among many others, the
following difficulties. The *object* for which Socrates states that it ought to be
instituted is evidently not established by the arguments which he uses.
Moreover, the end which he states as necessary for the city [*polis*] is
impracticable; and yet he gives no account of the lines on which it ought to be
interpreted. I have in mind here the idea, which Socrates takes as his premiss,
that the greatest possible unity of the whole city is the supreme good. Yet it is
obvious that a city which goes on becoming more and more of a unit, will
eventually cease to be a city at all. A city, by its nature, is some sort of plurality.
If it becomes more of a unit, it will first become a household instead of a city,
and them an individual instead of a household; for we should all call the
household more of a unit than the city, and the individual more of a unit than the
household. It follows that, even if we could, we ought not to achieve this object:
it would be the destruction of the city.

Not only is the city composed of a *number* of people: it is also composed of
different *kinds* of people, for a city cannot be composed of those who are like
one another.

◌   ◌   ◌

CHAPTER 3

Even if it were the supreme good of a political association that it should have the
greatest possible unity, this unity does not appear to follow from the formula of
'All men saying "Mine" and "Not mine" at the same time', which, in the view of
'Socrates', is the index of the perfect unity of a city. The word 'all' has a double
sense: if it means 'each separately', the object which 'Socrates' desires to realize
may perhaps be realized in a greater degree: each and all separately will then say
'My wife' (or 'My son') of one and the same person; and each and all separately
will speak in the same way of property, and of every other concern. But it is not
in the sense of 'each separately' that all who have children and women in
common will actually speak of them. They will all call them 'Mine'; but they
will do so collectively, and not individually. The same is true of property also;
[all will call it 'Mine'] but they will do so in the sense of 'all collectively', and
not in the sense of 'each separately'. It is therefore clear that there is a certain
fallacy in the use of the term 'all'. 'All' and 'both' and 'odd' and 'even' are

liable by their ambiguity to produce captious arguments even in reasoned discussions. We may therefore conclude that the formula of 'all men saying "Mine" of the same object' is in one sense something fine but impracticable, and in another sense does nothing to promote.

⌐ ⌐ ⌐

Even on Plato's system it is impossible to avoid the chance that some of the citizens might guess who are their brothers, or children, or fathers, or mothers. The resemblances between children and parents must inevitably lead to their drawing conclusions about one another. That this actually happens in real life is stated as fact by some of the writers on descriptive geography. They tell us that some of the inhabitants of upper Libya have their women in common; but the children born of such unions can still be distinguished by their resemblance to their fathers. Indeed there are some women, and some females in the animal world (mares, for instance, and cows), that show a strong natural tendency to produce offspring resembling the male parent.

⌐ ⌐ ⌐

CHAPTER 4

There are also other difficulties which those who construct such a community will not find it easy to avoid. We may take as examples cases of assault, homicide, whether unintentional or intentional, fighting, and slander. All these offences, when they are committed against father or mother or a near relative, differ from offences against people who are not so related, in being breaches of natural piety. Such offences must happen more frequently when men are ignorant of their relatives than when they know who they are; and when they do happen, the customary penance can be made if people know their relatives, but none can be made if they are ignorant of them. It is also surprising that, after having made sons common to all, he should simply forbid lovers from engaging in carnal intercourse. Nor does he forbid other familiarities which, if practised between son and father, or brother and brother, are the very height of indecency, all the more as this form of love [even if it is not expressed] is in itself indecent. It is surprising, too, that he should debar male lovers from carnal intercourse on the one ground of the excessive violence of the pleasure, and that he should think it a matter of indifference that the lovers may be father and son, or again that they may be brothers.

Community of women and children would seem to be more useful if it were practised among the farmers rather than among the guardians. The spirit of friendship is likely to exist to a lesser degree where women and children are common; and the governed class ought to have little of that spirit if it is to obey and not to attempt revolution. Generally, such a system must produce results directly opposed to those which a system of properly constituted laws should produce, and equally opposed to the very object for which, in the view of 'Socrates', this community of women and children ought to be instituted.

Friendship, we believe, is the chief good of cities, because it is the best safeguard against the danger of factional disputes. 'Socrates' himself particularly commends the ideal of the unity of the city; and that unity is commonly held, and expressly stated by him, to be the result of friendship. We may cite the argument of the discourses on love, where 'Aristophanes', as we know, speaks of lovers desiring out of friendship to grow together into a unity, and to be one instead of two. Now in that case it would be inevitable that both or at least one of them should cease to exist. But in the case of the political association there would be merely a watery sort of friendship: a father would be very little disposed to say 'Mine' of a son, and a son would be as little disposed to say 'Mine' of a father. Just as a little sweet wine, mixed so family feeling is diluted and tasteless when family names have as little meaning as they have in a constitution of this sort, and when there is so little reason for a father treating his sons as sons, or a son treating his father as a father, or brothers one another as brothers. There are two things which particularly move people to care for and love an object. One of these is that the object should belong to yourself: the other is that you should like it. Neither of these motives can exist among those who live under a constitution such as this.

The household, for Aristotle, is defined in terms of the city-state, which is its final cause, meaning that marriage laws and laws about the ownership of property are given in the constitution of the city-state and provide to men and women within the state the significance of their roles as husbands and wives. This is not say that the city occurs first historically—quite the contrary; for Aristotle, the more intimate relations of husband and wife, parent and child, master and slave, are more natural to us and certainly existed before there were ever cities. Nonetheless, claims Aristotle, in choosing a husband or wife, an individual presupposes certain political ideals, such as the kind of authority that husbands and/or wives should exert over each other.

According to Aristotle, the proper authority relation in marriage is constitutional rule of husbands over their wives. This differs from the royal rule that fathers should enjoy over children. A monarch, Aristotle claims, rules by virtue of his superior position over the ruled; i.e., there is a sort of natural absolute rule of parents over their children. The rule of the husband in marriage requires the consent of the wife. That one of them must rule consistently, according to Aristotle, is necessary for the smooth functioning of the household, and men are usually, he claims, better suited to rule than women. This is because of men's and women's differing natural tendencies towards virtue, implied by Aristotle in the foregoing passage from the *History of Animals*. Aristotle contrasts men's and women's courage as an example of these differences: a man's courage, he claims, is shown in command, a woman's in obedience. Clearly he is stating that both men and women can be courageous. However, the "rational fear" that constitutes courage is different for women and men, because their roles provide them with different things to fear.

Also of interest is Aristotle's criticism of the Socratic arguments for the community of women, presented above in the passages from the *Republic*. The relation of a husband to his wife, he implies, is meaningless; it loses all its distinct quality as a marital relationship if it does not differ from his relations to other women not his wife, i.e., if all women were equal to each other and to him under the law. To attain equality and justice by Socrates' means, claims Aristotle, would cost us the intimacy of the household, which he considers a necessary part of the good city-state. Woman's role as subject of her husband within the household is, according to Aristotle, a requirement of the political good.

THE FRIENDSHIP OF MEN AND WOMEN

The eighth and ninth books of Aristotle's *Nicomachean Ethics* are devoted to a discussion of friendship, which Aristotle thinks is crucial to human happiness, stating that "no one would choose to live without friends." One important friendship, as we might infer from the passages of the *Politics,* is the friendship of husband and wife.

THE NICOMACHAEN ETHICS

BOOK VIII

Now there are three forms of constitution, and also an equal number of perversions or corruptions of those forms. The constitutions are Kingship, Aristocracy, and thirdly, a constitution based on a property classification, which it seems appropriate to describe as timocratic, although most people are accustomed to speak of it merely as a constitutional government or Republic. The best of these constitutions is Kingship, and the worst Timocracy. The perversion of Kingship is Tyranny. Both are monarchies, but there is a very wide difference between them: a tyrant studies his own advantage, a king that of his subjects. For a monarch is not a king if he does not possess independent resources, and is not better supplied with goods of every kind than his subjects; but a ruler so situated lacks nothing, and therefore will not study his own interests but those of his subjects. (A king who is not independent of his subjects will be merely a sort of titular king.) Tyranny is the exact opposite in this respect, for the tyrant pursues his own good. The inferiority of Tyranny among the perversions is more evident than that of Timocracy among the constitutions, for the opposite of the best must be the worst.

When a change of constitution takes place, Kingship passes into Tyranny, because Tyranny is the bad form of monarchy, so that a bad king becomes a tyrant. Aristocracy passes into Oligarchy owing to badness in the rulers, who do not distribute what the State has to offer according to desert, but give all or most of its benefits to themselves, and always assign the offices to the same persons, because they set supreme value upon riches; thus power is in the hands of a few bad men, instead of being in the hands of the best men. Timocracy passes into Democracy, there being an affinity between them, inasmuch as the ideal of Timocracy also is government by the mass of the citizens, and within the property qualification all are equal. Democracy is the least bad of the perversions, for it is only a very small deviation from the constitutional form of government. These are the commonest ways in which revolutions occur in states, since they involve the smallest change, and come about most easily.

One may find likenesses and so to speak models of these various forms of constitution in the household. The relationship of father to sons is regal in type, since a father's first care is for his children's welfare. This is why Homer styles Zeus 'father,' for the ideal of kingship is paternal government. Among the Persians paternal rule is tyrannical, for the Persians use their sons as slaves. The relation of master to slaves is also tyrannic, since in it the master's interest is aimed at. The autocracy of a master appears to be right, that of the Persian father wrong; for different subjects should be under different forms of rule. The relation of husband to wife seems to be in the nature of an aristocracy: the husband rules in virtue of fitness, and in matters that belong to a man's sphere; matters suited to a woman he hands over to his wife. When the husband controls everything, he transforms the relationship into an oligarchy, for the governs in violation of fitness, and not in virtue of superiority. And sometimes when the wife is an heiress it is she who rules. In these cases then authority goes not by virtue but by wealth and power, as in an oligarchy. The relation between brothers constitutes a sort of timocracy; they are equals, save in so far as they differ in age; hence, if the divergence in age be great, the friendship between them cannot be of the fraternal type.

⌐ ⌐ ⌐

The friendship between husband and wife appears to be a natural instinct; since man is by nature a pairing creature even more than he is a political creature, inasmuch as the family is an earlier and more fundamental institution than the State, and the procreation of offspring a more general characteristic of the animal creation. So whereas with the other animals the association of the sexes aims only at continuing the species, human beings cohabit not only for the sake of begetting children but also to provide the needs of life; for with the human race division of labour begins at the outset, and man and woman have different functions; thus they supply each other's wants, putting their special capacities into the common stock. Hence the friendship of man and wife seems to be one of utility and pleasure combined. But it may also be based on virtue, if the partners be of high moral character; for either sex has its special virtue, and this may be the ground of attraction. Children, too, seem to be a bond of union, and therefore childless marriages are more easily dissolved; for children are a good possessed by both parents in common, and common property holds people together.

Here, Aristotle repeats the claims that the rule of husband over wife is "constitutional" (here he calls it "aristocratic"), but here he is not implying just that the wife's consent is required, but that the wife should consent out of a particular sort of friendship in order for the marriage to be happy. The best marriage, beyond just being consensual by law and based on a sort of equality, must be between friends, in the sense that the husband and wife must wish each other well and share a life together. Thus, here in the happy marriage, Aristotle implies that there could be a strict equality between men and women, enabling such a husband and wife to achieve a "perfect" kind of friendship—a friendship of virtue. These claims seem to be in stark contrast to those he makes in the *Politics*. However, in a perfect friendship, Aristotle claims, two people's lives are really shared; one's true friend is like "another self," as he puts it. This is more common, or easier, Aristotle implies, when the friends are the same sex. We might assume it would be easier, on the face of it, to share things with someone more like oneself. While it is possible for men and women to share such a friendship and such a life, it is not, according to Aristotle, a common occurrence and it cannot be legislated.

5. ST. PAUL
(Tarsinian (Present-Day Turkey),
?–Approx. 67 C.E.)

Born Saul, a Jew from Tarsus in Cilicia, St. Paul was originally an outspoken critic of Christianity. Acts 9 tells the story of Saul's conversion to Christianity: on his way from Damascus to Jerusalem to arrest Christians, he was blinded by a vision of Christ and instructed that he would become the "chosen instrument to bring [Christ's] name before the nations and their kings." (Acts 9: 15) Recovering his sight by a laying on of hands, Saul was baptized into the Christian church and became its most passionate defender.

Paul's arguments for Christianity are contained in the letters he wrote to the leaders of various cities, and in those letters he also teaches the proper practice of Christianity and distinguishes Christian practice from Jewish. Many of the rules for Christian living that he outlines in the letters became the core of Christian doctrine. Thus, in order to discover what Christianity has to say about the proper role of women, (or any question of fundamental Christian policy) one of the first places to turn is to the letters of St. Paul. The primary passages on sexuality and gender are to be found in his first letter to the Corinthians and in his letter to the Ephesians.

1 CORINTHIANS

In this letter, Paul establishes his role as an authority on Christian practice, and offers a guide to the unification of the Christian factions in Corinth and a response to the Corinthians' questions regarding Christian dicta. In order to establish a unified Christian congregation in Corinth, Paul outlines moral rules for, among other things, marriage and sexuality.

> **5** I actually hear reports of sexual immorality among you, immorality such as even pagans do not tolerate: the union of a man with his father's wife. And you can still be proud of yourselves! You ought to have gone into mourning; a man who has done such a deed should have been rooted out of your company. For my

part, though I am absent in body, I am present in spirit, and my judgement upon the man who did this thing is already given, as if I were indeed present: you all being assembled in the name of our Lord Jesus, and I with you in spirit, with the power of our Lord Jesus over us, this man is to be consigned to Satan for the destruction of the body, so that his spirit may be saved on the Day of the Lord.

☙ ☙ ☙

6 Make no mistake: no fornicator or idolater, none who are guilty either of adultery or of homosexual perversion, no thieves or grabbers or drunkards or slanderers or swindlers, will possess the kingdom of God. Such were some of you. But you have been through the purifying waters; you have been dedicated to God and justified through the name of the Lord Jesus and the Spirit of our God.

'I am free to do anything', you say. Yes, but not everything is for my good. No doubt I am free to do anything, but I for one will not let anything make free with me. 'Food is for the belly and the belly for food', you say. True; and one day God will put an end to both. But it is not true that the body is for lust; it is for the Lord—and the Lord for the body. God not only raised our Lord from the dead; he will also raise us by his power. Do you not know that your bodies are limbs and organs of Christ? Shall I then take from Christ his bodily parts and make them over to a harlot? Never! You surely know that anyone who links himself with a harlot becomes physically one with her (for Scripture says, 'The pair shall become one flesh'); but he who links himself with Christ is one with him, spiritually. Shun fornication. Every other sin that a man can commit is outside the body; but the fornicator sins against his own body. Do you not know that your body is a shrine of the indwelling Holy Spirit, and the Spirit is God's gift to you? You do not belong to yourselves; you were bought at a price. Then honour God in your body.

7 And now for the matters you wrote about.

It is a good thing for a man to have nothing to do with women; but because there is so much immorality, let each man have his own wife and each woman her own husband. The husband must give the wife what is due to her, and the wife equally must give the husband his due. The wife cannot claim her body as her own; it is her husband's. Equally, the husband cannot claim his body as his own; it is his wife's. Do not deny yourselves to one another, except when you agree upon a temporary abstinence in order to devote yourselves to prayer; afterwards you may come together again; otherwise for lack of self-control, you may be tempted by Satan.

All this I say by way of concession, not command. I should like you all to be as I am myself; but everyone has the gift God has granted him, one this gift and another that.

To the unmarried and to widows I say this: it is a good thing if they stay as I am myself; but if they cannot control themselves, they should marry. Better be married than burn with vain desire.

To the married I give this ruling, which is not mine but the Lord's: a wife must not separate herself from her husband; if she does, she must either remain unmarried or be reconciled to her husband; and the husband must not divorce his wife.

To the rest I say this, as my own word, not as the Lord's: if a Christian has a heathen wife, and she is willing to live with him, he must not divorce her; and a woman who has a heathen husband willing to live with her must not divorce her husband. For the heathen husband now belongs to God through his Christian wife, and the heathen wife through her Christian husband. Otherwise your children would not belong to God, whereas in fact they do. If on the other hand the heathen partner wishes for a separation, let him have it. In such cases the Christian husband or wife is under no compulsion; but God's call is a call to live in peace. Think of it: as a wife you may be your husband's salvation; as a husband you may be your wife's salvation.

However that may be, each one must order his life according to the gift the Lord has granted him and his condition when God called him. That is what I teach in all our congregations. Was a man called with the marks of circumcision on him? Let him not remove them. Was he uncircumcised when he was called? Let him not be circumcised. Circumcision or uncircumcision is neither here nor there; what matters is to keep God's commands.

⪽ ⪽ ⪽

On the question of celibacy, I have no instructions from the Lord, but I give my judgement as one who by God's mercy is fit to be trusted.

It is my opinion, then, that in a time of stress like the present this is the best way for a man to live—it is best for a man to be as he is. Are you bound in marriage? Do not seek a dissolution. Has your marriage been dissolved? Do not seek a wife. If, however, you do marry, there is nothing wrong in it; and if a virgin marries, she has done no wrong. But those who marry will have pain and grief in this bodily life, and my aim is to spare you.

What I mean, my friends, is this. The time we live in will not last long. While it lasts, married men should be as if they has no wives; mourners should be as if they had nothing to grieve them, the joyful as if they did not rejoice; buyers must not count on keeping what they buy, nor those who use the world's wealth on using it to the full. For the whole frame of this world is passing away.

I want you to be free from anxious care. The unmarried man cares for the Lord's business; his aim is to please the Lord. But the married man cares for worldly things; his aim is to please his wife; and he has a divided mind. The unmarried or celibate woman cares for the Lord's business; her aim is to be dedicated to him in body as in spirit; but the married woman cares for worldly things; her aim is to please her husband.

In saying this I have no wish to keep you on a tight rein. I am thinking simply of your own good, of what is seemly, and of your freedom to wait upon the Lord without distraction.

But if a man has a partner in celibacy and feels that he is not behaving properly towards her, if, that is, his instincts are too strong for him, and something must be done, he may do as he pleases; there is nothing wrong in it; let them marry. But if a man is stead-fast in his purpose, being under no compulsion, and has complete control of his own choice; and if he has decided in his own mind to preserve his partner in her virginity, he will do well. Thus, he who marries his partner does well, and he who does not will do better.

A wife is bound to her husband as long as he lives. But if the husband die, she is free to marry whom she will, provided the marriage is within the Lord's fellowship. But she is better off as she is; that is my opinion, and I believe that I too have the Spirit of God.

In contrast to the egalitarianism of Plato, or the biological naturalism that we have seen in Aristotle, Paul represents sexual behavior itself as sinful, because our bodies are not our own to dispose of as we please, but instead belong to God. The morally best course of action with regard to sex is celibacy. Following this line of reasoning, or so it seems, Paul understands marriage as a way of curbing and ordering the desires that lead human beings to sin. Marriage, then, is not an ideal state, but it can help train spouses in self-control, which in turn directs them to God. Consequently, for Paul, all sexual behavior other than that which is condoned as a part of marriage is sinful and justly punished. Within marriage, Paul claims that the wife's body belongs to her husband and the husband's to his wife, and spouses in this way are each other's helpmeets against temptation.

This belonging to one's spouse is paralleled in Chapter 11, but without the egalitarian gesture made by Paul in the preceding passages. Women, he claims here, should always cover their heads, because they are subordinate to men as men are subordinate to God.

EPHESIANS

The authenticity of Paul's letter to the Ephesians has been disputed by scholars; some believe that it is the work of a follower of Paul and written after his death. For our purposes, however, the similarities between this letter and others written by Paul, and its place in Christian scripture, ensure its relevance whoever may be its original author. In this letter, St. Paul stresses the unity of the Church and the consequent community of Christians.

5 In a word, as God's dear children, try to be like him, and live in love as Christ loved you, and gave himself up on your behalf as an offering and sacrifice whose fragrance is pleasing to God.

Fornication and indecency of any kind, or ruthless greed, must not be so much as mentioned among you, as befits the people of God. No coarse, stupid, or flippant talk; these things are out of place; you should rather be thanking God. For be very sure of this: no one given to fornication or indecency, or the greed which makes an idol of gain, has any share in the kingdom of Christ and of God.

⤸ ⤸ ⤸

Be subject to one another out of reverence for Christ.

Wives, be subject to your husbands as to the Lord; for the man is the head of the woman, just as Christ also is the head of the church. Christ is, indeed, the Saviour of the body; but just as the church is subject to Christ, so must women be to their husbands in everything.

Husbands, love your wives, as Christ also loved the church and gave himself up for it, to consecrate it, cleansing it by water and word, so that he might present the church to himself all glorious, with no stain or wrinkle or anything of the sort, but holy and without blemish. In the same way men also are bound to love their wives, as they love their own bodies. In loving his wife a man loves himself. For no one ever hated his own body: on the contrary, he provides and cares for it; and that is how Christ treats the church because it is his body, of which we are living parts. Thus it is that (in the words of Scripture) 'a man shall leave his father and mother and shall be joined to his wife, and the two shall become one flesh'. It is a great truth that is hidden here. I for my part refer it to Christ and to the church, but it applies also individually: each of you must love his wife as his very self; and the woman must see to it that she pays her husband all respect.

It would seem from this letter that the community of Christians is achieved in large part through Christian love of one another. In his claims that a man's wife is "another self," a part of his own body, St. Paul echoes the claims made by Aristotle in the *Ethics* and *Politics*. However, love, in this Christian context, is represented as a vehicle of subjection, a part of every Christian's submission to God and to the Church. This notion of love bears a striking resemblance to the definitions offered by Aristophanes and Socrates in Plato's *Symposium,* excerpted earlier in this chapter. Love here, as in that dialogue, appears to put the lover in an abject position with regard to his or her beloved. The ultimate "beloved" for St. Paul, however, is God, and marriage is a kind of metaphor for the relation of the Church to Christ.

SUGGESTED READINGS—PART TWO

Adkins, Arthur. *Merit and Responsibility: A Study in Greek Values.* Oxford: Clarendon Press, 1960.

Aeschylus. *The Complete Greek Tragedies, Vol. I: Aeschylus.* D. Grene and R. Lattimore (eds). Chicago: University of Chicago Press, 1959.

Annas, Julia. *The Morality of Happiness.* Oxford: Oxford University Press, 1993.

———. "Plato's *Republic* and Feminism." *Philosophy* 51: 307–321, 1976.

Aristotle. *Generation of Animals.* A.L. Peck (trans). Cambridge, Harvard University Press, 1953.

———. *History of Animals.* Cambridge, Harvard University Press, 1965, 1970, 1991.

———. *Nicomachean Ethics.* H. Rackham (trans.) Cambridge, Harvard University Press, 1962.

————. *Politics.* Cambridge, Harvard University Press, 1932.

Bar On, Bat-Ami (ed). *Engendering Origins.* Albany: State University of New York Press, 1994.

Barnes, Jonathan. *Aristotle.* Oxford: Oxford University Press, 1982.

———— (ed). *The Cambridge Companion to Aristotle.* Cambridge: Cambridge University Press, 1995.

Barnes, Jonathan, M. Schofield, and R. Sorabji (eds). *Articles on Aristotle, Vol. II: Ethics and Politics.* New York: St. Martin's Press, 1978.

Blundell, Mary W. *Helping Friends and Harming Enemies: A Study in Sophocles and Greek Ethics.* Cambridge: Cambridge University Press, 1989.

Broadie, Sarah. *Ethics With Aristotle.* Oxford: Oxford University Press, 1991.

Brown, Wendy. "Supposing 'Truth Were a Woman': Plato's Subversion of Masculine Discourse." *Political Theory* 16: 594–616, 1988.

Cohen, David. *Law, Sexuality and Society: The Enforcement of Morals in Classical Athens.* Cambridge: Cambridge University Press, 1991.

Dickason, Anne. "Anatomy and Destiny: The Role of Biology in Plato's Views of Women." *Philosophical Forum* 5: 45–53, 1973.

Dodds, E.R. *The Greeks and the Irrational.* Berkeley: University of California Press, 1951.

Dover, K.J. *Greek Homosexuality.* Cambridge: Harvard University Press, 1978.

————. *Greek Popular Morality in the Time of Plato and Aristotle.* Berkeley: University of California Press, 1974.

Else, G.F. *The Origin and Early Form of Greek Tragedy.* Cambridge: Harvard University Press, 1965.

Euben, J.P. (ed). *Greek Tragedy and Political Theory.* Berkeley: University of California Press, 1986.

Fortenbaugh, W.W. "On Plato's Feminism in *Republic V.*" *Apeiron* 9: 1–4, 1975.

Foxhall, Lin. "Household, Gender and Property in Classical Athens." *The Classical Quarterly* 39: 22–44, 1989.

Gagarin, Michael. *Aeschylean Drama.* Berkeley: University of California Press, 1976.

Goldhill, S. *Language, Sexuality, Narrative: The Oresteia.* Cambridge: Cambridge University Press, 1984.

Gouldner, Alvin. *Enter Plato: Classical Greece and the Origin of Social Theory.* New York: Basic Books, 1965.

Green, Judith. "Aristotle on Necessary Verticality, Body Heat and Gendered Proper Places in the *Polis:* A Feminist Critique." *Hypatia* 7(1): 70–96, 1992.

Hall, Edith. *Inventing the Barbarian: Greek Self-Definition Through Tragedy.* Oxford: Clarendon Press, 1989.

Halprin, David. "Why is Diotima a Woman?" in *One Hundred Years of Homosexuality.* New York: Routledge, 1990.

Hartourni, Valerie A. "Antigone's Dilemma: A Problem in Political Membership." *Hypatia* 1: 3–20, 1986.

Hill, Christopher (ed). *The Person and the Human Mind: Issues in Ancient and Modern Philosophy.* Oxford: Oxford University Press, 1990.

Irigaray, Luce. *An Ethics of Sexual Difference.* C. Burke and G. C. Gill (trans.) Ithaca: Cornell University Press, 1993.

Irwin, Terence. *Aristotle's First Principles.* Oxford: Clarendon Press, 1988.

———— (ed). *Classical Philosophy: Collected Papers Vol. II: Socrates and his Contemporaries.* New York: Garland, 1995.

———— (ed). *Classical Philosophy: Collected Papers Vol. III: Plato's Ethics.* New York: Garland, 1995.

————— (ed). *Classical Philosophy: Collected Papers Vol. V: Aristotle's Ethics.* New York: Garland, 1995.

—————. *Plato's Ethics.* Oxford: Oxford University Press, 1995.

Just, Roger.*Women in Athenian Law and Life.* New York: Routledge, 1989.

Keuls, Eva. *The Reign of the Phallus.* New York: Harper and Row,1985.

Knox, Bernard. *Essays Ancient and Modern.* Baltimore: Johns Hopkins University Press, 1989.

—————. *The Heroic Temper: Studies in Sophoclean Tragedy.* Berkeley: University of California Press, 1964.

—————. *The Oldest Dead White European Males and Other Reflections on the Classics.* New York: Norton, 1993.

—————. *Word and Action: Essays on the Ancient Theater.* Baltimore: Johns Hopkins University Press, 1979.

Kraut, Richard. *Aristotle on the Human Good.* Princeton: Princeton University Press, 1989.

————— (ed). *The Cambridge Companion to Plato.* Cambridge: Cambridge University Press, 1992.

Lacey, W.K. *The Family in Classical Greece.* Ithaca: Cornell University Press, 1968.

Lear, Jonathan. *Aristotle: The Desire to Understand.* Cambridge: Cambridge University Press, 1988.

Lesser, Harry. "Plato's Feminism." *Philosophy* 54: 113–117, 1979.

Macleod, C.W. *Collected Essays.* Oxford: Oxford University Press, 1983.

Matthews, Gareth B. "Gender and Essence in Aristotle." *The Australasian Journal of Philosophy* 64: 16–25, 1986.

Nussbaum, Martha. *The Fragility of Goodness: Luck and Ethics in Greek Tragedy and Philosophy.* Cambridge: Cambridge University Press, 1986.

Okin, Susan Moller. "Philosopher Queens and Private Wives: Plato on Women and the Family." *Philosophy and Public Affairs:* 345–369, 1977.

Osborne, Martha Lee. "Plato's Unchanging View of Woman: A Denial That Anatomy Spells Destiny." *Philosophical Forum* 6: 447–452, 1975.

Plato. *Collected Dialogues.* E. Hamilton and H. Cairnes (eds). Princeton: Prineton University Press, 1961.

—————. *Plato's Republic.* G.M.A. Grube (trans). Indianapolis: Hackett, 1974.

Podlecki, A.J. *The Political Background of Aeschylean Tragedy.* Ann Arbor: University of Michigan Press, 1966.

Price, Anthony W. *Love and Friendship in Plato and Aristotle.* Oxford: Clarendon Press, 1989.

Pritchard, Annie. "Antigone's Mirrors: Reflections on Moral Madness." *Hypatia* 7(3): 126–137, 1992.

Rorty, Amelie O. (ed). *Essays on Aristotle's Ethics.* Berkeley: University of California Press, 1980.

Schaps, David. *Economic Rights of Women in Ancient Greece.* Edinburgh: University Press, 1979.

Schott, Robin. "Aristotle on Women." *Kinesis* 11: 69–84, 1982.

Shaw, M. "Female Intruder: Women in Fifth Century Drama." *Classical Philology* 70: 255–266, 1975.

Smith, Nicholas D. "Plato and Aristotle on the Nature of Women." *Journal of the History of Philosophy* 21: 467–478, 1983.

Sophocles. *The Complete Greek Tragedies, Vol. II: Sophocles.* D. Grene and R. Lattimore (eds). Chicago: University of Chicago Press, 1959.

Steiner, George. *Antigones.* Oxford: Oxford University Press, 1984.

Strauss, Barry S. *Fathers and Sons in Athens: Ideology and Society in the Era of the Pelopennesian War.* Princeton: Princeton University Press, 1993.

Tyrell, William. *Amazons: A Study in Athenian Myth Making.* Baltimore: Johns Hopkins University Press, 1984.

Vlastos, Gregory (ed). *Plato: A Collection of Critical Essays.* South Bend: Notre Dame University Press, 1978.

———. *Platonic Studies.* Princeton: Princeton University Press, 1981.

———. *Studies in Greek Philosophy Vol. II: Socrates, Plato and Their Tradition.* Princeton: Princeton University Press, 1995.

Wender, Dorothea. "Plato: Misogynist, Paedophile and Feminist." *Arethusia* 6: 75–80, 1973.

Wider, Kathleen. "Women Philosophers of the Ancient Greek World: Donning the Mantle." *Hypatia* 1: 21–62, 1986.

Winkler, J.J. and F.I. Zeittin (eds). *Nothing to Do With Dionysos?: Athenian Drama and its Social Context.* Princeton: Princeton University Press, 1990.

PART THREE

EARLY MODERNITY:
THE DEVELOPING CONFLICT
WITHIN "HUMANISM"

Shakespeare, Milton, Descartes, Hobbes,
Locke, Rousseau, Wollstonecraft

INTRODUCTION

WHAT IS MODERNITY?

The notion of the "postmodern," mentioned in the Introduction to this book, has become fashionable today, not just in academia, but in popular culture as well. Despite its popularity, or even its essential role in defining our own age, it is not altogether clear what the contemporary buzzword "postmodernity" means. This is because it is often not clear what is meant by the "modern" to which the "postmodern" opposes itself. As evidence of this, we might look to the contemporary French thinker Jean-Francois Lyotard, one of the "fathers" of "postmodernism," who defines it in the following way:

> "It is undoubtedly a part of the modern. All that has been received, if only yesterday . . . must be suspected. . . . A work can become modern only if it is first postmodern. Postmodernism thus understood is not modernism at its end, but in the nascent state, and this state is constant."[1]

As Lyotard implies, and like so many of the oppositions in Part One, the modern and the postmodern are as intimately connected as they are distinct from each other. The postmodern poses itself as a radical reaction against its historical predecessor, modernity, which it perceives to have been stagnant, rigid, and politically repressive;

---

[1] Jean-Francois Lyotard, *The Postmodern Condition: A Report on Knowledge*.
(Minneapolis: University of Minnesota Press, 1984).

yet at the same time, as Lyotard describes, it inevitably yields a renewed modernity. But this is exactly how modernity posed itself—as a radical movement (or rather, a set of radical movements in lots of different disciplines and activities) against what it perceived as the rigidity and oppressiveness of the medieval world, itself yielding another—and to our mind, perhaps quite rigid—set of values. Thus, modernity and postmodernity share a spirit of radicalism and novelty, as well a sense of paradox. They have left us in a rather curious historical position: we are the heirs to a five hundred-year-old tradition of trying to escape tradition.

Postmodernity and modernity do differ, of course, in how they understand the faults of their ancestors and in how they have envisioned correcting those faults. To understand modernity, then, it is important to understand both how thinkers in the modern age understood the strict traditionalism of medieval life, and how what they envisioned as an escape from that structured worldview could seem from our perspective so rigid in its own right. The period we have come to call "modernity" began in the late sixteenth and early seventeenth centuries, and stemmed from the discoveries of what we have come to call "the scientific revolution" (those of Copernicus, Galileo, etc.), as well as from the beginning of the economic and social exploitation by Western Europe of the New World, and from the threats posed to the religious hierarchy of the Christian Church—which had immeasurable authority in Europe in the Middle Ages—by the Reformation. As a friend claimed to Descartes (who is excerpted in this section and often thought to be the seminal figure in modern philosophy), "it is easy to prove that the excessive respect maintained for antiquity is an error which is extremely prejudicial to the advancement of the sciences."[2]

For hundreds of years in the Western World, the Christian Church had had authority over all aspects of life: religious, of course, but also political, economic, cultural, and scientific. Together, and combined with continuing political and economic revisions to the feudal system, the various scientific and religious challenges to this authority placed Western Europe in a revolutionary mode across almost all aspects of society and culture. The twentieth-century Spanish philosopher, Jose Ortega y Gasset, describes the spirit of the "modern age" as inherently revolutionary and associates its radicalism with the philosophical movement called "rationalism." (Descartes, whom we just mentioned, was a rationalist.)

> *The convergence of the features of this spiritual state produced the sensibility which is specifically "modern." Mistrust and contempt for everything spontaneous and immediate. Enthusiasm for all the constructions of reason. . . . Accordingly [a "modern"] will consider all traditional political institutions stupid and unjust. As opposed to them, he believes he has discovered a definitive social order arrived at deductively by means of reason. It is a schematically perfect constitution in which it is assumed that men are rational entities and nothing else. . . . This is the temper which produces revolutions.[3]*

---

[2] Rene Descartes, *The Passions of the Soul*. Translated by Stephen H. Voss. (Indianapolis: Hackett, 1989). p. 7.

[3] Jose Ortega y Gasset, *The Modern Theme,* translated by James Cleugh. (NY: Harper Torchbooks, 1961) p. 34.

We have come to call modernity the "Age of Reason" in order to contrast it to the Medieval "Age of Faith"; but we might as easily oppose to the faithful age an age of *doubt,* of questioning faith, and modernity therefore as an age characterized by freedom and imagination, but also by anxiety and skepticism. The character of modernity can be attributed to the slow reorientation from what we might call the medieval's "god-centered outlook"—in which nature, political society, and human good were understood primarily through a prior faith in the rationality, power, and goodness of God—to what we might call the modern's "human-centered out-look"—in which natural science, politics, and ethics were all thought to be based in some prior notion of human nature and knowledge. In other words, the "reason" re-ferred to in the "Age of Reason" is *human,* not divine, rationality, and thus the "Age of Reason" is a fundamentally humanist age. But human beings, and thus the products of human reason, are changeable, often conflicted and fleeting things; hence while this humanist turn tended to make science and politics more accessible, more fair, and more manageable, it also tended to make them less authoritative, less trustworthy, and less stable.

However, as Ortega implies in the passage just quoted, this multitude of chal-lenges to the stable medieval perspective did not strike modern thinkers as unnat-ural or of dubious worth. On the contrary, the various scientific discoveries, economic restructuring, and protestant religious reforms all seemed to indicate to the modern mind that there existed a new, underlying, and as yet hidden *natural* au-thority, which, if tapped, might supersede the authority of the Church. Thus, we could characterize modern thought as an effort to firmly establish this natural au-thority and to ground it in human reason, for the ultimate purpose of bettering human life and society. From a contemporary perspective, this effort to establish, within the sphere of human reason, a foundation for science and politics more firm than the medieval's faith in God may seem profoundly rigid and intellectually fore-closed. To us, the effortfulness of these modern thinkers gives the impression of both innovation and anxiety—both freedom and disorientation, both progress and stagnation. But to modern thinkers, it seemed as if over a thousand years' worth of obstacles to the perfection of human wisdom and life were finally being removed.

HUMANISM, INDIVIDUALISM, AND THE PRIMACY OF METHOD

The modern challenge to the authority of the church manifested itself primarily through the success of new "methods" of obtaining knowledge. The humanist trend of modern thought promised that knowledge was within the grasp of human reason; in other words, it promoted the idea that there were natural or absolute truths, and that they could be known by every human being, insofar as he or she was a human being—i.e., insofar as he or she was rational. Humanism claims that human beings share a nature that is rational and therefore capable of perfect knowledge of the nat-ural world. Individualism claims that each human being is importantly different from every other, and that each human being retains his or her independent authority in any disagreement. The individualist trend that resulted from humanism promised each individual an autonomy over his or her own beliefs and decisions. Since, how-ever, individual beliefs and decisions differ, sometimes quite radically, from person to person, the presupposition of individual autonomy results in a plethora of seemingly irresolvable conflicts. These conflicts may indeed be the identifying mark of the modern sensibility, a mark with which we still brand ourselves today.

The methods of study used in the church-run universities during the Middle Ages (known at its high point as "scholasticism") were part of a well-entrenched tradition of thought among highly educated church members. The new discoveries of the scientific revolution, which challenged church doctrine, were the results of modern scientific or hypothetical method; in other words, they resulted at least in part from observations collected by an experimenter. These observations could be and were made by individuals independent of the authority of the church or the dictates of scripture; they were, in a sense, private—the modern scientist could work alone in his or her laboratory, or even conduct "thought experiments" within his or her private reflections—and they put the experimenter into a direct relationship with the objects of knowledge (truth, or God, or nature) not requiring the mediation of tradition, doctrine, or priests. The successes of scientific methods had profound significance across the spectrum of modern academic disciplines, prompting heated debate everywhere about how certain knowledge was actually to be achieved.

In particular, the new methods seemed to give the ordinary individual an "autonomy"—an independent right—over his or her decisions and the knowledge on which they were based. The various sects resulting from the Protestant Reformation asserted the rights of individuals to interpret scripture freely according to their own lights, and in the extreme, to enter into personal relationships with God, unmediated by the Catholic church. In political economics, individuals acquired throughout the sixteenth and seventeenth centuries more and more rights over the products of their labor, and consequently more political power. Following on the heels of the high Renaissance, the art of early modernity availed itself of the rediscovered ancient Greek notions of individual character, and of the beauty of the natural individual human body, turning away from formulaic symbolic art and towards unique depictions of individual characters, events, and stories. By the late seventeenth century, the humanistic spirit of the artistic renaissance of the fourteenth to sixteenth centuries had become more of a theory of the nature and limits of the human individual. By the eighteenth century, the period known as the Enlightenment (and which provided the philosophical context for the French and American revolutions), this trend had developed into a number of doctrines of individual rights. Thus, the "human-centered" worldview of early modernity gave birth to a modern notion of the individual as a political, moral, economic, scientific, and aesthetic unit. While this modern notion of the individual was a liberating one, that spawned the democratic rights and freedoms essential to so many modern Western nations, it is philosophically problematic. There is, it seems, an inherent conflict within humanism, between the belief that we are all alike, rational, and capable of possessing truth and the belief that we are all different and unable to resolve intellectual disagreements.

Philosophers faced with this inherent conflict within humanism tended to give priority to questions of method. To understand why, consider a contemporary example. Suppose you and a teacher have a dispute about your grade in a course. Under the conflicting assumptions, which we share with our modern predecessors, that both you and the teacher in question have autonomy over your judgments, and on the other hand, that there is a right grade for your assignment, it is likely that you and your teacher would begin by finding out what *procedure* your school has outlined for dealing with such disputes. Whatever the school policy—that you get the opinion of another teacher, or that you see a negotiator, or that you go to an appeals board—the notion that procedure, or a *method* of approaching the question, is a fair and objective authority in the dispute, is an inheritance from early modernity. The only way to preserve the conflicting beliefs that human beings in general are capable of scientific and political knowledge and that human beings have individual autonomy over their assertions is to suggest that every individual can somehow independently reach agreement with every other, if only he or she would follow the same fair and objective procedure. Thus, many modern philosophers gave priority to questions of method, trying to establish, before pursuing the truth of a claim, how to pursue truth in the most reliable, unimpeachable manner possible.

This sentiment is very clearly discernable in Descartes and summed up very nicely in the opening of his *Discourse on the Method of Rightly Conducting One's Reason and for Seeking Truth in the Sciences:*

> [T]he power of judging rightly and of distinguishing the true from the false (which, properly speaking, is what people call good sense or reason) is naturally equal in all men. Thus the diversity of our opinions does not arise from the fact that some people are more reasonable than others, but simply from the fact that we conduct our thoughts along different lines and do not consider the same things. For it is not enough to have a good mind; the main thing is to use it well.[4]

This question of *how to use one's mind well* or, in other words, of how to find certain knowledge of the truth, becomes the overriding question of early modernity, characterizing the age as one first and foremost concerned with "epistemological" questions, questions about the nature and marks of knowledge.

METHOD, NATURE, AND GENDER

This conflict within humanism also expresses itself in a new and somewhat paradoxical modern notion of "nature" and of its relation to human reason. In the ancient world, nature was understood as an ordered, rational, whole—external to human beings, who stood towards nature as parts to a whole. The medievals took a similar view, casting the order and rationality of nature as attributes of God, knowable through God. This view of nature, however, seemed to the thinkers of the sixteenth to eighteenth centuries to be increasingly inconsistent with the humanist orientation of their modern age. The modern scientific method of verifying hypotheses through observation presupposed that the underlying regularities of nature were law-like and absolute, as ordered and certain as mathematical theorems; yet it

---

[4] Rene Descartes, *Discourse on Method and Meditations on First Philosophy*, 3rd ed.. Translated by Donald A. Cress (Indianapolis: Hackett, 1993). p. 1

also presupposed that these regularities were hidden from the observer, requiring the repeated verification of empirical data. Thus, the developments of the scientific revolution, partly in combination with medieval views about God's perfection, left as a legacy a vision of nature—including human nature—as absolutely logical and law-like, yet somehow hidden from ordinary understanding or debased by poor understanding and use.

For instance, Newtonian physics indicated that the movements of material objects obeyed physical laws that were absolute and eternal and could be expressed in mathematical terms with perfect precision. For instance, there is a law-like truth, or nature, they would claim, regarding the movement of a ball rolling down a hill. Two different observers of this ball, however, will perceive its speed and direction differently if they are standing at different distances from it. Their perceptions of the ball rolling down the hill may change as they walk around, or the sun may go down and their view may be impaired, etc., and so these perceptions do not seem very law-like or reliable at all. Hence it seemed to modern philosophers that there was a truth about nature, perfectly accessible both to reason and to observation, which nonetheless normally evaded human understanding.

Even in physics, the notion that there is a "nature" to material objects and their motions may cause some intellectual difficulties; but in religion, morality, and politics, this notion raises profound philosophical problems. The integration of science, morality, religion, and politics that marked the curriculum in the medieval universities was not wholly abandoned in the modern age; hence, it was thought that social and moral questions, like scientific ones, could be answered with law-like authority through the proper application of philosophical method. The possibility of natural laws of human behavior and divine command rested on the belief that "human nature" was a definite and knowable essence whose character was the same in every instance and which gave the law to human action. Human nature, however, like the laws of physics, is also hidden from us, misunderstood or debased by different people because of their different conditions and impaired perceptions. Thus, according to this modern perspective, people do not always behave as nature dictates, but this is paradoxical. We normally think of natural laws, in this modern sense, as being absolutely binding—we cannot, for instance, choose to disobey the law of gravity. So, if human nature is law-like in this way, then we ought never to be able to behave otherwise than how our nature dictates. It is obvious, however, that people do act otherwise than "human": they sometimes behave like animals, for instance.

Obviously, this problematical reasoning comes to the fore in modern questions about gender, sex, and sexual role. Modern claims about male and female natures seek scientific accuracy and authority and an explanation for any variance from the regularities of nature. For instance, if it is knowable to reason, through the application of the proper method, that woman's nature is soft, lovely, and obedient, (as Rousseau will claim in his *Emile,* some of which appears in this chapter), then a rational marriage law would seek the husband's pleasure and the wife's protection. Therefore, if a woman is harsh and belligerent (like, for instance, Katherine in Shakespeare's *The Taming of the Shrew,* our next excerpt) she may be accused, according to this modern sensibility, of behaving unnaturally, and the state is legitimate in treating her as an anomaly, perhaps arranging a marriage in which she is not protected.

In each of their different ways, the authors represented in this section are struggling with questions about the scientific "truths" of sexual conduct and passion, the "nature" of the two sexes, the "natural" ways for men and women to behave, and the "natural" rights and obligations of men and women in political society. As a consequent of this search, these modern thinkers will all tend to make a wide distinction between "nature" and "culture" as sources of human behavior. This is not unlike the *nomos/physis* distinction made by the ancient Athenian thinkers in the last section; the tone, however, is different. Where the Greeks primarily investigated the relation between nature and culture and attempted to derive moral laws that would culturally approximate nature, the moderns are more interested in the distinction itself, as well as in the absolute authority of natural law over conventional law. They offer very different, sometimes surprising, sometimes perhaps exasperating resolutions to these modern quandaries, exploring in different ways the possibilities opened up by the gradual abandonment of medieval traditions of marriage, family, and work, even as they seek new and sometimes rigid natural limits on human freedom.

1. WILLIAM SHAKESPEARE
(English, 1564–1616)

Generally thought to be the greatest poet of the English language, Shakespeare would inform our thinking about gender in any of his plays, but because of limitations of space, here are excerpted only two, whose struggles with the gender issues of modernity are particularly clear: *The Taming of the Shrew* and *Macbeth*.

THE TAMING OF THE SHREW (1594)

This play is the story of an opportunist (Petruccio) who woos and marries a rich and, according to the other characters in the play, "unmarriageable" young woman (Katherine). The story of Katherine and Petruccio, however, is a play within a play, presented to a character named Christopher Sly, a drunk.

In this opening scene, called "The Induction" (like an induction into a club, it readies us for the role we are about to play as audience members), Sly, a drunken tinker, is found by the lord of the nearby manor sleeping outside a tavern. The nobleman decides to play a practical joke on Sly when the latter wakes up. The nobleman and all his servants pretend that Sly is the Lord of the manor, their master, who has been in a state of amnesia for a very long time. The jokesters are a kind of an acting troupe—in fact, they perform the "Katherine and Petruccio" play for Sly—and they in essence transform Christopher Sly. By treating him like a nobleman, they lead him to imagine that he is one.

Shakespeare focuses our attention on the questions of sex and gender role by having the Lord cast one of his male servants in the role of "Lady Sly," who pretends to be "Lord" Sly's long-suffering, devoted wife. In Shakespeare's own time, there were few female actors; women's characters were often played by young boys, whose voices had not yet broken. Here, the nobleman's servants do precisely the same thing. If, the scene implies, theatrical makeup and costuming can turn young boys into women adequately for an evening's entertainment on the stage, what makes us so attached to the notion that men and women have immutable natures in real life? If, as Shakespeare himself wrote, "all the world's a stage," then how can we be certain there is any human "reality" at all?

This is essentially the same manipulation that Petruccio will use on Katherine; he will make her marriageable by marrying her, make her gentle by pretending to be an ogre. Petruccio's work is also art, and also a practical joke. The Induction, then, prepares us to ponder the thematic puzzle of the play, a puzzle about human nature, the possibilities of art, and the sociology of gender roles. What is the real difference, we are being asked, between a nobleman and a tinker, or between a gentlewoman and a shrew? Is there a natural difference, or are our roles merely products of our own and others' imaginations?

KATHERINE AND BIANCA

The motivating problem in the play is that Baptista, a rich gentleman of Padua (where the play is set) wants to arrange a marriage for his lovely and well-mannered youngest daughter, Bianca. In the following scene, however, Baptista makes clear to Bianca's two main suitors, Hortensio and Gremio, that Bianca cannot marry before her older sister Katherine, who on account of her arrogant and churlish temper has no suitors on the horizon. Lucientio, a visitor to Padua, observes the scene and falls in love with Bianca.

BAPTISTA: Gentlemen, importune me no farther,
  For how I firmly am resolved you know:
  That is, not to bestow my youngest daughter
  Before I have a husband for the elder.
  If either of you both love Katherina,
  Because I know you well and love you well
  Leave shall you have to court her at your pleasure.

GREMIO: To cart her rather. She's too rough for me.
  There, there, Hortensio. Will you any wife?

KATHERINE (*to* BAPTISTA): I pray you, sir, is it your will
  To make a stale of me amongst these mates?

HORTENSIO: 'Mates', maid? How mean you that? No mates for you
  Unless you were of gentler, milder mould.
KATHERINE: I'faith, sir, you shall never need to fear.
  Iwis it is not half-way to her heart,

But if it were, doubt not her care should be
To comb your noddle with a three-legged stool,
And paint your face, and use you like a fool.

HORTENSIO: From all such devils, good Lord deliver us.

GREMIO: And me too, good Lord.

TRANIO (*aside to* LUCENTIO): Husht, master, here's some good pastime toward.
That wench is stark mad or wonderful froward.

LUCENTIO (*aside to* TRANIO): But in the other's silence do I see
Maid's mild behaviour and sobriety.
Peace, Tranio.

TRANIO (*aside to* LUCENTIO): Well said, master. Mum, and gaze your fill.

BAPTISTA: Gentlemen, that I may soon make good
What I have said—Bianca, get you in.
And let it not displease thee, good Bianca,
For I will love thee ne'er the less, my girl.

KATHERINE: A pretty peat! It is best
Put finger in the eye, an she knew why.

BIANCA: Sister, content you in my discontent.
(*To* BAPTISTA) Sir, to your pleasure humbly I subscribe.
My books and instruments shall be my company,
On them to look and practise by myself.

LUCENTIO (*aside to* TRANIO): Hark, Tranio, thou mayst hear Minerva speak.

HORTENSIO: Signor Baptista, will you be so strange?
Sorry am I that our good will effects
Bianca's grief.

GREMIO: Why will you mew her up,
Signor Baptista, for this fiend of hell,
And make her bear the penance of her tongue?

BAPTISTA: Gentlemen, content ye. I am resolved.
Go in, Bianca.   *Exit* BIANCA
And for I know she taketh most delight
In music, instruments, and poetry,
Schoolmaster will I keep within my house
Fit to instruct her youth. If you, Hortensio,
Or, Signor Gremio, you know any such,
Prefer them hither; for to cunning men
I will be very kind, and liberal
To mine own children in good bringing up.
And so farewell. Katherina, you may stay,
For I have more to commune with Bianca.   *Exit*

KATHERINE: Why, and I trust I may go too, may I not?
　　What, shall I be appointed hours, as though belike I
　　knew not what to take and what to leave? Ha!　*Exit*

⌒ ⌒ ⌒

LUCENTIO: . . . Sacred and sweet was all I saw in her.

TRANIO (*aside*): Nay, then 'tis time to stir him from his trance.
　　(*To* LUCENTIO) I pray, awake, sir. If you love the maid,
　　Bend thoughts and wits to achieve her. Thus it stands:
　　Her elder sister is so curst and shrewd
　　That till the father rid his hands of her,
　　Master, your love must live a maid at home,
　　And therefore has he closely mewed her up
　　Because she will not be annoyed with suitors.

LUCENTIO: Ah, Tranio, what a cruel father's he!
　　But art thou not advised he took some care
　　To get her cunning schoolmasters to instruct her?

TRANIO: Ay, marry am I, sir, and now 'tis plotted.

LUCENTIO: I have it, Tranio.

TRANIO: Master, for my hand,
　　Both our inventions meet and jump in one.

LUCENTIO: Tell me thine first.

TRANIO: You will be schoolmaster
　　And undertake the teaching of the maid.
　　That's your device.

LUCENTIO: It is. May it be done?

TRANIO: Not possible; for who shall bear your part,
　　And be in Padua here Vincentio's son,
　　Keep house, and ply his book, welcome his friends,
　　Visit his countrymen, and banquet them?

LUCENTIO: *Basta*, content thee, for I have it full.
　　We have not yet been seen in any house,
　　Nor can we be distinguished by our faces
　　For man or master. Then it follows thus:
　　Thou shalt be master, Tranio, in my stead;
　　Keep house, and port, and servants, as I should.
　　I will some other be, some Florentine,
　　Some Neapolitan, or meaner man of Pisa.
　　Tis hatched, and shall be so. Tranio, at once
　　Uncase thee. Take my coloured hat and cloak.

When Biondello comes he waits on thee,
But I will charm him first to keep his tongue.

TRANIO: So had you need.

[They exchange clothes]

In brief, sir, sith it your pleasure is,
And I am tied to be obedient—
For so your father charged me at our parting,
'Be serviceable to my son,' quoth he,
Although I think 'twas in another sense—
I am content to be Lucentio
Because so well I love Lucentio.

LUCENTIO: Tranio, be so, because Lucentio loves,
And let me be a slave t'achieve that maid
Whose sudden sight hath thralled my wounded eye.[5]

Katherine's "shrewishness" at least partially consists of her quick wit and self-assertiveness. She is not represented by Shakespeare as an unattractive woman, nor as an unskilled homemaker; neither is she represented as particularly violent or dangerous. Rather, she is outspoken, loud, and sharp-tongued. She is "wild," while Bianca—who loves music and poetry and is disciplined in her speech and conduct—is "tame." But things are not what they seem: Katherine's indignation is at least partly jealousy and loneliness; she does not seem to enjoy the alienation she has experienced on account of her character. She seems to long to be "tamed" as will be shown in later scenes. Similarly, Lucientio's scheme, outlined here—to pretend to be Tranio's (and Bianca's) servant—seems to appeal to Bianca's desire to be "masterful" like her sister, as this opening scene of Act II reveals, and as will be verified at the close of the play.

2.1 *Enter* KATHERINA *and* BIANCA, *her hands bound*

BIANCA: Good sister, wrong me not, nor wrong yourself
To make a bondmaid and a slave of me.
That I disdain, but for these other goods,
Unbind my hands, I'll pull them off myself,
Yea, all my raiment to my petticoat,
Or what you will command me will I do,
So well I know my duty to my elders.

KATHERINE: Of all thy suitors here I charge thee tell
Whom thou lov'st best. See thou dissemble not.

---

[5] All excerpts from Shakespeare's *The Taming of the Shrew* are taken from *The Complete Oxford Shakespeare II: Comedies.* General editors Stanley Wells and Gary Taylor (New York: Oxford U. Press, 1987) pp. 481-515.

BIANCA: Believe me, sister, of all the men alive
I never yet beheld that special face
Which I could fancy more than any other.

KATHERINE: Minion, thou liest. Is't not Hortensio?

BIANCA: If you affect him, sister, here I swear
I'll plead for you myself but you shall have him.

KATHERINE: O then, belike you fancy riches more.
You will have Gremio to keep you fair.

BIANCA: Is it for him you do envy me so?
Nay, then, you jest, and now I well perceive
You have but jested with me all this while.
I prithee, sister Kate, untie my hands.

KATHERINE (*strikes her*): If that be jest, then all the rest was so.

Enter BAPTISTA

BAPTISTA: Why, how now, dame, whence grows this insolence?
Bianca, stand aside.—Poor girl, she weeps.—
Go ply thy needle, meddle not with her.
(*To Katherine*) For shame, thou hilding of a devilish spirit,
Why dost thou wrong her that did ne'er wrong thee?
When did she cross thee with a bitter word?

KATHERINE: Her silence flouts me, and I'll be revenged.

She flies after BIANCA

BAPTISTA: What, in my sight? Bianca, get thee in. *Exit* BIANCA

KATHERINE: What, will you not suffer me? Nay, now I see
She is your treasure, she must have a husband.
I must dance barefoot on her wedding day,
And for your love to her lead apes in hell.
Talk not to me. I will go sit and weep
Till I can find occasion of revenge. *Exit*

PETRUCCIO AND KATHERINE

Meanwhile, Petruccio has arrived in Padua from Verona to visit Hortensio and has heard about the situation. Petruccio could use a generous dowry.

HORTENSIO:

⤶ ⤶ ⤶

And tell me now, sweet friend, what happy gale
Blows you to Padua from old Verona?

PETRUCCIO: Such wind as scatters young men through the world
    To seek their fortunes farther than at home,
    Where small experience grows. But in a few,
    Signor Hortensio, thus it stands with me:
    Antonio, my father, is deceased,
    And I have thrust myself into this maze
    Happily to wive and thrive as best I may.
    Crowns in my purse I have, and goods at home,
    And so am come abroad to see the world.

HORTENSIO: Petruccio, shall I then come roundly to thee
    And wish thee to a shrewd, ill-favored wife?
    Thou'dst thank me but a little for my counsel,
    And yet I'll promise thee she shall be rich,
    And very rich. But thou'rt too much my friend,
    And I'll not wish thee to her.

PETRUCCIO: Signor Hortensio, 'twixt such friends as we
    Few words suffice; and therefore if thou know
    One rich enough to be Petruccio's wife—
    As wealth is burden of my wooing dance—
    Be she as foul as was Florentius' love,
    As old as Sibyl, and as curst and shrewd
    As Socrates' Xanthippe or a worse,
    She moves me not—or not removes at least
    Affection's edge in me, were she as rough
    As are the swelling Adriatic seas.
    I come to wive it wealthily in Padua;
    If wealthily, then happily in Padua.

Petruccio lets the competition for Bianca take its course as he pursues his own plan. In the following scene, Petruccio makes a businesslike arrangement with Baptista and introduces himself to his new fiancee.

GREMIO: Good morrow, neighbour Baptista.

BAPTISTA: Good morrow, neighbour Gremio. God save you, gentlemen.

PETRUCCIO: And you, good sir. Pray, have you not a daughter
    Called Katherina, fair and virtuous?

BAPTISTA: I have a daughter, sir, called Katherina.

GREMIO: You are too blunt. Go to it orderly.

PETRUCCIO: You wrong me, Signor Gremio. Give me leave.
    (*To* BAPTISTA) I am a gentleman of Verona, sir,
    That hearing of her beauty and her wit,
    Her affability and bashful modesty,

Her wondrous qualities and mild behaviour,
Am bold to show myself a forward guest
Within your house to make mine eye the witness
Of that report which I so oft have heard.

⌒ ⌒ ⌒

PETRUCCIO: I see you do not mean to part with her,
Or else you like not of my company.

BAPTISTA: Mistake me not, I speak but as I find.
Whence are you, sir? What may I call your name?

PETRUCCIO: Petruccio is my name, Antonio's son,
A man well known throughout all Italy.

BAPTISTA: I know him well. You are welcome for his sake.

⌒ ⌒ ⌒

PETRUCCIO: Signor Baptista, my business asketh haste,
And every day I cannot come to woo.
You knew my father well, and in him me,
Left solely heir to all his lands and goods,
Which I have bettered rather than decreased.
Then tell me, if I get your daughter's love,
What dowry shall I have with her to wife?

BAPTISTA: After my death the one half of my lands,
And in possession twenty thousand crowns.

PETRUCCIO: And for that dowry I'll assure her of
Her widowhood, be it that she survive me,
In all my lands and leases whatsover.
Let specialties be therefore drawn between us,
That covenants may be kept on either hand.

⌒ ⌒ ⌒

Exeunt all but PETRUCCIO

⌒ ⌒ ⌒

Enter KATHERINA

PETRUCCIO: Good morrow, Kate, for that's your name, I hear.

KATHERINE: Well have you heard, but something hard of hearing.
They call me Katherine that do talk of me.

PETRUCCIO:You lie, in faith, for you are called plain Kate,
And bonny Kate, and sometimes Kate the curst,
But Kate, the prettiest Kate in Christendom,
Kate of Kate Hall, my super-dainty Kate—

For dainties are all cates, and therefore 'Kate'—
Take this of me, Kate of my consolation:
Hearing thy mildness praised in every town,
Thy virtues spoke of, and thy beauty sounded—
Yet not so deeply as to thee belongs—
Myself am moved to woo thee for my wife.

KATHERINE: Moved? In good time. Let him that moved you hither
Re-move you hence. I knew you at the first
You were a movable.

PETRUCCIO: Why, what's a movable?

KATHERINE: A joint-stool.

PETRUCCIO: Thou hast hit it. Come, sit on me.

KATHERINE: Assess are made to bear, and so are you.

PETRUCCIO: Women are made to bear, and so are you.

KATHERINE: No such jade as you, if me you mean.

PETRUCCIO: Alas, good Kate, I will not burden thee,
For knowing thee to be but young and light.

KATHERINE: Too light for such a swain as you to catch,
And yet as heavy as my weight should be.

PETRUCCIO: Should be?—should buzz.

KATHERINE: Well ta'en, and like a buzzard.

PETRUCCIO: O slow-winged turtle, shall a buzzard take thee?

KATHERINE: Ay, for a turtle, as he takes a buzzard.

PETRUCCIO: Come, come, you wasp, i'faith you are too angry.

KATHERINE: If I be waspish, best beware my sting.

PETRUCCIO: My remedy is then to pluck it out.

KATHERINE: Ay, if the fool could find it where it lies.

PETRUCCIO: Who knows not where a wasp does wear his sting?
In his tail.

KATHERINE: In his tongue.

PETRUCCIO: Whose tongue?

KATHERINE: Yours, if you talk of tales, and so farewell.

PETRUCCIO: What, with my tongue in your tail? Nay, come again,
Good Kate, I am a gentleman.

KATHERINE: That I'll try.

She strikes him

PETRUCCIO: I swear I'll cuff you if you strike again.

KATHERINE: So may you lose your arms.
　　If you strike me you are no gentleman,
　　And if no gentleman, why then, no arms.

PETRUCCIO: A herald, Kate? O, put me in thy books.

KATHERINE: What is your crest—a coxcomb?

PETRUCCIO: A combless cock, so Kate will be my hen.

KATHERINE: No cock of mine. You crow too like a craven.

PETRUCCIO: Nay, come, Kate, come. You must not look so sour.

KATHERINE: It is my fashion when I see a crab.

PETRUCCIO: Why, here's no crab, and therefore look not sour.

KATHERINE: There is, there is.

PETRUCCIO: Then show it me.

KATHERINE: Had I a glass I would.

PETRUCCIO: What, you mean my face?

KATHERINE: Well aimed, of such a young one.

PETRUCCIO: Now, by Saint George, I am too young for you.

KATHERINE: Yet you are withered.

PETRUCCIO: 'Tis with cares.

KATHERINE: I care not.

PETRUCCIO: Nay, hear you, Kate. In sooth, you scape not so.

KATHERINE: I chafe you if I tarry. Let me go.

PETRUCCIO: No, not a whit. I find you passing gentle.
　　'Twas told me you were rough, and coy, and sullen,
　　And now I find report a very liar,
　　For thou art pleasant, gamesome, passing courteous,
　　But slow in speech, yet sweet as springtime flowers.
　　Thou canst not frown. Thou canst not look askance,
　　Nor bite the lip, as angry wenches will,
　　Nor hast thou pleasure to be cross in talk,
　　But thou with mildness entertain'st thy wooers,
　　With gentle conference, soft, and affable.

Why does the world report that Kate doth limp?
O sland'rous world! Kate like the hazel twig
Is straight and slender, and as brown in hue
As hazelnuts, and sweeter than the kernels.
O let me see thee walk. Thou dost not halt.

KATHERINE: Go, fool, and whom thou keep'st command.

PETRUCCIO: Did ever Dian so become a grove
As Kate this chamber with her princely gait?
O, be thou Dian, and let her be Kate,
And then let Kate be chaste and Dian sportful.

KATHERINE: Where did you study all this goodly speech?

PETRUCCIO: It is extempore, from my mother-wit.

KATHERINE: A witty mother, witless else her son.

PETRUCCIO: Am I not wise?

KATHERINE: Yes, keep you warm.

PETRUCCIO: Marry, so I mean, sweet Katherine, in thy bed.
And therefore setting all this chat aside,
Thus in plain terms: your father hath consented
That you shall be my wife, your dowry 'greed on,
And will you, nill you, I will marry you.
Now, Kate, I am a husband for your turn,
For by this light, whereby I see thy beauty—
Thy beauty that doth make me like thee well—
Thou must be married to no man but me,

> *Enter* BAPTISA, GREMIO, *and* TRANIO *as*
> LUCENTIO

For I am he am born to tame you, Kate,
And bring you from a wild Kate to a Kate
Conformable as other household Kates.
Here comes your father. Never make denial.
I must and will have Katherine to my wife.

BAPTISTA: Now, Signor Petruccio, how speed you with my daughter?

PETRUCCIO: How but well, sir, how but well?
It were impossible I should speed amiss.

BAPTISTA: Why, how now, daughter Katherine—in your dumps?

KATHERINE: Call you me daughter? Now I promise you
You have showed a tender fatherly regard,
To wish me wed to one half-lunatic,

> A madcap ruffian and a swearing Jack,
> That thinks with oaths to face the matter out.

PETRUCCIO: Father, 'tis thus: yourself and all the world
> That talked of her have talked amiss of her.
> If she be curst, it is for policy,
> For she's not froward, but modest as the dove.
> She is not hot, but temperate as the morn.
> For patience she will prove a second Grissel,
> And Roman Lucrece for her chastity.
> And to conclude, we have 'greed so well together
> That upon Sunday is the wedding day.

KATHERINE: I'll see thee hanged on Sunday first.

GREMIO: Hark, Petruccio, she says she'll see thee hanged first.

TRANIO: Is this your speeding? Nay then, goodnight our part.

PETRUCCIO: Be patient, gentlemen. I choose her for myself.
> If she and I be pleased, what's that to you?
> Tis bargained 'twixt us twain, being alone,
> That she shall still be curst in company.
> I tell you, 'tis incredible to believe
> How much she loves me. O, the kindest Kate!
> She hung about my neck, and kiss on kiss
> She vied so fast, protesting oath on oath,
> That in a twink she won me to her love.
> O, you are novices. 'Tis a world to see
> How tame, when men and women are alone,
> A meacock wretch can make the curstest shrew.
> Give me thy hand, Kate. I will unto Venice,
> To buy apparel 'gainst the wedding day.
> Provide the feast, father, and bid the guests.
> I will be sure my Katherine shall be fine.

It is interesting in this scene just how well-matched Petruccio and Katherine do seem to be; how each manages to reveal insincere and sincere emotions at the same time. Indeed, they genuinely and pleasantly surprise each other: both are strong-willed, sharp-witted people, unused to the invigoration the other presents. They come to the meeting expecting to dislike each other and are surprised how much they enjoy their little battle. Thus, we see that Petruccio is vulnerable and Katherine is marriageable, but only when each is faced with an equal in strength and intelligence.

Petruccio puts his plan to "tame" Katherine into effect on their wedding day. He is late for the wedding and has obviously been living prodigally while he has been away. This shocks everyone, including Katherine, whose sincerity of interest in Petruccio is made clear in this scene. Katherine's patience is tried still further when he takes her to her new home, and again, she passes his test.

Enter BAPTISTA, GREMIO, TRANIO *as*
LUCENTIO, KATHERINE, BIANCA, *and*
others, attendants

BAPTISTA (*to* TRANIO): Signor Lucentio, this is the 'pointed day
That Katherine and Petruccio should be married,
And yet we hear not of our son-in-law.
What will be said, what mockery will it be,
To want the bridegroom when the priest attends
To speak the ceremonial rites of marriage?
What says Lucentio to this shame of ours?

KATHERINE: No shame but mine. I must forsooth be forced
To give my hand opposed against my heart
Unto a mad-brain rudesby full of spleen,
Who wooed in haste and means to wed at leisure.
I told you, I, he was a frantic fool,
Hiding his bitter jests in blunt behaviour,
And to be noted for a merry man
He'll woo a thousand, 'point the day of marriage,
Make friends, invite them, and proclaim the banns,
Yet never means to wed where he hath wooed.
Now must the world point at poor Katherine
And say 'Lo, there is mad Petruccio's wife,
If it would please him come and marry her.'

TRANIO: Patience, good Katherine, and Baptista, too.
Upon my life, Petruccio means but well.
Whatever fortune stays him from his word,
Though he be blunt, I know him passing wise;
Though he be merry, yet withal he's honest.

KATHERINE: Would Katherine had never seen him, though.

Exit weeping

BAPTISTA: Go, girl. I cannot blame thee now to weep.
For such an injury would vex a very saint,
Much more a shrew of thy impatient humour.

⌐ ⌐ ⌐

Enter PETRUCCIO *and* GRUMIO,
fantastically dressed

PETRUCCIO: Come, where be these gallants? Who's at home?

BAPTISTA: You are welcome, sir.

PETRUCCIO: And yet I come not well.

BAPTISTA: And yet you halt not.

TRANIO: Not so well apparelled as I wish you were.

PETRUCCIO: Were it not better I should rush in thus—
  But where is Kate? Where is my lovely bride?
  How does my father? Gentles, methinks you frown.
  And wherefore gaze this goodly company
  As if they saw some wondrous monument,
  Some comet or unusual prodigy?

BAPTISTA: Why, sir, you know this is your wedding day.
  First were we sad, fearing you would not come;
  Now sadder that you come so unprovided.
  Fie, doff this habit, shame to your estate,
  An eyesore to our solemn festival.

TRANIO: And tell us what occasion of import
  Hath all so long detained you from your wife
  And sent you hither so unlike yourself?

PETRUCCIO: Tedious it were to tell, and harsh to hear.
  Sufficeth I am come to keep my word,
  Though in some part enforced to digress,
  Which at more leisure I will so excuse
  As you shall well be satisfied withal.
  But where is Kate? I stay too long from her.
  The morning wears, 'tis time we were at church.

TRANIO: See not your bride in these unreverent robes.
  Go to my chamber, put on clothes of mine.

PETRUCCIO: Not I, believe me. Thus I'll visit her.

BAPTISTA: But thus, I trust, you will not marry her.

PETRUCCIO: Good sooth, even thus. Therefore ha' done with words.
  To me she's married, not unto my clothes.
  Could I repair what she will wear in me
  As I can change these poor accoutrements,
  'Twere well for Kate and better for myself.
  But what a fool am I to chat with you
  When I should bid good morrow to my bride,
  And seal the title with a lovely kiss!

Exit [*with* GRUMIO]

ෙ ෙ ෙ

[All exit]

[*Enter* LUCENTIO *as* CAMBIO, *and* TRANIO
as LUCENTIO]

TRANIO: And is the bride and bridegroom coming home?

GREMIO: A bridegroom, say you? 'Tis a groom indeed—
A grumbling groom, and that the girl shall find.

TRANIO: Curster than she? Why, 'tis impossible.

GREMIO: Why, he's a devil, a devil, a very fiend.

TRANIO: Why, she's a devil, a devil, the devil's dam.

GREMIO: Tut, she's a lamb, a dove, a fool to him.
I'll tell you, Sir Lucentio: when the priest
Should ask if Katherine should be his wife,
'Ay, by Gog's woun's,' quoth he, and swore so loud
That all amazed the priest let fall the book,
And as he stooped again to take it up
This mad-brained bridegroom took him such a cuff
That down fell priest, and book, and book, and priest.
'Now take them up,' quoth he, 'if any list.'

TRANIO: What said the vicar when he rose again?

GREMIO: Trembled and shook, forwhy he stamped and swore
As if the vicar meant to cozen him.
But after many ceremonies done
He calls for wine. 'A health,' quoth he, as if
He had been aboard, carousing to his mates
After a storm; quaffed off the muscatel
And threw the sops all in the sexton's face,
Having no other reason
But that his beard grew thin and hungerly
And seemed to ask him sops as he was drinking.
This done, he took the bride about the neck
And kissed her lips with such a clamorous smack
That at the parting all the church did echo,
And I seeing this came thence for very shame,
And after me, I know, the rout is coming.
Such a mad marriage never was before.

Music plays

Hark, hark, I hear the minstrels play.

Enter PETRUCCIO, KATHERINE, BIANCA,
HORTENSIO *as* LICIO, BAPTISTA, GRUMIO,
and others, attendants

PETRUCCIO: Gentlemen and friends, I thank you for your pains.
I know you think to dine with me today,
And have prepared great store of wedding cheer.
But so it is my haste doth call me hence,
And therefore here I mean to take my leave.

BAPTISTA: Is't possible you will away tonight?

PETRUCCIO: I must away today, before night come.
Make it no wonder. If you knew my business,
You would entreat me rather go than stay.
And, honest company, I thank you all
That have beheld me give away myself
To this most patient, sweet, and virtuous wife.
Dine with my father, drink a health to me,
For I must hence; and farewell to you all.

TRANIO: Let us entreat you stay till after dinner.

PETRUCCIO: It may not be.

GREMIO: Let me entreat you.

PETRUCCIO: It cannot be.

KATHERINE: Let me entreat you.

PETRUCCIO: I am content.

KATHERINE: Are you content to stay?

PETRUCCIO: I am content you shall entreat me stay,
But yet not stay, entreat me how you can.

KATHERINE: Now, if you love me, stay.

PETRUCCIO: Grumio, my horse.

GRUMIO: Ay, sir, they be ready. The oats have eaten the horses.

KATHERINE: Nay, then, do what thou canst, I will not go today,
No, nor tomorrow—not till I please myself.
The door is open, sir, there lies your way.
You may be jogging whiles your boots are green.
For me, I'll not be gone till I please myself.
'Tis like you'll prove a jolly, surly groom,
That take it on you at the first so roundly.

PETRUCCIO: O Kate, content thee. Prithee, be not angry.

KATHERINE: I will be angry. What hast thou to do?
Father, be quiet. He shall stay me leisure.

GREMIO: Ay, marry, sir. Now it begins to work.

KATHERINE: Gentlemen, forward to the bridal dinner.
  I see a woman may be made a fool
  If she had not a spirit to resist.

PETRUCCIO: They shall go forward, Kate, at thy command.
  Obey the bride, you that attend on her.
  Go to the feast, revel and domineer,
  Carouse full measure to her maidenhead.
  Be mad and merry, or go hang yourselves.
  But for my bonny Kate, she must with me.
  Nay, look not big, nor stamp, nor stare, nor fret.
  I will be master of what is mine own.
  She is my goods, my chattels. She is my house,
  My household-stuff, my field, my barn,
  My horse, my ox, my ass, my anything,
  And here she stands, touch her whoever dare.
  I'll bring mine action on the proudest he
  That stops my way in Padua. Grumio,
  Draw forth thy weapon, we are beset with thieves.
  Rescue thy mistress if thou be a man.
  Fear not, sweet wench. They shall not touch thee, Kate.

CURTIS: All ready, and therefore, I pray thee, news.

GRUMIO: First, know my horse is tired, my master and mistress fallen out.

CURTIS: How?

GRUMIO: Out of their saddles into the dirt, and thereby hangs a tale.

CURTIS: Let's ha't, good Grumio.

GRUMIO: Lend thine ear.

CURTIS: Here.

GRUMIO: (*cuffing him*) There.

CURTIS: This 'tis to feel a tale, not to hear a tale.

GRUMIO: And therefore 'tis called a sensible tale, and this cuff was but to knock
  at your ear and beseech listening. Now I begin. *Inprimis*, we came down a
  foul hill, my master riding behind my mistress.

CURTIS: Both of one horse?

GRUMIO: What's that to thee?

CURTIS: Why, a horse.

GRUMIO: Tell thou the tale. But hadst thou not crossed me thou shouldst have heard how her horse fell and she under her horse; thou shouldst have heard in how miry a place, how she was bemoiled, how he left her with the horse upon her, how he beat me because her horse stumbled, how she waded through the dirt to pluck him off me, how he swore, how she prayed that never prayed before, how I cried, how the horses ran away, how her bridle was burst, how I lost my crupper, with many things of worthy memory which now shall die in oblivion, and thou return unexperienced to thy grave.

CURTIS: By this reckoning he is more shrew than she.

Enter PETRUCCIO *and* KATHERINE

PETRUCCIO: Where be these knaves? What, no man at door
  To hold my stirrup nor to take my horse?
  Where is Nathaniel, Gregory, Philip?

ALL SERVANTS: Here, here sir, here sir.

PETRUCCIO: Here sir, here sir, here sir, here sir!
  You logger-headed and unpolished grooms,
  What! No attendance! No regard! No duty!

(*Kicking a servant*) Take that, and mend the plucking of the other.
  Be merry, Kate. (*Calling*) Some water, here. What, hoa!

Enter one with water

Where's my spaniel Troilus? Sirrah, get you hence,
And bid my cousin Ferdinand come hither—
One, Kate, that you must kiss and be acquainted with.
(*Calling*) Where are my slippers? Shall I have some water?
Come, Kate, and wash, and welcome heartily.

[A servant drops water]

You whoreson villain, will you let it fall?

KATHERINE: Patience, I pray you, 'twas a fault unwilling.

PETRUCCIO: A whoreson, beetle-headed, flap-eared knave.
  Come, Kate, sit down, I know you have a stomach.
  Will you give thanks, sweet Kate, or else shall I?
  What's this—mutton?

FIRST SERVINGMAN: Ay.

PETRUCCIO: Who brought it?

PETER: I.

PETRUCCIO: 'Tis burnt, and so is all the meat.
What dogs are these? Where is the rascal cook?
How durst you villains bring it from the dresser
And serve it thus to me that love it not?
There, (*throwing food*) take it to you, trenchers, cups, and all,
You heedless jolt-heads and unmannered slaves.
What, do you grumble? I'll be with you straight.

He chases the servants away

KATHERINE: I pray you, husband, be not so disquiet.
The meat was well, if you were so contented.

PETRUCCIO: I tell thee, Kate, 'twas burnt and dried away,
And I expressly am forbid to touch it,
For it engenders choler, planteth anger,
And better 'twere that both of us did fast,
Since of ourselves ourselves are choleric,
Than feed it with such overroasted flesh.
Be patient, tomorrow't shall be mended,
And for this night we'll fast for company.
Come, I will bring there to thy bridal chamber. *Exeunt*

Enter servants severally

NATHANIEL: Peter, didst ever see the like?

PETER: He kills her in her own humour.

Enter CURTIS, *a servant*

GRUMIO: Where is he?

CURTIS: In her chamber,
Making a sermon of continency to her,
And ralls, and swears, and rates, that she, poor soul,
Knows not which way to stand, to look, to speak,
And sits as one new risen from a dream.
Away, away, for he is coming hither.   *Exeunt*

Enter PETRUCCIO

PETRUCCIO: Thus have I politicly begun my reign,
And 'tis my hope to end successfully.
My falcon now is sharp and passing empty,
And till she stoop she must not be full-gorged,
For then she never looks upon her lure.
Another way I have to man my haggard,
To make her come and know her keeper's call—

That is, to watch her as we watch these kites
That bate and beat, and will not be obedient.
She ate no meat today, nor none shall eat.
Last night she slept not, nor tonight she shall not.
As with the meat, some undeserved fault
I'll find about the making of the bed,
And here I'll fling the pillow, there the bolster,
This way the coverlet, another way the sheets,
Ay, and amid this hurly I intend
That all is done in reverent care of her,
And in conclusion she shall watch all night,
And if she chance to nod I'll rall and brawl
And with the clamour keep her still awake.
This is a way to kill a wife with kindness,
And thus I'll curb her mad and headstrong humour.
He that knows better how to tame a shrew,
Now let him speak. 'Tis charity to show.   *Exit*

When Katherine's "training" has progressed, Petruccio makes plans to show off his triumph to her father and the others. As they near home, the audience, too, can witness Petruccio's success.

Enter KATHERINE *and* GRUMIO

KATHERINE: The more my wrong, the more his spite appears.
What, did he marry me to famish me?
Beggars that come unto my father's door
Upon entreaty have a present alms,
If not, elsewhere they meet with charity.
But I, who never knew how to entreat,
Nor never needed that I should entreat,
Am starved for meat, giddy for lack of sleep,
With oaths kept waking and with brawling fed,
And that which spites me more than all these wants,
He does it under name of perfect love,
As who should say if I should sleep or eat
'Twere deadly sickness, or else present death.
I prithee, go and get me some repast.
I care not what, so it be wholesome food.

GRUMIO: What say you to a neat's foot?

KATHERINE: 'Tis passing good. I prithee, let me have it.

GRUMIO: I fear it is too choleric a meat.
How say you to a fat tripe finely broiled?

KATHERINE: I like it well. Good Grumio, fetch it me.

GRUMIO: I cannot tell, I fear 'tis choleric.
What say you to a piece of beef, and mustard?

KATHERINE: A dish that I do love to feed upon.

GRUMIO: Ay, but the mustard is too hot a little.

KATHERINE: Why then, the beef, and let the mustard rest.

GRUMIO: Nay, then I will not. You shall have the mustard,
Or else you get no beef of Grumio.

KATHERINE: Then both, or one, or anything thou wilt.

GRUMIO: Why then, the mustard without the beef.

KATHERINE: Go, get thee gone, thou false, deluding slave,
(*Beating him*) That feed'st me with the very name of meat.
Sorrow on thee and all the pack of you,
That triumph thus upon my misery.
Go, get thee gone, I say.

> *Enter* PETRUCCIO *and* HORTENSIO, *with*
> *meat*

PETRUCCIO: How fares my Kate? What, sweeting, all amort?

HORTENSIO: Mistress, what cheer?

KATHERINE: Faith, as cold as can be.

PETRUCCIO: Pluck up thy spirits, look cheerfully upon me.
Here, love, thou seest how diligent I am
To dress thy meat myself and bring it thee.
I am sure, sweet Kate, this kindness merits thanks.
What, not a word? Nay then, thou lov'st it not,
And all my pains is sorted to no proof.
Here, take away this dish.

KATHERINE: I pray you, let it stand.

PETRUCCIO: The poorest service is repaid with thanks,
And so shall mine before you touch the meat.

KATHERINE: I thank you, sir.

HORTENSIO: Signor Petruccio, fie, you are to blame.
Come, Mistress Kate, I'll bear you company.

PETRUCCIO (*aside*): Eat it up all, Hortensio, if thou lov'st me.
(*To* KATHERINE) Much good do it unto thy gentle heart.
Kate, eat apace; and now, my honey love,
Will we return unto thy father's house,

And revel it as bravely as the best,
With silken coats, and caps, and golden rings,
With ruffs, and cuffs, and farthingales, and things,
With scarves, and fans, and double change of bravery,
With amber bracelets, beads, and all this knavery.
What, hast thou dined? The tailor stays thy leisure,

Enter TAILOR *with a gown*

Come, tailor, let us see these ornaments.
Lay forth the gown.

Enter HABERDASHER *with a cap*

What news with you, sir?

HABERDASHER: Here is the cap your worship did bespeak.

PETRUCCIO: Why, this was moulded on a porringer—
A velvet dish. Fie, fie, 'tis lewd and filthy.
Why, 'tis a cockle or a walnut-shell,
A knack, a toy, a trick, a baby's cap.
Away with it! Come, let me have a bigger.

KATHERINE: I'll have no bigger. This doth fit the time,
And gentlewomen wear such caps as these.

PETRUCCIO: When you are gentle you shall have one, too,
And not till then.

HORTENSIO (*aside*): That will not be in haste.

KATHERINE: Why, sir, I trust I may have leave to speak,
And speak I will. I am no child, no babe.
Your betters have endured me say my mind,
And if you cannot, best you stop your ears.
My tongue will tell the anger of my heart,
Or else my heart concealing it will break,
And rather than it shall I will be free
Even to the uttermost as I please in words.

PETRUCCIO: Why, thou sayst true. It is a paltry cap,
A custard-coffin, a bauble, a silken pie.
I love thee well in that thou like'st it not.   .

KATHERINE: Love me or love me not, I like the cap
And it I will have, or I will have none.

[*Exit* HABERDASHER]

PETRUCCIO: Thy gown? Why, ay. Come, tailor, let us see't.
O mercy, God, what masquing stuff is here?

What's this—a sleeve? 'Tis like a demi-cannon.
What, up and down carved like an apple-tart?
Here's snip, and nip, and cut, and slish and slash,
Like to a scissor in a barber's shop.
Why, what o'devil's name, tailor, call'st thou this?

HORTENSIO (*aside*): I see she's like to have nor cap nor gown.

TAILOR: You bid me make it orderly and well,

☙ ☙ ☙

Exit TAILOR

PETRUCCIO: Well, come, my Kate. We will unto your father's
Even in these honest, mean habiliments.
Our purses shall be proud, our garments poor,
For 'tis the mind that makes the body rich,
And as the sun breaks through the darkest clouds,
So honour peereth in the meanest habit.
What, is the jay more precious than the lark
Because his feathers are more beautiful?
Or is the adder better than the eel
Because his painted skin contents the eye?
O no, good Kate, neither art thou the worse
For this poor furniture and mean array.
If thou account'st it shame, lay it on me,
And therefore frolic; we will hence forthwith
To feast and sport us at thy father's house.
Go call my men, and let us straight to him,
And bring our horses unto Long Lane end.
There will we mount, and thither walk on foot.
Let's see, I think 'tis now some seven o'clock,
And well we may come there by dinner-time.

☙ ☙ ☙

Exeunt

☙ ☙ ☙

Enter PETRUCCIO, KATHERINE, HORTENSIO,
and SERVANTS

PETRUCCIO: Come on, I' God's name. Once more toward our father's.
Good Lord, how bright and goodly shines the moon!

KATHERINE: The moon?—the sun. It is not moonlight now.

PETRUCCIO: I say it is the moon that shines so bright.

KATHERINE: I know it is the sun that shines so bright.

PETRUCCIO: Now, by my mother's son—and that's myself—
    It shall be moon, or star, or what I list
    Or ere I journey to your father's house.
    Go on, and fetch our horses back again.
    Evermore crossed and crossed, nothing but crossed.

HORTENSIO (*to* KATHERINE): Say as he says or we shall never go.

KATHERINE: Forward, I pray, since we have come so far,
    And be it moon or sun or what you please,
    And if you please to call it a rush-candle
    Henceforth I vow it shall be so for me.

PETRUCCIO: I say it is the moon.

KATHERINE: I know it is the moon.

PETRUCCIO: Nay then you lie, it is the blessed sun.

KATHERINE: Then God be blessed, it is the blessed sun,
    But sun it is not when you say it is not,
    And the moon changes even as your mind.
    What you will have it named, even that it is,
    And so it shall be still for Katherine.

HORTENSIO: Petruccio, go thy ways. The field is won.

MARRIAGES COMPARED

Petruccio and Katherine arrive in Padua just as Lucentio reveals to Baptista that he
and Bianca have eloped; Hortensio, on the "rebound" over Bianca, has married a
wealthy Paduan widow. Thus, the play closes (as do many Shakespearean comedies
and romances) with a wedding party.

> *Enter* BAPTISTA, VINCENTIO, GREMIO, THE
> PEDANT, LUCENTIO *and* BIANCA,
> PETRUCCIO, KATHERINE, *and* HORTENSIO,
> TRANIO, BIONDELLO, GRUMIO, *and* THE
> WIDOW, THE SERVINGMEN *with* TRANIO
> *bringing in a banquet*

LUCENTIO: While I with selfsame kindness welcome thine.
    Brother Petruccio, sister Katherina,
    And thou, Hortensio, with thy loving widow,
    Feast with the best, and welcome to my house.
    My banquet is to close our stomachs up
    After our great good cheer. Pray you, sit down,
    For now we sit to chat as well as eat.

They sit

PETRUCCIO: Nothing but sit, and sit, and eat, and eat.

BAPTISTA: Padua affords this kindness, son Petruccio.

PETRUCCIO: Padua affords nothing but what is kind.

HORTENSIO: For both our sakes I would that word were true.

PETRUCCIO: Now, for my life, Hortensio fears his widow.

WIDOW: Then never trust me if I be afeard.

PETRUCCIO: You are very sensible, and yet you miss my sense.
    I mean Hortensio is afeard of you.

WIDOW: He that is giddy thinks the world turns round.

PETRUCCIO: Roundly replied.

KATHERINE: Mistress, how mean you that?

WIDOW: Thus I conceive by him.

PETRUCCIO: Conceives by me! How likes Hortensio that?

HORTENSIO: My widow says thus she conceives her tale.

PETRUCCIO: Very well mended. Kiss him for that, good widow.

KATHERINE: 'He that is giddy thinks the world turns round'—
    I pray you tell me what you meant by that.

WIDOW: Your husband, being troubled with a shrew,
    Measures my husband's sorrow by his woe.
    And now you know my meaning.

KATHERINE: A very mean meaning.

WIDOW: Right, I mean you.

KATHERINE: And I am mean indeed respecting you.

PETRUCCIO: To her, Kate!

HORTENSIO: To her, widow!

PETRUCCIO: A hundred marks my Kate does put her down.

HORTENSIO: That's my office.

PETRUCCIO: Spoke like an officer! Ha' to thee, lad.

He drinks to HORTENSIO

BAPTISTA: How likes Gremio these quick-witted folks?

GREMIO: Believe me, sir, they butt together well.

BIANCA: Head and butt? An hasty-witted body
   Would say your head and butt were head and horn.

VINCENTIO: Ay, mistress bride, hath that awakened you?

BIANCA: Ay, but not frighted me, therefore I'll sleep again.

PETRUCCIO: Nay, that you shall not. Since you have begun,
   Have at you for a better jest or two.

BIANCA: Am I your bird? I mean to shift my bush,
   And then pursue me as you draw your bow.
   You are welcome all.

> *Exit* BIANCA *with* KATHERINE *and the*
> WIDOW

PETRUCCIO: She hath prevented me here, Signor Tranio.
   This bird you aimed at, though you hit her not.
   Therefore a health to all that shot and missed.

TRANIO: O sir, Lucentio slipped me like his greyhound,
   Which runs himself and catches for his master.

PETRUCCIO: A good swift simile, but something currish.

TRANIO: 'Tis well, sir, that you hunted for yourself.
   'Tis thought your deer does hold you at a bay.

BAPTISTA: O, O, Petruccio, Tranio hits you now.

LUCENTIO: I thank thee for that gird, good Tranio.

HORTENSIO: Confess, confess, hath he not hit you here?

PETRUCCIO: A has a little galled me, I confess,
   And as the jest did glance away from me
   'Tis ten to one it maimed you two outright.

BAPTISTA: Now in good sadness, son Petruccio,
   I think thou hast the veriest shrew of all.

PETRUCCIO: Well, I say no.—And therefore, Sir Assurance,
   Let's each one send unto his wife,
   And he whose wife is most obedient
   To come at first when he doth send for her
   Shall win the wager which we will propose.

HORTENSIO: Content. What's the wager?

LUCENTIO: Twenty crowns.

PETRUCCIO: Twenty crowns!
  I'll venture so much of my hawk or hound,
  But twenty times so much upon my wife.

LUCENTIO: A hundred, then.

HORTENSIO: Content.

PETRUCCIO: A match, 'tis done.

HORTENSIO: Who shall begin?

LUCENTIO: That will I.
  Go, Biondello, bid your mistress come to me.

BIONDELLO: I go.   *Exit*

BAPTISTA: Son, I'll be your half Bianca comes.

LUCENTIO: I'll have no halves, I'll bear it all myself.

Enter BIONDELLO

  How now, what news?

BIONDELLO: Sir, my mistress sends you word
  That she is busy and she cannot come.

PETRUCCIO: How? She's busy and she cannot come?
  Is that an answer?

GREMIO: Ay, and a kind one, too.
  Pray God, sir, your wife send you not a worse.

PETRUCCIO: I hope, better.

HORTENSIO: Sirrah Biondello,
  Go and entreat my wife to come to me forthwith.

Exit BIONDELLO

PETRUCCIO: O ho, 'entreat' her—nay, then she must needs come.

HORTENSIO: I am afraid, sir, do what you can,

Enter BIONDELLO

  Yours will not be entreated. Now, where's my wife?

BIONDELLO: She says you have some goodly jest in hand.
  She will not come. She bids you come to her.

PETRUCCIO: Worse and worse! She will not come—O vile,
  Intolerable, not to be endured!
  Sirrah Grumio, go to your mistress.
  Say I command her come to me.   *Exit* GRUMIO

HORTENSIO: I know her answer.

PETRUCCIO: What?

HORTENSIO: She will not.

PETRUCCIO: The fouler fortune mine, and there an end.

Enter KATHERINE

BAPTISTA: Now by my halidom, here comes Katherina.

KATHERINE (*to* PETRUCCIO): What is your will, sir, that you send for me?

PETRUCCIO: Where is your sister and Hortensio's wife?

KATHERINE: They sit conferring by the parlour fire.

PETRUCCIO: Go, fetch them hither. If they deny to come,
    Swinge me them soundly forth unto their husbands.
    Away, I say, and bring them hither straight.

Exit KATHERINE

LUCENTIO: Here is a wonder, if you talk of wonders.

HORTENSIO: And so it is. I wonder what it bodes.

PETRUCCIO: Marry, peace it bodes, and love, and quiet life;
    An aweful rule and right supremacy,
    And, to be short, what not that's sweet and happy.

BAPTISTA: Now fair befall thee, good Petruccio,
    The wager thou hast won, and I will add
    Unto their losses twenty thousand crowns,
    Another dowry to another daughter,
    For she is changed as she had never been.

PETRUCCIO: Nay, I will win my wager better yet,
    And show more sign of her obedience,
    Her new-built virtue and obedience.

Enter KATHERINE, BIANCA, *and the* WIDOW

See where she comes, and brings your froward wives
As prisoners to her womanly persuasion.
Katherine, that cap of yours becomes you not.
Off with that bauble, throw it underfoot.

KATHERINE *throws down her cap*

WIDOW: Lord, let me never have a cause to sigh
    Till I be brought to such a silly pass.

BIANCA: Fie, what a foolish duty call you this?

LUCENTIO: I would your duty were as foolish, too.
>   The wisdom of your duty, fair Bianca,
>   Hath cost me a hundred crowns since supper-time.

BIANCA: The more fool you for laying on my duty.

PETRUCCIO: Katherine, I charge thee tell these headstrong women
>   What duty they do owe their lords and husbands.

WIDOW: Come, come, you're mocking. We will have no telling.

PETRUCCIO: Come on, I say, and first begin with her.

WIDOW: She shall not.

PETRUCCIO: I say she shall: and first begin with her.

KATHERINE: Fie, fie, unknit that threat'ning, unkind brow,
>   And dart not scornful glances from those eyes
>   To wound thy lord, thy king, thy governor.
>   It blots thy beauty as frosts do bite the meads,
>   Confounds thy fame as whirlwinds shake fair buds,
>   And in no sense is meet or amiable.
>   A woman moved is like a fountain troubled,
>   Muddy, ill-seeing, thick, bereft of beauty,
>   And while it is so, none so dry or thirsty
>   Will deign to sip or touch one drop of it.
>   Thy husband is thy lord, thy life, thy keeper,
>   Thy head, thy sovereign, one that cares for thee,
>   And for thy maintenance commits his body
>   To painful labour both by sea and land,
>   To watch the night in storms, the day in cold,
>   Whilst thou liest warm at home, secure and safe,
>   And craves no other tribute at thy hands
>   But love, fair looks, and true obedience,
>   Too little payment for so great a debt.
>   Such duty as the subject owes the prince,
>   Even such a woman oweth to her husband,
>   And when she is froward, peevish, sullen, sour,
>   And not obedient to his honest will,
>   What is she but a foul contending rebel,
>   And graceless traitor to her loving lord?
>   I am ashamed that women are so simple
>   To offer war where they should kneel for peace,
>   Or seek for rule, supremacy, and sway
>   When they are bound to serve, love, and obey.
>   Why are our bodies soft, and weak, and smooth,
>   Unapt to toil and trouble in the world,

> But that our soft conditions and our hearts
> Should well agree with our external parts?
> Come, come, you froward and unable worms,
> My mind hath been as big as one of yours,
> My heart as great, my reason haply more,
> To bandy word for word and frown for frown;
> But now I see our lances are but straws,
> Our strength as weak, our weakness past compare,
> That seeming to be most which we indeed least are.
> Then vail your stomachs, for it is no boot,
> And place your hands below your husband's foot,
> In token of which duty, if he please,
> My hand is ready, may it do him ease.

PETRUCCIO: Why, there's a wench! Come on, and kiss me, Kate.

They kiss

LUCENTIO: Well, go thy ways, old lad, for thou shalt ha't.

VINCENTIO: 'Tis a good hearing when children are toward.

LUCENTIO: But a harsh hearing when women are froward.

PETRUCCIO: Come, Kate, we'll to bed.
> We three are married, but you two are sped.
> 'Twas I won the wager, though (*to* LUCENTIO) you hit the white,
> And being a winner, God give you good night,

Exit PETRUCCIO *with* KATHERINE

Of the three marriages, Petruccio's to Katherine is represented as the most blessed, and of the three wives, Katherine appears the most faithful and loving. On the one hand, this point is made merely as a sort of "word to the wise" on Shakespeare's part, regarding the unpredictability and inevitable trials of marriage; more importantly, however, it is made through a comparison of the lesser characters to Katherine and Petruccio. Indeed, because of the foreshadowings present in earlier scenes, we can see that Bianca and Katherine have always had the potential that they enact here.

Katherine, in particular, effects a tremendous transformation of character, while yet retaining her strength of will; indeed, she remains a "shrew" towards everyone but Petruccio. Katherine's closing speech is thought-provoking, leading the audience to inquire into the "nature" vs. the "conventions" of women's character. Would a less willful character than Katherine be capable of the devotion she demonstrates here? Is her turnaround a masquerade, or has Petruccio changed her nature? Perhaps most perplexing is Shakespeare's willingness to leave these questions unanswered, implying perhaps that the issue of Katherine's sincerity, or in other words, of her "nature" as opposed to her behavior in marriage, is less important than we might like to think.

MACBETH (1606)

In the great tragedy *Macbeth,* Shakespeare gives us a darker, and indeed a more philosophically profound working of the puzzles of human nature and culture and of the capacities of femininity and masculinity than in the "Shrew." In this story—an historical fiction—Macbeth, a general in the Scottish army, kills King Duncan of Scotland in order to usurp the throne. But the violent action of the play is of secondary importance compared to the spiritual agonies of Macbeth himself. The play is in essence a study of the submission of a noble character to evil influences and inclinations.

THE WITCHES (THE "WEIRD SISTERS")

The play begins with a show of King Duncan's nobility and largess: he decides, on account of their heroism, to promote Captain Macbeth and his compatriot Captain Banquo, to the generalship. In contrast to the straightforward and honorable King Duncan, early scenes present us with the eerie machinations and predictions of three witches, boding ill for Macbeth and Duncan.

ACT FIRST
SCENE I.—[*A wild, open place.*]

> *Thunder and lightning. Enter the* THREE WITCHES.

FIRST WITCH: When shall we three meet again? In thunder, lightning, or in rain?

SECOND WITCH: When the hurlyburly's done, When the battle's lost and won.

THIRD WITCH: That will be ere the set of sun.

FIRST WITCH: Where the place?

SEC. WITCH: Upon the heath.

THIRD WITCH: There to meet with Macbeth.

FIRST WITCH: I come, Graymalkin.

[SEC. WITCH.] Paddock calls.

[THIRD WITCH.] Anon!

ALL: Fair is foul, and foul is fair;
    Hover through the fog and filthy air.

> *Exeunt.*

SCENE II.—[*A camp near Forres.*]

> *Alarum within. Enter* KING DUNCAN, MALCOLM, DONALBAIN, LENNOX, *with* ATTENDANTS, *meeting a bleeding* CAPTAIN.

≈ ≈ ≈

CAP: . . . Mark, King of Scotland, mark;—
No sooner justice had, with valour arm'd,
Compell'd these skipping kerns to trust their heels,
But the Norweyan lord, surveying vantage,
With furbish'd arms and new supplies of men,
Began a fresh assault.

DUN: Dismay'd not this
Our captains, Macbeth and Banquo?

CAP: Yes,
As sparrows eagles, or the hare the lion.
If I say sooth, I must report they were
As cannons overcharg'd with double cracks; so they
Doubly redoubled strokes upon the foe.

≈ ≈ ≈

[*Exit* CAPTAIN, *attended.*]
Enter ROSS *and* ANGUS.

MAL: The worthy thane of Ross

LEN: What a haste looks through his eyes! So should he look
That seems to speak things strange.

ROSS: God save the king!

DUN: Whence cam'st thou, worthy thane?

ROSS: From Fife, great king,
Where the Norweyan banners flout the sky
And fan our people cold. Norway himself,
With terrible numbers,
Assisted by that most disloyal traitor
The thane of Cawdor, began a dismal conflict,
Till that Bellona's bridegroom, lapp'd in proof,
Confronted him with self-comparisons,
Point against point rebellious, arm gainst arm,
Curbing his lavish spirit; and, to conclude,
The victory fell on us.

DUN: Great happiness!

ROSS: That now
Sweno, the Norways' king, craves composition;
Nor would we deign him burial of his men
Till he disbursed at Saint Colme's Inch
Ten thousand dollars to our general use.

DUN: No more that thane of Cawdor shall deceive
Our bosom interest. Go pronounce his present death,
And with his former title greet Macbeth.

ROSS: I'll see it done.

DUN: What he hath lost noble Macbeth hath won.

Exeunt.

SCENE III.—[*A heath near Forres.*]

Thunder. Enter the THREE WITCHES.

FIRST WITCH: Where hast thou been, sister?

SEC. WITCH: Killing swine.

THIRD WITCH: Sister, where thou?

FIRST WITCH: A sailor's wife had chestnuts in her lap,
And munch'd, and munch'd, and munch'd:—'Give me,' quoth I:
'Aroint thee, witch!' the rump-fed ronyon cries.
Her husband's to Aleppo gone, master o' the Tiger:
But in a sieve I'll thither sail,
And, like a rat without a tail,
I'll do, I'll do, and I'll do.

SEC. WITCH: I'll give thee a wind.

FIRST WITCH: Thou 'rt kind.

THIRD WITCH: And I another.

FIRST WITCH: I myself have all the other,
And the very ports they blow,
All the quarters that they know
I' the shipman's card.
I will drain him dry as hay:
Sleep shall neither night nor day
Hang upon his pent-house lid;
He shall live a man forbid:
Weary se'nnights nine times nine
Shall he dwindle, peak and pine:
Though his bark cannot be lost,
Yet it shall be tempest-tost.
Look what I have.

SEC. WITCH: Show me, show me.

FIRST WITCH: Here I have a pilot's thumb,
Wreck'd as homeward he did come.

Drum within.

THIRD WITCH: A drum, a drum!
 Macbeth doth come.

ALL: The weird sisters, hand in hand,
 Posters of the sea and land,
 Thus do go about, about:
 Thrice to thine and thrice to mine
 And thrice again, to make up nine.

[Dance.]

Peace! the charm's wound up.

Enter MACBETH *and* BANQUO.

MACB: So foul and fair a day I have not seen.

BAN: How far is't call'd to Forres? What are these
 So wither'd and so wild in their attire,
 That look not like the inhabitants o' the earth,
 And yet are on't? Live you? or are you aught
 That man may question? You seem to understand me,
 By each at once her choppy finger laying
 Upon her skinny lips. You should be women,
 And yet your beards forbid me to interpret
 That you are so.

MACB: Speak, if you can: what are you?

FIRST WITCH: All hail, Macbeth! hail to thee, thane of Glamis!

SEC. WITCH: All hail, Macbeth! hail to thee, thane of Cawdor!

THIRD WITCH: All hail, Macbeth, that shalt be king hereafter!

BAN: Good sir, why do you start, and seem to fear
 Things that do sound so fair? I' the name of truth,
 Are ye fantastical, or that indeed
 Which outwardly ye show? My noble partner
 You greet with present grace and great prediction
 Of noble having and of royal hope,
 That he seems rapt withal; to me you speak not.
 If you can look into the seeds of time,
 And say which grain will grow and which will not,
 Speak then to me, who neither beg nor fear
 Your favours nor your hate.

FIRST WITCH: Hail!

SEC. WITCH: Hail!

THIRD WITCH: Hail!

FIRST WITCH: Lesser than Macbeth, and greater.

SEC. WITCH: Not so happy, yet much happier.

THIRD WITCH: Thou shalt get kings, though thou be none:
  So all hail, Macbeth and Banquo!

FIRST WITCH: Banquo and Macbeth, all hail!

MACB: Stay, you imperfect speakers, tell me more.
  By Sinel's death I know I am thane of Glamis;
  But how of Cawdor? The thane of Cawdor lives,
  A prosperous gentleman; and to be king
  Stands not within the prospect of brief,
  No more than to be Cawdor. Say from whence
  You owe this strange intelligence? or why
  Upon this blasted heath you stop our way
  With such prophetic greeting? Speak, I charge you.

WITCHES vanish.

BAN: The earth hath bubbles, as the water has,
  And these are of them. Whither are they vanish'd?

MACB: Into the air; and what seem'd corporal melted
  As breath into the wind. Would they had stay'd!

BAN: Were such things here as we do speak about?
  Or have we eaten on the finsane root
  That takes the reason prisoner?

MACB: Your children shall be kings.

BAN: You shall be king.

MACB: And thane of Cawdor too: went it not so?

BAN: To the selfsame tune and words. Who's here?

Enter ROSS and ANGUS.

ROSS: The king hath happily receiv'd, Macbeth,
  The news of thy success; and when he reads
  Thy personal venture in the rebels' fight,
  His wonders and his praises do contend
  Which should be thine or his. Silenc'd with that,
  In viewing o'er the rest o' the selfsame day,
  He finds thee in the stout Norweyan ranks,
  Nothing afeard of what thyself didst make,
  Strange images of death. As thick as tale

    Came post with post; and every one did bear
    Thy praises in his kingdom's great defence,
    And pour'd them down before him.

ANG: We are sent
    To give thee from our royal master thanks,
    Only to herald thee into his sight,
    Not pay thee.

ROSS: And, for an earnest of a greater honour,
    He bade me, from him, call thee thane of Cawdor:
    In which addition, hail, most worthy thane!
    For it is thine.

BAN: What, can the devil speak true?

MACB: The thane of Cawdor lives: why do you dress me
    In borrow'd robes?

ANG: Who was the thane lives yet;
    But under heavy judgement bears that life
    Which he deserves to lose. Whether he was combin'd
    With those of Norway, or did line the rebel
    With hidden help and vantage, or that with both
    He labour'd in his country's wreck, I know not;
    But treasons capital, confess'd and prov'd,
    Have overthrown him.

MACB. [*Aside.*]: Glamis, and thane of Cawdor!
    The greatest is behind.   [*To* ROSS *and* ANGUS.]
    Thanks for your pains.
    [*To* BAN.] Do you not hope your children shall be kings,
    When those that gave the thane of Cawdor to me
    Promis'd no less to them?

BAN: That trusted home
    Might yet enkindle you unto the crown,
    Besides the thane of Cawdor. But 'tis strange;
    And oftentimes, to win us to our harm,
    The instruments of darkness tell us truths,
    Win us with honest trifles, to betray's
    In deepest consequence.
    Cousins, a word, I pray you.

MACB: [*Aside.*] Two truths are told,
    As happy prologues to the swelling act
    Of the imperial theme.   [*To* ROSS *and* ANGUS.]
    I thank you, gentlemen.
    [*Aside.*] This supernatural soliciting

Cannot be ill; cannot be good. If ill,
Why hath it given me earnest of success,
Commencing in a truth? I am thane of Cawdor.
If good, why do I yield to that suggestion
Whose horrid image doth unfix my hair,
And make my seated heart knock at my ribs.
Against the use of nature? Present fears
Are less than horrible imaginings:
My thought, whose murder yet is but fantastical,
Shakes so my single state of man that function
Is smother'd in surmise, and nothing is
But what is not.

BAN: Look, how our partner's rapt.

MACB: [*Aside.*] If chance will have me king,
why, chance may crown me,
Without my stir.

BAN: New honours come upon him,
Like our strange garments, cleave not to their mould
But with the aid of use.

MACB: [*Aside.*] Come what come may,
Time and the hour runs through the roughest day.

BAN: Worthy Macbeth, we stay upon your leisure.

MACB: Give me your favour: my dull brain was wrought
With things forgotten. Kind gentlemen, your pains
Are register'd where every day I turn
The leaf to read them. Let us toward the king.
Think upon what hath chanced, and, at more time,
The interim having weigh'd it, let us speak
Our free hearts each to other.

BAN: Very gladly.

MACB: Till then, enough. Come, friends.

Exeunt.

SCENE IV.—[*Forres. the palace*]

⌒ ⌒ ⌒

DUN: My plenteous joys,
Wanton in fulness, seek to hide themselves
In drops of sorrow. Sons, kinsmen, thane, as
And you whose places are the nearest, know

We will establish our estate upon
Our eldest, Malcolm, whom we name hereafter
The Prince of Cumberland; which honour must
Not unaccompanied invest him only,
But signs of nobleness, like stars, shall shine
On all deservers. From hence to Inverness,
And bind us further to you.

MACB: The rest is labour, which is not us'd for you.
I'll be myself the harbinger and make joyful
The hearing of my wife with your approach,
So humbly take my leave.

DUN: My worthy Cawdor!

MACB: [*Aside.*] The Prince of Cumberland!
That is a step
On which I must fall down, or else o'erleap,
For in my way it lies. Stars, hide your fires;
Let not light see my black and deep desires:
The eye wink at the hand; yet let that be,
Which the eye fears, when it is done, to see.

Exit.[6]

Who are the Witches, and of what exactly do their powers consist? Certainly, the Witches know the future, and yet they speak of it in broken, cryptic ways. This they share with other female characters we have seen in earlier sections, such as Cassandra. But the Witches are both mischievous and powerful, causing real trouble for Macbeth and their other victims. Yet clearly they do not have power over life and death, nor over Macbeth's actions. Indeed, it is quite clear that Macbeth is responsible for his decisions, and that he, not the Weird Sisters, is the author of the scheme to kill Duncan.

Some gender themes from earlier works, then, are being reiterated here: female characters bring evil and trouble to men, they are allied to the knowledge of past and future, they come in pluralities; a male character is involved in a struggle between morally ambiguous forces, he must make decisions without adequate knowledge, and he is a lone individual representing humanity generally. On the other hand, the Witches' knowledge, unlike that of Cassandra, Athena, or Diotima, is not of fate or of the gods' will, but of secret *natural* forces, apparently including the secrets of human nature. The Witches are magicians, not prophetesses; they are able to use—perhaps to pervert—natural forces, by an eerie kind of science. This new, modern, sense of "nature" is represented most simply here, in that these female characters live out in the woods—they are unallied to a man or men, and they do

---

[6] All excerpts from Shakespeare's *Macbeth* are taken from *Ten Plays of Shakespeare*. Edited by Tucker Brooke and Henry Noble MacCracken. (New York: The Century Co. 1927).

not mark a city or home to which men may return as to their mothers. They are allied with a "nature" wholly sundered from "culture," one that can be understood by men only through cryptic signs and at the Witches' whim.

MACBETH AND LADY MACBETH

Lady Macbeth, perhaps the most infamous female character in western literature, has more ambition for the throne than her husband himself seems to have. In the following scene, she reacts to her husband's description of the Witches' pronouncements, and to her husband's victorious return home from battle.

SCENE V.—[*Inverness. Macbeth's castle.*]

> *Enter Lady Macbeth, reading a letter.*

LADY M: 'They met me in the day of success: and I have learned by the
　　perfectest report, they have more in them than mortal knowledge. When I
　　burned in desire to question them further, they made themselves air, into
　　which they vanished. Whiles I stood rapt in the wonder of it, came missives
　　from the king, who all-hailed me "Thane of Cawdor;" by which title, before,
　　these weird sisters saluted me, and referred me to the coming on of time, with
　　"Hail, king that shalt be!" This have I thought good to deliver thee, my
　　dearest partner of greatness, that thou mightst not lose the dues of rejoicing,
　　by being ignorant of what greatness is promised thee. Lay it to thy heart, and
　　farewell.'
　　Glamis thou art, and Cawdor; and shalt be
　　What thou art promis'd: yet do I fear thy nature;
　　It is too full o' the milk of human kindness
　　To catch the nearest way. Thou wouldst be great;
　　Art not without ambition, but without
　　The illness should attend it. What thou wouldst highly,
　　That wouldst thou holily; wouldst not play false,
　　And yet wouldst wrongly win. Thou'ldst have, great Glamis,
　　That which cries 'Thus thou must do, if thou have it,'
　　And that which rather thou dost fear to do
　　Than wishest should be undone. Hie thee hither,
　　That I may pour my spirits in thine ear,
　　And chastise with the valour of my tongue
　　All that impedes thee from the golden round,
　　Which fate and metaphysical aid doth seem
　　To have thee crown'd withal.

> *Enter a* MESSENGER.

　What is your tidings?

MESS: The king comes here to-night.

LADY M: Thou'rt mad to say it!
   Is not thy master with him? who, were't so,
   Would have inform'd for preparation.

MESS: So please you, it is true. Our thane is coming;
   One of my fellows had the speed of him,
   Who, almost dead for breath, had scarcely more
   Than would make up his message.

LADY M: Give him tending;
   He brings great news.

Exit MESSENGER.

   The raven himself is hoarse
   That croaks the fatal entrance of Duncan
   Under my battlements. Come, you spirits
   That tend on mortal thoughts, unsex me here,
   And fill me from the crown to the toe topfull
   Of direst cruelty! make thick my blood;
   Stop up the access and passage to remorse,
   That no compunctious visitings of nature
   Shake my fell purpose, nor keep peace between
   The effect and it! Come to my woman's breasts,
   And take my milk for gall, you murdering ministers,
   Wherever in your sightless substances
   You wait on nature's mischief! Come, thick night,
   And pall thee in the dunnest smoke of hell,
   That my keen knife see not the wound it makes,
   Nor heaven peep through the blanket of the dark,
   To cry 'Hold, hold!'

Enter MACBETH.

   Great Glamis! worthy Cawdor!
   Greater than both, by the all-hail hereafter!
   Thy letters have transported me beyond
   This ignorant present, and I feel now
   The future in the instant.

MACB: My dearest love,
   Duncan comes here to-night.

LADY M: And when goes hence?

MACB: To-morrow, as he purposes.

LADY M: O, never
   Shall sun that morrow see!
   Your face, my thane, is as a book where men
   May read strange matters. To beguile the time,

Look like the time. Bear welcome in your eye,
Your hand, your tongue; look like the innocent flower,
But be the serpent under 't. He that's coming
Must be provided for; and you shall put
This night's great business into my dispatch,
Which shall to all our nights and days to come
Give solely sovereign sway and masterdom.

MACB: We will speak further.

LADY M: Only look up clear;
To alter favour ever is to fear:
Leave all the rest to me.

Exeunt.

SCENE VI.—[*Before Macbeth's castle.*]

Hautboys and torches. Enter DUNCAN,
MALCOLM, DONALBAIN, BANQUO, LENNOX,
MACDUFF, ROSS, ANGUS, *and* ATTENDANTS.

Enter LADY MACBETH.

⌒ ⌒ ⌒

DUN: . . . Fair and noble hostess,
We are your guest to-night.

LADY M: Your servants ever
Have theirs, themselves and what is theirs, in compt,
To make their audit at your highness' pleasure,
Still to return your own.

DUN: Give me your hand;
Conduct me to mine host. We love him highly,
And shall continue our graces towards him.
By your leave, hostess.

Exeunt.

SCENE VII.—[*Macbeth's castle.*]

Hautboys and torches. Enter a SEWER,
and divers SERVANTS *with dishes and
service, [and pass] over the stage. Then
enter* MACBETH.

MACB: If it were done when 'tis done, then 'twer well
It were done quickly. If the assassination
Could trammel up the consequence, and catch

With his surcease success; that but this blow
Might be the be-all and the end-all here,
But here, upon this bank and shoal of time,
We'ld jump the life to come. But in these cases
We still have judgement here; that we but teach
Bloody instructions, which, being taught, return
To plague the inventor: this even-handed justice
Commends the ingredients of our poison'd chalice
To our own lips. He's here in double trust;
First, as I am his kinsman and his subject,
Strong both against the deed; then, as his host,
Who should against his murderer shut the door,
Not bear the knife myself. Besides, this Duncan
Hath borne his faculties so meek, hath been
So clear in his great office, that his virtues
Will plead like angels, trumpet-tongu'd, against
The deep damnation of his taking-off;
And pity, like a naked new-born babe,
Striding the blast, or heaven's cherubim, hors'd
Upon the sightless couriers of the air,
Shall blow the horrid deed in every eye,
That tears shall drown the wind. I have no spur
To prick the sides of my intent, but only
Vaulting ambition, which o'erleaps itself,
And falls on the other.—

Enter LADY MACBETH.

How now! what news?

LADY M: He has almost supp'd: why have you left the chamber?

MACB: We will proceed no further in this business.
He hath honour'd me of late; and I have bought
Golden opinions from all sorts of people,
Which would be worn now in their newest gloss,
Not cast aside so soon.

LADY M: Was the hope drunk
Wherein you dress'd yourself? Hath it slept since?
And wakes it now, to look so green and pale
At what it did so freely? From this time
Such I account thy love. Art thou afeard
To be the same in thine own act and valour
As thou art in desire? Wouldst thou have that
Which thou esteem'st the ornament of life,
And live a coward in thine own esteem,

Letting 'I dare not' wait upon 'I would,'
Like the poor cat i' the adage?

MACB: Prithee, peace:
I dare do all that may become a man;
Who dares do more is none.

LADY M: What beast was't, then,
That made you break this enterprise to me?
When you durst do it, then you were a man;
And, to be more than what you were, you would
Be so much more the man. Nor time nor place
Did then adhere, and yet you would make both.
They have made themselves, and that their fitness now
Does unmake you. I have given suck, and know
How tender 'tis to love the babe that milks me;
I would, while it was smiling in my face,
Have pluck'd my nipple from his boneless gums,
And dash'd the brains out, had I so sworn as you
Have done to this.

MACB: If we should fail?

LADY M: We fail!
But screw your courage to the sticking-place,
And we'll not fail. When Duncan is asleep—
Whereto the rather shall his day's hard journey
Soundly invite him—his two chamberlains
Will I with wine and wassail so convince
That memory, the warder of the brain,
Shall be a fume, and the receipt of reason
A limbeck only. When in swinish sleep
Their drenched natures lie as in a death,
What cannot you and I perform upon
The unguarded Duncan? what not put upon
His spongy officers, who shall bear the guilt
Of our great quell?

MACB: Bring forth men-children only;
For thy undaunted mettle should compose
Nothing but males. Will it not be receiv'd,
When we have mark'd with blood those sleepy two
Of his own chamber and us'd their very daggers,
That they have done't?

LADY M: Who dares receive it other,
As we shall make our griefs and clamour roar
Upon his death?

MACB: I am settled, and bend up
  Each corporal agent to this terrible feat.

⌐ ⌐ ⌐

ACT SECOND
SCENE II

Enter LADY MACBETH.

LADY M: That which hath made them drunk hath made me bold;
  What hath quench'd them hasth given me fire.
  Hark! Peace!
  It was the owl that shriek'd, the fatal bellman,
  Which give the stern'st good-night. He is about it:
  The doors are open; and the surfeited grooms
  Do mock their charge with snores: I have drugg'd their possets,
  That death and nature do contend about them,
  Whether they live or die.

MACB: [*Within.*] Who's there? what ho!

LADY M: Alack, I am afraid they have awak'd,
  And 'tis not done. The attempt and not the dead
  Confounds us. Hark! I laid their daggers ready;
  He could not miss 'em. Had he not resembled
  My father as he slept, I had done't.

Enter MACBETH.

  My husband!

MACB: I have done the deed. Didst thou not hear a noise?

LADY M: I heard the owl scream and the crickets cry.
  Did not you speak?

MACB: When?

LADY M: Now.

MACB: As I descended?

LADY M: Ay.

MACB: Hark!
  Who lies i' the second chamber?

LADY M: Donalbain.

MACB: This is a sorry sight.

[Looking on his hands.]

LADY M: A foolish thought, to say a sorry sight.

MACB: There's one did laugh in's sleep, and one cried 'Murder!'
That they did wake each other. I stood and heard them;
But they did say their prayers, and address'd them
Again to sleep.

LADY M: There are two lodg'd together.

MACB: One cried 'God bless us!' and 'Amen' the other,
As they had seen me with these hangman's hands.
Listening their fear, I could not say 'Amen,'
When they did say 'God bless us!'

LADY M: Consider it not so deeply.

MACB: But wherefore could not I pronounce 'Amen'?
I had most need of blessing, and 'Amen'
Stuck in my throat.

LADY M: These deeds must not be thought
After these ways; so, it will make us mad.

MACB: Methought I heard a voice cry 'Sleep no more!
Macbeth does murder sleep,'—the innocent sleep.
Sleep that knits up the ravell'd sleave of care,
The death of each day's life, sore labour's bath,
Balm of hurt minds, great nature's second course,
Chief nourisher in life's feast,—

LADY M: What do you mean?

MACB: Still it cried 'Sleep no more!' to all the house:
'Glamis hath murder'd sleep, and therefore Cawdor
Shall sleep no more; Macbeth shall sleep no more.'

LADY M: Who was it that thus cried? Why, worthy thane,
You do unbend your noble strength, to think
So brainsickly of things. Go get some water,
And wash this filthy witness from your hand.
Why did you bring these daggers from the place?
They must lie there; go carry them, and smear
The sleepy grooms with blood.

MACB: I'll go no more.
I am afraid to think what I have done;
Look on't again I dare not.

LADY M: Infirm of purpose!
Give me the daggers. The sleeping and the dead
Are but as pictures; 'tis the eye of childhood

That fears a painted devil. If he do bleed,
I'll gild the faces of the grooms withal,
For it must seem their guilt.

Exit. Knocking within.

MACB: Whence is that knocking?
How is't with me, when every noise appals me?
What hands are here? Ha! they pluck out mine eyes.
Will all great Neptune's ocean wash this blood
Clean from my hand? No, this my hand will rather
The multitudinous seas incarnadine,
Making the green one red.

Enter LADY MACBETH.

LADY M: My hands are of your colour; but I shame
To wear a heart so white. (*Knocking within.*)
I hear a knocking.
At the south entry: retire we to our chamber.
A little water clears us of this deed:
How easy is it, then! Your constancy
Hath left you unattended. (*Knocking within.*)
Hark! more knocking.
Get on your nightgown, lest occasion call us,
And show us to be watchers. Be not lost
So poorly in your thoughts.

MACB: To know my deed, 'twere best not know myself.

(*Knocking within.*)

Wake Duncan with thy knocking! I would thou couldst!

Exeunt.

Once again, familiar gender themes from earlier works are manipulated in surprising ways by Shakespeare here. The dynastic household represents at once its leader and its city; the household contains within it morally ambiguous forces that come to the fore when opportunity and temptation present themselves, just as does Macbeth himself as an individual. The household is held and kept by a faithful woman; a courageous man returns home to her after military adventures. Like Jocasta and Electra, Lady Macbeth fights against Macbeth's conscience and curiosity. Like Clytaemnestra and the Furies, Lady Macbeth seems to champion here a kind of "natural" right, coded as feminine, and Macbeth a "civil" right—of entitlement to the throne.

But again, through modern reflections on "nature," Shakespeare challenges and perhaps even perverts these themes. As Macbeth expresses second thoughts to his wife, she behaves almost as if she were a voice within him, prodding and daring him to do what he now thinks—or fears—he ought not do. Lady Macbeth speaks as if she were the representative of Macbeth's own innermost and secret desires, his own irrational passions. Her motivations, on the other hand, are hard to discern. It is not clear that Lady Macbeth acts as an individual at all, that she makes or acts upon any conscious decision; her ambition, seemingly, is her husband's. Like the Witches, she seems to represent a powerful but secret nature, ever present but also ever mysterious, a nature that is not expressed in civil or moral codes, not discernable to men. This secret natural force, represented by female characters, is wholly divorced from culture, civility, and goodness, or—in other words—from "nature" in the sense of purity and essence. These females are "unnatural," "supernatural," "mysterious," "irrational," alongside—perhaps even because of—their association with nature; they are below the rational, moral, world of culture and civility, but they are also beyond its scope.

MACBETH AND BANQUO'S MURDERERS

Macbeth's fate is unravelled by his friend Banquo, who, having himself met the Witches and heard their predictions, suspects Macbeth. Banquo then, like Macbeth and Lady Macbeth, knows the hidden and evil nature within the human spirit, but he is able to resist it. This "royalty of nature," as Macbeth admits in the speech below, is Macbeth's greatest fear. Thus, Banquo too is like a voice inside Macbeth, a voice of conscience, country, morality with which Macbeth struggles as he weighs his own actions.

ACT THIRD
SCENE I.—[*Forres. The palace.*]

☙ ☙ ☙

MACB: Let every man be master of his time
    Till seven at night, to make society
    The sweeter welcome. We will keep ourself
    Till supper-time alone; while then, God be with you!

                  Exeunt all but MACBETH, *and a* SERVANT.

    Sirrah, a word with you: attend those men
    Our pleasure?

SERV: They are, my lord, without the palace gate.

MACB: Bring them before us.   *Exit* SERVANT.
    To be thus is nothing;
    But to be safely thus.—Our fears in Banquo
    Stick deep; and in his royalty of nature
    Reigns that which would be fear'd: 'tis much he dares;
    And, to that dauntless temper of his mind,

He hath a wisdom that doth guide his valour
To act in safety. There is none but he
Whose being I do fear: and, under him,
My Genius is rebuk'd, as, it is said,
Mark Antony's was by Cæsar. He chid the sisters
When first they put the name of king upon me,
And bade them speak to him. Then prophet-like
They hail'd him father to a line of kings.
Upon my head they placed a fruitless crown,
And put a barren sceptre in my gripe,
Thence to be wrench'd with an unlineal hand,
No son of mine succeeding. If't be so,
For Banquo's issue have I fil'd my mind;
For them the gracious Duncan have I murder'd;
Put rancours in the vessel of my peace
Only for them; and mine eternal jewel
Given to the common enemy of man,
To make them kings, the seed of Banquo kings!
Rather than so, come fate into the list,
And champion me to the utterance! Who's there?

Enter SERVANT *and two* MURDERERS.

Now go to the door, and stay there till we call.

Exit SERVANT.

Was it not yesterday we spoke together?

FIRST MUR: It was, so please your highness.

MACB: Well then, now
Have you consider'd of my speeches? Know
That it was he in the times past which held you
So under fortune, which you thought had been
Our innocent self. This I made good to you
In our last conference, pass'd in probation with you,
How you were borne in hand, how cross'd, the instruments,
Who wrought with them, and all things else that might
To half a soul and to a notion craz'd
Say 'Thus did Banquo.'

FIRST MUR: You made it known to us.

MACB: I did so, and went further, which is now
Our point of second meeting. Do you find
Your patience so predominant in your nature
That you can let this go? are you so gospell'd
To pray for this good man and for his issue,

Whose heavy hand hath bow'd you to the grave
And beggar'd yours for ever?

FIRST MUR: We are men, my liege.

MACB: Ay, in the catalogue ye go for men;
As hounds and greyhounds, mongrels, spaniels, curs,
Shoughs, water-rugs and demi-wolves are clept
All by the name of dogs; the valued file
Distinguishes the swift, the slow, the subtle,
The housekeeper, the hunter, every one
According to the gift which bounteous nature
Hath in him clos'd, whereby he does receive
Particular addition, from the bill
That writes them all alike: and so of men.
Now, if you have a station in the file,
Not i' the worst rank of manhood, say't;
And I will put that business in your bosoms,
Whose execution takes your enemy off,
Grapples you to the heart and love of us,
Who wear our health but sickly in his life,
Which in his death were perfect.

SEC. MUR: I am one, my liege,
Whom the vile blows and buffets of the world
Have so incens'd that I am reckless what
I do to spite the world.

FIRST MUR: And I another
So weary with disasters, tugg'd with fortune,
That I would set my life on any chance,
To mend it, or be rid on't.

MACB: Both of you
Know Banquo was your enemy.

BOTH MUR: True, my lord.

MACB: So is he mine; and in such bloody distance,
That every minute of his being thrusts
Against my near'st of life; and though I could
With barefac'd power sweep him from my sight
And bid my will avouch it, yet I must not,
For certain friends that are both his and mine,
Whose loves I may not drop, but will his fall
Who I myself struck down; and thence it is,
That I to your assistance do make love,
Masking the business from the common eye
For sundry weighty reasons.

SEC. MUR: We shall, my lord,
 Perform what you command us.

FIRST MUR: Though our lives—

MACB: Your spirits shine through you. Within this hour at most
 I will advise you where to plant yourselves;
 Acquaint you with the perfect spy o' the time.
 The moment on't; for't must be done to-night,
 And something from the palace; always thought
 That I require a clearness; and with him—
 To leave no rubs nor botches in the work—
 Fleance his son, that keeps him company,
 Whose absence is no less material to me
 Than is his father's, must embrace the fate
 Of that dark hour. Resolve yourselves apart
 I'll come to you anon.

BOTH MUR: We are resolv'd, my lord.

Note the role of the two murderers and its contrast to the Witches. Dank and unpleasant as both sets of characters are, the murderers are represented as pawns of
Macbeth's, entirely within his control and understanding (he is even sympathetic to
them) where the Witches are far beyond Macbeth's ken. According to the murderers
themselves, they are "men," and as such, lowly creatures unable not to do what
they are commanded. Thus, Macbeth compares them, precisely in their humanity, to
animals. Thus, these henchmen represent a manhood not very different from that of
Macbeth himself, one that is riddled by weighty forces it tries to control; and they,
like Macbeth, have lost command of themselves and given in to the worst of their
passions. Their murder of Banquo, at the bidding of Macbeth, symbolizes this: the
best of masculinity, the royalty of spirit that is commanded only by reason and loyalty, is killed by its own worst elements.

RETURN OF THE WITCHES, AND HECATE

In the woods, the Witches have met with their "leader," Hecate. Hecate is the Greek
goddess of nature and the underworld, to whom sacrifices are made, and by whom
rewards and punishments are dealt to men. In the scene preceding the one represented below, Hecate has taken the Witches to task for spending too much time on
Macbeth, and for acting on their own initiative in doing so, instead of yielding to
her authority. Thus, the three witches are depicted as "rogues" within their own
mischievous ranks, becoming too involved in human affairs.
   In the scene depicted here, the Witches, at Hecate's instruction, correct their failing. Through a series of apparitions predicting Macbeth's ruin, they make clear that
Macbeth has acted on his own responsibility.

ACT FOURTH

SCENE I.—[*A cavern. in the middle, a boiling cauldron.*]

Thunder. Enter the three WITCHES.

FIRST WITCH: Thrice the brinded cat hath mew'd.

SEC. WITCH: Thrice and once the hedge-pig whin'd.

THIRD WITCH: Harpier cries. 'Tis time, 'tis time.

FIRST WITCH: Round about the cauldron go;
    In the poison'd entrails throw.
    Toad, that under cold stone
    Days and nights has thirty one
    Swelter'd venom sleeping got,
    Boil thou first i' the charmed pot.

ALL: Double, double toil and trouble;
    Fire burn, and cauldron bubble.

SEC. WITCH: Fillet of a fenny snake,
    In the cauldron boil and bake;
    Eye of newt and toe of frog,
    Wool of bat and tongue of dog,
    Adder's fork and blind-worm's sting,
    Lizard's leg and howlet's wing,
    For a charm of powerful trouble,
    Like a hell-broth boil and bubble.

ALL: Double, double toil and trouble;
    Fire burn and cauldron bubble.

THIRD WITCH: Scale of dragon, tooth of wolf,
    Witches' mummy, maw and gulf
    Of the ravin'd salt-sea shark,
    Root of hemlock digg'd i' the dark,
    Liver of blaspheming Jew,
    Gall of goat, and slips of yew
    Sliver'd in the moon's eclipse,
    Nose of Turk and Tartar's lips,
    Finger of birth-strangled babe
    Ditch-deliver'd by a drab,
    Make the gruel thick and slab:
    Add thereto a tiger's chaudron,
    For the ingredients of our cauldron.

ALL: Double, double toil and trouble;
    Fire burn and cauldron bubble.

SEC. WITCH: Cool it with a baboon's blood,
    Then the charm is firm and good.

                Enter HECATE *[to] the other three*
                WITCHES.

HEC: O, well done! I commend your pains;
    And every one shall share i' the gains:
    And now about the cauldron sing,
    Like elves and fairies in a ring,
    Enchanting all that you put in.

                [*Dance*] *Music and song:* 'Black spirits,'
                &c.

                [*Exit* HECATE.]

SEC. WITCH: By the pricking of my thumbs,
    Something wicked this way comes.
    Open, locks,
    Whoever knocks!

                Enter MACBETH.

MACB: How now, you secret, black, and mid-night hags!
    What is't you do?

ALL: A deed without a name.

MACB: I cónjure you, by that which you profess,
    Howe'er you come to know it, answer me:
    Though you untie the winds and let them fight
    Against the churches; though the yesty waves
    Confound and swallow navigation up;
    Though bladed corn be lodg'd and trees blown down;
    Though castles topple on their warders' heads;
    Though palaces and pyramids do slope
    Their heads to their foundations; though the treasure
    Of nature's germens tumble all together.
    Even till destruction sicken; answer me
    To what I ask you.

FIRST WITCH: Speak.

SEC. WITCH: Demand.

THIRD WITCH: We'll answer.

FIRST WITCH: Say, if thou'dst rather hear it from our mouths,
    Or from our masters?

MACB: Call 'em; let me see 'em.

FIRST WITCH: Pour in sow's blood, that hath eaten
    Her nine farrow; grease that's sweaten
    From the murderer's gibbet throw
    Into the flame.

ALL: Come, high or low;
    Thyself and office deftly show!

                    Thunder. FIRST APPARITION: *an armed*
                    HEAD.

MACB: Tell me, thou unknown power,—

FIRST WITCH: He knows thy thought:
    Hear his speech, but say thou nought.

FIRST APP: Macbeth! Macbeth! Macbeth! beware Macduff;
    Beware the thane of Fife. Dismiss me.
    Enough.   *He descends.*

MACB: Whate'er thou art, for thy good caution, thanks.
    Thou hast harp'd my fear aright. But one word more,—

FIRST WITCH: He will not be commanded. Here's another,
    More potent than the first.

                    Thunder. SECOND APPARITION: *a bloody*
                    CHILD.

SEC. APP: Macbeth! Macbeth! Macbeth!

MACB: Had I three ears, I'ld hear thee.

SEC. APP: Be bloody, bold, and resolute; laugh to scorn
    The power of man, for none of woman born
    Shall harm Macbeth.   *Descends.*

MACB: Then live, Macduff: what need I fear of thee?
    But yet I'll make assurance double sure,
    And take a bond of fate: thou shalt not live;
    That I may tell pale-hearted fear it lies,
    And sleep in spite of thunder.

                    Thunder. THIRD APPARITION: *a* CHILD
                    crowned, with a tree in his hand.

What is this
That rises like the issue of a king,
And wears upon his baby-brow the round
And top of sovereignty?

ALL: Listen, but speak not to't.

THIRD APP: Be lion-mettled, proud, and take no care
　　Who chafes, who frets, or where conspirers are.
　　Macbeth shall never vanquish'd be until
　　Great Birnam wood to high Dunsinane hill
　　Shall come against him.　　　　　　*Descends.*

MACB: That will never be:
　　Who can impress the forest, bid the tree
　　Unfix his earth-bound root? Sweet bodements! good!
　　Rebellion's head, rise never till the wood
　　Of Birnam rise, and our high-plac'd Macbeth
　　Shall live the lease of nature, pay his breath
　　To time and mortal custom. Yet my heart
　　Throbs to know one thing: tell me, if your art
　　Can tell so much: shall Banquo's issue ever
　　Reign in this kingdom?

ALL: Seek to know no more.

MACB: I will be satisfied: deny me this
　　And an eternal curse fall on you! Let me know,
　　Why sinks that cauldron? and what noise is this?　　　　*Hautboys.*

FIRST WITCH: Show!

SEC. WITCH: Show!

THIRD WITCH: Show!

ALL: Show his eyes, and grieve his heart;
　　Come like shadows, so depart!

> *A show of* EIGHT KINGS, *[the last with a
> glass in his hand;* BANQUO'S GHOST
> *following].*

MACB: Thou art too like the spirit of Banquo; down!
　　Thy crown does sear mine eye-balls. And thy hair,
　　Thou other gold-bound brow, is like the first.
　　A third is like the former. Filthy hags!
　　Why do you show me this? A fourth! Start, eyes!
　　What, will the line stretch out to the crack of doom?
　　Another yet! A seventh! I'll see no more:
　　And yet the eighth appears, who bears a glass
　　Which shows me many more; and some I see
　　That two-fold balls and treble sceptres carry:
　　Horrible sight! Now, I see, 'tis true;
　　For the blood-bolter'd Banquo smiles upon me,
　　And points at them for his. [*Apparitions vanish.*] What, is this so?

FIRST WITCH: Ay, sir, all this is so: but why
    Stands Macbeth thus amazedly?
    Come, sisters, cheer we up his sprites,
    And show the best of our delights:
    I'll charm the air to give a sound,
    While you perform your antic round,
    That this great king may kindly say,
    Our duties did his welcome pay.

Music. The WITCHES *dance, and vanish.*

MACB: Where are they? Gone? Let this pernicious hour
    Stand aye accursed in the calendar!
    Come in, without there!

Enter LENNOX.

LEN: What's your grace's will?

MACB: Saw you the weird sisters?

LEN: No, my lord.

MACB: Came they not by you?

LEN: No, indeed, my lord.

MACB: Infected be the air whereon they ride;
    And damn'd all those that trust them! I did hear
    The galloping of horse: who was't came by?

LEN: 'Tis two or three, my lord, that bring you word
    Macduff is fled to England.

MACB: Fled to England!

LEN: Ay, my good lord.

MACB: Time, thou anticipatest my dread exploits:
    The flighty purpose never is o'ertook
    Unless the deed go with it. From this moment
    The very firstlings of my heart shall be
    The firstlings of my hand. And even now,
    To crown my thoughts with acts, be it thought and done:
    The castle of Macduff I will surprise;
    Seize upon Fife; give to the edge o' the sword
    His wife, his babes, and all unfortunate souls
    That trace him in his line. No boasting like a fool;
    This deed I'll do before this purpose cool.
    But no more sights!—Where are these gentlemen?

☙ ☙ ☙

CLIMAX AND RESOLUTION

Macbeth makes good the new plan he has laid in fear and confusion about the apparition's predictions, and sends his murdering henchmen to kill Macduff's family while Macduff is in England. Ross, bringing the news to Macduff, compares the deed to the death of Scotland itself, and Macbeth's now rampant evil to Scotland's fatal disease. Macduff and Malcolm (Duncan's son and heir to the throne) make plans to avenge themselves against Macbeth. Macbeth is slain by Macduff and Lady Macbeth takes her own life.

ROSS: Alas, poor country!
    Almost afraid to know itself. It cannot
    Be call'd our mother, but our grave; where nothing,
    But who knows nothing, is once seen to smile;
    Where sighs and groans and shrieks that rend the air
    Are made, not mark'd; where violent sorrow seems
    A modern ecstasy. The dead man's knell
    Is there scarce ask'd for who; and good men's lives
    Expire before the flowers in their caps,
    Dying or ere they sicken.

MACD: O, relation
    Too nice, and yet too true!

MAL: What's the newest grief?

ROSS: That of an hour's age doth hiss the speaker:
    Each minute teems a new one.

MACD: How does my wife?

ROSS: Why, well.

MACD: And all my children?

ROSS: Well too.

MACD: The tyrant 'has not batter'd at their peace?

ROSS: No, they were well at peace when I did leave 'em.

MACD: Be not a niggard of your speech; how goes't?

ROSS: When I came hither to transport the tidings,
    Which I have heavily borne, there ran a rumour
    Of many worthy fellows that were out;
    Which was to my belief witness'd the rather,
    For that I saw the tyrant's power a-foot:
    Now is the time of help; your eye in Scotland
    Would create soldiers, make our women fight,
    To doff their dire distresses.

MAL: Be't their comfort
We are coming thither: gracious England hath
Lent us good Siward and ten thousand men;
An older and a better soldier none
That Christendom gives out.

ROSS: Would I could answer
This comfort with the like! But I have words
That would be howl'd out in the desert air,
Where hearing should not latch them.

MACD: What concern they?
The general cause? or is it a fee-grief
Due to some single breast?

ROSS: No mind that's honest
But in it shares some woe; though the main part
Pertains to you alone.

MACD: If it be mine,
Keep it not from me, quickly let me have it.

ROSS: Let not your ears despise my tongue for ever,
Which shall possess them with the heaviest sound
That ever yet they heard.

MACD: Hum! I guess at it.

ROSS: Your castle is surpris'd; your wife and babes
Savagely slaughter'd: to relate the manner,
Were, on the quarry of these murder'd deer,
To add the death of you.

MAL: Merciful heaven!
What, man! ne'er pull your hat upon your brows;
Give sorrow words: the grief that does not speak
Whispers the o'er-fraught heart and bids it break.

MACD: My children too?

ROSS: Wife, children, servants, all
That could be found.

MACD: And I must be from thence!

ROSS: I have said.

MAL: Be comforted.
Let's make us medicines of our great revenge,
To cure this deadly grief.

MACD: He has no children. All my pretty ones?
Did you say all? O hell-kite! All?

What, all my pretty chickens and their dam
At one fell swoop?

MAL: Dispute it like a man.

MACD: I shall do so;
But I must also feel it as a man:
I cannot but remember such things were,
That were most precious to me. Did heaven look on,
And would not take their part? Sinful Macduff,
They were all struck for thee! Naught that I am,
Not for their own demerits, but for mine,
Fell slaughter on their souls. Heaven rest them now!

MAL: Be this the whetstone of your sword: let grief
Convert to anger; blunt not the heart, enrage it.

MACD: O, I could play the woman with mine eyes
And braggart with my tongue! But, gentle heavens,
Cut short all intermission; front to front
Bring thou this fiend of Scotland and myself;
Within my sword's length set him; if he 'scape,
Heaven forgive him too!

MAL: This tune goes manly.
Come, go we to the king; our power is ready;
Our lack is nothing but our leave. Macbeth
Is ripe for shaking, and the powers above
Put on their instruments. Receive what cheer you may:
The night is long that never finds the day.

Exeunt.

ACT FIFTH
SCENE III.—[*Dunsinane. A room in the castle.*]

Enter MACBETH, DOCTOR, *and*
ATTENDANTS.

MACB: Bring me no more reports; let them fly all;
Till Birnam wood remove to Dunsinane,
I cannot taint with fear. What's the boy Malcolm?
Was he not born of woman? The spirits that know
All mortal consequences have pronounced me thus:
'Fear not, Macbeth; no man that's born of woman
Shall e'er have power upon thee.' Then fly, false thanes,
And mingle with the English epicures:
The mind I sway by and the heart I bear
Shall never sag with doubt nor shake with fear.

Enter a SERVANT.

The devil damn thee black, thou cream-fac'd loon!
Where got'st thou that goose look?

SERV: There is ten thousand—

MACB: Geese, villain?

SERV: Soldiers, sir.

MACB: Go prick thy face, and over-red thy fear,
Thou lily-liver'd boy. What soldiers, patch?
Death of thy soul! those linen checks of thine
Are counsellors to fear.

MACB: How does your patient, doctor?

DOCT: Not so sick, my lord,
As she is troubled with thick-coming fancies,
That keep her from her rest.

MACB: Cure her of that.
Canst thou not minister to a mind diseas'd,
Pluck from the memory a rooted sorrow,
Raze out the written troubles of the brain
And with some sweet oblivious antidote
Cleanse the stuff'd bosom of that perilous stuff
Which weighs upon the heart?

DOCT: Therein the patient
Must minister to himself.

SCENE V.—[*Dunsinane. Within the castle.*]

MACB: I have almost forgot the taste of fears.
The time has been, my senses would have cool'd
To hear a night-shriek; and my fell of hair
Would at a dismal treatise rouse and stir
As life were in't. I have supp'd full with horrors;
Direness, familiar to my slaughterous thoughts,
Cannot once start me.

[*Re-enter* SEYTON.]

SEY: The queen, my lord, is dead.

MACB: She should have died hereafter;
    There would have been a time for such a word.
    To-morrow, and to-morrow, and to-morrow,
    Creeps in this petty pace from day to day
    To the last syllable of recorded time,
    And all our yesterdays have lighted fools
    The way to dusty death. Out, out, brief candle!
    Life's but a walking shadow, a poor player
    That struts and frets his hour upon the stage
    And then is heard no more: it is a tale
    Told by an idiot, full of sound and fury,
    Signifying nothing.

∝ ∝ ∝

SCENE VIII.—[*Another part of the field.*]

                                Enter MACBETH.

MACB: Why should I play the Roman fool, and die
    On mine own sword? Whiles I see lives, the gashes
    Do better upon them.

                              Enter MACDUFF.

MACD: Turn, hell-hound, turn!

MACB: Of all men else I have avoided thee:
    But get thee back; my soul is too much charg'd
    With blood of thine already.

MACD: I have no words:
    My voice is in my sword: thou bloodier villain
    Than terms can give thee out!

                          They fight. Alarum.

MACB: Thou losest labour:
    As easy mayst thou the intrenchant air
    With thy keen sword impress as make me bleed.
    Let fall thy blade on vulnerable crests;
    I bear a charmed life, which must not yield
    To one of woman born.

MACD: Despair thy charm;
    And let the angel whom thou still hast serv'd
    Tell thee, Macduff was from his mother's wormb
    Untimely ripp'd.

MACB: Accursed be that tongue that tells me so,
    For it hath cow'd my better part of man!
    And be these juggling fiends no more believ'd,

That palter with us in a double sense;
That keep the word of promise to our ear,
And break it to our hope. I'll not fight with thee.

MACD: Then yield thee, coward,
And live to be the show and gaze o' the time.
We'll have thee, as our rarer monsters are,
Painted upon a pole, and underwrit:
'Here may you see the tyrant.'

MACB: I will not yield,
To kiss the ground before young Malcom's feet,
And to be baited with the rabble's curse.
Though Birnam wood be come to Dunsinane,
And thou oppos'd, being of no woman born,
Yet I will try the last. Before my body
I throw my warlike shield. Lay on, Macduff,
And damn'd be him that first cries 'Hold, enough!'

Exeunt, fighting. Alarums.

Enter fighting, and MACBETH *slain.*

Two gender-related themes from the closing scenes are worthy of reflection. First, note how Macduff satisfies the criterion stated by the first apparition to mark Macbeth's murderer; he is "not of woman born." Surely there is something about Macduff—who is able to vanquish the evil passions that lie hidden in the human heart—which escapes the cycle of mortality and moral ambiguity inherent to human nature. This is represented by his having escaped the natural cycle of birth and death, which in both its "natural" and in its "evil" character is "of woman." Second, note the character of Lady Macbeth's insanity, and Macbeth's reaction to her death. Macbeth's unnatural visions were real, as was his act; Lady Macbeth's however, are hallucinated, as was her contribution to the murders. Yet her thoughts have led her to her death as certainly and really as Macbeth's deeds have to his. Surely Lady Macbeth has been represented throughout the play as being as powerful as her husband, even though—perhaps because—he does the act. Lady Macbeth seems to share with the Witches—and, to compare this to the Induction to the "Shrew," with art—some magical skill through which fantasy is made potent.

2. JOHN MILTON
(English, 1608–1674)

Milton was one of the most outspoken literary champions of "modernity" as it has been described in the introduction to this chapter. In addition to his poetry, Milton wrote many essays on politics, religion, and history, expressing his revolutionary views.

PARADISE LOST (1667)

In his famous poem *Paradise Lost,* Milton reworks the biblical stories of creation, of Satan's and Adam's fall, and of the divine ordering of the universe. In this, he was greatly influenced by the Greek myths, especially the story of Prometheus. Thus, Milton's retelling, in addition to the revival of ancient Greek themes typical of the high renaissance, also secularizes and naturalizes the traditional religious stories, making *Paradise Lost* an almost paradigmatically "modern" poem. Filled as it is with investigations of the nature of the divine and the human, the poem provides material relevant to our study of gender, almost throughout. Here, we will look at just a few of the most provocative passages.

SATAN'S FALL

The first of the twelve books of *Paradise Lost* prepares the ground for the original sin of humans in the fall of the Angel Satan from Heaven. As Milton depicts Heaven, God, and Satan, they are reminiscent of Hesiod's creation stories; the poet invokes the Muses, Heaven and Hell derive from Chaos, Satan's disobedience is his defiance of, and consequent threat to, God's power. Further, though, through his reinterpretation of Christian themes, Milton enriches both the biblical and the Greek stories, constructing a pan-historical analogy that relates to one another the characters of Prometheus, Achilles, Satan, and Adam.

BOOK I

Of Man's First Disobedience, and the Fruit
Of that Forbidden Tree, whose mortal taste
Brought Death into the World, and all our woe,
With loss of *Eden*, till one greater Man
Restore us, and regain the blissful Seat,
Sing Heav'nly Muse, that on the secret top
Of *Oreb,* or of *Sinai,* didst inspire
That Shepherd, who first taught the chosen Seed,
In the Beginning how the Heav'ns and Earth
Rose out of *Chaos:* Or if *Sion* Hill
Delight thee more, and *Siloa's* Brook that flow'd
Fast by the Oracle of God; I thence
Invoke thy aid to my advent'rous Song.

የ የ የ

    Say first, for Heav'n hides nothing from thy view
Nor the deep Tract of Hell, say first what cause
Mov'd our Grand Parents in that happy State,
Favour'd of Heav'n so highly, to fall off
From thir Creator, and transgress his Will
For one restraint, Lords of the World besides?

Who first seduc'd them to that foul revolt?
Th' infernal Serpent; he it was, whose guile
Stirr'd up with Envy and Revenge, deceiv'd
The Mother of Mankind, what time his Pride
Had cast him out from Heav'n, with all his Host
Of Rebel Angels, by whose aid aspiring
To set himself in Glory above his Peers,
He trusted to have equall'd the most High,
If he oppos'd; and with ambitious aim
Against the Throne and Monarchy of God
Rais'd impious War in Heav'n and Battle proud
With vain attempt. Him the Almighty Power
Hurl'd headlong flaming from th' Ethereal Sky
With hideous ruin and combustion down
To bottomless perdition, there to dwell
In Adamantine Chains and penal Fire,
Who durst defy th' Omnipotent to Arms.
Nine times the Space that measures Day and Night
To mortal men, he with his horrid crew
Lay vanquisht, rolling in the fiery Gulf
Confounded though immortal: But his doom
Reserv'd him to more wrath; for now the thought
Both of lost happiness and lasting pain
Torments him; round he throws his baleful eyes
That witness'd huge affliction and dismay
Mixt with obdúrate pride and steadfast hate:
At once as far as Angels ken he views
The dismal Situation waste and wild,
A Dungeon horrible, on all sides round
As one great Furnace flam'd, yet from those flames
No light, but rather darkness visible
Serv'd only to discover sights of woe,
Regions of sorrow, doleful shades, where peace
And rest can never dwell, hope never comes
That comes to all; but torture without end
Still urges, and a fiery Deluge, fed
With ever-burning Sulphur unconsum'd:
Such place Eternal Justice had prepar'd
For those rebellious, here their Prison ordained
In utter darkness, and thir portion set
As far remov'd from God and light of Heav'n
As from the Centre thrice to th' utmost Pole.
O how unlike the place from whence they fell
There the companions of his fall, o'erwhelm'd
With Floods and Whirlwinds of tempestuous fire,

He soon discerns, and welt'ring by his side
One next himself in power, and next in crime,
Long after known in *Palestine,* and nam'd
Beëlzebub. To whom th' Arch-Enemy,
And thence in Heav'n call'd Satan, with bold words
Breaking the horrid silence thus began.
    If thou beest he; But O how fall'n! how chang'd
From him, who in the happy Realms of Light
Cloth'd with transcendent brightness didst outshine
Myriads though bright: If he whom mutual league,
United thoughts and councels, equal hope,
And hazard in the Glorious Enterprise,
Join'd with me once, now misery hath join'd
In equal ruin: into what Pit thou seest
From what highth fall'n, so much the stronger prov'd
He with his Thunder: and till then who knew
The force of those dire Arms? yet not for those,
Nor what the Potent Victor in his rage
Can else inflict, do I repent or change,
Though chang'd in outward iustre; that fixt mind
And high disdain, from sense of injur'd merit,
That with the mightiest rais'd me to contend,
And to the fierce contention brought along
Innumerable force of Spirits arm'd
That durst dislike his reign, and me preferring,
His utmost power with adverse power oppos'd
In dubious Battle on the Plains of Heav'n,
And shook his throne. What though the field be lost?
All is not lost; the unconquerable Will,
And study of revenge, immortal hate,
And courage never to submit or yield:
And what is else not to be overcome?
That Glory never shall his wrath or might
Extort from me. To bow and sue for grace
With suppliant knee, and deify his power
Who from the terror of this Arm so late
Doubted his Empire, that were low indeed,
That were an ignominy and shame beneath
This downfall; since by Fate the strength of Gods
And this Empyreal substance cannot fail,
Since through experience of this great event
In Arms not worse, in foresight much advanc't,
We may with more successful hope resolve
To wage by force or guile eternal War
Irreconcilable, to our grand Foe,

Who now triumphs, and in th' excess of joy
Sole reigning holds the Tyranny of Heav'n.
　So spake th' Apostate Angel, though in pain,
Vaunting aloud, but rackt with deep despair:

☞　☞　☞

　Is this the Region, this the Soil, the Clime,
Said then the lost Arch-Angel, this the seat
That we must change for Heav'n, this mournful gloom
For that celestial light? Be it so, since hee
Who now is Sovran can dispose and bid
What shall be right: fardest from him is best
Whom reason hath equll'd, force hath made supreme
Above his equals. Farewell happy Fields
Where Joy for ever dwells: Hail horrors, hail
Infernal world, and thou profoundest Hell
Receive thy new Possessor: One who brings
A mind not to be chang'd by Place or Time.
The mind is its own place, and in itself
Can make a Heav'n of Hell, a Hell of Heav'n.

☞　☞　☞

What matter where, if I be still the same,
And what I should be, all but less than hee
Whom Thunder hath made greater? Here at least
We shall be free; th' Almighty hath not built
Here for his envy, will not drive us hence:
Here we may reign secure, and in my choice
To reign is worth ambition though in Hell:
Better to reign in Hell, than serve in Heav'n.

☞　☞　☞

　They heard, and were abasht, and up they sprung
Upon the wing, as when men wont to watch
On duty, sleeping found by whom they dread,
Rouse and bestir themselves ere well awake.
Nor did thy not perceive the evil plight
In which they were, or the fierce pains not feel;
Yet to thir General's Voice they soon obey'd
Innumerable.

☞　☞　☞

First *Moloch,* horrid King besmear'd with blood
Of human sacrifice, and parents' tears,
Though for the noise of Drums and Timbrels loud

Thir children's cries unheard, that past through fire
To his grim Idol. Him the *Ammonite*
Worshipt in *Rabba* and her wat'ry Plain,
In *Argob* and in *Basan,* to the stream
Of utmost *Arnon.* Nor content with such
Audacious neighbourhood, the wisest heart
Of *Solomon* he led by fraud to build
His Temple right against the Temple of God
On that opprobrious Hill, and made his Grove
The Pleasant Valley of *Hinnom, Tophet* thence
And black *Gehenna* call'd, the Type of Hell.
Next *Chemos,* th' obscene dread of *Moab's* Sons,
From *Aroar* to *Nebo*, and the wild
Of Southmost *Abarim;* in *Hesebon*
And *Horonaim, Seon's* Realm, beyond
The flow'ry Dale of *Sibma* clad with Vines,
And *Eleale* to th' *Asphaltic* Pool.
Peor his other Name, when he entic'd
Israel in *Sittim* on thir march from *Nile*
To do him wanton rites, which cost them woe.
Yet thence his lustful Orgies he enlarg'd
Even to that Hill of scandal, by the Grove
Of *Moloch* homicide, lust hard by hate;
Till good *Josiah* drove them thence to Hell.
With these came they, who from the bord'ring flood
Of old *Euphrates* to the Brook that parts
Egypt from *Syrian* ground, had general Names
Of *Badim* and *Ashtaroth,* those male,
These Feminine. For Spirits when they please
Can either Sex assume, or both; so soft
And uncompounded is thir Essence pure,
Not ti'd or manacl'd with joint or limb,
Nor founded on the brittle strength of bones,
Like cumbrous flesh; but in what shape they choose
Dilated or condens't, bright or obscure,
Can execute their aery purposes,
And works of love or enmity fulfil.

                                    ◿ ◿ ◿

    Thus far these beyond
Compare of mortal prowess, yet observ'd
Thir dread commander: he above the rest
In shape and gesture proudly eminent
Stood like a Tow'r; his form had yet not lost
All her Original brightness, nor appear'd

Less then Arch Angel ruin'd, and th' excess
Of Glory obscur'd: As when the Sun new ris'n
Looks through the Horizontal misty Air
Shorn of his Beams, or from behind the Moon
In dim Eclipse disastrous twilight sheds
On half the Nations, and with fear of change
Perplexes Monarchs. Dark'n'd so, yet shone
Above them all th' Arch Angel: but his face
Deep scars of Thunder had intrencht, and care
Sat on his faded cheek, but under Brows
Of dauntless courage, and considerate Pride
Waiting revenge: cruel his eye, but cast
Signs of remorse and passion to behold
The fellows of his crime, the followers rather
(Far other once beheld in bliss) condemn'd
For ever now to have thir lot in pain. [7]

Satan is depicted as a powerful, brilliant, and in that sense, an heroic, figure here; but a figure whose heroism, though recognizable, is perverted by rage, passion, and pride into an abomination, no longer welcome in Heaven. His ghastly army of evil spirits, however, is gathered under its leader first and foremost out of his pain and confusion at being cast out of Heaven and denied the favor of God with which he had grown familiar. The pridefulness, the freedom, in whose exercise the forces of Hell are glorying, requires of them a commitment to eternal torment. Satan, like Prometheus, recognizes the superior power of Heaven, and takes his only refuge in the spiteful enjoyment of his punishment. His is an evil born, as much as anything, of frustration at his own weakness, and riddled with pain and confusion at his situation.

We should also consider the notion of divinity implied here. Satan has supposedly been created "in the image and likeness of God." Yet his creator has abandoned him, and done so without explaining to Satan His reasons. Here, through Satan's understanding of God, we are given a picture of our own human condition, fallen away from God and cast out of the garden. That we should react to such a parent with the vicious resentment of Satan, though forbidden and foolish, is understandable. Thus, Satan, while superhuman, nonetheless presents us with paradigms of humanity. It is in this role as a model of human failings, that Satan evokes the images of Prometheus, Achilles, and Adam. Is Satan, then, a wholly masculine character? Certainly he sees himself as, above all, a ruler or a military leader. But Milton's Satan, an image of modernity, sees his most salient characteristic as his freedom, a freedom that finds its source in the mind, which "in itself/Can make a Heav'n of Hell, a Hell of Heav'n." Satan tells us that a pure Spirit "Can either Sex assume, or both; so soft/And uncompounded is [its] Essence pure." Here, then,

---

[7] All excerpts from Milton's *Paradise Lost* are taken from the edition by Marritt Y. Hughes (New York: Odyssey Press, 1935).

Milton implies that our sex is not "essential" to us, that our spirits are free to pick and choose their sex; rather sex, for Milton, insofar as it exerts control over us, does so by virtue of our materiality, our flesh and blood. Thus, in this sense, only embodied creatures may be male or female.

ADAM AND EVE

All the central books of *Paradise Lost* are involved in a retelling of the Adam and Eve story from Genesis, though it is based in the Christian interpretation of the story, developed over a long history, in which the doctrine of original sin plays a primary role. In Milton's retelling, central focus is given to the serpent's (Satan's) motivation for tempting Eve, the groundwork for which is laid in the opening books. But Milton also fleshes out in great detail—far more than does the biblical story—the motivations of Adam and Eve and the differences between them.

BOOK IV

                          ☙ ☙ ☙

Satan now first inflam'd with rage, came down,
The Tempter ere th' Accuser of man-kind,
To wreck on innocent frail man his loss
Of that first Battle, and his flight to Hell:

                          ☙ ☙ ☙

The lower still I fall, only Supreme
In misery; such joy Ambition finds.
But say I could repent and could obtain
By Act of Grace my former state; how soon
Would highth recall high thoughts, how soon unsay
What feign'd submission swore: ease would recant
Vows made in pain, as violent and void.
For never can true reconcilement grow
Where wounds of deadly hate have pierc'd so deep:
Which would but lead me to a worse relapse,
And heavier fall: so should I purchase dear
Short intermission bought with double smart.
This knows my punisher; therefore as far
From granting hee, as I from begging peace:
All hope excluded thus, behold instead
Of us out-cast, exil'd, his new delight,
Mankind created, and for him this World.
So farewell Hope, and with Hope farewell Fear,
Farewell Remorse: all Good to me is lost;
Evil be thou my Good: by thee at least

Divided Empire with Heav'n's King I hold
By thee, and more than half perhaps will reign;
As Man ere long, and this new World shall know.

⌐ ⌐ ⌐

So clomb this first grand Thief into God's Fold:
So since into his Church lewd Hirelings climb.
Thence up he flew, and on the Tree of Life,
The middle Tree and highest there that grew,
Sat like a Cormorant; yet not true Life
Thereby regain'd, but sat devising Death
To them who liv'd; nor on the virtue thought
Of that life-giving Plant, but only us'd
For prospect, what well us'd had been the pledge
Of immortality. So little knows
Any, but God alone, to value right
The good before him, but perverts best things
To worst abuse, or to thir meanest use.
Beneath him with new wonder now he views
To all delight of human sense expos'd
In narrow room Nature's whole wealth, yea more,
A Heaven on Earth: for blissful Paradise
Of God the Garden was, by him in the East
Of *Eden* planted;

⌐ ⌐ ⌐

From this *Assyrian* Garden, where the Fiend
Saw undelighted all delight, all kind
Of living Creatures noew to sight and strange:
Two of far nobler shape erect and tall,
Godlike erect, with native Honour clad
In naked Majesty seem'd Lords of all,
And worthy seem'd, for in thir looks Divine
The image of thir glorious Maker shone,
Truth, Wisdom, Sanctitude severe and pure,
Severe, but in true filial freedom plac't;
Whence true autority in men; though both
Not equal, as their sex not equal seem'd;
For contemplation hee and valour form'd,
For softness shee and sweet attractive Grace,
Hee for God only, shee for God in him:
His fair large Front and Eye sublime declar'd
Absolute rule; and Hyacinthine Locks
Round from his parted forelock manly hung
Clust'ring, but not beneath his shoulders broad:

Shee as a veil down to the slender waist
Her unadorned golden tresses wore
Dishevell'd, but in wanton ringlets wav'd
As the Vine curls her tendrils, which impli'd
Subjection, but requir'd with gentle sway,
And by her yielded, by him best receiv'd,
Yielded with coy submission, modest pride,
And sweet reluctant amorous delay.
Nor those mysterious parts were then conceal'd,
Then was not guilty shame: dishonest shame
Of nature's works, honour dishonorable,
Sin-bred, how have ye troubl'd all mankind
With shows instead, mere shows of seeming pure,
And banisht from man's life his happiest life,
Simplicity and spotless innocence.
So pass'd they naked on, nor shunn'd the sight
Of God or Angel, for they thought no ill:
So hand in hand they pass'd, the loveliest pair
That ever since in love's imbraces met.
Adam the goodliest man of men since born
His Sons, the fairest of her Daughters *Eve.*
Under a tuft of shade that on a green
Stood whispering soft, by a fresh Fountain side
They sat them down, and after no more toil
Of thir sweet Gard'ning labour than suffic'd
To recommend cool *Zephyr,* and made ease
More easy, wholesome thirst and appetite
More grateful, to thir Supper Fruits they fell,

◠ ◠ ◠

O Hell! what do mine eyes with grief behold,
Into our room of bliss thus high advanc't
Creatures of other mould, earth-born perhaps,
Not Spirits, yet to heav'nly Spirits bright
Little inferior; whom my thoughts pursue
With wonder, and could love, so lively shines
In them Divine resemblance, and such grace
The hand that form'd them on thir shape hath pour'd.
Ah gentle pair, yee little think how nigh
Your change approaches, when all these delights
Will vanish and deliver ye to woe,
More woe, the more your taste is now of joy;
Happy, but for so happy ill secur'd
Long to continue, and this high seat your Heav'n
Ill fenc't for Heav'n to keep out such a foe

As now is enter'd; yet no purpos'd foe
To you whom I could pity thus forlorn
Though I unpitied: League with you I seek,
And mutual amity so strait, so close,
That I with you must dwell, or you with me
Henceforth; my dwelling haply may not please
Like this fair Paradise, your sense, yet such
Accept your Maker's work; he gave it me,
Which I as freely give; Hell shall unfold,
To entertain you two, her widest Gates,
And send forth all her Kings; there will be room,
Not like these narrow limits, to receive
Your numerous offspring; if no better place,
Thank him who puts me loath to this revenge
On you who wrong me not for him who wrong'd.
And should I at your harmless innocence
Melt, as I do, yet public reason just,
Honour and Empire with revenge enlarg'd,
By conquering this new World, compels me now
To do what else though damn'd I should abhor.

$$\approx \quad \approx \quad \approx$$

Sole partner and sole part of all these joys,
Dearer thyself than all; needs must the Power
That made us, and for us this ample World
Be infinitely good, and of his good
As liberal and free as infinite,
That rais'd us from the dust and plac't us here
In all this happiness, who at his hand
Have nothing merited, nor can perform
Aught whereof hee hath need, hee who requires
From us no other service than to keep
This one, this easy charge, of all the Trees
In Paradise that bear delicious fruit
So various, not to taste that only Tree
Of knowledge, planted by the Tree of Life,
So near grows Death to Life, whate'er Death is,
Some dreadful thing no doubt; for well thou know'st
God hath pronounc't it death to taste that Tree,
The only sign of our obedience left
Among so many signs of power and rule
Conferr'd upon us, and Dominion giv'n
Over all other Creatures that possess
Earth, Air, and Sea. Then let us not think hard
One easy prohibition, who enjoy

Free leave so large to all things else, and choice
unlimited of manifold delights:
But let us ever praise him, and extol
His bounty, following our delightful task
To prune these growing Plants, and tend these Flow'rs,
Which were it toilsome, yet with thee were sweet.
    To whom thus *Eve* repli'd. O thou for whom
And from whom I was form'd flesh of thy flesh,
And without whom am to no end, my Guide
And Head, what thou hast said is just and right.
For wee to him indeed all praises owe,
And daily thanks, I chiefly who enjoy
So far the happier Lot, enjoying thee
Preëminent by so much odds, while thou
Like consort to thyself canst nowhere find.
That day I oft remember, when from sleep
I first awak't, and found myself repos'd
Under a shade on flow'rs, much wond'ring where
And what I was, whence thither brought, and how.
Not distant far from thence a murmuring sound
Of waters issu'd from a Cave and spread
Into a liquid Plain, then stood unmov'd
Pure as th' expanse of Heav'n; I thither went
With unexperienc't thought, and laid me down
On the green bank, to look into the clear
Smooth Lake, that to me seem'd another Sky.
As I bent down to look, just opposite,
A Shape within the wat'ry gleam appear'd
Bending to look on me, I started back,
It started back, but pleas'd I soon return'd,
Pleas'd it return'd as soon with answering looks
Of sympathy and love; there I had fixt
Mine eyes till now, and pin'd with vain desire,
Had not a voice thus warn'd me, What thou seest,
What there thou seest fair Creature is thyself,
With thee it came and goes: but follow me,
And I will bring thee where no shadow stays
Thy coming, and thy soft imbraces, hee
Whose image thou art, him thou shall enjoy
Inseparably thine, to him shalt bear
Multitudes like thyself, and thence be call'd
Mother of human Race: what could I do,
But follow straight, invisibly thus led?
Till I espi'd thee, fair indeed and tall,
Under a Platan, yet methought less fair,

Less winning soft, less amiably mild,
Than that smooth wat'ry image; back I turn'd,
Thou following cri'd'st aloud, Return fair *Eve*,
Whom fli'st thou? whom thou fli'st, of him thou art,
His flesh, his bone; to give thee being I lent
Out of my side to thee, nearest my heart
Substantial Life, to have thee by my side
Henceforth an individual solace dear;
Part of my Soul I seek thee, and thee claim
My other half: with that thy gentle hand
Seiz'd mine, I yielded, and from that time see
How beauty is excell'd by manly grace
And wisdom, which alone is truly fair.
    So spake our general Mother, and with eyes
Of conjugal attraction unreprov'd,
And meek surrender, half imbracing lean'd
On our first Father, half her swelling Breast
Naked met his under the flowing Gold
Of her loose tresses hid: he in delight
Both of her Beauty and submissive Charms
Smil'd with superior Love, as *Jupiter*
On *Juno* smiles, when he impregns the Clouds
That shed *May* Flowers; and press'd her Matron lip
With kisses pure: aside the Devil turn'd
For envy, yet with jealous leer malign
Ey'd them askance,

⸺ ⸺ ⸺

    In shadier Bower
More sacred and sequester'd, though but feign'd,
Pan or *Silvanus* never slept, nor Nymph,
Nor *Faunus* haunted. Here in close recess
With Flowers, Garlands, and sweet-smelling Herbs
Expoused *Eve* deckt first her nuptial Bed,
And heav'nly Quires the Hymenæan sung,
What day the genial Angel to our Sire
Brought her in naked beauty more adorn'd
More lovely than *Pandora*, whom the Gods
Endow'd with all thir gifts, and O too like
In sad event, when to the unwiser Son
Of *Japhet* brought by *Hermes,* she ensnar'd
Mankind with her fair looks, to be aveng'd
On him who had stole *Jove's* authentic fire.
    Thus at thir shady Lodge arriv'd, both stood,
Both turn'd, and under op'n Sky ador'd

The God that made both Sky, Air, Earth and Heav'n
Which they beheld, the Moon's resplendent Globe
And starry Pole: Thou also mad'st the Night,
Maker Omnipotent, and thou the Day,
Which we in our appointed work imploy'd
Have finisht happy in our mutual help
And mutual love, the Crown of all our bliss
Ordain'd by thee, and this delicious place
For us too large, where thy abundance wants
Partakers, and uncropt falls to the ground.
But thou hast promis'd from us two a Race
To fill the Earth, who shall with us extol
Thy goodness infinite, both when we wake,
And when we seek, as now, thy gift of sleep.
      This said unanimous, and other Rites
Observing none, but adoration pure
Which God likes best, into thir inmost bower
Handed they went; and eas'd the putting off
These troublesome disguises which wee wear,
Straight side by side were laid, nor turn'd I ween
Adam from his fair Spouse, nor *Eve* the Rites
Mysterious of connubial Love refus'd:
Whatever Hypocrites austerely talk
Of purity and place and innocence,
Defaming as impure what God declares
Pure, and commands to some, leaves free to all.
Our Maker bids increase, who bids abstain
But our destroyer, foe to God and Man?
Hail wedded Love, mysterious Law, true source
Of human offspring, sole propriety,
In Paradise of all things common else.
By thee adulterous lust was driv'n from men
Among the bestial herds to range, by thee
Founded in Reason, Loyal, Just, and Pure,
Relations dear, and all the Charities
Of Father, Son, and Brother first were known.
Far be it, that I should write thee sin or blame,
Or think thee unbefitting holiest place,
Perpetual Fountain of Domestic sweets,
Whose bed is undefil'd and chaste pronounc't,
Present, or past, as Saints and Patriarchs us'd.
Here Love his golden shafts imploys, here lights
His constant Lamp, and waves his purple wings,
Reigns here and revels; not in the bought smile

Of Harlots, loveless, joyless, unindear'd,
Casual fruition, nor in Court Amours,
Mixt Dance, or wanton Mask, or Midnight Ball,
Or Serenate, which the starv'd Lover sings
To his proud fair, best quitted with disdain.
These lull'd by Nightingales imbracing slept,
And on thir naked limbs the flow'ry roof
Show'r'd Roses, which the Morn repair'd. Sleep on,
Blest pair; and O yet happiest if ye seek
No happier state, and know to know no more.

Adam and Eve, before their fall, are here depicted as blissfully happy and fulfilled, and this is demonstrated primarily through descriptions of their physical
beauty and sexuality. Indeed, Satan finds himself, for all his power, jealous of their
sexuality and of the happiness it brings them. It is clear, of course, that their physical state puts Adam and Eve in need of protection; it is a fragile beauty, as is the
happiness that it engenders. Several gender-related claims are noteworthy. One,
Milton does not revise the biblical claim that Eve was created from Adam's side,
despite his willingness elsewhere to invoke the findings of modern science within
the biblical context. It is quite clear that Milton maintains Adam's priority as both
the first and the archetypical human creature. Second, and perhaps because of
Adam's position, Milton describes Eve as receiving her divinity *through* Adam.
Thus, Eve would seem to be an image of the image of God, whose own understanding of God's will and commandments is mediated by Adam. This, combined with
her beauty, will influence Satan's decision to approach Eve with his temptations.
Third, Milton's comparison of Eve to Pandora, and by association of Satan and
Adam to Prometheus, color our understanding of the biblical story. Obviously this
foreshadows their fall and comparesAdam to Satan through the Prometheus allusion; in addition, it characterizes Eve as a back-handed gift to Adam.

Lastly, Milton is clearly at pains to argue that original sin does not consist in the
sexual act. Adam and Eve's innocent sexuality and sexual activity is characterized as
commanded and sanctified by God as a part of their obligation to bear fruit. Thus,
here again, we see the modern ambivalence regarding nature and the natural human
state—our original state, the state of nature, is innocent and pure, beloved of God and
fully present to Him, but for some reason (here, on account of the fall) our nature is
hidden from us, sullied and confounded and far distanced from us. This "natural
law," like the law of gravity, is represented by Milton as fully rational, fully disclosed
by God to the human spirit; yet, like the law of gravity, it is hidden from us and must
be rediscovered with great effort by reflection upon ourselves and our weaknesses.

These themes are reiterated in later books, where Adam is instructed by the
angel Raphael regarding his state, the universe, and the power of God. Thus, God
arms Adam against Satan by giving Adam knowledge of his origins and nature.
Adam expresses his gratitude and demonstrates his partial understanding by
retelling his own experiences.

BOOK VIII

⌒ ⌒ ⌒

    Adam clear'd of doubt, repli'd.
How fully hast thou satisfi'd me, pure
Intelligence of Heav'n, Angel serene,
And freed from intricacies, taught to live
The easiest way, nor with perplexing thoughts
To interrupt the sweet of Life, from which
God hath bid dwell far off all anxious cares,
And not molest us, unless we ourselves
Seek them with wand'ring thoughts, and notions vain.
But apt the Mind or Fancy is to rove
Uncheckt, and of her roving is no end;
Till warn'd, or by experience taught, she learn
That not to know at large of things remote
From use, obscure and subtle, but to know
That which before us lies in daily life,
Is the prime Wisdom.

⌒ ⌒ ⌒

So spake the Godlike Power, and thus our Sire.
For Man to tell how human Life began
Is hard: for who himself beginning knew?
Desire with thee still longer to converse
Induc'd me. As new wak't from soundest sleep
Soft on the flow'ry herb I found me laid
In Balmy Sweat, which with his Beams the Sun
Soon dri'd, and on the reeking moisture fed.

⌒ ⌒ ⌒

Pensive I sat me down; there gentle sleep
First found me, and with soft oppression seiz'd
My drowsed sense, untroubl'd, though I thought
I then was passing to my former state
Insensible, and forthwith to dissolve:
When suddenly stood at my Head a dream,
Whose inward apparition gently mov'd
My fancy to believe I yet had being,
And liv'd: One came, methought, of shape Divine,
And said, they Mansion wants thee, *Adam,* rise,
First Man, of Men innumerable ordain'd
First Father, call'd by thee I come thy Guide
To the Garden of bliss, thy seat prepar'd.

⌒ ⌒ ⌒

This Paradise I give thee, count it thine
To Till and keep, and of the Fruit to eat:
Of every Tree that in the Garden grows
Eat freely with glad heart; fear here no dearth:
But of the Tree whose operation brings
knowledge of good and ill, which I have set
The Pledge of thy Obedience and thy Faith,
Amid the Garden by the Tree of Life,
Remember what I warn thee, shun to taste,
And shun the bitter consequence: for know,
The day thou eat'st thereof, my sole command
Transgrest, inevitably thou shalt die;
From that day mortal, and this happy State
Shalt lose, expell'd from hence into a World
Of woe and sorrow. Sternly he pronounc'd
The rigid interdiction, which resounds
Yet dreadful in mine ear, though in my choice
Not to incur; but soon his clear aspect
Return'd and gracious purpose thus renew'd.
Not only these fair bounds, but all the Earth
To thee and to thy Race I give; as Lords
Possess it, and all things that therein live,
Or live in Sea, or Air, Beast, Fish, and Fowl.
In sign whereof each Bird and Beast behold
After thir kinds; I bring them to receive
From thee thir Names, and pay thee fealty
With low subjection; understand the same
Of Fish within thir wat'ry residence,
Not hither summon'd, since they cannot change
Thir Element to draw the thinner Air.

Let not my words offend thee, Heav'nly Power,
My Maker, be propitious while I speak.
Hast thou not made me here thy substitute,
And these inferior far beneath me set?
Among unequals what society
Can sort, what harmony or true delight?
Which must be mutual, in proportion due
Giv'n and receiv'd; but in disparity
The one intense, the other still remiss
Cannot well suit with either, but soon prove
Tedious alike: Of fellowship I speak
Such as I seek, fit to participate
All rational delight, wherein the brute
Cannot be human consort

⌒ ⌒ ⌒

He ceas'd, I lowly answer'd. To attain
The highth and depth of thy Eternal ways
All human thoughts come short, Supreme of things;
Thou in thyself art perfect, and in thee
Is no deficience found; not so is Man,
But in degree, the cause of his desire
By conversation with his like to help,
Or solace his defects. No need that thou
Shouldst propagate, already infinite;
And through all numbers absolute, though One;
But Man by number is to manifest
His single imperfection, and beget
Like of his like, his Image multipli'd,
In unity defective, which requires
Collateral love, and dearest amity.
Thou in thy secrecy although alone,
Best with thyself accompanied, seek'st not
Social communication, yet so pleas'd,
Canst raise thy Creature to what highth thou wilt
Of Union or Communion, deifi'd;
I by conversing cannot these erect
From prone, nor in thir ways complacence find.
Thus I embold'n'd spake, and freedom us'd
Permissive, and acceptance found, which gain'd
This answer from the gracious voice Divine.
      Thus far to try thee, *Adam*, I was pleas'd,
And find thee knowing not of Beasts alone,
Which thou hast rightly nam'd, but of thyself,
Expressing well the spirit within thee free,
My Image, not imparted to the Brute,
Whose fellowship therefore unmeet for thee.
Good reason was thou freely shouldst dislike,
And be so minded still; I, ere thou spak'st,
Knew it not good for Man to be alone,
And no such company as then thou saw'st
Intended, thee, for trial only brought,
To see how thou couldst judge of fit and meet:
What next I bring shall please thee, be assur'd,
Thy likeness, thy fit help, thy other self,
Thy wish, exactly to thy heart's desire.
      Hee ended, or I heard no more, for now
My earthly by his Heav'nly overpower'd,
Which it had long stood under, strain'd to the highth
In that celestial Colloquy sublime,

As with an object that excels the sense,
Dazzl'd and spent, sunk down, and sought repair
Of sleep, which instantly fell on me, call'd
By Nature as in aid, and clos'd mine eyes.
Mine eyes he clos'd, but op'n left the Cell
Of Fancy my internal sight, by which
Abstract as in a trance methought I saw,
Though sleeping, where I lay, and saw the shape
Still glorious before whom awake I stood;
Who stooping op'n'd my left side, and took
From thence a Rib, with cordial spirits warm,
And Life-blood streaming fresh; wide was the wound,
But suddenly with flesh fill'd up and heal'd:
The Rib he form'd and fashion'd with his hands;
Under his forming hands a Creature grew,
Manlike, but different sex, so lovely fair,
That what seem'd fair in all the World, seem'd now
Mean, or in her summ'd up, in her contain'd
And in her looks, which from that time infus'd
Sweetness into my heart, unfelt before,
And into all things from her Air inspir'd
The spirit of love and amorous delight.
Shee disappear'd, and left me dark, I wak'd
To find her, or for ever to deplore
Her loss, and other pleasures all abjure:
When out of hope, behold her, not far off,
Such as I saw her in my dream, adorn'd
With what all Earth or Heaven could bestow
To make her amiable: On she came,
Led by her Heav'nly Maker, though unseen,
And guided by his voice, nor uninform'd
Of nuptial Sanctity and marriage Rites:
Grace was in all her steps, Heav'n in her Eye,
In every gesture dignity and love.
I overjoy'd could not forbear aloud.
      This turn hath made amends; thou hast fulfill'd
Thy words, Creator bounteous and benign,
Giver of all things fair, but fairest this
Of all thy gifts, nor enviest. I now see
Bone of my Bone, Flesh of my Flesh, my Self
Before me; Woman is her Name, of Man
Extracted; for this cause he shall forgo
Father and Mother, and to his Wife adhere;
And they shall be one Flesh, one Heart, one Soul.

Milton depicts the sexes as having certain weaknesses and strengths by their very natures, natures that suit them for particular roles. Yet these essential natures of men and women are not universally binding like the law of gravity; they may be disobeyed, and when one disobeys them—when one acts "unnaturally" for one's sex—one sets in motion a whole chain of immoral action, distancing oneself and others from God, from human nature, and from reason. Milton is an excellent example, then, of the "modern" paradoxes discussed above: in his attempt to replace the rigid medieval traditions regulating sex and marriage with more rational, more scientific notions of human nature and individual freedom, he further rigidifies his ideas of morality and social role.

3. RENE DESCARTES
(French, 1596–1650)

Descartes is often credited with fathering modern philosophy, partly because his theories, more than those of almost any other thinker of his era, effected the kind of humanist "turnaround"—referred to in the Introduction to this section—from a god-centered philosophy to a human-centered one. As was also stated before, Descartes was the first "rationalist." Renowned as well for his contributions to mathematics, (he was the first to do what is now called "analytic geometry"), Descartes sought through rationalism to give all human knowledge the same certainty and precision as occurred in that discipline. He claimed that this certainty and precision could be achieved only by stringent application of a skeptical method, which has come to be called "hypothetical doubt."

THE MEDITATIONS (1641)

Probably the most widely read of Descartes's works, The *Meditations* applies the skeptical method in an attempt to identify the most certain and precise truths of natural reason (called by Descartes "clear and distinct ideas") and to use them to legitimate the scientific study of the external world. As was indicated in the Introduction to this chapter, this goal was at odds with the Church dicta, and so placed Descartes in a dangerous position. Note, in that regard, that Descartes begins his defense of empirical science by denying the reliability of empirical observation through sense experience. The famous and almost infinitely provocative "stages of hypothetical doubt" through which Descartes effects this enterprise are given in the first two of the six meditations. Although his arguments in the first two meditations do not deal directly with the question of gender, they provide a relevant background for that issue, and are summarized here.

THE COGITO AND HYPOTHETICAL DOUBT

The famous realization to which Descartes comes in the second meditation, "I think, therefore I am" (called the *cogito,* after the original Latin), is a pivotal moment, both in the *Meditations* and in the history of philosophy. After trying to doubt every claim that he formerly thought was true, Descartes decides that he cannot doubt that he himself exists. As he puts it:

MEDITATION TWO: CONCERNING THE NATURE OF THE HUMAN MIND: THAT THE MIND IS MORE KNOWN THAN THE BODY

But I have persuaded myself that there is nothing at all in the world: no heaven, no earth, no minds, no bodies. Is it not then true that I do not exist? But certainly I should exist, if I were to persuade myself of some thing. But there is a deceiver (I know not who he is) powerful and sly in the highest degree, who is always purposely deceiving me. Then there is no doubt that I exist, if he deceives me. And deceive me as he will, he can never bring it about that I am nothing so long as I shall think that I am something. Thus it must be granted that, after weighing everything carefully and sufficiently, one must come to the considered judgment that the statement "I am, I exist" is necessarily true every time it is uttered by me or conceived in my mind.

Thus, the *cogito* is a very spare claim both about human nature and about truth; Descartes does not get very much when he gets the indubitability of his own existence. But the spareness of this claim is one reason why it is so important.

First, the *cogito* effects a sort of "Copernican" revolution in the theory of knowledge, since Descartes claims in it that he knows *himself* truly and before all other things. Thus, while he will claim later in the *Meditations* that he knows God far more clearly than he knows himself, he can only access his idea of God as one among the various ideas he thinks, and thus, in a sense, he comes to the idea of God *second*. Thus, the *cogito* encapsulates the modern shift from a "god-centered" worldview to a "human-centered" one. Second, the *cogito*—and the stages of doubt that lead up to it, establish in the definition of human nature the clear priority of consciousness or thought over what we perceive through our bodily senses. Descartes claims that I know about the existence of my body only through sense experience, but he establishes the unreliability of sense experience. For instance, claims Descartes (in the first stage of hypothetical doubt), sometimes a tower we see far in the distance looks like a tiny rectangle instead of a large cylinder, or (as he claims in the second stage, or "dream hypothesis"), sometimes it turns out that I've been dreaming very vividly, and what I dreamed seemed at the time to be real; then, when I wake up, I realize it was only a dream.

MEDITATION ONE

How often has my evening slumber persuaded me of such customary things as these: that I am here, clothed in my dressing gown, seated at the fireplace, when in fact I am lying undressed between the blankets! But right now I certainly am gazing upon this piece of paper with eyes wide awake. This head which I am moving is not heavy with sleep. I extend this hand consciously and deliberately and I feel it. These things would not be so distinct for one who is asleep. But this all seems as if I do not recall having been deceived by similar thoughts on other

occasions in my dreams. As I consider these cases more intently, I see so plainly
that there are no definite signs to distinguish being awake from being asleep that
I am quite astonished, and this astonishment almost convinces me that I am
sleeping.

Let us say, then, for the sake of argument, that we are sleeping and that such
particulars as these are not true: that we open our eyes, move our heads, extend
our hands. Perhaps we do not even have these hands, or any such body at all.

How do I know for sure, asks Descartes, that I'm not dreaming right now? Because I could be dreaming everything I sense to be true, he claims, I could be
dreaming the existence of my body. Hence, while the existence of conscious thinking can be known, the existence of bodies—mine and those of other people—cannot, according to Descartes, be certainly known. Hence, consciousness or mind
(which ultimately, for Descartes, does include sensing and feeling), has a priority
over the existence of one's body in the definition of human nature, according to
Descartes.

But what then am I? A thing that thinks. What is that? A thing that doubts,
understands, affirms, denies, wills, refuses, and which also imagines and senses.

It is truly no small matter if all of these things pertain to me. But why should
they not pertain to me? Is it not I who now doubt almost everything, I who
nevertheless understand something, I who affirm that this one thing is true, I
who deny other things, I who desire to know more things, I who wish not to be
deceived, I who imagine many things against my will, I who take note of many
things as if coming from the senses? Is there anything in all of this which is not
just as true as it is that I am, even if I am always dreaming or even if the one
who created me tries as hard as possible to delude me? Are any of these
attributes distinct from my thought? What can be said to be separate from
myself? For it is so obvious that it is I who doubt, I who understand, I who will,
that there is nothing through which it could be more evidently explicated. But
indeed I am also the same one who imagines; for, although perhaps as I
supposed before, no imagined thing would be wholly true, the very power of
imagining does really exist, and constitutes a part of my thought. Finally, I am
the same one who senses or who takes note of bodily things as if through the
senses. For example, I now see a light, I hear a noise, I feel heat. These are false,
since I am asleep. But I certainly seem to see, hear, and feel. This cannot be
false: properly speaking, this is what is called "sensing" in me. But this is, to
speak precisely, nothing other than thinking.

On account of these features of the *cogito,* Descartes has been interpreted by
many contemporary feminists philosophers, such as Susan Bordo and Genevieve
Lloyd (listed in the suggested readings for this chapter), to be giving a philosophical foundation for male authority. On the one hand, it would seem that Descartes
lays the philosophical groundwork for a liberal position in which all human beings
are considered equal and treated as such. Since human nature is here associated first

and foremost with consciousness or thought, and since men and women are both equally conscious entities, male and female consciousness ought to be equally human and treated equally as such. On the other hand, to the extent that moderns still accept the ancient binary oppositions between say, earth and sky or matter and spirit, and to the extent that the side of these oppositions associated with earth and matter are also associated with femininity and the side associated with sky and spirit are also associated with masculinity, Descartes' *cogito* establishes the priority of masculine qualities in the essence of humanity.

MEDITATION SIX

Nowhere can one find more justifications for this reading than in Descartes' sixth meditation. There, Descartes establishes a strict metaphysical *dualism*—i.e., he claims that there exist in the universe two wholly distinct substances—mind and body. No matter what one concludes about the implications of the *cogito* for sexual politics, it cannot be denied that in the sixth meditation Descartes makes one of the most strict distinctions between mind and body of any philosopher in any time period. Neither can it be denied that this claim is a very problematic one.

In the sixth meditation, Descartes claims that every substance has a distinct nature that clearly and fully defines it as the kind of thing that it is, and that this "nature" or "essence" is that by which each substance is known. In other words, the nature or essence of a thing is *the idea of it,* and it is through the ideas of things that knowledge is gained. Descartes claims that only natures or essences can be known truly—i.e., "clearly and distinctly"—and thus, when the mind has a clear and distinct idea of something, it knows that thing truly. This notion of "essence" is the foundation of Descartes's defense of modern science. Through it, minds can know fully about the "external," or physical, world. Bodies, then, are the proper object of scientific investigation, and the mind can know all about them and their motions— through something like Newtonian mechanics. In that sense, then, again the mind is superior to the body, because bodies are subject to natural laws while minds are free to know these laws and to know bodies through them.

In the following passages, Descartes establishes distinct natures for mind and body.

MEDITATION SIX

First, because I know that all the things that I clearly and distinctly understand can be made by God exactly as I understand them, it is enough that I can clearly and distinctly understand one thing without the other in order for me to be certain that the one thing is different from the other, because at least God can establish them separately. The question of the power by which this takes place is not relevant to their being thought to be different. For this reason, from the fact that I know that I exist, and that meanwhile I judge that nothing else clearly belongs to my nature or essence except that I am a thing that thinks, I rightly conclude that my essence consists in this alone: that I am only a thing that thinks. Although perhaps (or rather, as I shall soon say, to be sure) I have a body that is very closely joined to me, nevertheless, because on the one hand I have a clear and distinct idea of myself—insofar as I am a thing that thinks and not an extended thing—and because on the other hand I have a distinct idea of a body—insofar as it is merely an extended thing, and not a thing that thinks—it is therefore certain that I am truly distinct from my body, and that I can exist without it.

Moreover, I find in myself faculties endowed with certain special modes of thinking—namely the faculties of imagining and sensing—without which I can clearly and distinctly understand myself in my entirety, but not vice versa: I cannot understand them clearly and distinctly without me, that is, without the knowing substance to which they are attached. For in their formal concept they include an act of understanding; thus I perceive that they are distinguished from me just as modes are to be distinguished from the thing of which they are modes. I also recognize certain other faculties—like those of moving from one place to another, of taking on various shapes, and so on—that surely no more can be understood without the substance to which they are attached than those preceding faculties; for that reason they cannot exist without the substance to which they are attached. But it is clear that these faculties, if in fact they exist, must be attached to corporeal or extended substances, but not to a knowing substance, because extension—but certainly not understanding—is contained in a clear and distinct concept of them.

Now, first, I realize at this point that there is a great difference between a mind and a body, because the body, by its very nature, is something divisible, whereas the mind is plainly indivisible. Obviously, when I consider the mind, that is, myself insofar as I am only a thing that thinks, I cannot distinguish any parts in me; rather, I take myself to be one complete thing. Although the whole mind seems to be united to the whole body, nevertheless, were a foot or an arm or any other bodily part amputated, I know that nothing would be taken away from the mind; nor can the faculties of willing, sensing, understanding, and so on be called its "parts," because it is one and the same mind that wills, senses, and understands. On the other hand, no corporeal or extended thing can be thought by me that I did not easily in thought divide into parts; in this way I know that it is divisible. If I did not yet know it from any other source, this consideration alone would suffice to teach me that the mind is wholly different from the body.

Next, I observe that my mind is not immediately affected by all the parts of the body, but merely by the brain, or perhaps even by just one small part of the brain—namely, by that part in which the "common sense" is said to be found. As often as it is disposed in the same manner, it presents the same thing to the mind, although the other parts of the body can meanwhile orient themselves now this way, now that way, as countless experiments show—none of which need be reviewed here.

I also notice that the nature of the body is such that none of its parts can be moved by another part a short distance away, unless it is also moved in the same direction by any of the parts that stand between them, even though this more distant part does nothing. For example, in the cord ABCD, if the final part D is pulled, the first part A would be moved in exactly the same direction as it could be moved if one of the intermediate parts, B or C, were pulled and the last part D remained motionless. Just so, when I sense pain in the foot, physics teaches me that this feeling took place because of nerves scattered throughout the foot. These nerves, like cords, are extended from that point all the way to the brain; when they are pulled in the foot, they also pull on the inner parts of the brain to which they are stretched, and produce a certain motion in these parts of the brain. This motion has been constituted by nature so as to affect the mind with a feeling of pain, as if it existed in the foot. But because these nerves need to pass through the tibia, thigh, loins, back, and neck, with the result that they extend from the foot to the brain, it can happen that the part that is in the foot is not stretched; rather, one of the intermediate parts is thus stretched, and obviously the same movement will occur in the brain that happens when the foot was badly affected. The necessary result is that the mind feels the same pain. And we must believe the same regarding any other sense.

Finally, I observe that, since each of the motions occurring in that part of the brain that immediately affects the mind occasions only one sensation in it, there is no better way to think about this than that it occasions the sensation that, of all that could be occasioned by it, is most especially and most often conducive to the maintenance of a healthy man. Moreover, experience shows that such are all the senses bestowed on us by nature; therefore, clearly nothing is to be found in them that does not bear witness to God's power and goodness. Thus, for example, when the nerves in the foot are violently and unusually agitated, their motion, which extends through the marrow of the spine to the inner reaches of the brain, gives the mind at that point a sign to feel something—namely, the pain as if existing in the foot. This pain provokes it to do its utmost to move away from the cause, since it is harmful to the foot. But the nature of man could have been so constituted by God that this same motion in the brain might have displayed something else to the mind: either the motion itself as it is in the brain, or as it is in the foot, or in some place in between—or somewhere else entirely different. But nothing else serves so well the maintenance of the body. Similarly, when we need a drink, a certain dryness arises in the throat that moves its nerves, and, by means of them, the inner recesses of the brain. This motion affects the mind with a feeling of thirst, because in this situation nothing is more useful for us to know than that we need a drink to sustain our health; the same holds for the other matters.

Having established his strict dualism, Descartes must explain how it is that these two wholly different substances can act together in human experience. For instance, willing something, according to Descartes's definition, is a mental quality, an idea in consciousness. But it seems that in ordinary human experience, one's limbs move when one wills them to do so, and the movement of one's limbs is a quality of body. Similarly, it seems in ordinary experience that when one stubs one's toe—an interaction of bodies—one feels pain, which is a moment of consciousness. Descartes claims to solve these problems, while saving his dualism, by a theory called "causal interactionism." In the foregoing passage, Descartes claims that Mind-substance can *cause* something to occur in Body-substance, and vice versa (and that we call the causation in the first direction, "will" and in the second direction—from body to mind—"perception.")

The theory of "causal interaction" between mind and body is famously insufficient. However, for anyone who finds Descartes's mind–body dualism acceptable, it seems the only way to solve the problems posed by our experience of will and perception. Thus, in a sense, the awkwardness of causal interactionism is a paradigm of the paradoxes of modern humanism, and of the uncomfortable mix of presuppositions within which moderns think about gender. Human nature on the Cartesian model is consciousness bound unnecessarily and uncomfortably to a body. Our physical differences, then, including the differences between males and females, are inessential to our human nature, yet crucially important to our human experience.

Gender differences are also, on this model, the proper objects of natural science—not of philosophy or religion or morality. Hence, natural science is given the job of distinguishing the "natures" of male and female. To the extent that one accepts the gender associations of this dualism, scientific investigation, as a mental function, is masculine. Thus, the image presented in Descartes's dualism is of a male authority defining its own distinction from femininity, and defining it as something feminine—i.e., as a physical distinction. The female, then, on this model, is given the sole responsibility for causing sexual difference; men will have a human nature, and women will have a sexual nature. While this may seem to be quite a stretch from the dualism outlined above, it is in fact the way many philosophers and scientists will come to talk about gender differences in the eighteenth and nineteenth centuries, as several contemporary feminist thinkers have pointed out (see, for instance, Sandra Harding's and Evelyn Fox-Keller's work in the suggested readings at the end of this chapter).

THE PASSIONS OF THE SOUL (1649)

Descartes's last, though not his most famous work, *The Passions of the Soul,* discusses human beings' emotional nature and draws out some of the consequences of causal interactionism. As such, it is noteworthy and relevant for our purposes for several reasons. First, it is the only Cartesian work that discusses human relationships. Second, it is the work in which Descartes lays out in the greatest detail the interrelation between the human Mind and the human Body. Third, it does this work on the assumption that the body is a proper object of science, subject wholly to physical laws, while mind is a free agent of scientific practice.

The book begins with a set of letters between Descartes and a friend of his, which discuss the overall purpose of the work. One of the letters—from the friend to Descartes—perfectly summarizes the spirit of Descartes's work.

And there are three points above all that I'd want you to get everyone to understand rightly. The first is that there is an infinity of things to find out in Physics which can be extremely useful to life; the second, that there is excellent reason to expect the discovery of these things from you; and the third, that the more opportunity you have to carry out a great number of experiments, the more of them you'll be able to find out. It is appropriate for people to be informed of the first point because the greater part of mankind think nothing better can be found in the sciences than what was found by the ancients, and many do not even understand what Physics is or what it can be good for. Now it is easy to prove that the excessive respect maintained for antiquity is an error which is extremely prejudicial to the advancement of the sciences. For we see that the savage peoples of America—and many others as well who inhabit places not so far away—have a lot fewer of the comforts of life than we do, and yet have an origin as ancient as ours, so that they have as much cause as we to say that they are content with the wisdom of their forefathers, and believe no one can teach them anything better than what's been known and practiced among them from the most ancient times. This opinion is so prejudicial that, so long as it is not given up, it's certain that no new capacity can be acquired. Thus experience shows us that the peoples in whose minds it is most deeply rooted are those who have remained the most ignorant and uncouth. And since it's still very common among us, it can serve as a proof that we are a very long way from knowing all we are capable of knowing. This can also be proven quite clearly by many very useful inventions, like the use of the compass, the art of printing, telescopes, and the like, which though they seem easy enough now to those who understand them, have only been devised in the most recent times. But nowhere is our need to acquire new learning more apparent than in things that concern Medicine. For though no one doubts that God has provided this Earth with all things necessary for men to be preserved in perfect health to an extreme old age, and though there is nothing whatever so desirable as the knowledge of these things, so that in olden times it was the principal study of Kings and Sages, nevertheless experience shows that we are still so far from having all of [that knowledge] that we're often bedridden with little illnesses which all the most learned Physicians cannot understand, and only aggravate by their remedies when they undertake to dispel them. The deficiency of their art and the need to perfect it are so plain herein that it is sufficient to tell those who do not understand what Physics is that it is the science which ought to teach people to understand so perfectly the nature of man and all things capable of serving him as nourishment or as remedy, that it would be easy for him to free himself from all sorts of sicknesses by its means.

ABOUT THE PASSIONS IN GENERAL

The main text is divided into three parts. In the first part, "About the Passions in General, and Incidentally about the Entire Nature of Man," Descartes gives an analysis of passion itself, essentially extending his mind/body dualism and his causal interactionism to this question.

FIRST PART

ABOUT THE PASSIONS IN GENERAL, *and Incidentally about the Entire Nature of Man*

Article 1.   That what is a Passion with respect to a subject is always an Action in some other respect.

The defectiveness of the sciences we inherit from the ancients is nowhere more apparent than in what they wrote about the Passions. For even though this is a topic about which knowledge has always been vigorously sought, and though it does not seem to be one of the most difficult—because, as everyone feels them in himself, one need not borrow any observation from elsewhere to discover their nature—nevertheless what the Ancients taught about them is so little, and for the most part so little believable, that I cannot hope to approach the truth unless I forsake the paths they followed. For this reason I shall be obliged to write here as though I were treating a topic which no one before me had ever described. To begin with, I take into consideration that whatever is done or happens afresh is generally called by the Philosophers a Passion with respect to the subject it happens to, and an Action with respect to what makes it happen. Thus, even though the agent and the patient are often quite different, the Action and the Passion are always a single thing, which has these two names in accordance with the two different subjects it may be referred to.

Article 2.   That in order to understand the Passions of the soul we need to distinguish its functions from those of the body.

Then I also take into consideration that we notice no subject that acts more immediately upon our soul than the body it is joined to, and that consequently we ought to think that what is a Passion in the former is commonly an Action in the latter. So there is no better path for arriving at an understanding of our Passions than to examine the difference between the soul and the body, in order to understand to which of the two each of the functions within us should be attributed.

Article 3.   What rule must be followed to achieve this end.

One will find no great difficulty in doing that if one bears this in mind: everything we find by experience to be in us which we see can also be in entirely inanimate bodies must be attributed to our body alone; on the other hand, everything in us which we conceive entirely incapable of belonging to a body must be attributed to our soul.

Article 4.   That the heat and movement of the members proceed from the body, and thoughts from the soul.

Thus, because we do not conceive the body to think in any way, we do right to believe that every kind of thought within us belongs to the soul. And because we have no doubt that there are inanimate bodies which can move in as many different ways as ours, or more, and which have as much heat, or more (experience shows this in [the case of] flame, which in itself has much more heat and motion than any of our members), we must believe that all the heat and all the movements which are in us, insofar as they do not depend on thought, belong to the body alone.

ᴇ ᴇ ᴇ

Article 18.   About volition.

Again, our volitions are of two sorts. For the first are actions of the soul which have their terminus in the soul itself, as when we will to love God or in general to apply our thought to some object that is not material. The others are actions which have their terminus in our body, as when, from the mere fact that we have the volition to take a walk, it follows that our legs move and we walk.

Article 19.   About Perception.

Our perceptions are also of two sorts, and the first have the soul as cause, the others the body. Those which have the soul as cause are the perceptions of our volitions, and of the imaginations or other thoughts that depend on them. For it is certain that we could not will anything unless we perceived by the same means that we willed it. And though with respect to our soul it is an action to will something, it can be said that it is also a passion within it to perceive that it wills. Nevertheless, because this perception and this volition are really only a single thing, the denomination is always made by the loftier one, and so it is not usually named a passion, but an action only.

Article 20.   About imaginations and other thoughts that are formed by the soul.

When our soul applies itself to imagine something which does not exist—as to represent to itself an enchanted palace or a chimera—and also when it applies itself to attend to something which is solely intelligible and not imaginable—for example to attend to its own nature—the perceptions it has of these things depend principally upon the volition that makes it perceive them. That is why they are usually regarded as actions rather than passions.

ᴇ ᴇ ᴇ

Article 47.   What the struggles consist in that people customarily imagine between the lower part of the soul and the higher.

And all the struggles that people customarily imagine between the lower part of the soul, which is called sensitive, and the higher, which is rational, or between the natural appetites and the will, consist only in the opposition between the movements which the body by its spirits and the soul by its will tend to excite simultaneously in the gland. For there is only a single soul in us, and this soul has within itself no diversity of parts; the very one that is sensitive is rational, and all its appetites are volitions. The error which has been committed in having it play different characters, usually opposed to one another, arises only from the fact that its functions have not been rightly distinguished from those of the body, to which alone must be attributed everything to be found in us that is opposed to our reason.

෴ ෴ ෴

This is what has given people occasion to imagine two powers within [the soul] which struggle against one another. All the same, a certain struggle can still be conceived, in that often the same cause which excites some passion in the soul also excites certain movements in the body, to which the soul does not contribute and which it stops or tries to stop as soon as it perceives them, as we experience when what excites fear also makes the spirits enter the muscles that move the legs to flee, and our volition to be bold stops them.

ABOUT THE NUMBER AND ORDER OF THE PASSIONS

In the second part of the work, "About the Number and Order of the Passions, and the Explanation of the Six Primitives," Descartes discusses in detail the various passions to which human nature is subject. According to him, all human feelings are ultimately derivable from six "primitive" passions: Wonder, Love, Hatred, Desire, Joy, and Sadness. Thus, Descartes will handle the analysis of human nature according to the same presuppositions he applied to the analysis of knowledge—that there are certain passions which are, in a sense, "axiomatic" to all others, just as there are certain ideas—for instance the idea of God—from which he believes all other ideas are derived. In the case of the passions, the "primitives" are those strong passions which constitute the basic ways our soul is excited by "external" stimuli. Love and desire are of most interest to our discussion of gender.

Article 69.   That there are only six primitive Passions.

But the number of those which are simple and primitive is not very large. For by carrying out a review of all those I have enumerated, one can discover with ease that only six of them are of this kind—namely Wonder, Love, Hatred, Desire, Joy, and Sadness—and that all the others are composed of some of these six or are species of them. This is why, so that their multiplicity may not perplex readers, I shall treat the six primitives separately here, and show later in what way all the others originate from them.

෴ ෴ ෴

Article 79.   The definitions of Love and Hatred.

Love is an excitation of the soul, caused by the motion of the spirits, which incites it to join itself in volition to the objects that appear to be suitable to it. And Hatred is an excitation, caused by the spirits, which incites the soul to will to be separated from the objects that are presented to it as harmful. I say these excitations are caused by the spirits in order to distinguish Love and Hatred, which are passions and depend on the body, both from judgments which also incline the soul to join itself in volition with the things it deems good and to separate itself from those it deems bad, and from excitations which these judgments excite by themselves in the soul.

Article 80.   What it is to join or separate oneself in volition.

Moreover, by the phrase "in volition" I do not intend here to speak of desire, which is a passion by itself and has reference to the future, but of the consent by which we consider ourselves from the present as joined with what we love, in such a way that we imagine a whole of which we think ourselves to be only one part and the thing loved another. So, on the other hand, in hatred we consider ourselves alone as a whole, entirely separated from the thing for which we have the aversion.

Article 81.   About the distinction customarily made between the Love of concupiscence and that of benevolence.

Now two sorts of Love are commonly distinguished, of which one is named the Love of benevolence—that is, that which incites us to will the good of what we love, the other is named the Love of concupiscence—that is, that which makes us desire the thing we love. But it seems to me that this distinction concerns only the effects of Love and not its essence. For as soon as we have joined ourselves in volition to some object, whatever its nature may be, we have benevolence for it; that is, we also join to it in volition the things we believe to be suitable to it— which is one of the principal effects of Love. And if we judge it to be a good to possess it or to be associated with it in some other manner than in volition, we desire it—which is likewise one of the most common effects of love.

Article 82.   How very different passions agree in that they participate in Love.

Nor is there any need to distinguish as many species of Love as there are different objects which may be loved. For, e.g., although the passions an ambitious person has for glory, an avaricious person for money, a drunkard for wine, a brutish man for a woman he wants to violate, a man of honor for his friend or his mistress, and a good father for his children may be very different from one another, they are nevertheless similar in that they participate in Love. But the first four have Love only for the possession of the objects their passion has reference to, and have none whatever for the objects themselves, for which they have only desire mixed with other particular passions. On the other hand, a good father's Love for his children is so pure that he desires to have nothing from them, and wills neither to possess them otherwise than he does nor to be joined to them more closely than he already is; instead, considering them each as another himself, he seeks their good as his own or with even greater solicitude, because, representing to himself that he and they make up a whole of which he is not the best part, he often prefers their interests to his, and is not afraid to lose himself in order to save them. The affection people of honor have for their friends is of this same nature, though it is rarely so perfect, and that which they have for their mistress participates greatly in it, but also participates a little in the other.

Love, according to Descartes, is a species of volition, or will—i.e., it is a causal interaction from mind to body, which occurs on the occasion of a causal interaction from body to mind (a perception) of something to which the agent mentally attaches him or herself. Thus, love is defined as a sort of enlarged self-definition (as is hatred), through which one adds the idea of an external object and the idea of oneself into a single idea (or, in the case of hatred, distinguishes the idea of an external object from the idea of oneself). Love, then, is a result of an agent's free, wholly mental or conscious, will, not—as the ancients might have claimed—of the agent's good judgment or reason, or of fate. Thus, with regard to the passions, we see another aspect of Descartes's "humanistic" turn; human beings, as agents, bear moral responsibility for their emotional attachments. This is discussed further in the third part of the essay.

Descartes claims that "high" love and "low" love (a distinction made also by medieval thinkers and suggested in Plato's *Symposium,* excerpted in Part Two) are not essentially different, and that they are only distinguished by their "effects." Desire is an entirely separate emotion, which is understood here as one of the common "effects" of love. In desire, the agent (mentally) wills to (physically) possess the objects to which he or she is attached. Thus, desire is also a kind of enlarged vision of self, an enlarged idea of one's body, of its physical possession of another body. Sexuality, then, is also "humanized" here; it is a mental quality in which the idea of an external body is added to the idea of the agent's body. Consequently, desire is envisioned here as the desire *for* actual physical possession of the desired object by the agent, but *within* the mind.

Human desire, then, would have to be wholly different from animals' sexuality. Indeed, Descartes believed that only human beings had minds at all. Non-human animals, he claimed, were nothing but machines—they had no consciousness. Here, we see that animals must on that account have no passions either. Thus, what ancients and medievals conceived as human beings' most "animal" characteristic, one that allied human beings with other creatures—sexual desire—is understood by Descartes to be especially human, and nothing like other creatures' experience. Thus, even the "lowest," simplest forms of consciousness, according to Descartes, are completely alienated from bodily existence, and special to the human race.

ABOUT THE PARTICULAR PASSIONS

The third part of the essay, "About the Particular Passions," is ultimately an explanation of how passions affect human action. Complex emotions, derived from the primitives and from our opinions about right and wrong, constitute something like "moral feelings." As Descartes describes them, they can be "used" to self-reflect on one's other passions, squelching some and encouraging others.

Jealousy is one of these emotions, and Descartes claims it can be either honorable or blameworthy depending, like love, on its objects and effects. In his discussion of its blameworthiness, we see both a good example of how Descartes understands these complex emotions and a vision of how he would apply this theory of the emotions to relations between the sexes.

Article 169. Wherein it is blameworthy.

But an avaricious person is mocked when he is jealous of his treasure, that is, when he devours it with his eyes and is never willing to leave it for fear he will be robbed of it; for money is not worth being watched over with such solicitude. And a man who is jealous of his wife is scorned, because this is a sign that he does not love her as he should, and has a bad opinion of himself or her. I say he does not love her as he should, for if he had a true Love for her, he would have no inclination to distrust her. It is not even she that he loves, properly speaking; it is only the good he imagines to consist in having sole possession for her, and he would not be apprehensive about losing this good if he did not judge that he was unworthy of it or that his wife was unfaithful. Finally, this Passion has reference only to suspicions and distrustings, for it is not, properly speaking, being jealous to try to avoid some evil when one has just cause to be apprehensive about it.

Descartes closes the essay with "a general remedy for the passions." Essentially, moral action is achieved through each person's engagement in the kind of scientific and philosophical investigations that Descartes has performed, here and in the *Meditations*. Thus, even in the internal world of consciousness, or mind, Descartes envisions a struggle of "mental" thoughts to overpower "physical" thoughts; i.e., of reason and perception. Here, as in others of his works, Descartes is a "rationalist," claiming that withholding one's judgment until one can apply the "axioms" of pure reason (for Descartes, ultimately contained in the idea of God) to the ideas of sense experience is the only way to establish their truth or falsity. Here, he shows it is the only way to establish their moral goodness as well.

Article 211. A general remedy for the Passions.

And now that we understand them all, we have much less reason to fear them than we had before. For we see that they are all in their nature good, and that we have nothing to avoid but misuses or excesses of them, for which the remedies I have explained could suffice if everyone had enough interest in putting them into practice. But because I have included among these remedies the forethought and skill by which we can correct our constitutional deficiencies, in applying ourselves to separate within us the movements of the blood and spirits from the thoughts to which they are usually joined, I grant that there are few people who are sufficiently prepared in this way against all sorts of contingencies, and that these movements, excited in the blood by the objects of the Passions, immediately follow so swiftly from mere impressions formed in the brain and from the disposition of the organs, even though the soul may in no way contribute to them, that there is no human wisdom capable of withstanding them when one is insufficiently prepared for them. Thus many cannot abstain from laughing when tickled, even though they derive no pleasure from it. For, in spite of themselves, the impression of Joy and surprise which previously made them laugh for the same reason, being awakened in their fantasy, makes their lungs suddenly swell with the blood that the heart sends there. And so those who are strongly inclined by their constitution to the excitations of Joy, Pity, Fear, or Anger cannot keep from fainting, crying, trembling, or having their blood all stirred up just as though they had a fever, when their fantasy is greatly affected by the object of one of these Passions. But what can always be done on such an occasion, and what I think I can set down here as the most general remedy for all the excesses of the Passions and the easiest to put into practice, is this: when one feels the blood stirred up like that, one should take warning, and recall that everything presented to the imagination tends to deceive the soul, and to make the reasons for favoring the object of its Passion appear to it much stronger than they are, and those for opposing it much weaker. And when the Passion favors only things whose execution admits of some delay, one must abstain from making any immediate judgment about them, and distract oneself by other thoughts until time and rest have completely calmed the excitation in the blood. Finally, when it incites one to actions requiring one to reach some resolution at once, the will must be inclined above all to take into consideration and to follow the reason opposed to those the Passion represents, even though they appear less strong.

SOCIAL CONTRACT THEORY

The next three philosophers from whose works readings appear are all practitioners of a kind of political philosophizing called "contractarianism," or "social contract theory." There are many very different political arguments that are offered by contractarians; indeed, Hobbes, Locke, and Rousseau, the three most famous modern contractarians, promote very different political views, as you will see. All social contract theorists, however, share the same *method*. All three of the following thinkers derive their notions of the good political state by investigating human life in a hypothetical condition prior to or outside of any political community, which they called the "state of nature."

The contractarian's notion of the "state of nature" is philosophical, not anthropological; in other words, none of these thinkers did any scientific studies of "primitive" societies, or anything of the sort (although all of them were influenced in part by the example of the new American, and other, colonies). In this vein, Rousseau was famous for his remark, "[l]et us . . . begin by putting aside all the facts, for they have no bearing on the question."[8] Rather, the "state of nature" is a kind of a

---

[8] Jean-Jacques Rousseau, *Discourse on the Origin of Inequality*, from *The Basic Political Writings*. Translated by Donald A. Cress. (Indianapolis: Hackett, 1987), p. 38.

"thought experiment," inspired by the new empirical sciences but purely philosoph-ical. In this, the "state of nature" is similar to Descartes's "hypothetical doubt"; it is a methodological tool, through which, it was hoped, political disagreements could be resolved.

The "state of nature" hypothesis can also be compared to Descartes's hypothe-ses, and to other modern methodologies, in its "humanist" and "revolutionary" as-pects, and consequently it will share with Descartes's humanism and liberalism many of their problematic implications for notions of gender. Contractarianism is specifically designed to "tear down to the foundations" of all the traditional me-dieval political systems, or at least their theoretical justifications, and to reestablish political societies on a more "scientific" basis, by appeal to a more "natural" au-thority. But this "natural" foundation is not the power and justice of God, but the needs and capacities of *human beings.* Thus, in contractarian treatments of gender we will again see a search for "natural" sex differences, here as a justification for the treatment men and women should receive in an ideal political system.

On this account, contractarianism will provide the clearest and most explicit modern discussion of the "nature–culture" distinction, and consequently of the nat-ural or cultural foundations of the social roles of men and women. Different con-tractarians hold different views about the relative values of culturally prescribed and naturally prescribed roles; for instance, Hobbes argues that because the "state of nature" is so terrible, government is legitimate in almost anything it asks of citi-zens, while Rousseau argues that because the "state of nature" is so idyllic, govern-ment is only legitimate when it rests in the citizens' hands. But whatever view a particular social contract theorist may have about the legitimacy of the state, his or her arguments will have to be bolstered by clear distinctions between "natural" and "artificial" human characteristics.

4. THOMAS HOBBES
(English, 1588–1679)

Along with Descartes one of the first great modern philosophers, Thomas Hobbes was a radical political scientist, psychologist, and theologian. In *Leviathan,* his best-known work, from which the following passages are taken, Hobbes offers one of the earliest versions of social contract theory, in which he argues that govern-ments are necessitated by the almost unbearable insecurity of human life in the "state of nature."

LEVIATHAN (1651)

The name of Hobbes's most famous work is a biblical reference: the Leviathan is a great sea monster to which "no power on earth can be compared" (Job 41: 33). Hobbes claimed that the political power of a government was a monster of this kind, hence his "leviathan" is the modern political state. Hobbes is a *materialist,* meaning that he believes consciousness is a result of bodily mechanisms, and not the work of a spirit or soul or mind. In other words, Hobbes disagrees completely with Descartes's and others' claim that human nature is a combination of mind and body; in fact, Hobbes denies entirely the existence of any non-material mental "stuff." In fact, in accordance with this materialist philosophy, Hobbes opens the work with an analogy between a human body and the "body" of the state. His political theory, as we will see, is based largely on this analogy.

OF MAN

In the first part of *Leviathan*, Hobbes gives a rather full materialist discussion of human psychology. Following is a list of definitions of various emotions, something like Descartes's list in *The Passions of the Soul*. Note, however, that for Hobbes, all these emotions are rather dry, simple mechanisms, such as any animal would feel.

> Of pleasures or delights, some arise from the sense of an object present, and those may be called *pleasures of sense* (the word *sensual*, as it is used by those only that condemn them, having no place till there be laws). Of this kind are all onerations and exonerations of the body, as also all that is pleasant in the *sight, hearing, smell, taste, or touch.* Others arise from the expectation that proceeds from foresight of the end or consequence of things, whether those things in the sense please or displease. And these are *pleasures of the mind* of him that draweth those consequences, and are generally called Joy. In the like manner displeasures are some in the sense, and called PAIN; others in the expectation of consequences, and are called GRIEF.
>
> These simple passions, called *appetite, desire, love, aversion, hate, joy,* and *grief,* have their names for diverse considerations diversified. As first, when they one succeed another, they are diversely called from the opinion men have of the likelihood of attaining what they desire Secondly, from the object loved or hated. Thirdly, from the consideration of many of them together. Fourthly, from the alteration or succession itself.
>
> ℮ ℮ ℮
>
> *Love* of persons for society, KINDNESS.
> *Love* of persons for pleasing the sense only, NATURAL LUST.
> *Love* of the same, acquired from rumination, that is, imagination of pleasure past, LUXURY.
> *Love* of one singularly, with desire to be singularly beloved, THE PASSION OF LOVE. The same, with fear that the love is not mutual, JEALOUSY.
> *Desire*, by doing hurt to another, to make him condemn some fact of his own, REVENGEFULNESS.
> *Desire* to know why, and how, CURIOSITY, such as is in no living creature but *man,* so that man is distinguished, not only by his reason, but also by this singular passion from other *animals,* in whom the appetite of food and other pleasures of sense by predominance take away the care of knowing causes,

which is a lust of the mind that by a perseverance of delight in the continual and indefatigable generation of knowledge exceedeth the short vehemence of any carnal pleasure.

Fear of power invisible, feigned by the mind, or imagined from tales publicly allowed, RELIGION; not allowed, SUPERSTITION. And when the power imagined is truly such as we imagine, TRUE RELIGION.

Thus, if we were to evaluate Hobbes's treatment of the mind/body distinction and its implications for gender, as we did Descartes, we would find him far more egalitarian on account of his materialism. Since, for Hobbes, consciousness is nothing but the machinations of a body, all human beings are defined first and foremost as bodies.

OF THE COMMONWEALTH

Central to Hobbes's political philosophy is his claim that the "state of nature"—i.e., human life without the protection of government—is a state of constant mortal fear, or, as he describes it in an oft-quoted line, "solitary, poor, nasty, brutish, and short." Thus, for Hobbes, the natural instability of human life made the institution of government—he called the "commonwealth"—not only legitimate but absolutely vital to citizens' survival. In the following passages, Hobbes describes the "state of nature" and gives his arguments for the legitimacy of the state.

CHAPTER XIII

OF THE NATURAL CONDITION *OF* MANKIND,
AS CONCERNING THEIR FELICITY, AND MISERY

Nature hath made men so equal in the faculties of body and mind as that, though there be found one man sometimes manifestly stronger in body or of quicker mind than another, yet when all is reckoned together the difference between man and man is not so considerable as that one man can thereupon claim to himself any benefit to which another may not pretend as well as he. For as to the strength of body, the weakest has strength enough to kill the strongest, either by secret machination, or by confederacy with others that are in the same danger with himself.

And as to the faculties of the mind—setting aside the arts grounded upon words, and especially that skill of proceeding upon general and infallible rules called science (which very few have, and but in few things), as being not a native faculty (born with us), nor attained (as prudence) while we look after somewhat else—I find yet a greater equality amongst men than that of strength. For prudence is but experience, which equal time equally bestows on all men in those things they equally apply themselves unto. That which may perhaps make such equality incredible is but a vain conceit of one's own wisdom, which almost all men think they have in a greater degree than the vulgar, that is, than all men but themselves and a few others whom, by fame or for concurring with themselves, they approve. For such is the nature of men that howsoever they may acknowledge many others to be more witty, or more eloquent, or more learned, yet they will hardly believe there be many so wise as themselves. For they see their own wit at hand, and other men's at a distance. But this proveth rather that men are in that point equal, than unequal. For there is not ordinarily a greater sign of the equal distribution of anything than that every man is contented with his share.

From this equality of ability ariseth equality of hope in the attaining of our ends. And therefore, if any two men desire the same thing, which nevertheless they cannot both enjoy, they become enemies; and in the way to their end, which is principally their own conservation, and sometimes their delectation only, endeavour to destroy or subdue one another. And from hence it comes to pass that, where an invader hath no more to fear than another man's single power, if one plant, sow, build, or possess a convenient seat, others may probably be expected to come prepared with forces united, to dispossess and deprive him, not only of the fruit of his labour, but also of his life or liberty. And the invader again is in the like danger of another.

And from this diffidence of one another, there is no way for any man to secure himself so reasonable as anticipation, that is, by force or wiles to master the persons of all men he can, so long till he see no other power great enough to endanger him. And this is no more than his own conservation requireth, and is generally allowed. Also, because there be some that taking pleasure in contemplating their own power in the acts of conquest, which they pursue farther than their security requires, if others (that otherwise would be glad to be at ease within modest bounds) should not by invasion increase their power, they would not be able, long time, by standing only on their defence, to subsist. And by consequence, such augmentation of dominion over men being necessary to a man's conservation, it ought to be allowed him.

Hereby it is manifest that during the time men live without a common power to keep them all in awe, they are in that condition which is called war, and such a war as is of every man against every man. For War consisteth not in battle only, or the act of fighting, but in a tract of time wherein the will to contend by battle is sufficiently known. And therefore, the notion of *time* is to be considered in the nature of war, as it is in the nature of weather. For as the nature of foul weather lieth not in a shower or two of rain, but in an inclination thereto of many days together, so the nature of war consisteth not in actual fighting, but in the known disposition thereto during all the time there is no assurance to the contrary. All other time is PEACE.

Whatsoever therefore is consequent to a time of war, where every man is enemy to every man, the same is consequent to the time wherein men live without other security than what their own strength and their own invention shall furnish them withal. In such condition there is no place for industry, because the fruit thereof is uncertain, and consequently, no culture of the earth, no navigation, nor use of the commodities that may be imported by sea, no commodious building, no instruments of moving and removing such things as require much force, no knowledge of the face of the earth, no account of time, no arts, no letters, no society, and which is worst of all, continual fear and danger of violent death, and the life of man, solitary, poor, nasty, brutish, and short.

⌐ ⌐ ⌐

CHAPTER XIV

Of the First and Second Natural Laws *and of* Contracts

The Right of Nature, which writers commonly call *jus naturale,* is the liberty each man hath to use his own power, as he will himself, for the preservation of his own nature, that is to say, of his own life, and consequently of doing anything which, in his own judgment and reason, he shall conceive to be the aptest means thereunto.

By Liberty is understood, according to the proper signification of the word, the absence of external impediments, which impediments may oft take away part of a man's power to do what he would, but cannot hinder him from using the power left him, according as his judgment and reason shall dictate to him.

A Law of Nature (*lex naturalis*) is a precept or general rule, found out by reason, by which a man is forbidden to do that which is destructive of his life or taketh away the means of preserving the same, and to omit that by which he thinketh it may be best preserved.

⌐ ⌐ ⌐

And because the condition of man (as hath been declared in the precedent chapter) is a condition of war of everyone against everyone (in which case everyone is governed by his own reason and there is nothing he can make use of that may not be a help unto him in preserving his life against his enemies), it followeth that in such a condition every man has a right to everything, even to one another's body. And therefore, as long as this natural right of every man to everything endureth, there can be no security to any man (how strong or wise soever he be) of living out the time which nature ordinarily alloweth men to live. And consequently it is a precept, or general rule, of reason *that every man ought to endeavour peace, as far as he has hope of obtaining it, and when he cannot obtain it, that he may seek and use all helps and advantages of war.* The first branch of which rule containeth the first and fundamental law of nature, which is *to seek peace, and follow it.* The second, the sum of the right of nature, which is *by all means we can, to defend ourselves.*

From this fundamental law of nature, by which men are commanded to endeavour peace, is derived this second law: *that a man be willing, when others*

*are so too, as far-forth as for peace and defence of himself he shall think it
necessary, to lay down this right to all things, and be contented with so much
liberty against other men, as he would allow other men against himself.* For as
long as every man holdeth this right of doing anything he liketh, so long are all
men in the condition of war. But if other men will not lay down their right as
well as he, then there is no reason for anyone to divest himself of his; for that
were to expose himself to prey (which no man is bound to), rather than to
dispose himself to peace.

Hobbes claims that all people are equal in the "state of nature." Note, however,
the basis for this equality: everyone is equal, Hobbes claims, because everyone is
able, whether by force or by conniving, to kill anyone else. And since, according to
Hobbes, everyone naturally wants something that someone else has, the threat people pose to one another's lives in the state of nature is real and constant. It is reasonable to assume, even though Hobbes uses the masculine pronoun, that because
physical strength is not the only way people threaten other's lives, women are included in this equality. This will be supported by passages excerpted below. Thus,
even though, as Hobbes will claim, it is more common for men to rule commonwealths, it is in women's best interest that someone rule the commonwealth, and if
a man, then a man.

But the legitimacy of government, as is already implied, will reside in its ability
to protect the lives of citizens and keep the peace. According to Hobbes, the citizens are entitled to revolt if, but only if, their lives are threatened by their government. Thus, if women have an equal stake in the social contract that they make with
other citizens to be governed, then women, too, would have a right to revolt if their
lives are threatened.

Any disagreement among rulers weakens the government, and so the strongest
government will avoid such disagreements by resting its rulership—which Hobbes
calls "Sovereignty"—in a single individual, i.e., in a monarch. The Sovereign, according to Hobbes, performs such a valuable service to the citizens—protecting
them from killing one another—that they owe the Sovereign absolute obedience in
anything it asks of them, as long as the Sovereign Power keeps its end of the bar-
gain, and never allows citizens' lives to be threatened.

The only way to erect such a common power as may be able to defend them
from the invasion of foreigners and the injuries of one another, and thereby to
secure them in such sort as that by their own industry, and by the fruits of the
earth, they may nourish themselves and live contentedly, is to confer all their
power and strength upon one man, or upon one assembly of men, that may
reduce all their wills, by plurality of voices, unto one will, which is as much as
to say, to appoint one man or assembly of men to bear their person, and every
one to own and acknowledge himself to be author of whatsoever he that so
beareth their person shall act, or cause to be acted, in those things which concern
the common peace and safety, and therein to submit their wills, every one to his
will, and their judgments, to his judgment. This is more than consent, or

concord; it is a real unity of them all, in one and the same person, made by covenant of every man with every man, in such manner as if every man should say to every man *I authorise and give up my right of governing myself to this man, or to this assembly of men, on this condition, that thou give up thy right to him, and authorize all his actions in like manner.* This done, the multitude so united in one person is called a COMMONWEALTH, in Latin CIVITAS. This is the generation of that great LEVIATHAN, or rather (to speak more reverently) of that *Mortal God* to which we owe, under the *Immortal God,* our peace and defence. For by this authority, given him by every particular man in the commonwealth, he hath the use of so much power and strength conferred on him that by terror thereof he is enabled to conform the wills of them all to peace at home and mutual aid against their enemies abroad. And in him consisteth the essence of the commonwealth, which (to define it) is *one person, of whose acts a great multitude, by mutual covenants one with another, have made themselves every one the author, to the end he may use the strength and means of them all, as he shall think expedient, for their peace and common defence.*

And he that carrieth this person is called SOVEREIGN, and said to have *Sovereign Power,* and every one besides, his SUBJECT.

CHAPTER XVIII

OF THE RIGHTS *OF SOVEREIGNS BY INSTITUTION*

First, because they covenant, it is to be understood they are not obliged by former covenant to anything repugnant hereunto. And consequently they that have already instituted a commonwealth, being thereby bound by covenant to own the actions and judgments of one, cannot lawfully make a new covenant amongst themselves to be obedient to any other, in any thing whatsoever, without his permission. And therefore, they that are subjects to a monarch cannot without his leave cast off monarchy and return to the confusion of a disunited multitude, nor transfer their person from him that beareth it to another man, or other assembly of men; for they are bound, every man to every man, to own, and be reputed author of, all that he that already is their sovereign shall do and judge fit to be done; so that, any one man dissenting, all the rest should break their covenant made to that man, which is injustice. And they have also every man given the sovereignty to him that beareth their person; and therefore if they depose him, they take from him that which is his own, and so again it is injustice.

Fourthly, because every subject is by this institution author of all the actions and judgments of the sovereign instituted, it follows that, whatsoever he doth, it can be no injury to any of his subjects, nor ought he to be by any of them accused of injustice. For he that doth anything by authority from another doth therein no injury to him by whose authority he acteth; but by this institution of a commonwealth every particular man is author of all the sovereign doth; and consequently he that complaineth of injury from his sovereign complaineth of that whereof he himself is author, and therefore ought not to accuse any man but himself; no nor himself of injury, because to do injury to one's self is impossible. It is true that they that have sovereign power may commit iniquity, but not injustice, or injury in the proper signification.

Since monarchy is, according to Hobbes, the best kind of government, it is important to understand its nature and to distinguish it from the leadership of a dynastic household with which it is often—and according to Hobbes, wrongly—confused. It is here that Hobbes clearly compares and contrasts political rule to family rule, and argues against the necessity of paternal authority.

CHAPTER XX

OF DOMINION PATERNAL *AND* DESPOTICAL

A *commonwealth by acquisition* is that where the sovereign power is acquired by force; and it is acquired by force when men singly (or many together by plurality of voices) for fear of death or bonds do authorize all the actions of that man or assembly that hath their lives and liberty in his power.

And this kind of dominion or sovereignty differeth from sovereignty by institution only in this, that men who choose their sovereign do it for fear of one another, and not of him whom they institute; but in this case they subject themselves to him they are afraid of. In both cases they do it for fear, which is to be noted by them that hold all such covenants as proceed from fear of death or violence void; which, if it were true, no man in any kind of commonwealth could be obliged to obedience.

⌒ ⌒ ⌒

Dominion is acquired two ways: by generation and by conquest. The right of dominion by generation is that which the parent hath over his children, and is called PATERNAL. And is not so derived from the generation as if therefore the parent had dominion over his child because he begat him, but from the child's consent, either express or by other sufficient arguments declared. For as to the generation, God hath ordained to man a helper, and there be always two that are equally parents; the dominion therefore over the child should belong equally to both, and he be equally subject to both, which is impossible; for no man can obey two masters. And whereas some have attributed the dominion to the man only, as being of the more excellent sex, they misreckon in it. For there is not always that difference of strength or prudence between the man and the woman as that the right can be determined without war. In commonwealths this controversy is decided by the civil law, and for the most part (but not always) the sentence is in favour of the father, because for the most part commonwealths have been erected by the fathers, not by the mothers of families.

But the question lieth now in the state of mere nature, where there are supposed no laws of matrimony, no laws for the education of children, but the law of nature, and the natural inclination of the sexes, one to another, and to their children. In this condition of mere nature either the parents between themselves dispose of the dominion over the child by contract, or do not dispose thereof at all. If they dispose thereof, the right passeth according to the contract. We find in history that the *Amazons* contracted with the men of the neighbouring countries, to whom they had recourse for issue, that the issue male should be sent back, but the female remain with themselves, so that the dominion of the females was in the mother.

If there be no contract, the dominion is in the mother. For in the condition of mere nature, where there are no matrimonial laws, it cannot be known who is the father unless it be declared by the mother; and therefore the right of dominion over the child dependeth on her will, and is consequently hers. Again, seeing the infant is first in the power of the mother, so as she may either nourish or expose it, if she nourish it, it oweth its life to the mother, and is therefore obliged to obey her rather than any other, and by consequence the dominion over it is hers. But if she expose it, and another find and nourish it, the dominion is in him that nourisheth it. For it ought to obey him by whom it is preserved, because preservation of life being the end for which one man becomes subject to another, every man is supposed to promise obedience to him in whose power it is to save or destroy him.

If the mother be the father's subject, the child is in the father's power; and if the father be the mother's subject (as when a sovereign queen marrieth one of her subjects), the child is subject to the mother, because the father also is her subject.

If a man and woman, monarchs of two several kingdoms, have a child, and contract concerning who shall have the dominion of him, the right of the dominion passeth by the contract. If they contract not, the dominion followeth the dominion of the place of his [sc. the child's] residence. For the sovereign of each country hath dominion over all that reside therein.

He that hath the dominion over the child hath dominion also over the children of the child, and over their children's children. For he that hath dominion over the person of a man hath dominion over all that is his, without which dominion were but a title, without the effect.

The right of succession to paternal dominion proceedeth in the same manner as doth the right of succession to monarchy, of which I have already sufficiently spoken in the precedent chapter.

Dominion acquired by conquest, or victory in war, is that which some writers call DESPOTICAL, from *despotes,* which signifieth a *lord* or *master,* and is the dominion of the master over his servant. And this dominion is then acquired to the victor when the vanquished, to avoid the present stroke of death, covenanteth either in express words, or by other sufficient signs of the will, that so long as his life and the liberty of his body is allowed him, the victor shall have the use thereof, at his pleasure. And after such covenant made, the vanquished is a Servant, and not before; for by the word *servant* (whether it be derived from *servire,* to serve, or from *servare,* to save, which I leave to grammarians to dispute) is not meant a captive (which is kept in prison or bonds till the owner of him that took him, or bought him of one that did, shall consider what to do with him; for such men, commonly called slaves, have no obligation at all, but may break their bonds or the prison, and kill or carry away captive their master, justly), but one that, being taken, hath corporal liberty allowed him, and upon promise not to run away, nor to do violence to his master, is trusted by him.

It is not therefore the victory that giveth the right of dominion over the vanquished, but his own covenant. Nor is he obliged because he is conquered (that is to say, beaten, and taken or put to flight), but because he cometh in, and submitteth to the victor; nor is the victor obliged by an enemy's rendering himself (without promise of life) to spare him for this his yielding to discretion, which obliges not the victor longer than in his own discretion he shall think fit.

OF RELIGION

As a part of his political philosophy, and a response to the then-current notion that kings ruled by divine right, Hobbes offered a thick and sometimes obscure theology and biblical interpretation. While little of Hobbes's religious philosophy is relevant to the topic of gender, the following passages do touch on the question. They relate Hobbes's views on witches and witchcraft, which was an important issue of his day (the famous witch trials in the American colony of Salem took place about forty years after *Leviathan* was published).

The issue of witches was a political one, tied essentially to the political issues surrounding modern philosophy. The popularity of the practice of witchcraft—and its apparent power—was a threat to the authority of the church and to the governments of the religious states dominant in the period. Further, since most practitioners were women, it was a threat as well to the patriarchal authority of both of these European institutions. For Hobbes (as for other modern thinkers, like Descartes, as we have seen), religious questions, like psychological ones, were best answered by scientific methods and best based on a scientific foundation. Thus, Hobbes proposed that there is a "true" religion, which was consistent with reason and scientific methodology, and that religious belief in anything not consistent with reason—like the belief in modern miracles or in divine revelation—was "superstition." However, Hobbes also claimed that in order to safely avoid civil war (such as the English Civil War, which occurred during Hobbes's lifetime and greatly influenced his work), the government ought to be able to dictate a state religion to citizens, which citizens would be obliged by law to practice. Thus, questions about religious practice are, for Hobbes, always also political and scientific questions, and it is with this in mind that he discusses witchcraft.

From that which I have here set down of the nature and use of a miracle, we may define it thus: *A* MIRACLE *is a work of God (besides his operation by the way of nature, ordained in the creation), done for the making manifest to his elect the mission of an extraordinary minister for their salvation.*

And from this definition we may infer: first, that in all miracles the work done is not the effect of any virtue in the prophet, because it is the effect of the immediate hand of God (that is to say, God hath done it without using the prophet therein as a subordinate cause).

Secondly, that no devil, angel, or other created spirit, can do a miracle. For it must either be by virtue of some natural science or by incantation, that is, by virtue of words. For if the enchanters do it by their own power independent, there is some power that proceedeth not from God, which all men deny; and if they do it by power given them, then is the work not from the immediate hand of God, but natural, and consequently no miracle.

There be some texts of Scripture that seem to attribute the power of working wonders (equal to some of those immediate miracles wrought by God himself) to certain arts of magic and incantation. As, for example, when we read that after the rod of Moses, being cast on the ground, became a serpent, "the magicians of Egypt did the like by their enchantments" (Exod. 7:11); and that after Moses had turned the waters of the Egyptian streams, rivers, ponds, and pools of water into blood, "the magicians of Egypt did so likewise with their enchantments" (Exod. 7:22); and that after Moses had by the power of God brought frogs upon the land, "the magicians also did so with their enchantments" (Exod. 8:7), and brought up frogs upon the land of Egypt. Will not a man be apt to attribute miracles to enchantments (that is to say, to the efficacy of the sound of words), and think the same very well proved out of this and other such places?

And yet there is no place of Scripture that telleth us what an enchantment is. If, therefore, enchantment be not, as many think it, a working of strange effects by spells and words, but imposture and delusion, wrought by ordinary means, and so far from supernatural as the impostors need not the study so much as of natural causes, but the ordinary ignorance, stupidity, and superstition of mankind, to do them, those texts that seem to countenance the power of magic, witchcraft, and enchantment must needs have another sense than at first sight they seem to bear.

Note how in all these passages, witchcraft is treated as being of a piece with other more "ordinary" superstitions and heresies. In other words, Hobbes, far from being shocked and appalled by the practice, believed it offered persuasive claims that warranted a philosophical criticism. In this way, Hobbes demystified witchcraft in the same way he sought to demystify other superstitions, which policy, while sternly opposed to the practice, also accorded it an unusual respect. This fits well with his treatment of female sovereignty as an unusual, but often rational and always respectworthy occurrence, as well as with his materialism.

5. JOHN LOCKE
(English, 1632–1704)

John Locke was an important figure in both political philosophy and in epistemology and metaphysics. With regard to the latter, Locke was one of the first modern "empiricists"; in other words, he argued, against rationalists like Descartes, that knowledge originates in sense perception, or experience. He argued, for instance, that there were no such things as "innate" ideas of pure reason.

   Both Locke's political and metaphysical work were influential; his political treatises, for instance, were an influence on Thomas Jefferson and so on the ideals on which were founded the United States. However Locke, unlike Descartes and Hobbes, does not seem to have made an effort to derive his political or moral philosophy from his epistemology, or even to have applied the same methodology to both. In fact, the *Essay on Human Understanding* (his epistemological work) and the *Two Treatises of Government* (his political theory, excerpted here) do not seem to cohere with each other very well—in places, they even seem inconsistent. In particular, Locke bases his notion of the good political society on a notion of "natural law," which would seem more consistent with a rationalist philosophy.

THE SECOND TREATISE OF GOVERNMENT (1698)

The first of Locke's two treatises is primarily a criticism of other political thinkers of his day. The second, "An Essay Concerning the True Original, Extent, and End of Civil Government" is far more widely read and more philosophical.

ON THE RIGHTS AND LAWS OF NATURE

Like Hobbes, Locke founds the legitimacy of political power in a hypothetical notion of the "state of nature." However, Locke's idea of the character of this state is quite different from Hobbes's. While he shares with Hobbes the notion that all people are fully equal and free in the state of nature, he claims that they are also rational in this state, and that reason, as a Law of Nature, obliges people to behave in certain ways.

CHAPTER II

OF THE STATE OF NATURE

4. To understand political power aright, and derive it from its original, we must consider what estate all men are naturally in, and that is, a state of perfect freedom to order their actions, and dispose of their possessions and persons as they think fit, within the bounds of the law of Nature, without asking leave or depending upon the will of any other man.

   A state also of equality, wherein all the power and jurisdiction is reciprocal, no one having more than another, there being nothing more evident than that creatures of the same species and rank, promiscuously born to all the same advantages of Nature, and the use of the same faculties, should also be equal one amongst another, without subordination or subjection, unless the lord and master of them all should, by any manifest declaration of his will, set one above another, and confer on him, by an evident and clear appointment, an undoubted right to dominion and sovereignty.

6. But though this be a state of liberty, yet it is not a state of licence; though man in that state have an uncontrollable liberty to dispose of his person or possessions, yet he has not liberty to destroy himself, or so much as any creature in his possession, but where some nobler use than its bare preservation calls for it. The state of Nature has a law of Nature to govern it, which obliges every one, and reason, which is that law, teaches all mankind who will but consult it, that being all equal and independent, no one ought to harm another in his life, health, liberty or possessions; for men being all the workmanship of one omnipotent and infinitely wise Maker; all the servants of one sovereign Master, sent into the world by His order and about His business; they are His property, whose workmanship they are made to last during His, not one another's pleasure. And, being furnished with like faculties, sharing all in one community of Nature, there cannot be supposed any such subordination among us that may authorise us to destroy one another, as if we were made for one another's uses, as the inferior ranks of creatures are for ours. Every one as he is bound to preserve himself, and not to quit his station willfully, so by the like reason, when his own preservation comes not in competition, ought he as much as he can to preserve the rest of mankind, and not unless it be to do justice on an offender, take away or impair the life, or what tends to the preservation of the life, the liberty, health, limb, or goods of another.

CHAPTER III

OF THE STATE OF WAR

17. And hence it is that he who attempts to get another man into his absolute power does thereby put himself into a state of war with him; it being to be understood as a declaration of a design upon his life. For I have reason to conclude that he who would get me into his power without my consent would use me as he pleased when he had got me there, and destroy me too when he had a fancy to it; for nobody can desire to have me in his absolute power unless it be to compel me by force to that which is against the right of my freedom—*i.e.* make me a slave. To be free from such force is the only security of my preservation, and reason bids me look on him as an enemy to my preservation

who would take away that freedom which is the fence to it; so that he who makes an attempt to enslave me thereby puts himself into a state of war with me.

CHAPTER IV

OF SLAVERY

21. The natural liberty of man is to be free from any superior power on earth, and not to be under the will or legislative authority of man, but to have only the law of Nature for his rule. The liberty of man in society is to be under no other legislative power but that established by consent in the commonwealth, nor under the dominion of any will, or restraint of any law, but what that legislative shall enact according to the trust put in it.[9]

The Law of Nature does a lot of work for Locke. Not least of its qualities is that it establishes a fairly low threshold of abuses above which citizens are justified in revolution against their government. Essentially, any government is illegitimate, according to Locke, if it offers citizens a worse life than they would find in the state of nature. This strong notion of civil rights follows from Locke's vision of the state of nature; this state, far from being the dog-eat-dog struggle for survival that Hobbes describes, is for Locke a staid and reasonable condition in which people consider themselves morally obligated to one another and empowered to punish those who do not meet these obligations. In fact, as Locke describes it, the social contract is entered into by individuals only out of convenience, because it provides a court of appeals for disputes.

This very different view of human nature and of civil government stems in large part from the importance to Locke of human freedom. According to Locke (and Hobbes also claimed this), joining together into a society under a civil government requires citizens to give up rights and freedoms that they enjoy in the state of nature. But, where for Hobbes, the freedom of human beings in the state of nature is only a freedom to continue the state of war, for Locke, human freedom is the freedom to exercise a set of "positive" rights recognized by reason, such as the "pursuit of life, health, liberty, and possessions." Thus, for Locke, freedom is a positive and valuable possession that a rational person would exchange only for something of equal or greater value.

ON PROPERTY AND PATERNITY

Locke's positive notion of freedom is founded in his theory of property—a theory which Locke himself considered his greatest achievement. According to Locke,

---

[9] This and the following passages of Locke are taken from John Locke, *Two Treatises of Civil Government, Book II: An Essay Concerning the True Original Extent and End of Civil Government.* London: J.M. Dent and Sons (Everyman's Library), 1924.

there are several different kinds of legitimate rule or authority (in this he follows Aristotle) which are legitimate only so long as they are freely chosen by their subjects; i.e., so long as each subject retains his or her natural freedom. Any authority which is absolute—i.e., which leaves subjects entirely unfree—is tantamount to the imposition of slavery and is therefore illegitimate. But Locke's notion of slavery and its opposite depend on a vision of human freedom as inherently "ownership of one's self." Indeed, Locke claimed that all people own, first and foremost, their own bodies. Freedom, then, consists in the ability to dispose of one's property however one decides, and all people by nature are equal in that, by nature —i.e., inalienably—each owns his or her own body. This is one of the fundamental claims of liberalism on which, for instance, some arguments for abortion rights are based.

In addition, Locke believed that human beings could naturally increase their property through their work. In other words, conventional law is not the foundation of property relations; rather, they hold in the state of nature. Thus, in the modern debate over where to draw the line between nature and culture, Locke gives a great deal of territory to nature, including in it a kind of natural economy and a set of natural rights and obligations. One might imagine, then, that Locke would also found gender differences and the notion of the proper work or roles of men and women in nature, but the case is quite the contrary. For Locke, everyone in the state of nature—including a woman—is free, and so everyone has a set of natural rights whose breach by a political authority constitutes grounds for revolt.

CHAPTER V

OF PROPERTY

☞ ☞ ☞

26. Though the earth and all inferior creatures be common to all men, yet every man has a "property" in his own "person." This nobody has any right to but himself. The "labour" of his body and the "work" of his hands, we may say, are properly his. Whatsoever, then, he removes out of the state that Nature hath provided and left it in, he hath mixed his labour with it, and joined to it something that is his own, and thereby makes it his property. It being by him removed from the common state Nature placed it in, it hath by this labour something annexed to it that excludes the common right of other men. For this "labour" being the unquestionable property of the labourer, no man but he can have a right to what that is once joined to, at least where there is enough, and as good left in common for others.

☞ ☞ ☞

44. From all which it is evident, that though the things of Nature are given in common, man (by being master of himself, and proprietor of his own person, and the actions or labour of it) had still in himself the great foundation of property; and that which made up the great part of what he applied to the support or comfort of his being, when invention and arts had improved the conveniences of life, was perfectly his own, and did not belong in common to others.

45. Thus labour, in the beginning, gave a right of property, wherever any one was pleased to employ it, upon what was common, which remained a long while, the far greater part, and is yet more than mankind makes use of. Men at first, for the most part, contented themselves with what unassisted Nature offered to their necessities; and though afterwards, in some parts of the world, where the increase of people and stock, with the use of money, had made land scarce, and so of some value, the several communities settled the bounds of their distinct territories, and, by laws, within themselves, regulated the properties of the private men of their society, and so, by compact and agreement, settled the property which labour and industry began.

CHAPTER VI

OF PATERNAL POWER

56. Adam was created a perfect man, his body and mind in full possession of their strength and reason, and so was capable from the first instance of his being to provide for his own support and preservation, and govern his actions according to the dictates of the law of reason God had implanted in him. From him the world is peopled with his descendants, who are all born infants, weak and helpless, without knowledge or understanding. But to supply the defects of this imperfect state till the improvement of growth and age had removed them, Adam and Eve, and after them all parents were, by the law of Nature, under an obligation to preserve, nourish and educate the children they had begotten, not as their own workmanship, but the workmanship of their own Maker, the Almighty, to whom they were to be accountable for them.

64. But what reason can hence advance this care of the parents due to their offspring into an absolute, arbitrary dominion of the father, whose power reaches no farther than by such a discipline as he finds most effectual to give such strength and health to their bodies, such vigour and rectitude to their minds, as may best fit his children to be most useful to themselves and others, and, if it be necessary to his condition, to make them work when they are able for their own subsistence; but in this power the mother, too, has her share with the father.

65. Nay, this power so little belongs to the father by any peculiar right of Nature, but only as he is guardian of his children, that when he quits his care of them he loses his power over them, which goes along with their nourishment and education, to which it is inseparably annexed, and belongs as much to the foster-father of an exposed child as to the natural father of another. So little power does the bare act of begetting give a man over his issue, if all his care ends there, and this be all the title he hath to the name and authority of a father. And what will become of this paternal power in that part of the world where one woman hath more than one husband at a time? or in those parts of America

where, when the husband and wife part, which happens frequently, the children are all left to the mother, follow her, and are wholly under her care and provision? And if the father die whilst the children are young, do they not naturally everywhere owe the same obedience to their mother, during their minority, as to their father, were he alive?

⌐ ⌐ ⌐

CHAPTER VII

OF POLITICAL OR CIVIL SOCIETY

77. God, having made man such a creature that, in His own judgment, it was not good for him to be alone, put him under strong obligations of necessity, convenience, and inclination, to drive him into society, as well as fitted him with understanding and language to continue and enjoy it. The first society was between man and wife, which gave beginning to that between parents and children, to which, in time, that between master and servant came to be added. And though all these might, and commonly did, meet together, and make up but one family, wherein the master or mistress of it had some sort of rule proper to a family, each of these, or all together, came short of "political society," as we shall see if we consider the different ends, ties, and bounds of each of these.

78. Conjugal society is made by a voluntary compact between man and woman, and though it consist chiefly in such a communion and right in one another's bodies as is necessary to its chief end, procreation, yet it draws with it mutual support and assistance, and a communion of interests too, as necessary not only to unite their care and affection, but also necessary to their common offspring, who have a right to be nourished and maintained by them till they are able to provide for themselves.

79. For the end of conjunction between male and female being not barely procreation, but the continuation of the species, this conjunction betwixt male and female ought to last, even after procreation, so long as is necessary to the nourishment and support of the young ones, who are to be sustained by those that got them till they are able to shift and provide for themselves. This rule, which the infinite wise Maker hath set to the works of His hands, we find the inferior creatures steadily obey. In those vivaporous animals which feed on grass the conjunction between male and female lasts no longer than the very act of copulation, because the teat of the dam being sufficient to nourish the young till it be able to feed on grass, the male only begets, but concerns not himself for the female or young, to whose sustenance he can contribute nothing. But in beasts of prey the conjunction lasts longer, because the dam, not being able well to subsist herself and nourish her numerous offspring by her own prey alone (a more laborious as well as more dangerous way of living than by feeding on grass), the assistance of the male is necessary to the maintenance of their common family, which cannot subsist till they are able to prey for themselves,

but by the joint care of male and female. The same is observed in all birds (except some domestic ones, where plenty of food excuses the cock from feeding and taking care of the young brood), whose young, needing food in the nest, the cock and hen continue mates till the young are able to use their wings and provide for themselves.

80. And herein, I think, lies the chief, if not the only reason, why the male and female in mankind are tied to a longer conjunction than other creatures— viz., because the female is capable of conceiving, and, *de facto,* is commonly with child again, and brings forth too a new birth, long before the former is out of a dependency for support on his parents' help and able to shift for himself, and has all the assistance due to him from his parents, whereby the father, who is bound to take care for those he hath begot, is under an obligation to continue in conjugal society with the same woman longer than other creatures, whose young, being able to subsist of themselves before the time of procreation returns again, the conjugal bond dissolves of itself, and they are at liberty till Hymen, at his usual anniversary season, summons them again to choose new mates.

82. But the husband and wife, though they have but one common concern, yet having different understandings, will unavoidably sometimes have different wills too. It therefore being necessary that the last determination (*i.e.,* the rule) should be placed somewhere, it naturally falls to the man's share as the abler and the stronger. But this, reaching but to the things of their common interest and property, leaves the wife in the full and true possession of what by contract is her peculiar right, and at least gives the husband no more power over her than she has over his life; the power of the husband being so far from that of an absolute monarch that the wife has, in many cases, a liberty to separate from him where natural right or their contract allows it, whether that contract be made by themselves in the state of Nature or by the customs or laws of the country they live in, and the children, upon such separation, fall to the father or mother's lot as such contract does determine.

83. For all the ends of marriage being to be obtained under politic government, as well as in the state of Nature, the civil magistrate doth not abridge the right or power of either, naturally necessary to those ends—viz., procreation and mutual support and assistance whilst they are together, but only decides any controversy that may arise between man and wife about them. If it were otherwise, and that absolute sovereignty and power of life and death naturally belonged to the husband, and were necessary to the society between man and wife, there could be no matrimony in any of these countries where the husband is allowed no such absolute authority. But the ends of matrimony requiring no such power in the husband, it was not at all necessary to it. The condition of conjugal society put it not in him; but whatsoever might consist with procreation and support of the children till they could shift for themselves—mutual assistance, comfort, and maintenance—might be varied and regulated by that contract which first united them in that society, nothing being necessary to any society that is not necessary to the ends for which it is made.

Hence, while Locke founds the difference between the sexes and their obligations to each other in nature, reason, and God—similarly in some ways to Descartes and Milton, excerpted earlier, and Rousseau, excerpted next—unlike these other modern thinkers, he is not led to make on this basis a political or economic distinction between them. Though men and women may have "different wills," according to Locke, both contribute equally to their common labor of raising children, and both are equally free, as citizens, to defend their life and property.

6. JEAN-JACQUES ROUSSEAU
(Native Swiss, But French Resident, 1712–1778)

Where Locke's writings were influential upon the formation of the new American United States and the revolution through which they were given birth, Rousseau's were influential upon the French Revolution and the resulting French Republic, and one might say that Rousseau bears to Locke a similar relationship as does the French to the American revolution. Among the very most influential and fervent of modern political texts, Rousseau's treatises are the epitome of the paradoxes of humanism as described in the Introduction to this section. Rousseau was a pillar of the French Enlightenment, a *philosophe,* the name history has given to the French liberal thinkers of his day.

Yet Rousseau has been interpreted both as a great defender of freedom and democracy and as an apologist for totalitarianism. Somewhat like John Stuart Mill, some of whose work appears in the next chapter, Rousseau's apparent inconsistencies stem from his twofold commitment to social reform and to economic and scientific progress. (Scientific method and the system of capitalism were both developing during this period.) Thus, while some of Rousseau's claims may seem inconsistent, they are unified by his always liberal and progressive spirit. Thus, while Rousseau follows Hobbes and Locke in his contractarian method, he differs vastly from them in many of his claims. He also differs from them in his claim that both the physical and sexual characteristics of men and women are fundamentally different.

Rousseau's most famous works are the two political treatises, *Discourse on the Origins of Inequality* and *On the Social Contract.* Since these treatises deliver Rousseau's fundamental political theory, and since they discuss the development of marriage and the family, it is worth taking a moment with them before turning our attention to Rousseau's theory of education, in which he explicitly discusses the nature of the typical or perfect woman.

THE DISCOURSE ON INEQUALITY (1754)

In the "Second Discourse" (On the Origins of Inequality), Rousseau describes his version of the "State of Nature" and of the development of civil society from it. For Rousseau, this development is essentially a degeneration from a delightful to a depraved existence.

For it is no light undertaking to separate what is original from what is artificial in the present nature of man, and to have a proper understanding of a state which no longer exists, which perhaps never existed, which probably never will exist, and yet about which it is necessary to have accurate notions in order to judge properly our own present state.

෧ ෧ ෧

These investigations, so difficult to carry out and so little thought about until now, are nevertheless the only means we have left of removing a multitude of difficulties that conceal from us the knowledge of the real foundations of human society. It is this ignorance of the nature of man which throws so much uncertainty and obscurity on the true definition of natural right.

෧ ෧ ෧

But as long as we are ignorant of natural man, it is futile for us to attempt to determine the law he has received or which is best suited to his constitution. All that we can see very clearly regarding this law, is that, for it to be law, not only must the will of him who is obliged by it be capable of knowing submission to it, but also, for it to be natural, it must speak directly by the voice of nature.

Leaving aside therefore all the scientific books which teach us only to see men as they have made themselves, and meditating on the first and most simple operations of the human soul, I believe I perceive in it two principles that are prior to reason, of which one makes us ardently interested in our well being and our self-preservation, and the other inspires in us a natural repugnance to seeing any sentient being, especially our fellow man, perish or suffer. It is from the conjunction and combination that our mind is in a position to make regarding these two principles, without the need for introducing that of sociability, that all the rules of natural right appear to me to flow; rules which reason is later forced to reestablish on other foundations, when, by its successive developments, it has succeeded in smothering nature.

෧ ෧ ෧

DISCOURSE ON THE ORIGIN AND FOUNDATIONS OF INEQUALITY AMONG MEN

෧ ෧ ෧

I conceive of two kinds of inequality in the human species: one which I call natural or physical, because it is established by nature and consists in the difference of age, health, bodily strength, and qualities of mind or soul. The other may be called moral or political inequality, because it depends on a kind of convention and is established, or at least authorized by the consent of men. This latter type of inequality consists in the different privileges enjoyed by some at the expense of others, such as being richer, more honored, more powerful than they, or even causing themselves to be obeyed by them.

There is no point in asking what the source of natural inequality is, because the answer would be found enunciated in the simple definition of the word. There is still less of a point in asking whether there would not be some essential connection between the two inequalities, for that would amount to asking whether those who command are necessarily better than those who obey, and whether strength of body or mind, wisdom or virtue are always found in the same individuals in proportion to power or wealth. Perhaps this is a good question for slaves to discuss within earshot of their masters, but it is not suitable for reasonable and free men who seek the truth.

Precisely what, then, is the subject of this discourse? To mark, in the progress of things, the moment when, right taking the place of violence, nature was subjected to the law. To explain the sequence of wonders by which the strong could resolve to serve the weak, and the people to buy imaginary repose at the price of real felicity.

Thus, without having recourse to the supernatural knowledge we have on this point, and without taking note of the changes that must have occurred in the internal as well as the external conformation of man, as he applied his limbs to new purposes and nourished himself on new foods, I will suppose him to have been formed from all time as I see him today: walking on two feet, using his hands as we use ours, directing his gaze over all of nature, and measuring with his eyes the vast expanse of the heavens.

When I strip that being, thus constituted, of all the supernatural gifts he could have received and of all the artificial faculties he could have acquired only through long progress; when I consider him, in a word, as he must have left the hands of nature, I see an animal less strong than some, less agile than others, but all in all, the most advantageously organized of all. I see him satisfying his hunger under an oak tree, quenching his thirst at the first stream, finding his bed at the foot of the same tree that supplied his meal; and thus all his needs are satisfied.

When the earth is left to its natural fertility and covered with immense forests that were never mutilated by the axe, it offers storehouses and shelters at every step to animals of every species. Men, dispersed among the animals, observe and imitate their industry, and thereby raise themselves to the level of animal instinct, with the advantage that, whereas each species has only its own instincts, man, who may perhaps have none that belongs to him, appropriates all of them to himself, feeds himself equally well on most of the various foods which the other animals divide among themselves, and consequently finds his sustenance more easily than any of the rest can.

There are other, more formidable enemies, against which man does not have the same means of self-defense: natural infirmities, childhood, old age, and illnesses of all kinds—sad signs of our weakness, of which the first two are common to all animals, with the last belonging principally to man living in society. On the subject of childhood, I even observe that a mother, by carrying her child everywhere with her can feed it much more easily than females of several animal species, which are forced to be continually coming and going, with great fatigue, to seek their food and to suckle or feed their young. It is true that if a woman were to perish, the child runs a considerable risk of perishing with her. But this danger is common to a hundred other species, whose young are for quite some time incapable of going off to seek their nourishment for themselves.

The first [reflection] that presents itself is to imagine how languages could have become necessary; for since men had no communication among themselves nor any need for it, I fail to see either the necessity of this invention or its possibility, if it were not indispensable. I might well say, as do many others, that languages were born in the domestic intercourse among fathers, mothers, and children. But aside from the fact that this would not resolve the difficulties, it would make the mistake of those who, reasoning about the state of nature, intrude into it ideas from society. They always see the family gathered in one and the same dwelling, with its members maintaining among themselves a union as intimate and permanent as exists among us, where so many common interests unite them. But the fact of the matter is that in that primitive state, since nobody had houses or huts or property of any kind, each one bedded down in some random spot and often for only one night. Males and females came together fortuitously as a result of chance encounters, occasion, and desire, without there being any great need for words to express what they had to say to one another. They left one another with the same nonchalance. The mother at first nursed children for her own need, then, with habit having endeared them to her, she later nourished them for their own need. Once they had the strength to look for their food, they did not hesitate to leave the mother herself.

Instead of the sublime maxim of reasoned justice, *Do unto others as you would have them do unto you,* pity inspires all men with another maxim of natural goodness, much less perfect but perhaps more useful than the preceding one: *Do what is good for you with as little harm as possible to others.*

Among the passions that agitate the heart of man, there is an ardent, impetuous one that renders one sex necessary to the other: a terrible passion which braves all dangers, overcomes all obstacles, and which in its fury, seems fitted to destroy the human race it is designed to preserve. What would become of men, victimized by this unrestrained and brutal rage, without modesty and self-control, fighting everyday over the object of their passion at the price of their blood?

There must first be agreement that the more violent the passions are, the more necessary that laws are to contain them. But over and above the fact that the disorders and the crimes these passions cause daily in our midst show quite well the insufficiency of the laws in this regard, it would still be good to examine whether these disorders did not come into being with the laws themselves; for then, even if they were capable of repressing them, the least one should expect of them would be that they call a halt to an evil that would not exist without them.

Let us begin by distinguishing between the moral and the physical aspects of the sentiment of love. The physical aspect is that general desire which inclines one sex to unite with the another. The moral aspect is what determines this desire and fixes it exclusively on one single object, or which at least gives it a greater degree of energy for this preferred object. Now it is easy to see that the moral aspect of love is an artificial sentiment born of social custom and extolled by women with so much skill and care in order to establish their hegemony and make dominant the sex that ought to obey. Since this feeling is founded on certain notions of merit or beauty that a savage is not in a position to have, and on comparisons he is incapable of making, it must be almost non-existent for him. For since his mind could not form abstract ideas of regularity and proportion, his heart is not susceptible to sentiments of admiration and love, which, even without its being observed come into being from the application of these ideas. He pays exclusive attention to the temperament he has received from nature and not to the taste [aversion] he has been unable to acquire; any woman suits his purpose.

☙ ☙ ☙

Let us conclude that, wandering in the forests, without industry, without speech, without dwelling, without war, without relationships, with no need for his fellow men, and correspondingly with no desire to do them harm, perhaps never even recognizing any of them individually, savage man, subject to few passions and self-sufficient, had only the sentiments and enlightenment appropriate to that state; he felt only his true needs, took notice of only what he believed he had an interest in seeing; and that his intelligence made no more progress than his vanity. If by chance he made some discovery, he was all the less able to communicate it to others because he did not even know his own children. Art perished with its inventor. There was neither education nor progress; generations were multiplied to no purpose. Since each one always began from the same point, centuries went by with all the crudeness of the first ages; the species was already old, and man remained a child.

☙ ☙ ☙

PART TWO

☙ ☙ ☙

The first developments of the heart were the effect of a new situation that united the husbands and wives, fathers and children in one common habitation. The habit of living together gave rise to the sweetest sentiments known to men;

conjugal love and paternal love. Each family became a little society all the better united because mutual attachment and liberty were its only bonds; and it was then that the first difference was established in the lifestyle of the two sexes, which until then had had only one. Women became more sedentary and grew accustomed to watch over the hut and the children, while the man went to seek their common subsistence. With their slightly softer life the two sexes also began to lose something of their ferocity and vigor. But while each one separately became less suited to combat savage beasts, on the other hand it was easier to assemble in order jointly to resist them.

⌐ ⌐ ⌐

As for paternal authority, from which several have derived absolute government and all society, it is enough, without having recourse to the contrary proofs of Locke and Sidney, to note that nothing in the world is farther from the ferocious spirit of despotism than the gentleness of that authority which looks more to the advantage of the one who obeys than to the utility of the one who commands; that by the law of nature, the father is master of the child as long as his help is necessary for him; that beyond this point they become equals, and the son, completely independent of the father, then owes him merely respect and not obedience; for gratitude is clearly a duty that must be rendered, but not a right that can be demanded. Instead of saying that civil society derives from paternal power, on the contrary it must be said that it is from civil society that this power draws its principal force. An individual was not recognized as the father of several children until the children remained gathered about him. The goods of the father, of which he is truly the master, are the goods that keep his children in a state of dependence toward him, and he can cause their receiving a share in his estate to be consequent upon the extent to which they will have well merited it from him by continuous deference to his wishes. Now, far from having some similar favor to expect from their despot (since they belong to him as personal possessions—they and all they possess—or at least he claims this to be the case), subjects are reduced to receiving as a favor what he leaves them of their goods. He does what is just when he despoils them; he does them a favor when he allows them to live.

Both Rousseau's stirring enthusiasm for natural rights and his disturbing and ob- tuse delineation of the state of nature are evident in the Second Discourse. While Rousseau is at pains, for instance, to argue that in the state of nature, men and women are equally free and unencumbered by children, he nonetheless also goes out of his way to argue that paternal authority over children is natural. Further, while he is consistent in his claims that in the state of nature all people are completely free and equal, including women, he adds an unnecessary inconsistency by claiming that there are both physical and *emotional* differences between men and women that are natural and that properly found different political status for the sexes.

These odd inconsistencies stem from Rousseau's ambiguous position with regard to the state of nature in general. On the one hand, Rousseau seems to want to argue, against Hobbes, that the state of nature is wonderful and bountiful, and that people in the state of nature are both happy and kind to each other (this is the gist of his claim that in the state of nature, people have only the emotions of pity and self-protection, with no higher faculties). Following this line, Rousseau intimates that all succeeding levels of civilization plunge the race further into degeneracy and injustice. On the other hand, Rousseau maintains, at points throughout his argument, that there are cultural institutions that are "natural" in their spirit and that therefore ought to be cultivated further—conjugal and paternal love, for instance, and mutual cooperation.

It is this second line that is the foundation of the possibility of the social contract, in which, according to Rousseau's account of contractarianism, certain "natural" goods and rights are to be rediscovered and protected in law, according to mutual agreement in the community. If there were not some culturally derived goods, which demonstrated the ability of civil institutions to concede to citizens the goods of the state of nature, then no good political society would ever be possible. So Rousseau does need this "second" line of argument in the *Discourse on Inequality.* What remains obscure in its rationale, however, is the basis for Rousseau's choices regarding which early civil institutions are "natural" and which are not. And it is crucially important for our purposes that Rousseau places sexual differences in this more "natural" category.

ON THE SOCIAL CONTRACT

This mystery also affects Rousseau's theory of the legitimate state, in *On the Social Contract,* to which we will now turn briefly.

CHAPTER 6

"Find a form of association which defends and protects with all common forces the person and goods of each associate, and by means of which each one, while uniting with all, nevertheless obeys only himself and remains as free as before?" This is the fundamental problem for which the social contract provides the solution.

The clauses of this contract are so determined by the nature of the act that the least modification renders them vain and ineffectual, that, although perhaps they have never been formally promulgated, they are everywhere the same, everywhere tacitly accepted and acknowledged. Once the social compact is violated, each person then regains his first rights and resumes his natural liberty, while losing the conventional liberty for which he renounced it.

These clauses, properly understood, are all reducible to a single one, namely, the total alienation of each associate together with all of his rights, to the entire community. For first of all, since each person gives himself whole and entire, the condition is equal for everyone: and since the condition is equal for everyone, no one has an interest in making it burdensome for the others.

Moreover, since the alienation is made without reservation, the union is as perfect as possible, and no associate has anything further to demand. For if some rights remained with private individuals, in the absence of any common superior who could decide between them and the public, each person would eventually claim to be his own judge in all things, since he is on some point his own judge. The state of nature would subsist and the association would necessarily become tyrannical or hollow.

Finally, in giving himself to all, each person gives himself to no one. And since there is no associate over whom he does not acquire the same right that he would grant others over himself, he gains the equivalent of everything he loses, along with a greater amount of force to preserve what he has.

If, therefore, one eliminates from the social compact whatever is not essential to it, one will find that it is reducible to the following terms. *Each of us places his person and all his power in common under the supreme direction of the general will; and as one we receive each member as an indivisible part of the whole.*

At once, in place of the individual person of each contracting party, this act of association produces a moral and collective body composed of as many members as there are voices in the assembly, which receives from this same act its unity, its common *self,* its life and its will. This public person, formed thus by union of all the others formerly took the name *city,* and at present takes the name *republic* or *body politic,* which is called *state* by its members when it is passive, *sovereign* when it is active, *power* when compared to others like itself. As to the associates, they collectively take the name *people;* individually they are called *citizens,* insofar as participants in the sovereign authority, and *subjects,* insofar as they are subjected to the laws of the state.

ᑺ ᑺ ᑺ

CHAPTER 7

As soon as this multitude is thus united in a body, one cannot harm one of the members without attacking the whole body. It is even less likely that the body can be harmed without the members feeling it. Thus duty and interest equally obligate the two parties to come to one another's aid, and the same men should seek to combine in this two-fold relationship all the advantages that result from it.

For since the sovereign is formed entirely from the private individuals who make it up, it neither has nor could have an interest contrary to theirs. Hence, the sovereign power has no need to offer a guarantee to its subjects, since it is impossible for a body to want to harm all of its members, and, as we will see later, it cannot harm any one of them in particular. The sovereign, by the mere fact that it exists, is always all that it should be.

But the same thing cannot be said of the subjects in relation to the sovereign, for which, despite their common interest, their commitments would be without substance if it did not find ways of being assured of their fidelity.

In fact, each individual can, as a man, have a private will contrary to or different from the general will that he has as a citizen. His private interest can speak to him in an entirely different manner than the common interest. His absolute and naturally independent existence can cause him to envisage what he owes the common cause as a gratuitous contribution, the loss of which will be less harmful to others than its payment is burdensome to him. And in viewing the moral person which constitutes the state as a being of reason because it is not a man, he would enjoy the rights of a citizen without wanting to fulfill the duties of a subject, an injustice whose growth would bring about the ruin of the body politic.

Thus, in order for the social compact to avoid being an empty formula, it tacitly entails the commitment—which alone can give force to the others—that whoever refuses to obey the general will be forced to do so by the entire body. This means merely that he will be forced to be free. For this is the sort of condition that, by giving each citizen to the homeland, guarantees him against all personal dependence—a condition that produces the skill and the performance of the political machine, and which alone bestows legitimacy upon civil commitments. Without it such commitments would be absurd, tyrannical and subject to the worst abuses.

Rousseau's famous (or infamous) claim, that a citizen in disagreement with the general will may be "forced to be free" epitomizes the paradoxes within Rousseau that enable so many different interpretations of his work. The claim follows, of course, from Rousseau's rather obscure notion of the "general will," with which, Rousseau assumes, all rational citizens simply do agree. Thus, his is a notion of a free commonwealth in which there is, essentially and by nature, no dissent or civil unrest of any kind. Thus, the rare citizen who does not recognize his own nature in the general will is, in a sense, irrational, and the civil society then has a right to protect itself from him.

Whatever the fascinating consequences for pure political theory of the notion of the general will, it is also formative of Rousseau's theories on education, and especially on the education and political status of women. In it is the kernel of a human being's recognition of his or her own nature and its incumbent freedoms. Thus, in the general will is encapsulated the idea that human nature is something that, under less than ideal political conditions, one may *not* recognize, and so one may not be able to exercise his or her own natural freedoms. Since, as Rousseau claims, the society of his day was so far from this ideal as to be inherently unjust, reform of contemporary society and the ultimate institution of the social contract would require moral reform as its foundation; essentially, people needed to be educated *into* their own natural and free condition.

EMILE

Rousseau's famous treatise on moral education, *Emile,* is founded on the claim that man is naturally good, and that, if allowed to follow his own natural inclinations— his curiosity, his sympathy, his athleticism, his scientific spirit—he will become the ideal and perfectly happy citizen. The work begins similarly to *On the Social Contract:* "God makes all things good; man meddles with them and they become evil."[10] The last section of the book is devoted to the proper education of Sophy, the perfect citizen's perfect wife.

NATURAL SEX DIFFERENCES AND EDUCATION

SOPHY, OR WOMAN

Sophy should be as truly a woman as Emile is a man, *i.e.,* she must possess all those characters of her sex which are required to enable her to play her part in the physical and moral order. Let us inquire to begin with in what respects her sex differs from our own.

But for her sex, a woman is a man; she has the same organs, the same needs, the same faculties. The machine is the same in its construction; its parts, its working, and its appearance are similar. Regard it as you will the difference is only in degree.

Yet where sex is concerned man and woman are unlike; each is the complement of the other; the difficulty in comparing them lies in our inability to decide, in either case, what is a matter of sex, and what is not. General differences present themselves to the comparative anatomist and even to the superficial observer; they seem not to be a matter of sex; yet they are really sex differences, though the connection eludes our observation. How far such differences may extend we cannot tell; all we know for certain is that where man and woman are alike we have to do with the characteristics of the species; where they are unlike, we have to do with the characteristics of sex. Considered from these two standpoints, we find so many instances of likeness and unlikeness that it is perhaps one of the greatest of marvels how nature has contrived to make two beings so like and yet so different.

These resemblances and differences must have an influence on the moral nature; this inference is obvious, and it is confirmed by experience; it shows the vanity of the disputes as to the superiority or the equality of the sexes; as if each sex, pursuing the path marked out for it by nature, were not more perfect in that very divergence than if it more closely resembled the other. A perfect man and a perfect woman should no more be alike in mind than in face, and perfection admits of neither less nor more.

In the union of the sexes each alike contributes to the common end, but in different ways. From this diversity springs the first difference which may be observed between man and woman in their moral relations. The man should be strong and active; the woman should be weak and passive; the one must have both the power and the will; it is enough that the other should offer little resistance.

---

[10] All passages from *Emile* are from Jean-Jacques Rousseau, *Emile.* Translated by Barbara Foxley. (London: Everyman, J.M. Dent, 1911 (1993)).

When this principle is admitted, it follows that woman is specially made for man's delight. If man in his turn ought to be pleasing in her eyes, the necessity is less urgent, his virtue is in his strength, he pleases because he is strong. I grant you this is not the law of love, but it is the law of nature, which is older than love itself.

If woman is made to please and to be in subjection to man, she ought to make herself pleasing in his eyes and not provoke him to anger; her strength is in her charms, by their means she should compel him to discover and use his strength. The surest way of arousing this strength is to make it necessary by resistance. Thus pride comes to the help of desire and each exults in the other's victory. This is the origin of attack and defence, of the boldness of one sex and the timidity of the other, and even of the shame and modesty with which nature has armed the weak for the conquest of the strong.

[T]he stronger party seems to be master, but is as a matter of fact dependent on the weaker, and that, not by any foolish custom of gallantry, nor yet by the magnanimity of the protector, but by an inexorable law of nature. For nature has endowed woman with a power of stimulating man's passions in excess of man's power of satisfying those passions, and has thus made him dependent on her goodwill, and compelled him in his turn to endeavour to please her, so that she may be willing to yield to his superior strength. Is it weakness which yields to force, or is it voluntary self-surrender? This uncertainty constitutes the chief charm of the man's victory, and the woman is usually cunning enough to leave him in doubt. In this respect the woman's mind exactly resembles her body; far from being ashamed of her weakness, she is proud of it; her soft muscles offer no resistance, she professes that she cannot lift the lightest weight; she would be ashamed to be strong. And why? Not only to gain an appearance of refinement; she is too clever for that; she is providing herself beforehand with excuses, with the right to be weak if she chooses.

The mutual duties of the two sexes are not, and cannot be, equally binding on both. Woman do wrong to complain of the inequality of man-made laws; this inequality is not of man's making, or at any rate it is not the result of mere prejudice, but of reason. She to whom nature has entrusted the care of the children must hold herself responsible for them to their father. No doubt every breach of faith is wrong, and every faithless husband, who robs his wife of the sole reward of the stern duties of her sex, is cruel and unjust; but the faithless wife is worse; she destroys the family and breaks the bonds of nature; when she gives her husband children who are not his own, she is false both to him and them, her crime is not infidelity but treason. To my mind, it is the source of dissension and of crime of every kind. Can any position be more wretched than that of the unhappy father who, when he clasps his child to his breast, is haunted by the suspicion that this is the child of another, the badge of his own dishonour, a thief who is robbing his own children of their inheritance. Under such circumstances the family is little more than a group of secret enemies, armed against each other by a guilty woman, who compels them to pretend to love one another.

Thus it is not enough that a wife should be faithful; her husband, along with his friends and neighbours, must believe in her fidelity; she must be modest, devoted, retiring; she should have the witness not only of a good conscience, but of a good reputation. In a word, if a father must love his children, he must be able to respect their mother. For these reasons it is not enough that the woman should be chaste, she must preserve her reputation and her good name. From these principles there arises not only a moral difference between the sexes, but also a fresh motive for duty and propriety, which prescribes to women in particular the most scrupulous attention to their conduct, their manners, their behaviour. Vague assertions as to the equality of the sexes and the similarity of their duties are only empty words; they are no answer to my argument.

☙ ☙ ☙

Woman is worth more as a woman and less as a man; when she makes a good use of her own rights, she has the best of it; when she tries to usurp our rights, she is our inferior. It is impossible to controvert this, except by quoting exceptions after the usual fashion of the partisans of the fair sex.

To cultivate the masculine virtues in women and to neglect their own is evidently to do them an injury. Women are too clear-sighted to be thus deceived; when they try to usurp our privileges they do not abandon their own; with this result: they are unable to make use of two incompatible things, so they fall below their own level as women, instead of rising to the level of men. If you are a sensible mother you will take my advice. Do not try to make your daughter a good man in defiance of nature. Make her a good woman, and be sure it will be better both for her and us.

☙ ☙ ☙

Worth alone will not suffice, a woman must be thought worthy; nor beauty, she must be admired; nor virtue, she must be respected. A woman's honour does not depend on her conduct alone, but on her reputation, and no woman who permits herself to be considered vile is really virtuous. A man has no one but himself to consider, and so long as he does right he may defy public opinion; but when a woman does right her task is only half finished, and what people think of her matters as much as what she really is. Hence her education must, in this respect, be different from man's education. 'What will people think' is the grave of a man's virtue and the throne of a woman's.

☙ ☙ ☙

Boys and girls have many games in common, and this is as it should be; do they not play together when they are grown up? They have also special tastes of their own. Boys want movement and noise, drums, tops, toy-carts; girls prefer things which appeal to the eye, and can be used for dressing-up-mirrors, jewellery, finery, and specially dolls. The doll is the girl's special plaything; this shows her instinctive bent towards her life's work. The art of pleasing finds its physical basis in personal adornment, and this physical side of the art is the only one which the child can cultivate.

Here is a little girl busy all day with her doll; she is always changing its clothes, dressing and undressing it, trying new combinations of trimmings well or ill matched; her fingers are clumsy, her taste is crude, but there is no mistaking her bent; in this endless occupation time flies unheeded, the hours slip away unnoticed, even meals are forgotten. She is more eager for adornment than for food. 'But she is dressing her doll, not herself,' you will say. Just so; she sees her doll, she cannot see herself; she cannot do anything for herself, she has neither the training, nor the talent, nor the strength; as yet she herself is nothing, she is engrossed in her doll and all her coquetry is devoted to it. This will not always be so; in due time she will be her own doll.

We have here a very early and clearly-marked bent; you have only to follow it and train it. What the little girl most clearly desires is to dress her doll, to make its bows, its tippets, its sashes, and its tuckers; she is dependent on other people's kindness in all this, and it would be much pleasanter to be able to do it herself. Here is a motive for her earliest lessons, they are not tasks prescribed, but favours bestowed. Little girls always dislike learning to read and write, but they are always ready to learn to sew. They think they are grown up, and in imagination they are using their knowledge for their own adornment.

The way is open and it is easy to follow it; cutting out, embroidery, lace-making follow naturally.

̅ ̅ ̅

If I object to little boys being made to learn to read, still more do I object to it for little girls until they are able to see the use of reading; we generally think more of our own ideas than theirs in our attempts to convince them of the utility of this art. After all, why should a little girl know how to read and write? Has she a house to manage? Most of them make a bad use of this fatal knowledge, and girls are so full of curiosity that few of them will fail to learn without compulsion. Possibly cyphering should come first; there is nothing so obviously useful, nothing which needs so much practice or gives so much opportunity for error as reckoning. If the little girl does not get the cherries for her lunch without an arithmetical exercise, she will soon learn to count.

Thus far, Rousseau's claims about women seem to be derived from haphazard observation, and to follow in a stream-of-consciousness fashion. But he does seem to have an argument; he wants to claim that girls' education should strengthen their natural weaknesses and curb their natural faults. But many of these "natural" feminine qualities are, at least on the face of it, inconsistent with each other. Young women should be deceitful yet honest, coquettish yet genuinely virtuous; they are better spoken than men, and seemingly more intelligent, yet they cannot make moral judgments for themselves, or choose or evaluate their own religion.

Show the sense of the tasks you set your little girls, but keep them busy. Idleness and insubordination are two very dangerous faults, and very hard to cure when once established. Girls should be attentive and industrious, but this is not enough by itself; they should early be accustomed to restraint. This misfortune, if such it be, is inherent in their sex, and they will never escape from it, unless to endure more cruel sufferings. All their life long, they will have to submit to the strictest and most enduring restraints, those of propriety. They must be trained to bear the yoke from the first, so that they may not feel it, to master their own caprices and to submit themselves to the will of others. If they were always eager to be at work, they should sometimes be compelled to do nothing. Their childish faults, unchecked and unheeded, may easily lead to dissipation, frivolity, and inconstancy. To guard against this, teach them above all things self-control. Under our senseless conditions, the life of a good woman is a perpetual struggle against self; it is only fair that woman should bear her share of the ills she has brought upon man.

⌐ ⌐ ⌐

Just because they have, or ought to have, little freedom, they are apt to indulge themselves too fully with regard to such freedom as they have; they carry everything to extremes, and they devote themselves to their games with an enthusiasm even greater than that of boys. This is the second difficulty to which I referred. This enthusiasm must be kept in check, for it is the source of several vices commonly found among women, caprice and that extravagant admiration which leads a woman to regard a thing with rapture to-day and to be quite indifferent to it to-morrow. This fickleness of taste is as dangerous as exaggeration; and both spring from the same cause. Do not deprive them of mirth, laughter, noise, and romping games, but do not let them tire of one game and go off to another; do not leave them for a moment without restraint. Train them to break off their games and return to their other occupations without a murmur. Habit is all that is needed, as you have nature on your side.

⌐ ⌐ ⌐

What is, is good, and no general law can be bad. This special skill with which the female sex is endowed is a fair equivalent for its lack of strength; without it woman would be man's slave, not his helpmeet. By her superiority in this respect she maintains her equality with man, and rules in obedience. She has everything against her, our faults and her own weakness and timidity; her beauty and her wiles are all that she has. Should she not cultivate both? Yet beauty is not universal; it may be destroyed by all sorts of accidents, it will disappear with years, and habit will destroy its influence. A woman's real resource is her wit; not that foolish wit which is so greatly admired in society, a wit which does nothing to make life happier; but that wit which is adapted to her condition, the art of taking advantage of our position and controlling us through our own strength.

⌐ ⌐ ⌐

The education of our girls is, in this respect, absolutely topsy-turvy. Ornaments are promised them as rewards, and they are taught to delight in elaborate finery. 'How lovely she is!' people say when she is most dressed up. On the contrary, they should be taught that so much finery is only required to hide their defects, and that beauty's real triumph is to shine alone. The love of fashion is contrary to good taste, for faces do not change with the fashion, and while the person remains unchanged, what suits it at one time will suit it always.

If I saw a young girl decked out like a little peacock, I should show myself anxious about her figure so disguised, and anxious what people would think of her; I should say, 'She is over-dressed with all those ornaments; what a pity!'

☙ ☙ ☙

Do not be afraid to educate your women as women; teach them a woman's business, that they be modest, that they may know how to manage their house and look after their family; the grand toilet will soon disappear, and they will be more tastefully dressed.

Growing girls perceive at once that all this outside adornment is not enough unless they have charms of their own. They cannot make themselves beautiful, they are too young for coquetry, but they are not too young to acquire graceful gestures, a pleasing voice, a self-possessed manner, a light step, a graceful bearing, to choose whatever advantages are within their reach. The voice extends its range, it grows stronger and more resonant, the arms become plumper, the bearing more assured, and they perceive that it is easy to attract attention however dressed. Needlework and industry suffice no longer, fresh gifts are developing and their usefulness is already recognised.

I know that stern teachers would have us refuse to teach little girls to sing or dance, or to acquire any of the pleasing arts. This strikes me as absurd: Who should learn these arts—our boys? Are these to be the favourite accomplishments of men or women? Of neither, say they; profane songs are simply so many crimes, dancing is an invention of the Evil One; her tasks and her prayers are all the amusement a young girl should have. What strange amusements for a child of ten! I fear that these little saints who have been forced to spend their childhood in prayers to God will pass their youth in another fashion; when they are married they will try to make up for lost time. I think we must consider age as well as sex; a young girl should not live like her grandmother; she should be lively, merry, and eager; she should sing and dance to her heart's content, and enjoy all the innocent pleasures of youth; the time will come, all too soon, when she must settle down and adopt a more serious tone.

But is this change in itself really necessary? Is it not merely another result of our own prejudices? By making good women the slaves of dismal duties, we have deprived marriage of its charm for men. Can we wonder that the gloomy silence they find at home drives them elsewhere, or inspires little desire to enter a state which offers so few attractions?

☙ ☙ ☙

Women have ready tongues; they talk earlier, more easily, and more pleasantly than men. They are also said to talk more; this may be true, but I am prepared to reckon it to their credit; eyes and mouth are equally busy and for the same cause. A man says what he knows, a woman says what will please; the one needs knowledge, the other taste; utility should be the man's object; the woman speaks to give pleasure. There should be nothing in common but truth.

You should not check a girl's prattle like a boy's by the harsh question, 'What is the use of that?' but by another question at least as difficult to answer, 'What effect will that have?' At this early age when they know neither good nor evil, and are incapable of judging others, they should make this their rule and never say anything which is unpleasant to those about them; this rule is all the more difficult to apply because it must always be subordinated to our first rule, 'Never tell a lie.'

꙰ ꙰ ꙰

If boys are incapable of forming any true idea of religion, much more is it beyond the grasp of girls; and for this reason I would speak of it all the sooner to little girls, for if we wait till they are ready for a serious discussion of these deep subjects we should be in danger of never speaking of religion at all. A woman's reason is practical, and therefore she soon arrives at a given conclusion, but she fails to discover it for herself. The social relation of the sexes is a wonderful thing. This relation produces a moral person of which woman is the eye and man the hand, but the two are so dependent on one another that the man teaches the woman what to see, while she teaches him what to do. If women could discover principles and if men had as good heads for detail, they would be mutually independent, they would live in perpetual strife, and there would be an end to all society. But in their mutual harmony each contributes to a common purpose; each follows the other's lead, each commands and each obeys.

As a woman's conduct is controlled by public opinion, so is her religion ruled by authority. The daughter should follow her mother's religion, the wife her husband's. Were that religion false, the docility which leads mother and daughter to submit to nature's laws would blot out the sin of error in the sight of God. Unable to judge for themselves they should accept the judgment of father and husband as that of the church.

꙰ ꙰ ꙰

When the guests are gone, husband and wife talk over the events of the evening. He relates what was said to him, what was said and done by those with whom he conversed. If the lady is not always quite exact in this respect, yet on the other hand she perceived what was whispered at the other end of the room; she knows what so-and-so thought, and what was the meaning of this speech or that gesture; there is scarcely a change of expression for which she has not an explanation in readiness, and she is almost always right.

The same turn of mind which makes a woman of the world such an excellent hostess, enables a flirt to excel in the art of amusing a number of suitors. Coquetry, cleverly carried out, demands an even finer discernment than courtesy.

☙ ☙ ☙

If you want to see a man in a quandary, place him between two women with each of whom he has a secret understanding, and see what a fool he looks. But put a woman in similar cricumstances between two men, and the results will be even more remarkable; you will be astonished at the skill with which she cheats them both, and makes them laugh at each other. Now if that woman were to show the same confidence in both, if she were to be equally familiar with both, how could they be deceived for a moment? If she treated them alike, would she not show that they both had the same claims upon her? Oh, she is far too clever for that; so far from treating them just alike, she makes a marked difference between them, and she does it so skilfully that the man she flatters thinks it is affection, and the man she ill uses thinks it is spite. So that each of them believes she is thinking of him, when she is thinking of no one but herself.

☙ ☙ ☙

Self-possession, penetration, delicate observation, this is a woman's science; the skill to make use of it is her chief accomplishment.

This is what is, and we have seen why it is so. It is said that women are false. They become false. They are really endowed with skill not duplicity; in the genuine inclinations of their sex they are not false even when they tell a lie. Why do you consult their words when it is not their mouths that speak? Consult their eyes, their colour, their breathing, their timid manner, their slight resistance, that is the language nature gave them for your answer. The lips always say 'No,' and rightly so; but the tone is not always the same, and that cannot lie.

☙ ☙ ☙

The more modest a woman is, the more art she needs, even with her husband. Yes, I maintain that coquetry, kept within bounds, becomes modest and true, and out of it springs a law of right conduct.

After describing in detail the proper education for girls, Rousseau describes its results: the full-grown Sophy, perfect wife for Emile.

SOPHY

Sophy is well born and she has a good disposition; she is very warm-hearted, and this warmth of heart sometimes makes her imagination run away with her. Her mind is keen rather than accurate, her temper is pleasant but variable, her person pleasing though nothing out of the common, her countenance bespeaks a soul and it speaks true; you may meet her with indifference, but you will not leave her without emotion. Others possess good qualities which she lacks; others possess her good qualities in a higher degree, but in no one are these qualities better blended to form a happy disposition. She knows how to make the best of her very faults, and if she were more perfect she would be less pleasing.

Sophy is not beautiful; but in her presence men forget the fairer women, and the latter are dissatisfied with themselves. At first sight she is hardly pretty; but the more we see her the prettier she is; she wins where so many lose, and what she wins she keeps. Her eyes might be finer, her mouth more beautiful, her stature more imposing; but no one could have a more graceful figure, a finer complexion, a whiter hand, a daintier foot, a sweeter look, and a more expressive countenance. She does not dazzle; she arouses interest; she delights us, we know not why.

Sophy is fond of dress, and she knows how to dress; her mother has no other maid; she has taste enough to dress herself well; but she hates rich clothes; her own are always simple but elegant. She does not like showy but becoming things. She does not know what colours are fashionable, but she makes no mistake about those that suit her. No girl seems more simply dressed, but no one could take more pains over her toilet; no article is selected at random, and yet there is no trace of artificiality. Her dress is very modest in appearance and very coquettish in reality; she does not display her charms, she conceals them, but in such a way as to enhance them. When you see her you say, 'That is a good modest girl,' but while you are with her, you cannot take your eyes or your thoughts off her, and one might say that this very simple adornment is only put on to be removed bit by bit by the imagination.

Sophy has natural gifts; she is aware of them, and they have not been neglected; but never having had a chance of much training she is content to use her pretty voice to sing tastefully and truly; her little feet step lightly, easily, and gracefully, she can always make an easy graceful courtesy. She has had no singing master but her father, no dancing mistress but her mother; a neighbouring organist has given her a few lessons in playing accompaniments on the spinet, and she has improved herself by practice. At first she only wished to show off her hand on the dark keys; then she discovered that the thin clear tone of the spinet made her voice sound sweeter; little by little she recognised the charms of harmony; as she grew older she at last began to enjoy the charms of expression, to love music for its own sake. But she has taste rather than talent; she cannot read a simple air from notes.

Needlework is what Sophy likes best; and the feminine arts have been taught her most carefully, even those you would not expect, such as cutting out and dressmaking. There is nothing she cannot do with her needle, and nothing that she does not take a delight in doing; but lace-making is her favourite occupation, because there is nothing which requires such a pleasing attitude, nothing which calls for such grace and dexterity of finger. She has also studied all the details of housekeeping; she understands cooking and cleaning; she knows the prices of food, and also how to choose it; she can keep accounts accurately, she is her mother's house-keeper. Some day she will be the mother of a family; by managing her father's house she is preparing to manage her own; she can take the place of any of the servants and she is always ready to do so.

⌐ ⌐ ⌐

. . . Nothing could be more revolting than a dirty woman, and a husband who tires of her is not to blame. She insisted so strongly on this duty when Sophy was little, she required such absolute cleanliness in her person, clothing, room, work, and toilet, that use has become habit, till it absorbs one half of her time and controls the other; so that she thinks less of how to do a thing than of how to do it without getting dirty.

Yet this has not degenerated into mere affectation and softness; there is none of the over refinement of luxury. Nothing but clean water enters her room; she knows no perfumes but the scent of flowers, and her husband will never find anything sweeter than her breath. In conclusion, the attention she pays to the outside does not blind her to the fact that time and strength are meant for greater tasks; either she does not know or she despises that exaggerated cleanliness of body which degrades the soul. Sophy is more than clean, she is pure.

Sophy's mind is pleasing but not brilliant, and thorough but not deep; it is the sort of mind which calls for no remark, as she never seems cleverer or stupider than oneself. When people talk to her they always find what she says attractive, though it may not be highly ornamental according to modern ideas of an educated woman; her mind has been formed not only by reading, but by conversation with her father and mother, by her own reflections, and by her own observations in the little world in which she has lived.

Sophy is too sensitive to be always good humoured, but too gentle to let this be really disagreeable to other people; it is only herself who suffers. If you say anything that hurts her she does not sulk, but her heart swells; she tries to run away and cry. In the midst of her tears, at a word from her father or mother she returns at once laughing and playing, secretly wiping her eyes and trying to stifle her sobs.

Yet she has her whims; if her temper is too much indulged it degenerates into rebellion, and then she forgets herself. But give her time to come round and her way of making you forget her wrong-doing is almost a virtue. If you punish her she is gentle and submissive, and you see that she is more ashamed of the fault than the punishment. If you say nothing, she never fails to make amends, and she does it so frankly and so readily that you cannot be angry with her. She would kiss the ground before the lowest servant and would make no fuss about it; and as soon as she is forgiven, you can see by her delight and her caresses that a load is taken off her heart. In a word, she endures patiently the wrong-doing of others, and she is eager to atone for her own. This amiability is natural to her sex when unspoiled. Woman is made to submit to man and to endure even injustice at his hands.

Rousseau incorporates into Sophy's nature, seemingly, everything he likes in a woman. The result is not an entirely consistent personality, nor one that seems particularly easily or "naturally" mastered by anyone. And yet this fits perfectly with the paradoxes of "nature" throughout Rousseau's works; a "nature" which is perfect and yet had been defiled irreparably by culture; a "nature" which is an admitted fiction yet to be made legally binding upon us; a "nature" which is less than beautiful yet mysteriously and compellingly attractive. In addition, Rousseau's Sophy incorporates within her many of our traditional and paradoxical expectations of women. Indeed, she is not really very different from the television moms of the 1950s and 1960s, nor perhaps from today's ideals, both for young men and young women. Thus, Rousseau, whatever one's reaction to his work—and, as discussed above, such reaction runs the philosophical gamut—his is an exceptionally informative set of theories about the modern tradition of thinking on the subject of gender.

7. MARY WOLLSTONECRAFT
(English, 1759–97)

Mary Wollstonecraft was a staunch and eloquent early feminist, journalist, and political activist. Her most famous work is *A Vindication of the Rights of Woman,* from which all the following excerpts are taken. It is a sequel of sorts to her pamphlet, *A Vindication of the Rights of Man,* which had argued against Edmund Burke's condemnation of the French revolution. Thus, we can see that Wollstonecraft set her feminist work within the framework of a general liberal political theory, somewhat akin to Rousseau's; in other words, the "rights" that she wanted to vindicate for women were the "enlightenment" ideals of freedom, individualism, and equality. As we will see, Wollstonecraft's feminist spin on modern political theory does not rid it of the kinds of paradoxes that befell her predecessors.

A VINDICATION OF THE RIGHTS OF WOMAN

Wollstonecraft dedicated this work to Tallyrand, who had shortly before written in favor of educating little girls in public schools with boys, at least until they were about eight years old when, he claimed, they should return home for instruction in household management. Wollstonecraft's response is essentially a plea that Tallyrand's basic thesis be adopted and revised to include the equal education of women and men throughout their schooling. Thus, while in spirit Wollstonecraft shares much with Rousseau, in this particular work she strongly takes issue with him.

WHY WOMEN'S EDUCATION

The focus of the work, then, is women's education. In her Introduction, Wollstonecraft argues that the weaknesses and moral failings of women have been the result of their inequality with men, and not its natural cause. In this way, Wollstonecraft anticipates and undermines the objections of her detractors, that educating women similarly to men, and thereby making women "masculine," would be undesirable. Rather, claims Wollstonecraft, the so-called "feminine" traits that are cultivated in women by not educating them equally with men, are really weaknesses that will prevent women from achieving virtue and greatness. Wollstonecraft holds instead that the virtues inculcated in men by virtue of their modern liberal education are human virtues with which everyone should be honored if they possibly can.

INTRODUCTION

. . . I have turned over various books written on the subject of education, and patiently observed the conduct of parents and the management of schools; but what has been the result?—a profound conviction that the neglected education of my fellow-creatures is the grand source of the misery I deplore; and that women, in particular, are rendered weak and wretched by a variety of concurring causes, originating from one hasty conclusion. The conduct and manners of women, in fact, evidently prove that their minds are not in a healthy state; for, like the flowers which are planted in too rich soil, strength and usefulness are sacrificed to beauty; and the flaunting leaves, after having pleased a fastidious eye, fade, disregarded on the stalk, long before the season when they ought to have arrived at maturity.—One cause of this barren blooming I attribute to a false system of education, gathered from the books written on this subject by men who, considering females rather as women than human creatures, have been more anxious to make them alluring mistresses than rational wives; and the understanding of the sex has been so bubbled by this specious homage, that the civilized women of the present century, with a few exceptions, are only anxious to inspire love; when they ought to cherish a nobler ambition, and by their abilities and virtues exact respect.

In a treatise, therefore, on female rights and manners, the works which have been particularly written for their improvement must not be overlooked; especially when it is asserted, in direct terms, that the minds of women are enfeebled by false refinement; that the books of instruction, written by men of genius, have had the same tendency as more frivolous productions; and that, in the true style of Mahometanism, they are only considered as females, and not as a part of the human species, when improvable reason is allowed to be the dignified distinction which raises men above the brute creation, and puts a natural scepter in a feeble hand.

Yet, because I am a woman, I would not lead my readers to suppose that I mean violently to agitate the contested question respecting the equality or inferiority of the sex; but as the subject lies in my way, and I cannot pass it over without subjecting the main tendency of my reasoning to misconstruction, I shall stop a moment to deliver, in a few words, my opinion.—In the government of the physical world it is observable that the female, in general, is inferior to the male. The male pursues, the female yields—this is the law of nature; and it does not appear to be suspended or abrogated in favour of woman. This physical superiority cannot be denied—and it is a noble prerogative! But not content with this natural pre-eminence, men endeavour to sink us still lower, merely to render us alluring objects for a moment; and women, intoxicated by the adoration which men, under the influence of their senses, pay them, do not seek to obtain a durable interest in their hearts, or to become the friends of the fellow creatures who find amusement in their society.

I am aware of an obvious inference:—from every quarter have I heard exclamations against masculine women; but where are they to be found? If by this appellation men mean to inveigh against their ardour in hunting, shooting, and gaming, I shall most cordially join in the cry; but if it be against the imitation of manly virtues, or, more properly speaking, the attainment of those talents and virtues, the exercise of which ennobles the human character, and which raise females in the scale of animal being, when they are comprehensively termed mankind;—all those who view them with a philosophical eye must, I should think, wish with me, that they may every day grow more and more masculine.

 ⌐ ⌐ ⌐

My own sex, I hope, will excuse me, if I treat them like rational creatures, instead of flattering their *fascinating* graces, and viewing them as if they were in a state of perpetual childhood, unable to stand alone. I earnestly wish to point out in what true dignity and human happiness consists—I wish to persuade women to endeavour to acquire the strength, both of mind and body, and to convince them that the soft phrases, susceptibility of heart, delicacy of sentiment, and refinement of taste, are almost synonymous with epithets of weakness, and that those beings who are only the objects of pity and that kind of love, which has been termed its sister, will soon become objects of contempt.

Dismissing then those pretty feminine phrases, which the men condescendingly use to soften our slavish dependence, and despising that weak elegancy of mind, exquisite sensibility, and sweet docility of manners, supposed to be the sexual characteristics of the weaker vessel, I wish to shew that elegance is inferior to virtue, that the first object of laudable ambition is to obtain a character as a human being, regardless of the distinction of sex; and that secondary views should be brought to this simple touchstone.

⌐ ⌐ ⌐

The education of women, has, of late, been more attended to than formerly; yet they are still reckoned a frivolous sex, and ridiculed or pitied by the writers who endeavour by satire or instruction to improve them. It is acknowledged that they spend many of the first years of their lives in acquiring a smattering of accomplishments: meanwhile strength of body and mind are sacrificed to libertine notions of beauty, to the desire of establishing themselves,—the only way women can rise in the world,—by marriage. And this desire making mere animals of them, when they marry they act as such children may be expected to act:—they dress; they paint, and nickname God's creatures.—Surely these weak beings are only fit for a seraglio!—Can they govern a family, or take care of the poor babes whom they bring into the world?

If then it can be fairly deduced from the present conduct of the sex, from the prevalent fondness for pleasure which takes place of ambition and those nobler passions that open and enlarge the soul; that the instruction which women have received has only tended, with the constitution of civil society, to render them insignificant objects of desire—mere propagators of fools!—if it can be proved that in aiming to accomplish them, without cultivating their understandings, they are taken out of their sphere of duties, and made ridiculous and useless when the short-lived bloom of beauty is over, I presume that *rational* men will excuse me for endeavouring to persuade them to become more masculine and respectable.

Indeed the word masculine is only a bugbear: there is little reason to fear that women will acquire too much courage or fortitude; for their apparent inferiority with respect to bodily strength, must render them, in some degree, dependent on men in the various relations of life; but why should it be increased by prejudices that give a sex to virtue, and confound simple truths with sensual reveries?

Women are, in fact, so much degraded by mistaken notions of female excellence, that I do not mean to add a paradox when I assert, that this artificial weakness produces a propensity to tyrannize, and gives birth to cunning, the natural opponent of strength, which leads them to play off those contemptible infantile airs that undermine esteem even whilst they excite desire. Do not foster these prejudices, and they will naturally fall into their subordinate, yet respectable station, in life.[11]

It is already apparent in the Introduction that Wollstonecraft plans to take a humanist line, at least in an enlightenment version for women's rights. Her claim here is that there are certain human rights attendant upon certain human virtues which, as human, are available to everyone, if only each is provided with the right education. This claim, by itself, is almost identical to Rousseau's claims in his political treatises; human beings are thought by Wollstonecraft to be perfectly endowed by God with all that is required to lead an ideal human life and yet to have been corrupted by life in civil society such that their virtue is now almost unrecognizable. Wollstonecraft assumes here, as she will clarify in the body of the text, that the proper virtues for all human beings are those which modern political states ("modern" in the sense of "eighteenth-century" or "enlightenment" states) ascribe to male citizens; in other words, her argument is basically that modern political states have corrupted women far more than they have men, and that the only adequate cure for this corrupt state is to educate women for the achievement of human ideals. Thus, although in other places Wollstonecraft will argue that there are other natural inequalities between the sexes, here she echoes Plato in her assumption that there is no difference of character between men and women, only a difference in physical strength; she also echoes Rousseau in her claim that corrupted, yet naturally perfect, human beings must be "educated into" their own natures. Her dispute with Rousseau is only in her claim that women's natures, and thus their education, be identical to men's. Wollstonecraft's humanism, then, is thorough: she goes so far as to claim that there really is no such thing as masculinity (nor therefore, femininity), but only humanity. This is argued explicitly in her, still introductory, first chapter:

---

[11] All excepts are taken from Mary Wollstonecraft, *A Vindication of the Rights of Woman,* London: Source Book Press, 1971 unabridged reprinting of the 1792 London edition.

CHAP. I

THE RIGHTS AND INVOLVED DUTIES OF MANKIND CONSIDERED

. . . In what does man's pre-eminence over the brute creation consist? The answer is as clear as that a half is less than the whole: in Reason.

What acquirement exalts one being above another? Virtue; we spontaneously reply.

For what purpose were the passions implanted? That man by struggling with them might attain a degree of knowledge denied to the brutes; whispers Experience.

Consequently the perfection of our nature and capability of happiness, must be estimated by the degree of reason, virtue, and knowledge, that distinguish the individual, and direct the laws which bind society: and that from the exercise of reason, knowledge and virtue naturally flow, is equally undeniable, if mankind be viewed collectively.

ON SEXUAL CHARACTER

In Chapters II and III, "The Prevailing Idea of a Sexual Character Discussed," Wollstonecraft goes into some greater detail with regard to what capacities and virtues women possess; her claim, as could be surmised from her introduction, is that they possess essentially the same ones as men. It may be interesting to compare Wollstonecraft's use of Milton's *Paradise Lost* as a foil for her argument, to Milton himself, and to that of her daughter—Mary Shelley—whose work is excerpted in the next section, and who was also influenced by Milton.

Wollstonecraft's principle objection, of course, is to Rousseau's claim that the natures of men and women differ, and more specifically, to his claim that woman's nature and therefore the goal of her education, is to please man. As Wollstonecraft understands it, femininity and masculinity are essentially only inventions of corrupt inegalitarian societies: gender is one of the tools tyrants use in the oppression of their citizens. Feminine ideals—like beauty, elegance, docility, and charm—as she understands them, are an accident of hundreds of years of unenlightened governments. A reformed government established to recapture an ideal human community will surely encourage the same virtues—strength, freedom, intelligence, and autonomy—in all its citizens.

CHAP. II

THE PREVAILING OPINION OF A SEXUAL CHARACTER DISCUSSED

To account for, and excuse the tyranny of man, many ingenious arguments have been brought forward to prove, that the two sexes, in the acquirement of virtue, ought to aim at attaining a very different character: or, to speak explicit, women are not allowed to have sufficient strength of mind to acquire what really deserves the name of virtue. Yet it should seem, allowing them to have souls, that there is but one way appointed by Providence to lead *mankind* to either virtue or happiness.

If then women are not a swarm of ephemeron triflers, why should they be kept in ignorance under the specious name of innocence? Men complain, and with reason, of the follies and caprices of our sex, when they do not keenly satirize our headstrong passions and groveling vices.—Behold, I should answer, the natural effect of ignorance! The mind will ever be unstable that has only prejudices to rest on, and the current will run with destructive fury when there are no barriers to break its force. Women are told from their infancy, and taught by the example of their mothers, that a little knowledge of human weakness, justly termed cunning, softness of temper, *outward* obedience, and a scrupulous attention to a puerile kind of propriety, will obtain for them the protection of man; and should they be beautiful, every thing else is needless, for, at least, twenty years of their lives.

᭡   ᭡   ᭡

Children, I grant, should be innocent; but when the epithet is applied to men, or women, it is but a civil term for weakness. For if it be allowed that women were destined by Providence to acquire human virtues, and by the exercise of their understandings, that stability of character which is the firmest ground to rest our future hopes upon, they must be permitted to turn to the fountain of light, and not forced to shape their course by the twinkling of a mere satellite. Milton, I grant, was of a very different opinion; for he only bends to the indefeasible right of beauty, though it would be difficult to render two passages which I now mean to contrast, consistent. But into similar inconsistencies are great men often led by their senses.

> *To whom thus* Eve *with* perfect beauty *adorn'd.*
> *My Author and Disposer, what thou bidst*
> Unargued *I obey; so God ordains;*
> *God is* thy law, thou mine: *to know no more*
> *Is* Woman's *happiest knowledge and her* praise.

᭡   ᭡   ᭡

Yet in the following lines Milton seems to coincide with me; when he makes Adam thus expostulate with his Maker.

> *Hast thou not made me here thy substitute,*
> *And these inferior far beneath me set?*
> *Among* unequals *what society*
> *Can sort, what harmony or true delight?*
> *Which must be mutual, in proportion due*
> *Giv'n and receiv'd; but in* disparity
> *The one intense, the other still remiss*
> *Cannot well suit with either, but soon prove*
> *Tedious alike: of* fellowship *I speak*
> *Such as I seek, fit to participate*
> *All rational delight—*

In treating, therefore, of the manners of women, let us, disregarding sensual arguments, trace what we should endeavour to make them in order to co-operate, if the expression be not too bold, with the supreme Being.

[T]he most perfect education, in my opinion, is such an exercise of the understanding as is best calculated to strengthen the body and form the heart. Or, in other words, to enable the individual to attain such habits of virtue as will render it independent. In fact, it is a farce to call any being virtuous whose virtues do not result from the exercise of its own reason. This was Rousseau's opinion respecting men: I extend it to women, and confidently assert that they have been drawn out of their sphere by false refinement, and not by an endeavour to acquire masculine qualities. Still the regal homage which they receive is so intoxicating, that till the manners of the times are changed, and formed on more reasonable principles, it may be impossible to convince them that the illegitimate power which they obtain, by degrading themselves, is a curse, and that they must return to nature and equality, if they wish to secure the placid satisfaction that unsophisticated affections impart. But for this epoch we must wait—wait, perhaps, till kings and nobles, enlightened by reason, and, preferring the real dignity of man to childish state, throw off their gaudy hereditary trappings; and if then women do not resign the arbitrary power of beauty—they will prove that they have *less* mind than man.

Many are the causes that, in the present corrupt state of society, contribute to enslave women by cramping their understandings and sharpening their sense. One, perhaps, that silently does more mischief than all the rest, is their disregard of order.

To do every thing in an orderly manner, is a most important precept, which women, who, generally speaking, receive only a disorderly kind of education, seldom attend to with that degree of exactness that men, who from their infancy are broken into method, observe. This negligent kind of guesswork, for what other epithet can be used to point out the random exertions of a sort of instinctive common sense, never brought to the test of reason? prevents their generalizing matters of fact—so they do to-day, what they did yesterday, merely because they did it yesterday.

This contempt of the understanding in early life has more baneful consequences than is commonly supposed; for the little knowledge which women of strong minds attain, is, from various circumstances, of a more desultory kind than the knowledge of men, and it is acquired more by sheer observations on real life, than from comparing what has been individually observed with the results of experience generalized by speculation. Led by their dependent situation and domestic employments more into society, what they learn is rather by snatches; and as learning is with them, in general, only a secondary thing, they do not pursue any one branch with that persevering ardour necessary to give vigour to the faculties, and clearness to the judgment. In the present state of society, a little learning is required to support the character of a gentleman; and boys are obliged to submit to a few years of discipline. But in the education of women, the cultivation of the understanding is always subordinate to the acquirement of some corporeal accomplishment; even while enervated by confinement and false notions of modesty, the body is prevented from attaining that grace and beauty which relaxed half-formed limbs never exhibit. Besides, in youth their faculties are not brought forward by emulation; and having no serious scientific study, if they have natural sagacity it is turned too soon on life and manners. They dwell on effects, and modifications, without tracing them back to causes; and complicated rules to adjust behaviour, are a weak substitute for simple principles.

As a proof that education gives this appearance of weakness to females, we may instance the example of military men, who are, like them, sent into the world before their minds have been stored with knowledge or fortified by principles. The consequences are similar; soldiers acquire a little superficial knowledge, snatched from the muddy current of conversation, and, from continually mixing with society, they gain, what is termed a knowledge of the world; and this acquaintance with manners and customs has frequently been confounded with a knowledge of the human heart. But can the crude fruit of casual observation, never brought to the test of judgment, formed by comparing speculation and experience, deserve such a distinction? Soldiers, as well as women, practise the minor virtues with punctilious politeness. Where is then the sexual difference, when the education has been the same? All the difference that I can discern, arises from the superior advantage of liberty, which enables the former to see more of life.

☞ ☞ ☞

Standing armies can never consist of resolute, robust men; they may be well disciplined machines, but they will seldom contain men under the influence of strong passions, or with very vigorous faculties. And as for any depth of understanding, I will venture to affirm, that it is as rarely to be found in the army as amongst women; and the cause, I maintain, is the same. It may be further observed, that officers are also particularly attentive to their persons, fond of dancing, crowded rooms, adventures, and ridicule. Like the *fair* sex, the business of their lives is gallantry.—They were taught to please, and they only live to please. Yet they do not lose their rank in the distinction of sexes, for they are still reckoned superior to women, though in what their superiority consists, beyond what I have just mentioned, it is difficult to discover.

The great misfortune is this, that they both acquire manners before morals, and a knowledge of life before they have, from reflection, any acquaintance with the grand ideal outline of human nature.

☞ ☞ ☞

Strengthen the female mind by enlarging it, and there will be an end to blind obedience; but, as blind obedience is ever sought for by power, tyrants and sensualists are in the right when they endeavour to keep women in the dark, because the former only want slaves, and the latter a play-thing. The sensualist, indeed, has been the most dangerous of tyrants, and women have been duped by their lovers, as princes by their ministers, whilst dreaming that they reigned over them.

I now principally allude to Rousseau, for his character of Sophia is, undoubtedly, a captivating one, though it appears to me grossly unnatural; however, it is not the superstructure, but the foundation of her character, the principles on which her education was built, that I mean to attack; nay, warmly as I admire the genius of that able writer, whose opinions I shall often have occasion to cite, indignation always takes place of admiration, and the rigid frown of insulted virtue effaces the smile of complacency, which his eloquent periods are wont to raise, when I read his voluptuous reveries.

Wollstonecraft's analogy between the lady and the army officer, through which she means to argue against Rousseau for the classical education of women, is an intriguing one, which shares with Rousseau many of the paradoxes of the modern age. She has in mind, of course, the career military man, but this image evokes for her and her readers, not a wily or brave fighter for his country, but rather a frivolous man educated to please wealthy or aristocratic ladies, thereby to establish a position in the upper class. The ancient soldier, like Achilles, who epitomized human virtue, has been replaced by a sycophantic and presumably effeminate social climber created by a history of corrupt government. The virtue which the ancient soldier represented has been replaced by a rather unclear ideal. On the one hand, Wollstonecraft praises strength, freedom, dignity—all the traits of the enlightened individual as characterized by Rousseau and other modern political theorists—for the sake of political and economic equality. On the other hand, however, she here praises strict discipline and passionlessness. Thus, the freedom for which she so passionately argues is not a freedom to act in accordance with one's passions; in fact it is ultimately a freedom to discipline oneself as was formerly the purview of one's government. In this, Wollstonecraft nicely echoes Rousseau's injunction that an irrational person be "forced to be free."

Further, the analogy to the army officer also makes clear the kind of feminism Wollestonecraft champions—it is essentially one in which all characteristics thought to be "feminine" are eradicated by education, such that all citizens possess the characteristics traditionally thought "masculine." This is the argument she pursues in the rest of the chapters.

Let it not be concluded that I wish to invert the order of things; I have already granted, that, from the constitution of their bodies, men seem to be designed by Providence to attain a greater degree of virtue. I speak collectively of the whole sex; but I see not the shadow of a reason to conclude that their virtues should differ in respect to their nature. In fact, how can they, if virtue has only one eternal standard? I must therefore, if I reason consequentially, as strenuously maintain that they have the same simple direction, as that there is a God.

It follows then that cunning should not be opposed to wisdom, little cares to great exertions, nor insipid softness, varnished over with the name of gentleness, to that fortitude which grand views alone can inspire.

⤳ ⤳ ⤳

Youth is the season for love in both sexes; but in those days of thoughtless enjoyment provision should be made for the more important years of life, when reflection takes place of sensation. But Rousseau, and most of the male writers who have followed his steps, have warmly inculcated that the whole tendency of female education ought to be directed to one point:—to render them pleasing.

Let me reason with the supporters of this opinion who have any knowledge of human nature, do they imagine that marriage can eradicate the habitude of life? The woman who has only been taught to please will soon find that her charms are oblique sunbeams, and that they cannot have much effect on her husband's heart when they are seen every day, when the summer is passed and gone. Will she then have sufficient native energy to look into herself for comfort, and cultivate her dormant faculties? or, is it not more rational to expect that she will try to please other men; and, in the emotions raised by the expectation of new conquests, endeavour to forget the mortification her love or pride has received? When the husband ceases to be a lover—and the time will inevitably come, her desire of pleasing will then grow languid, or become a spring of bitterness; and love, perhaps, the most evanescent of all passions, gives place to jealously or vanity.

⤳ ⤳ ⤳

Women ought to endeavour to purify their heart; but can they do so when their uncultivated understandings make them entirely dependent on their senses for employment and amusement, when no noble pursuit sets them above the little vanities of the day, or enables them to curb the wild emotions that agitate a reed over which every passing breeze has power? To gain the affections of a virtuous man is affection necessary? Nature has given woman a weaker frame than man, but, to ensure her husband's affections, must a wife, who by the exercise of her mind and body whilst she was discharging the duties of a daughter, wife, and mother has allowed her constitution to retain its natural strength, and her nerves a healthy tone, is she, I say, to condescend to use art and feign a sickly delicacy in order to secure her husband's affection? Weakness may excite tenderness, and gratify the arrogant power of man; but the lordly caresses of a protector will not gratify a noble mind that pants for, and deserves to be respected. Fondness is poor substitute for friendship!

In a seraglio, I grant, that all these arts are necessary; the epicure must have his palate tickled, or he will sink into apathy; but have women so little ambition as to be satisfied with such a condition?

⤳ ⤳ ⤳

In fact, if we revert to history, we shall find that the women who have distinguished themselves have neither been the most beautiful nor the most gentle of their sex.

This is, must be, the course of nature:—friendship or indifference inevitably succeeds love.—And this constitution seems perfectly to harmonize with the system of government which prevails in the moral world. Passions are spurs to action, and open the mind; but they sink into mere appetites, become a personal and momentary gratification, when the object is gained, and the satisfied mind rests in enjoyment. The man who had some virtue whilst he was struggling for a crown, often becomes a voluptuous tyrant when it graces his brow; and, when the lover is not lost in the husband, the dotard, a prey to childish caprices, and fond jealousies, neglects the serious duties of life, and the caresses which should excite confidence in his children are lavished on the overgrown child, his wife.

In order to fulfill the duties of life, and to be able to pursue with vigour the various employments which form the moral character, a master and mistress of a family ought not to continue to love each other with passion. I mean to say, that they ought not to indulge those emotions which disturb the order of society, and engross the thoughts that should be otherwise employed. The mind that has never been engrossed by one object wants vigour—if it can long be so, it is weak.

A mistaken education, a narrow, uncultivated mind, and many sexual prejudices, tend to make women more constant than men; but, for the present, I shall not touch on this branch of the subject. I will go still further, and advance, without dreaming of a paradox, that an unhappy marriage is often very advantageous to a family, and that the neglected wife is, in general, the best mother. And this would almost always be the consequence if the female mind was more enlarged: for, it seems to be the common dispensation of Providence, that what we gain in present enjoyment should be deducted from the treasure of life, experience; and that when we are gathering the flowers of the day and revelling in pleasure, the solid fruit of toil and wisdom should not be caught at the same time. The way lies before us, we must turn to the right or left; and he who will pass life away in bounding from one pleasure to another, must not complain if he neither acquires wisdom nor respectability of character.

I own it frequently happens that women who have fostered a romantic unnatural delicacy of feeling, waste their lives in *imagining* how happy they should have been with a husband who could love them with a fervid increasing affection every day, and all day. But they might as well pine married as single— and would not be a jot more unhappy with a bad husband than longing for a good one. That a proper education; or, to speak with more precision, a well stored mind, would enable a woman to support a single life with dignity, I grant; but that she should avoid cultivating her taste, lest her husband should occasionally shock it, is quitting a substance for a shadow.

But to view the subject in another point of view. Do passive indolent women make the best wives? Confining our discussion to the present moment of existence, let us see how such weak creatures perform their part? Do the women who, by the attainment of a few superficial accomplishments, have strengthened the prevailing prejudice, merely contribute to the happiness of their husbands? Do they display their charms merely to amuse them? And have women, who have early imbibed notions of passive obedience, sufficient character to manage a family or educate children? So far from it, that, after surveying the history of women, I cannot help, agreeing with the severest satirist, considering the sex as the weakest as well as the most oppressed half of the species. What does history disclose but marks of inferiority, and how few women have emancipated themselves from the galling yoke of sovereign man?—So few, that the exceptions remind me of an ingenious conjecture respecting Newton: that he was probably a being of a superior order, accidentally caged in a human body. In the same style I have been led to imagine that the few extraordinary women who have rushed in eccentrical directions out of the orbit prescribed to their sex, were *male* spirited, confined by mistake in a female frame. But if it be not philosophical to think of sex when the soul is mentioned, the inferiority must depend on the organs; or the heavenly fire, which is to ferment the clay, is not given in equal portions.

But avoiding, as I have hitherto done, any direct comparison of the two sexes collectively, or frankly acknowledging the inferiority of woman, according to the present appearance of things, I shall only insist that men have increased that inferiority till women are almost sunk below the standard of rational creatures. Let their faculties have room to unfold, and their virtues to gain strength, and then determine where the whole sex must stand in the intellectual scale. Yet let it be remembered, that for a small number of distinguished women I do not ask a place.

It is difficult for us purblind mortals to say to what height human discoveries and improvements may arrive when the gloom of despotism subsides, which makes us stumble at every step; but, when morality shall be settled on a more solid basis, then, without being gifted with a prophetic spirit, I will venture to predict that woman will be either the friend or slave of man.

. . .—Thanks to that Being who impressed them on my soul, and gave me sufficient strength of mind to dare to exert my own reason, till, becoming dependent only on him for the support of my virtue, I view, with indignation, the mistaken notions that enslave my sex.

I love man as my fellow; but his scepter, real, or usurped, extends not to me, unless the reason of an individual demands my homage; and even then the submission is to reason, and not to man. In fact, the conduct of an accountable being must be regulated by the operations of its own reason; or on what foundation rests the throne of God?

It appears to me necessary to dwell on these obvious truths, because females have been insulated, as it were; and, while they have been stripped of the virtues that should clothe humanity, they have been decked with artificial graces that enable them to exercise a short-lived tyranny. Love, in their bosoms, taking place of every nobler passion, their sole ambition is to be fair, to raise emotion instead of inspiring respect; and this ignoble desire, like the servility in absolute monarchies, destroys all strength of character. Liberty is the mother of virtue, and if women are, by their very constitution, slaves, and not allowed to breathe the sharp invigorating air of freedom, they must ever languish like exotics, and be reckoned beautiful flaws in nature;—let it also be remembered, that they are the only flaw.

As to the argument respecting the subjection in which the sex has ever been held, it retorts on man. The many have always been enthralled by the few; and monsters, who scarcely have shewn any discernment of human excellence, have tyrannized over thousands of their fellow creatures. Why have men of superior endowments submitted to such degradation? For, is it not universally acknowledged that kings, viewed collectively, have ever been inferior, in abilities and virtue, to the same number of men taken from the common mass of mankind—yet, have they not, and are they not still treated with a degree of reverence that is an insult to reason? China is not the only country where a living man has been made a God. *Men* have submitted to superior strength to enjoy with impunity the pleasure of the moment—*women* have only done the same, and therefore till it is proved that the courtier, who servilely resigns the birthright of a man, is not a moral agent, it cannot be demonstrated that woman is essentially inferior to man because she has always been subjugated.

Brutal force has hitherto governed the world, and that the science of politics is in its infancy, is evident from philosophers scrupling to give the knowledge most useful to men that determinate distinction.

In her argument against Rousseau, whose descriptions of "Sophy" foreshadowed romantic notions about marriage (see, for instance, discussion of marriage in Part Four), Wollstonecraft apparently feels compelled to argue against romantic love in marriage. She does not argue, however, against the institution of marriage: on the contrary, she champions the virtues of good motherhood and household management, which she believes fall to women only under the protection of marriage. However, Wollstonecraft believes that while certain "natural" virtues are engendered by the institution of marriage, many artificial and vicious traits, falsely named "virtues" by husbands who benefit from the submissiveness of their wives, are cultivated by the visions that modern men and women attach to the institution. The vices of adultery, child neglect, and injustice, Wollstonecraft argues, are the results of seeking passion and beauty in marriage instead of friendship, health, comfort, and independence. Fascinatingly, other than her independence from her husband and her unflirtatiousness, Wollstonecraft's "perfect wife" is very similar to Rousseau's "Sophy": she is a warm and loving mother, a devoted friend, an unadorned and healthy beauty, etc. Thus, like so many of the modern philosophers in this section, Wollstonecraft makes a rationalist objection to the precedent culture that she envisions as tyrannically oppressive, but she offers in its place sometimes quite vague and paradoxical ideals.

SUGGESTED READINGS—PART THREE

Adelman, Janet. "Born of Woman: Fantasies of Maternal Power in Macbeth." *Cannibals, Witches and Divorce: Estranging the Renaissance: Selected Papers From the English Institute,* 1985. M. Garber (ed). Baltimore: The Johns Hopkins University Press, 1987.

Amoros, Celia. "Cartesianism and Feminism: What Reason Has Forgotten, Reasons for Forgetting." *Hypatia* 9: 147–163, 1994.

Arnaud, A.J. (ed). *Women's Rights and the Rights of Man.* Oxford: Aberdeen, 1990.

Bamber, Linda. *Comic Women, Tragic Men: a Study of Gender and Genre in Shakespeare.* Palo Alto: Stanford University Press, 1982.

Baumlin, Tita French. "Petruccio the Sophist and Language as Creation in the Taming of the Shrew." *Studies in English Literature, 1500–1900* 29: 237–257, 1989.

Bordo, Susan. "The Cartesian Masculinization of Thought." *Signs* 11: 439–456, 1986.

———. "Feminist Skepticism and the "Maleness" of Philosophy."*Journal of Philosophy* 85: 619–29, 1988.

Boucher, D. and P. Kelly (eds). *The Social Contract from Hobbes to Rawls.* New York: Routledge, 1992.

Brown, John Russell (ed). *Focus on Macbeth.* Boston: Routledge and Kegan Paul, 1982.

Cavell, Stanley. *Disowning Knowledge in Six Plays of Shakespeare.* Cambridge: Cambridge University Press, 1987.

Chandler, John. "Feminism and Epistemology." *Metaphilosophy* 21: 367–81, 1990.

Chappell, Vere (ed). *The Cambridge Companion to Locke.* Cambridge: Cambridge University Press, 1994.

——— (ed). *Essays on Early Modern Philosophers Vol. I: Rene Descartes.* Hamden: Garland, 1992.

——— (ed). *Essays on Early Modern Philosophers Vol. V: Thomas Hobbes.* Hamden: Garland, 1992.

——— (ed). *Essays on Early Modern Philosophers Vol. IX: John Locke— Political Philosophy.* Hamden: Garland, 1992.

Claridge, Laura and Elizabeth Langland (eds). *Out of Bounds.* Amherst: University of Massachusetts Press, 1990.

Clark, Corenne. "Women and John Locke: Or, Who Owns the Apples in the Garden of Eden?" *Canadian Journal of Philosophy* 7: 699–724, 1977.

Cottingham, John (ed). *The Cambridge Companion to Descartes.* Cambridge: Cambridge University Press, 1992.

Cranston, M. and R.S. Peters (eds). *Hobbes and Rousseau: A Collection of Critical Essays.* Garden City: Anchor, 1972.

Dash, Irene. *Wooing, Wedding and Power: Women in Shakespeare Plays.* New York: Columbia University Press, 1981.

Davies, Stephen. *The Feminine Reclaimed: The Idea of Woman in Spenser, Shakespeare and Milton.* Lexington: University of Kentucky Press, 1986.

Descartes, Rene. *Discourse on Method and Meditations on First Philosophy.* Donald A. Cress (trans). Indianapolis: Hackett, 1993.

————. *The Passions of the Soul.* Stephen H. Voss (trans). Indianapolis: Hackett, 1989.

Di Stefano, Christine.*Configurations of Masculinity: A Feminist Perspective on Modern Political Theory.* Ithaca: Cornell University Press, 1991.

Doney, Willis (ed). *Descartes: A Collection of Critical Essays.* New York: Anchor, 1967.

Dusinberre, Juliet. *Shakespeare and the Nature of Women.* New York: Barnes and Noble, 1975.

Farwell, Marilyn R. "Eve, the Separation Scene, and the Renaissance Idea of Androgyny." *Milton Studies* 16: 3–20, 1982.

Ferrara, Alassandro. *Modernity and Authenticity: A Study in the Social and Ethical Thought of Jean-Jacques Rousseau.* Albany: State University of New York Press, 1993.

Fineman, Joel. *The Subjectivity Effect in Western Literary Tradition: Essays Toward the Release of Shakespeare's Will.* Cambridge: MIT Press, 1991.

Flexner, Eleanor. *Mary Wollstonecraft: A Biography.* New York: Coward, McCann and Geoghegan, 1972.

Frankfurt, Harry G. *Demons, Dreamers and Madmen: The Defense of Reason in Descartes' Meditations.* Indianapolis: Bobbs-Merrill, 1970.

Flathman, Richard E. *Thomas Hobbes: Skepticism, Individuality and Chastened Politics.* Newberry Park: Sage, 1993.

Fresch, Cheryl. "And Brought Her Unto the Man: The Wedding in Paradise Lost," *Milton Studies* 16: 21–33, 1982.

Gatens, Moira. "Rousseau and Wollstonecraft: Nature vs. Reason." *Australasian Journal of Philosophy* 64: 1–15, 1986.

Gay, Peter. *The Enlightenment: An Interpretation.* New York: Vintage, 1966.

Gobetti, Daniela. *Private and Public: Individuals, Households, and Body Politic in Locke and Hutcheson.* New York: Routledge, 1992.

Gould, Carol C. and M. W. Wartofsky (eds). *Women and Philosophy.* New York: G.P. Putnam and Sons, 1976.

Graves, Robert. *The White Goddess.* New York: Creative Age Press, 1948.

Green, Karen. "Christine dePizan and Thomas Hobbes." *Philosophical Quarterly* 44: 456–475, 1994.

Greene, James J. "Macbeth: Masculinity as Murder." *American Imago* 41: 155–80, 1984.

Grene, Marjorie. *Descartes.* Minneapolis: University of Minnesota Press, 1985.

Grimshaw, Jean. "Mary Wollstonecraft and the Tensions in Feminist Philosophy,"*Radical Philosophy* 52: 11–17, 1989.

Harding, Sandra.*The Science Question in Feminism.* Ithaca: Cornell University Press, 1986.

Heilman, Robert B. "The Taming Untamed, or, The Return of the Shrew." *Modern Language Quarterly* 27: 147–61, 1966.

Henze, Richard. "Role Playing in The Taming of the Shrew." *Shakespeare Review* 4: 231–40, 1970.

Hobbes, Thomas. *Leviathan.* New York: Dutton,1950.

Huyssen, Andrea. "Mapping the Postmodern." *Feminism/Postmodernism,* edited by Linda Nicholson. 1989.

Johnson, Claudia L. *Equivocal Beings: Politics, Gender and Sentimentality in the 1790s.* Chicago: University of Chicago Press, 1995.

Kahn, Coppelia (ed). *Man's Estate: Masculine Identity in Shakespeare.* California: University of California Press, 1981.

Keller, Evelyn Fox. "The Gender/Science System: Or Is Sex to Gender as Nature Is to Science?" *Hypatia* 2: 37–89, 1987.

Keohane, Nannerl. " 'But For Her Sex': The Domestication of Sophie." *Revue de l'Universite D'Ottowa* 49: 390–400, 1979.

Kimbrough, Robert. "Macbeth: Prisoner of Gender." *Shakespeare Studies* 16 : 175–90, 1983.

Kofman, Sarah. "Rousseau's Phallocratic Ends." *Hypatia* 3: 123–136, 1989.

Korsmeyer, Carolyn. "Reason and Moral in the Early Feminist Movement: Mary Wollstonecraft." *Philosophical Forum* 5: 97–111, 1973.

Landes, Joan B. *Women and the Public Sphere in the Age of the French Revolution.* Ithaca: Cornell University Press, 1988.

Landy, Marcia."Kinship and the Role of Women in Paradise Lost," *Milton Studies* 4: 3–18, 1972.

Levine, Andrew. *The General Will: Rousseau, Marx and Communism.* Cambridge: Cambridge University Press, 1993.

Lewalski, Barbara K. "Milton on Women—Yet Once More." *Milton Studies* 6: 3–20, 1974.

Lloyd, Genevieve. *The Man of Reason: "Male" and "Female" in Western Philosophy.* Minneapolis: University of Minnesota Press, 1984.

Locke, John. *Two Treatises of Government.* Peter Laslett (ed). Cambridge: Cambridge University Press, 1988.

Mackenzie, Catriana. "Reason and Sensibility: The Ideal of Women's Self-Governance in the Writings of Mary Wollstonecraft." *Hypatia* 8(4): 35–55, 1993.

Macpherson, C.B. *Political Theory of Possessive Individualism: Hobbes to Locke.* Oxford: Oxford University Press, 1988.

McColley, Diane K. *Milton's Eve.* Champaign: University of Illinois Press, 1983.

Mellor, Anne. *The Proper Lady and the Woman Writer: Ideology as Style in the Works of Mary Wollstonecraft, Mary Shelley, and Jane Austen.* Chicago: University of Chicago Press, 1984.

Merchant, Caroline. *The Death of Nature.* San Francisco: Harper & Row, 1980.

Milton, John. *Paradise Lost.* New York: The Odyssey Press, 1935.

Misenheimer, Helen Evans. *Rousseau on the Education of Women.* Lanham: University Press of America, 1981.

Novy, Marianne. *Love's Argument: Gender Relations in Shakespeare.* Chapel Hill: University of North Carolina Press, 1984.

Ortega y Gassett, Jose.*The Modern Theme.* New York: Harper & Row, 1961.

Perret, Marian D. "Petruchio: The Model Wife." *Studies in English Literature, 1500–1900.* 23: 223–235, 1983.

Pateman, Carol. *The Sexual Contract.* Palo Alto: Stanford University Press, 1988.

Plumwood, Val. "Nature, Self, and Gender: Feminism, Environmental Philosophy, and the Critique of Rationalism." *Hypatia* 6(1): 3–27,1991.

Rapaczynski, Andrzej. *Nature and Politics: Liberalism in the Philosophies of Hobbes, Locke and Rousseau.* Ithaca: Cornell University Press, 1987.

Rappaport, Elizabeth. "On the Future of Love: Rousseau and the Radical Feminists." *Philosphical Forum* 5: 185–205, 1973.

Roach, Catherine. "Loving Your Mother: On the Woman–Nature Relationship." *Hypatia* 6(1): 46– 59, 1991.

Rogers, G.A.J. and A. Ryan. *Perspectives on Thomas Hobbes.* Oxford: Clarendon Press, 1988.

Rorty, Amelie O. *Essays on Descartes' Meditations.* Berkeley: University of California Press, 1986.

Rossi, Alice (ed).*The Feminist Papers: From Adams to deBeauvoir.* Boston: Northeastern University Press, 1973.

Rousseau, Jean-Jacques. *The Basic Political Writings.* Donald A. Cress (trans). Indianapolis: Hackett, 1987.

———. *Emile.* Barbara Foxley (trans). London: J.M. Dent, 1993.

Sapiro, Virginia. *A Vindication of Political Virtue: The Political Theory of Mary Wollstonecraft.* Chicago: University of Chicago Press, 1992.

Shakespeare, William. *The Riverside Shakespeare.* Evans, G. Blakemore (ed.). Boston: HM, 1974.

Strong, Tracy B. *Jean-Jacques Rousseau: The Politics of the Ordinary.* Thousand Oaks: Sage, 1994.

Todd, Janet. *A Wollstonecraft Anthology.* New York: Columbia University Press, 1989.

Turner, James. *One Flesh: Paradisal Marriage and Sexual Relations in the Age of Milton.* Oxford: Oxford University Press, 1987.

Walker, Julia (ed). *Milton and the Idea of Woman.* Urbana: University of Illinois Press, 1988.

Webber, Joan Malory. "The Politics of Poetry: Feminism and Paradise Lost," *Milton Studies* 14: 3–24, 1980.

Weiss, Penny A. *Gendered Community: Rousseau, Sex and Politics.* New York: NYU Press, 1993.

Williams, Bernard. *Descartes: The Project of Pure Enquiry.* Atlantic Highlands: Humanities Press, 1978.

Wittreich, Joseph. *Feminist Milton.* Ithaca: Cornell University Press, 1987.

Wollstonecraft, Mary. *A Vindication of the Rights of Woman.* New York: Norton, 1967.

PART FOUR

THE NINETEENTH CENTURY: LIBERALISM AND ROMANTICISM

Hegel, Shelley, Mill, Marx and Engels,
Kierkegaard and Nietzsche

INTRODUCTION

THE SCIENTIFIC VS. THE INDUSTRIAL REVOLUTION

When contemporary philosophers delineate the periods of the history of Western philosophy—say, when they decide how to break it up into a series of courses—they customarily set off the nineteenth century as an era unto itself. As we saw in the last section, early moderns thought themselves quite radically distinct from their medieval forebears; yet towards the end of the eighteenth century, there began to develop a far more overwhelming set of social, political, economic, and philosophical changes than the early moderns had imagined. What had seemed to the early moderns to be the final unveiling of the secrets of nature—the discoveries of the scientific revolution—began towards the nineteenth century to bear fruit in the inventions of new technologies—the products of the industrial revolution. But these inventions—new machines, new consumer goods, new buildings, new systems of labor, new gadgets and gizmos of every kind—affected everyday human affairs in a way that the pure discoveries of scientists like Galileo and Copernicus could never have done. The nineteenth century manifested more than just a shift in intellectual presuppositions and political organization: it wholly transformed the day-to-day quality of human life in an amazingly short period of time.

Where the early moderns argued for and against different scientific methods, the nineteenth century tested their applications in productive technologies. Where the early moderns championed the autonomy of the individual, the nineteenth century quantified and analyzed him or her for the purposes of social design. Where early modernity sought a set of new truths, the nineteenth century produced an enormity of new *things*. It was enamored not with the success of the sciences, but with the progress of technologies. Lewis Mumford, a well-known historian of technology, called the nineteenth century the "paleotechnic phase" of human history—fully, but primitively, machine-run—and referred to it as "the new barbarism":

> *Paleotechnic industry . . . arose out of the breakdown of European society and carried the process of disruption to a finish. There was a sharp shift in interest from life values to pecuniary values . . . It was no longer sufficient for industry to provide a livelihood: it must create an independent fortune: work was no longer a necessary part of living: it became an all-important end. . . . Here the break with the past was complete. People lived and died within sight of the coal pit or the cotton mill in which they spent from fourteen to sixteen hours of their daily life, lived and died without either memory or hope . . ."*[1]

Several of the axes along which Mumford characterizes the era are relevant to the ways its philosophers thought about gender, and about existence in general. Nineteenth-century philosophy could be described as increasingly oriented towards social or historical issues (as opposed to the natural-scientific focus of the early moderns), towards psychological explanations of phenomena, and towards dramatic writing styles that wove together philosophical and literary concerns. In other words, where the early moderns had sought a foundation for scientific knowledge in a notion of human nature, the thinkers of the nineteenth century increasingly understood human nature as founded within the predilection for scientific knowledge. This enterprise was productive of some novel and fascinating works in literature and philosophy, but this reversal of perspective on the nature of humanity turned the whole idea of knowledge, of scientific authority, on its head. Truth and knowledge were on the defensive.

NATURE AND CULTURE

One way of putting this reversal of perspective is this: where early modernity was taken up with the paradoxes of nature, the nineteenth century was taken up with the dichotomy between nature and culture. This dichotomy was a pervasive analytic tool for romantic poets and political philosophers alike, as we will see. As industrial scenery more and more overtook the landscape of Europe and America, it seemed more and more foreign to, and at odds with, the natural world out of which it arose. Further, life in this rapidly changing industrialized society seemed to put individuals at a greater and greater remove from the "state of nature" upon which early modern hypothesis these societies had been built. The industrial revolution alienated the natural world—including the world of human nature—from the social or cultural world to an extent unintended and unimagined by the thinkers of earlier centuries.

---

[1] Lewis Mumford, *Technics and Civilization*. (San Diego: Harcourt Brace Jovonovich, Publishers, 1962(1934)), pp. 153–4.

Thus, the clear delineation of the natural from the artificial appeared as a pressing problem, whether it was sought for the sake of technological advance or romantic nostalgia. This first strain, the distinction of nature from culture as part of the pursuit of cultural progress, was an intellectual ally of nineteenth-century liberalism. Thinkers like John Stuart Mill followed the liberal political theories of the seventeenth and eighteenth centuries in their desire for an improved human life of freedom and equality through the application of new scientific, political-economic, and educational theories. The latter strain, which distinguished nature from culture as part of a nostalgic investigation of a rapidly disappearing nature, was the intellectual ally of nineteenth-century romanticism. Writers like Mary Shelley and Nietzsche expressed remorse and some fear at the ugly and unvirtuous consequences of the scientific revolution, and waxed nostalgic for their respective visions of a more primordial state. Unlike the political "conservatism" and "liberalism" of today, however, the liberal and the romantic strains of nineteenth-century thought are neither mutually exclusive nor purely political. They often are intertwining strains even within a single author's work, and they combine literary, political, and philosophical aspects in almost any author of the period.

With regard to the question of gender, the nature/culture distinction foreshadows the contemporary debate among feminists known as "essentialism vs. inessentialism." Today's "essentialist" claims that there are natural feminine and masculine qualities that account for sex differences between men and women, which no amount of social or cultural reform can erase. The nineteenth-century analogue to the "essentialist" would claim that women's behavior, or "femininity" (or men's behavior, or "masculinity") is a product of nature and therefore must be accepted by culture no matter how technologically advanced it becomes. Some versions of this claim might even extend to someone who believed that technology was powerful enough to change or eradicate nature, but that it should not do so, as a matter of morality or prudence. Today's "inessentialist" would claim that masculinity and femininity are nothing but social constructs, an internalization by individuals of what are really just socially prescribed roles. The nineteenth-century predecessor of the "inessentialist" would claim that women's or men's behavior is entirely a product of culture and can be changed whenever a society decides to change its cultural habits. This position is not necessarily associated with political liberalism. Certain passages of Nietzsche, for instance, as we will see, seem to evoke a sort of "inessentialist nostalgia," a belief that while everything we are is a social construction, people should nonetheless return to the roles of earlier eras.

The philosophical distinction between the "natural" and the "cultural" that pervaded nineteenth-century thought shared all the paradoxes of "nature" of early modernity. With such powerful industrialism, for instance, it is not clear that what is "natural" cannot, on that account, be changed. Nonetheless, many thinkers of the period, Mill for instance, are at pains to show that, say, women's lives can and should be made better, because there is *nothing natural* about women's subordination to men. Others, however, like Marx and Engels, arguing for a similar social reform—the economic equality of women and men—base their claim on the *natural* sexual equality of earlier periods in history. Thus, the distinction seems in many thinkers to be of desperate importance, yet there is little consensus among them about how to draw the line between nature and culture, or about why one would want to do so.

HISTORICISM AND A RETURN TO OPPOSITIONS

In addition to foreshadowing contemporary debates, this nature/culture dichotomy harks back to some of the ancient concerns we saw in Parts Two and Three, in particular the "*nomos/physis*" debate of the Athenian Sophists. For many nineteenth-century writers, this was a deliberate reference. The concern over the progressive or degenerative effect of technology was an inherently historical issue: progress and degeneration happen only over time. The classical education common at the time included ancient Greek and Latin, and so many authors naturally turned to comparisons and contrasts between these ancient cultures and the seemingly so different industrial Europe and America. Many found surprising similarities between these periods and their own.

In particular, nineteenth-century thinkers seemed to find in ancient Greece, in concerns such as theirs over the nominal or natural origins of moral standards, a notion of human life as inherently conflicted, anguished by and yet indebted to its own internal oppositions. Without the inherent conflict between good and evil, for instance, with which each human being must struggle, neither vice nor great achievements of virtue would have any meaning for us. Similarly, noted some nineteenth-century thinkers, many great political goods could not have been achieved without the horrors of war or revolution. Humanity itself seemed to many of these thinkers, as it had to many of the ancient Greeks, to be inherently both natural and cultural, both good and bad, both divine and animal; indeed these notions themselves seemed interdependent. What is the meaning of culture, devoid of its contrast to nature, for instance? Or, what is the meaning of a good will, other than its rejection of evil? Nineteenth-century thinkers seemed to find in the ancient Greeks a sort of spiritual ally, a culture seeking to explain and evaluate human history itself, and finding the source of history—the wellspring of human change and the cultures that manifest it—in these conflicts themselves. The idea that human life is itself paradoxical—that human nature is cultural and human culture is natural—was an inspiration for many thinkers of the period, as they tried to accommodate the enormity of the changes brought on by the industrial revolution.

Thus was revived the ancient Greek notion that change is *dialectical*—i.e., that it originates in and perpetuates conflicts between opposing forces—not just between nature and culture, but between a whole series of dichotomous oppositions. Thus, we will see in the period a kind of a return to binarism, including the notion that binary opposites interact with each other dialectically over time. Indeed, some of the philosophers in this chapter themselves claimed explicitly that a return to binarism was a part of the "spirit of the age." Marx, for instance, claimed that industrial capitalism reduced a formerly complex class system to a bald dichotomy between owners and workers. However, for thinkers of the nineteenth century, the unification of these opposites tended not to be found in God or in eternal forms, but in human existence itself, as a conflicted agent faced with its own paradoxes. Thus, it was common to lay out these problems of binary oppositions in historical, or at least temporal, terms—time and history being the unifying forces underlying the conflicts of human existence. Thinkers of the period addressed problems, including the problems of gender, in large, dramatic terms—pan-historical generalizations, interdisciplinary modes of thought, sweeping metaphors, in which human conflict is the theme and human history is the setting.

THE NEW IMPORTANCE OF WORK

Perhaps the most salient feature of nineteenth century social life was the growing dominance of industrial capitalism. Responsible for both the greatest wealth and the most abject poverty that the world had witnessed to date, the factory system of labor in the great industrialized nations of the West changed dramatically the nature and purpose of human labor in human life. Certain features that had been characteristic of human labor since antiquity were radically altered as the industrial age dawned. 1) Work was no longer a direct interaction with raw materials resulting in property—as Locke, for instance, little more than a hundred years earlier, had described it. Increasingly, nineteenth-century workers interacted directly only with machines, perhaps never even seeing, certainly not owning, the products of their labor. 2) Work was no longer primarily agricultural or rural. Most workers migrated to the cities, which added to their status as cultural hubs a new reputation as centers of production and of working-class life. In the cities in particular, not least because of the large populations which filled their relatively small space, the bald dichotomies of wealth and poverty, owner and worker, educated and uneducated, etc., were particularly grossly manifested. Thus, the nature/culture dichotomy was often an abstraction of a country/city dichotomy, which was an increasingly salient geographic and cultural distinction. 3) For the majority, work was no longer performed directly for sustenance, nor for its intrinsic rewards, but for pay. This fact necessitated the quantification of labor, usually in terms of time spent upon it. Thus, the very meaning of the word "work" underwent a shift in this period to mean "paid labor." Unpaid labor was increasing relegated to the status of "hobby," or "moral duty," or "relaxation," etc.

These changes in the nature of work, together with the increasing importance of paid labor in establishing social position, social status, character, etc., has marked effects on the relations between the sexes, and on the philosophy of gender which took them as its subject of study. The distinction between labor done in and outside of the home grew more marked as the one was unpaid and the other paid, the one considered "natural" and the other "cultural." While many women worked in the factories, particularly in England, the association of women with the household—already well established in the ancient texts of earlier chapters of this book—became more static, more entrenched, than ever. Thus, the notion of the "proper" work for women and men became the prevalent line of analysis for questions about gender, and has remained a fundamental issue for feminists and others to the present day.

1. GEORG WILHELM FRIEDRICH HEGEL
(German, 1770–1831)

G.W.F. Hegel's work was the predominant influence in European philosophy for the entire nineteenth century. Hegel is responsible for the reinterpretation of the notion of *dialectic* which his predecessor, Immanuel Kant, had revived from the Greeks. Although his work is largely outside the scope of this book, some background on the theory of Kant (German, 1724–1804), the culminating thinker of the early modern period and a pivotal figure in the history of philosophy, will be useful in understanding nineteenth-century theories of gender, some of which—starting with Hegel—involved reactions to Kantian philosophy.

A WORD ABOUT KANT

Kant had apparently resolved the epistemological problems of early modernity, claiming that the nature of the human mind was fully rational and ordered and that the mind provided order and intelligibility to the "external world." In other words, Kant had claimed that the human mind was an active participant in the rational order of the world of its experience. Kant's notion of human reason or consciousness, then, was of an active, productive force—this was very different from the sort of "passive receptor" of knowledge that earlier thinkers like Descartes and Hobbes had supposed it. As a consequence, Kant claimed, our knowledge of the external world was always colored by the categories of our own mind. Kant claimed that these categories of experience were the same for every human being, and so were objective and absolute. "Things in themselves"—i.e., the external world untouched by human experience of it—was, however, unknowable; we could know *that* something existed outside our experience, and we could know *how* we must all necessarily experience it, but we could not know anything else about the external world.

Thus, Kant claimed that objective truth was possible, but that it was objective and true only of universal human experience (or,"phenomena") and not of the external world by itself. This was echoed in his moral, political, and aesthetic thought, in all of which the human being was positioned as both the ultimate object and the striving subject of value or knowledge. Kant's notion of truth then was radically humanized, and although he himself had claimed that universal objective knowledge was possible for every rational person, he opened the door for a set of relativist critics, philosophers who claimed that, and how, existence was ultimately relative to the differences in human thought over different time periods and cultures. Kant's critics also tended to be "idealists"—philosophers who claimed that reality is dependent on or interdependent with the mind—despite Kant's rejection of idealism. Kant had claimed that the categories of the mind constituted *experience,* but not the whole of reality itself.

HEGEL'S HISTORICISM

Perhaps the most stunning of Hegel's claims was that truth was by its very nature *historical.* All ideas, he claimed, were dependent upon or outgrowths of their historical predecessors, critical appropriations of the ideas of the past. Truth was envisioned by Hegel as a dynamic, developing relationship between mind and world which, according to him, were integrally bound together. For Hegel, human history, and not individual or autonomous human thought, was the medium of truth and of consciousness. Individuals were swept up in and bound by the general standards of human thought and achievement of their era.

Thus, what counts as the truth at any particular historical period is, according to Hegel, really only a partial truth, relative to its particular moment in history. The "whole" truth, or "Absolute Knowledge," as Hegel called it, would consist of all the partial truths of all periods in history—in other words, the absolute truth contained the whole of human history and thus could only exist at its end. While Hegel had a kind of a relativist view of truth, then, he did not claim that any truth claim was as good as any other; rather, a "larger," historically later, more encompassing standard of truth was closer to the whole ("Absolute Knowledge") and so could be said to be *truer* or *better* than the more partial standards of truth of earlier periods in history. Thus, for Hegel, truth was a force which *progressed* over history; improving, broadening, and deepening itself over time. The notion of a progress of knowledge over history presupposes a goal or an end towards which it progresses, and according to Hegel, this goal was "The Absolute," which, though it was never achieved in history, must be presupposed by Reason.

THE HISTORICAL DIALECTIC

According to Hegel, truth—the progressive integration of mind and world—is the unfolding of self-consciousness. In other words, for Hegel, because mind and world are interdependent, they are both constitutive of, and constituted by, consciousness. In this sense, then, Hegel is an "idealist," sometimes referred to by scholars as one of a group of "German Idealists." The standards of truth at any particular period in history, according to Hegel, are the results of consciousness's reflections upon and development of itself, such that "Absolute Knowledge" or the whole of truth is also the moment of complete and thorough self-consciousness. As Hegel states, "In the kinds of certainty hitherto considered, the truth for consciousness is something other than consciousness itself. The conception, however, of this truth vanishes in the course of our experience of it."[2] In other words, our *experience* of knowledge (or the "phenomenological" character of knowledge—hence the title of the work) tells us that when we are conscious, we are always conscious *of ourselves*.

In order to know itself, if only partially, consciousness must be self-divided into knower and thing known, subject and object. According to Hegel, truth at any particular moment is the totality of ways that consciousness is able to resolve its inherent conflicts. Knower and thing known, in a sense, "negotiate" between themselves a settlement, which is expressed in a claim to truth; but this truth claim is itself the

---

[2] G.W.F. Hegel, *The Phenomenology of Mind*. Translated by J.B. Baillie, with introduction and notes by George Lichtheim. (New York: Harper Colophon Books, 1967, Reprinted by arrangement with George Allen and Unwin, Ltd., London and the Humanities Press, New York), p. 218.

object of reflection for a new subjective consciousness that stands in opposition to it. As an example of Hegel's point, suppose you are trying to figure out a math problem. As a math *problem,* the question itself, once you've read it and understood that you're supposed to solve it, appears to you as the *kind of thing* that has a *right* answer and several *wrong* answers. Suppose you try to do the problem one way, say the way you remember your teacher doing a similar problem in class. You come up with an answer this way, and for a while you are satisfied with it, but soon you come at this answer from a different viewpoint and see clearly that it must be wrong. So you critically analyze your first answer—i.e., oppose it—in order to figure out what you did wrong, and then come up with a new answer. This will go on until you get the right answer; i.e., your answers will get better and better through the inherent conflict in your own consciousness of the problem. For Hegel, this dialectic of knowledge and good but mistaken belief is what goes on on a grand scale in science, politics, religion, and art. Over history, consciousness progresses and enlarges itself through an historical *dialectic* somewhat similar to the dialectical oppositions that were the source of change according to Plato and the preSocratic thinkers discussed in Parts Two and Three, and they will have similar relevance to the question of sex difference.

THE PHENOMENOLOGY OF SPIRIT (1807)

In *The Phenomenology of Spirit,* Hegel gives his own history of thought, outlining in rather large terms the stages along the evolution of self-consciousness, and then he projects the future stages necessary in order to reach Absolute Knowledge. Because the progress of consciousness is dialectical, each new stage retains the traces of its past—notions of truth that, though obsolete, are distinct influences on present-day knowledge. Thus our beginnings, the most primal conflict from which the first knowledge in history originated, is always with us, however far we progress. In our example above, for instance, the right answer that you eventually find is still an answer to the original problem, and it still carries a sense of your initial insight that your answer could be wrong.

THE MASTER–SLAVE DICHOTOMY

According to Hegel, the first conflict of consciousness in history is—at least in general outline—the first confrontation between two moments of consciousness. The inherent division in consciousness, he claimed, cannot be recognized until it presents itself to consciousness in the person of another consciousness. In other words, knowledge, for Hegel, is an inherently social enterprise—it cannot get off the ground until two conscious selves confront each other. And this confrontation, when it does occur, is the beginning of history and of knowledge. According to Hegel, the original conflict in consciousness occurs between "two desiring selves"—i.e., when two people both want the same thing, but cannot both have it. The resolution of this first conflict is the first stage of consciousness which he claimed was consciousness divided into *master* [Lord] and *slave* [Bondsman].

Self-consciousness exists in itself and for itself, in that, and by the fact that it exists for another self-consciousness; that is to say, it *is* only by being acknowledged or "recognized". The conception of this its unity in its duplication, of infinitude realizing itself in self-consciousness, has many sides to it and encloses within it elements of varied significance.

Self-consciousness has before it another self-consciousness; it has come outside itself. This has a double significance. First it has lost its own self, since it finds itself as an *other* being; secondly, it has thereby sublated that other, for it does not regard the other as essentially real, but sees its own self in the other.

It must cancel this its other. To do so is the sublation of that first double meaning, and is therefore a second double meaning. First, it must set itself to sublate the other independent being, in order thereby to become certain of itself as true being, secondly, it thereupon proceeds to sublate its own self, for this other is itself.

The first does not have the object before it only in the passive form characteristic primarily of the object of desire, but as an object existing independently for itself, over which therefore it has no power to do anything for its own behoof, if that object does not *per se* do what the first does to it. The process then is absolutely the double process of both self-consciousnesses. Each sees the other do the same as itself; each itself does what it demands on the part of the other, and for that reason does what it does, only so far as the other does the same. Action from one side only would be useless, because what is to happen can only be brought about by means of both.

While *qua* consciousness, it no doubt comes outside itself, still, in being outside itself, it is at the same time restrained within itself, it exists for itself, and its self-externalization is for consciousness. *Consciousness* finds that it immediately is and is not another consciousness, as also that this other is for itself only when it cancels itself as existing for itself, and has self-existence only in the self-existence of the other. Each is the mediating term to the other, through which each mediates and unites itself with itself; and each is to itself and to the other an immediate self-existing reality, which, at the same time, exists thus for itself only through this mediation. They recognize themselves as mutually recognizing one another.

Self-consciousness is primarily simple existence for self, self-identity by exclusion of every other from itself. It takes its essential nature and absolute object to be Ego; and in this immediacy, in this bare fact of its self-existence, it is individual. That which for it is other stands as unessential object, as object with the impress and character of negation. But the other is also a self-consciousness; an individual makes its appearance in antithesis to an individual. Appearing thus in their immediacy, they are for each other in the manner of ordinary objects.

ᕰ ᕰ ᕰ

Each is indeed certain of its own self, but not of the other, and hence its own certainty of itself is still without truth. For its truth would be merely that its own individual existence for itself would be shown to it to be an independent object, or, which is the same thing, that the object would be exhibited as this pure certainty of itself.

ᕰ ᕰ ᕰ

The process of bringing all this out involves a twofold action—action on the part of the other and action on the part of itself. In so far as it is the other's action, each aims at the destruction and death of the other. But in this there is implicated also the second kind of action, self-activity; for the former implies that it risks its own life. The relation of both self-consciousnesses is in this way so constituted that they prove themselves and each other through a life-and-death struggle. They must enter into this struggle, for they must bring their certainty of themselves, the certainty of being for themselves, to the level of objective truth, and make this a fact both in the case of the other and in their own case as well. And it is solely by risking life that freedom is obtained.

ᕰ ᕰ ᕰ

This trial by death, however, cancels both the truth which was to result from it, and therewith the certainty of self altogether. For just as life is the natural "position" of consciousness, independence without absolute negativity, so death is the natural "negation" of consciousness, negation without independence, which thus remains without the requisite significance of actual recognition.

ᕰ ᕰ ᕰ

In this experience self-consciousness becomes aware that *life* is as essential to it as pure self-consciousness. In immediate self-consciousness the simple ego is absolute object, which, however, is for us or in itself absolute mediation, and has as its essential moment substantial and solid independence. The dissolution of that simple unity is the result of the first experience; through this there is posited a pure self-consciousness, and a consciousness which is not purely for itself, but for another, i.e. as an existent consciousness, consciousness in the form and shape of thinghood. Both moments are essential, since, in the first instance, they are unlike and opposed, and their reflexion into unity has not yet come to light, they stand as two opposed forms or modes of consciousness. The one is independent, and its essential nature is to be for itself; the other is dependent, and its essence is life or existence for another. The former is the Master, or Lord, the latter the Bondsman.

The master is the consciousness that exists *for itself;* but no longer merely the general notion of existence for self. Rather, it is a consciousness existing on its own account which is mediated with itself through an other consciousness, i.e. through an other whose very nature implies that it is bound up with an independent being or with thinghood in general. The master brings himself into relation to both these moments, to a thing as such, the object of desire, and to the consciousness whose essential character is thinghood. And since the master, is (*a*) *qua* notion of self-consciousness, an immediate relation of self-existence, but (*b*) is now moreover at the same time mediation, or a being-for-self which is for itself only through an other—he [the master] stands in relation (*a*) immediately to both (*b*) mediately to each through the other. The master relates himself to the bondsman mediately through independent existence, for that is precisely what keeps the bondsman in thrall; it is his chain, from which he could not in the struggle get away, and for that reason he proved himself to be dependent, to have his independence in the shape of thinghood. The master, however, is the power controlling this state of existence for he has shown in the struggle that he holds it to be merely something negative. Since he is the power dominating existence, while this existence again is the power controlling the other [the bondsman], the master holds, *par consequence,* this other in subordination. In the same way the master relates himself to the thing mediately through the bondsman. The bondsman being a self-consciousness in the broad sense, also takes up a negative attitude to things and cancels them; but the thing is, at the same time, independent for him, and, in consequence, he cannot, with all his negating, get so far as to annihilate it outright and be done with it; that is to say, he merely works on it. To the master, on the other hand, by means of this mediating process, belongs the immediate relation, in the sense of the pure negation of it, in other words he gets the enjoyment.

In these two moments, the master gets his recognition through an other consciousness, for in them the latter affirms itself as unessential, both by working upon the thing, and, on the other hand, by the fact of being dependent on a determinate existence; in neither case can this other get the mastery over existence, and succeed in absolutely negating it. We have thus here this moment of recognition, viz. that the other consciousness cancels itself as self-existent, and *ipso facto,* itself does what the first does to it. In the same way we have the other moment, that this action on the part of the second is the action proper of the first; for what is done by the bondsman is properly an action on the part of the master. The latter exists only for himself, that is his essential nature; he is the negative power without qualification, a power to which the thing is naught. And he is thus the absolutely essential act in this situation, while the bondsman is not so, he is an unessential activity. But for recognition proper there is needed the moment that what the master does to the other he should also do to himself, and what the bondsman does to himself, he should do to the other also. On that account a form of recognition has arisen that is one sided and unequal.

In all this, the unessential consciousness is, for the master, the object which embodies the truth of his certainty of himself. But it is evident that this object does not correspond to its notion[.]

ᴄ ᴄ ᴄ

The truth of the independent consciousness is accordingly the consciousness of the bondsman. This doubtless appears in the first instance outside itself, and not as the truth of self-consciousness. But just as lordship showed its essential nature to be the reverse of what it wants to be, so, too, bondage will, when completed, pass into the opposite of what it immediately is: being a consciousness repressed within itself, it will enter into itself, and change round into real and true independence.

ᴄ ᴄ ᴄ

It has been in that experience melted to its inmost soul, has trembled throughout its every fibre, and all that was fixed and steadfast has quaked within it. This complete perturbation of its entire substance, this absolute dissolution of all its stability into fluent continuity, is, however, the simple, ultimate nature of self-consciousness[.]

ᴄ ᴄ ᴄ

By serving he cancels in every particular aspect his dependence on and attachment to natural existence, and by his work removes this existence away.

ᴄ ᴄ ᴄ

. . . Desire has reserved to itself the pure negating of the object and thereby unalloyed feeling of self. This satisfaction, however, just for that reason is itself only a state of evanescence, for it lacks objectivity or subsistence. Labour, on the other hand, is desire restrained and checked, evanescence delayed and postponed; in other words, labour shapes and fashions the thing. The negative relation to the object passes into the *form* of the object, into something that is permanent and remains; because it is just for the labourer that the object has independence. This negative mediating agency, this activity giving shape and form, is at the same time the individual existence, the pure self-existence of that consciousness, which now in the work it does is externalized and passes into the condition of permanence. The consciousness that toils and serves accordingly attains by this means the direct apprehension of that independent being as its self.

Although Hegel's "master–slave dialectic" is not intended as an analytic schema for gender relations, it has been many times adapted to that purpose, and so plays an important role in our investigation. It is, for many later philosophers, the paradigm for all dichotomous political and social relations. As it is described above, the master–slave relationship is the result of a fight to the death between two selves who originally desire the same thing. Were it not for this conflict—i.e., if people's desires never clashed—there would be no interaction and no relationship between them. In this sense, the foundation of human society is thought by Hegel to be a binary opposition, and the result of the conflict between these opposites gives humanity its social or political character. In all human society, in other words, there are traces of mastery and slavery, command and service, power and subordination. Hence, later thinkers concerned with the subordination of women to men will often try to find in the relation between the sexes the traces of Hegel's master and slave.

In the beginning, the character of the two selves is not socially differentiated. The one who will become the master does so because he or she is willing to die to get what he or she wants. In other words, according to Hegel, the motivation for mastery is the love of one's freedom above even one's own life. The one who will become the slave does so because he or she is ultimately unwilling to risk his or her life in order to get the things he or she desires—in other words, he or she will surrender the battle in order to save his or her life. But to surrender in the battle is to submit to the other—in yielding the prize, the self who gives up puts him or herself at the mercy of the victor. Thus, the master character, after the fight, centers his or her life on the exercise of his or her freedom, while the slave character is unfree, and focuses his or her attention on preserving his or her own life.

In order to preserve his or her own life, however, the slave must serve the master, doing all the work usual for a slave and necessary for the master—the slave cooks and farms and makes clothes and utensils etc. for the master and for him or herself. Similarly, in order for the master to exercise his or her freedom by satisfying desires and demonstrating power over others, the master must be master *over* the slave. So the master must preserve the slave's life if the master is to retain his or her character as master. In this way, the master and the slave, though distinct moments of consciousness and distinct parts of society, are from the beginning dependent on each other, and on the distinction between them. Thus, both are responsible for the maintenance of these positions. According to Hegel, then, the master-consciousness exists primarily "for-itself" but recognizes and depends upon the other, while the slave-consciousness exists primarily "for-another" but recognizes itself and maintains itself. Each needs the other in order to exist in the way each does, and in this interdependence each recognizes itself and its own needs.

Eventually, according to Hegel, the conflict between master and slave will give way, from its own weaknesses, to another social stage. As the primal relationship between these two continues, the master's dependence on the slave will begin to outweigh his or her desire for freedom; similarly, the slave's desire to be free of his or her master will begin to outweigh his or her fear for his or her own life. When this occurs, there will be a new "battle," whose resolution will result in a new social form with a new pair of opposing forces. According to Hegel, society will evolve through a primarily "natural," or raw emotional existence, to an "ethical" existence, in which society holds itself to legal and moral standards, and after several more stages, human consciousness will evolve towards Absolute Knowledge.

THE FAMILY

In the "ethical" stage, the primary social structure is the family, according to Hegel; the family exists in order to create an individual who is ethically structured. Hence, as with the master–slave relationship, the self and the other in the ethical world are interdependent, and the community that they create is at once constitutive of their individual character. This family structure that first appears in an ethically constituted world is the first in which the distinction between the sexes plays a social role. In the family, there are brother and sister, husband and wife, and these roles are integral to the nature of an ethical world.

In the first place, because the ethical element is the intrinsically universal element, the *ethical* relation between the members of the family is not that of sentiment or the relationship of love. The ethical element in this case seems bound to be placed in the relation of the individual member of the family to the *entire* family as the real substance, so that the purpose of his action and the content of his actuality are taken from this substance, are derived solely from the family life. But the conscious purpose which dominates the action of this whole, so far as that purpose concerns that whole, is itself the individual member.

⌐ ⌐ ⌐

The divine law which holds sway in the family has also on its side distinctions within itself, the relations among which make up the living process of its realization. Amongst the three relationships, however, of husband and wife, parents and children, brothers and sisters, the relationship of husband and wife is to begin with the primary and immediate form in which one consciousness recognizes itself in another, and in which each knows that reciprocal recognition.

⌐ ⌐ ⌐

In a household of the ethical kind, a woman's relationships are not based on a reference to this particular husband, this particular child, but to *a* husband, to children *in general,*—not to feeling, but to the universal. The distinction between her ethical life (*Sittlichkeit*) (while it determines her particular existence and brings her pleasure) and that of her husband consists just in this, that it has always a directly universal significance for her, and is quite alien to the impulsive condition of mere particular desire. On the other hand, in the husband these two aspects get separated; and since he possesses, as a citizen, the self-conscious power belonging to the universal life, the life of the social whole, he acquires thereby the rights of desire, and keeps himself at the same time in detachment from it. So far, then, as particularity is implicated in this relationship in the case of the wife, her ethical life is not purely ethical; so far, however, as it is ethical, the particularity is a matter of indifference, and the wife is without the moment of knowing herself as *this* particular self in and through an other.

⌐ ⌐ ⌐

. . . The sister, however, becomes, or the wife remains, director of the home and the preserver of the divine law. In this way both the sexes overcome their merely natural being, and become ethically significant, as diverse forms dividing between them the different aspects which the ethical substance assumes.

Thus, the family relation retains, in some faded way, the primitive relation of master and slave and the early relations of the emotional life, but it reinterprets these relations through the ethical structure of the family. Within the family the sexes come to have social importance, marking the universal relations of parent-to-child, husband-to-wife, and brother-to-sister. In order to mark their world as the ethical one, family members must maintain the structure of the family, and so mark home as distinct from the outer community. The marking of the home as such, according to Hegel, falls to women, while the marking of the larger community as such falls to men; and again, since the larger community at this stage of human history is essentially an aggregate of families, these roles are interdependent. It is interesting to note that Hegel in many places cites Sophocles' *Antigone* (excerpted in Part Two) as evidence of the woman's relation to the family and to divine law in the ethical world. To Hegel, Antigone's devotion to divine right and her humility in its face perfectly exemplifies his vision of the ethical consciousness.

2. MARY SHELLEY
(English, 1797–1851)

Daughter of Mary Wollstonecraft, the early feminist whose work is excerpted in the preceding chapter, and William Godwin, a well-known radical social theorist, and wife of the great English Romantic poet, Percy Bysshe Shelley, Mary Shelley was destined to be a prominent literary figure. Mary Shelley's *Frankenstein,* excerpted here, has provoked the imagination of readers—and even of movie-viewers and of the general population—since its first publication in 1816. *Frankenstein* is on one level simply a great horror story, but it is also a profound and eerie investigation of humanity, its rebellious drive against God and nature, and its quest to overcome its mortality.

FRANKENSTEIN, OR, THE MODERN PROMETHEUS (1816)

The basic story of *Frankenstein* is at this point familiar to most readers. Victor Frankenstein, the protagonist of the story and perhaps the greatest of "mad scientists," discovers the secret of creating life out of lifeless organic matter, and demonstrates his scientific theories by building a living creature out of the remains of the dead. As soon as his creation comes to life, however, Frankenstein judges it a monstrosity and abandons it. The creature, lonely and innocent, searches for his creator in the hopes of finding companionship and peace; when his hopes are dashed, he takes revenge on Frankenstein by killing his family and closest friends, ultimately reducing the scientist to the solitary grief of his creature. Frankenstein lives out his days following the monster to the ends of the earth (they wind up eventually near the North Pole) in order to kill that which he brought into the world.

The subtitle Shelley chose for her horror story, "the modern Prometheus," encapsulates the Romantic vision that is its focus. Evoking the Prometheus story of ancient Greek mythology (Hesiod's version is excerpted in Part One) marks the obsessive scientist as a rebel against the gods for the sake of humankind, stealing the secret of life as Prometheus stole fire. Like Prometheus, Victor is a morally ambiguous figure—he is motivated at least in part by raw courage and a desire to improve the lot of his fellows, but he has other less admirable motivations as well. He is a mighty and talented fighter for his ends—which he achieves—but the means he employs and the consequences of his achievement are awful and ungodly, putting human beings at an even further remove from their creator. Victor's obsessive desire for knowledge clouds his moral judgment so that he, like Prometheus, fails to anticipate the effects his actions will have upon himself and on the world, and so fails to take responsibility for them.

In addition to Prometheus, Shelley makes repeated comparisons between her own and two other stories, both of which are also excerpted in earlier chapters of this book: the Adam and Eve story of the Bible, and Milton's Satan in *Paradise Lost*. Profoundly influenced by Milton (who as was mentioned compares his own Satan to Prometheus and Adam), Shelley is in essence following his vision, giving a Romantic retelling of the fall of humankind. Shelley's version manifests all the paradoxes and dichotomies typical of nineteenth-century Romanticism: a moral discomfort with the technological outgrowth of the scientific revolution; an obsession with the nature/culture distinction—played nostalgically as a distinction between the natural and the unnatural; a fascination with women's role and with the proper work for the two sexes; an aesthetic and moral concern over the effects of the industrial revolution on work habits and quality of life.

MOTHER, SISTER, WIFE—THE CREATION OF LIFE FROM DEATH

Frankenstein is an "epistolary" novel, meaning that Shelley uses a stylistic device of putting forward the novel as a series of letters supposedly written during an exploratory mission to the North Pole, from the ship's captain Walton to his sister at home in England. Victor Frankenstein, in grave ill-health, has been taken aboard Captain Walton's ship and has made friends with the Captain, to whom he has told the story of the monster; the Captain retells the story in his letters. In a sort of a novel-within-a-novel, Frankenstein's letters to his fiancee, Elizabeth, are transcribed from his testimony to Walton, into Walton's letters to his sister. Elizabeth, however, had been adopted by Frankenstein's parents—thus, she is, in a purely "cultural" or non-natural sense, Frankenstein's sister. That he intends to marry his "sister" is of course, "unnatural" in another sense.

Thus, in the very structure of the novel there exists a parallel between Frankenstein's situation and that of "everyman"—his listener, or the reader—one that places us all in a bind between the natural and the unnatural, represented through the family relationships of husband to wife and brother to sister. Such was, of course, the situation for the first man and woman in the garden of Eden—what is Eve to Adam? Does her role change after the Fall? By evoking these kinds of questions, Shelley sets the entire story of Frankenstein within the context of a gender symbolism. The women wait at home, marking the peaceful and practical, the ethical and natural life while the men roam far away, pursuing knowledge without regard to the consequences of their action. The men's relationship to the women, throughout the novel, wavers ambiguously between the natural and the unnatural, the godly and the ungodly, the safe and the dangerous, the known and the unknown.

This gender symbolism is taken to another level by Shelley, in her representation of Frankenstein's motivation for his obsessive pursuit of knowledge. His mother died giving birth to his youngest brother, and Frankenstein's actions are driven in large part by his grief over, and fascination with, this event. Metaphorically then, Shelley represents the human quest for knowledge in general as a quest for immortality, but in particular this quest for immortality is represented as a desire to return to our mother's bosom, or even womb, forever. Thus, Frankenstein's sister, his wife, the monster, all become figures for his lost mother.

CHAPTER 3

⌒ ⌒ ⌒

I need not describe the feelings of those whose dearest ties are rent by that most irreparable evil, the void that presents itself to the soul, and the despair that is exhibited on the countenance. It is so long before the mind can persuade itself that she whom we saw every day and whose very existence appeared a part of our own can have departed forever—that the brightness of a beloved eye can have been extinguished and the sound of a voice so familiar and dear to the ear can be hushed, never more to be heard. These are the reflections of the first days; but when the lapse of time proves the reality of the evil, then the actual bitterness of grief commences. Yet from whom has not that rude hand rent away some dear connection? And why should I describe a sorrow which all have felt, and must feel?

⌒ ⌒ ⌒

Partly from curiosity and partly from idleness, I went into the lecturing room, which M. Waldman entered shortly after.

⌒ ⌒ ⌒

After having made a few preparatory experiments, he concluded with a panegyric upon modern chemistry, the terms of which I shall never forget:

"The ancient teachers of this science," said he, "promised impossibilities and performed nothing. The modern masters promise very little.

⌒ ⌒ ⌒

They penetrate into the recesses of nature and show how she works in her hiding-places. They ascend into the heavens; they have discovered how the blood circulates, and the nature of the air we breathe. They have acquired new and almost unlimited powers; they can command the thunders of heaven, mimic the earthquake, and even mock the invisible world with its own shadows."

Such were the professor's words—rather let me say such the words of the fate—enounced to destroy me. As he went on I felt as if my soul were grappling with a palpable enemy; one by one the various keys were touched which formed the mechanism of my being; chord after chord was sounded, and soon my mind was filled with one thought, one conception, one purpose. So much has been done, exclaimed the soul of Frankenstein—more, far more, will I achieve; treading in the steps already marked, I will pioneer a new way, explore unknown powers, and unfold to the world the deepest mysteries of creation.

ᗍ ᗍ ᗍ

CHAPTER 4

To examine the causes of life, we must first have recourse to death. I became acquainted with the science of anatomy, but this was not sufficient; I must also observe the natural decay and corruption of the human body.

ᗍ ᗍ ᗍ

My attention was fixed upon every object the most insupportable to the delicacy of the human feelings. I saw how the fine form of man was degraded and wasted; I beheld the corruption of death succeed to the blooming check of life; I saw how the worm inherited the wonders of the eye and brain. I paused, examining and analysing all the minutiae of causation, as exemplified in the change from life to death, and death to life, until from the midst of this darkness a sudden light broke in upon me—a light so brilliant and wondrous, yet so simple, that while I became dizzy with the immensity of the prospect which it illustrated, I was surprised that among so many men of genius who had directed their inquiries towards the same science, that I alone should be reserved to discover so astonishing a secret.

ᗍ ᗍ ᗍ

I succeeded in discovering the cause of generation and life; nay, more, I became myself capable of bestowing animation upon lifeless matter.

The astonishment which I had at first experienced on this discovery soon gave place to delight and rapture.

ᗍ ᗍ ᗍ

Life and death appeared to me ideal bounds, which I should first break through, and pour a torrent of light into our dark world. A new species would bless me as its creator and source; many happy and excellent natures would owe their being to me. No father could claim the gratitude of his child so completely as I should deserve theirs. Pursuing these reflections, I thought that if I could bestow animation upon lifeless matter, I might in process of time (although I now found it impossible) renew life where death had apparently devoted the body to corruption.

❧ ❧ ❧

In a solitary chamber, or rather cell, at the top of the house, and separated from all the other apartments by a gallery and staircase, I kept my workshop of filthy creation; my eyeballs were starting from their sockets in attending to the details of my employment. The dissecting room and the slaughter-house furnished many of my materials; and often did my human nature turn with loathing from my occupation, whilst, still urged on by an eagerness which perpetually increased, I brought my work near to a conclusion.

❧ ❧ ❧

I am now convinced that he was justified in conceiving that I should not be altogether free from blame. A human being in perfection ought always to preserve a calm and peaceful mind and never to allow passion or a transitory desire to disturb his tranquillity. I do not think that the pursuit of knowledge is an exception to this rule. If the study to which you apply yourself has a tendency to weaken your affections and to destroy your taste for those simple pleasures in which no alloy can possibly mix, then that study is certainly unlawful, that is to say, not befitting the human mind.

❧ ❧ ❧

CHAPTER 5

It was on a dreary night of November that I beheld the accomplishment of my toils.

❧ ❧ ❧

I saw the dull yellow eye of the creature open; it breathed hard, and a convulsive motion agitated its limbs.

How can I describe my emotions at this catastrophe, or how delineate the wretch whom with such infinite pains and care I had endeavoured to form? His limbs were in proportion, and I had selected his features as beautiful. Beautiful! Great God!³

THE MONSTER'S STORY

Disgusted with his own action, Frankenstein abandons his creation. Although Frankenstein is sick with regret and fear about the creature, he makes no attempt to retrieve it, nor does he tell anyone about his work or its results, taking no responsibility for the "child" to which he has given birth. Sometime later, Frankenstein's youngest brother is murdered and his family's maid is convicted and executed for

---

³ This and all the following excerpts are taken from Mary Shelley, *Frankenstein, or the Modern Prometheus*. (New York: New American Library, 1965).

the crime. Frankenstein suspects that his creature is responsible, but says nothing. He returns home from the university to Geneva, Switzerland, to be with his family in their time of grief. On a walk in the mountains, he meets the monster, who recounts to his creator the sad story of his life, and asks a favor.

CHAPTER 10

≈ ≈ ≈

Alas! Why does man boast of sensibilities superior to those apparent in the brute; it only renders them more necessary beings. If our impulses were confined to hunger, thirst, and desire, we might be nearly free; but now we are moved by every wind that blows and a chance word or scene that word may convey to us.

≈ ≈ ≈

As I said this I suddenly beheld the figure of a man, at some distance, advancing towards me with superhuman speed. He bounded over the crevices in the ice, among which I had walked with caution; his stature, also, as he approached, seemed to exceed that of man. I was troubled; . . . it was the wretch whom I had created.

≈ ≈ ≈

"Devil," I exclaimed, "do you dare approach me? And do not you fear the fierce vengeance of my arm wreaked on your miserable head? Begone, vile insect! Or rather, stay, that I may trample you to dust! And, oh! That I could, with the extinction of your miserable existence, restore those victims whom you have so diabolically murdered!"

"I expected this reception," said the demon. "All men hate the wretched; how, then, must I be hated, who am miserable beyond all living things! Yet you, my creator, detest and spurn me, thy creature, to whom thou art bound by ties only dissoluble by the annihilation of one of us. You purpose to kill me. How dare you sport thus with life? Do your duty towards me, and I will do mine towards you and the rest of mankind. If you will comply with my conditions, I will leave them and you at peace; but if you refuse, I will glut the maw of death, until it be satiated with the blood of your remaining friends."

≈ ≈ ≈

He easily eluded me and said, "Be calm! I entreat you to hear me before you give vent to your hatred on my devoted head. Have I not suffered enough, that you seek to increase my misery? Life, although it may only be an accumulation of anguish, is dear to me, and I will defend it. Remember, thou hast made me more powerful than thyself; my height is superior to thine, my joints more supple. But I will not be tempted to set myself in opposition to thee. I am thy creature, and I will be even mild and docile to my natural lord and king if thou wilt also perform thy part, the which thou owest me. Oh, Frankenstein, be not equitable to every other and trample upon me alone, to whom thy justice, and even thy clemency and affection, is most due. Remember that I am thy creature; I ought to be thy Adam, but I am rather the fallen angel, whom thou drivest from joy for no misdeed. Everywhere I see bliss, from which I alone am irrevocably excluded. I was benevolent and good; misery made me a fiend. Make me happy, and I shall again be virtuous."

☙ ☙ ☙

I had hitherto supposed him to be the murderer of my brother, and I eagerly sought a confirmation or denial of this opinion. For the first time, also, I felt what the duties of a creator towards his creature were, and that I ought to render him happy before I complained of his wickedness. These motives urged me to comply with his demand.

☙ ☙ ☙

CHAPTER 11

☙ ☙ ☙

[The monster spoke.] . . . "I escaped to the open country and fearfully took refuge in a low hovel, quite bare, and making a wretched appearance after the palaces I had beheld in the village. This hovel, however, joined a cottage of a neat and pleasant appearance.

☙ ☙ ☙

"Here, then, I retreated and lay down happy to have found a shelter, however miserable, from the inclemency of the season, and still more from the barbarity of man.

☙ ☙ ☙

I heard a step, and looking through a small chink, I beheld a young creature, with a pail on her head, passing before my hovel. The girl was young and of gentle demeanour, unlike what I have since found cottagers and farmhouse servants to be. Yet she was meanly dressed, a coarse blue petticoat and a linen jacket being her only garb; her fair hair was plaited but not adorned: she looked patient yet sad.

☙ ☙ ☙

"On examining my dwelling, I found that one of the windows of the cottage had formerly occupied a part of it, but the panes had been filled up with wood. In one of these was a small and almost imperceptible chink through which the eye could just penetrate. Through this crevice a small room was visible, whitewashed and clean but very bare of furniture. In one corner, near a small fire, sat an old man, leaning his head on his hands in a disconsolate attitude.

The silver hair and benevolent countenance of the aged cottager won my reverence, while the gentle manners of the girl enticed my love. He played a sweet mournful air which I perceived drew tears from the eyes of his amiable companion, of which the old man took no notice, until she sobbed audibly; he then pronounced a few sounds, and the fair creature, leaving her work, knelt at his feet. He raised her and smiled with such kindness and affection that I felt sensations of a peculiar and over-powering nature; they were a mixture of pain and pleasure, such as I had never before experienced, either from hunger or cold, warmth or food; and I withdrew from the window, unable to bear these emotions.

CHAPTER 12

"This day was passed in the same routine as that which preceded it. The young man was constantly employed out of doors, and the girl in various laborious occupations within. The old man, whom I soon perceived to be blind, employed his leisure hours on his instrument or in contemplation. Nothing could exceed the love and respect which the younger cottagers exhibited towards their venerable companion. They performed towards him every little office of affection and duty with gentleness, and he rewarded them by his benevolent smiles.

"A considerable period elapsed before I discovered one of the causes of the uneasiness of this amiable family: it was poverty, and they suffered that evil in a very distressing degree. Their nourishment consisted entirely of the vegetables of their garden and the milk of one cow, which gave very little during the winter, when its masters could scarcely procure food to support it. They often, I believe, suffered the pangs of hunger very poignantly, especially the two younger cottagers, for several times they placed food before the old man when they reserved none for themselves.

"By degrees I made a discovery of still greater moment. I found that these people possessed a method of communicating their experience and feelings to one another by articulate sounds. I perceived that the words they spoke sometimes produced pleasure or pain, smiles or sadness, in the minds and countenances of the hearers. This was indeed a godlike science, and I ardently desired to become acquainted with it.

When they had retired to rest, if there was any moon or the night was star-light, I went into the woods and collected my own food and fuel for the cottage. When I returned, as often as it was necessary, I cleared their path from the snow and performed those offices that I had seen done by Felix. I afterwards found that these labours, performed by an invisible hand, greatly astonished them; and once or twice I heard them, on these occasions, utter the words 'good spirit,' 'wonderful'; but I did not then understand the signification of these terms.

I looked upon them as superior beings who would be the arbiters of my future destiny. I formed in my imagination a thousand pictures of presenting myself to them, and their reception of me. I imagined that they would be disgusted, until, by my gentle demeanour and conciliating words, I should first win their favour and afterwards their love.

"These thoughts exhilarated me and led me to apply with fresh ardour to the acquiring the art of language.

CHAPTER 13

"These wonderful narrations inspired me with strange feelings. Was man, indeed, at once so powerful, so virtuous, and magnificent, yet so vicious and base? He appeared at one time a mere scion of the evil principle and at another as all that can be conceived of noble and godlike. To be a great and virtuous man appeared the highest honour that can befall a sensitive being; to be base and vicious, as many on record have been, appeared the lowest degradation, a condition more abject than that of the blind mole or harmless worm.

Of my creation and creator I was absolutely ignorant, but I knew that I possessed no money, no friends, no kind of property. I was, besides, endued with a figure hideously deformed and loathsome; I was not even of the same nature as man. I was more agile than they and could subsist upon coarser diet; I bore the extremes of heat and cold with less injury to my frame; my stature far exceeded theirs. When I looked around I saw and heard of none like me. Was I, then, a monster, a blot upon the earth, from which all men fled and whom all men disowned?

"I cannot describe to you the agony that these reflections inflicted upon me; I tried to dispel them, but sorrow only increased with knowledge.

"Of what a strange nature is knowledge! It clings to the mind when it has once seized on it like a lichen on the rock. I wished sometimes to shake off all thought and feeling, but I learned that there was but one means to overcome the sensation of pain, and that was death—a state which I feared yet did not understand.

⌐ ⌐ ⌐

"Other lessons were impressed upon me even more deeply. I heard of the difference of sexes, and the birth and growth of children, how the father doted on the smiles of the infant, and the lively sallies of the older child, how all the life and cares of the mother were wrapped up in the precious charge, how the mind of youth expanded and gained knowledge, of brother, sister, and all the various relationships which bind one human being to another in mutual bonds.

"But where were my friends and relations? No father had watched my infant days, no mother had blessed me with smiles and caresses; or if they had, all my past life was now a blot, a blind vacancy in which I distinguished nothing. From my earliest remembrance I had been as I then was in height and proportion. I had never yet seen a being resembling me or who claimed any intercourse with me. What was I? The question again recurred, to be answered only with groans.

CHAPTER 16

"Cursed, cursed creator! Why did I live? Why, in that instant, did I not extinguish the spark of existence which you had so wantonly bestowed? I know not; despair had not yet taken possession of me; my feelings were those of rage and revenge.

⌐ ⌐ ⌐

[F]rom that moment I declared everlasting war against the species, and more than all, against him who had formed me and sent me forth to this insupportable misery.

⌐ ⌐ ⌐

CHAPTER 17

. . . "You must create a female for me with whom I can live in the interchange of those sympathies necessary for my being. This you alone can do, and I demand it of you as a right which you must not refuse to concede."

⌐ ⌐ ⌐

. . . I am malicious because I am miserable. Am I not shunned and hated by all mankind? You, my creator, would tear me to pieces and triumph; remember that, and tell me why I should pity man more than he pities me? You would not call it murder if you could precipitate me into one of those ice-rifts and destroy my frame, the work of your own hands. Shall I respect man when he contemns me? Let him live with me in the interchange of kindness, and instead of injury I would bestow every benefit upon him with tears of gratitude at his acceptance.

But that cannot be; the human senses are insurmountable barriers to our union. Yet mine shall not be the submission of abject slavery. I will revenge my injuries; if I cannot inspire love, I will cause fear, and chiefly towards you my arch-enemy, because my creator, do I swear inextinguishable hatred. Have a care; I will work at your destruction, nor finish until I desolate your heart, so that you shall curse the hour of your birth."

"What I ask of you is reasonable and moderate, I demand a creature of another sex, but as hideous as myself; the gratification is small, but it is all that I can receive, and it shall content me. It is true, we shall be monsters, cut off from all the world; but on that account we shall be more attached to one another. Our lives will not be happy, but they will be harmless and free from the misery I now feel. Oh! My creator, make me happy; let me feel gratitude towards you for one benefit! Let me see that I excite the sympathy of some existing thing; do not deny me my request!"

His words had a strange effect upon me. I compassionated him and sometimes felt a wish to console him, but when I looked upon him, when I saw the filthy mass that moved and talked, my heart sickened and my feelings were altered to those of horror and hatred.

"If I have no ties and no affections, hatred and vice must be my portion; the love of another will destroy the cause of my crimes, and I shall become a thing of whose existence everyone will be ignorant. My vices are the children of a forced solitude that I abhor, and my virtues will necessarily arise when I live in communion with an equal. I shall feel the affections of a sensitive being and become linked to the chain of existence and events from which I am now excluded."

The monster asks Frankenstein for a female companion of his species, just as Adam—on Shelley's interpretation—asked God. Indeed, it is the monster who now takes on the metaphorical role of Prometheus as well—cursing his creators and seeking a bold revenge. Where Frankenstein had stood as a Promethean figure, his creature now takes that role. Shelley is developing a chain of creation—not unreminiscent of Hesiod's "five generations" (excerpted in Part One)—in which creatures themselves become creators; and this of course is the ever-repeating human state. Here, men's "unnatural" chain of creation is unfavorably compared to the "natural" creation of children by women.

The monster's story, however, is particularly stunning, the most moving portion of the entire novel. Despite the parallels between Frankenstein and the monster, despite the "unnatural" origins of the monster, despite the monster's vengeful behavior, the monster is the fuller and more sympathetic character of the two. His is the more reflective, more responsible, more loving stance—and in his way, he is in the moral sense more human than his creator. Part of the monster's pathos stems from his loneliness, which itself is related to his great ugliness. To the extent that the monster "should be [Frankenstein's] Adam," he represents the first man and Frankenstein represents his god. The monster's loneliness, stemming from his physical ugliness, is like Adam's loneliness—surrounded by animals over which he had dominion, he still lacked a companion—and Victor's reaction represents a kind of moral ugliness, and demonstrates his inadequacy to his godlike position. Is Adam's dominion to be understood as his ugliness before God? Eve, perhaps, represents beauty, finally bestowed upon man and bringing him love and happiness. But she also brings him grief and mortality, his price to pay for an end to loneliness. Women represent beauty in *Frankenstein* in this way, a beauty which has as its price mortality, death (e.g., Frankenstein's mother's death during childbirth). By pursuing an end to mortality and victory over death, Frankenstein forsakes his home and the company of women that exists only there. The monster, however, in addition seems actually to believe that the companionship of a woman will make *him* appear beautiful: as if women *represent* beauty *to* men rather than *are really* beautiful in themselves. Women serve as the humanizing, beautifying force in this novel, a force that acts upon men rather than standing by itself.

FRANKENSTEIN'S PURSUIT OF THE MONSTER

Frankenstein's response to the monster will demonstrate whether he is able to meet the godlike responsibilities to which he has been called by his creative act. Throughout the novel, he has avoided his responsibilities: delaying his marriage to Elizabeth indefinitely as he attends to his researches, leaving the university, withholding his suspicions about the murder of his brother, abandoning his creation. It seems as if, moved by the entreaties of the monster, he will finally meet his obligations. In the end, however, he reverts to his irresponsible character, his imperfect humanity, refusing his creation what God in his greater justice had granted Adam. Frankenstein has achieved the power of God without the divine wisdom that would make his power just. This seems to be Shelley's vision of the human, or at least the male, state: by its very nature courting, yet never achieving, the super- or unnatural.

CHAPTER 20

. . . I was now about to form another being of whose dispositions I was alike ignorant; she might become ten thousand times more malignant than her mate and delight, for its own sake, in murder and wretchedness. He had sworn to quit the neighbourhood of man and hide himself in deserts, but she had not; and she, who in all probability was to become a thinking and reasoning animal, might refuse to comply with a compact made before her creation. They might even hate each other; the creature who already lived loathed his own deformity, and might he not conceive a greater abhorrence for it when it came before his eyes in the female form? She also might turn with disgust from him to the superior beauty of man; she might quit him, and he be again alone, exasperated by the fresh provocation of being deserted by one of his own species.

Even if they were to leave Europe and inhabit the deserts of the new
world, yet one of the first results of those sympathies for which the demon
thirsted would be children, and a race of devils would be propagated upon the
earth   who might make the very existence of the species of man a condition
precarious and full of terror. Had I right, for my own benefit, to inflict this curse
upon everlasting generations? I had before been moved by the sophisms of the
being I had created; I had been struck senseless by his fiendish threats; but now,
for the first time, the wickedness of my promise burst upon me; I shuddered to
think that future ages might curse me as their pest, whose selfishness had not
hesitated to buy its own peace at the price, perhaps, of the existence of the
whole human race.

I trembled and my heart failed within me, when, on looking up, I saw by the
light of the moon the demon at the casement. A ghastly grin wrinkled his lips as
he gazed on me, where I sat fulfilling the task which he had allotted to me. Yes,
he had followed me in my travels; he had loitered in forests, hid himself in
caves, or taken refuge in wide and desert heaths; and he now came to mark my
progress and claim the fulfillment of my promise.

As I looked on him, his countenance expressed the utmost extent of malice
and treachery. I thought with a sensation of madness on my promise of creating
another like to him, and trembling with passion, tore to pieces the thing on
which I was engaged. The wretch saw me destroy the creature on whose future
existence he depended for happiness, and with a howl of devilish despair and
revenge, withdrew.

⌒ ⌒ ⌒

I shuddered to think who might be the next victim sacrificed to his insatiate
revenge. And then I thought again of his words—"*I will be with you on your
wedding-night.*"

⌒ ⌒ ⌒

Everywhere I turn I see the same figure—her bloodless arms and relaxed
form flung by the murderer on its bridal bier. Could I behold this and live? Alas!
Life is obstinate and clings closest where it is most hated.

⌒ ⌒ ⌒

Know that, one by one, my friends were snatched away; I was left desolate.

⌒ ⌒ ⌒

All my speculations and hopes are as nothing, and like the archangel who
aspired to omnipotence, I am chained in an eternal hell. My imagination was
vivid, yet my powers of analysis and application were intense; by the union of
these qualities I conceived the idea and executed the creation of a man. Even
now I cannot recollect without passion my reveries while the work was
incomplete. I trod heaven in my thoughts, now exulting in my powers, now
burning with the idea of their effects. From my infancy I was imbued with high
hopes and a lofty ambition; but how am I sunk!

3. JOHN STUART MILL
(English, 1806–1873)

John Stuart Mill was profoundly influential on later moral and political philosophy. Following Jeremy Bentham and his father, James Mill, in his advocation of the moral theory called "utilitarianism," Mill was responsible for the paradigmatic defense of that philosophy, summarized in the "greatest happiness principle"—that right action consists in whatever will achieve the most pleasure and the least pain for the greatest number of people. In *On Liberty,* Mill gives another paradigmatic defense, this time of the political position that has come to be known as "libertarianism." Here, he argues for the "harm principle," that the government should never intervene in an individual's affairs except in the case of imminent real harm. While Mill's moral and political theories, in themselves, are not directly relevant to our topic, they do set the background for his feminism. One, they require as their prerequisite the equality of each individual's ranking of goods; two, by taking the good to be identical to "pleasure," Mill widens the field of moral participants in society. Mill is best known for his *Utilitarianism* (1861) and *On Liberty* (1859), but his famous defense of sexual equality, *The Subjection of Women,* from which all the following passages are taken, is also a fundamental work on its subject.

In all of his work, Mill was committed to social reform; although by and large he favors the system of industrial capitalism, he sought throughout his lifetime to rid it of its inequities and cruelties. Thus, while these three works seem on some specific points to be inconsistent, they are unified on a thematic level by Mill's liberal and progressive ideals. This is encapsulated in Mill's characteristically nineteenth-century stance on "scientific progress"; he is at once appalled at the horrors of the industrial revolution and devoted to furthering its achievements.

THE SUBJECTION OF WOMEN (1869)

Mill dedicated *On Liberty* to "the beloved and deplored memory of her who was the inspirer, and in part the author, of all that is best in my writings—the friend and wife whose exalted sense of truth and right was my strongest incitement, and whose approbation was my chief reward . . ."[4] Mill's best friend and strongest intellectual influence for twenty years before they married (she was married to someone else during this long Platonic friendship), Harriet Taylor Mill was acknowledged by Mill as a co-author of that important work and the inspiration for several others. The profound respect she inspired in Mill provides a rich background for both his utilitarian and libertarian theories: her influence was a guiding principle behind his political and moral theories. Harriet Taylor Mill's talent and insight were testimony, as Mill saw it, to the tremendous resources inherent in individuals that could be squelched by the tyrannical imposition upon them of the majority will.

---

[4] J. S. Mill, On Liberty, 1859. Dedication.

In *The Subjection of Women,* Mill lays out a methodical argument against all forms of legal discrimination against women. While once again, Mill remains sympathetic to many traditional claims about the social roles of men and women, his proposals in this work were tremendously controversial in his time, and most of them remain so. The compassion with which Mill describes woman's position is noteworthy throughout; this too may be in part attributable to the strong influence of Harriet Taylor Mill.

AN ARGUMENT FROM MORAL PROGRESS

Early in the essay, Mill draws an analogy on which he shall repeatedly rely: an analogy between the subjection of women and the possession of slaves. The enlightenment ideals of individual freedom and autonomy, he claimed, had almost eradicated slavery despite its long tradition. These same ideals should, it followed, eradicate the subordination of women to men, which Mill considered the most abject and inescapable of oppression.

CHAPTER 1

The object of this Essay is to explain as clearly as I am able, the grounds of an opinion which I have held from the very earliest period when I had formed any opinions at all on social or political matters, and which, instead of being weakened or modified, has been constantly growing stronger by the progress of reflection and the experience of life: That the principle which regulates the existing social relations between the two sexes—the legal subordination of one sex to the other—is wrong in itself, and now one of the chief hindrances to human improvement; and that it ought to be replaced by a principle of perfect equality, admitting no power or privilege on the one side, nor disability on the other.

The generality of a practice is in some cases a strong presumption that it is, or at all events once was, conducive to laudable ends. This is the case, when the practice was first adopted, or afterwards kept up, as a means to such ends, and was grounded on experience of the mode in which they could be most effectually attained. If the authority of men over women, when first established, had been the result of a conscientious comparison between different modes of constituting the government of society; if, after trying various other modes of social organization—the government of women over men, equality between the two, and such mixed and divided modes of governments as might be invented—it had been decided, on the testimony of experience, that the mode in which women are wholly under the rule of men, having no share at all in public concerns, and each in private being under the legal obligation of obedience to the man with whom she has associated her destiny, was the arrangement most conducive to the happiness and well being of both; its general adoption might then be fairly thought to be some evidence that, at the time when it was adopted, it was the best: though even then the considerations which recommended it may, like so many other primeval social facts of the greatest importance, have subsequently, in the course of ages, ceased to exist. But the state of the case is in every respect the reverse of this. In the first place, the opinion in favour of the present system, which entirely subordinates the weaker sex to the stronger, rests upon theory only; for there never has been trial made of any other: so that experience, in the sense in which it is vulgarly opposed to theory, cannot be pretended to have pronounced any verdict. And in the second place, the adoption of this system of inequality never was the result of deliberation, or forethought, or any social ideas, or any notion whatever of what conduced to the benefit of humanity or the good order of society. It arose simply from the fact that from the very earliest twilight of human society, every woman (owing to the value attached to her by men, combined with her inferiority in muscular strength) was found in a state of bondage to some man. Laws and systems of polity always begin by recognising the relations they find already existing between individuals. They convert what was a mere physical fact into a legal right, give it the sanction of society, and principally aim at the substitution of public and organized means of asserting and protecting these rights, instead of the irregular and lawless conflict of physical strength. Those who had already been compelled to obedience became in this manner legally bound to it. Slavery, from being a mere affair of force between the master and the slave, became regularized and a matter of compact among the masters.

By degrees such thinkers did arise: and (the general progress of society assisting) the slavery of the male sex has, in all the countries of Christian Europe at least thought, in one of them, only within the last few years been at length abolished, and that of the female sex has been gradually changed into a milder form of dependence. But this dependence, as it exists at present, is not an original institution, taking a fresh start from considerations of justice and social expediency—it is the primitive state of slavery lasting on, through successive mitigations and modifications occasioned by the same causes which have softened the general manners, and brought all human relations more under the control of justice and the influence of humanity. It has not lost the taint of its brutal origin. No presumption in its favour, therefore, can be drawn from the fact of its existence.

. . . people flatter themselves that the rule of mere force is ended; that the law of the strongest cannot be the reason of existence of anything which has remained in full operation down to the present time.

Less than forty years ago, Englishmen might still by law hold human beings in bondage as saleable property: within the present century they might kidnap them and carry them off, and work them literally to death. This absolutely extreme case of the law of force, condemned by those who can tolerate almost every other form of arbitrary power, and which, of all others, presents features the most revolting to the feelings of all who look at it from an impartial position, was the law of civilized and Christian England within the memory of persons now living.

≈ ≈ ≈

Whatever gratification of pride there is in the possession of power, and whatever personal interest in its exercise, is in this case not confined to a limited class, but common to the whole male sex. Instead of being, to most of its supporters, a thing desirable chiefly in the abstract, or, like the political ends usually contended for by factions, of little private importance to any but the leaders; it comes home to the person and hearth of every male head of a family, and of every one who looks forward to being so. The clodhopper exercises, or is to exercise, his share of the power equally with the highest nobleman.

Mill's prose is florid and persuasive. It is founded in the notions of freedom of choice and equality of persons put forward in *On Liberty* and *Utilitarianism* and in Mill's belief that moral progress does occur over history—though it still has a long way to go. Most of the civilized world has rightly abandoned slavery, he claims; yet the slavery of women has remained so entrenched and so invisible that most men refuse to recognize it as such, and so refuse to reform. Mill will use this argument that women's labor and life is akin to that of a slave throughout *The Subjection of Women*. Importantly, because of Mill's belief in moral progress, this is tantamount to an argument against women's subordination.

CHAPTER I: RESPONSES TO OBJECTIONS

The rest of Chapter One of *The Subjection of Women* is a tightly organized set of responses to objections that had already been leveled against the equality of women by Mill's predecessors. It is noteworthy that Mill frames these objections against a nature/culture distinction: in other words, he groups together a number of specific objections under the claim that women's subordination is natural, and responds to them by demonstrating that women's subordination is a cultural phenomenon, subject to revision on this account.

So true is it that unnatural generally means only uncustomary, and that everything which is usual appears natural. The subjection of women to men being a universal custom, any departure from it quite naturally appears unnatural. But how entirely, even in this case, the feeling is dependent on custom, appears by ample experience. Nothing so much astonishes the people of distant parts of the world, when they first learn anything about England, as to be told that it is under a queen: the thing seems to them so unnatural as to be almost incredible. To Englishmen this does not seem in the least degree unnatural, because they are used to it; but they do feel it unnatural that women should be soldiers or members of Parliament. In the feudal ages, on the contrary, war and politics were not thought unnatural to women, because not unusual[.]

‿ ‿ ‿

But, it will be said, the rule of men over women differs from all these others in not being a rule of force: it is accepted voluntarily; women make no complaint, and are consenting parties to it. In the first place, a great number of women do not accept it. Ever since there have been women able to make their sentiments known by their writings (the only mode of publicity which society permits to them), an increasing number of them have recorded protests against their present social condition: and recently many thousands of them, headed by the most eminent women known to the public, have petitioned Parliament for their admission to the Parliamentary Suffrage. The claim of women to be educated as solidly, and in the same branches of knowledge, as men, is urged with growing intensity, and with a great prospect of success; while the demand for their admission into professions and occupations hitherto closed against them, becomes every year more urgent.

‿ ‿ ‿

It must be remembered, also, that no enslaved class ever asked for complete liberty at once.

‿ ‿ ‿

It is a political law of nature that those who are under any power of ancient origin, never begin by complaining of the power itself, but only of its oppressive exercise. There is never any want of women who complain of ill usage by their husbands. There would be infinitely more, if complaint were not the greatest of all provocatives to a repetition and increase of the ill usage. It is this which frustrates all attempts to maintain the power but protect the woman against its abuses. In no other case (except that of a child) is the person who has been proved judicially to have suffered an injury, replaced under the physical power of the culprit who inflicted it. Accordingly wives, even in the most extreme and protracted cases of bodily ill usage, hardly ever dare avail themselves of the laws made for their protection: and if, in a moment of irrepressible indignation, or by the interference of neighbours, they are induced to do so, their whole effort afterwards is to disclose as little as they can, and to beg off their tyrant from his merited chastisement.

‿ ‿ ‿

They are so far in a position different from all other subject classes, that their masters require something more from them than actual service. Men do not want solely the obedience of women, they want their sentiments. All men, except the most brutish, desire to have, in the woman most nearly connected with them, not a forced slave but a willing one, not a slave merely, but a favourite.

The masters of women wanted more than simple obedience, and they turned the whole force of education to effect their purpose. All women are brought up from the very earliest years in the belief that their ideal of character is the very opposite to that of men; not self-will, and government by self-control, but submission, and yielding to the control of others.

When we put together three things—first, the natural attraction between opposite sexes; secondly, the wife's entire dependence on the husband, every privilege or pleasure she has being either his gift, or depending entirely on his will; and lastly, that the principal object of human pursuit, consideration, and all objects of social ambition, can in general be sought or obtained by her only through him, it would be a miracle if the object of being attractive to men had not become the polar star of feminine education and formation of character. And, this great means of influence over the minds of women having been acquired, an instinct of selfishness made men avail themselves of it to the utmost as a means of holding women in subjection, by representing to them meekness, submissiveness, and resignation of all individual will into the hands of a man, as an essential part of sexual attractiveness.

Neither does it avail anything to say that the *nature* of the two sexes adapts them to their present functions and position, and renders these appropriate to them. Standing on the ground of common sense and the constitution of the human mind, I deny that any one knows, or can know, the nature of the two sexes, as long as they have only been seen in their present relation to one another.

Hence, in regard to that most difficult question, what are the natural differences between the two sexes—a subject on which it is impossible in the present state of society to obtain complete and correct knowledge—while almost everybody dogmatizes upon it, almost all neglect and make light of the only means by which any partial insight can be obtained into it. This is, an analytic study of the most important department of psychology, the laws of the influence of circumstances on character. For, however great and apparently ineradicable the moral and intellectual differences between men and women might be, the evidence of their being natural differences could only be negative. Those only could be inferred to be natural which could not possibly be artificial—the residuum, after deducting every characteristic of either sex which can admit of being explained from education or external circumstances. The profoundest knowledge of the laws of the formation of character is indispensable to entitle any one to affirm even that there is any difference, much more what the difference is, between the two sexes considered as moral and rational beings;

and since no one, as yet, has that knowledge, (for there is hardly any subject which, in proportion to its importance, has been so little studied), no one is thus far entitled to any positive opinion on the subject.

It is only a man here and there who has any tolerable knowledge of the character even of the women of his own family. I do not mean, of their capabilities; these nobody knows, not even themselves, because most of them have never been called out. I mean their actually existing thoughts and feelings. Many a man thinks he perfectly understands women, because he has had amatory relations with several, perhaps with many of them. If he is a good observer, and his experience extends to quality as well as quantity, he may have learnt something of one narrow department of their nature—an important department, no doubt. But of all the rest of it, few persons are generally more ignorant, because there are few from whom it is so carefully hidden. The most favourable case which a man can generally have for studying the character of a woman, is that of his own wife: for the opportunities are greater, and the cases of complete sympathy not so unspeakably rare. And in fact, this is the source from which any knowledge worth having on the subject has, I believe, generally come. But most men have not had the opportunity of studying in this way more than a single case: accordingly one can, to an almost laughable degree, infer what a man's wife is like, from his opinions about women in general. To make even this one case yield any result, the woman must be worth knowing, and the man not only a competent judge, but of a character so sympathetic in itself, and so well adapted to hers, that he can either read her mind by sympathetic intuition, or has nothing in himself which makes her shy of disclosing it. Hardly anything, I believe, can be more rare than this conjunction.

When we further consider that to understand one woman is not necessarily to understand any other woman; that even if he could study many women of one rank, or of one country, he would not thereby understand women of other ranks or countries; and even if he did, they are still only the women of a single period of history; we may safely assert that the knowledge which men can acquire of women, even as they have been and are, without reference to what they might be, is wretchedly imperfect and superficial, and always will be so, until women themselves have told all that they have to tell.

On thing we may be certain of—that what is contrary to women's nature to do, they never will be made to do by simply giving their nature free play.

If women have a greater natural inclination for some things than for others, there is no need of laws or social inculcation to make the majority of them do the former in preference to the latter. Whatever women's services are most wanted for, the free play of competition will hold out the strongest inducements to them to undertake.

The general opinion of men is supposed to be, that the natural vocation of a woman is that of a wife and mother. I say, is supposed to be, because, judging from acts—from the whole of the present constitution of society—one might infer that their opinion was the direct contrary. They might be supposed to think that the alleged natural vocation of women was of all things the most repugnant to their nature; insomuch that if they are free to do anything else—if any other means of living, or occupation of their time and faculties, is open, which has any chance of appearing desirable to them—there will not be enough of them who will be willing to accept the condition said to be natural to them.

And here, I believe, is the clue to the feelings of those men, who have a real antipathy to the equal freedom of women. I believe they are afraid, not least women should be unwilling to marry, for I do not think that any one in reality has that apprehension; but lest they should insist that marriage should be on equal conditions; lest all women of spirit and capacity should prefer doing almost anything else, not in their own eyes degrading, rather than marry, when marrying is giving themselves a master, and a master too of all their earthly possessions. And truly, if this consequence were necessarily incident to marriage, I think that the apprehension would be very well founded.

The first objection to which Mill responds in Chapter One we might call the "voluntary submission" objection. Such a person claims that the fact of women's subordination over history indicates their willing consent to it. Mill responds in several ways. First, he claims that voluntary submission at least is not a universal phenomenon, because there have long been some women who have objected to their subjection. Second, he claims that women's objections to *particular abuses* of male authority should be taken as a first stage in their objection to male authority *per se.* He cites historical precedent for this claim, again invoking the analogy to slavery, claiming that slave rebellion always begins with individual complaints about particular abusive masters. Third, Mill very perceptively cites the fact that many women do not stand up for themselves out of fear of their husbands' retribution—hence, "statistics" about women's objections to their treatment are probably very inaccurate. Lastly, Mill comments that women's subjection is a special kind of power relation, because men so want to be loved by the women they subordinate. Hence, men require of women not just submission but apparently willing submission, as a sign of love. Once again, then, Mill shows that what seems like voluntary submission to male authority may be a misrepresentation of women's actual feelings.

The second objection to which Mill responds might be called the "argument from women's nature." This objection to women's equality is akin to Aristotle's claims (in Part Two of this book) and others', that women's natural virtue is to obey, not to rule. Mill's response is stern and very pertinent to our discussion: he claims that natural sex differences cannot be known, or at least that they cannot be known yet. Here, Mill's argument is similar to ones he offers in both *Utilitarianism* and *On Liberty,* that few authorities are in a position to make judgments of character about their subjects, and that therefore only individuals' own judgments of their character and happiness are reliable. In this case, men, because they are in a position of authority, are not very close to any women but their wives, and often are not close enough to their wives to gain reliable information about their wives' natures. Hence, men's claims about women's nature are never very reliable, and we would need to wait to hear from the women themselves before making a judgment.

Lastly, Mill responds to an objection from "social progress" or "natural functioning." This objection to women's equality is that women's traditional subordination helps insure that women achieve their own natural "calling"—being good wives and mothers—and so, in a sense, that subordination is for women's own good. But Mill's presupposition, here as in *On Liberty* and *Utilitarianism,* is that everyone naturally pursues his or her own good, and that legal or traditional regulations always more or less restrict human nature. Thus, he claims that whatever is really women's natural function would be better achieved by leaving women free to pursue it. Of course, Mill does not believe that being a wife or mother is women's natural function. Hence, he closes the chapter speculating that such an objector to women's equality "dost protest too much," that defenders of women's subjection must be afraid of the consequences of women's freedom—afraid that it will result in men's loneliness and subjection.

CHAPTER II: CRITICISM OF MARRIAGE LAWS

According to Mill, as for many thinkers of the period, the primary vehicle of women's subjection to men is marriage. Though Mill believes that marriage can be a genuinely hallowed state for both men and women, he believes that the nineteenth-century laws and traditions regarding marriage worked against its sanctity and for the subordination of women. He devotes all of Chapter Two to a criticism of marriage and marriage laws. This chapter is also organized as responses to objections, where in this case the objectors are defenders of marriage laws.

CHAPTER II

It will be well to commence the detailed discussion of the subject by the particular branch of it to which the course of our observations has led us: the conditions which the laws of this and all other countries annex to the marriage contract. Marriage being the destination appointed by society for women, the prospect they are brought up to, and the object which it is intended should be sought by all of them, except those who are too little attractive to be chosen by any man as his companion; one might have supposed that everything would have been done to make this condition as eligible to them as possible, that they might have no cause to regret being denied the option of any other. Society, however, both in this, and, at first, in all other cases, has preferred to attain its object by foul rather than fair means.

The two are called "one person in law," for the purpose of inferring that whatever is hers is his, but the parallel inference is never drawn that whatever is his is hers; the maxim is not applied against the man, except to make him responsible to third parties for her acts, as a master for the acts of his slaves or of his cattle. I am far from pretending that wives are in general no better treated than slaves; but no slave is a slave to the same lengths, and in so full a sense of the word, as a wife is. Hardly any slave, except one immediately attached to the master's person, is a slave at all hours and all minutes.

Above all, a female slave has (in Christian countries) an admitted right, and is considered under a moral obligation, to refuse to her master the last familiarity. Not so the wife: however brutal a tyrant she may unfortunately be chained to—though she may know that he hates her, though it may be his daily pleasure to torture her, and though she may feel it impossible not to loathe him—he can claim from her and enforce the lowest degradation of a human being, that of being made the instrument of an animal function contrary to her inclinations. While she is held in this worst description of slavery as to her own person, what is her position in regard to the children in whom she and her master have a joint interest? They are by law *his* children.

This is her legal state. And from this state she has no means of withdrawing herself. If she leaves her husband, she can take nothing with her, neither her children nor anything which is rightfully her own. If he chooses, he can compel her to return, by law, or by physical force; or he may content himself with seizing for his own use anything which she may earn, or which may be given to her by her relations.

Who doubts that there may be great goodness, and great happiness, and great affection, under the absolute government of a good man? Meanwhile, laws and institutions require to be adapted, not to good men, but to bad. Marriage is not an institution designed for a select few. Men are not required, as a preliminary to the marriage ceremony, to prove by testimonials that they are fit to be trusted with the exercise of absolute power.

When we consider how vast is the number of men, in any great country, who are little higher than brutes, and that this never prevents them from being able, through the law of marriage, to obtain a victim, the breadth and depth of human misery caused in this shape alone by the abuse of the institution swells to something appalling. Yet these are only the extreme cases. They are the lowest abysses, but there is a sad succession of depth after depth before reaching them. In domestic as in political tyranny, the case of absolute monsters chiefly illustrates the institution by showing that there is scarcely any horror which may not occur under it if the despot pleases, and thus setting in a strong light what must be the terrible frequency of things only a little less atrocious. Absolute fiends are as rare as angels, perhaps rarer: ferocious savages, with occasional touches of humanity, are however very frequent.

I know that there is another side to the question. I grant that the wife, if she cannot effectually resist, can at least retaliate; she, too, can make the man's life extremely uncomfortable, and by that power is able to carry many points which she ought, and many which she ought not, to prevail in. But this instrument of self-protection—which may be called the power of the scold, or the shrewish sanction—has the fatal defect, that it avails most against the least tyrannical superiors, and in favour of the least deserving dependents.

The wife's power of being disagreeable generally only establishes a counter-tyranny, and makes victims in their turn chiefly of those husbands who are least inclined to be tyrants.

What is it, then, which really tempers the corrupting effects of the power, and makes it compatible with such amount of good as we actually see? Mere feminine blandishments, though of great effect in individual instances, have very little effect in modifying the general tendencies of the situation; for their power only lasts while the woman is young and attractive, often only while her charm is new, and not dimmed by familiarity; and on many men they have not much influence at any time.

Accordingly, as things now are, those who act most kindly to their wives, are quite as often made worse, as better, by the wife's influence, in respect to all interests extending beyond the family. She is taught that she has no business with things out of that sphere; and accordingly she seldom has any honest and conscientious opinion on them; and therefore hardly ever meddles with them for any legitimate purpose, but generally for an interested one. She neither knows nor cares which is the right side in politics, but she knows what will bring in money or invitations, give her husband a title, her son a place, or her daughter a good marriage.

The real practical decision of affairs, to whichever may be given the legal authority, will greatly depend, as it even now does, upon comparative qualifications. The mere fact that he is usually the eldest, will in most cases give the preponderance to the man; at least until they both attain a time of life at which the difference in their years is of no importance. There will naturally also be a more potential voice on the side, whichever it is, that brings the means of support. Inequality from this source does not depend on the law of marriage, but on the general conditions of human society, as now constituted. The influence of mental superiority, either general or special, and of superior decision of character, will necessarily tell for much. It always does so at present. And this fact shows how little foundation there is for the apprehension that the powers and responsibilities of partners in life (as of partners in business), cannot be satisfactorily apportioned by agreement between themselves. They always are so apportioned, except in cases in which the marriage institution is a failure. Things never come to an issue of downright power on one side, and obedience on the other, except where the connexion altogether has been a mistake, and it would be a blessing to both parties to be relieved from it.

The equality of married persons before the law, is not only the sole mode in which that particular relation can be made consistent with justice to both sides, and conducive to the happiness of both, but it is the only means of rendering the daily life of mankind, in any high sense, a school of moral cultivation. Though the truth may not be felt or generally acknowledged for generations to come, the only school of genuine moral sentiment is society between equals.

The moral training of mankind will never be adapted to the conditions of the life for which all other human progress is a preparation, until they practise in the family the same moral rule which is adapted to the normal constitution of human society. Any sentiment of freedom which can exist in a man whose nearest and dearest intimacies are with those of whom he is absolute master, is not the genuine or Christian love of freedom, but, what the love of freedom generally was in the ancients and in the middle ages—an intense feeling of the dignity and importance of his own personality; making him disdain a yoke for himself, of which he has no abhorrence whatever in the abstract, but which he is abundantly ready to impose on others for his own interest or glorification.

. . . It is almost superfluous to say anything concerning the more special point included in the general one—a woman's right to her own property; for I need not hope that this treatise can make any impression upon those who need anything to convince them that a woman's inheritance or gains ought to be as much her own after marriage as before. The rule is simple: whatever would be the husband's or wife's if they were not married, should be under their exclusive control during marriage.

But the utmost latitude ought to exist for the adaptation of general rules to individual suitabilities; and there ought to be nothing to prevent faculties exceptionally adapted to any other pursuit, from obeying their vocation notwithstanding marriage: due provision being made for supplying otherwise any falling-short which might become inevitable, in her full performance of the ordinary functions of mistress of a family. These things, if once opinion were rightly directed on the subject, might with perfect safety be left to be regulated by opinion, without any interference of law.

Again, Mill relies upon the analogy to slavery, claiming that although wives have in general a better life than slaves, their freedom is as restricted, if not more so, than slaves. Thus, Mill begins the chapter with the empirical claim that marriage, while it is the destiny of most women, is inherently unfair to them. He then responds to a series of objections, each of which tries to justify this unfairness in some way. Thus, Mill will end the chapter having shown that since nothing justifies the inherent unfairness of the institution of marriage, it is in need of vast reform.

The first objection to which Mill responds might be called the "mountain out of a molehill" objection. This defender of marriage claims that few men abuse the legal authority that marriage laws permit them; i.e., most men are nicer to their wives than they legally could get away with. Mill grants that few men are as tyrannical over their wives as they could be but argues that, since law is inherently restrictive, its proper use is to restrict people's worst behavior, not—as this objector claims—to rely on people's best behavior. Marriage is not a privileged position for which one must prove oneself worthy; hence, under the laws of marriage as they stand, the worst men can terribly abuse their wives with impunity.

The second objection to which Mill here responds is one in which the defender of marriage claims that any unfair restrictions placed upon women by the institution of marriage are balanced by the unfair nagging and shrewishness that wives impose on their husbands. Against this, Mill argues, in the first place, that this retaliation on women's part is a pretty feeble force against civil law and long-standing social tradition. Further, in those marriages where wives do exert their authority in this way, they demean themselves and humiliate their husbands by doing so. Women's nagging is an expression of the weakness of their position—not its strength; no one, Mill implies, would resort to such dishonest tactics if he or she had legitimate means of exercising his or her rights.

After taking up these objections, Mill argues for legal reform to achieve legal equality in marriage. First, he claims that marriage is a social institution and should be organized like the ideal state. Since Mill's vision of such a utopia is one in which everyone has individual autonomy over his or her actions and an equal say about what makes him or her happy, Mill's vision of the best marriage is one in which husbands and wives are equal and autonomous. Further, in marriage—because at its best it is intimate and friendly—husbands and wives stand to benefit the most from mutual cooperation, the sharing of decisions, and moral education. Thus, he claims that the power in marriage should be shared, that the property should be held individually, and that husband and wife be allowed the freedom to pass on their best habits and aspirations to their children.

CHAPTER III: WOMEN'S WORK

In the next chapter of *The Subjection of Women,* Mill takes up the question of whether or not women should work outside the home, which, as we discussed in the introduction to this chapter, is of increasing importance to the question of gender in the nineteenth century. Mill's claim, of course, is that women should do any work for which they are qualified; however, he admits it is difficult to know—after so many years of women's subordination—exactly what great achievements women would contribute to society if they were free to do so.

CHAPTER III

On the other point which is involved in the just equality of women, their admissibility to all the functions and occupations hitherto retained as the monopoly of the stronger sex, I should anticipate no difficulty in convincing any one who has gone with me on the subject of the equality of women in the family. I believe that their disabilities elsewhere are only clung to in order to maintain their subordination in domestic life; because the generality of the male sex cannot yet tolerate the idea of living with an equal. Were it not for that, I think that almost every one, in the existing state of opinion in politics and political economy, would admit the injustice of excluding half the human race from the greater number of lucrative occupations, and from almost all high social functions; ordaining from their birth either that they are not, and cannot by any possibility become, fit for employments which are legally open to the stupidest and basest of the other sex, or else that however fit they may be, those employments shall be interdicted to them, in order to be preserved for the exclusive benefit of males.

It is not sufficient to maintain that women on the average are less gifted than men on the average, with certain of the higher mental faculties, or that a smaller number of women than of men are fit for occupations and functions of the highest intellectual character. It is necessary to maintain that no women at all are fit for them, and that the most eminent women are inferior in mental faculties to the most mediocre of the men on whom those functions at present devolve. For if the performance of the function is decided either by competition, or by any mode of choice which secures regard to the public interest, there needs be no apprehension that any important employments will fall into the hands of women inferior to average men, or to the average of their male competitors. The only result would be that there would be fewer women than men in such employments; a result certain to happen in any case, if only from the preference always likely to be felt by the majority of women for the one vocation in which there is nobody to compete with them. Now, the most determined depreciator of women will not venture to deny, that when we add the experience of recent times to that of ages past, women, and not a few merely, but many women, have proved themselves capable of everything, perhaps without a single exception, which is done by men, and of doing it successfully and creditably. The utmost that can be said is, that there are many things which none of them have succeeded in doing as well as they have been done by some men—many in which they have not reached the very highest rank. But there are extremely few, dependent only on mental faculties, in which they have not attained the rank next to the highest. Is not this enough, and much more than enough, to make it a tyranny to them, and a detriment to society, that they should not be allowed to compete with men for the exercise of these functions? Is it not a mere truism to say, that such functions are often filled by men far less fit for them than numbers of women, and who would be beaten by women in any fair field of competition?

And even if we could do without them, would it be consistent with justice to refuse to them their fair share of honour and distinction, or to deny to them the equal moral right of all human beings to choose their occupation (short of injury to others) according to their own preferences, at their own risk? Nor is the injustice confined to them: it is shared by those who are in a position to benefit by their services. To ordain that any kind of persons shall not be physicians, or shall not be advocates, or shall not be members of parliament, is to injure not them only, but all who employ physicians or advocates, or elect members of parliament, and who are deprived of the stimulating effect of greater competition on the exertions of the competitors, as well as restricted to a narrower range of individual choice.

. . . [W]omen require the suffrage, as their guarantee of just and equal consideration. This ought to be obvious even to those who coincide in no other of the doctrines for which I contend. Even if every woman were a wife, and if every wife ought to be a slave, all the more would these slaves stand in need of legal protection: and we know what legal protection the slaves have, where the laws are made by their masters.

With regard to the fitness of women, not only to participate in elections, but themselves to hold offices or practise professions involving important public responsibilities; I have already observed that this consideration is not essential to the practical question in dispute: since any woman, who succeeds in an open profession, proves by that very fact that she is qualified for it. And in the case of public offices, if the political system of the country is such as to exclude unfit men, it will equally exclude unfit women: while if it is not, there is no additional evil in the fact that the unfit persons whom it admits may be either women or men. As long therefore as it is acknowledged that even a few women may be fit for these duties, the laws which shut the door on those exceptions cannot be justified by any opinion which can be held respecting the capacities of women in general.

It cannot be inferred to be impossible that a woman should be a Homer, or an Aristotle, or a Michael Angelo, or a Beethoven, because no woman has yet actually produced works comparable to theirs in any of those lines of excellence. This negative fact at most leaves the question uncertain, and open to psychological discussion. But it is quite certain that a woman can be Queen Elizabeth, or a Deborah, or a Joan of Arc, since this is not inference, but fact. Now it is a curious consideration, that the only things which the existing law excludes women from doing, are the things which they have proved that they are able to do. There is no law to prevent a woman from having written all the plays of Shakspeare, or composed all the operas of Mozart. But Queen Elizabeth or Queen Victoria, had they not inherited the throne, could not have been intrusted with the smallest of the political duties, of which the former showed herself equal to the greatest.

If anything conclusive could be inferred from experience, without psychological analysis, it would be that the things which women are not allowed to do are the very ones for which they are peculiarly qualified; since their vocation for government has made its way, and become conspicuous, through the very few opportunities which have been given; while in the lines of distinction which apparently were freely open to them, they have by no means so eminently distinguished themselves. We know how small a number of reigning queens history presents, in comparison with that of kings. Of this smaller number a far larger proportion have shown talents for rule; though many of them have occupied the throne in difficult periods. It is remarkable, too, that they have, in a great number of instances, been distinguished by merits the most opposite to the imaginary and conventional character of women: they have been as much remarked for the firmness and vigour of their rule, as for its intelligence.

⋐ ⋐ ⋐

I shall presently show, that even the least contestable of the differences which now exist, are such as may very well have been produced merely by circumstances, without any difference of natural capacity. But, looking at women as they are known in experience, it may be said of them, with more truth than belongs to most other generalizations on the subject, that the general bent of their talents is towards the practical. This statement is conformable to all the public history of women, in the present and the past. It is no less borne out by common and daily experience. Let us consider the special nature of the mental capacities most characteristic of a woman of talent. They are all of a kind which fits them for practice, and makes them tend towards it. What is meant by a woman's capacity of intuitive perception? It means, a rapid and correct insight into present fact. It has nothing to do with general principles. Nobody ever perceived a scientific law of nature by intuition, nor arrived at a general rule of duty or prudence by it. These are results of slow and careful collection and comparison of experience; and neither the men nor the women of intuition usually shine in this department, unless, indeed, the experience necessary is such as they can acquire by themselves. For what is called their intuitive sagacity makes them peculiarly apt in gathering such general truths as can be collected from their individual means of observation. When, consequently, they chance to be as well provided as men are with the results of other people's experience, by reading and education, (I use the word chance advisedly, for, in respect to the knowledge that tends to fit them for the greater concerns of life, the only educated women are the self-educated) they are better furnished than men in general with the essential requisites of skilful and successful practice. Men who have been much taught, are apt to be deficient in the sense of present fact; they do not see, in the facts which they are called upon to deal with, what is really there, but what they have been taught to expect. This is seldom the case with women of any ability. Their capacity of "intuition" preserves them from it. With equality of experience and of general faculties, a woman usually sees much more than a man of what is immediately before her. Now this sensibility to the present, is the main quality on which the capacity for practice, as distinguished from theory, depends. To discover general principles, belongs to the speculative faculty: to discern and discriminate the particular cases in which they are and are not applicable, constitutes practical talent: and for this, women as they now are have a peculiar aptitude. I admit that there can be no good practice without principles, and that the predominant place which quickness of observation holds among a woman's faculties, makes her particularly apt to build over-hasty generalizations upon her own observation; though at the same time no less ready in rectifying those generalizations, as her observation takes a wider range. But the corrective to this defect, is access to the experience of the human race; general knowledge—exactly the thing which education can best supply.

But this gravitation of women's minds to the present, to the real, to actual fact, while in its exclusiveness it is a source of errors, is also a most useful counteractive of the contrary error. The principal and most characteristic aberration of speculative minds as such, consists precisely in the deficiency of this lively perception and ever-present sense of objective fact. For want of this, they often not only overlook the contradiction which outward facts oppose to their theories, but lose sight of the legitimate purpose of speculation altogether, and let their speculative faculties go astray into regions not peopled with real beings, animate or inanimate, even idealized, but with personified shadows created by the illusions of metaphysics or by the mere entanglement of words, and think these shadows the proper objects of the highest, the most transcendent, philosophy. Hardly anything can be of greater value to a man of theory and speculation who employs himself not in collecting materials of knowledge by observation, but in working them up by processes of thought into comprehensive truths of science and laws of conduct, than to carry on his speculations in the companionship, and under the criticism, of a really superior woman.

It will be said, perhaps, that the greater nervous susceptibility of women is a disqualification for practice, in anything but domestic life, by rendering them mobile, changeable, too vehemently under the influence of the moment, incapable of dogged perseverance, unequal and uncertain in the power of using their faculties. I think that these phrases sum up the greater part of the objections commonly made to the fitness of women for the higher class of serious business. Much of all this is the mere overflow of nervous energy run to waste, and would cease when the energy was directed to a definite end. Much is also the result of conscious or unconscious cultivation; as we see by the almost total disappearance of "hysterics" and fainting fits, since they have gone out of fashion. Moreover, when people are brought up, like many women of the higher classes (though less so in our own country than in any other) a kind of hot-house plants, shielded from the wholesome vicissitudes of air and temperature, and untrained in any of the occupations and exercises which give stimulus and development to the circulatory and muscular system, while their nervous system, especially in its emotional department, is kept in unnaturally active play; it is no wonder if those of them who do not die of consumption, grow up with constitutions liable to derangement from slight causes, both internal and external, and without stamina to support any task, physical or mental, requiring continuity of effort. But women brought up to work for their livelihood show none of these morbid characteristics.

To so ridiculous an extent are the notions formed of the nature of women, mere empirical generalizations, framed, without philosophy or analysis, upon the first instances which present themselves, that the popular idea of it is different in different countries, according as the opinions and social circumstances of the country have given to the women living in it any speciality of development or non-development. An Oriental thinks that women are by nature peculiarly voluptuous; see the violent abuse of them on this ground in Hindoo writings. An Englishman usually thinks that they are by nature cold. The sayings about women's fickleness are mostly of French origin; from the famous distich of Francis I, upward and downward.

For the artificial state superinduced by society disguises the natural tendencies of the thing which is the subject of observation, in two different ways: by extinguishing the nature, or by transforming it. In the one case there is but a starved residuum of nature remaining to be studied; in the other case there is much, but it may have expanded in any direction rather than that in which it would spontaneously grow.

Let us take, then, the only marked case which observation affords, of apparent inferiority of women to men, if we except the merely physical one of bodily strength. No production in philosophy, science, or art, entitled to the first rank, has been the work of a woman. Is there any mode of accounting for this, without supposing that women are naturally incapable of producing them?

In the first place, we may fairly question whether experience has afforded sufficient grounds for an induction. It is scarcely three generations since women, saving very rare exceptions, have begun to try their capacity in philosophy, science, or art. It is only in the present generation that their attempts have been at all numerous; and they are even now extremely few, everywhere but in England and France. It is a relevant question, whether a mind possessing the requisites of first-rate eminence in speculation or creative art could have been expected, on the mere calculation of chances, to turn up during that lapse of time, among the women whose tastes and personal position admitted of their devoting themselves to these pursuits. In all things which there has yet been time for—in all but the very highest grades in the scale of excellence, especially in the department in which they have been longest engaged, literature (both prose and poetry)—women have done quite as much, have obtained fully as high prizes and as many of them, as could be expected from the length of time and the number of competitors.

☞ ☞ ☞

It is in the fine arts, properly so called, that the *primâ facie* evidence of inferior original powers in women at first sight appears the strongest: since opinion (it may be said) does not exclude them from these, but rather encourages them, and their education, instead of passing over this department, is in the affluent classes mainly composed of it. Yet in this line of exertion they have fallen still more short than in many others, of the highest eminence attained by men. This shortcoming, however, needs no other explanation than the familiar fact, more universally true in the fine arts than in anything else; the vast superiority of professional persons over amateurs. Women in the educated classes are almost universally taught more or less of some branch or other of the fine arts, but not that they may gain their living or their social consequence by it. Women artists are all amateurs.

☞ ☞ ☞

The only one of the fine arts which women do follow, to any extent, as a profession, and an occupation for life, is the histrionic; and in that they are confessedly equal, if not superior, to men. To make the comparison fair, it should be made between the productions of women in any branch of art, and those of men not following it as a profession. In musical composition, for example, women surely have produced fully as good things as have ever been produced by male amateurs. There are now a few women, a very few, who practise painting as a profession, and these are already beginning to show quite as much talent as could be expected.

☞ ☞ ☞

There are other reasons, besides those which we have now given, that help to explain why women remain behind men, even in the pursuits which are open to both. For one thing, very few women have time for them. This may seem a paradox; it is an undoubted social fact. The time and thoughts of every woman have to satisfy great previous demands on them for things practical. There is, first, the superintendence of the family and the domestic expenditure, which occupies at least one woman in every family, generally the one of mature years and acquired experience; unless the family is so rich as to admit of delegating that task to hired agency, and submitting to all the waste and malversation inseparable from that mode of conducting it. The superintendence of a household, even when not in other respects laborious, is extremely onerous to the thoughts; it requires incessant vigilance, an eye which no detail escapes, and presents questions for consideration and solution, foreseen and unforeseen, at every hour of the day, from which the person responsible for them can hardly ever shake herself free. If a woman is of a rank and circumstances which relieve her in a measure from these cares, she has still devolving on her the management for the whole family of its intercourse with others—of what is called society, and the less the call made on her by the former duty, the greater is always the development of the latter: the dinner parties, concerts, evening parties, morning visits, letter writing, and all that goes with them. All this is over and above the engrossing duty which society imposes exclusively on women, of making themselves charming. A clever woman of the higher ranks finds nearly a sufficient employment of her talents in cultivating the graces of manner and the arts of conversation.

☞ ☞ ☞

There is another consideration to be added to all these. In the various arts and intellectual occupations, there is a degree of proficiency sufficient for living by it, and there is a higher degree on which depend the great productions which immortalize a name.

☞ ☞ ☞

Now, whether the cause be natural or artificial, women seldom have this eagerness for fame. Their ambition is generally confined within narrower bounds. The influence they seek is over those who immediately surround them. Their desire is to be liked, loved, or admired, by those whom they see with their eyes: and the proficiency in knowledge, arts, and accomplishments, which is sufficient for that, almost always contents them. This is a trait of character which cannot be left out of the account in judging of women as they are. I do not at all believe that it is inherent in women. It is only the natural result of their circumstances.

☞ ☞ ☞

As for moral differences, considered as distinguished from intellectual, the distinction commonly drawn is to the advantage of women. They are declared to be better than men; an empty compliment, which must provoke a bitter smile from every woman of spirit, since there is no other situation in life in which it is the established order, and considered quite natural and suitable, that the better should obey the worse. If this piece of idle talk is good for anything, it is only as an admission by men, of the corrupting influence of power; for that is certainly the only truth which the fact, if it be a fact, either proves or illustrates. And it *is* true that servitude, except when it actually brutalizes, though corrupting to both, is less so to the slaves than to the slave-masters.

≈ ≈ ≈

The complimentary dictum about women's superior moral goodness may be allowed to pair off with the disparaging one respecting their greater liability to moral bias. Women, we are told, are not capable of resisting their personal partialities: their judgment in grave affairs is warped by their sympathies and antipathies. Assuming it to be so, it is still to be proved that women are oftener misled by their personal feelings than men by their personal interests. The chief difference would seem in that case to be, that men are led from the course of duty and the public interest by their regard for themselves, women (not being allowed to have private interests of their own) by their regard for somebody else.

Mill's arguments in this chapter are allied to his claims about women's nature in his first chapter, as well as to his utilitarianism and libertarianism. First, he reiterates the cultural foundation of the problem: Mill claims it is only recently in human history, since the increased division of labor, that men's and women's work has been separated into the rigorous dichotomy of public and private labor that is common in modernity. Thus, the focus of Mill's arguments has to do with how a good society should distribute labor among men and women. He begins with a defense of women's suffrage, arguing that permitting women to exercise their right to vote for their leaders would also likely benefit society in general. Further, since political interests are founded in class and not in sex, there is no reason for men to fear that giving women the vote will lead to drastic changes in voting trends. In addition, Mill points to the great women leaders who have distinguished themselves in history and claims that women's demonstrated ability to rule indicates an ability to vote wisely as well.

With regard to employment, Mill basically relies upon the demands of a free market to regulate job performance. In other words, he believes that women's abilities to perform public functions—including governing—is an empirical matter; it cannot be judged until it has been tried. Mill argues that women should be given equal employment opportunity to that of men, and that the market should decide which individuals should do which jobs. On the face of it, Mill claims, we have no reason to assume that women cannot, at least case-for-case, do everything men can do. According to Mill (and this will foreshadow the liberal feminism of thinkers like Gilman, some of whose work appears in the next chapter), the system of industrial capitalism, free of government intervention, does lead to social progress. Hence, since under these classic economic presuppositions, a larger labor force with more competition always results in more and better products, and consequently in the general improvement of the conditions of life, adding women to the labor force can only benefit society.

The arts and the achievements of high culture are for Mill a particularly important case. Here, in a sense, he is responding to yet another objector, a person who would claim that while women may be able to do unskilled labor, artistic creation is the strict purview of men. According to Mill, however, it is in the arts that women have shown the most initiative and achievement to date, especially in literature.

Again, particular women's strengths and weaknesses cannot be known to be natural or universal, and society is obliged to judge each case on its own merits. In general, Mill's arguments here echo the reluctance he showed in his first chapter to make generalizations about men's and women's natures. Rather, Mill tries throughout *The Subjection of Women* to refrain from judgment until all the results of women's legal equality are in. Only when we have tried this great experiment will we be able to say whether or not women are the way men have for so long imagined them. This is the tone in which Mill ends the essay, in his fourth chapter.

CHAPTER IV

There remains a question, not of less importance than those already discussed, and which will be asked the most importunately by those opponents whose conviction is somewhat shaken on the main point. What good are we to expect from the changes proposed in our customs and institutions? Would mankind be at all better off if women were free? If not, why disturb their minds, and attempt to make a social revolution in the name of an abstract right?

When we consider the positive evil caused to the disqualified half of the human race by their disqualification—first in the loss of the most inspiriting and elevating kind of personal enjoyment, and next in the weariness, disappointment, and profound dissatisfaction with life, which are so often the substitute for it; one feels that among all the lessons which men require for carrying on the struggle against the inevitable imperfections of their lot on earth, there is no lesson which they more need, than not to add to the evils which nature inflicts, by their jealous and prejudiced restrictions on one another. Their vain fears only substitute other and worse evils for those which they are idly apprehensive of: while every restraint on the freedom of conduct of any of their human fellow creatures, (otherwise than by making them responsible for any evil actually caused by it), dries up *pro tanto* the principal fountain of human happiness, and leaves the species less rich, to an inappreciable degree, in all that makes life valuable to the individual human being.

4./5. KARL MARX
(German, 1818–1883)

AND FRIEDRICH ENGELS
(German, 1820–1895)

Karl Marx and his life-long friend and frequent collaborator, Friedrich Engels, offered the classic philosophical critique of industrial capitalism. They claimed that capitalism was a systematic immoral force that drained people of their fundamental humanity. In contrast to the basically congenial reforms advocated by Mill, Marx and Engels sought to hasten what they claimed was the inevitable destruction of capitalism by abolishing private property altogether through a communist revolution.

Although Marx believed that philosophers were far too distanced from the economic realities of the working class, and sought for actual social reforms instead of mere analysis, there is no question that Marx was first and foremost a philosopher. In fact, social reformers and revolutionaries who have tried to apply Marxist theories in modern-day communist nations have grappled (and as we know, sometimes unsuccessfully) with the difficulties of interpretation and application as much as with any theoretical philosophy. Here then, instigative as they are, we will look at these Marxist writings as philosophy and not as polemic.

POLITICAL ECONOMIES AND DIALECTICAL MATERIALISM

Marx's philosophy was deeply influenced by, yet fundamentally critical of, the philosophy of Hegel. Marx accepted Hegel's claims that philosophers should be inherently historical in their analyses, and that history moved along dialectically—through conflicts between opposing forces. However, Marx did not believe with Hegel that the dialectic of history was primarily a movement of consciousness. Rather, Marx claimed that history moved through a *material dialectic,* meaning that the conflicts that history struggles to resolve are always physically manifested. In other words, Marx believed that nature—even human nature—was inherently partly physical, and that our physical needs and limits and strengths inevitably play a part in the great movements of history.

Marx believed that politics and economics could not be legitimately distinguished from each other, that the physical conditions of human life were represented in economic terms and always accompanied their more abstract political ideals. Thus, for Marx, each era in history is marked by its own "material conditions of labor"—the technological and economic standards possible at the time—just as in Hegel's notion of history, "truth" was the standard of knowledge for any particular era. The material conditions of labor are basically the instruments and machines, the basic form of economic production (e.g., hunting/gathering vs. agriculture), and the standards of living available to people at that time.

Obviously, the material conditions of existence are not the same for everyone, even during the same historical time period. They are very different, for instance, for the poor than they are for the wealthy. This insight is integral to the dialectical aspect of Marxist theory: every political economy is defined, not just by the highest material conditions available to it, but also by the inherent class differences created by those material conditions. The opposing forces through whose conflict the dialectic of history progresses, according to Marx, always create a conflict among economic classes. The class-conflict of any particular historical stage characterized the weakness of that political economic system, and by playing itself out this conflict would inevitably lead to the destruction of that system. In this sense, Marx can be characterized as an economic "determinist," claiming that new political economies with new inherent class systems would take the place of the old over and over again, until a classless society could evolve that would end the dialectic of history.

ALIENATION AND THE PROLETARIAN REVOLUTION

The class-conflict that characterized industrial capitalism, according to Marx, was the most raw, dichotomous, and immoral of all political economies—that between the *Bourgeoisie,* or middle-class (those who owned the "means of production," the factories and machines), and the *Proletariat,* or working-class, who did all the labor in the society but owned nothing. The Bourgeois class, during the earlier era of national aristocracies, had been a revolutionary class whose displeasure with their political economic system had succeeded in bringing about its downfall. Under industrial capitalism, however, Marx claimed that the Bourgeoisie was no longer a revolutionary class. The owners' interest was in maintaining their position as owners, and so, in maintaining the system of industrial capitalism on which their position depended. Hence, Marx claimed the Proletariat was the only genuinely revolutionary class and that this class would inevitably bring about the abolition of private property and the destruction of capitalism. Only after the Proletarian revolution, claimed Marx, could there be a society in which human beings could achieve their fullest potential.

The inhumanity of capitalism was most cruelly manifested, Marx claimed, in its *alienation* of the worker from the fruits of his or her labor. Marx, like Locke (whose discussion of this topic appears in the preceding chapter) believed that a person's labor upon something gave both the worker and the product their value and significance—it is through labor that human beings both sustain themselves physically and make their personal mark upon the world. Since a person's own value is invested into the products of her or his labor, claimed Marx, that product becomes entwined with the worker's self-image and a reflection of it to the world; just as when that artist produces a painting we say that it is "a Rembrandt," everything a person produces is crucially representative of her or him. Under the system of industrial capitalism, however, both the means and the products of the worker's labor are owned by someone else—the Bourgeois capitalist. By giving up the fruits of her or his labor to the owner of the factory, the worker becomes a stranger to aspects of her or himself. In addition, by appropriating the labor of others instead of laboring him or herself, the owner also becomes a stranger to him or herself, never leaving his or her own mark upon the world directly. In this way, according to Marx, both owners and workers under capitalism are alienated from themselves and from each other. They are dehumanized, interacting only with machines and time-clocks, lost in a sea of meaningless work and profits.

The immorality of capitalism, for Marx, stems mostly from its inevitable alienation of people from their own humanity, or "species being." Marx's early writings give far more attention to this moral issue; his later works, such as *Capital,* are more oriented towards economic theory and analysis. Scholars disagree about the consistency of Marx's early writings with his later work. In both periods however—since the most primordial of human relations, according to Marx, is the sexual relation—he discusses the question of gender integrally to his theories. After Marx's death and following this theme, Engels wrote a famous and very provocative analysis of the interdependence of family structure and political economics. We will look at several of these analyses, concluding with Engels's *The Origin of the Family.*

THE ECONOMIC AND PHILOSOPHIC MANUSCRIPTS OF 1844

These early essays frame Marx against the background of Hegel and provide the most humanistic vision of Marxist theory. In them appears the most detailed discussion of alienation, and in particular of its effect on sexual relations.

[ESTRANGED LABOUR]

We have proceeded from the premises of political economy. We have accepted its language and its laws. We presupposed private property, the separation of labour, capital and land, and of wages, profit of capital and rent of land—likewise division of labour, competition, the concept of exchange-value, etc. On the basis of political economy itself, in its own words, we have shown that the worker sinks to the level of a commodity and becomes indeed the most wretched of commodities; that the wretchedness of the worker is in inverse proportion to the power and magnitude of his production; that the necessary result of competition is the accumulation of capital in a few hands, and thus the restoration of monopoly in a more terrible form; that finally the distinction between capitalist and land-rentier, like that between the tiller of the soil and the factory-worker, disappears and that the whole of society must fall apart into the two classes—the property-*owners* and the propertyless *workers*.

☞ ☞ ☞

The only wheels which political economy sets in motion are *avarice* and the *war amongst the avaricious—competition.*

☞ ☞ ☞

The worker becomes all the poorer the more wealth he produces, the more his production increases in power and range. The worker becomes an ever cheaper commodity the more commodities he creates. With the *increasing value* of the world of things proceeds in direct proportion the *devaluation* of the world of men. Labour produces not only commodities: it produces itself and the worker as a *commodity*—and does so in the proportion in which it produces commodities generally.

This fact expresses merely that the object which labour produces—labour's product—confronts it is *something alien,* as a *power independent* of the producer. The product of labour is labour which has been congealed in an object, which has become material: it is the *objectification* of labour. Labour's realization is its objectification. In the conditions dealt with by political economy this realization of labour appears as *loss of reality* for the workers; objectification as *loss of the object* and *object-bondage;* appropriation as *estrangement,* as *alienation.*

☞ ☞ ☞

All these consequences are contained in the definition that the worker is related to the *product of his labour* as to an *alien* object. For on this premise it is clear that the more the worker spends himself, the more powerful the alien objective world becomes which he creates over-against himself, the poorer he himself—his inner world—becomes, the less belongs to him as his own. It is the same in religion. The more man puts into God, the less he retains in himself. The worker puts his life into the object; but now his life no longer belongs to him but to the object.

⌐ ⌐ ⌐

Let us now look more closely at the *objectification,* at the production of the worker; and therein at the *estrangement,* the *loss* of the object, his product.

The worker can create nothing without *nature,* without the *sensuous external world.* It is the material on which his labour is manifested, in which it is active, from which and by means of which it produces.

But just as nature provides labour with the *means of life* in the sense that labour cannot *live* without objects on which to operate, on the other hand, it also provides the *means of life* in the more restricted sense—i.e., the means for the physical subsistence of the *worker* himself.

Thus the more the worker by his labour *appropriates* the external world, sensuous nature, the more he deprives himself of *means of life* in the double respect: first, that the sensuous external world more and more ceases to be an object belonging to his labour—to be his labour's *means of life;* and secondly, that it more and more ceases to be *means of life* in the immediate sense, means for the physical subsistence of the worker.

⌐ ⌐ ⌐

As a result, therefore, man (the worker) no longer feels himself to be freely active in any but his animal functions—eating, drinking, procreating, or at most in his dwelling and in dressing-up, etc.; and in his human functions he no longer feels himself to be anything but an animal. What is animal becomes human and what is human becomes animal.

Certainly eating, drinking, procreating, etc., are also genuinely human functions. But in the abstraction which separates them from the sphere of all other human activity and turns them into sole and ultimate ends, they are animal.

⌐ ⌐ ⌐

Man is a species being, not only because in practice and in theory he adopts the species as his object (his own as well as those of other things), but—and this is only another way of expressing it—but also because he treats himself as the actual, living species; because he treats himself as a *universal* and therefore a free being.

⌐ ⌐ ⌐

In estranging from man (1) nature, and (2) himself, his own active functions, his life-activity, estranged labour estranges the *species* from man. It turns for him the *life of the species* into a means of individual life. First it estranges the life of the species and individual life, and secondly it makes individual life in its abstract form the purpose of the life of the species, likewise in its abstract and estranged form.

For in the first place labour, *life-activity, productive life* itself, appears to man merely as a *means* of satisfying a need-the need to maintain the physical existence. Yet the productive life is the life of the species. It is life-engendering life. The whole character of a species—its species character—is contained in the character of its life-activity; and free, conscious activity is man's species character. Life itself appears only as a *means to life.*[5]

From this discussion, we can see how alienation, according to Marx, devalues human life and human labor. It also separates human beings from their natural goals, which include reproduction, community, and sexuality—or what Marx here refers to as "species life." For Marx, human beings are distinguished from other animals by their ability to universalize their actions, to understand themselves as members of a species with its own specific goals, of which the individual is a part. In this sense, then, the individual and the community are always interrelated, and anything that estranges a person from him or herself also estranges him or her from his or her community and species.

In the approach to *woman* as the spoil and handmaid of communal lust is expressed the infinite degradation in which man exists for himself, for the secret of this approach has its *unambiguous,* decisive, *plain* and undisguised expression in the relation of *man* to *woman* and in the manner in which the *direct* and *natural* procreative relationship is conceived. The direct, natural, and necessary relation of person to person is the *relation of man to woman.* In this *natural* relationship of the sexes man's relation to nature is immediately his relation to man, just as his relation to man is immediately his relation to nature—his own *natural* function. In this relationship, therefore, is *sensuously manifested,* reduced to an observable *fact,* the extent to which the human essence has become nature to man, or to which nature has to him become the human essence of man. From this relationship one can therefore judge man's whole level fo development. It follows from the character of this relationship how much *man* as a *species being,* as *man,* has come to be himself and to comprehend himself; the relation of man to woman is *the most natural* relation of human being to human being.

≈ ≈ ≈

Man is the immediate object of natural science: for immediate, *sensuous nature* for man is, immediately, human sensuousness (the expressions are identical)—presented immediately in the form of the *other* man sensuously

[5] This and the following selections from Karl Marx, *Economic and Philosophic Manuscripts of 1844.* Translated by Martin Milligan. (Moscow: Foreign Languages Publishing House, undated).

present for him. For his own sensuousness first exists as human sensuousness for himself through the *other* man. But *nature* is the immediate object of the *science of man:* the first object of man—man—is nature, sensuousness; and the particular human sensuous essential powers can only find their self-knowledge in the science of the natural world in general, since they can find their objective realization in *natural* objects only. The element of thought itself—the element of thought's living expression—*language*—is of a sensuous nature. The *social* reality of nature, and *human* natural science, or the *natural science about man,* are identical terms.

☞ ☞ ☞

. . . Besides, the opposition between political economy and ethics is only a *sham* opposition and just as much no opposition as it is an opposition. All that happens is that political economy expresses moral laws *in its own way.*

Needlessness as the principle of political economy is *most brilliantly* shown in its *theory of population.* There are *too many* people. Even the existence of men is a pure luxury; and if the worker is *"ethical,"* he will be *sparing* in procreation. (Mill suggests public acclaim for those who prove themselves continent in their sexual relations, and public rebuke for those who sin against such barrenness of marriage. . . . Is not this the ethics, the teaching of asceticism?) The production of people appears in the form of public misery.

☞ ☞ ☞

. . . Such things as smoking, drinking, eating, etc., are no longer means of contact or means that bring together. Company, association, and conversation, which again has society as its end, are enough for them; the brotherhood of man is no mere phrase with them, but a fact of life, and the nobility of man shines upon us from their work-hardened bodies.

When political economy claims that demand and supply always balance each other, it immediately forgets that according to its own claim (theory of population) the supply of *people* always exceeds the demand, and that, therefore, in the essential result of the whole production process—the existence of man—the disparity between demand and supply gets its most striking expression.

Marx's claim here is that, under capitalism, a person's "private life"—i.e., that which seems to be her or his own—is really dictated by the capitalist system just as much as is the worker's labor. The very most private of human, even of animal, processes—sexual relations—is subjected to the law of supply and demand like everything else. According to classical economics, as the demand for labor goes down, so must the supply; hence in a time of economic stagnation, claims Marx, workers are encouraged, under the guise of a moral obligation, to abstain from sex. Marx claims that morality and political economy are always in cahoots, both cogs in a system that runs on its own steam. In this way, sexual morality and the activities of individuals' personal lives get their character from the stage of political economy of which they are parts. Under industrial capitalism according to Marx, sexuality is raw, desperate, alienated; sex is cut off from the free human choices about beloveds, family size, and lifestyle that are its natural end and is left as nothing but a vague and inhuman desire of people to possess each other.

THE COMMUNIST MANIFESTO (1848)

The *Manifesto* is one of the most influential works in political philosophy, certainly the most often read of Marxist works. It was written by Marx and Engels as a mission statement for the Communist League, the radical German labor party at the time. Despite its provocative intent, however, the *Manifesto* is also a brilliantly concise statement of the early Marxist theories of dialectical materialism and economic critique.

I BOURGEOIS AND PROLETARIANS

The history of all hitherto existing society is the history of class struggles.

Freeman and slave, patrician and plebeian, lord and serf, guild-master and journeyman, in a word, oppressor and oppressed, stood in constant opposition to one another, carried on an uninterrupted, now hidden, now open fight, a fight that each time ended, either in a revolutionary reconstitution of society at large, or in the common ruin of the contending classes.

In the earlier epochs of history, we find almost everywhere a complicated arrangement of society into various orders, a manifold gradation of social rank. In ancient Rome we have patricians, knights, plebeians, slaves; in the Middle Ages, feudal lords, vassals, guild-masters, journeymen, apprentices, serfs; in almost all of these classes, again, subordinate gradations.

The modern bourgeois society that has sprouted from the ruins of feudal society has not done away with class antagonisms. It has but established new classes, new conditions of oppression, new forms of struggle in place of the old ones.

Our epoch, the epoch of the bourgeoisie, possesses, however, this distinctive feature: it has simplified the class antagonisms. Society as a whole is more and more splitting up into two great hostile camps, into two great classes directly facing each other: Bourgeoisie and Proletariat.

From the serfs of the Middle Ages sprang the chartered burghers of the earliest towns. From these burgesses the first elements of the bourgeoisie were developed.

The bourgeoisie, during its rule of scarce one hundred years, has created more massive and more colossal productive forces than have all preceding generations together. Subjection of Nature's forces to man, machinery, application of chemistry to industry and agriculture, steam-navigation, railways, electric telegraphs, clearing of whole continents for cultivation, canalisation of rivers, whole populations conjured out of the ground—what earlier century had even a presentiment that such productive forces slumbered in the lap of social labour?

We see then: the means of production and of exchange, on whose foundation the bourgeoisie built itself up, were generated in feudal society. At a certain stage in the development of these means of production and of exchange, the conditions under which feudal society produced and exchanged, the feudal organisation of agriculture and manufacturing industry, in one word, the feudal relations of property became no longer compatible with the already developed productive forces; they became so many fetters. They had to be burst asunder; they were burst asunder.

Into their place stepped free competition, accompanied by a social and political constitution adapted to it, and by the economical and political sway of the bourgeois class.

A similar movement is going on before our own eyes. Modern bourgeois society with its relations of production, of exchange and of property, a society that has conjured up such gigantic means of production and of exchange, is like the sorcerer, who is no longer able to control the powers of the nether world whom he has called up by his spells.

Society suddenly finds itself put back into a state of momentary barbarism; it appears as if a famine, a universal war of devastation had cut off the supply of every means of subsistence; industry and commerce seem to be destroyed; and why? Because there is too much civilisation, too much means of subsistence, too much industry, too much commerce.

The weapons with which the bourgeoisie felled feudalism to the ground are now turned against the bourgeoisie itself.

But not only has the bourgeoisie forged the weapons that bring death to itself; it has also called into existence the men who are to wield those weapons—the modern working class—the proletarians.

In proportion as the bourgeoisie, *i.e.,* capital, is developed, in the same proportion is the proletariat, the modern working class, developed—a class of labourers, who live only so long as they find work, and who find work only so long as their labour increases capital. These labourers, who must sell themselves piecemeal, are a commodity, like every other article of commerce, and are consequently exposed to all the vicissitudes of competition, to all the fluctuations of the market.

Masses of labourers, crowded into the factory, are organised like soldiers. As privates of the industrial army they are placed under the command of a perfect hierarchy of officers and sergeants. Not only are they slaves of the bourgeois class, and of the bourgeois State; they are daily and hourly enslaved by the machine, by the overlooker, and, above all, by the individual bourgeois manufacturer himself. The more openly this despotism proclaims gain to be its end and aim, the more petty, the more hateful and the more embittering it is.

The less the skill and exertion of strength implied in manual labour, in other words, the more modern industry becomes developed, the more is the labour of men superseded by that of women. Differences of age and sex have no longer any distinctive social validity for the working class. All are instruments of labour, more or less expensive to use, according to their age and sex.

No sooner is the exploitation of the labourer by the manufacturer, so far, at an end, and he receives his wages in cash, than he is set upon by the other portions of the bourgeoisie, the landlord, the shopkeeper, the pawnbroker, etc.

◌ ◌ ◌

Of all the classes that stand face to face with the bourgeoisie today, the proletariat alone is a really revolutionary class. The other classes decay and finally disappear in the face of Modern Industry; the proletariat is its special and essential product.

◌ ◌ ◌

II

◌ ◌ ◌

The bourgeois clap-trap about the family and education, about the hallowed co-relation of parent and child, becomes all the more disgusting, the more, by the action of Modern Industry, all family ties among the proletarians are torn asunder, and their children transformed into simple articles of commerce and instruments of labour.

But you Communists would introduce community of women, screams the whole bourgeoisie in chorus.

The bourgeois sees in his wife a mere instrument of production. He hears that the instruments of production are to be exploited in common, and, naturally, can come to no other conclusion than that the lot of being common to all will likewise fall to the women.

He has not even a suspicion that the real point aimed at is to do away with the status of women as mere instruments of production.

For the rest, nothing is more ridiculous than the virtuous indignation of our bourgeois at the community of women which, they pretend, is to be openly and officially established by the Communists. The Communists have no need to introduce community of women; it has existed almost from time immemorial.

Our bourgeois, not content with having the wives and daughters of their proletarians at their disposal, not to speak of common prostitutes, take the greatest pleasure in seducing each other's wives.

Bourgeois marriage is in reality a system of wives in common and thus, at the most, what the Communists might possibly be reproached with, is that they desire to introduce, in substitution for a hypocritically concealed, an openly legalised community of women. For the rest, it is self-evident that the abolition of the present system of production must bring with it the abolition of the community of women springing from that system, *i.e.* of prostitution both public and private.[6]

Here, Marx and Engels discuss marriage and sex differences as essentially defined by the political economy of which they are a part. We see here first an outline of the material dialectic, in the description of the evolution of capitalism out of Feudalism. Capitalism creates a blunt dichotomy between Bourgeois and Proletarian, into which all other social relations are subsumed, including the sexual relation. Women, children, neighbors, friends, devolve under capitalism into nothing more than fellow workers or fellow owners. They become empty of character. Thus, Marx and Engels imply, the further capitalism goes in its devaluation of human life, the more women will work outside of the home: far from being liberating, according to the *Manifesto,* this work will bind women into the exploitative system of capital. The inevitable outcome, however—fortunately for the laborer but not for the Bourgeois—is that women will be united with the proletarian class, making for a more unified, more powerful revolutionary force.

The Bourgeoisie claim that under communism there will be communality of wives, and that this will be immoral. However, counter Marx and Engels, the Bourgeoisie—through rampant but secret adulterous habits—have already established the communality of wives under capitalism. In reality, they claim, communism will dissolve marriage as it is currently manifested and will restore women to their natural equality with men, where they are no longer possessions, communal or otherwise. This point is further discussed by Engels in *The Origin of the Family.*

THE ORIGIN OF THE FAMILY (1884)

In this monograph, written by Engels after Marx's death, the analysis of marriage roughly outlined in the *Manifesto* is fully developed. Engels relies upon the anthropological theories of the development of the family available at the time, particularly that of Lewis H. Morgan (*Ancient Society,* 1877), in his claims that the modern European monogamous marriage and the family that results from it, far from being natural or universal, are recent historical developments with a relatively narrow sphere of practice. Further, he follows Morgan in his claim that monogamous marriage in most societies—according to Engels, including our own—does not hinder non-monogamous sexual relations, but rather, necessarily exists alongside them.

Following Morgan, Engels quickly outlines in the first part of the essay three kinds of family, corresponding to three historical stages of human development. The *group* or *consanguine* marriage, which existed during the period of savagery prior to organized civilization, was a basically tribal arrangement, in which husbands and

---

[6] Karl Marx and Friedrich Engels, *The Communist Manifesto.*
Translated by Samuel Moore, first published 1888.

wives were simply the adult members of the same generation within the tribal group. Thus, in this stage, brother–sister and husband–wife are essentially the same family relationship; this form of the family is of course extinct, Engels claims, but like all past social forms, its traces remain in later familial arrangements. In the second stage of civilization, which according to Engels is the stage of barbarism—an organized society that is not yet fully civilized—is found the *pairing* or *punaluan* marriage, according to Engels. In this form of family (the word is an Hawaiian one, where some groups still practiced this form of family in Engels's day) the relation of brother–sister was distinguished from the relation of husband–wife. This was a polygamous and polyandrous form of family—in other words, all men had more than one wife and all women more than one husband—and marriages still occurred between adult group members of the same generation, but marriages to one's biological brother or sister were forbidden. It is not until the third stage of historical development, i.e., the civilized world, that *monogamous* marriage first occurs, according to Engels. Monogamous marriage, he claims, is part and parcel of political economies that are founded in codified law—i.e., it is a purely legal relationship that has little to do with either sex or love.

Before the middle ages we cannot speak of individual sexlove.

☞ ☞ ☞

Our sexlove is essentially different from the simple sexual craving, the Eros, of the ancients. In the first place it presupposes mutual love. In this respect woman is the equal of man, while in the antique Eros her permission is by no means always asked. In the second place our sexlove has such a degree of intensity and duration that in the eyes of both parties lack of possession and separation appear as a great, if not the greatest, calamity.

☞ ☞ ☞

Thus it came about that the rising bourgeoisie more and more recognized the freedom of contracting in marriage.

☞ ☞ ☞

Marriage remained class marriage, but within the class a certain freedom of choice was accorded to the contracting parties. And on paper, in moral theory as in poetical description, nothing was more unalterably established than the idea that every marriage was immoral unless founded on mutual sexlove and perfectly free agreement of husband and wife.

☞ ☞ ☞

. . . Monogamy was the first form of the family not founded on natural, but on economic conditions, viz.: the victory of private property over primitive and natural collectivism. Supremacy of the man in the family and generation of children that could be his offspring alone and were destined to be the heirs of his wealth—these were openly avowed by the Greeks to be the sole objects of monogamy.

⌇ ⌇ ⌇

Monogamy, then, does by no means enter history as a reconciliation of man and wife and still less as the highest form of marriage. On the contrary, it enters as the subjugation of one sex by the other, as the proclamation of an antagonism between the sexes unknown in all preceding history. In an old unpublished manuscript written by Marx and myself in 1846, I find the following passage: "The first division of labor is that of man and wife in breeding children." And to-day I may add: The first class antagonism appearing in history coincides with the development of the antagonism of man and wife in monogamy, and the first class oppression with that of the female by the male sex. Monogamy was a great historical progress. But by the side of slavery and private property it marks at the same time that epoch which, reaching down to our days, takes with all progress also a step backwards, relatively speaking, and develops the welfare and advancement of one by the woe and submission of the other.

⌇ ⌇ ⌇

The old relative freedom of sexual intercourse by no means disappeared with the victory of the pairing or even of the monogamous family.

⌇ ⌇ ⌇

By hetaerism Morgan designates sexual intercourse of men with unmarried women outside of the monogamous family, flourishing, as is well known, during the whole period of civilization in many different forms and tending more and more to open prostitution. This hetaerism is directly derived from group marriage, from the sacrificial surrender of women for the purpose of obtaining the right to chastity.

⌇ ⌇ ⌇

Here monogamy, there hetaerism and its most extreme form, prostitution. Hetaerism is as much a social institution as all others. It continues the old sexual freedom—for the benefit of the men. In reality not only permitted, but also assiduously practised by the ruling class, it is denounced only nominally. Still in practice this denunciation strikes by no means the men who indulge in it, but only the women. These are ostracised and cast out by society, in order to proclaim once more the fundamental law of unconditional male supremacy over the female sex.

However, a second contradiction is thereby developed within monogamy itself. By the side of the husband, who is making his life pleasant by hetaerism, stands the neglected wife. And you cannot have one side of the contradiction without the other, just as you cannot have the whole apple after eating half of it. Nevertheless this seems to have been the idea of the men, until their wives taught them a lesson. Monogamy introduces two permanent social characters that were formerly unknown: the standing lover of the wife and the cuckold. The men had gained the victory over the women, but the vanquished magnanimously provided the coronation. In addition to monogamy and hetaerism, adultery became an unavoidable social institution—denounced, severely punished, but irrepressible.

The certainty of paternal parentage rested as of old on moral conviction at best, and in order to solve the unreconcilable contradiction, the code Napoléon decreed in its article 312: "L'enfant conçu pendant le mariage a pour père le mari;" the child conceived during marriage has for its father—the husband. This is the last result of three thousand years of monogamy.

⌒ ⌒ ⌒

Civil matrimony in our day is of two kinds. In Catholic countries, the parents provide a fitting spouse for their son as of old, and the natural consequence is the full development of the contradictions inherent to monogamy: voluptuous hetaerism on the man's part, voluptuous adultery of the woman. Probably the Catholic church has abolished divorce for the simple reason that it had come to the conclusion, there was as little help for adultery as for death. In Protestant countries, again, it is the custom to give the bourgeois son more or less liberty in choosing his mate. Hence a certain degree of love may be at the bottom of such a marriage and for the sake of propriety this is always assumed, quite in keeping with Protestant hypocrisy. In this case hetaerism is carried on less strenuously and adultery on the part of the woman is not so frequent. But as human beings remain under any form of marriage what they were before marrying, and as the citizens of Protestant countries are mostly philistines, this Protestant monogamy on the average of the best cases confines itself to the community of a leaden ennui, labeled wedded bliss.

⌒ ⌒ ⌒

In both cases the marriage is influenced by the class environment of the participants, and in this respect it always remains conventional. This conventionalism often enough results in the most pronounced prostitution— sometimes of both parties, more commonly of the women. She is distinguished from a courtisane only in that she does not offer her body for money by the hour like a commodity, but sells it into slavery for once and all.

⌒ ⌒ ⌒

Sexual love in man's relation to woman becomes and can become the rule among the oppressed classes alone, among the proletarians of our day—no matter whether this relation is officially sanctioned or not.

Here all the fundamental conditions of classic monogamy have been abolished. Here all property is missing and it was precisely for the protection and inheritance of this that monogamy and man rule were established. Hence all incentive to make this rule felt is wanting here. More still, the funds are missing. Civil law protecting male rule applies only to the possessing classes and their intercourse with proletarians. Law is expensive and therefore the poverty of the laborer makes it meaningless for his relation to his wife. Entirely different personal and social conditions decide in this case. And finally, since the great industries have removed women from the home to the labor market and to the factory, the last remnant of man rule in the proletarian home has lost its ground—except, perhaps, a part of the brutality against women that has become general since the advent of monogamy. Thus the family of the proletarian is no longer strictly monogamous, even with all the most passionate love and the most unalterable loyalty of both parties, and in spite of any possible clerical or secular sanction. Consequently the eternal companions of monogamy, hetaerism and adultery, play an almost insignificant role here. The woman has practically regained the right of separation, and if a couple cannot agree, they rather separate.

⌐ ⌐ ⌐

True, our jurists hold that the progress of legislation continually lessens all cause of complaint for women. The modern systems of civil law recognize, first that marriage, in order to be legal, must be a contract based on voluntary consent of both parties, and secondly that during marriage the relations of both parties shall be founded on equal rights and duties. These two demands logically enforced will, so they claim, give to women everything they could possibly ask.

⌐ ⌐ ⌐

The legal equality of man and woman in marriage is by no means better founded. Their legal inequality inherited from earlier stages of society is not the cause, but the effect of the economic oppression of women. In the ancient communistic household comprising many married couples and their children, the administration of the household entrusted to women was just as much a public function, a socially necessary industry, as the procuring of food by men. In the patriarchal and still more in the monogamous family this was changed. The administration of the household lost its public character. It was no longer a concern of society. It became a private service. The women became the first servant of the house, excluded from participation in social production. Only by the great industries of our time the access to social production was again opened for women—for proletarian women alone, however. This is done in such a manner that they remain excluded from public production and cannot earn anything, if they fulfill their duties in the private service of the family; or that they are unable to attend to their family duties, if they wish to participate in public industries and earn a living independently. . . . The modern monogamous family is founded on the open or disguised domestic slavery of women, and modern society is a mass composed of molecules in the form of monogamous families. . . . In the family, he is the bourgeois, the woman represents the proletariat.

⌐ ⌐ ⌐

The emancipation of women is primarily dependent on the re-introduction of the whole female sex into the public industries. To accomplish this, the monogamous family must cease to be the industrial unit of society.

⌐ ⌐ ⌐

What we may anticipate about the adjustment of sexual relations after the impending downfall of capitalist production is mainly of a negative nature and mostly confined to elements that will disappear. But what will be added? That will be decided after a new generation has come to maturity: a race of men who never in their lives have had any occasion for buying with money or other economic means of power the surrender of a women; a race of women who have never had any occasion for surrendering to any man for any other reason but love, or for refusing to surrender to their lover from fear of economic consequences. Once such people are in the world, they will not give a moment's thought to what we today believe should be their course. They will follow their own practice and fashion their own public opinion about the individual practice of every person—only this and nothing more.[7]

Modern monogamous marriage, then, according to Engels, is nothing more than a Bourgeois sham; it exists in order to maintain property relations and nothing else. Where property relations count for little—i.e., among the Proletariat—or after private property is entirely abolished, monogamous marriage as we know it will not exist. A more "natural" relation, based on love, attraction, and mutual respect will replace the crass conventions of capitalism, in which, according to Engels, marriage is nothing but a legitimated form of prostitution.

Notice how for Engels, the monogamous marriage carries with it all the (for him, more "natural") traces of earlier forms of sexual and familial relations. It always and necessarily retains—albeit under a cloud of social ostracism—polygamous and polyandrous relations in the practice of adultery. It is precisely because adultery is never really abolished under monogamous systems that Engels believes his claim is demonstrated that monogamous marriage is unrelated to either sex or love, whatever the romantic rhetoric used by the Bourgeoisie to enforce it. In this sense, the primordial Hegelian master–slave relationship still glimmers under the surface of the monogamous marriage, despite enlightened claims about legal equality and democracy. For Engels, monogamous marriage always of necessity enslaves or subordinates the wife to the husband, because her exclusive knowledge of the paternity of the child—who will inherit the family property—must be submitted to her husband so that property can run along the male line of the family.

In addition, Engels claims that because monogamous marriage is an inherently economic relation, it always carries within it the traces of the class conflicts of the society of which it is a part. Hence, under capitalism, the husband "is the Bourgeois, the woman represents the proletariat." Thus, for Engels, following Marx, whether the woman works outside the home is irrelevant to the question of her emancipation: by virtue of her marriage, she is necessarily part of an oppressed class. Hence, in disagreement with Mill's utilitarianism, Marxist theory claims that reform within the capitalist system will never achieve true equality for women. As long as the system exists, the raw class conflict between owner and worker will plague sexual relations. The entire system must fall, according to Engels, before any genuine love and happiness can take place between man and woman.

---

[7] Friedrich Engels, *The Origin of the Family, Private Property and the State*. Translated by Ernest Untermann (Chicago: Charles H. Kerr & Co., 1902).

6. SØREN KIERKEGAARD
(Danish, 1813–1855)

Generally acknowledged as the father of the philosophical movement called "existentialism," Kierkegaard was an exceptionally complicated author, consistently concerned over the irrational nature of faith and the obstacle that faith presents to a rational human nature. In all his works, Kierkegaard returns to the claim that human existence is *choice,* that one's character, one's values—indeed truth itself— is always a result of human decisions. Human choices, then, are fundamentally free, and as such, according to Kierkegaard, our choices are frightening, almost overwhelming. In our hurry to overcome the anxiety that our freedom elicits from us, human beings try, Kierkegaard claimed, to make their choices seem *rational, reasonable*—but this can only ever be an excuse, a masquerade through which we make ourselves seem more in control of the world than we really are. In this sense, since we are trying to escape our freedom, human beings can be said to desire to be slaves—but to pretend to be masters.

While many existentialists after Kierkegaard claimed that the belief in human freedom was inconsistent with religious faith, Kierkegaard believed that a genuine recognition of one's freedom inevitably leads to God. Ultimately, according to Kierkegaard, the various facades with which human beings cover over their freedom wear thin, and they are plunged into a state of despair. Many will revisit or remain in that despair for a lifetime, but, he claimed, some will finally find happiness in an irrational "leap of faith." Kierkegaard did not believe that there was any way to rationalize the choice of a religious life—in fact, he tried to show that the essence of religion was its paradox, that truly religious claims were self-contradictory and could not be rationally accommodated. Only this sort of paradox, he claimed, could demonstrate to human beings that despite our freedom and rationality we are fundamentally limited creatures, and only this would finally allay our anxiety in a meaningful way.

Kierkegaard exemplified these claims through a stylistic device of indirect authorship. He regularly takes on various characters—kinds of consciousness, or choices, or in other words *kinds of lives*—as pseudonyms. Through these he puts forward in the first person examples of lives for the reader to try out and reflect upon. In this way, Kierkegaard demonstrates that each individual is, inside, a multiplicity of characters, the choice among which is at any moment her or his own. The reader's choice need not be rationally motivated. Rather, Kierkegaard implies, the reader will experience the interior motivations of the character and will be comforted or disturbed by them, as is the pseudonymic narrator.

EITHER/OR (1843)

Either/Or, the only work of Kierkegaard's excerpted here, is throughout its two volumes, among other things, an investigation of the existential or symbolic significance of gender and of sexual relations. Its title indicates Kierkegaard's fundamental belief in the necessity of choice—existence presents to us an inescapable "either/or"—as well as a criticism of the Hegelian notion of truth in which opposing truths can exist together in the dialectical progress of history. Against Hegel, Kierkegaard indicates that the life of pleasure and desire, for instance, is not incorporated into the religious or ethical life; we cannot have both, but must choose between them.

The work is put across in a complicated mass of pseudonyms. At base, it is a comparison of two lives: the life of the aesthete (called "A")—a young Don Juan who doesn't do much of anything for a living—and the life of the ethical man (called "B")—a middle-aged judge. A's papers and diaries, and the series of letters written to him by B, have supposedly been found in an old desk drawer by the pretend-editor of the work, called Victor Eremita. In the last of B's letters to A is included a copy of sermon by an old friend of B's, a "pastor in Jutland." Thus, we have four male characters representing three lives—the aesthetic life, the ethical life, and the religious life—and their "editor," who brings them all together and reflects upon them. Each life is essentially identified by its relationship to women: seduction for the aesthete, marriage for the ethical man, and celibacy for the religious man. It seems that for Kierkegaard, one's stance towards women is a crucial determinant of one's life—the pretty young thing, the wife, and the symbol of abject devotion, all represented by women, are essential guides for men's choices. All of these characters, of course, are parts of Kierkegaard—and parts of us—as Victor Eremita indicates in his Preface:

THE PREFACE BY VICTOR EREMITA

> During my constant occupation with the papers, it dawned upon me that they might be looked at from a new point of view, by considering all of them as the work of one man. I know very well everything that can be urged against this view, that it is unhistorical, improbable, unreasonable, that one man should be the author of both parts, although the reader might easily be tempted to the play on words, that he who says A must also say B. However, I have not yet been able to relinquish the idea. Let us imagine a man who had lived through both of these phases, or who had thought upon both. A's papers contain a number of attempts to formulate an aesthetic philosophy of life. A single, coherent, aesthetic view of life can scarcely be carried out. B's papers contain an ethical view of life. As I let this thought sink into my soul, it became clear to me that I might make use of it in choosing a title. The one I have selected precisely expresses this.

We can see that A and B are not simply two characters hashing out their philosophies of life, but two stages of a single person's life. We will not be looking, then, at the pros and cons of certain life paths, so much as at the natural decline of one set of beliefs and one possible result of its self-destructiveness.

DIAPSALMATA

A's papers, which comprise volume one of *Either/Or,* consist of a set of essays, from two of which we take passages—the first, entitled *Diapsalmata* and the last, entitled *Diary of the Seducer.* Of the *Diapsalmata* (the name comes from that of the repeating refrains at the end of psalms) Victor Eremita writes: "It seems as if A had become afraid of [his own writing], as if it continued to terrify him, like a troubled dream when it is told."[8] In other words, Kierkegaard is telling the reader through his character Eremita that A's "aesthetic" life has not made A happy; quite the opposite. The *Diapsalmata,* as a "preface" for the *Diary,* encourages the reader to interpret A's lighthearted and amoral seduction critically.

> I lie stretched out, inactive; the only thing I see is emptiness, the only thing I move about in is emptiness. I do not even suffer pain. The vulture constantly devoured Prometheus' liver . . . that was at least an interruption, even though a monotonous one. Even pain has lost its refreshment for me. If I were offered all the glories of the world, or all its pain, the one would move me as little as the other.

෴ ෴ ෴

EITHER/OR

AN ECSTATIC LECTURE

If you marry, you will regret it; if you do not marry, you will also regret it; if you marry or do not marry, you will regret both; whether you marry or do not marry, you will regret both. Laugh at the world's follies, you will regret it; weep over them, you will also regret that; laugh at the world's follies or weep over them, you will regret both; whether you laugh at the world's follies or weep over them, you will regret both. Believe a woman, you will regret it, believe her not, you will also regret that; believe a woman, or believe her not, you will regret both; whether you believe a woman or believe her not, you will regret both. Hang yourself, you will regret it; do not hang yourself, and you will also regret that; hang yourself or do not hang yourself, you will regret both; whether you hang yourself or do not hang yourself, you will regret both.

In these despondent lines we see the existential results of choosing the aesthetic life: there is no coherence, no beginnings or ends, and no surprises for such a consciousness; because everything in this life is interesting and arranged for the achievement of the greatest pleasure, there is nothing that stands out of the ordinary. Everything is possible here, and everything is equally meaningless.

It is noteworthy that A's aesthetic "either/or"—(basically, that it doesn't ever matter which one chooses) is characterized first and repetitively in terms of choices about women. Through the rest of the work Kierkegaard will symbolize all human choices as choices about how men relate to women. In that sense the man—or the three men, in this case—for Kierkegaard, is the human being insofar as he is always the freely choosing agent, the one who must face the "either/or." However, the

---

[8] Søren Kierkegaard, *Either/Or*, vol. I, translated by David F. Swenson and Lillian Marvin Swenson; with revisions and a foreword by Howard A. Johnson. Princeton: Princeton University Press, 1959, p. 9.

character of a human life, its relation to or distance from the religious life, will be figured by Kierkegaard as its relation to women. As we will see, the seducer will engage in any relationship to a woman that he believes will result in an interesting experience; it's all the same to him—regrettable.

THE DIARY OF THE SEDUCER

The "Diary," a fascinating moment in philosophical literature, recounts and ruminates upon the seduction of a young girl, Cordelia. She is one in an indefinitely long series of such seductions, or so we are led to believe (after all, the seducer is supposedly writing to himself, and there remains the possibility that he is self-deluded). The diary contains several different kinds of writing: some of it is reportage about the progress of the seducer's plans—his first sight of Cordelia, his conniving to meet her, become engaged to her, leave her, etc.; some of it consists in his philosophical reflections upon the aesthetic life and the proper techniques of seduction, or upon women in particular or in general; and some of the diary consists in supposed copies of letters that the seducer has written to Cordelia, perhaps intended as practice exercises for aspiring Dons Juan. The letters are signed "Johannes," but as Victor Eremita notes in his preface, A has himself denied the authorship of the diary and claims to have "found" it; Eremita speculates that A may be ashamed of his aesthetic life, or regret it unbearably. The "Diary" is very long, and the passages that appear here emphasize the second of these categories—the ruminations upon seduction and women; some recounting is excerpted for the sake of coherence, but none of the letters.

> He who does not know how to compass a girl about so that she loses sight of everything which he does not wish her to see, he who does not know how to poetize himself in a girl's feelings so that it is from her that everything issues as he wishes it, he is and remains a bungler; I do not begrudge him his enjoyment. A bungler he is and remains, a seducer, something one can by no means call me. I am an aesthete, an eroticist, one who has understood the nature and meaning of love, who believes in love and knows it from the ground up, and only makes the private reservation that no love affair should last more than six months at the most, and that every erotic relationship should cease as soon as one has had the ultimate enjoyment.
>
> ⌒ ⌒ ⌒
>
> ### 3RD DAY.
>
> So now I am engaged; so is Cordelia, and that is about all she knows about the whole matter.
>
> ⌒ ⌒ ⌒
>
> What I now have to do is, on the one hand, to get everything in order for getting the engagement broken, thus assuring myself of a more beautiful and significant relation to Cordelia; on the other hand, I must improve the time to the

uttermost by enjoying all the charm, all the loveliness with which nature has so abundantly endowed her, enjoying myself in it, still with the self-limitation and circumspection that prevents any violation of it. When I have brought her to the point where she has learned what it is to love, and what it is to love me, then the engagement breaks like an imperfect mold, and she belongs to me. This is the point at which others become engaged, and have a good prospect of a boring marriage for all eternity. Well, let others have it.

Woman will always offer an inexhaustible fund of material for reflection, an eternal abundance for observation. The man who feels no impulse toward the study of woman may, as far as I am concerned, be what he will; one thing he certainly is not, he is no aesthetician. This is the glory and divinity of aesthetics, that it enters into relation only with the beautiful: it has to do essentially only with fiction and the fair sex. It makes me glad and causes my heart to rejoice when I represent to myself how the sun of feminine loveliness diffuses its rays into an infinite manifold, refracting itself in a confusion of tongues, where each individual woman has her little part of the whole wealth of femininity, yet so that her other characteristics harmoniously center about this point. In this sense feminine beauty is infinitely divisible.

Every woman has her share: the merry smile, the roguish glance, the wistful eye, the pensive head, the exuberant spirits, the quiet sadness, the deep foreboding, the brooding melancholy, the earthly homesickness, the unbaptized movements, the beckoning brows, the questioning lips, the mysterious forehead, the ensnaring curls, the concealing lashes, the heavenly pride, the earthly modesty, the angelic purity, the secret blush, the light step, the airy grace, the languishing posture, the dreamy yearning, the inexplicable sighs, the willowy form, the soft outlines, the luxuriant bosom, the swelling hips, the tiny foot, the dainty hand.

I shut up my fan, and gather the fragments into a unity, the parts into a whole. Then my soul is glad, my heart beats, my passion is aflame. This one woman, the only woman in all the world, she must belong to me, she must be mine.

Hence I shall now for variety's sake attempt, myself being cold, to think coldly of woman. I shall attempt to think of woman in terms of her category. Under what category must she be conceived? Under the category of being for another. But this must not be understood in the bad sense, as if the woman who is for me is also for another. Here as always in abstract thinking, it is essential to refrain from every reference to experience; for otherwise, as in the present case, I should find, in the most curious manner, that experience is both for me and against me.

Woman is therefore being for another. Here again, but from another side, it will be necessary not to let oneself be disturbed by experience, which teaches that it is a rare thing to find a woman who is in truth a being for another, since a great many are in general absolutely nothing, either for themselves or for others. Woman shares this category with Nature, and, in general, with everything feminine. Nature as a whole exists only for another; not in the teleological sense, so that one part of Nature exists for another part, but so that the whole of Nature is for an Other—for the Spirit. In the same way with the particulars. The life of the plant, for example, unfolds in all naïvetè its hidden charms and exists only for another. In the same way a mystery, a charade, a secret, a vowel, and so on, has being only for another. And from this it can be explained why, when God created Eve, he caused a deep sleep to fall upon Adam; for woman is the dream of man.

She became flesh and blood, but this causes her to be included under the category of Nature, which is essentially being for another. She awakens first at the touch of love, before that time she is a dream. Yet in her dream life we can distinguish two stages: in the first love dreams about her; in the second, she dreams about love.

As being for another, woman is characterized by pure virginity. Virginity is, namely, a form of being, which, in so far as it is a being for itself, is really an abstraction, and only reveals itself to another. The same characterization also lies in the concept of female innocence. It is therefore possible to say that woman in this condition is invisible. As is well known, there existed no image of Vesta, the goddess who most nearly represented feminine virginity. This form of existence is, namely, jealous for itself aesthetically, just as Jehovah is ethically, and does not desire that there should be any image or even any notion of one. This is the contradiction, that the being which is for another *is* not, and only becomes visible, as it were, by the interposition of another.

This being of woman (for the word *existence* is too rich in meaning, since woman does not persist in and through herself) is rightly described as charm, an expression which suggests plant life, she is a flower, as the poets like to say, and even the spiritual in her is present in a vegetative manner. She is wholly subject to Nature, and hence only aesthetically free. In a deeper sense she first becomes free by her relation to man, and when man courts her properly, there can be no question of a choice. Woman chooses, it is true, but if this choice is thought of as the result of a long deliberation, then this choice is unfeminine. Hence it is, that it is a humiliation to receive a refusal, because the individual in question has rated himself too high, has desired to make another free without having the power.—In this situation there is deep irony. That which merely exists for another has the appearance of being predominant: man sues, woman chooses.

The very concept of woman requires that she be the vanquished, the concept of man, that he be the victor; and yet the victor bows before the vanquished. And yet this is quite natural, and it is only boorishness, stupidity, and lack of erotic sensibility to take no notice of that which immediately yields in this fashion. It has also a deeper ground. Woman is, namely, substance, man is reflection. She does not therefore choose independently; man sues, she chooses. But man's courtship is a question, and her choice only an answer to a question. In a certain sense man is more than woman, in another sense he is infinitely less.

This being for another is the true virginity. If it makes an attempt to be a being for itself, in relation to another being which is being for it, then the opposition reveals itself in an absolute coyness; but this opposition shows at the same time that woman's essential being is being for another. The diametrical opposite to absolute devotion is absolute coyness, which in a converse sense is invisible as the abstraction against which everything breaks, without the abstraction itself coming to life. Femininity now takes on the character of an abstract cruelty, the caricature in its extreme form of the intrinsic feminine brittleness.

Thus, the more I reflect on this matter, I see that my practice is in perfect harmony with my theory. My practice has always been impregnated with the theory that woman is essentially a being for another. Hence it is that the moment has here such infinite significance; for a being for another is always the matter of a moment.

I know very well that husbands say that the woman is also in another sense a being for another, that she is everything to her husband through life. One must make allowance for husbands. I really believe that it is something which they mutually delude one another into thinking.

SEPT. 24

Everything is symbol, I myself am a myth about myself, for is it not as a myth that I hasten to this meeting? Who I am has nothing to do with it.

Her development was my handiwork—soon I shall enjoy my reward.—How much I have gathered into this one moment which now draws nigh.

SEPT. 25

Still, it is over now, and I hope never to see her again. When a girl has given away everything, then she is weak, then she has lost everything.

⌐ ⌐ ⌐

I will have no farewell scene with her; nothing is more disgusting to me than a woman's tears and a woman's prayers, which alter everything, and yet really mean nothing. I have loved her, but from now on she can no longer engross my soul. If I were a god, I would do for her what Neptune did for a nymph: I would change her into a man.

In essence, the seducer seeks in every instance the most interesting experience possible. This indicates that the aesthetic life is inherently a literary one, in which real people and their decisions become mere representations of feelings. In other words, the aesthetic principle, according to Kierkegaard, is to denude one's life of its individual character, of its agency and its activity, in order to fill it with feeling. Thus, the aesthetic life, like the other lives investigated in *Either/Or,* requires a wholehearted devotion to its ideals—in this case, the heightened feelings of being interested, pleased, even pained. The seducer claims that girls are the perfect tool for this endeavor, like catalysts for the aesthete's feelings—as the seducer claims, the girl's are the substance that the aesthete skillfully reflects.

It is therefore according to this "symbolic" or "poeticized" psychology that we should interpret the seducer's analysis of women in the long ruminative passage above. Woman is "being for another," and as such she represents "Nature, and, in general . . . everything feminine." Thus, it seems that woman for the seducer represents femininity, and not vice versa as an ethical thinker might claim. It is noteworthy as well that the seducer uses the nature–culture dichotomy to spell out the genders here, where the seducer is like an artist who uses "nature"—women—as raw material, but also as inspiration. Indeed, the seducer often writes as if his manipulation of Cordelia—in eliciting a "free" choice on her part—helps her to become a more masculine being, a freer agent. The implication is that sexual relations—at least according to the aesthetic mode of thinking—change the character of the parties involved, and "mix" their sexuality. The seducer also figures all this in terms of virginity, that femininity is somehow equated by him with virginity, such that once deflowered, a woman becomes more like a man.

Indeed, that she become a man is the seducer's last wish for Cordelia, once he has had his way with her. She is, it seems, no longer of any use to him as a woman, since for him women are nothing but the promise of excitement. The closing passage implies that, from the point of view of the aesthete, the ethical life is nothing but the attempt to live with a woman after she has been used and changed by her first sexual experience with a man. For Johannes, this idea is foolish and distasteful, but in principle his view is reminiscent of Hegel's in which the "ethical" stage is that of the family. By showing us the aesthete's disdain for the ethical life, Kierkegaard demonstrates that from the "existential" point of view, the ethical life is not at all a natural development from the life of desire. It must be adopted by a conscious choice, a choice that an aesthete is likely not to make. It is irresponsible, Kierkegaard implies, to underestimate the aesthete or to assume that he will see the "error" of his ways and choose an ethical life.

EQUILIBRIUM

B, the "ethical man," tries in his letters to A precisely to make A "see the error of his ways." The second volume of *Either/Or* consists entirely of B's three letters to A, the first two of which are farcically long. Their titles, "The Aesthetic Validity of Marriage" and "Equilibrium Between the Aesthetical and the Ethical in the Composition of the Personality," indicate Kierkegaard's idea of the logic of the ethical life. In contrast to the dramatic, descriptive style of A, which is geared either to make his choice of the aesthetic life appealing or disgusting on its own artistic merits, B tries at length to argue with A that there is *aesthetic* value to the *ethical* life. In other words, B is a Hegelian by Kierkegaard's interpretation; he believes that traces of an earlier, incomplete aesthetic existence can be retained within the ethical one that progresses rationally from it. We already know from Volume I of course, (A's writings) that these rational appeals carry no weight whatsoever with the aesthete. Thus, despite B's earnest efforts, Kierkegaard makes readers evaluate the ethical life existentially, by deciding whether we experience B's first-person narrative as happy or unhappy.

All of the second volume of *Either /Or* is taken up with question of the meaning of marriage. The passage below is taken from the second letter, in which B describes the wonders of marriage from the ethical point of view. He wants to show that married life is an improvement over the aesthetic life by any standard, because it retains everything good about the latter.

So then one either has to live aesthetically or one has to live ethically.

My either/or does not in the first instance denote the choice between good and evil; it denotes the choice whereby one chooses good *and* evil/or excludes them. Here the question is under what determinants one would contemplate the whole of existence and would himself live. That the man who chooses good and evil chooses the good is indeed true, but this becomes evident only afterwards; for the aesthetical is not the evil but neutrality, and that is the reason why I affirmed that it is the ethical which constitutes the choice. It is, therefore, not so much a question of choosing between willing the good *or* the evil, as of choosing to will, but by this in turn the good and evil are posited.

The ethical view that it is every man's duty to work in order to live has accordingly two advantages over the aesthetical view. In the first place, it is consonant with reality and explains something universal in it, whereas the aesthetical view propounds something accidental and explains nothing. In the second place, it construes man with a view to his perfection, sees him in his true beauty.

Our hero, then, is willing to work, not because it is for him a *dura necessitas,* but because he regards it as the most beautiful thing and the most perfect.

But precisely because he is willing to work, his occupation can be work and not slave-labor.

And then what next? You will smile, you think I have something up my sleeve. You already shudder at my prosaic intention, for you say, "Now it comes to nothing less than getting him married."

. . . What is it that marriage does? Does it deprive him of anything, does it take away from her any beauty, does it abolish one single difference? By no means. But it shows to him all these things as accidents so long as marriage is external to him, and only when he gives to the difference the universal expression is he in secure possession of it. The ethical teaches him that this relationship is the absolute, For the relationship is the ordinary and universal. It deprives him of the vain joy of being the extraordinary in order to give him the true joy of being the universal. It brings him into harmony with existence as a whole, teaching him to rejoice in this.

So the ethical view of marriage has several advantages over every aesthetic interpretation of love. It elucidates the universal, not the accidental. It does not show how a couple of very singular people with extraordinary traits might become happy, but how every married couple may become so. It regards the relationship as the absolute, and so does not apprehend the differences as guarantees but comprehends them as tasks. It regards the relationship as the absolute and hence beholds love with a view to its beauty, that is, its freedom; it understands historical beauty.

. . . You so often deride the other sex. I have often admonished you to desist. Regard, if you will, a young girl as an incomplete being; I should like to say to you, however, "My good wise man, go to the ant and become wise, learn from a girl how to make time pass, for in this she has an innate virtuosity." Perhaps she has no conception such as a man has of severe and persistent labor, but she is never idle, is always occupied, time is never long for her.

In general woman has an innate talent, a primitive gift and an absolute virtuosity for explaining finiteness. When man was created he stood there as the master and lord of all nature; nature's pomp and splendor, the entire wealth of finiteness awaited only his beck and call, but he did not comprehend what he was to do with it all.

⌐ ⌐ ⌐

Thus he stood, an imposing figure, thoughtfully absorbed in himself, and yet comic, for one must indeed smile at this rich man who did not know how to use his wealth—but also tragic, for he could not use it. Then was woman created. She was in no embarrassment, she knew at once how one had to handle this affair; without fuss, without preparation, she was ready at once to begin. This was the first comfort bestowed upon man. She drew near to him, humble as a child, joyful as a child, pensive as a child. She wanted only to be a comfort to him, to make up for his lack (a lack which she did not comprehend, having no suspicion that she was supplying it), to abbreviate for him the intervals. And, lo, her humble comfort became life's richest joy, her innocent pastimes life's most beautiful adornment, her childish play life's deepest meaning.

A woman comprehends finiteness, she understands it from the bottom up, therefore she is beauteous (essentially regarded, every woman is beauteous), therefore she is charming (and that no man is), therefore she is happy (happy as no man is or should be), therefore she is in harmony with existence (as no man is or should be). Therefore one may say that her life is happier than that of man; for finiteness can perhaps make a human being happy, infinitude as such can never do so. She is more perfect than man, for surely one who can explain something is more perfect than one who is in pursuit of an explanation. Woman explains finiteness, man is in chase of infinitude. So it should be, and each has one's own pain; for woman bears children with pain, but man conceives ideas with pain and woman does not have to know the anguish of doubt or the torment of despair, she is not obliged to stand outside the idea, but she has it at secondhand. But because woman thus explains finiteness she is man's deepest life, but a life which should always be concealed and hidden as the root of life always is. For this reason I hate all talk about the emancipation of woman.

⌐ ⌐ ⌐

Let man give up the claim to be the lord and master of nature, let him yield this place to woman, she is its mistress, it understands her, and she understands it, everything of hers it follows. For this reason she is everything to man, for she bestows upon him finiteness, without her he is an unstable spirit, an unhappy creature who cannot find rest, has no abiding place. I have often had joy in viewing woman in this light; to me she is a symbol of the congregation, and the spirit is in great embarrassment when it has not a congregation to dwell in, and when it dwells in the congregation it is the spirit of the congregation.

The ethical man's life is filled with a logic of compromise, self-sacrifice, and or-dinariness. He tries to argue with A that marriage, which for both A and B seems al-ways to accompany a regular job, is not so much a sacrifice of pleasure as it is a fulfillment of the emptiness in which the life of pleasure inevitably results, and we have seen that the aesthetic life does indeed have its empty and lonely aspect. B certainly appears self-satisfied, but is this the same as his being happy?

Of interest for our purposes, of course, are the similarities and differences between A's and B's views regarding what woman represents. B focuses on two themes in the ethical view of women. First, B stresses that marriage both universalizes and concretizes the husband and wife, whereas the aesthetic life leaves both parties in a figurative, neither universal nor concrete, world. In other words, he claims that marriage, as a social institution with historical roots that individuals live out in the present in their own particular way, gives concrete lived reality to an ideal. In this way, marriage represents the logic of all ethical behavior, in which human beings really try to act in accordance with long-standing moral ideals. The aesthetic life, he implies, is an essentially disorganized, distracted life, which makes its practitioner feel like several people and like no one at the same time. The ethical life, he claims, integrates one's experience and makes one into an individual person who can be blamed or credited for his action. As B describes it, this organization of a life is provided by the "finiteness" that only wives can bring to men's experience. This, it may be noted, is in disagreement with the preSocratic Greek figurations we saw in Part One, and is allied more with the biblical view. It would seem that the man who decides to marry brings the universal element into his life, and his wife, in yielding to that decision, brings the concrete element.

Second, B claims that a wife "fills up time," which is therefore "never long for her." This element of work, happy or unhappy, simply does not enter into the aesthetic life, whereas we see that for B, both husband and wife are essentially defined in relation to work, and that work characterizes the relation of each to time. The decision to marry, then, is inherently the decision to think of one's life as continuing over time. The aesthete, from B's point of view, lives only for the present and consequently lives only *in* the present; A, according to B, has no historical sense, no sense of his own future, no preparation for his old age, etc. For B, this seems a very unrealistic way to conduct one's life. Rather, B quite reasonably chooses to acknowledge the past and plan for the future, and he presents his wife as an important part of his formula for doing so.

Clearly, despite the social legitimacy with which he would admit marriage endows women, Kierkegaard no more advocates the ethical life than he does the aesthetic. Indeed, in his own life Kierkegaard decided not to marry, despite his devotion and a short-lived engagement to a woman named Regina Olsen. Both A and B have a certain logic to their actions, and both present a life with a certain appeal; yet both also leave the reader with a sense of uneasiness, a distrust of the praises that each man's sings about his choice in life.

ULTIMATUM

In contrast to these two lengthy narratives of lives is the short sermon with which Kierkegaard ends *Either/Or.* B presents it in his last letter to A, supposedly having been moved by it and wanting to share its message with A. Since B does not provide his usual lengthy analysis of the sermon, we may imagine that he has taken it seriously; perhaps he has no more to say in the person of the ethical man, having finally chosen to follow the religious life. Perhaps, on the other hand, the ball is simply being left in the reader's court.

The sermon, entitled "The Edification Implied in the Thought that As Against God We Are Always in the Wrong," presented in the letter called "Ultimatum," does not mention woman or women at all. It is, in a literary sense, "chaste." Rather, it presents the experience of abject devotion to a beloved—a kind of love we have seen in neither A nor B—as the edifying experience that marks the religious life. The gender signification here, then, is to be decided by the reader's own gender identification with the experience described.

Let us strive to set them at rest by meditating upon

THE EDIFICATION IMPLIED IN THE THOUGHT THAT
AS AGAINST GOD WE ARE ALWAYS IN THE WRONG.

Being in the wrong—can any feeling be thought of more painful than this? And do we not see that men would rather suffer anything than admit that they are in the wrong?

⌒ ⌒ ⌒

Yet it is not by this we would quiet doubt and allay concern, but by reflecting upon the edification implied in the thought that we are always in the wrong. Can, then, this opposite consideration have the same effect?

Your life brings you into manifold relationships with other people, to some of whom you are drawn by a more heartfelt love than you feel for others. Now if such a man who was the object of your love were to do you a wrong, it would pain you deeply, would it not? You would carefully rehearse everything that had occurred—but then would you say, I know of myself that I am in the right, this thought shall tranquilize me? Oh, if you loved him, this thought would not tranquilize you, you would explore anew every possibility. You would not be able to come to any other conclusion but that he was in the wrong, and yet this certainty would disquiet you, you would wish that you might be in the wrong, you would try to find something which might speak in his defense, and if you did not find it, you would first find comfort in the thought that you were in the wrong.

⌒ ⌒ ⌒

So it is painful to be in the wrong, and the more painful the more frequently it occurs; it is edifying to be in the wrong, and the more edifying the more frequently it occurs! That is clearly a contradiction.

⌒ ⌒ ⌒

Hence, to wish to be in the wrong is the expression for an infinite relationship; to wish to be in the right or to find it painful to be in the wrong is the expression for a finite relationship! So, then, it is edifying always to be in the wrong, for only the infinite edifies, not the finite!

7. FRIEDRICH NIETZSCHE
(German, 1844–1900)

Berated by some contemporary feminists for his explicit misogynist statements and championed by others as a first proponent of an alternate and possibly "feminine" view of truth and knowledge, Nietzsche is a crucially important but frustratingly ambiguous figure in the history of thinking about gender. Nietzsche, unlike Hegel, did not believe that the standards of truth progressed over history, or that there was any absolute standard presupposed in human reason. Rather, Nietzsche claimed that truth was "an error" and that there were infinitely many equally true *interpretations* of the world available to an individual consciousness at any time.

The interpretation one chooses, according to Nietzsche, has nothing to do with reasons or logic, but only with the set of presupposed *values* that guide one's choices. Thus, Nietzsche subsumed philosophy under a study of psychological motivations. Rather than inquiring into whether a claim, say the claim that God exists, is true, Nietzsche always asks why someone would believe such a thing; what *kind of person* would claim that there is a God, etc. As Nietzsche saw it, most people's choices about what to believe are motivated by weaknesses—fear, loneliness, hatred, loss—and as such, always indicate a slavish temperament. The value system to which one attaches oneself, within which a particular claim is true or false, is always a kind of master over one—but it is also a strategic alliance; one's values become a protective force that strengthen one's position. For instance, Nietzsche interpreted some people's belief in God as their invocation of an all-powerful bully who will take revenge on their enemies.

Since everybody human must have some system of values and make some claims to truth, Nietzsche believed that humanity, as a species, was inherently weak and insidious, by its very nature slavish. All the great achievements in religion, science, and philosophy were by his reckoning just so much foolish servitude to unworthy ideals. In his work *Thus Spake Zarathustra,* passages of which are excerpted here, Nietzsche prophesies that a far better, stronger kind of individual—which he famously called the *Superman*—would overcome humanity and its weaknesses. Claims such as these have been interpreted in wildly disparate ways.[9] This is exactly as Nietzsche would have had it; as we will see, his writing—whose implicit theory of truth has been called "perspectivism"—is calculated to yield varied interpretations. We may say however, generously, that Nietzsche sought ultimately to incite people to lead better lives, to be free and strong and honorable. Thus, he often writes to provoke readers to question themselves as readers, to identify their values and to choose those that are glorious and lively rather than anonymous and sniveling. As Nietzsche put it, his "formula" or goal was "a revaluation of all values."

Ironically, despite this apparent progressivism, Nietzsche was a profoundly nostalgic thinker. Trained in Greek philology, the value system that Nietzsche seemed to

---

[9] including, notoriously, as a program for Nazi intellectuals.

find the most appealing was the preHomeric "honor" culture of the ancient Greeks, much of whose character can be gleaned from readings in Parts One and Two.

It may already be apparent how ambivalent is Nietzsche's view of women and the differences between the sexes. Nietzsche follows the tradition, similar in many of the readings thus far, that the man represents humanity as a whole. But we can see that Nietzsche is not very enamored with either humanity or with men. On the other hand, he was not enamored of the idea of truth, and he claims in *Beyond Good and Evil* and *The Gay Science* that "truth is woman. . . ." His writings are riddled with scathing analyses of woman's character; yet, as with men, he finds something hopeful in them.

In a general sense, however, we may say that Nietzsche's ambivalence about women is his ambivalence about values. He tends to figure men as human, and therefore as weak, slavish, and incomplete; and to figure men's goals and ideals—knowledge, truth, science, strength—as feminine or as women. Since these goals are often vicious or unworthy masters, and yet as such, they often take the kind of disdainful position that Nietzsche admires, Nietzsche figures women as both horrifying and wonderful, depending on the context—or sometimes in the same context.[10]

THE BIRTH OF TRAGEDY (PUBL. 1872/ REVISED 1886)

Nietzsche's first book, to which he added an "attempt at a self-criticism" for the second edition, is in many ways his most traditional. In it, he lays out a theory of artistic creativity as the dialectical resolution of a conflict between two artistic forces. Since his interest is in the development of Greek tragedy—which he nostalgically took to be the high point of great art—he named these two forces after two Greek gods—Apollo and Dionysus. Early in the work, Nietzsche makes explicit the analogy between artistic creation and sexual reproduction.

SECTION 1

1

We shall have gained much for the science of aesthetics, once we perceive not merely by logical inference, but with the immediate certainty of vision, that the continuous development of art is bound up with the *Apollinian* and *Dionysian* duality—just as procreation depends on the duality of the sexes, involving perpetual strife with only periodically intervening reconciliations. The terms Dionysian and Apollinian we borrow from the Greeks, who disclose to the discerning mind the profound mysteries of their view of art, not, to be sure, in concepts, but in the intensely clear figures of their gods.

---

[10] It may be of interest that Nietzsche grew up with a pervasive female influence in his life. Except for Nietzsche's father, who died when Nietzsche was young, the rest of the members of his household were women.

In order to grasp these two tendencies, let us first conceive of them as the separate art worlds of *dreams* and *intoxication*. These physiological phenomena present a contrast analogous to that existing between the Apollinian and the Dionysian. It was in dreams, says Lucretius, that the glorious divine figures first appeared to the souls of men; in dreams the great shaper beheld the splendid bodies of superhuman beings.

ॐ ॐ ॐ

. . . Thus the aesthetically sensitive man stands in the same relation to the reality of dreams as the philosopher does to the reality of existence; he is a close and willing observer, for these images afford him an interpretation of life, and by reflecting on these processes he trains himself for life.

ॐ ॐ ॐ

This joyous necessity of the dream experience has been embodied by the Greeks in their Apollo: Apollo, the god of all plastic energies, is at the same time the soothsaying god. He, who (as the etymology of the name indicates) is the "shining one," the deity of light, is also ruler over the beautiful illusion of the inner world of fantasy. The higher truth, the perfection of these states in contrast to the incompletely intelligible everyday world, this deep consciousness of nature, healing and helping in sleep and dreams, is at the same time the symbolical analogue of the soothsaying faculty and of the arts generally, which make life possible and worth living.

ॐ ॐ ॐ

. . . [W]e might call Apollo himself the glorious divine image of the *principium individuationis,* through whose gestures and eyes all the joy and wisdom of "illusion," together with its beauty, speak to us.

ॐ ॐ ॐ

If we add to this terror the blissful ecstasy that wells from the innermost depths of man, indeed of nature, at this collapse of the *principium individuationis,* we steal a glimpse into the nature of the *Dionysian,* which is brought home to us most intimately by the analogy of intoxication.

Either under the influence of the narcotic draught, of which the songs of all primitive men and peoples speak, or with the potent coming of spring that penetrates all nature with joy, these Dionysian emotions awake, and as they grow in intensity everything subjective vanishes into complete self-forgetfulness.

ॐ ॐ ॐ

2

Thus far we have considered the Apollinian and its opposite, the Dionysian, as artistic energies which burst forth from nature herself, *without the mediation of the human artist*—energies in which nature's art impulses are satisfied in the most immediate and direct way—first in the image world of dreams, whose completeness is not dependent upon the intellectual attitude or the artistic culture of any single being; and then as intoxicated reality, which likewise does not heed the single unit, but even seeks to destroy the individual and redeem him by a mystic feeling of oneness. With reference to these immediate art-states of nature, every artist is an "imitator," that is to say, either an Apollinian artist in dreams, or a Dionysian artist in ecstasies, or finally—as for example in Greek tragedy—at once artist in both dreams and ecstasies; so we may perhaps picture him sinking down in his Dionysian intoxication and mystical self-abnegation, alone and apart from the singing revelers, and we may imagine how, through Apollinian dream-inspiration, his own state, i.e., his oneness with the inmost ground of the world, is revealed to him in *symbolical dream image.*

The horrible "witches' brew" of sensuality and cruelty becomes ineffective; only the curious blending and duality in the emotions of the Dionysian revelers remind us—as medicines remind us of deadly poisons—of the phenomenon that pain begets joy, that ecstasy may wring sounds of agony from us. At the very climax of joy there sounds a cry of horror or a yearning lamentation for an irretrievable loss. In these Greek festivals, nature seems to reveal a sentimental trait; it is as if she were heaving a sigh at her dismemberment into individuals. The song and pantomime of such dually-minded revelers was something new and unheard-of in the Homeric-Greek world; and the Dionysian *music* in particular excited awe and terror. If music, as it would seem, had been known previously as an Apollinian art, it was so, strictly speaking, only as the wave beat of rhythm, whose formative power was developed for the representation of Apollinian states. . . .

The distinction between the Apollinian and the Dionysian is something like a form/content distinction; the Apollinian is orderly, structured, accessible, bearable—it is best represented as the dream or illusory element in art, that which brings the artwork to intelligible expression. Nietzsche refers to the Apollinian element as the "principium individuationis," the "principle of individuation" through which an otherwise chaotic whirl is brought to articulation. Thus, in a sense the human individual, insofar as he or she thinks of him or herself as an individual, is Apollinian, and some feminists have associated this tendency with masculinity. Certainly Nietzsche, by calling Nature "she" and associating it with the opposite or Dionysian tendency, adds support to this interpretation, and he adds further support for it in later books. The Dionysian is represented by drunkenness, as inarticulate and confused force that brings the tremendous emotional element to art. In the Dionysian ritual the sense of individuality is lost, and there is instead a unity with nature, with the gods, with death, with all that is not human. If the Dionysian tendency is feminine, then Nietzsche's theory of art places femininity at the edge of humanity, at the border between humanity and the frightening but glorious world of the gods.

THE GAY SCIENCE (PUBL. 1882, REVISED ED. 1887)

Nietzsche referred to this as "the most personal" of all his books, taking on as it did a criticism of philosophy, science, and religion. In this work Nietzsche first made his famous claim that "God is dead," (that idea is developed further in *Thus Spoke Zarathustra*). Like much of Nietzsche's work, it is put forth in short, variously interpretable aphorisms in five books plus a preface, a prelude, and appendix; the latter two of which consist of poems. Certain aphorisms scattered throughout the work take up the questions of women, sex, and sexuality.

FROM BOOK TWO:

68

Will and willingness.—Someone took a youth to a sage and said: "Look, he is being corrupted by women." The sage shook his head and smiled. "It is men," said he, "that corrupt women; and all the failings of women should be atoned by and improved in men. For it is man who creates for himself the image of woman, and woman forms herself according to this image."

"You are too kindhearted about women," said one of those present; "you do not know them." The sage replied: "Will is the manner of men; willingness that of women. That is the law of the sexes—truly, a hard law for women. All of humanity is innocent of its existence; but women are doubly innocent. Who could have oil and kindness enough for them?"

"Damn oil! Damn kindness!" someone else shouted out of the crowd; "women need to be educated better!"—"Men need to be educated better," said the sage and beckoned to the youth to follow him.—The youth, however, did not follow him.

☞ ☞ ☞

72

Mothers.—Animals do not think about females as men do; they consider the female the productive being. Paternal love does not exist among them; merely something like love for the children of a beloved and a kind of getting used to them. The females find in their children satisfaction for their desire to dominate, a possession, an occupation, something that is wholly intelligible to them and can be chattered with: the sum of all this is what mother love is; it is to be compared with an artist's love for his work. Pregnancy has made women kinder, more patient, more timid, more pleased to submit; and just so does spiritual pregnancy produce the character of the contemplative type, which is closely related to the feminine character: it consists of male mothers.—Among animals the male sex is considered the beautiful sex.

FROM BOOK FOUR:

339

Vita femina.—For seeing the ultimate beauties of a work no knowledge or good will is sufficient; this requires the rarest of lucky accidents: The clouds that veil these peaks have to lift for once so that we see them glowing in the sun. Not only do we have to stand in precisely the right spot in order to see this but the unveiling must have been accomplished by our own soul because it needed some external expression and parable, as if it were a matter of having something to hold on to and retain control of itself. But it is so rare for all of this to coincide that I am inclined to believe that the highest peaks of everything good, whether it be a work, a deed, humanity, or nature, have so far remained concealed and veiled from the great majority and even from the best human beings. But what does unveil itself for us, *unveils itself for us once only.*

The Greeks, to be sure, prayed: "Everything beautiful twice and even three times!" They implored the gods with good reason, for ungodly reality gives us the beautiful either not at all or once only. I mean to say that the world is overfull of beautiful things but nevertheless poor, very poor when it comes to beautiful moments and unveilings of these things. But perhaps this is the most powerful magic of life: it is covered by a veil interwoven with gold, a veil of beautiful possibilities, sparkling with promise, resistance, bashfulness, mockery, pity, and seduction. Yes, life is a woman.

FROM BOOK FIVE:

363

How each sex has its own prejudice about love.—Despite all the concessions that I am willing to make to the prejudice in favor of monogamy, I will never admit the claim that man and woman have *equal* rights in love; these do not exist. For man and woman have different conceptions of love; and it is one of the conditions of love in both sexes that neither sex presupposes the same feeling and the same concept of "love" in the other. What woman means by love is clear enough: total devotion (not mere surrender) with soul and body, without any consideration or reserve, rather with shame and horror at the thought of a devotion that might be subject to special clauses or conditions. In this absence of conditions her love is a *faith;* woman has no other faith.

Man, when he loves a woman, wants precisely this love from her and is thus himself as far as can be from the presupposition of feminine love. Supposing, however, that there should also be men to whom the desire for total devotion is not alien; well, then they simply are—not men. A man who loves like a woman becomes a slave; while a woman who loves like a woman becomes *a more perfect woman.*

A woman's passion in its unconditional renunciation of rights of her own presupposes precisely that on the other side there is no equal pathos, no equal will to renunciation; for if both partners felt impelled by love to renounce themselves, we should then get—I do not know what; perhaps an empty space?

Woman wants to be taken and accepted as a possession, wants to be absorbed into the concept of possession, possessed. Consequently, she wants someone who *takes,* who does not give himself or give himself away; on the contrary, he is supposed to become richer in "himself"—through the accretion of strength, happiness, and faith given him by the woman who gives herself. Woman gives herself away, man acquires more—I do not see how one can get around this natural opposition by means of social contracts or with the best will in the world to be just, desirable as it may be not to remind oneself constantly how harsh, terrible, enigmatic, and immoral this antagonism is. For love, thought of in its entirety as great and full, is nature, and being nature it is in all eternity something "immoral."

Nietzsche's deliberate inconsistencies regarding women and their relationship to men are vastly provocative. It is first worth mentioning that most of Nietzsche's claims seem to have more to do with the *figure* or *symbol* of woman and man *for* masculinity and femininity. Nietzsche seems unconcerned with what real women and men are like or with what they should do—as an "immoralist" who rejects the legitimacy of all value systems, he could hardly claim to do such a thing. Rather, he elucidates the effect on one's character of playing certain masculine or feminine roles. These roles themselves, however, admit of vastly different interpretations, just as an actor's role can be "played" many different ways. Throughout these aphorisms, Nietzsche paints masculinity and femininity in terms of several different dichotomies, each a kind of aesthetic opposition between "masculine" and "feminine" *styles* or approaches to life: will vs. willingness, expression vs. hiddenness, stability or death vs. life, possession vs. devotion, respectively. Several of these dichotomies evoke early Greek oppositions (see Parts One and Two of this book), but sometimes only in order to reverse or manipulate them. In this way, Nietzsche provokes readers both to be aware of their traditions and habits of thinking, and to reevaluate them.

BEYOND GOOD AND EVIL (PUBL. 1886)

This book, written by Nietzsche between his authorship of the third and fourth parts of *Zarathustra,* covers an enormous variety of topics, once again in the form of pithy aphorisms, in nine parts plus a preface and epode (epilogue). As the title implies, it takes a critical view of the very concepts of value and belief. The entire project is prefaced by the supposition that truth is woman:

> *Supposing truth to be a woman—what? is the suspicion not well founded that all philosophers, when they have been dogmatists, have had little understanding of women? that the gruesome earnestness, the clumsy importunity with which they have hitherto been in the habit of approaching truth have been inept and improper means for winning a wench? Certainly she has not let herself be won— and today every kind of dogmatism stands sad and discouraged.*

By supposing truth to be a woman, Nietzsche lets the woman stand as a figure for whatever it is—in any context—that human beings (figured as men) seek. This symbolic use of femininity—which we have already seen in Kierkegaard—will be repeated in many "existentialist" works (several are excerpted here), many of which were strongly influenced by Nietzsche. Kinds of lives—i.e., human choices—are characterized here by the ideals towards which they are oriented, and these ideals are depicted as women. Thus, women themselves take on a dichotomous signification here—as both the ideal of man and his repetitive defeat.

In one aphorism in Part Seven (entitled "Our Virtues"), Nietzsche offers a brutal commentary on women who fight against this dual signification of woman as man's unconquerable ideal.

232

Woman wants to be independent: and to that end she is beginning to enlighten men about 'woman as such'—*this* is one of the worst developments in the general *uglification* of Europe. For what must these clumsy attempts on the part of female scientificality and self-exposure not bring to light! Woman has so much reason for shame; in woman there is concealed so much pedanticism, superficiality, schoolmarmishness, petty presumption, petty unbridledness and petty immodesty—one needs only to study her behaviour with children!—which has fundamentally been most effectively controlled and repressed hitherto by *fear* of man. Woe when the 'eternal-boring in woman'—she has plenty of that!—is allowed to venture forth! When she begins radically and on principle to forget her arts and best policy: those of charm, play, the banishing of care, the assuaging of grief and taking lightly, together with her subtle aptitude for agreeable desires! Already female voices are raised which, by holy Aristophanes! make one tremble; there are threatening and medically explicit statements of what woman *wants* of man. Is it not in the worst of taste when woman sets about becoming scientific in that fashion? Enlightenment in this field has hitherto been the affair and endowment of men—we remained 'among ourselves' in this; and whatever women write about 'woman' we may in the end reserve a good suspicion as to whether woman really *wants* or *can* want enlightenment about herself . . . Unless a woman is looking for a new *adornment* for herself in this way—self-adornment pertains to the eternal-womanly, does it not?—she is trying to inspire fear of herself—perhaps she is seeking dominion. But she does not *want* truth: what is truth to a woman! From the very first nothing has been more alien, repugnant, inimical to woman than truth—her great art is the lie, her supreme concern is appearance and beauty. Let us confess it, we men: it is precisely *this* art and *this* instinct in woman which we love and honour: we who have a hard time and for our refreshment like to associate with creatures under whose hands, glances and tender follies our seriousness, our gravity and profundity appear to us almost as folly. Finally I pose the question: has any woman ever conceded profundity to a woman's mind or justice to a woman's heart? And is it not true that on the whole 'woman' has hitherto been slighted most by woman herself—and not at all by us?

⁀ ⁀ ⁀

237

Seven Proverbs for Women
How the slowest tedium flees when a man comes on his knees!
Age and scientific thought give even virtue some support.
Sober garb and total muteness dress a woman with—astuteness.
Who has brought me luck today? God!—and my *couturier.*
Young: a cavern decked about. Old: a dragon sallies out.
Noble name, a leg that's fine, man as well: oh were *he* mine!
Few words, much meaning—slippery ground, many a poor she-ass has found!

Men have hitherto treated women like birds which have strayed down to them
from the heights: as something more delicate, more fragile, more savage,
stranger, sweeter, soulful—but as something which has to be caged up so that it
shall not fly away.

⁀ ⁀ ⁀

239

. . . She wants more, she learns to demand, in the end she finds this tribute of
respect almost offensive, she would prefer competition for rights, indeed a real
stand-up fight: enough, woman loses in modesty. Let us add at once that she also
loses in taste. She unlearns *fear* of man: but the woman who 'unlearns fear'
sacrifices her most womanly instincts. That woman should venture out when the
fear-inspiring in man, let us put it more precisely and say the *man* in man, is no
longer desired and developed, is fair enough, also comprehensible enough; what
is harder to comprehend is that, through precisely this fact—woman degenerates.
This is what is happening today: let us not deceive ourselves! Wherever the spirit
of industry has triumphed over the military and aristocratic spirit woman now
aspires to the economic and legal independence of a clerk: 'woman as clerk'
stands inscribed on the portal of the modern society now taking shape. As she
thus seizes new rights, looks to become 'master', and inscribes the 'progress' of
woman on her flags and banners, the reverse is happening with dreadful clarity:
woman is retrogressing. Since the French Revolution the influence of woman in
Europe has grown *less* in the same proportion as her rights and claims have
grown greater; and the 'emancipation of woman', in so far as it has been
demanded and advanced by women themselves (and not only by male shallow-
pates), is thus revealed as a noteworthy symptom of the growing enfeeblement
and blunting of the most feminine instincts. There is *stupidity* in this movement,
an almost masculine stupidity, of which a real woman—who is always a clever
woman—would have to be ashamed from the very heart. To lose her sense for
the ground on which she is most sure of victory; to neglect to practise the use of
her own proper weapons; to let herself go before the man, perhaps even 'to the

extent of producing a book', where formerly she kept herself in check and in subtle cunning humility; to seek with virtuous assurance to destroy man's belief that a fundamentally different ideal is *wrapped up* in a woman, that there is something eternally, necessarily feminine; emphatically and loquaciously to talk man out of the idea that woman has to be maintained, cared for, protected, indulged like a delicate, strangely wild and often agreeable domestic animal; the clumsy and indignant parade of all of slavery and bondage that woman's position in the order of society has hitherto entailed and still entails (as if slavery were a counter-argument and not rather a condition of every higher culture, of every enhancement of culture)—what does all this mean if not a crumbling of the feminine instinct, a defeminizing? To be sure, there are sufficient idiotic friends and corrupters of woman among the learned asses of the male sex who advise woman to defeminize herself in this fashion and to imitate all the stupidities with which 'man' in Europe, European 'manliness', is sick—who would like to reduce woman to the level of 'general education', if not to that of newspaper reading and playing at politics. Here and there they even want to turn women into free-spirits and *literati:* as if a woman without piety would not be something utterly repellent or ludicrous to a profound and godless man—; almost everywhere her nerves are being shattered by the most morbid and dangerous of all the varieties of music (our latest German music), and she is being rendered more and more hysterical with every day that passes and more and more incapable of her first and last profession, which is to bear strong children. There is a desire to make her in general more 'cultivated' and, as they say to make the 'weak sex' *strong* through culture: as if history did not teach in the most emphatic manner possible that making human beings 'cultivated' and making them weaker—that is to say, enfeebling, fragmenting, contaminating, the *force of the will,* have always gone hand in hand, and that the world's most powerful and influential women (most recently the mother of Napoleon) owed their power and ascendancy over men precisely to the force of their will—and not to school-masters! That in woman which inspires respect and fundamentally fear is her *nature,* which is more 'natural' than that of the man, her genuine, cunning, beast-of-prey suppleness, the tiger's claws beneath the glove, the naïvety of her egoism, her ineducability and inner savagery, and how incomprehensible, capacious and prowling her desires and virtues are.

☞ ☞ ☞

The passages, of course, admit of wide interpretation, but it would seem that Nietzsche wants to claim that becoming an agent—a subject who seeks an object—would be a step down for woman, who already exists *as* the object sought. His repetition here that *want* characterizes masculinity implies that masculinity—or humanity—by its nature lacks fulfillment and full expression, implying that women who seek entitlements are creating a weakness in themselves that they did not formerly suffer from. To the extent that women represent beauty, this diminution of themselves represents "uglification." This theme, that for women equality with men is a degradation, will reappear in later Nietzschean and existentialist works.

THUS SPAKE ZARATHUSTRA (I AND II PUBL. 1883, III PUBL. 1884, IV PUBL. 1892)

In this work, Nietzsche's character Zarathustra comes out of solitude in order to announce his prophesies of the death of God and the coming of the Superman. As a prophet of an entirely new ideal, and of a new race of individuals to assert it, Zarathustra's style mimics religious texts—a series of "discourses" and "discussions" directed at the individual who will push towards this new dawn. It would seem that, for Nietzsche, the knowledge of the death of God will lead human beings finally to abandon their shackles to old "values" and "truths" and to freely assert their will *as* the truth. Hence, Zarathustra says of "readers" and "writers:"

> *Untroubled, scornful, outrageous—that is how wisdom wants us to be: she is a woman and never loves anyone but a warrior.*

Two of the "Discourses" in Part One are devoted to the topic of gender:

OF OLD AND YOUNG WOMEN

. . . Today as I was going my way alone, at the hour when the sun sets, a little old woman encountered me and spoke thus to my soul:

'Zarathustra has spoken much to us women, too, but he has never spoken to us about woman.'

And I answered her: 'One should speak about women only to men.'

'Speak to me too of woman,' she said; 'I am old enough soon to forget it.'

And I obliged the little old woman and spoke to her thus:

Everything about woman is a riddle, and everything about woman has one solution: it is called pregnancy.

For the woman, the man is a means: the end is always the child. But what is the woman for the man?

The true man wants two things: danger and play. For that reason he wants woman, as the most dangerous plaything.

Man should be trained for war and woman for the recreation of the warrior: all else is folly.

The warrior does not like fruit that is too sweet. Therefore he likes woman; even the sweetest woman is still bitter.

Woman understands children better than a man, but man is more childlike than woman.

A child is concealed in the true man: it wants to play. Come, women, discover the child in man!

Let woman be a plaything, pure and fine like a precious stone illumined by the virtues of a world that does not yet exist.

Let the flash of a star glitter in your love! Let your hope be: 'May I bear the Superman!'

⌒ ⌒ ⌒

Let man fear woman when she loves. Then she bears every sacrifice and every other thing she accounts valueless.

Let man fear woman when she hates: for man is at the bottom of his soul only wicked, but woman is base.

Whom does woman hate most?—thus spoke the iron to the magnet: 'I hate you most, because you attract me, but are not strong enough to draw me towards you.'

The man's happiness is: I will. The woman's happiness is: He will.

'Behold, now the world has become perfect!'—thus thinks every woman when she obeys with all her love.

And woman has to obey and find a depth for her surface. Woman's nature is surface, a changeable, stormy film upon shallow waters.

But a man's nature is deep, its torrent roars in subterranean caves: woman senses its power but does not comprehend it.

Then the little old woman answered me: 'Zarathustra has said many nice things, especially for those who are young enough for them.

'It is strange, Zarathustra knows little of women and yet he is right about them! Is this because with women nothing is impossible?

☞ ☞ ☞

Thus spoke Zarathustra.

OF MARRIAGE AND CHILDREN

. . . Marriage: that I call the will of two to create the one who is more than those who created it. Reverence before one another, as before the willers of such a will—that I call marriage.

Let this be the meaning and the truth of your marriage. But that which the many-too-many, the superfluous, call marriage—ah, what shall I call it?

Ah, this poverty of soul in partnership! Ah, this filth of soul in partnership! Ah, this miserable ease in partnership!

All this they call marriage; and they say their marriages are made in Heaven.

☞ ☞ ☞

Do not laugh at such marriages! What child has not had reason to weep over its parents?

☞ ☞ ☞

This man set forth like a hero in quest of truth and at last he captured a little dressed-up lie. He calls it his marriage.

That man used to be reserved in his dealings and fastidious in his choice. But all at once he spoilt his company once and for all: he calls it his marriage.

That man sought a handmaiden with the virtues of an angel. But all at once he became the handmaiden of a woman, and now he needs to become an angel too.

I have found all buyers cautious, and all of them have astute eyes. But even the most astute man buys his wife while she is still wrapped.

ᕦ ᕦ ᕦ

A creator's thirst, arrow, and longing for the Superman: speak, my brother, is
this your will to marriage?

I call holy such a will and such a marriage.

Thus spoke Zarathustra.

There is much to be said—perhaps some of it self-contradictory—about these
cryptic and disturbing passages. Why, for instance, should one speak about women
only to men, and why is the Old Woman an exception to this? In some lines, Nietzsche seems to return to themes that are by now familiar: woman is what(ever) man
wants or desires, she is the surface that brings his depth to expression, woman is attractive to men but men are not strong enough to attract her to them, marriage signifies the commitment to an ideal or value, the good marriage is one in which the
woman and man make fuller individuals out of each other or properly fear each
other, and the bad marriage is an error or lie, etc. However, these lines and others in
the discourses remain unclear, changeable. It is not obvious, for instance, the extent
to which we should understand Zarathustra himself, despite his status as a prophet,
as a "mere" man, nor consequently the extent to which we should take his comments with a grain of salt. Nor is it clear that "speaking" about women is the only
way to have or show knowledge of them, or whether it is just a man's way.

ECCE HOMO (PUBL. 1908)

This book, subtitled "How One Becomes What One Is," was one of the author's
last, written in 1888, the year prior to a mental collapse that left him hospitalized
for the rest of his life. *Ecce Homo* is a charming, witty book in which Nietzsche reflects upon his own works, giving incisive criticism of each one and of himself. In
the section entitled "Why I Write Such Good Books"—in which the actual critical
commentaries on the works appear—Nietzsche attributes at least some of his "success" to his knowledge of women and of "the eternal feminine."

THE ETERNAL FEMININE

5

That a psychologist without equal speaks from my writings, is perhaps the first
insight reached by a good reader—a reader as I deserve him.

ᕦ ᕦ ᕦ

One has to sit firmly upon *oneself,* one must stand bravely on one's own two
legs, otherwise one is simply *incapable* of loving. Ultimately, women know that
only too well: they don't give a damn about selfless, merely objective men.

May I here venture the surmise that I *know* women? That is part of my
Dionysian dowry. Who knows? Perhaps I am the first psychologist of the

eternally feminine. They all love me—and old story—not counting *abortive* females, the "emancipated" who lack the stuff for children.—Fortunately, I am not willing to be torn to pieces: the perfect woman tears to pieces when she loves.—I know these charming maenads.—Ah, what a dangerous, creeping, subterranean little beast of prey she is! And yet so agreeable!—A little woman who pursues her revenge would run over fate itself.—Woman is indescribably more evil than man; also cleverer: good nature is in a woman a form of degeneration.—In all so-called "beautiful souls" something is physiologically askew at bottom; I do not say everything, else I should become medi-cynical. The fight for equal rights is actually a symptom of a disease: every physician knows that.—Woman, the more she is a woman, resists rights in general hand and foot: after all, the state of nature, the eternal war between the sexes, gives her by far the first rank.

Has my definition of love been heard? It is the only one worthy of a philosopher. Love—in its means, war; at bottom, the deadly hatred of the sexes.

Has my answer been heard to the question how one *cures* a woman— "redeems" her? One gives her a child. Woman needs children, a man is for her always only a means: thus spoke *Zarathustra*.

"Emancipation of women"—that is the instinctive hatred of the abortive woman, who is incapable of giving birth, against the woman who is turned out well—the fight against the "man" is always a mere means, pretext, tactic. By raising themselves higher, as "woman in herself," as the "higher woman," as a female "idealist," they want to lower the level of the general rank of woman; and there is no surer means for that than higher education, slacks, and political voting-cattle rights. At bottom, the emancipated are anarchists in the world of the "eternally feminine," the underprivileged whose most fundamental instinct is revenge.

Nietzsche's self-evaluation brings up fundamental questions regarding the nature of language for Nietzsche—its strengths and weaknesses, it usefulness and its failure. Language can be understood as itself representing what Nietzsche sees as the uncomfortable position of being human. In language, human beings struggle to express their will, under the guise of delivering an objective description of the world. One possible implication of his claims here, then, is that language itself, or at least its use to date, is masculine. This line of Nietzschean thought has been an influence on later feminists, such as Cixous, some of whose work appears in Part Six.

SUGGESTED READINGS—PART FOUR

Agacinski, Sylviane. *Aparte: Conceptions and Deaths of Søren Kierkegaard.* K. Newmark (trans). Gainesville: University Presses of Florida, 1988.

Allison, David B. (ed). *The New Nietzsche.* New York: Dell, 1977.

Annas, Julia. "Mill and the Subjection of Women." *Philosophy* 52: 179–94, 1977.

Ansell-Pearson, Keith. *Nietzsche Contra Rousseau: A Study of Nietzsche's Moral and Political Thought.* Cambridge: Cambridge University Press, 1991.

Ansell-Pearson, Keith, and Howard Caugill, (eds). *The Fate of the New Nietzsche.* Brookfield: Avebury, 1993.

Armstrong, Hugh and Pat Armstrong. "Beyond Sexless Class and Classless Sex: Towards Feminist Marxism." *Studies in Political Economy* 10: 7–44, 1983.

Avineri, Schlomo. *Hegel's Theory of the Modern State.* Cambridge: Cambridge University Press, 1972.

———. *The Social and Political Thought of Karl Marx.* Cambridge: Cambridge University Press, 1968.

Barber, Benjamin R. "Spirits Phoenix and History's Owl or the Incoherence of Dialectics in Hegel's Account of Women." *Political Theory* 16: 5–28, 1988.

Barrett, Michele. *The Politics of Truth from Marx to Foucault.* Palo Alto: Stanford University Press, 1991.

Brennan, Teresa, and Carole Pateman. "'Mere Auxiliaries to the Commonwealth': Women and the Origins of Liberalism." *Political Studies* 27: 183–200, 1979.

Carver, Terrell (ed). *The Cambridge Companion to Marx.* Cambridge: Cambridge University Press, 1991.

———. "Engels' Feminism." *The History of Political Thought.* 6(3), 1985.

Coole, Diana (ed). *Women and Political Theory.* Boulder: Lynne Reiner Publishers, 1993.

Cooper, W.E., K. Nielsen, and S.C. Patten (eds). *New Essays on John Stuart Mill and Utilitarianism.* Guelph: Canadian Association for Publishing in Philosophy, 1979.

Cornell, G.B. and C.S. Evans (eds). *Foundations of Kierkegaard's Vision of Community.* Atlantic Highlands: Humanities Press, 1992.

Diprose, Rosalyn. "Nietzsche, Ethics and Sexual Difference." *Radical Philosophy* 52: 27–33, 1989.

Easton, Susan. "Slavery and Freedom: A Feminist Reading of Hegel." *Politics* vol. 5(2), 1985.

Eisenstein, Zillah (ed). *Capitalist Patriarchy and the Case for Socialist Feminism.* New York: Longman, 1981.

Elshtain, Jean Bethke. *Public Man, Private Woman: Women in Social and Political Thought.* Princeton: Princeton University Press, 1981.

Firestone, Shulamith. *The Dialectic of Sex: The Case for Feminist Revolution.* London: Women's Press, 1979.

Gatens, Moira. "A Critique of the Sex/Gender Distinction." in *Beyond Marxism?* J. Allen and P. Patton (eds). Leichhardt: Intervention Publications, 1985.

Goldstein, Leslie. "Mill, Marx, and Women's Liberation." *Journal of the History of Philosophy* 18(3), 1980.

Gould, Carol C. *Marx's Social Ontology: Individuality and Community in Marx's Theory of Social Reality.* Cambridge: MIT Press, 1978.

Hardimon, Michael O. *Hegel's Social Philosophy: The Project of Reconciliation.* Cambridge: Cambridge University Press, 1994.

Hartmann, Heidi. "The Family as the Locus of Gender, Class and Political Struggle: the Example of Housework." *Signs* 6: 366–94, 1981.

Hatab, Lawrence J. "Nietzsche on Woman." *Southern Journal of Philosophy* 19: 33–346, 1981.

Hayim, Gila J. "Hegel's Critical Theory and Feminist Concerns." *Philosophy and Social Criticism* 16: 1–21, 1990.

Hearn, Jeff. *The Gender of Oppression: Men, Masculinity and the Critique of Marxism.* New York: St. Martin's Press, 1987.

Hekman, Susan. "John Stuart Mill's *The Subjection of Women:* The Foundations of Liberal Feminism." *History of European Ideas* 15: 681–686, 1992.

Hegel, G.W.F. *The Phenomenology of Mind.* J.B. Baillie (trans). New York: Harper Colophon,1967.

———. *The Phenomenology of Spirit.* A.V. Miller (trans). Oxford: Oxford University Press, 1977.

Held, Virginia. "Marx, Sex and the Transformation of Society." *Philosophical Forum* 5: 168–184, 1973.

Higgins, Kathleen M. *Nietzsche's "Zarathustra."* Philadelphia: Temple University Press, 1987.

Hughes, P. "The Reality vs.the Ideal: John Stuart Mill's Treatment of Women, Workers and Private Property."*Canadian Journal of Political Science* 12, 523–42.

Kain, Philip J. *Marx and Modern Political Theory: From Hobbes to Contemporary Feminism.* Lanham: Rowman and Littlefield, 1993.

Kierkegaard, Søren. *Either/Or.* Vols. I and II. David Swenson and L. M. Swenson (trans. vol. I) and W. Lowrie (trans. vol. II) Princeton: Princeton University Press, 1972.

Kuhn, Annette and Ann Marie Wolpe (eds). *Feminism and Materialism: Women and Modes of Production.* London: Routledge and Kegan Paul, 1978.

Lamb, David (ed). *Hegel and Modern Philosophy* London: Croom Helm, 1987.

Lewis, Jane. "The Debate on Sex and Class," *New Left Review* 149: 108–20, 1985.

MacIntyre, Alasdair (ed). *Hegel: A Collection of Critical Essays.* Garden City: Anchor, 1972.

Mackey, Louis. *Kierkegaard: A Kind of Poet.* Philadelphia: University of Pennsylvania Press, 1971.

———. *Points of View: Readings of Kierkegaard.* Gainesville: University Presses of Florida, 1986.

Marcuse, Herbert. *Reason and Revolution: Hegel and the Rise of Social Theory.* Boston: Beacon, 1960.

Marx, Karl. *Capital.* Vols. 1–3. Ben Fowkes (trans vol.1), and David Fernbach (trans. vols. 2 & 3) New York: Random House, 1977.

———. *Early Writings.* T. Bottomore (trans). New York, McGraw-Hill, 1963.

Marx, Karl, and Friedrich Engels.*The Communist Manifesto.* S. Moore (trans). Great Britain: Penguin, 1967.

———. *The Marx–Engels Reader.* Robert C. Tucker (ed). New York: Norton, 1972.

McKinnon, Catharine. "Feminism, Marxism, Method and the State: An Agenda for Theory." *Signs* 7: 515–530,1982.

Mill, John Stuart. *On Liberty.* Indianapolis: Hackett Publishing Co., 1978.

———. *Utilitarianism.* George Sher (ed).Indianapolis: Hackett, 1979.

———. *The Subjection of Women.* Susan M. Okin (ed). Indianapolis: Hackett, 1988

Mills, P.J. "Hegel's *Antigone.*" *Owl of Minerva* 17: 131–152, 1986.

Nehemas, Alexander. *Nietzsche: Life as Literature.* Cambridge: Harvard University Press, 1985.

O'Brien, Mary. *The Politics of Reproduction.* London: Routledge and Kegan Paul, 1981.

Panidras, George (ed). *Marx Analyzed: Philosophical Essays on the Thought of Karl Marx.* Lanham: University Press of America, 1985.

Patton, Paul (ed). *Nietzsche, Feminism and Political Theory.* New York: Routledge, 1993.

Perkius, Robert C. (ed). *The Sickness Unto Death.* Macon: Mercer University Press, 1987.

Poovy, Mary. *The Proper Lady and the Woman Writer: The Ideology of Style in the Works of Mary Wollstonecraft, Mary Shelley, and Jane Austen.* Chicago: University of Chicago Press, 1984.

Raaven, Heidi M. "Has Hegel Anything to Say to Feminists?" *The Owl of Minerva* 19: 49–68, 1988.

Rabine, Leslie. "Searching for the Connection: Marxist-Feminists and Women's Studies." *Humanities in Society* 6: 195–221, 1983.

Rudd, Anthony. *Kierkegaard and the Limits of the Ethical.* Oxford: Clarendon Press, 1993.

Sargent, Lydia (ed). *Women and Revolution: A Discussion of the Unhappy Marriage of Marxism and Feminism.* London: Pluto Press, 1981.

Sayers, Janet, M. Evans and N. Redclif (eds). *Engels Revisited: New Feminist Essays.* London: Tavistock, 1987.

Schneewind, J.B. (ed). *Mill: A Collection of Critical Essays.* South Bend: Notre Dame University Press, 1969.

Shapiro, Gary. *Alcyone: Nietzsche on Gifts, Noise, and Women.* Albany: State University of New York Press, 1991.

Smart, J.J.C. and B. Williams. *Utilitarianism: For and Against.* Cambridge: Cambridge University Press, 1973.

Solomon, Robert C. *In the Spirit of Hegel.* Oxford: Oxford University Press, 1983.

Solomon, Robert C., and Kathleen Higgins. *Reading Nietzsche.* New York: Oxford University Press, 1988.

Steinberger, Peter. "Hegel on Marriage and Politics." *Political Studies* 34(4), 1986.

Sunstein, Emily W. *Mary Shelley: Romance and Reality.* Boston: Little, Brown, 1989.

Taylor, Mark C. *Kierkegaard's Pseudonymous Authorship: A Study of Time and the Self.* Princeton: Princeton University Press, 1975.

Thompson, Josiah. *Kierkegaard: A Collection of Essays.* Garden City: Anchor Books, 1972.

Tilly, Louise. "Paths of Proletarianization: Organization of Production, Sexual Division of Labor and Women's Collective Action." *Signs* 7: 100–17, 1981.

Veeder, William. *Mary Shelley and Frankenstein: The Fate of Androgyny.* Chicago: University of Chicago Press, 1988.

Vogel, Lise. *Marxism and the Oppression of Women: Toward a Unitary Theory.* New Brunswick: Rutgers University Press, 1983.

Warren, Mark. *Nietzsche and Political Thought.* Cambridge: MIT Press, 1988.

Wood, Allen. *Hegel's Ethical Theory.* Cambridge University Press, 1990.

PART FIVE

THE EARLY TWENTIETH CENTURY: SCIENTISM AND MORALISM

Freud, Gilman, Woolf, Jung, Horney, Mead, Sartre, De Beauvoir

INTRODUCTION

THE WORLD WARS AND THE ASCENDENCE OF THE UNITED STATES

During the nineteenth century industrial growth and technological evolution made for a growing distinction between "developed"—i.e., industrialized—and "underdeveloped" nations, conflating political issues with economic and technological ones and affecting the framework within which world power relations were to be assessed. This, combined with the century's Romanticism about "pre-civilized" or "natural" regional characters, contributed to a pervasive spirit of nationalism in the industrialized countries around the world. But as Romanticism gave way to Decadence, this nationalism inevitably gave way to internationalism; as the fervor of national pride swelled in various countries around the world, so did the awareness of the international arena in which these nations competed. Adding to this growing internationalism was the increasing importance of the United States in world politics. The youth, vigor, and success of the United States—both military and economic—gave this country an exemplary status around the world.

There is perhaps nothing so indicative of the incipient spirit of the twentieth century, then, as the First World War and its outcome. As the historian John Lukacs put it:

> It is wrong to believe that the Great War of 1914 caused the decline of Europe. In many ways that war was a consequence, not a cause. . . . In many ways, there was no such thing as Europe before 1914. . . . The utopians, the pacifists, the self-professed pioneers of a united Europe or of a united world were . . .

stimulated by the American example, as indeed were the business practices of the more enterprising bourgeois.[1]

With the turn of the century came a growing sense that the political world was itself subject to technological manipulation. Far beyond the early Modern ideal of creating enlightened liberal states based on a knowledge of human nature, there was in the twentieth century the growing belief that national borders could be re-drawn, cultural traditions redesigned, international economies tinkered with, indeed even the national character of individuals renovated according to the "best scien-tific hypotheses" of the day. In a sense, nineteenth-century faith in technological progress turned into a sort of devotion to it, to the point of asking technology to do political and moral work. Accompanying this was the heir to the Romantic nostal-gia of the nineteenth century—a kind of anti-technology characterized mostly by the fear of its unreckoned consequences.

Of course, one of the main—and one of the most fearworthy—applications of technology to politics is in the development of the machines and techniques of war. Thus, in that we might say, with Lukacs, that the First World War gave paradig-matic expression to the technological and internationalist trends of the age, we might add that the Second World War brought these trends to their climax, leaving the world with confusing and sometimes frightening repercussions that it still grap-ples to understand. In this chapter, we will focus on theories of gender from the period between roughly the turn of the century and the end of the "post-World-War-Two" era, or the 1960s. Despite the fact that the readings included do not deal di-rectly with questions of war or even of politics, it is worth keeping in the back of one's mind that the two world wars are fundamental to the background against which these authors' works stand out. The internationalism, the world-wide interde-pendence of technology and human action, and the underlying fear of a disintegrat-ing world politic and a technology out of control, are important motivators for even these more philosophical and literary authors. In addition, it is noteworthy that our first American authors appear in this chapter.

THE INTERNALIZATION OF NATURE AND THE "MASS"

As technological production increased, scientific explanation focused more and more on the abstract objects of the human mind. Similarly, as markets for the new products of scientific technology were exhausted, production and consumption also took on the more internal, abstract character of the mental world. Ready-to-wear fashions and household products for women increasingly exploited the interior of the home for the purposes of national economic expansion. More and more prod-ucts aimed at creating subtle, essentially psychological, differences of taste and sta-tus among their consumers. Theories of art and morality were increasingly posed in terms of the agent's psychological processes, such as was foreshadowed by

---

[1] John Lukacs, *The Passing of the Modern Age.* (New York: Harper Torchbooks, 1970), pp. 21–23.

Kierkegaard and Nietzsche. Western philosophy focused inward on human experience and language. Even political questions were drawn along the more personal and abstract issue of the individual's role in national and even international policies and actions. These and other factors of encroaching twentieth-century life helped to build a worldview with an increasingly "internal" landscape, one in which the natural causes or consequences of events were attributed to the psyche. As Lukacs remarked, "We live in a time when there is developing an increasing intrusion of mental processes into the structure of events."[2]

In essence, this internal turn was a redirection of the technological energies of the nineteenth century inward to the human personality and character. Scientists, economic producers, national policy-makers, philosophers, and of course psychologists sought increasingly to transform human behavior, to apply their theories to the quality and moral substance of human life. Thus, where in nineteenth century authors, as we have seen, there was a tendency to interweave literature and philosophy, the twentieth-century authors whose works appear in this chapter will tend to combine these styles with a psychologistic perspective, one that takes not only scientific understanding but also cultural or moral change as its sphere. Moral improvement was taken to be the realistic goal of a scientifically founded technology.

Hence, the nature/culture dichotomy that had so consumed thinkers of the nineteenth century leaves its traces on the twentieth, but in a changed form. The world external to the human psyche seemed so saturated with cultural artifacts, with technological improvements, that the secrets of nature were imagined to appear in their "pure" form only in the hidden recesses of the mind. Since, however, the mind itself is of course the source of technological change and scientific investigation, the turn inward seemed to many thinkers of the time to be foiled, disappointed, even futile. Thus, the internalization of the twentieth-century worldview was often posed as an inherently confused and possibly self-defeating enterprise.

Perhaps surprisingly, this internalized, individualized orientation accompanied what we might call a "mass" orientation. The various scientific, economic, and political techniques that took human mental processes as their object of study and/or policy-making adopted of necessity abstract theoretical constructs for the human individual, which applied identically to everyone. This, added to the population explosions of the industrial revolution, and the growing internationalism mentioned above, created a sociological discourse that was often posed in terms of masses of roughly identical individuals. As the products and policies that structured people's lives increasingly relied on the notion of the "mass," individuals increasingly envisioned their own lives in terms of their participation in mass movements, mass media, and mass production. Thus, while the technology of the era entered more deeply into the human psyche, it seemed to empty the psyche of what had been thought to be its traditional contents—its passions, its desires, its choices. These were projected onto an equally abstract but wholly external entity called the "mass."

---

[2] Ibid., p. 5.

The habits of daily life, then, required a certain disorientation, a certain inner schism, among twentieth-century individuals, between their "internal" perspective on themselves and their "mass" perspective. According to Paul Valery, the famous poet and social critic of the era, the result of this was "chaos"; he described this "politics of the mind" in the following way.

> *Everyone tacitly agrees that the* man *in question in constitutional or civil law, the pawn in political speculations and maneuvers—the* citizen, *the* voter, *the* candidate, *the* taxpayer, *the* common man—*is perhaps not quite the same as the man defined by contemporary biology, psychology or even psychiatry. A strange contrast is the result. We look on the same individual as both responsible and irresponsible; we sometimes consider him irresponsible and treat him as responsible, depending on which of these fictions we adopt at the moment, whether we are in a juridical or an objective frame of mind. In the same way, we find that in many minds, faith coexists with atheism, anarchy of feeling and doctrinal views.*

☞ ☞ ☞

> *In short, we are faced with confusion in the social system, in the verbal material and in the myths of all kinds inherited from our ancestors, and in the conditions in which we live—conditions that are intellectual in origin, quite artificial, and moreover essentially unstable, for they are dependent on further and ever more numerous creations of the intellect. Here we are, then, prey to this confused mixture of* boundless hopes (justified by our incredible achievements) *and* immense disappointments *or* sinister expectations (equally justified by our incredible failures and catastrophes).[3]

SEX, FREEDOM, AND RESPONSIBILITY

Because of the confusing character of the internal landscape towards which these thinkers turned, concepts that had formerly been understood in terms of natural and cultural elements came increasingly to be understood in terms of their free and determined elements. As people's lives and decisions became more dependent on technological forces, which controlled the movements of individuals not always by their consent, intellectuals of the period often focused their analyses on the nature of control and of its opposite, freedom. Individuals seemed increasingly to envision themselves as struggling for freedom amidst masses of coercive forces, not all of which were obvious or tangible. For some, freedom consisted primarily in the freedom to choose which forces, which mass movements, or which mass-produced products, to ally themselves with. For others, freedom was depicted as a kind of mysterious escape from the whole range of impending controls, including the internalized, unconscious moral ideals to which most ordinary people found themselves beholden.

---

[3] Paul Valery, "Politics of the Mind," [1932]. Collected in *The Outlook for Intelligence,* vol. X of the Collected Works of Paul Valery, Bollingen Series #XLV. Translated by Denise Folliot and Jackson Matthews (Princeton: Bollingen Series, 1962), pp. 92-94.

Of course, this dichotomy is a development from the master/slave opposition so prevalent in the discourse of the nineteenth century. But the pervasiveness of mass-produced technology, international or mass political movements and the mass media, and the horrifying consequences of their use—e.g., the rise of fascism, as well as the world war required to defeat it and the atomic bomb that ended that war—led thinkers to characterize the concrete image of master and slave in new, more abstract terms. For with free action comes responsibility, and under the seemingly uncontrollable conditions of twentieth-century life, the attribution of responsibility took on heroic proportions.

As in the nineteenth century, different thinkers in the twentieth century held differing opinions about the relations between free and determined actions and natural and cultural elements. For some, the existentialists, freedom was depicted as the natural and frightening human fate, from which cultural habits and institutions were feeble attempts at escape. For others, liberal economists like Gilman, human freedom was best represented by full participation in social institutions such as elections and paid labor outside the home. For still others, such as the psychoanalysts, human freedom was always inscribed by naturally determined physical or unconscious forces, and it consisted mostly in gaining knowledge and control of these forces. In general, however, thinkers of this period faced what they found to be unjust, unhappy or confusing circumstances by trying to attribute responsibility—sometime in terms of the scientifically discovered cause and sometimes in terms of moral agency—and thereafter to exercise the freedom to change the situation. Surrounded by such pervasive and oppressive technological achievements, effecting change seemed both possible and desirable to many people—but the consequences and value of these rapid changes seemed increasingly to elude clear understanding.

Among the circumstances that twentieth-century thinkers sought to transform, and in line with the general internalized focus of the period, were sexual drives and sex differences. The Nineteenth Amendment to the U.S. Constitution, insuring women's suffrage in this country, was passed in 1920, and for a short time before and after that, the women's movement seemed to be occupied primarily with the right to vote. Equal suffrage, however, in the larger context of the whole century, was only one part of the intellectual and political activities that concerned themselves with the question of sexuality and the social technologies of increased freedom and responsibility. Are human sexual habits freely chosen or physically determined? Are we responsible for our drives or helpless pawns of them? What is responsible for the different roles that men and women play in society—physical, natural differences; social constraints; or free choices? These and questions like them defined the early twentieth-century debates about gender, and the thinkers included in this chapter have widely varying answers. In many ways, the discourse on sex in the early years of this century are an unbroken development from nineteenth-century treatments: the influence of Nietzsche, Marx, and other nineteenth-century philosophers upon the thinkers in the present chapter will be very easily recognized. However, the development of twentieth- from nineteenth-century thought on gender is taken to a kind of shocking extreme in many cases. It is an extreme born of the convoluted, quickly moving, artificial, sometimes disappointing, and even violent circumstances of the age.

1. SIGMUND FREUD
(Austrian, 1856–1939)

Like Nietzsche's before him, Sigmund Freud's work has faced the wrath of some feminists and the idolization of others. Whether one takes him as a foil or a champion, however, one cannot engage responsibly in a study of twentieth-century notions of gender without reading some Freud, a pivotal thinker in the study of sex and gender. In order to understand both the early theory of femininity and the later developments within it, it will be helpful to have a quick overview of the basics of Freudian theory.

Freud's therapeutic method of "free-association" (early on, he called it "the talking cure") was an attempt to elicit from patients the underlying, unconscious sources of their neuroses, by asking them to say whatever came into their heads in relation to certain important ideas culled from their childhoods or their dreams or their dysfunctional daily habits. Perhaps this is responsible for his enduring appeal for literary critics and philosophers—even during periods of relative disdain among psychologists and other scientists. Many of the philosophers of a more literary bent, such as deconstructionists, some of whose work appears in Part Six, take their intellectual cue from a combination of Freudian and Nietzschean theory.

THE ORGANIZATION OF MENTAL PROCESSES

Perhaps Freud's most important contribution to the history of thought was his theory of the *unconscious*. Freud claimed that the human mind was constantly active on an unconscious level, even when one is asleep. The content of the mind, both conscious and unconscious, was, according to Freud, ideas: but, he claimed, first, that ideas carried a sort of mental "weight" or "value," regardless of their objective truth or of the beliefs of the individual thinker; and second, that not all ideas have an equal value within the psyche of a particular individual. Rather, each person is invested more in some ideas and less in others—Freud's translators use a Greek derivative, *cathexis,* for this phenomenon of investing mental energy in an idea, of developing an emotional attachment to it. Cathected ideas, Freud claimed, are ideas to that one is strongly attached, and which one always has somewhere in one's thoughts, even if one doesn't think consciously about them very often. Freud believed that there was a kind of commerce of ideas between the different mental functions. Through a kind of "exchange" between consciousness and unconsciousness, an idea that was formerly conscious may now be unconscious—for instance, one may have forgotten it or refocused one's attention—and an idea that had been unconscious may now be conscious—as when one remembers something, or articulates something to oneself.

Freud claimed—and this was a part of his theory that was revised several times—that there are three main kinds of mental functioning. There is the *id,* which is a wellspring of ideas, full of primitive desires, needs, and appetites that it strives endlessly to express; there is the *superego,* which is an internalized code of morality or social acceptability, or even an internalized ideal person, which passes judgment on one's ideas; and there is the *ego,* which is responsible for directing one's behavior and personality so as to satisfy the demands of both the id and the superego, to the greatest extent possible. Thus, the ego is responsible for the personality that shows itself to the world—for the upshot of the negotiations among various competing demands within the self. The compromise that the ego negotiates often takes the form of encoding or symbolizing id desires, making them palatable to the superego. Thus, Freud claimed that human nature is inherently conflicted, and that the speech and behavior an individual presents to others— whether healthy or neurotic—are often only baroque symbolizations for his or her deeply buried desires.

There are some ideas—usually, according to Freud, sexual ones—which are either too extremely embarrassing or distasteful, or too much socially ostracized, for one to think about consciously. These ideas, Freud claimed, must be *repressed;* i.e., kept unconscious. This repression requires an effort, especially if the idea to be repressed is very highly cathected. Thus, much of a typical adult's unconscious consisted, according to Freud, of repressed ideas; and neuroses, he claimed, were usually the results of the efforts necessary to repress them. Thus, neurotic behavior could be cured, he believed, by relieving the patient of his or her burden by bringing the repressed ideas to his or her consciousness.

THEORY OF HUMAN DEVELOPMENT

According to Freud, the most highly cathected ideas for most people are those relating to their childhood sexual development. On this account, since so much of our external discourse is a kind of hidden or encoded expression of such ideas, Freud tended to believe that the vast majority of human discourse and behavior had an underlying or symbolic sexual content. Hence, Freud's crucial position in the study of gender: he found sexual significance in an enormous array of human endeavor.

According to Freud, everything associated with the seeking of pleasure or the avoidance of pain—i.e., according to him, the motivation for almost everything we do—is essentially sexual: it is directed towards satisfying physical desires and needs. This general motivating force he called the "libido," meaning the "sexual drive," but also the "life force." In infancy, according to Freud, a person has an unrefined libido, innocently seeking pleasure and avoiding pain, with no conflict or restraint. Soon, however, a child faces certain obstacles to his or her libido, and must accommodate them somehow. For instance, his or her mother may not be available to feed him or her anytime he or she wants to be fed. Thus, for Freud, growing up consists mainly in negotiating or facing the various impediments to one's libidinal instincts. In other words, for Freud, psychological development is founded in sexual development.

The libido by itself seeks all pleasure equally, and so is inherently bisexual. According to Freud, there are three crucial stages to childhood (i.e., pre-adolescent) sexual development, which eventually direct the libido towards certain objects and activities and away from others. First is the *oral* stage, in which pleasure and pain are associated essentially with the mouth, with food and hunger. Since one's mother is primarily responsible for providing the infant with food, she is, according to

Freud, every child's first love object: one's mother is always the original and most fundamental source of pleasure. After this is the *anal* phase, in which pain and pleasure are associated primarily with the anus, with controlling one's own bodily functions and so establishing autonomy from one's parents and others. Finally, there is the *genital* phase, in which pleasure and pain are associated primarily with the genitals, and during which most children, according to Freud, come to take the opposite-sex parent as a love-object. Freud claimed that during the oral and anal phases, boys and girls undergo similar or identical sexual development, and in that sense, all adult men and women will carry traces of bisexuality and sexual similarity to one another throughout their lives. It is only in the genital phase—the first time they must actually accommodate their physical differences and the social unacceptability of homosexual or same-sex love objects—that boys' and girls' sexual developments diverge, and sex differences are manifested in their behavior.

The genital phase is accomplished through a resolution of what Freud called the "Oedipal conflict," in which young boys, like Oedipus in the Greek myth, must face their sexual desire for their mothers and their jealous resentment of their fathers on that account. Young boys maintain the same love-object through the Oedipal conflict; they simply find acceptable female symbolic substitutes for their mother. Young girls, however, according to Freud, have a more complicated sexual development, because they must change, or seem to change, the sex of their primary love object. Thus, according to Freud, psychological sex differences are accounted for by the different resolutions of the Oedipal conflict that initiates maturation to the genital phase.

"ON NARCISSISM: AN INTRODUCTION" (1914)

In this essay, Freud proposes that a theory of narcissism (i.e., a tendency towards self-love) be added to his "libido theory" (according to which everyone eventually chooses a love-object external to him or herself). The theory of narcissism, like the original libido theory, is based on observations of neurotic patients in therapy; but Freud claims that the neurotic narcissism which one finds in these patients is just an extension of a normal self-preservative instinct. In the second section, from which the following passages are taken, Freud speculates that these two different tendencies in object-choice (of others or of oneself) correspond respectively to masculine and feminine sexual styles.

> . . . We have recognized our mental apparatus as being first and foremost a device designed for mastering excitations which would otherwise be felt as distressing or would have pathogenic effects. Working them over in the mind helps remarkably towards an internal draining away of excitations which are incapable of direct discharge outwards, or for which such a discharge is for the moment undesirable.

☙ ☙ ☙

. . . The first autoerotic sexual satisfactions are experienced in connection with vital functions which serve the purpose of self-preservation. The sexual instincts are at the outset attached to the satisfaction of the ego-instincts; only later do they become independent of these, and even then we have an indication of that original attachment in the fact that the persons who are concerned with a child's feeding, care, and protection become his earliest sexual objects: that is to say, in the first instance his mother or a substitute for her. Side by side, however, with this type and source of object-choice, which may be called the 'anaclitic' or 'attachment' type, psycho-analytic research has revealed a second type, which we were not prepared for finding. We have discovered, especially clearly in people whose libidinal development has suffered some disturbance, such as perverts and homosexuals, that in their later choice of love-objects they have taken as a model not their mother but their own selves. They are plainly seeking *themselves* as a love-object, and are exhibiting a type of object-choice which must be termed 'narcissistic'.

We have, however, not concluded that human beings are divided into two sharply differentiated groups, according as their object-choice conforms to the anaclitic or to the narcissistic type; we assume rather that both kinds of object-choice are open to each individual, though he may show a preference for one or the other. We say that a human being has originally two sexual objects—himself and the woman who nurses him—and in doing so we are postulating a primary narcissism in everyone, which may in some cases manifest itself in a dominating fashion in his object-choice.

A comparison of the male and female sexes then shows that there are fundamental differences between them in respect of their type of object-choice, although these differences are of course not universal. Complete object-love of the attachment type is, properly speaking, characteristic of the male. It displays the marked sexual overvaluation which is doubtless derived from the child's original narcissism and thus corresponds to a transference of that narcissism to the sexual object. This sexual overvaluation is the origin of the peculiar state of being in love, a state suggestive of a neurotic compulsion, which is thus traceable to an impoverishment of the ego as regards libido in favour of the love-object. A different course is followed in the type of female most frequently met with, which is probably the purest and truest one. With the onset of puberty the maturing of the female sexual organs, which up till then have been in a condition of latency, seems to bring about an intensification of the original narcissism, and this is unfavourable to the development of a true object-choice with its accompanying sexual overvaluation. Women, especially if they grow up with good looks, develop a certain self-contentment which compensates them for the social restrictions that are imposed upon them in their choice of object. Strictly speaking, it is only themselves that such women love with an intensity comparable to that of the man's love for them. Nor does their need lie in the direction of loving, but of being loved; and the man who fulfils this condition is the one who finds favour with them. The importance of this type of woman for the erotic life of mankind is to be rated very high. Such women have the greatest fascination for men, not only for aesthetic reasons, since as a rule they are the most beautiful, but also because of a combination of interesting psychological factors. For it seems very evident that another person's narcissism has a great attraction for those who have renounced part of their own narcissism and are in search of object-love. The charm of a child lies to a great extent in his narcissism, his self-contentment and inaccessibility, just as does the charm of certain animals which seem not to concern themselves about us, such as cats and the large beasts of prey. Indeed, even great criminals and humorists, as they are represented in literature, compel our interest by the narcissistic consistency with which they manage to keep away from their ego anything that would diminish it. It is as if we envied them for maintaining a blissful state of mind—an unassailable libidinal position which we ourselves have since abandoned. The great charm of narcissistic women has, however, its reverse side; a large part of the lover's dissatisfaction, of his doubts of the woman's love, of his complaints of her enigmatic nature, has its root in this incongruity between the types of object-choice.

Perhaps it is not out of place here to give an assurance that this description of the feminine form of erotic life is not due to any tendentious desire on my part to depreciate women. Apart from the fact that tendentiousness is quite alien to me, I know that these different lines of development correspond to the differentiation of functions in a highly complicated biological whole; further, I am ready to admit that there are quite a number of women who love according to the masculine type and who also develop the sexual overvaluation proper to that type.

Even for narcissistic women, whose attitude towards men remains cool, there is a road which leads to complete object-love. In the child which they bear, a part of their own body confronts them like an extraneous object, to which, starting out from their narcissism, they can then give complete object-love. There are other women, again, who do not have to wait for a child in order to take the step in development from (secondary) narcissism to object-love. Before puberty they feel masculine and develop some way along masculine lines; after this trend has been cut short on their reaching female maturity, they still retain the capacity of longing for a masculine ideal—an ideal which is in fact a survival of the boyish nature that they themselves once possessed.

What I have so far said by way of indication may be concluded by a short summary of the paths leading to the choice of an object.

A person may love:—

(1) According to the narcissistic type:
   (*a*) what he himself is (i.e. himself),
   (*b*) what he himself was,
   (*c*) what he himself would like to be,
   (*d*) someone who was once part of himself.

(2) According to the anaclitic (attachment) type:
    (a) the woman who feeds him,
    (b) the man who protects him,

and the succession of substitutes who take their place.

Note how Freud's claims about femininity are more hesitantly put forward than his remarks about male sexual life. He makes it clear even in these early stages of his theory of sex difference that it is based on a male model and that it should be challenged, and if necessary revised, on the basis of observations of women. Although Freud did revise the theory himself a number of times, he remained fairly steadfast in his claim that female sexuality was a complication or inversion of what he took to be the "normal" male type. Here, he claims that the narcissistic object-choice common to women almost always appears in a less developed form in men, and that the typically male "anaclitic" object choice is similarly found in women, and is brought out boldly in a mother's love for her child.

Although Freud finds several good things to say about the narcissistic state—he claims that it plays a vital and constructive role in human social life—it is certainly noteworthy that both the "pros and cons" of narcissism that Freud cites are described in terms of their effect on men. Whatever we may think of Freud's basic claim that the sexes can be psychologically differentiated by their different kinds of object-choice, we need not adopt this evaluative stance. In fact, one of the contributions of female psychoanalysts following Freud—some of whose work appears later—is an ongoing attempt to revise these evaluations and to add a woman's introspective or empirical findings to Freud's. Not all these critiques challenged the claim that narcissism is feminine, though many have tried to explain a similar phenomenon in different terms, claiming for instance that women tend to "identify" with their love objects, or that women place themselves in a position of "personal responsibility" for others.

THREE ESSAYS ON THE THEORY OF SEXUALITY
(1905—REVISED 1910, 1915, 1920, 1922, 1925)

The Three Essays are pivotal texts in Freud's theories regarding sex differences, and as can be seen from the publication dates given above, they underwent many revisions as his thinking on this issue changed. Freud's more settled opinions on female development and sexuality appear in the 1930s, even after the last revision, but the "Three Essays" remain very informative about the Freudian theory of sex differences.

In these passages, we will see examples of two Freudian themes, which take up issues ongoing in earlier thinkers and reinterpret or rethink them. First, while Freud bases sexuality in biology, he claims that human biological organisms and organs are not as clear and singular in their functions as we normally think. Hence, while sex differences are founded in the different genitalia of men and women, the differences between male and female genitalia are not clear-cut—members of both sexes share aspects of the other's reproductive system. Hence, the physical differences between men and women, on which the psychological differences between masculine and feminine characters are based, are not clear enough to base the claim that there *are* such things as men and women, in the strictest sense of the term, at all: we are all simply more or less one than the other.

Second, for Freud, concepts that seem to the conscious mind to be opposites are always more alike in the unconscious than they are different. In one essay he calls this concept "negation"—meaning that the negation of a claim is psychologically equivalent to its assertion; e.g., "I love ice cream" indicates the same psychological content to the analyst as does "I hate ice cream." Heterosexual object choice for instance, always, perhaps unconsciously or symbolically, carries some degree of homosexual object choice; masochism always carries some degree of sadistic impulses. This is because the so-called "perverse" practices or impulses are, according to Freud, only excessive degrees or expressions of the normal human state, which he believes to be bisexual and naturally aggressive.

II. INFANTILE SEXUALITY

In the Second Essay, Freud discusses the sexual development, naive theories, and practices of children. One important observation Freud makes, now commonplace, is that children have sexual impulses at a very young age. Because of this, Freud believed that children are curious about sex and about their bodies very early on and conduct researches into the question, coming up with wholly fictional, but surprisingly acute theories about sex. As they grow up, their impulses are repressed in various ways and to varying degrees, and their theories develop, in normal children, more closely to the truth. As their sexual impulses are further and further checked, children learn more and more to "sublimate"—or re-direct—their sexual energies into non-sexual pursuits. As this happens, their love-objects change, and the symbolizations through which these objects represent their original—the child's parents and him or herself—become more complex.

II. INFANTILE SEXUALITY

[1]   THE PERIOD OF SEXUAL LATENCY IN CHILDHOOD AND ITS INTERRUPTIONS

. . . There seems no doubt that germs of sexual impulses are already present in the new-born child and that these continue to develop for a time, but are then overtaken by a progressive process of suppression; this in turn is itself interrupted by periodical advances in sexual development or may be held up by individual peculiarities. Nothing is known for certain concerning the regularity and periodicity of this oscillating course of development. It seems, however, that the sexual life of children usually emerges in a form accessible to observation round about the third or fourth year of life.

SEXUAL INHIBITIONS

It is during this period of total or only partial latency that are built up the mental forces which are later to impede the course of the sexual instinct and, like dams, restrict its flow—disgust, feelings of shame and the claims of aesthetic and moral ideals. One gets an impression from civilized children that the construction of these dams is a product of education, and no doubt education has much to do with it. But in reality this development is organically determined and fixed by heredity, and it can occasionally occur without any help at all from education.

REACTION-FORMATION AND SUBLIMATION

What is it that goes to the making of these constructions which are so important for the growth of a civilized and normal individual? They probably emerge at the cost of the infantile sexual impulses themselves.

Historians of civilization appear to be at one in assuming that powerful components are acquired for every kind of cultural achievement by this diversion of sexual instinctual forces from sexual aims and their direction to new ones—a process which deserves the name of 'sublimation'. To this we would add, accordingly, that the same process plays a part in the development of the individual and we would place its beginning in the period of sexual latency of childhood.

[5]   THE SEXUAL RESEARCHES OF CHILDHOOD

THE INSTINCT FOR KNOWLEDGE

At about the same time as the sexual life of children reaches its first peak, between the ages of three and five, they also begin to show signs of the activity which may be ascribed to the instinct for knowledge or research.

Its relations to sexual life, however, are of particular importance, since we have learn from psycho-analysis that the instinct for knowledge in children is attracted unexpectedly early and intensively to sexual problems and is in fact possibly first aroused by them.

THE RIDDLE OF THE SPHINX

... And this history of the instinct's origin is in line with the fact that the first problem with which it deals is not the question of the distinction between the sexes but the riddle of where babies come from. (This, in a distorted form which can easily be rectified, is the same riddle that was propounded by the Theban Sphinx.) On the contrary, the existence of two sexes does not to begin with arouse any difficulties or doubts in children. It is self-evident to a male child that a genital like his own is to be attributed to everyone he knows, and he cannot make its absence tally with his picture of these other people.

CASTRATION COMPLEX AND PENIS ENVY

This conviction is energetically maintained by boys, is obstinately defended against the contradictions which soon result from observation, and is only abandoned after severe internal struggles (the castration complex). The substitutes for this penis which they feel is missing in women play a great part in determining the form taken by many perversions.

The assumption that all human beings have the same (male) form of genital is the first of the many remarkable and momentous sexual theories of children. It is of little use to a child that the science of biology justifies his prejudice and has been obliged to recognize the female clitoris as a true substitute for the penis.

Little girls do not resort to denial of this kind when they see that boys' genitals are formed differently from their own. They are ready to recognize them immediately and are overcome by envy for the penis—an envy culminating in the wish, which is so important in its consequences, to be boys themselves.

TYPICAL FAILURE OF INFANTILE SEXUAL RESEARCHES

We can say in general of the sexual theories of children that they are reflections of their own sexual constitution, and that in spite of their grotesque errors the theories show more understanding of sexual processes than one would have given their creators credit for.

𝒞 𝒞 𝒞

There are, however, two elements that remain undiscovered by the sexual researches of children: the fertilizing role of semen and the existence of the female sexual orifice—the same elements, incidentally, in which the infantile organization is itself undeveloped. It therefore follows that the efforts of the childish investigator are habitually fruitless, and end in a renunciation which not infrequently leaves behind it a permanent injury to the instinct for knowledge.

𝒞 𝒞 𝒞

[6]   THE PHASES OF DEVELOPMENT OF THE SEXUAL ORGANIZATION

The characteristics of infantile sexual life which we have hitherto emphasized are the facts that it is essentially autoerotic (i.e. that it finds its object in the infant's own body) and that its individual component instincts are upon the whole disconnected and independent of one another in their search for pleasure.

The final outcome of sexual development lies in what is known as the normal sexual life of the adult, in which the pursuit of pleasure comes under the sway of the reproductive function and in which the component instincts, under the primacy of a single erotogenic zone, form a firm organization directed towards a sexual aim attached to some extraneous sexual object.

PREGENITAL ORGANIZATION

⌐ ⌐ ⌐

We shall give the name of 'pregenital' to organizations of sexual life in which the genital zones have not yet taken over their predominant part. We have hitherto identified two such organizations, which almost seem as though they were harking back to early animal forms of life.

The first of these is the oral or, as it might be called, cannibalistic pregenital sexual organization. Here sexual activity has not yet been separated from the ingestion of food; nor are opposite currents within the activity differentiated. The *object* of both activities is the same; the sexual *aim* consists in the incorporation of the object.

⌐ ⌐ ⌐

A relic of this constructed phase of organization, which is forced upon our notice by pathology, may be seen in thumb-sucking, in which the sexual activity, detached from the nutritive activity, has substituted for the extraneous object one situated in the subject's own body.

A second pregenital phase is that of the sadistic-anal organization. Here the opposition between two currents, which runs through all sexual life, is already developed: they cannot yet, however, be described as 'masculine' and 'feminine', but only as 'active' and 'passive'. The *activity* is put into operation by the instinct for mastery through the agency of the somatic musculature; the organ which, more than any other, represents the *passive* sexual aim is the erotogenic mucous membrane of the anus. Both of these currents have objects, which, however, are not identical. Alongside these, other component instincts operate in an auto-erotic manner. In this phase, therefore, sexual polarity and an extraneous object are already observable. But organization and subordination to the reproductive function are still absent.

Freud's claim that boys' and girls' early sexual development is the same boils down, for him, to the claim that *both* develop as little *boys* until the Oedipal conflict. Both boys and girls believe themselves and everyone else to have a penis, Freud claims, and upon finding that the little girl's is missing, both believe it to have been lost by castration. This leads to Freud's famous claim that girls and women are motivated in their behavior by "penis envy," a claim that has received tremendous criticism—even ridicule—from later thinkers, though many others still hold to it.

In this essay, however Freud adds another to the "oppositions" that he claims can be psychologically equivalent to each other: the opposition between self and other—or, which is the same for Freud, between narcissistic and anaclitic object choice. He claims here that as the child changes his or her love object from the mother's breast to his or her own body—say, to his or her thumb—and as the child changes love-objects again after the Oedipal conflict to someone else external to him or her, that the other becomes symbolized in the self, and vice versa. For instance, the mother's breast becomes symbolized in the child's thumb, and both may be symbolized in some quality or physical characteristic of the child's adult love-objects. Thus, again, in the love-objects of heterosexual individuals, some degree of homosexual object-choice is symbolized, according to Freud.

III. TRANSFORMATIONS OF PUBERTY

The last of the Three Essays discusses adult sexual life, and the repercussions of pre-adolescent sexuality therein.

III. THE TRANSFORMATIONS OF PUBERTY

. . . Now, however, a new sexual aim appears, and all the component instincts combine to attain it, while the erotogenic zones become subordinated to the primacy of the genital zone. Since the new sexual aim assigns very different functions to the two sexes, their sexual development now diverges greatly. That of males is the more straight-forward and the more understandable, while that of females actually enters upon a kind of involution. A normal sexual life is only assured by an exact convergence of the affectionate current and the sensual current both being directed towards the sexual object and sexual aim.

From the vantage-point of psycho-analysis we can look across a frontier, which we may not pass, at the activities of narcissistic libido, and may form some idea of the relation between it and object-libido. Narcissistic or ego-libido seems to be the great reservoir from which the object-cathexes are sent out and into which they are withdrawn once more; the narcissistic libidinal cathexis of the ego is the original state of things, realized in earliest childhood, and is merely covered by the later extrusions of libido, but in essentials persists behind them.

☞ ☞ ☞

[4]   THE DIFFERENTIATION BETWEEN MEN AND WOMEN

As we all know, it is not until puberty that the sharp distinction is established between the masculine and feminine characters. From that time on, this contrast has a more decisive influence than any other upon the shaping of human life. It is true that the masculine and feminine dispositions are already easily recognizable in childhood. The development of the inhibitions of sexuality (shame, disgust, pity, etc.) takes place in little girls earlier and in the face of less resistance than in boys; the tendency to sexual repression seems in general to be greater; and, where the component instincts of sexuality appear, they prefer the passive form. The auto-erotic activity of the erotogenic zones is, however, the same in both sexes, and owing to this uniformity there is no possibility of a distinction between the two sexes such as arises after puberty. So far as the auto-erotic and masturbatory manifestations of sexuality are concerned, we might lay it down that the sexuality of little girls is of a wholly masculine character. Indeed, if we were able to give a more definite connotation to the concepts of 'masculine' and 'feminine', it would even be possible to maintain that libido is invariably and necessarily of a masculine nature, whether it occurs in men or in women and irrespectively of whether its object is a man or a woman.

LEADING ZONES IN MEN AND WOMEN

The leading erotogenic zone in female children is located at the clitoris, and is thus homologous to the masculine genital zone of the glans penis. All my experience concerning masturbation in little girls has related to the clitoris and not to the regions of the external genitalia that are important in later sexual functioning. I am even doubtful whether a female child can be led by the influence of seduction to anything other than clitoridal masturbation.

Puberty, which brings about so great an accession of libido in boys, is marked in girls by a fresh wave of *repression,* in which it is precisely clitoridal sexuality that is affected. What is thus overtaken by repression is a piece of masculine sexuality. The intensification of the brake upon sexuality brought about by pubertal repression in women serves as a stimulus to the libido in men and causes an increase of its activity. Along with this heightening of libido there is also an increase of sexual overvaluation which only emerges in full force in relation to a woman who holds herself back and who denies her sexuality.

Before this transference can be effected, a certain interval of time must often elapse, during which the young woman is anaesthetic.

When erotogenic susceptibility to stimulation has been successfully transferred by a woman from the clitoris to the vaginal orifice, it implies that she has adopted a new leading zone for the purposes of her later sexual activity. A man, on the other hand, retains his leading zone unchanged from childhood. The fact that women change their leading erotogenic zone in this way, together with the wave of repression at puberty, which as it were, puts aside their childish masculinity, are the chief determinants of the greater proneness of women to neurosis and especially to hysteria. These determinants, therefore, are intimately related to the essence of femininity.

[5]   *THE FINDING OF AN OBJECT*

☞ ☞ ☞

At a time at which the first beginnings of sexual satisfaction are still linked with the taking of nourishment, the sexual instinct has a sexual object outside the infant's own body in the shape of his mother's breast.

☞ ☞ ☞

There are thus good reasons why a child sucking at his mother's breast has become the prototype of every relation of love. The finding of an object is in fact a refinding of it.

THE SEXUAL OBJECT DURING EARLY INFANCY

. . . A child's intercourse with anyone responsible for his care affords him an unending source of sexual excitation and satisfaction from his erotogenic zones. This is especially so since the person in charge of him, who, after all, is as a rule his mother, herself regards him with feelings that are derived from her own sexual life: she strokes him, kisses him, rocks him and quite clearly treats him as a substitute for a complete sexual object. A mother would probably be horrified if she were made aware that all her marks of affection were rousing her child's sexual instinct and preparing for its later intensity. She regards what she does as asexual, 'pure' love, since, after all, she carefully avoids applying more excitations to the child's genitals than are unavoidable in nursery care. As we know, however, the sexual instinct is not aroused only by direct excitation of the genital zone. What we call affection will unfailingly show its effects one day on the genital zones as well. Moreover, if the mother understood more of the high importance of the part played by instincts in mental life as a whole—in all its ethical and psychical achievements—she would spare herself any self-reproaches even after her enlightenment. She is only fulfilling her task in teaching the child to love.

THE BARRIER AGAINST INCEST

. . . Among these tendencies the first place is taken with uniform frequency by the child's sexual impulses towards his parents, which are as a rule already differentiated owing to the attraction of the opposite sex—the son being drawn towards his mother and the daughter towards her father. At the same time as these plainly incestuous phantasies are overcome and repudiated, one of the most significant, but also one of the most painful, psychical achievements of the pubertal period is completed: detachment from parental authority, a process that alone makes possible the opposition, which is so important for the progress of civilization, between the new generation and the old.

☞ ☞ ☞

[There are some,] mostly girls, who, to the delight of their parents, have persisted in all their childish love far beyond puberty. It is most instructive to find that it is precisely these girls who in their later marriage lack the capacity to give their husbands what is due to them; they make cold wives and remain sexually anaesthetic.

~ ~ ~

AFTER-EFFECTS OF INFANTILE OBJECT-CHOICE

Even a person who has been fortunate enough to avoid an incestuous fixation of his libido does not entirely escape its influence. It often happens that a young man falls in love seriously for the first time with a mature woman, or a girl with an elderly man in a position of authority; this is clearly an echo of the phase of development that we have been discussing, since these figures are able to re-animate pictures of their mother or father. There can be no doubt that every object-choice whatever is based, though less closely, on these prototypes.

Here, Freud is struggling to account for adult sex differences in love-object choices and sexuality, and to understand and explain female sexual development. He remains committed to the claim that the original and generically human sexual-ity is male sexuality, here going so far as to imply that libido itself is masculine and its repression, feminine. In order to enter into puberty, Freud claims, the boy keeps his primary love object (his mother, or symbols of her) and his primary erogenous zone (the penis); the little girl, however, must change her primary love-object from her mother to her father (and symbols of him) and change her primary erogenous zone. According to Freud, this cannot be achieved by her without a repression of the original instincts, to such an extent that the adult woman's sexuality is always partly repressed, always retaining traces of her necessary pubescent repression. In addition, Freud claims that adult women's sexuality—like all repressed instincts— is complicated and multi-leveled, unlike the straightforward libido of men.

In the Three Essays, despite continuing revision of his theories, Freud lays out the basics of a theory of femininity against which succeeding generations of female psychoanalysts and feminists, in different ways and to varying degrees, have ar-gued: penis envy, mysterious and complex sexuality, derivativeness from male norms, masochism and narcissism. Freud paints a picture of women's psychology that, by his own admission, begs for further investigation.

"FEMININITY" (1932)

This essay, the culmination of Freud's thought on the matter, was one of his series of *New Introductory Lectures on Psychoanalysis,* intended for a broad, non-techni-cal audience. Here, Freud is bolder than elsewhere in his arguments that there are general social, psychological, and even moral differences between the sexes. Many of these differences he attributes to "penis-envy" on the part of women, stemming from the special female version of the "castration complex," in which Freud claims little girls unconsciously blame their mothers for their lack of a penis. It is noteworthy that Freud here makes broad, relatively unsupported, claims about feminine types, about happy marriages for women, about women's social inadequacy, etc.—which stand out as rather unusual in his work, normally cautiously limited to empirical findings in particular patients or examples from mythology or literature.

Among the claims, however, that Freud attributes strictly to psychoanalytic data from women patients is his "seduction hypothesis," briefly discussed here. Many of his neurotic women patients, he claimed, revealed in analysis that they had been seduced when very young by their fathers. Originally, Freud took these claims to be literally true, but by the time of the writing of "Femininity," he had decided that these patients were very likely describing infantile fantasies and not real occurrences. There has been considerable debate among Freud scholars, both about the true frequency of father–daughter incest, and about the sincerity of Freud's decision not to take these patients' claims seriously. In addition, there is vehement current debate regarding the decisions of some contemporary therapists, and even law enforcers, to take the patient's memory of incestuous incidents, recalled during therapy sessions, as true without further analysis.

Other points about femininity upon which Freud touches in this essay received serious review by psychoanalysts and psychologists following him—excerpts from some of which appear later—thinkers who rejected some of these bald claims and reinterpreted others. The claims, e.g., that women are more envious or more masochistic than men, and that women have fewer moral and social principles than men, or that women are emotionally more ambivalent than men, are not themes new to Freud. They appear in various forms, for instance, in several of the readings from earlier periods selected in this book. If nothing else (and many would claim he contributed nothing else), Freud at least offered what he claimed was rational scientific support for some of these age-old beliefs, giving succeeding generations a framework within which to revise or argue against them, instead of merely accepting or rejecting them according to their affinities. Once again, for Freud, as for many philosophers, the ultimate test of his explanations was to be found in the reader's own introspection and in further empirical study, both of which Freud calls for, here and elsewhere in his work.

LECTURE XXXIII

FEMININITY

. . . When you meet a human being, the first distinction you make is 'male or female?' and you are accustomed to make the distinction with unhesitating certainty.

⌐ ⌐ ⌐

Science next tells you something that runs counter to your expectations and is probably calculated to confuse your feelings. It draws your attention to the fact that portions of the male sexual apparatus also appear in women's bodies, though in an atrophied state, and vice versa in the alternative case. It regards their occurrence as indications of *bisexuality*, as though an individual is not a man or a woman but always both—merely a certain amount more the one than the other. You will then be asked to make yourselves familiar with the idea that the proportion in which masculine and feminine are mixed in an individual is subject to quite considerable fluctuations.

∂ ∂ ∂

In conformity with its peculiar nature, psycho-analysis does not try to describe what a woman is—that would be a task it could scarcely perform—but sets about enquiring how she comes into being, how a woman develops out of a child with a bisexual disposition.

∂ ∂ ∂

A comparison with what happens with boys tells us that the development of a little girl into a normal woman is more difficult and more complicated, since it includes two extra tasks, to which there is nothing corresponding in the development of a man.

∂ ∂ ∂

The difference in the structure of the genitals is accompanied by other bodily differences which are too well known to call for mention. Differences emerge too in the instinctual disposition which give a glimpse of the later nature of women. A little girl is as a rule less aggressive, defiant and self-sufficient; she seems to have a greater need for being shown affection and on that account to be more dependent and pliant.

∂ ∂ ∂

One gets an impression, too, that little girls are more intelligent and livelier than boys of the same age; they go out more to meet the external world and at the same time form stronger object-cathexes. I cannot say whether this lead in development has been confirmed by exact observations, but in any case there is no question that girls cannot be described as intellectually backward. These sexual differences are not, however, of great consequence: they can be outweighed by individual variations. For our immediate purposes they can be disregarded.

Both sexes seem to pass through the early phases of libidinal development in the same manner. It might have been expected that in girls there would already have been some lag in aggressiveness in the sadistic-anal phase, but such is not the case. Analysis of children's play has shown our women analysts that the aggressive impulses of little girls leave nothing to be desired in the way of abundance and violence.

∂ ∂ ∂

We are entitled to keep to our view that in the phallic phase of girls the clitoris is the leading erotogenic zone. But it is not, of course, going to remain so. With the change to femininity the clitoris should wholly or in part hand over its sensitivity, and at the same time its importance, to the vagina. This would be one of the two tasks which a woman has to perform in the course of her development, whereas the more fortunate man has only to continue at the time of his sexual maturity the activity that he has previously carried out at the period of the early efflorescence of his sexuality.

. . . Let us now turn to the second task with which a girl's development is burdened. A boy's mother is the first object of his love, and she remains so too during the formation of his Oedipus complex and, in essence, all through his life. For a girl too her first object must be her mother (and the figures of wet-nurses and foster-mothers that merge into her).

In the course of time, therefore, a girl has to change her erotogenic zone and her object—both of which a boy retains. The question then arises of how this happens: in particular, how does a girl pass from her mother to an attachment to her father? or, in other words, how does she pass from her masculine phase to the feminine one to which she is biologically destined?

We shall be glad, then, to know the nature of the girl's libidinal relations to her mother. The answer is that they are of very many different kinds. Since they persist through all three phases of infantile sexuality, they also take on the characteristics of the different phases and express themselves by oral, sadistic-anal and phallic wishes. These wishes represent active as well as passive impulses; if we relate them to the differentiation of the sexes which is to appear later—though we should avoid doing so as far as possible—we may call them masculine and feminine. Besides this, they are completely ambivalent, both affectionate and of a hostile and aggressive nature.

It is not always easy to point to a formulation of these early sexual wishes; what is most clearly expressed is a wish to get the mother with child and the corresponding wish to bear her a child—both belonging to the phallic period and sufficiently surprising, but established beyond doubt by analytic observation.

For instance, we discover the fear of being murdered or poisoned, which may later form the core of a paranoic illness, already present in this pre-Oedipus period, in relation to the mother. Or another case: you will recall an interesting episode in the history of analytic research which caused me many distressing hours. In the period in which the main interest was directed to discovering infantile sexual traumas, almost all my women patients told me that they had been seduced by their father. I was driven to recognize in the end that these reports were untrue and so came to understand that hysterical symptoms are derived from phantasies and not from real occurrences. It was only later that I was able to recognize in this phantasy of being seduced by the father the expression of the typical Oedipus complex in women. And now we find the phantasy of seduction once more in the pre-Oedipus prehistory of girls; but the seducer is regularly the mother. Here, however, the phantasy touches the ground of reality, for it was really the mother who by her activities over the child's bodily hygiene inevitably stimulated, and perhaps even roused for the first time, pleasurable sensations in her genitals.

We will now turn our interest on to the single question of what it is that brings this powerful attachment of the girl to her mother to an end. This, as we know, is its usual fate: it is destined to make room for an attachment to her father.

The turning away from the mother is accompanied by hostility; the attachment to the mother ends in hate. A hate of that kind may become very striking and last all through life; it may be carefully overcompensated later on; as a rule one part of it is overcome while another part persists.

An abundant source of a child's hostility to its mother is provided by its multifarious sexual wishes, which alter according to the phase of the libido and which cannot for the most part be satisfied. The strongest of these frustrations occur at the phallic period, if the mother forbids pleasurable activity with the genitals—often with severe threats and every sign of displeasure—activity to which, after all, she herself had introduced the child. One would think these were reasons enough to account for a girl's turning away from her mother.

It might be thought indeed that this first love-relation of the child's is doomed to dissolution for the very reason that it is the first, for these early object-cathexes are regularly ambivalent to a high degree.

Or the idea that there is an original ambivalence such as this in erotic cathexes may be rejected, and it may be pointed out that it is the special nature of the mother-child relation that leads, with equal inevitability, to the destruction of the child's love; for even the mildest upbringing cannot avoid using compulsion and introducing restrictions, . . . but an objection suddenly emerges which forces our interest in another direction. All these factors—the slights, the disappointments in love, the jealousy, the seduction followed by prohibition— are, after all, also in operation in the relation of a *boy* to his mother and are yet unable to alienate him from the maternal object. Unless we can find something that is specific for girls and is not present or not in the same way present in boys, we shall not have explained the termination of the attachment of girls to their mother.

I believe we have found this specific factor, and indeed where we expected to find it, even though in a surprising form. Where we expected to find it, I say, for it lies in the castration complex. After all, the anatomical distinction [between the sexes] must express itself in psychical consequences. It was, however, a surprise to learn from analyses that girls hold their mother responsible for their lack of a penis and do not forgive her for their being thus put at a disadvantage.

As you hear, then, we ascribe a castration complex to women as well.

The castration complex of girls is also started by the sight of the genitals of the other sex. They at once notice the difference and, it must be admitted, its significance too. They feel seriously wronged, often declare that they want to 'have something like it too', and fall a victim to 'envy for the penis', which will leave ineradicable traces on their development and the formation of their character and which will not be surmounted in even the most favourable cases without a severe expenditure of psychical energy. The girl's recognition of the fact of her being without a penis does not by any means imply that she submits to the fact easily.

One cannot very well doubt the importance of envy for the penis. You may take it as an instance of male injustice if I assert that envy and jealousy play an even greater part in the mental life of women than of men. It is not that I think these characteristics are absent in men or that I think they have no other roots in women than envy for the penis; but I am inclined to attribute their greater amount in women to this latter influence.

The discovery that she is castrated is a turning-point in a girl's growth. Three possible lines of development start from it: one leads to sexual inhibition or to neurosis, the second to change of character in the sense of a masculinity complex, the third, finally, to normal femininity. We have learnt a fair amount, though not everything, about all three.

The essential content of the first is as follows: the little girl has hitherto lived in a masculine way, has been able to get pleasure by the excitation of her clitoris and has brought this activity into relation with her sexual wishes directed towards her mother, which are often active ones; now, owing to the influence of her penis-envy, she loses her enjoyment in her phallic sexuality. Her self-love is mortified by the comparison with the boy's far superior equipment and in consequence she renounces her masturbatory satisfaction from her clitoris, repudiates her love for her mother and at the same time not infrequently represses a good part of her sexual trends in general.

⌇ ⌇ ⌇

Along with the abandonment of clitoridal masturbation a certain amount of activity is renounced.

⌇ ⌇ ⌇

If too much is not lost in the course of it through repression, this femininity may turn out to be normal. The wish with which the girl turns to her father is no doubt originally the wish for the penis which her mother has refused her and which she now expects from her father. The feminine situation is only established, however, if the wish for a penis is replaced by one for a baby, if, that is, a baby takes the place of a penis in accordance with an ancient symbolic equivalence.

⌇ ⌇ ⌇

In this way the ancient masculine wish for the possession of a penis is still faintly visible through the femininity now achieved. But perhaps we ought rather to recognize this wish for a penis as being *par excellence* a feminine one.

With the transference of the wish for a penis-baby on to her father, the girl has entered the situation of the Oedipus complex. Her hostility to her mother, which did not need to be freshly created, is now greatly intensified, for she becomes the girl's rival, who receives from her father everything that she desires from him.

⌇ ⌇ ⌇

In a boy the Oedipus complex, in which he desires his mother and would like to get rid of his father as being a rival, develops naturally from the phase of his phallic sexuality. The threat of castration compels him, however, to give up that attitude. Under the impression of the danger of losing his penis, the Oedipus complex is abandoned, repressed and, in the most normal cases, entirely destroyed, and a severe super-ego is set up as its heir. What happens with a girl is almost the opposite. The castration complex prepares for the Oedipus complex instead of destroying it; the girl is driven out of her attachment to her mother through the influence of her envy for the penis and she enters the Oedipus situation as though into a haven of refuge. In the absence of fear of castration the chief motive is lacking which leads boys to surmount the Oedipus complex. Girls remain in it for an indeterminate length of time; they demolish it late and, even so, incompletely. In these circumstances the formation of the super-ego must suffer; it cannot attain the strength and independence which give it its cultural significance, and feminists are not pleased when we point out to them the effects of this factor upon the average feminine character.

To go back a little. We mentioned as the second possible reaction to the discovery of female castration the development of a powerful masculinity complex.

⌇ ⌇ ⌇

The extreme achievement of such a masculinity complex would appear to be the influencing of the choice of an object in the sense of manifest homosexuality. Analytic experience teaches us, to be sure, that female homosexuality is seldom or never a direct continuation of infantile masculinity. Even for a girl of this kind it seems necessary that she should take her father as an object for some time and enter the Oedipus situation. But afterwards, as a result of her inevitable disappointments from her father, she is driven to regress into her early masculinity complex.

＠ ＠ ＠

Regressions to the fixations of the pre-Oedipus phases very frequently occur; in the course of some women's lives there is a repeated alternation between periods in which masculinity or femininity gains the upper hand. Some portion of what we men call 'the enigma of women' may perhaps be derived from this expression of bisexuality in women's lives. . . . We have called the motive force of sexual life 'the libido'. Sexual life is dominated by the polarity of masculine-feminine; thus the notion suggests itself of considering the relation of the libido to this antithesis. It would not be surprising if it were to turn out that each sexuality had its own special libido appropriated to it, so that one sort of libido would pursue the aims of a masculine sexual life and another sort those of a feminine one. But nothing of the kind is true. There is only one libido, which serves both the masculine and the feminine sexual functions. To it itself we cannot assign any sex; if, following the conventional equation of activity and masculinity, we are inclined to describe it as masculine, we must not forget that it also covers trends with a passive aim.

＠ ＠ ＠

We do not lay claim to more than an average validity for these assertions; nor is it always easy to distinguish what should be ascribed to the influence of the sexual function and what to social breeding. Thus, we attribute a larger amount of narcissism to femininity, which also affects women's choice of object, so that to be loved is a stronger need for them than to love. The effect of penis-envy has a share, further, in the physical vanity of women, since they are bound to value their charms more highly as a late compensation for their original sexual inferiority. Shame, which is considered to be a feminine characteristic *par excellence* but is far more a matter of convention than might be supposed, has as its purpose, we believe, concealment of genital deficiency.

＠ ＠ ＠

The determinants of women's choice of an object are often made unrecognizable by social conditions. Where the choice is able to show itself freely, it is often made in accordance with the narcissistic ideal of the man whom the girl had wished to become. If the girl has remained in her attachment to her father—that is, in the Oedipus complex—her choice is made according to the paternal type. Since, when she turned from her mother to her father, the hostility of her ambivalent relation remained with her mother, a choice of this kind should guarantee a happy marriage. But very often the outcome is of a kind that presents a general threat to such a settlement of the conflict due to ambivalence.

⌒ ⌒ ⌒

So it may easily happen that the second half of a woman's life may be filled by the struggle against her husband, just as the shorter first half was filled by her rebellion against her mother. When this reaction has been lived through, a second marriage may easily turn out very much more satisfying. Another alteration in a woman's nature, for which lovers are unprepared, may occur in a marriage after the first child is born. Under the influence of a woman's becoming a mother herself, an identification with her own mother may be revived, against which she had striven up till the time of her marriage, and this may attract all the available libido to itself, so that the compulsion to repeat reproduces an unhappy marriage between her parents. The difference in a mother's reaction to the birth of a son or a daughter shows that the old factor of lack of a penis has even now not lost its strength. A mother is only brought unlimited satisfaction by her relation to a son; this is altogether the most perfect, the most free from ambivalence of all human relationships.

⌒ ⌒ ⌒

A woman's identification with her mother allows us to distinguish two strata: the pre-Oedipus one which rests on her affectionate attachment to her mother and takes her as a model, and the later one from the Oedipus complex which seeks to get rid of her mother and take her place with her father. We are no doubt justified in saying that much of both of them is left over for the future and that neither of them is adequately surmounted in the course of development. But the phase of the affectionate pre-Oedipus attachment is the decisive one for a woman's future: during it preparations are made for the acquisition of the characteristics with which she will later fulfil her role in the sexual function and perform her invaluable social tasks.

⌒ ⌒ ⌒

The fact that women must be regarded as having little sense of justice is no doubt related to the predominance of envy in their mental life; for the demand for justice is a modification of envy and lays down the condition subject to which one can put envy aside. We also regard women as weaker in their social interests and as having less capacity for sublimating their instincts than men. The former is no doubt derived from the dissocial quality which unquestionably characterizes all sexual relations. Lovers find sufficiency in each other, and families too resist inclusion in more comprehensive associations. The aptitude for sublimation is subject to the greatest individual variations. On the other hand I cannot help mentioning an impression that we are constantly receiving during analytic practice. A man of about thirty strikes us as a youthful, somewhat unformed individual, whom we expect to make powerful use of the possibilities for development opened up to him by analysis. A woman of the same age, however, oftens frightens us by her psychical rigidity and unchangeability. Her libido has taken up final positions and seems incapable of exchanging them for others. There are no paths open to further development; it is as though the whole process had already run its course and remains thenceforward insusceptible to influence—as though, indeed, the difficult development to femininity had exhausted the possibilities of the person concerned. As therapists we lament this state of things, even if we succeed in putting an end to our patient's ailment by doing away with her neurotic conflict.

2. CHARLOTTE PERKINS GILMAN
(American, 1860–1935)

Charlotte Perkins Gilman was the leading intellectual figure in the women's movement in the United States in the early part of this century. Exceptionally determined, stoic, and physically fit for a woman of her time, she wrote and lectured extensively throughout her adult life. She considered herself a sociologist, not a feminist, who sought women's full equality in the industrial workforce as a matter of rational, progressive social design. In all her work, she argued a socialist, but non-Marxist position, somewhat similar to that of John Stuart Mill, in which women's equality rested in equal labor opportunities for men and women. This made Gilman a fundamental thinker in what we might today call "liberal feminism." Her best-known work, *Women and Economics,* from which all the following passages are taken, supports this liberal feminist position by appeal to the Social Darwinist principles popular in her day.

WOMEN AND ECONOMICS (1898)

Women and Economics enjoyed immediate and sustained popularity, going into a second edition just a year after the first. As much a call for reform as an intellectual analysis, the work is strong in its language and a little dramatic in its scientific and historical gestures. It is devoted to an argument against what Gilman calls the "sexuo-economic" relation—the association of sexual and economic relationships in love and marriage. Gilman claimed that while sexual selection did improve the human species, women should be the selectors of men, and not vice versa.

She argues extensively for women's economic independence from men; in other words, that women be free to participate in the nation's productive workforce so that their love relations to men can be disentangled from men's financial support of them. This, Gilman claims, will allow sex-love relationships to flourish unhindered by economic concerns, and it will allow economic progress to go forward unhindered by the conservative force of romantic attachments.

THE OPENING ARGUMENT

In the first chapter, Gilman puts forward the fundamental premise that in our present society, economics and sex are linked by virtue of women's virtually complete dependence on men for financial support. Gilman claims, through a series of responses to hypothetical objections, similar to Mill's strategy of argument, that this linkage is unnatural, unjust, and shameful. It is unnatural, she claims, because it appears only in human cultures. That it is unjust and shameful, she argues, is shown by the fact that efforts to justify women's financial support by men inevitably and rather obviously fail.

CHAPTER 1

. . . We are the only animal species in which the female depends on the male for food, the only animal species in which the sex-relation is also an economic relation. With us an entire sex lives in a relation of economic dependence upon the other sex, and the economic relation is combined with the sex-relation. The economic status of the human female is relative to the sex-relation.

The economic status of the human race in any nation, at any time, is governed mainly by the activities of the male: the female obtains her share in the racial advance only through him.

None can deny these patent facts,—that the economic status of women generally depends upon that of men generally, and that the economic status of women individually depends upon that of men individually, those men to whom they are related. But we are instantly confronted by the commonly received opinion that, although it must be admitted that men make and distribute the wealth of the world, yet women earn their share of it as wives. This assumes either that the husband is in the position of employer and the wife as employee, or that marriage is a "partnership," and the wife an equal factor with the husband in producing wealth.

The claim that marriage is a partnership, in which the two persons married produce wealth which neither of them, separately, could produce, will not bear examination.

Man and wife are partners truly in their mutual obligation to their children,— their common love, duty, and service. But a manufacturer who marries, or a doctor, or a lawyer, does not take a partner in his business, when he takes a partner in parenthood, unless his wife is also a manufacturer, a doctor, or a lawyer.

↩ ↩ ↩

If the wife is not, then, truly a business partner, in what way does she earn from her husband the food, clothing, and shelter she receives at his hands? By house service, it will be instantly replied. This is the general misty idea upon the subject,—that women earn all they get, and more, by house service. Here we come to a very practical and definite economic ground. Although not producers of wealth, women serve in the final processes of preparation and distribution. Their labor in the household has a genuine economic value.

↩ ↩ ↩

The labor of women in the house, certainly, enables men to produce more wealth than they otherwise could; and in this way women are economic factors in society. But so are horses. The labor of horses enables men to produce more wealth than they otherwise could. The horse is an economic factor in society. But the horse is not economically independent, nor is the woman.

↩ ↩ ↩

But the salient fact in this discussion is that, whatever the economic value of the domestic industry of women is, they do not get it. The women who do the most work get the least money, and the women who have the most money do the least work. Their labor is neither given nor taken as a factor in economic exchange. It is held to be their duty as women to do this work; and their economic status bears no relation to their domestic labors, unless an inverse one.

↩ ↩ ↩

The ground that women earn their living by domestic labor is instantly forsaken, and we are told that they obtain their livelihood as mothers.

↩ ↩ ↩

In treating of an economic exchange, asking what return in goods or labor given them,—either to the race collectively or to their husbands individually,—what payment women make for their clothes and shoes and furniture and food and shelter, we are told that the duties and services of the mother entitle her to support.

If this is so, if motherhood is an exchangeable commodity given by women in payment for clothes and food, then we must of course find some relation between the quantity or quality of the motherhood and the quantity and quality of the pay. This being true, then the women who are not mothers have no economic status at all; and the economic status of those who are must be shown to be relative to their motherhood. This is obviously absurd.

↩ ↩ ↩

Visibly, and upon the face of it, women are not maintained in economic prosperity proportioned to their motherhood. Motherhood bears no relation to their economic status.

The claim of motherhood as a factor in economic exchange is false to-day. But suppose it were true. Are we willing to hold this ground, even in theory? Are we willing to consider motherhood as a business, a form of commercial exchange? Are the cares and duties of the mother, her travail and her love, commodities to be exchanged for bread?

It is revolting so to consider them; . . . —what remains to those who deny that women are supported by men?

Because of her maternal duties, the human female is said to be unable to get her own living. As the maternal duties of other females do not unfit them for getting their own living and also the livings of their young, it would seem that the human maternal duties require the segregation of the entire energies of the mother to the service of the child during her entire adult life, or so large a proportion of them that not enough remains to devote to the individual interests of the mother.

. . . Do we see before us the human race, with all its females segregated entirely to the uses of motherhood, consecrated, set apart, specially developed, spending every power of their nature on the service of their children?

In spite of her supposed segregation to maternal duties, the human female, the world over, works at extra-maternal duties for hours enough to provide her with an independent living, and then is denied independence on the ground that motherhood prevents her working!

The working power of the mother has always been a prominent factor in human life. She is the worker *par excellence,* but her work is not such as to affect her economic status. Her living, all that she gets,—food, clothing, ornaments, amusements, luxuries,—these bear no relation to her power to produce wealth, to her services in the house, or to her motherhood. These things bear relation only to the man she marries, the man she depends on,—to how much he has and how much he is willing to give her.

ANALYSIS AND CRITICISM

In succeeding chapters, Gilman offers her own explanation of the sexuo-economic relation and how it came about, giving critical analyses of its failures as well as a sympathetic interpretation of its underlying logic. Her basic argument is that the sexuo-economic relation had its social benefits, but that it has outgrown its use-fulness. As a rhetorical choice, she begins the argument by identifying the many detrimental effects of women's economic dependence on men. Essentially, Gilman claims that linking sexual relations to women's economic survival both creates an undue social emphasis on sex and sex differences, and demoralizes sex-love relationships for both women and men.

CHAPTER 3

Woman's femininity—and "the eternal feminine" means simply the eternal sexual—is more apparent in proportion to her humanity than the femininity of other animals in proportion to their caninity or felinity or equinity. "A feminine hand" or "a feminine foot" is distinguishable anywhere. We do not hear of "a feminine paw" or "a feminine hoof." A hand is an organ of prehension, a foot an organ of locomotion: they are not secondary sexual characteristics. The comparative smallness and feebleness of woman is a sex-distinction. We have carried it to such an excess that women are commonly known as "the weaker sex."

⌐ ⌐ ⌐

. . . Sex has been made to dominate the whole human world,—all the main avenues of life marked "male," and the female left to be a female, and nothing else.

But while with the male the things he fondly imagined to be "masculine" were merely human, and very good for him, with the female the few things marked "feminine" were feminine, indeed; and her ceaseless reiteration of one short song, however sweet, has given it a conspicuous monotony. In garments whose main purpose is unmistakably to announce her sex; with a tendency to ornament which marks exuberance of sex-energy, with a body so modified to sex as to be grievously deprived of its natural activities; with a manner and behavior wholly attuned to sex-advantage, and frequently most disadvantageous to any human gain; with a field of action most rigidly confined to sex-relations; with her overcharged sensibility, her prominent modesty, her "eternal femininity,"—the female of genus homo is undeniably oversexed.

This excessive distinction shows itself again in a marked precocity of development. Our little children, our very babies, show signs of it when the young of other creatures are serenely asexual in general appearance and habit. We eagerly note this precocity. We are proud of it. We carefully encourage it by precept and example, taking pains to develop the sex-instinct in little children, and think no harm. One of the first things we force upon the child's dawning consciousness is the fact that he is a boy or that she is a girl, and that, therefore, each must regard everything from a different point of view. They must be dressed differently, not on account of their personal needs, which are exactly similar at this period, but so that neither, they nor anyone beholding them, may for a moment forget the distinction of sex.

⌐ ⌐ ⌐

CHAPTER 4

. . . The mother ape, with her maternal function well fulfilled, flees leaping through the forest,—plucks her fruit and nuts, keeps up with the movement of the tribe, her young one on her back or held in one strong arm. But the mother woman, enslaved, could not do this.

⌒ ⌒ ⌒

. . . To this day—save, indeed, for the increasing army of women wage-earners, who are changing the face of the world by their steady advance toward economic independence—the personal profit of women bears but too close a relation to their power to win and hold the other sex. From the odalisque with the most bracelets to the debutante with the most bouquets, the relation still holds good,—woman's economic profit comes through the power of sex-attraction.

⌒ ⌒ ⌒

All this human progress has been accomplished by men. Women have been left behind, outside, below, having no social relation whatever, merely the sex-relation, whereby they lived. Let us bear in mind that all the tender ties of family are ties of blood, of sex-relationship. A friend, a comrade, a partner,—this is a human relative. Father, mother, son, daughter, sister, brother, husband, wife,—these are sex-relatives. Blood is thicker than water, we say. True. But ties of blood are not those that ring the world with the succeeding waves of progressive religion, art, science, commerce, education, all that makes us human. Man is the human creature. Woman has been checked, starved, aborted in human growth; and the swelling forces of race-development have been driven back in each generation to work in her through sex-functions alone.

CHAPTER 5

. . . Because of our abnormal sex-development, the whole field has become something of an offence,—a thing to be hidden and ignored, passed over without remark or explanation. Hence this amazing paradox of mothers ashamed of motherhood, unable to explain it, and—measure this well—lying to their children about the primal truths of life,—mothers lying to their own children about motherhood!

The pressure under which this is done is an economic one. The girl must marry: else how live? The prospective husband prefers the girl to know nothing. He is the market, the demand. She is the supply.

⌒ ⌒ ⌒

. . . It is just as humanly natural for a woman as for a man to want wealth. But, when her wealth is made to come through the same channels as her love, she is forbidden to ask for it by her own sex-nature and by business honor. Hence the millions of mismade marriages with "anybody, good Lord!" Hence the million broken hearts which must let all life pass, unable to make any attempt to stop it. Hence the many "maiden aunts," elderly sisters and daughters, unattached women everywhere, who are a burden on their male relatives and society at large. This is changing for the better, to be sure, but changing only through the advance of economic independence for women.

෧ ෧ ෧

Since women are viewed wholly as creatures of sex even by one another, and since everything is done to add to their young powers of sex-attraction; since they are marriageable solely on this ground, unless, indeed, "a fortune" has been added to their charms,—failure to marry is held a clear proof of failure to attract, a lack of sex-value. And, since they have no other value, save in a low order of domestic service, they are quite naturally despised. What else is the creature good for, failing in the functions for which it was created? The scorn of male and female alike falls on this sexless thing: she is a human failure.

෧ ෧ ෧

. . . The girl who marries the rich old man or the titled profligate is condemned by the popular voice; and the girl who marries the poor young man, and helps him live his best, is still approved by the same great arbiter. And yet why should we blame the woman for pursuing her vocation? Since marriage is her only way to get money, why should she not try to get money in that way? Why cast the weight of all self-interest on the "practical" plane so solidly against the sex-interest of the individual and of the race? The mercenary marriage is a perfectly natural consequence of the economic dependence of women.

෧ ෧ ෧

. . . In no other animal species is the female economically dependent on the male. In no other animal species is the sex-relation for sale. A coincidence. Where, on the one hand, every condition of life tends to develop sex in women, to crush out the power and the desire for economic production and exchange, and to develop also the age-long habit of seeking all earthly good at a man's hands and of making but one return; where, on the other hand, man inherits the excess in sex-energy, and is never blamed for exercising it, and where he develops also the age-long habit of taking what he wants from women, for whose helpless acquiescence he makes an economic return,—what should naturally follow? Precisely what has followed. We live in a world of law, and humanity is no exception to it. We have produced a certain percentage of females with inordinate sex-tendencies and inordinate greed for material gain. We have produced a certain percentage of males with inordinate sex-tendencies and a cheerful willingness to pay for their gratification.

෧ ෧ ෧

CHAPTER 6

Besides this maintenance of primeval individualism in the growing collectivity of social economic process and the introduction of the element of sex-combat into the narrowing field of industrial competition, there is another side to the evil influence of the sexuo-economic relation upon social development. This is in the attitude of woman as a non-productive consumer.

. . . To consume food, to consume clothes, to consume houses and furniture and decorations and ornaments and amusements, to take and take and take forever,—from one man if they are virtuous, from many if they are vicious, but always to take and never to think of giving anything in return except their womanhood,—this is the enforced condition of the mothers of the race.

. . . The sexuo-economic relation in its effect on the constitution of the individual keeps alive in us the instincts of savage individualism which we should otherwise have well outgrown. It sexualizes our industrial relation and commercializes our sex-relation. And, in the external effect upon the market, the over-sexed woman, in her unintelligent and ceaseless demands, hinders and perverts the economic development of the world.

Gilman's social critique foreshadows many of the concerns of later philosophers that arose from the preponderance of mass media and mass production. Her vision is that women, as economic beings, will pursue to the best of their abilities whatever avenues are made available to them for their economic security and gain. A number of unnatural and morally distasteful practices result, according to Gilman, from society's allowing women to support themselves only through their sexual relationships to men. Not least of these, she argues, is the unnaturally numerous and elaborate sex differences among humans, more than those found in other animals. This overemphasis of our differences distracts us, she claims, from attending to our underlying human characteristics—identical in men and women—which are the foundation of our social success. In addition, of course, Gilman argues that the sexuo-economic relation reduces marriage essentially to prostitution, encouraging greediness in both women and men, and that mothers who must attend so exclusively to their sexual attractiveness cannot help but set a bad example for their children. These arguments are quite similar to some later Marxist-feminist social critiques, in their insistence that there is always an economic basis for social progress and social decline, including that which regards the position of women.

FEMININITY AS A SOCIAL FORCE, AND A PROGRESSIVE PROGRAM

In Chapter 7 of *Women and Economics,* Gilman offers a sort of genealogy of the sexuo-economic relation as we know it today. Here, she seems to claim that despite the false elaboration of sex differences in our society, there are real sex differences—or at least, gender differences between masculinity and femininity—that have worked together to create the society in which we live. The feminine social force she characterizes as "maternal energy," and she believes it is responsible for preservation and sustenance and as such is naturally superior to masculinity. The masculine social force, however, is characterized as strong and progressive, responsible for social change. These two forces have combined to create the sexuo-economic relations in society, as they have all other social trends. In the chapters following, Gilman argues that although this relation was useful, it is time to change.

CHAPTER 7

Maternal energy is the force through which have come into the world both love and industry. It is through the tireless activity of this desire, the mother's wish to serve the young, that she began the first of the arts and crafts whereby we live. While the male savage was still a mere hunter and fighter, expressing masculine energy, the katabolic force, along its essential line, expanding, scattering, the female savage worked out in equally natural ways the conserving force of female energy. She gathered together and saved nutrition for the child, as the germ-cell gathers and saves nutrition in the unconscious silences of nature.

ᕫ ᕫ ᕫ

Maternal energy, working externally through our elaborate organism, is the source of productive industry, the main current of social life.

But not until this giant force could ally itself with others and work cooperatively, overcoming the destructive action of male energy in its blind competition, could our human life enter upon its full course of racial evolution. This is what was accomplished through the suppression of the free action of maternal energy in the female and its irresistible expression through the male.

ᕫ ᕫ ᕫ

The subjection of woman has involved to an enormous degree the maternalizing of man. Under its bonds he has been forced into new functions, impossible to male energy alone. He has had to learn to love and care for some one besides himself. He has had to learn to work, to serve, to be human.

ᕫ ᕫ ᕫ

. . . It was not well for the race to have the conservative processes of life so wholly confined to the female, the male being merely a temporary agent in reproduction and of no further use. His size, strength, and ferocity—admirable qualities in maintaining the life of an individual animal—were not the most desirable to develop the human race. We needed most the quality of coordination,—the facility in union, the power to make and to save rather than to spend and to destroy. These were female qualities.

ᕫ ᕫ ᕫ

. . . Race-preservation has been almost entirely a female function, sometimes absolutely so. But it has been proven better for the race to have two highly developed parents rather than to have one. Therefore, sexual equality has been slowly evolved, not only by increasing the importance of the male element in reproduction, but by developing race-qualities in the male, so long merely a reproductive agent. The last step of this process has been the elevation of the male of genus homo to full racial equality with the female, and this has involved her temporary subjection. Both her physical and psychical tendencies have been transplanted into the organism of the male. He has been made the working mother of the world. The sexuo-economic relation was necessary to raise and broaden, to deepen and sweeten, to make more feminine, and so more human, the male of the human race. If the female had remained in full personal freedom and activity, she would have remained superior to him, and both would have remained stationary.

            ☞ ☞ ☞

The expansive and variable male energy, struggling under its new necessity for constructive labor, has caused that labor to vary and progress more than it would have done in feminine hands alone. Out of her wealth of power and patience, liking to work, to give, she toils on forever in the same primitive industries. He, impatient of obstacles, not liking to work, desirous to get rather than to give, splits his task into a thousand specialties, and invents countless ways to lighten his labors. Male energy made to expend itself in performing female functions is what has brought our industries to their present development. Without the economic dependence of the female, the male would still be merely the hunter and fighter, the killer, the destroyer; and she would continue to be the industrious mother, without change or progress.

            ☞ ☞ ☞

. . . Many, reassured by this frank admission, will ask, if it is so clear that the subjection of woman was useful, that this evil-working, monstrous sexuo-economic relation was after all of racial advantage, how we know that it is time to change. Principally, because we are changing.

            ☞ ☞ ☞

The common consciousness of humanity, the sense of social need and social duty, is making itself felt in both men and women. The time has come when we are open to deeper and wider impulses than the sex-instinct; the social instincts are strong enough to come into full use at last. This is shown by the twin struggle that convulses the world to-day,—in sex and economics,—the "woman's movement" and the "labor movement."

            ☞ ☞ ☞

Sociologically, these conditions, which some find so painful and alarming, mean but one thing,—the increase of social consciousness.

            ☞ ☞ ☞

With this higher growth of individual consciousness, and forming a part of it, comes the commensurate growth of social consciousness. We have grown to care for one another.

The woman's movement rests not alone on her larger personality, with its tingling sense of revolt against injustice, but on the wide, deep sympathy of women for one another.

⌒ ⌒ ⌒

In our present stage of social evolution it is increasingly difficult and painful for women to endure their condition of economic dependence, and therefore they are leaving it.

⌒ ⌒ ⌒

CHAPTER 10

Economic independence for women necessarily involves a change in the home and family relation. But, if that change is for the advantage of individual and race, we need not fear it. It does not involve a change in the marriage relation except in withdrawing the element of economic dependence, nor in the relation of mother to child save to improve it. But it does involve the exercise of human faculty in women, in social service and exchange rather than in domestic service solely. This will of course require the introduction of some other form of living than that which now obtains. It will render impossible the present method of feeding the world by means of millions of private servants, and bringing up children by the same hand.

⌒ ⌒ ⌒

Marriage and "the family" are two institutions, not one, as is commonly supposed. We confuse the natural result of marriage in children, common to all forms of sex-union, with the family,—a purely social phenomenon. Marriage is a form of sex-union recognized and sanctioned by society. It is a relation between two or more persons, according to the custom of the country, and involves mutual obligations. Although made by us an economic relation, it is not essentially so, and will exist in much higher fulfillment after the economic phase is outgrown.

⌒ ⌒ ⌒

Human love, as it rises to an ever higher grade, looks more and more for such companionship. But the economic status of marriage rudely breaks in upon love's young dream. On the economic side, apart from all the sweetness and truth of the sex-relation, the woman in marrying becomes the house-servant, or at least the housekeeper, of the man. Of the world we may say that the intimate personal necessities of the human animal are ministered to by woman. Married lovers do not work together. They may, if they have time, rest together: they may, if they can, play together; but they do not make beds and sweep and cook together, and they do not go down town to the office together. They are economically on entirely different social planes, and these constitute a bar to any higher, truer union than such as we see about us. Marriage is not perfect unless it is between class equals. There is no equality in class between those who do their share in the world's work in the largest, newest, highest ways and those who do theirs in the smallest, oldest, lowest ways.

Granting squarely that it is the business of women to make the home life of the world true, healthful, and beautiful, the economically dependent woman does not do this, and never can. The economically independent woman can and will.

☞ ☞ ☞

CHAPTER 11

If there should be built and opened in any of our large cities to-day a commodious and well-served apartment house for professional women with families, it would be filled at once. The apartments would be without kitchens; but there would be a kitchen belonging to the house from which meals could be served to the families in their rooms or in a common dining-room, as preferred. It would be a home where the cleaning was done by efficient workers, not hired separately by the families, but engaged by the manager of the establishment; and a roof-garden, day nursery, and kindergarten, under well-trained professional nurses and teachers, would insure proper care of the children. The demand for such provision is increasing daily, and must soon be met, not by a boarding-house or a lodging-house, a hotel, a restaurant, or any makeshift patching together of these; but by a permanent provision for the needs of women and children, of family privacy with collective advantage. This must be offered on a business basis to prove a substantial business success; and it will so prove, for it is a growing social need.

☞ ☞ ☞

CHAPTER 14

It is worth while for us to consider the case fully and fairly, that we may see what it is that is happening to us, and welcome with open arms the happiest change in human condition that ever came into the world. To free an entire half of humanity from an artificial position; to release vast natural forces from a strained and clumsy combination, and set them free to work smoothly and easily as they were intended to work; to introduce conditions that will change humanity from within, making for better motherhood and fatherhood, better babyhood and childhood, better food, better homes, better society,—this is to work for human improvement along natural lines. It means enormous racial advance, and that with great swiftness; for this change does not wait to create new forces, but sets free those already potentially strong, so that humanity will fly up like a released spring. And it is already happening. All we need do is to understand and help.[4]

---

[4] All the above excerpts are from Charlotte Perkins Gilman, *Women and Economics: A Study of the Economic Relation Between Men and Women as a Factor in Social Evolution*. Originally published in 1898 by Small, Maynard & Co., Boston.

It would appear that Gilman considers maternal energy to be a socially conservative but morally superior historical force, and masculinity a socially progressive but morally retrograde one. Gilman seems to claim that maternal energy has played the larger role in the development of modern society, leading to a very advanced culture that has reached a plateau in its social and moral development. Gilman wants to balance what she calls the "maternalization of men" that has so advanced throughout human history with what we might call a "fraternalization of women," in which women cooperate with men in all kinds of work and so effect a social advance.

In intervening chapters, which because of limits of space could not be reproduced here, Gilman adds support to her general argument through the investigation of a number of specific employments—the upbringing of children, the preparation of food, the cleaning and decoration of the home, etc. Achievement in these vitally necessary social functions, Gilman claims, has been retarded by their alliance with the sexuo-economic relation. By exclusively assigning these jobs to women but distributing them to all women indiscriminately, society has, according to Gilman, denied these employments the economic benefits of specialization, fair market competition, and professional development. Hence, Gilman claims, we have come to a point where families receive maternal care, food, and home life far below the standards of other services.

Gilman advocates social changes not unlike the sorts of programs championed by contemporary liberals; indeed she allies herself with their predecessors, the women's and labor movements. In essence, she seeks a sort of political, moral, and personal utopia based on social-scientific principles. As she sees it, human society is by its nature always advancing, always growing better as it grows older. Hence, while Gilman retains many of the nineteenth-century concerns over the distinctions between nature and culture and the deleterious effects of certain cultural institutions, she does not share the nineteenth-century's romanticism, its nostalgia, or its fear of scientific domination. Rather, Gilman seems to believe in a kind of social technology, a harnessing of natural feminine and masculine forces in the creation of idyllic society.

3. VIRGINIA WOOLF
(British, 1882–1941)

One of the great literary figures of modern times, Virginia Woolf was a sensitive critic and essayist as well as an innovative novelist of the first calibre. Along with her sisters and brother, she was a founding figure in the free-thinking intellectual circle later to be called the "Bloomsbury Group" (after the area of London in which they lived), with which several prominent intellectuals of the period were associated. Although Woolf participated only nominally in feminist activities, many of her works, both fictional and non-fictional, take up the questions of women's interior life and artistic creativity, and of the intellectual and emotional quality of the relationships between men and women.

A ROOM OF ONE'S OWN (1929)

A Room of One's Own, from which all the following passages are taken, is a long essay based on two lectures on the topic of "women and fiction" that Woolf delivered in 1928. The title indicates her primary claim with regard to this issue, namely that a woman writer requires above all a private, quiet place to write. Woolf, like Gilman, believes that one prerequisite for women's creative productivity is their economic independence. However, Woolf's concern is not with social progress, but with the productive activity of the creative intellect. The busy life of most women, who have been forced to depend on men for their support, Woolf claims, leaves them without the time and peace of mind necessary to art.

THE MIRROR

Woolf's reflections on women and fiction are delivered through a narrative depicting Woolf's experiences doing research for the lectures. Her investigation is based on her intuition that women writers have been rare primarily because they have lacked economic independence from men.

CHAPTER TWO

. . . Why did men drink wine and women water? Why was one sex so prosperous and the other so poor? What effect has poverty on fiction? What conditions are necessary for the creation of works of art?—a thousand questions at once suggested themselves. But one needed answers, not questions; and an answer was only to be had by consulting the learned and the unprejudiced, who have removed themselves above the strife of tongue and the confusion of body and issued the result of their reasoning and research in books which are to be found in the British Museum.

Have you any notion how many books are written about women in the course of one year? Have you any notion how many are written by men? Are you aware that you are, perhaps, the most discussed animal in the universe?

Even the names of the books gave me food for thought. Sex and its nature might well attract doctors and biologists; but what was surprising and difficult of explanation was the fact that sex—woman, that is to say—also attracts agreeable essayists, light-fingered novelists, young men who have taken the M.A. degree; men who have taken no degree; men who have no apparent qualification save that they are not women. Some of these books were, on the face of it, frivolous and facetious; but many, on the other hand, were serious and prophetic, moral and hortatory. Merely to read the titles suggested innumerable schoolmasters, innumerable clergymen mounting their platforms and pulpits and holding forth with a loquacity which far exceeded the hour usually allotted to such discourse on this one subject. It was a most strange phenomenon; and apparently—here I consulted the letter M—one confined to male sex. Women do not write books about men—a fact that I could not help welcoming with relief, for if I had first to read all that men have written about women, then all that women have written about men, the aloe that flowers once in a hundred years would flower twice before I could set pen to paper.

. . . Why are women, judging from this catalogue, so much more interesting to men than men are to women? A very curious fact it seemed, and my mind wandered to picture the lives of men who spend their time in writing books about women; whether they were old or young, married or unmarried, red-nosed or humpbacked—anyhow, it was flattering, vaguely, to feel oneself the object of such attention, provided that it was not entirely bestowed by the crippled and the infirm—

⌒ ⌒ ⌒

Professors, schoolmasters, sociologists, clergymen, novelists, essayists, journalists, men who had no qualification save that they were not women, chased my simple and single question—Why are women poor?—until it became fifty questions.

. . . Are they capable of education or incapable? Napoleon thought them incapable. Dr. Johnson thought the opposite. Have they souls or have they not souls? Some savages say they have none. Others, on the contrary, maintain that women are half divine and worship them on that account. Some sages hold that they are shallower in the brain; others that they are deeper in the consciousness. Goethe honoured them; Mussolini despises them. Wherever one looked men thought about women and thought differently. It was impossible to make head or tail of it all.

⌒ ⌒ ⌒

. . . In my listlessness, in my desperation, been drawing a picture where I should, like my neighbour, have been writing a conclusion. I had been drawing a face, a figure. It was the face and the figure of Professor von X. engaged in writing his monumental work entitled *The Mental, Moral, and Physical Inferiority of the Female Sex*. He was not in my picture a man attractive to women. He was heavily built; he had a great jowl; to balance that he had very small eyes; he was very red in the face. His expression suggested that he was labouring under some emotion that made him jab his pen on the paper as if he were killing some noxious insect as he wrote, but even when he had killed it that did not satisfy him; he must go on killing it; and even so, some cause for anger and irritation remained. Could it be his wife, I asked, looking at my picture. Was she in love with a cavalry officer? Was the cavalry officer slim and elegant and dressed in astrachan? Had he been laughed at, to adopt the Freudian theory, in his cradle by a pretty girl? For even in his cradle the professor, I thought, could not have been an attractive child. Whatever the reason, the professor was made to look very angry and very ugly in my sketch, as he wrote his great book upon the mental, moral and physical inferiority of women. Drawing pictures was an idle way of finishing an unprofitable morning's work. Yet it is in our idleness, in our dreams, that the submerged truth sometimes comes to the top. A very elementary exercise in psychology, not to be dignified by the name of psycho-analysis, showed me, on looking at my notebook, that the sketch of the angry professor had been made in anger. Anger had snatched my pencil while I dreamt. But what was anger doing there? Interest, confusion, amusement, boredom—all these emotions I could trace and name as they succeeded each other throughout the morning. Had anger, the black snake, been lurking among them? Yes, said the sketch, anger had. It referred me unmistakably to the one book, to the one phrase, which had roused the demon; it was the professor's statement about the mental, moral and physical inferiority of women. My heart had leapt. My cheeks had burnt. I had flushed with anger. There was nothing specially remarkable, however foolish, in that. One does not like to be told that one is naturally the inferior of a little man—I looked at the student next me—who breathes hard, wears a ready-made tie, and has not shaved this fortnight. One has certain foolish vanities.

Soon my own anger was explained and done with; but curiosity remained. How explain the anger of the professors? Why were they angry? For when it came to analysing the impression left by these books there was always an element of heat. This heat took many forms; it showed itself in satire, in sentiment, in curiosity, in reprobation.

To judge from its odd effects, it was anger disguised and complex, not anger simple and open.

. . . The most transient visitor to this planet, I thought, who picked up this paper could not fail to be aware, even from this scattered testimony, that England is under the rule of a patriarchy. Nobody in their senses could fail to detect the dominance of the professor. His was the power and the money and the influence. He was the proprietor of the paper and its editor and sub-editor. He was the Foreign Secretary and the Judge. He was the cricketer; he owned the race-horses and the yachts. He was the director of the company that pays two hundred per cent to its shareholders. He left millions to charities and colleges that were ruled by himself. He suspended the film actress in mid-air. He will decide if the hair on the meat axe is human; he it is who will acquit or convict the murderer, and hang him, or let him go free. With the exception of the fog he seemed to control everything. Yet he was angry.

If he had written dispassionately about women, had used indisputable proofs to establish his argument and had shown no trace of wishing that the result should be one thing rather than another, one would not have been angry either.

One would have accepted the fact, as one accepts the fact that a pea is green or a canary yellow. So be it, I should have said. But I had been angry because he was angry. Yet it seemed absurd, I thought, turning over the evening paper, that a man with all this power should be angry. Or is anger, I wondered, somehow, the familiar, the attendant sprite on power?

☞ ☞ ☞

Possibly they were not "angry" at all; often, indeed, they were admiring, devoted, exemplary in the relations of private life. Possibly when the professor insisted a little too emphatically upon the inferiority of women, he was concerned not with their inferiority, but with his own superiority. That was what he was protecting rather hot-headedly and with too much emphasis, because it was a jewel to him of the rarest price. Life for both sexes—and I looked at them, shouldering their way along the pavement—is arduous, difficult, a perpetual struggle. It calls for gigantic courage and strength. More than anything, perhaps, creatures of illusion as we are, it calls for confidence in oneself. Without self-confidence we are as babes in the cradle. And how can we generate this imponderable quality, which is yet so invaluable, most quickly? By thinking that other people are inferior to oneself.

☞ ☞ ☞

Women have served all these centuries as looking-glasses possessing the magic and delicious power of reflecting the figure of man at twice its natural size. Without that power probably the earth would still be swamp and jungle. The glories of all our wars would be unknown.

☞ ☞ ☞

That serves to explain in part the necessity that women so often are to men. And it serves to explain how restless they are under her criticism; how impossible it is for her to say to them this book is bad, this picture is feeble, or whatever it may be, without giving far more pain and rousing far more anger than a man would do who gave the same criticism. For if she begins to tell the truth, the figure in the looking-glass shrinks; his fitness for life is diminished. How is he to go on giving judgement, civilising natives, making laws, writing books, dressing up and speechifying at banquets, unless he can see himself at breakfast and at dinner at least twice the size he really is? So I reflected, crumbling my bread and stirring my coffee and now and again looking at the people in the street. The looking-glass vision is of supreme importance because it charges the vitality; it stimulates the nervous system. Take it away and man may die, like the drug fiend deprived of his cocaine.

☞ ☞ ☞

My aunt, Mary Beton, I must tell you, died by a fall from her horse when she was riding out to take the air in Bombay. The news of my legacy reached me one night about the same time that the act was passed that gave votes to women. A

solicitor's letter fell into the post-box and when I opened it I found that she had
left me five hundred pounds a year for ever. Of the two—the vote and the
money—the money, I own, seemed infinitely the more important.

Food, house, and clothing are mine for ever. Therefore not merely do effort
and labour cease, but also hatred and bitterness. I need not hate any man; he
cannot hurt me. I need not flatter any man; he has nothing to give me. So
imperceptibly I found myself adopting a new attitude towards the other half of
the human race. It was absurd to blame any class or any sex, as a whole. Great
bodies of people are never responsible for what they do. They are driven by
instincts which are not within their control. They too, the patriarchs, the
professors, had endless difficulties, terrible drawbacks to contend with.

And, as I realised these drawbacks, by degrees fear and bitterness modified
themselves into pity and toleration; and then in a year or two, pity and toleration
went, and the greatest release of all came, which is freedom to think of things
in themselves.

Behind the paradoxes of men's writing about women, Woolf finds a kind of unified male psychology—a need to be superior, which men seek to satisfy through
women. In the history books, then, appear only the oversized "reflections" of man's
greatness that women helped to create. In this way, Woolf explains as well men's
general personal dependence on women, despite their complete misunderstanding
of them. As a reflection of themselves, women provide to men a kind of smaller,
derivative, but quite *masculine* identity. Just as one's focus on one's reflection in
the surface of a window prevents one from seeing the interior of the room behind it,
this self-absorbed position of men towards women prevents them from any genuine
investigations of women's characters or lives. Woolf's view of men's social and
economic power, based on this image, is of a great civilization based on the foundation of a rather pathetic emotional dependence. Thus, Woolf tends in general to explain social phenomena—men's social power, the vast number of books derogating
women, women's historical invisibility, the dearth of women writers—by appeal to
psychological phenomena.

SHAKESPEARE'S SISTER

One of the most famous and effective of Woolf's images in this essay is the story of
Shakespeare's fictional "sister."

CHAPTER THREE

. . . It is a perennial puzzle why no woman wrote a word of that extraordinary
literature when every other man, it seemed, was capable of song or sonnet. What

were the conditions in which women lived, I asked myself; for fiction, imaginative work that is, is not dropped like a pebble upon the ground, as science may be; fiction is like a spider's web, attached ever so lightly perhaps, but still attached to life at all four corners.

☞ ☞ ☞

I went, therefore, to the shelf where the histories stand and took down one of the latest, Professor Trevelyan's *History of England.* Once more I looked up Women, found "position of," and turned to the pages indicated. "Wife-beating," I read, "was a recognised right to man, and was practised without shame by high as well as low. . . . Similarly," the historian goes on, "the daughter who refused to marry the gentleman of her parents' choice was liable to be locked up, beaten and flung about the room, without any shock being inflicted on public opinion.

☞ ☞ ☞

That was about 1470, soon after Chaucer's time. The next reference to the position of women is some two hundred years later, in the time of the Stuarts.

☞ ☞ ☞

Yet even so," Professor Trevelyan concludes, "neither Shakespeare's women nor those of authentic seventeenth-century memories, like the Verneys and the Hutchinsons, seem wanting in personality and character." Certainly, if we consider it, Cleopatra must have had a way with her; Lady Macbeth, one would suppose, had a will of her own; Rosalind, one might conclude, was an attractive girl. Professor Trevelyan is speaking no more than the truth when he remarks that Shakespeare's women do not seem wanting in personality and character. Not being a historian, one might go even further and say that women have burnt like beacons in all the works of all the poets from the beginning of time— Clytemnestra, Antigone, Cleopatra, Lady Macbeth, Phedre, Cressida, Rosalind, Desdemona, the Duchess of Malfi, among the dramatists; then among the prose writers: Millamant, Clarissa, Becky Sharp, Anna Karenina, Emma Bovary, Madame de Guermantes—the names flock to mind, nor do they recall women "lacking in personality and character." Indeed, if woman had no existence save in the fiction written by men, one would imagine her a person of the utmost importance; very various; heroic and mean; splendid and sordid; infinitely beautiful and hideous in the extreme; as great as a man, some think even greater. But this is woman in fiction. In fact, as Professor Trevelyan points out, she was locked up, beaten and flung about the room.

☞ ☞ ☞

Here am I asking why women did not write poetry in the Elizabethan age, and I am not sure how they were educated; whether they were taught to write; whether they had sitting-rooms to themselves; how many women had children before they were twenty-one; what, in short, they did from eight in the morning till eight at night. They had no money evidently; according to Professor

Trevelyan they were married whether they liked it or not before they were out of the nursery, at fifteen or sixteen very likely. It would have been extremely odd, even upon this showing, had one of them suddenly written the plays of Shakespeare, I concluded , and I thought of that old gentleman, who is dead now, but was a bishop, I think, who declared that it was impossible for any woman, past, present, or to come, to have the genius of Shakespeare.

⸎ ⸎ ⸎

Be that as it may, I could not help thinking, as I looked at the works of Shakespeare on the shelf, that the bishop was right at least in this; it would have been impossible, completely and entirely, for any woman to have written the plays of Shakespeare in the age of Shakespeare. Let me imagine, since facts are so hard to come by, what would have happened had Shakespeare had a wonderfully gifted sister, called Judith, let us say. Shakespeare himself went, very probably—his mother was an heiress—to the grammar school, where he may have learnt Latin—Ovid, Virgil and Horace—and the elements of grammar and logic. He was, it is well known, a wild boy who poached rabbits, perhaps shot a deer, and had, rather sooner than he should have done, to marry a woman in the neighbourhood, who bore him a child rather quicker than was right. That escapade sent him to seek his fortune in London. He had, it seemed, a taste for the theatre; he began by holding horses at the stage door. Very soon he got work in the theatre, became a successful actor, and lived at the hub of the universe, meeting everybody, knowing everybody, practising his art on the boards, exercising his wits in the streets, and even getting access to the palace of the queen. Meanwhile his extraordinarily gifted sister, let us suppose, remained at home. She was as adventurous, as imaginative, as agog to see the world as he was. But she was not sent to school. She had no chance of learning grammar and logic, let alone of reading Horace and Virgil. She picked up a book now and then, one of her brother's perhaps, and read a few pages. But then her parents came in and told her to mend the stockings or mind the stew and not moon about with books and papers. They would have spoken sharply but kindly, for they were substantial people who knew the conditions of life for a woman and loved their daughter—indeed, more likely than not she was the apple of her father's eye. Perhaps she scribbled some pages up in an apple loft on the sly, but was careful to hide them or set fire to them. Soon, however, before she was out of her teens, she was to be betrothed to the son of a neighbouring wool-stapler. She cried out that marriage was hateful to her, and for that she was severely beaten by her father. Then he ceased to scold her. He begged her instead not to hurt him, not to shame him in this matter of her marriage. He would give her a chain of beads or a fine petticoat, he said; and there were tears in his eyes. How could she disobey him? How could she break his heart? The force of her own gift alone drove her to it. She made up a small parcel of her belongings, let herself down by a rope one summer's night and took the road to London. She was not seventeen. The birds that sang in the hedge were not more musical than she was. She had the quickest fancy, a gift like her brother's, for the tune of words. Like him, she had a taste for the theatre. She stood at the stage door; she wanted to act, she said. Men laughed in her face. The manager—a fat, loose-lipped man—guffawed. He bellowed something about poodles dancing and women acting—no woman, he said, could possibly be an actress. He hinted—you can imagine what. She could get no training in her craft. Could she even seek her dinner in a tavern or roam the streets at midnight? Yet her genius was for fiction and lusted to feed abundantly upon the lives of men and women and the study of their ways. At last—for she was very young, oddly like Shakespeare the poet in her face, with the same grey eyes and rounded brows—at last Nick Greene the actor-manager took pity on her; she found herself with child by that gentleman and so—who shall measure the heat and violence of the poet's heart when caught and tangled in a woman's body?—killed herself one winter's night and lies buried at some cross-roads where the omnibuses now stop outside the Elephant and Castle.

That, more or less, is how the story would run, I think, if a woman in Shakespeare's day had had Shakespeare's genius. But for my part, I agree with the deceased bishop, if such he was—it is unthinkable that any woman in Shakespeare's day should have had Shakespeare's genius.

ᕗ ᕗ ᕗ

That woman, then, who was born with a gift of poetry in the sixteenth century, was an unhappy woman, a woman at strife against herself. All the conditions of her life, all her own instincts, were hostile to the state of mind which is needed to set free whatever is in the brain. But what is the state of mind that is most propitious to the act of creation, I asked. Can one come by any notion of the state that furthers and makes possible that strange activity? Here I opened the volume containing the Tragedies of Shakespeare. What was Shakespeare's state of mind, for instance, when he wrote *Lear* and *Antony and Cleopatra*? It was certainly the state of mind most favourable to poetry that there has ever existed. But Shakespeare himself said nothing about it.

"Judith" Shakespeare serves in the essay as a kind of philosophical hypothesis to show that the conditions of a woman's life, and not her innate capacity, prevent her from producing works of art. This will contribute to Woolf's overall thesis that women need, above all, "five hundred a year . . . and rooms of our own" to produce fiction. Financial dependence on men, Woolf claims, similarly to Gilman, forces women to occupy themselves otherwise than by writing. In addition, the unique social pressures with which women find themselves surrounded—the emotional dependence of their fathers and husbands upon them, the advantages taken of them by men and the resulting and continual spectre of pregnancy and of having to raise children—has throughout history made life as an artist nearly impossible for a woman.

Note Woolf's discussion of Shakespeare himself, however. This greatest of poets, she claims, in company with other great male artists, portrays women as the equals of men, for better and for worse. Note as well Woolf's rather sympathetic portrayal of "Judith's" father, and her picturesque portrayal of the theater manager and others, as well as her depiction of "Judith" herself as in spirit similar to our idea of the male artist in her devotion to her art and her energetic pursuit of it. Woolf's own writing certainly demonstrates therefore the claim she wants to make, using Shakespeare, about the sexual fairness of artists as compared to other men. What is it about a great artist, she wonders, that allows him or her to overcome the failings and forego the needs that she has found in the writings of male historians and scientists? To solve this new puzzle, Woolf investigates the artistic process itself.

THE ARTIST'S CONSCIOUSNESS

In the closing chapter of *A Room of One's Own,* Woolf ponders the question of "women and fiction" in tandem with the question, raised earlier, about the sexual equilibrium of the artist as compared to other men. This fruitful combination of interests leads Woolf to a sort of general literary theory regarding gender and the artist's consciousness.

CHAPTER SIX

The sight was ordinary enough; what was strange was the rhythmical order with which my imagination had invested it; and the fact that the ordinary sight of two people getting into a cab had the power to communicate something of their own seeming satisfaction. The sight of two people coming down the street and meeting at the corner seems to ease the mind of some strain, I thought, watching the taxi turn and make off. Perhaps to think, as I had been thinking these two days, of one sex as distinct from the other is an effort. It interferes with the unity of the mind. Now that effort had ceased and that unity had been restored by seeing two people come together and get into a taxi-cab. The mind is certainly a very mysterious organ, I reflected, drawing my head in from the window, about which nothing whatever is known, though we depend upon it so completely. Why do I feel that there are severances and oppositions in the mind, as there are strains from obvious causes on the body? What does one mean by "the unity of the mind," I pondered, for clearly the mind has so great a power of concentrating at any point at any moment that it seems to have no single state of being. It can separate itself from the people in the street, for example, and think of itself as apart from them, at an upper window looking down on them.

Again if one is a woman one is often surprised by a sudden splitting off of consciousness, say in walking down Whitehall, when from being the natural inheritor of that civilisation, she becomes, on the contrary, outside of it, alien and critical. Clearly the mind is always altering its focus, and bringing the world into different perspectives. But some of these states of mind seem, even if adopted spontaneously, to be less comfortable than others. In order to keep oneself continuing in them one is unconsciously holding something back, and gradually the repression becomes an effort. But there may be some state of mind in which one could continue without effort because nothing is required to be held back.

One has a profound, if irrational, instinct in favour of the theory that the union of man and woman makes for the greatest satisfaction, the most complete happiness. But the sight of the two people getting into the taxi and the satisfaction it gave me made me also ask whether there are two sexes in the mind corresponding to the two sexes in the body, and whether they also require to be united in order to get complete satisfaction and happiness. And I went on amateurishly to sketch a plan of the soul so that in each of us two powers preside, one male, one female; and in the man's brain, the man predominates over the woman, and in the woman's brain, the woman predominates over the man. The normal and comfortable state of being is that when the two live in harmony together, spiritually co-operating. If one is a man, still the woman part of the brain must have effect; and a woman also must have intercourse with the man in her. Coleridge perhaps meant this when he said that a great mind is androgynous. It is when this fusion takes place that the mind is fully fertilised and uses all its faculties. Perhaps a mind that is purely masculine cannot create, any more than a mind that is purely feminine, I thought. But it would be well to test what one meant by man-womanly, and conversely by woman-manly, by pausing and looking at a book or two.

. . . He meant, perhaps, that the androgynous mind is resonant and porous; that it transmits emotion without impediment; that it is naturally creative, incandescent and undivided. In fact one goes back to Shakespeare's mind as the type of the androgynous, of the man-womanly mind, though it would be impossible to say what Shakespeare thought of women. And if it be true that it is one of the tokens of the fully developed mind that it does not think specially or separately of sex, how much harder it is to attain that condition now than ever before. Here I came to the books by living writers, and there paused and wondered if this fact were not at the root of something that had long puzzled me. No age can ever have been as stridently sex-conscious as our own; those innumerable books by men about women in the British Museum are a proof of it. The Suffrage campaign was no doubt to blame. It must have roused in men an extraordinary desire for self-assertion; it must have made them lay an emphasis upon their own sex and its characteristics which they would not have troubled to think about had they not been challenged.

Do what she will a woman cannot find . . . that fountain of perpetual life which the critics assure her is there. It is not only that they celebrate male virtues, enforce male values and describe the world of men; it is that the emotion with which these books are permeated is to a woman incomprehensible.

⌒ ⌒ ⌒

For the emotion which is so deep, so subtle, so symbolical to a man moves a woman to wonder. So with Mr. Kipling's officers who turn their backs; and his Sowers who sow the Seed; and his Men who are alone with their Work; and the Flag—one blushes at all these capital letters as if one had been caught eavesdropping at some purely masculine orgy. The fact is that neither Mr. Galsworthy nor Mr. Kipling has a spark of the woman in him. Thus all their qualities seem to a woman, if one may generalise, crude and immature. They lack suggestive power. And when a book lacks suggestive power, however hard it hits the surface of the mind it cannot penetrate within.

⌒ ⌒ ⌒

However, the blame for all this, if one is anxious to lay blame, rests no more upon one sex than upon the other. All seducers and reformers are responsible, . . . All who have brought about a state of sex-consciousness are to blame, and it is they who drive me, when I want to stretch my faculties on a book, to seek it in that happy age, . . . One must turn back to Shakespeare then, for Shakespeare was androgynous; and so was Keats and Sterne and Cowper and Lamb and Coleridge. Shelley perhaps was sexless. Milton and Ben Jonson had a dash too much of the male in them. So had Wordsworth and Tolstoi. In our time Proust was wholly androgynous, if not perhaps a little too much of a woman.

⌒ ⌒ ⌒

Even so, the very first sentence that I would write here, I said, crossing over to the writing-table and taking up the page headed Women and Fiction, is that it is fatal for any one who writes to think of their sex. It is fatal to be a man or woman pure and simple; one must be woman-manly or man-womanly. It is fatal for a woman to lay the least stress on any grievance; to plead even with justice any cause; in any way to speak consciously as a woman. And fatal is no figure of speech; for anything written with that conscious bias is doomed to death. It ceases to be fertilised. Brilliant and effective, powerful and masterly, as it may appear for a day or two, it must wither at nightfall; it cannot grow in the minds of others. Some collaboration has to take place in the mind between the woman and the man before the act of creation can be accomplished. Some marriage of opposites has to be consummated. The whole of the mind must lie wide open if we are to get the sense that the writer is communicating his experience with perfect fullness. There must be freedom and there must be peace. Not a wheel must grate, not a light glimmer. The curtains must be close drawn. The writer, I thought, once his experience is over, must lie back and let his mind celebrate its nuptials in darkness.

⌒ ⌒ ⌒

If we live another century or so—I am talking of the common life which is the real life and not of the little separate lives which we live as individuals—and have five hundred a year each of us and rooms of our own . . . if we face the fact, for it is a fact, that there is no arm to cling to, but that we go alone and that our relation is to the world of reality and not only to the world of men and women, then the opportunity will come and the dead poet who was Shakespeare's sister will put on the body which she has so often laid down.

ᙍ ᙍ ᙍ

. . . I maintain that she would come if we worked for her, and that so to work, even in poverty and obscurity, is worth while.

The misogyny of the men whose books appeared on the shelves of the British Museum Library, and of the lesser male writers whom she cites, is not attributable, Woolf claims, to their having been men, but rather to their having written solely *as* men. Similarly to Freud, Woolf claims that each of us has within us both masculine and feminine capabilities and characteristics, implying, again like Freud, that the genders are naturally distinct, but psychologically and socially intertwined. The conception of great ideas that occurs in great art, she supposes, requires the internal intercourse of these masculine and feminine parts of our consciousness. Ultimately, Woolf contends that there is rarely if ever a full androgyny in art; rather she claims, the artistic process always maintains to some degree the sexuality that it partly overcomes. It can only do so, however, living the life of peace and freedom requisite for art. It is these conditions—freedom and peace—that come with a "room of one's own," and unfortunately, most women have not been able to acquire these crucial commodities because of their economic and social position. Women artists, she claims, need to be freed, not so much of men but of the *cares* of most women's lives. Thus, this freedom and the peace are not, as Woolf envisions them, social conditions so much as they are conditions of consciousness. Even so, the artist's thinking is "like a spider's web . . . still attached to life at all four corners."

4. CARL GUSTAVE JUNG
(Swiss, 1875–1961)

Longtime friend and follower of Sigmund Freud, Jung broke with Freud over a bitter disagreement between the two about the basis and function of psychoanalysis. Jung founded his own school of analytic psychology, which attributed to the individual personality essentially spiritual and historical elements, a claim which Freud had refused to accept. Jung posited the existence of what he called the "collective unconscious," a set of mythic archetypes that Jung claimed all individuals brought unconsciously to their understanding of the world. Freud, of course, had used myths to represent psychological phenomena, but always only with the understanding that myths gained their significance as the products of a psyche such as was discovered empirically by psychoanalysis. Jung, on the other hand, claimed that the mythic symbols themselves were universal forces which were merely represented in individual psyches.

According to Jung, the personality is composed of three parts, roughly analogous to Freud's superego, id, and ego, respectively, called the "persona," the "shadow," and the "ego." The persona is a set of internalized social restrictions on the psyche, similar to the superego. The shadow is the personal unconscious, similar to the id, which develops, according to Jung, as the individual matures. It exists in the unconscious in addition to the collective unconscious, which Jung claimed is fully developed in every individual from the beginning of life. The ego is the set of ideas that are presented to consciousness, similarly to Freud's ego.

However, according to Jung, those ideas which the ego has taken from the unconscious are not, as Freud had claimed, made palatable to consciousness by the ego's individual effort to symbolize and codify them, but rather by the unconscious's universal practice of "projecting" these symbols outward. Thus, in a sense, an individual's conscious understanding of the world is always accomplished through the "lens" of the unconscious will. The projections of the shadow, or personal unconscious, are of an alter-ego, or "other person," qualities and emotions the individual possesses on an unconscious level, but refuses to accept into the conscious picture of him or herself, and so projects onto another. The projections of the collective unconscious, on the other hand, are acceptable to consciousness as projections of archetypical love-objects, which Jung called the *anima* and the *animus*. The feminine anima is the projection of an ideal female archetype within the male psyche; the masculine animus is the projection of an ideal male archetype within the female psyche. In this way Jung, like Freud, provided for a kind of innate bisexuality in everyone, but for Jung this is not made acceptable to consciousness through repression, as Freud had claimed, but through idealization. The anima, for instance, consists in the feminine qualities of a man, known by him only as the image of the ideal woman. In *Aion: Researches Into the Phenomenology of the Self,* from which the passage below is taken, Jung calls the anima and the animus together, the "syzygy," meaning that they are paired, or joined, opposites, like the poles of a planet. For Jung, then, the mythological and ancient religious frameworks of human culture, including the kinds of mythical paradigms in Chapter One of this book, at once characterized the internal life of every individual, and so could be used to analyze a personality.

AION III: THE SYZYGY: ANIMA AND ANIMUS

What, then, is this projection-making factor? . . . The enveloping, embracing, and devouring element points unmistakably to the mother, that is, to the son's relation to the real mother, to her imago, and to the woman who is to become a mother for him. His Eros is passive like a child's; he hopes to be caught, sucked in, enveloped, and devoured. He seeks, as it were, the protecting, nourishing, charmed circle of the mother, the condition of the infant released from every care, in which the outside world bends over him and even forces happiness upon him. No wonder the real world vanishes from sight!

If this situation is dramatized, as the unconscious usually dramatizes it, then there appears before you on the psychological stage a man living regressively, seeking his childhood and his mother, fleeing from a cold cruel world which denies him understanding. Often a mother appears beside him who apparently shows not the slightest concern that her little son should become a man, but who, with tireless and self-immolating effort, neglects nothing that might hinder him from growing up and marrying. You behold the secret conspiracy between mother and son, and how each helps the other to betray life.

Where does the guilt lie? With the mother, or with the son? Probably with both. The unsatisfied longing of the son for life and the world ought to be taken seriously. There is in him a desire to touch reality, to embrace the earth and fructify the field of the world. But he makes no more than a series of fitful starts, for his initiative as well as his staying power are crippled by the secret memory that the world and happiness may be had as a gift—from the mother. The fragment of world which he, like every man, must encounter again and again is never quite the right one, since it does not fall into his lap, does not meet him half way, but remains resistant, has to be conquered, and submits only to force. It makes demands on the masculinity of a man, on his ardour, above all on his courage and resolution when it comes to throwing his whole being into the scales. For this he would need a faithless Eros, one capable of forgetting his mother and undergoing the pain of relinquishing the first love of his life. The mother, foreseeing this danger, has carefully inculcated into him the virtues of faithfulness, devotion, loyalty, so as to protect him from the moral disruption which is the risk of every life adventure. He has learnt these lessons only too well, and remains true to his mother. This naturally causes her the deepest anxiety (when, to her greater glory, he turns out to be a homosexual, for example) and at the same time affords her an unconscious satisfaction that is positively mythological. For, in the relationship now reigning between them, there is consummated the immemorial and most sacred archetype of the marriage of mother and son.

☞ ☞ ☞

This myth, better than any other, illustrates the nature of the collective unconscious. At this level the mother is both old and young, Demeter and Persephone, and the son is spouse and sleeping suckling rolled into one. The imperfections of real life, with its laborious adaptations and manifold disappointments, naturally cannot compete with such a state of indescribable fulfillment.

In the case of the son, the projection-making factor is identical with the mother-imago, and this is consequently taken to be the real mother. The projection can only be dissolved when the son sees that in the realm of his psyche there is an image not only of the mother but of the daughter, the sister, the beloved, the heavenly goddess, and the chthonic Baubo. Every mother and every beloved is forced to become the carrier and embodiment of this omnipresent and ageless image, which corresponds to the deepest reality in a man. It belongs to him, this perilous image of Woman; she stands for the loyalty which in the interests of life he must sometimes forgo; she is the much needed compensation for the risks, struggles, sacrifices that all end in disappointment; she is the solace for all the bitterness of life. And, at the same time, she is the great illusionist, the seductress, who draws him into life with her Maya—and not only into life's reasonable and useful aspects, but into its frightful paradoxes and ambivalences where good and evil, success and ruin, hope and despair, counterbalance one another. Because she is his greatest danger she demands from a man his greatest, and if he has it in him she will receive it.

☞ ☞ ☞

The projection-making factor is the anima, or rather the unconscious as represented by the anima. Whenever she appears, in dreams, visions, and fantasies, she takes on personified form, thus demonstrating that the factor she embodies possesses all the outstanding characteristics of a feminine being. She is not an invention of the conscious, but a spontaneous product of the unconscious. Nor is she a substitute figure for the mother. On the contrary, there is every likelihood that the numinous qualities which make the mother-imago so dangerously powerful derive from the collective archetype of the anima, which is incarnated anew in every male child.

Since the anima is an archetype that is found in men, it is reasonable to suppose that an equivalent archetype must be present in women; for just as the man is compensated by a feminine element, so woman is compensated by a masculine one.

☞ ☞ ☞

Just as the mother seems to be the first carrier of the projection-making factor for the son, so is the father for the daughter. Practical experience of these relationships is made up of many individual cases presenting all kinds of variations on the same basic theme. A concise description of them can, therefore, be no more than schematic.

Woman is compensated by a masculine element and therefore her unconscious has, so to speak, a masculine imprint. This results in a considerable psychological difference between men and women, and accordingly I have called the projection-making factor in women the animus, which means mind or spirit. The animus corresponds to the paternal Logos just as the anima corresponds to the maternal Eros. But I do not wish or intend to give these two intuitive concepts too specific a definition. I use Eros and Logos merely as conceptual aids to describe the fact that woman's consciousness is characterized more by the connective quality of Eros than by the discrimination and cognition associated with Logos. In men, Eros, the function of relationship, is usually less developed than Logos. In women, on the other hand, Eros is an expression of their true nature, while their Logos is often only a regrettable accident. It gives rise to misunderstandings and annoying interpretations in the family circle and among friends. This is because it consists of *opinions* instead of reflections, and by opinions I mean *a priori* assumptions that lay claim to absolute truth. Such assumptions, as everyone knows, can be extremely irritating. As the animus is partial to argument, he can best be seen at work in disputes where both parties know they are right. Men can argue in a very womanish way, too, when they are anima-possessed and have thus been transformed into the animus of their own anima. With them the question becomes one of personal vanity and touchiness (as if they were females); with women it is a question of power, whether of truth or justice or some other "ism"—for the dressmaker and hairdresser have already taken care of their vanity. The "Father" (i.e., the sum of conventional opinions) always plays a great role in female argumentation.

෧ ෧ ෧

This singular fact is due to the following circumstance: when animus and anima meet, the animus draws his sword of power and the anima ejects her poison of illusion and seduction. The outcome need not always be negative, since the two are equally likely to fall in love (a special instance of love at first sight). The language of love is of astonishing uniformity, using the well-worn formulas with the utmost devotion and fidelity, so that once again the two partners find themselves in a banal collective situation. Yet they live in the illusion that they are related to one another in a most individual way.

In both its positive and its negative aspects the anima/animus relationship is always full of "animosity," i.e., it is emotional, and hence collective. Affects lower the level of the relationship and bring it closer to the common instinctual basis, which no longer has anything individual about it. Very often the relationship runs its course heedless of its human performers, who afterwards do not know what happened to them.

Whereas the cloud of "animosity" surrounding the man is composed chiefly of sentimentality and resentment, in woman it expresses itself in the form of opinionated views, interpretations, insinuations, and misconstructions, which all have the purpose (sometimes attained) of severing the relation between two human beings. The woman, like the man, becomes wrapped in a veil of illusions by her demon-familiar, and, as the daughter who alone understands her father (that is, is eternally right in everything), she is translated to the land of sheep, where she is put to graze by the shepherd of her soul, the animus.

Like the anima, the animus too has a positive aspect. Through the figure of the father he expresses not only conventional opinion but—equally—what we call "spirit," philosophical or religious ideas in particular, or rather the attitude resulting from them. Thus the animus is a psychopomp, a mediator between the conscious and the unconscious and a personification of the latter. Just as the anima becomes, through integration, the Eros of consciousness, so the animus becomes a Logos; and in the same way that the anima gives relationship and relatedness to a man's consciousness, the animus gives to woman's consciousness a capacity for reflection, deliberation, and self-knowledge.

The effect of anima and animus on the ego is in principle the same. This effect is extremely difficult to eliminate because, in the first place, it is uncommonly strong and immediately fills the ego-personality with an unshakable feeling of rightness and righteousness. In the second place, the cause of the effect is projected and appears to lie in objects and objective situations. Both these characteristics can, I believe, be traced back to the peculiarities of the archetype.

⌐ ⌐ ⌐

As I said, it is easier to gain insight into the shadow than into the anima or animus. With the shadow, we have the advantage of being prepared in some sort by our education, which has always endeavoured to convince people that they are not one-hundred-per-cent pure gold. So everyone immediately understands what is meant by "shadow," "inferior personality," etc. And if he has forgotten, his memory can easily be refreshed by a Sunday sermon, his wife, or the tax collector. With the anima and animus, however, things are by no means so simple. Firstly, there is no moral education in this respect, and secondly, most people are content to be self-righteous and prefer mutual vilification (if nothing worse!) to the recognition of their projections. Indeed, it seems a very natural state of affairs for men to have irrational moods and women irrational opinions. Presumably this situation is grounded on instinct and must remain as it is to ensure that the Empedoclean game of the hate and love of the elements shall continue for all eternity.

⌐ ⌐ ⌐

The autonomy of the collective unconscious expresses itself in the figures of anima and animus. They personify those of its contents which, when withdrawn from projection, can be integrated into consciousness. To this extent, both figures represent *functions* which filter the contents of the collective unconscious through to the conscious mind. They appear or behave as such, however, only so long as the tendencies of the conscious and unconscious do not diverge too greatly. Should any tension arise, these functions, harmless till then, confront the conscious mind in personified form and behave rather like systems split off from the personality, or like part souls. This comparison is inadequate in so far as nothing previously belonging to the ego-personality has split off form it; on the contrary, the two figures represent a disturbing accretion. The reason for their behaving in this way is that though the *contents* of anima and animus can be integrated they themselves cannot, since they are archetypes. As such they are the foundation stones of the psychic structure, which in its totality exceeds the limits of consciousness and therefore can never become the object of direct cognition. Though the effects of anima and animus can be made conscious, they themselves are factors transcending consciousness and beyond the reach of perception and volition. Hence they remain autonomous despite the integration of their contents, and for this reason they should be borne constantly in mind.

⌐ ⌐ ⌐

Both these archetypes, as practical experience shows, possess a fatality that can on occasion produce tragic results. They are quite literally the father and mother of all the disastrous entanglements of fate and have long been recognized as such by the whole world. Together they form a divine pair, one of whom, in accordance with his Logos nature, is characterized by *pneuma* and *nous,* rather like Hermes with his ever-shifting hues, while the other, in accordance with her Eros nature, wears the features of Aphrodite, Helen (Selene), Persephone, and Hecate. Both of them are unconscious powers, "gods" in fact, as the ancient world quite rightly conceived them to be. To call them by this name is to give them that central position in the scale of psychological values which has always been theirs whether consciously acknowledged or not; for their power grows in proportion to the degree that they remain unconscious.

◌ ◌ ◌

. . . The shadow can be realized only through a relation to a partner, and anima and animus only through a relation to the opposite sex, because only in such a relation do their projections become operative. The recognition of anima or animus gives rise, in a man, to a triad, one third of which is transcendent: the masculine subject, the opposing feminine subject, and the transcendent anima. With a woman the situation is reversed. The missing fourth element that would make the triad a quaternity is, in a man, the archetype of the Wise Old Man, which I have not discussed here, and in a woman the Chthonic Mother. These four constitute a half immanent and half transcendent quaternity, an archetype which I have called the *marriage quaternio.* The marriage quaternio provides a schema not only for the self but also for the structure of primitive society with its cross-cousin marriage, marriage classes, and division of settlements into quarters. The self, on the other hand, is a God-image, or at least cannot be distinguished from one.

In a sense, Jung claims that individuals are at least partly the pawns of an ongoing mythical drama, in which masculinity and femininity are ideal characters. Each individual brings these characters to life by playing out his or her unconscious projections in conscious interactions with others. The animus, the projected unconscious masculinity of a woman, Jung associates with the Greek idea of *logos*—thinking or opinion or argument. The feminine anima he associates with Greek *eros*—desire or love. A woman with a strong animus, he claims, will be a vehement but empty arguer, and so will likely be an irritating or unpleasant person for herself and others. A man with a strong anima will be a vain and emotional arguer, and so be confusing to himself and others. Each archetype has a good and a bad side—a happy or functional element and a disruptive or unhappy element—which it brings into the life of the individual in greater or lesser degree, depending on his or her object choice and relation to it. Hence, Jung implies, if a woman with a strong animus marries a man without a strong anima to balance it, hers may be an unhappy marriage. Though some of these misfortunes can be avoided or restrained through psychotherapy, these universal spiritual forces, Jung claims, are largely out of our control.

5. KAREN HORNEY
(German, 1885–1952)

Karen Horney was one of several early female analysts who added pioneering work to Freud's own. She is especially noted for her criticisms of Freud's theory of female sexual development. Horney's versions of the female castration complex, of female masochism, and of female envy rework these basic Freudian insights in the light of extensive observations of women patients, and of course through a female analyst's perspective. Through her new observations and insights, Horney also extended the horizons of psychoanalytic research, identifying newly several feminine character types and several common female neuroses, as well as reevaluating the Freudian interpretation of certain male affects. In particular, Horney stressed the social contribution to the individual personality, particularly in women, a theme to which Freud had many times alluded, but which he had insufficiently developed. A considerable portion of Horney's work is devoted to the questions of female development and sex differences; what follows is a smattering of relevant claims from three short essays.

"THE FLIGHT FROM WOMANHOOD" (1926)

In this essay, subtitled, "The Masculinity Complex in Women as Viewed by Men and Women," Horney criticizes the Freudian theory of penis-envy, which he had claimed characterized feminine psychology through adulthood.

> . . . Like all sciences and all valuations, the psychology of women has hitherto been considered only from the point of view of men. It is inevitable that the man's position of advantage should cause objective validity to be attributed to his subjective, effective relations to the woman, and according to Delius the psychology of women hitherto actually represents a deposit of the desired and disappointments of men.
>
> And additional and very important factor in the situation is that women have adapted themselves to the wishes of men and felt as if their adaptation were their true nature. That is, they see or saw themselves in the way that their men's wishes demanded of them; unconsciously they yielded to the suggestion of masculine thought.

       ↶ ↶ ↶

> If we look at the matter from this point of view our first impression is a surprising one. The present analytical picture of feminine development (whether that picture be correct or not) differs in no case by a hair's breadth from the typical ideas that the boy has of the girl.

       ↶ ↶ ↶

THE BOY'S IDEAS	OUR IDEAS OF FEMININE DEVELOPMENT
Naïve assumption that girls as well as boys possess a penis	*For both sexes it is only the male genital which plays any part*
Realization of the absence of the penis	*Sad discovery of the absence of the penis*
Idea that the girl is a castrated, mutilated boy	*Belief of the girl that she once possessed a penis and lost it by castration*
Belief that the girl has suffered punishment that also threatens him	*Castration is conceived of as the infliction of punishment*
The girl is regarded as inferior	*The girl regards herself as inferior. Penis envy*
The boy is unable to imagine how the girl can ever get over this loss or envy	*The girl never gets over the sense of deficiency and inferiority and has constantly to master afresh her desire to be a man*
The boy dreads her envy	*The girl desires throughout life to avenge herself on the man for possessing something which she lacks*

The existence of this over-exact agreement is certainly no criterion of its objective correctness.

☞ ☞ ☞

Now, if we try to free our minds from this masculine mode of thought, nearly all the problems of feminine psychology take on a different appearance.

The first thing that strikes us is that it is always, or principally, the genital difference between the sexes which has been made the cardinal point in the analytical conception and that we have left out of consideration the other great biological difference, namely, the different parts played by men and by women in the function of reproduction.

☞ ☞ ☞

But from the biological point of view woman has in motherhood, or in the capacity for motherhood, a quite indisputable and by no means negligible physiological superiority. This is most clearly reflected in the unconscious of the male psyche in the boy's intense envy of motherhood. We are familiar with this envy as such, but it has hardly received due consideration as a dynamic factor. When one begins, as I did, to analyze men only after a fairly long experience of analyzing women, one receives a most surprising impression of the intensity of this envy of pregnancy, childbirth, and motherhood, as well as of the breasts and of the act of suckling.

In the light of this impression derived from analysis, one must naturally inquire whether an unconscious masculine tendency to depreciation is not expressing itself intellectually in the above mentioned view of motherhood.

. . . [T]he masculine envy is clearly capable of more successful sublimation than the penis envy of the girl, and that it certainly serves as one, if not as the essential, driving force in the setting up of cultural values.

Language itself points to this origin of cultural productivity. In the historic times that are known to us, this productivity has undoubtedly been incomparably greater in men than in women. Is not the tremendous strength in men of the impulse to creative work in every field precisely due to their feeling of playing a relatively small part in the creation of living beings, which constantly impels them to an overcompensation in achievement?

In favor of the greater intensity of the man's envy we might point out that an actual anatomical disadvantage on the side of the woman exists only from the point of view of the pregenital levels of organization. From that of the genital organization of adult women there is no disadvantage, for obviously the capacity of women for coitus is not less but simply other than that of men. On the other hand, the part of the man in reproduction is ultimately less than that of the woman.

Further, we observe that men are evidently under a greater necessity to depreciate women than conversely.

From beginning to end, my experience has proved to me with unchanging clearness that the Oedipus complex in women leads not only in extreme cases where the subject has come to grief, but *regularly* to a regression to penis envy naturally in every possible degree and shade. The difference between the outcome of the male and the female Oedipus complexes seems to me in average cases to be as follows. In boys the mother as a sexual object is renounced owing to the fear of castration, but the male role itself is not only affirmed in further development but is actually overemphasized in the reaction to the fear of castration. We see this clearly in the latency and prepubertal period in boys and generally in later life as well. Girls, on the other hand, not only renounce the father as a sexual object but simultaneously recoil from the feminine role altogether.

The female genital anxiety, like the castration dread of boys, invariably bears the impress of feelings of guilt and it is to them that it owes its lasting influence.

Under the pressure of this anxiety the girl now takes refuge in a fictitious male role.

What is the economic gain of this flight? Here I would refer to an experience that all analysts have probably had: The find that the desire to be a man is generally admitted comparatively willingly and that when once it is accepted, it is clung to tenaciously, the reason being the desire to avoid the realization of libidinal wishes and fantasies in connection with the father. Thus the wish to be a man subserves the repression of these feminine wishes or the resistance against their being brought to light. This constantly recurring, typical experience compels us, if we are true to analytical principles, to conclude that the fantasies of being a man were at an earlier period devised for the very purpose of securing the subject against libidinal wishes in connection with the father. The fiction of maleness enabled the girl to escape from the female role now burdened with guilt and anxiety. It is true that this attempt to deviate from her own line to that of the male inevitably brings about a sense of inferiority, for the girl begins to measure herself by pretensions and values that are foreign to her specific biological nature and confronted with which she cannot but feel herself inadequate.

Although this sense of inferiority is very tormenting, analytical experience emphatically shows us that the ego can tolerate it more easily than the sense of guilt associated with the feminine attitude, and hence it is undoubtedly a gain for the ego when the girl flees from the Scylla of the sense of guilt to the Charybdis of the sense of inferiority.

☙ ☙ ☙

There is one further consideration. Owing to the hitherto purely masculine character of our civilization, it has been much harder for women to achieve any sublimation that would really satisfy their nature, for all the ordinary professions have been filled by men. This again must have exercised an influence upon women's feelings of inferiority, for naturally they could not accomplish the same as men in these masculine professions and so it appeared that there was a basis in fact for their inferiority. It seems to me impossible to judge to how great a degree the unconscious motives for the flight from womanhood are reinforced by the actual social subordination of women. One might conceive of the connection as an interaction of psychic and social factors.

Horney consistently argues, not against Freud's claims wholesale, but only against those claims of Freud's that she believes exhibit a male bias on his part. For instance, she agrees with Freud's claims about the true bisexuality of the libido, but claims that this logically necessitates that there be a similar resolution of the Oedi-pal conflict in both boys and girls, not a different one, as Freud had claimed. As elsewhere, she argues that both women and men experience pleasure, instinctual drives towards the opposite-sex parent, envy, and guilt. This, she believes, is a view that avoids the clearly narrow male perspective on female development which she claims had dominated psychoanalysis. She exemplifies this more egalitarian view of the libido in her claim that women, particularly after puberty, are in an enviable sexual position, not a pitiable one at all.

Horney explains adult women's penis envy and its accompanying feelings of in-feriority to men as a regression to childhood feelings of guilt (over the little girl's original—not secondary—attraction to her father) aroused in adult life by real social factors that put her in an inferior position. In this way, Horney introduces two themes that characterize much of her work. 1) She stresses the emotional motivations that accompany biological drives. For instance, guilt and envy play more integral roles in Horney's notion of the psychological dynamic than they did in Freud's, taking on identities of their own as emotions, rather than merely marking the disappointment of the libidinal drive in its vehicle of expression. 2) Horney consistently takes a holistic approach to the understanding of psychological conditions, always looking to the interaction of social and psychological factors on their development. Here, for instance, she argues that real social inhibitions on women's expression of their drive encourages them to feel envious of and inferior to men.

"THE DREAD OF WOMAN" (1932)

In the following essay, subtitled, "Observations on a Specific Difference in the Dread Felt by Men and by Women Respectively for the Opposite Sex," Horney gives her account of the castration anxiety experienced by men. In essence, she claims that men clearly exhibit a desire to be women, a desire that parallels the penis-envy of women, and that the inevitable disappointment of this desire results in anxiety and dread.

... Men have never tired of fashioning expressions for the violent force by which man feels himself drawn to the woman, and side by side with his longing, the dread that through her he might die and be undone.

To primitive sensibilities the woman becomes doubly sinister in the presence of the bloody manifestations of her womanhood. Contact with her during menstruation is fatal: men lose their strength, the pastures wither away, the fisherman and the huntsman take nothing. Defloration involves the utmost danger to the man.

Is it not really remarkable (we ask ourselves in amazement), when one considers the overwhelming mass of this transparent material, that so little recognition and attention are paid to the fact of men's secret dread of women?

The man on his side has in the first place very obvious strategic reasons for keeping his dread quiet. But he also tries by every means to deny it even to himself. This is the purpose of the efforts to which we have alluded, to "objectify" it in artistic and scientific creative work. We may conjecture that even his glorification of women has its source not only in his cravings for love, but also in his desire to conceal his dread. A similar relief, however, is also sought and found in the disparagement of women that men often display ostentatiously in their attitudes. The attitude of love and adoration signifies:

"There is no need for me to dread a being so wonderful, so beautiful, nay, so saintly." That of disparagement implies: "It would be too ridiculous to dread a creature who, if you take her all round, is such a poor thing." This last way of allaying his anxiety has a special advantage for the man: It helps to support his masculine self-respect.

⌐ ⌐ ⌐

Only *anxiety* is a strong enough motive to hold back from his goal a man whose libido is assuredly urging him on to union with the woman. But Freud's account fails to explain this anxiety. A boy's castration anxiety in relation to his father is not an adequate reason for his dread of a being to whom this punishment has already happened. Besides the dread of the father, there must be a further dread, the object of which is the woman or the female genital.

⌐ ⌐ ⌐

All analysts are familiar with dreams of this sort and I need only give the merest outline of them: e.g., a motorcar is rushing along and suddenly falls into a pit and is dashed to pieces; a boat is sailing in a narrow channel and is suddenly sucked into a whirlpool; there is a cellar with uncanny, blood-stained plants and animals; one is climbing a chimney and is in danger of falling and being killed.

⌐ ⌐ ⌐

. . . Are love and death more closely bound up with one another for the male than for the female, in whom sexual union potentially produces a new life? Does the man feel, side by side with his desire to conquer, a secret longing for extinction in the act of reunion with the woman (mother)? Is it perhaps this longing that underlies the "death-instinct"? And is it his will to live that reacts to it with anxiety?

⌐ ⌐ ⌐

. . . [T]here are various reasons why it seems to me improbable that the existence of a specific female opening should remain "undiscovered." On the one hand, of course, a boy will automatically conclude that everyone else is made like himself; but on the other hand his phallic impulses surely bid him instinctively to search for the appropriate opening in the female body—an opening, moreover, that he himself lacks, for the one sex always seeks in the other that which is complementary to it or of a nature different from its own. If we seriously accept Freud's dictum that the sexual theories formed by children are modeled on their own sexual constitution, it must surely mean in the present connection that the boy, urged on by his impulses to penetrate, pictures in fantasy a complementary female organ. And this is just what we should infer from all the material I quoted at the outset in connection with the masculine dread of the female genital.

It is not at all probable that this anxiety dates only from puberty.

◔ ◔ ◔

Moreover, the grotesque character of the anxiety, as we meet with it in the symbolism of dreams and literary productions, points unmistakably to the period of early infantile fantasy.

At puberty a normal boy has already acquired a conscious knowledge of the vagina, but what he fears in women is something uncanny, unfamiliar, and mysterious. If the grown man continues to regard woman as the great mystery, in whom is a secret he cannot divine, this feeling of his can only relate ultimately to one thing in her: the mystery of motherhood. Everything else is merely the residue of his dread of this.

◔ ◔ ◔

. . . The anatomical differences between the sexes lead to a totally different situation in girls and in boys, and really to understand both their anxiety and the diversity of their anxiety we must take into account first of all *the children's real situation* in the period of their early sexuality. The girl's nature as biologically conditioned gives her the desire to receive, to take into herself; she feels or knows that her genital is too small for her father's penis and this makes her react to her own genital wishes with direct anxiety; she dreads that if her wishes were fulfilled, she herself or her genital would be destroyed.

The boy, on the other hand, feels or instinctively judges that his penis is much too small for his mother's genital and reacts with the dread of his own inadequacy, of being rejected and derided. Thus his anxiety is located in quite a different quarter from the girl's; his original dread of women is not castration anxiety at all, but a reaction to the menace to his self-respect.

◔ ◔ ◔

. . . Thus, if it is first made distasteful to him by its association with wounded self-regard, it will by a secondary process (by way of frustration anger) become an object of castration anxiety. And probably this is very generally reinforced when the boy observes traces of menstruation.

Very often this latter anxiety in its turn leaves a lasting mark on the man's attitude to women, as we learn from the examples already given at random from very different periods and races. But I do not think that it occurs regularly in all men in any considerable degree, and certainly it is not a *distinctive* characteristic of the man's relation to the other sex.

◔ ◔ ◔

On the other hand I think that the anxiety connected with his self-respect leaves more or less distinct traces in every man and gives his general attitude toward women a particular stamp that either does not exist in women's attitude to men, or if it does, is acquired secondarily.

◔ ◔ ◔

> According to my experience, the dread of being rejected and derided is a typical ingredient in the analysis of every man.

☞   ☞   ☞

> Once we realize that masculine castration anxiety is very largely the ego's response to the *wish to be a woman,* we cannot altogether share Freud's conviction that bisexuality manifests itself more clearly in the female than in the male. We must leave it an open question.

Horney is apparently able, on the basis of her studies of women and her own, perhaps feminine, insights, to give an explanation for commonly observed male feelings of sexual inadequacy (e.g., men's anxious concern over penis-size) as well as of their common protestations against women, both of which earlier psychoanalysts had overlooked. Here again, she gives a parallel explanation of boys' and girls' development, claiming that boys' castration anxiety, like girls', is very strongly felt and associated with their mothers, or with female figures, not with a fear of their fathers. In addition, she again ties in social factors—here as a result, rather than a cause (as above) of psychological developments—claiming that men's cultural achievements and their disparagement of women (which has affected women's social position) is a compensation for their feelings of sexual inadequacy.

"THE OVERVALUATION OF LOVE" (1934)

The subtitle of this essay is "A Study of a Common Present-Day Feminine Type." In it, Horney tries to make sense of the odd combination of symptoms she observed in a growing number of female patients: a rampant obsession with men, love, and sex; a strong but often unrealistic professional ambition; a feeling of inadequacy in work and love; and expressions of resentment against their female therapist. The data from analysis indicates to Horney that these women have had similar childhood experiences, whose effects are manifested in this particular way because of particular, twentieth-century social circumstances.

> Woman's efforts to achieve independence and an enlargement of her field of interests and activities are continually met with a skepticism which insists that such efforts should be made only in the face of economic necessity, and that they run counter to her inherent character and her natural tendencies.

☞   ☞   ☞

> . . . It is comprehensible, therefore—speaking solely from the sociological standpoint—that women who nowadays obey the impulse to the independent development of their abilities are able to do so only at the cost of a struggle against both external opposition and such resistances within themselves as are created by an intensification of the traditional ideal of the exclusively sexual function of woman.

☞   ☞   ☞

. . . The present report is based upon seven analyses of my own, and upon a number of additional cases familiar to me through analytic conferences.

. . . The first impression did not yield much more than the fact that for these women their relation to men was of great importance to them, but that they had never succeeded in establishing a satisfactory relationship of any duration. Either attempts to form a relationship had failed outright, or there had been a series of merely evanescent relationships, broken off either by the man in question or the patient—relationships that more over often showed a certain lack of selectivity.

The transference situation relative to a woman analyst was dominated throughout by two attitudes: by rivalry, and by recourse to activity in relations with men.

. . . Desperate complaints of discouragement barely veiled the obstinate wish to discourage the analyst.

In a word, they wanted to prove that the analyst could not do anything.

The other transference attitude consists in this, that, as in life too, the relation to men is pushed into the foreground, and this with conspicuous frequency in the form of acting out. Often one man after another plays a part, ranging from mere approaches to sexual relations; while accounts of what he has done or not done, whether he loves or disappoints them, and of how they have reacted to him, take up at times the greater part of the hour and are tirelessly spun out to the smallest detail.

In the previous histories of these women there is one factor that is striking in the regularity of its occurrence and the marked affect with which it is characterized: All these women in childhood had come off second best in competition for a man (father or brother). Conspicuously often—in seven cases out of thirteen—there was, above all, an older *sister* who was able by various means to command a place in the sun, that is, in the favor of the father, or in one case that of an older brother, in another of a younger.

The analysis brought to light a tremendous anger against these sisters.

It prevents the patient's own development in this direction, in the sense of a complete repudiation of feminine wiles; thus she refrains from wearing attractive clothes, dancing, and participation in general in anything in the sphere of the erotic.

⌒ ⌒ ⌒

In the fact that such a struggle brings in its train a permanent and destructive attitude of rivalry with women, the same psychology is evident as holds true of every competitive situation—the vanquished feels lasting anger toward the victor, suffers injury to his self-esteem, will consequently be in a less favorable psychological position in subsequent competitive situations, and will ultimately feel either consciously or unconsciously that his only chance of success lies in the death of his opponent. Exactly the same consequences can be traced in the cases under discussion: a feeling of being downtrodden, a permanent feeling of insecurity with regard to feminine self-esteem, and a profound anger with their more fortunate rivals.

⌒ ⌒ ⌒

The most frequent form that these doubts assume in consciousness is the conviction that the patient is ugly and therefore cannot possibly be attractive to men. This conviction is quite independent of whatever the actual facts may be; it may be found, for example, even in girls who are unusually pretty. The feeling is referred to some real or imaginary defect—straight hair, large hands or feet, too stout a figure, too large or small a stature, their age, or a poor complexion.

⌒ ⌒ ⌒

The insult to their femininity drives these women, both directly and *via* the fear of not being normal, to prove their feminine potency to themselves; but since this goal is never reached on account of the self-depreciation that instantly occurs, such a technique leads of necessity to a rapid change from one relationship to another. Their interest in a man, such as may even amount to an illusion of being tremendously in love with him, vanishes as a rule as soon as he is "conquered"— that is, as soon as he has become emotionally dependent on them.

⌒ ⌒ ⌒

For the patient there is but one way out of a situation so totally unsatisfactory, namely, by means of achievement, of esteem of ambition. These women without exception seek this way out, in that they all develop tremendous ambition. They are motivated by powerful impulses emanating from wounded feminine self-esteem and from an exaggerated sense of rivalry.

⌒ ⌒ ⌒

However, they are foredoomed to failure along this path as well as in the erotic sphere.

⌒ ⌒ ⌒

This feeling of an inability to achieve anything, which is just as tormenting here as in the erotic sphere from which it originates, is as rule maintained with equal tenacity. The patient is determined to prove to herself and to others, and above all to the analyst, that she is incompetent to do anything.

≈ ≈ ≈

. . . This is, as it were, a magic appeal to their pity. The function of this masochistic attitude is therefore a neurotically distorted means of attaining a heterosexual goal, which these patients believe they cannot reach in any other way.

To put it simply, one might say that the solution of the problem of their feeling of inhibition in regard to work lies in these cases in their inability to bring to the work in question a sufficient amount of interest.

≈ ≈ ≈

Every reader will in all probability have noticed that the type of woman depicted here occurs frequently today in less exaggerated form, at any rate in our middle-class intellectual circles. At the outset I expressed the opinion that this is largely determined by social reasons, reasons that lie in the social narrowing of women's sphere of work. In the cases described here, however, the particular neurotic entanglement nevertheless arises clearly from an unfortunate individual development.

This description might give the impression that the two sets of forces, social and individual, are separated from each other. This is certainly not the case. I believe that I can show in each instance that the type of woman described can only result in this form on the basis of individual factors, and I assume that the *frequency* of the type is explained by the fact that, given the social factors, relatively slight difficulties in personal development suffice to drive women in the direction of this type of womanhood.

The character type Horney describes exhibits several difficulties that commonly face women today. Inordinate concern and feelings of inadequacy over appearance and weight, a confusing sense of competitiveness with other women, professional ambition combined with a lack of fulfillment in work, desperate but unsatisfactory love affairs—these seem to be predecessors of the concerns expressed on the covers of today's women's magazines and by the participants in talk shows (eating disorders, the quandary of the "bitch" at work, disillusion with "having it all," disappointments resulting in "serial monogamy"). Horney finds the causes of these difficulties in relationships whose further study Freud had very much advocated: the female–female relationships of sisters with each other and of daughters with their mothers. As Horney understands it, these relationships, even among healthy women, are fraught with envy and resentment, as well as with sexual desire. While the relationships themselves have their own psychological integrity, and would have these characteristics in any time or culture, Horney believes that women's new professional opportunities have directed them in ways that are not adequately understood and for which women may not be prepared—a cycle of ambition and disappointment of a wholly feminine type.

6. MARGARET MEAD
(American, 1901–1978)

Margaret Mead was one of the most prominent anthropologists of all time, making groundbreaking discoveries and insightful theoretical analyses about many cultures, particularly peoples of the Pacific. She was a pioneer in the field of cultural ethnology and in its anthropological methods, making several visits to the areas which she studied—rather than just one, as was common in her day—and stressing over and over the importance of accepting from the participants in a culture their own frameworks of analysis and self-understanding, rather than imposing the scientist's ready-made framework upon them. One ongoing interest of Mead's was the way different societies organized sex-differences; she demonstrated in several of her studies that sex distinctions could be drawn in vastly different ways from that of the modern West. This was the single focus of the work excerpted here.

SEX AND TEMPERAMENT IN THREE PRIMITIVE SOCIETIES (1935)

The research for this book was conducted in three societies within a hundred miles of one another in eastern New Guinea—the peaceful Arapesh, the violent Mundugumor, and the artistic Tchambuli. Mead's discoveries in these nearby yet vastly different societies led her to revise the hypotheses with which she had begun her work: originally proposed as a study of sex differences, the research turned out to reveal more about the sexual distribution of temperamental differences, which Mead came to believe could be accomplished by different societies in enormously various ways. The experience clarified for Mead that "each of us belongs to a sex and has a temperament, a temperament shared with others of our own sex *and* others of the opposite sex."[5]

Mead came increasingly to believe that American and European systems of sex-temperament attribution—both those of traditionalists and those of reformers—had missed the social point of such attributions, and would lead increasingly to social disservice. "To insist that there are no sex differences in a society that has always believed in them and depended upon them," she writes in her conclusion to this work, "may be as subtle a form of standardizing personality as to insist that there are many sex differences."[6] Though the majority of the book is taken up with descriptive reports on the three societies, the Introduction and Conclusion develop Mead's more general theories of sex-temperament attribution, and of the implications of these theories to our own society. It is consequently only with these passages that we will be concerned.

---

[5] Margaret Mead, *Sex and Temperament in Three Primitive Societies*. (New York: William Morrow and Co., 1963), preface to the 1950 edition.

[6] Ibid, pp. 314-315.

INTRODUCTION

Here, Mead sets up the distinction between sex and temperament that will be the analytic framework for her claims about the Arapesh, Mundugumor, and Tchambuli.

. . . Each simple, homogeneous culture can give scope to only a few of the varied human endowments, disallowing or penalizing others too antithetical or too unrelated to its major emphases to find room within its walls. Having originally taken its values from the values dear to some human temperaments and alien to others, a culture embodies these values more and more firmly in its structure, in its political and religious systems, in its art and its literature; and each new generation is shaped, firmly and definitely, to the dominant trends.

Now as each culture creates distinctively the social fabric in which the human spirit can wrap itself safely and intelligibly, sorting, reweaving, and discarding threads in the historical tradition that it shares with many neighbouring peoples, it may bend every individual born within it to one type of behaviour, recognizing neither age, sex, nor special disposition as points for differential elaboration. Or a culture may seize upon the very obvious facts of difference in age, in sex, in strength, in beauty, or the unusual variations, such as a native propensity to see visions or dream dreams, and make these dominant cultural themes.

This study is not concerned with whether there are or are not actual and universal differences between the sexes, either quantitative or qualitative. It is not concerned with whether women are more variable than men, which was claimed before the doctrine of evolution exalted variability, or less variable, which was claimed afterwards. It is not a treatise on the rights of women, nor an inquiry into the basis of femininism. It is, very simply, an account of how three primitive societies have grouped their social attitudes towards temperament about the very obvious facts of sex-difference.

. . . All discussion of the position of women, of the character and temperament of women, the enslavement or the emancipation of women, obscures the basic issue—the recognition that the cultural plot behind human relations is the way in which the roles of the two sexes are conceived, and that the growing boy is shaped to a local and special emphasis as inexorably as is the growing girl.

. . . While every culture has in some way institutionalized the roles of men and women, it has not necessarily been in terms of contrast between the prescribed personalities of the two sexes, nor in terms of dominance or submission. With the paucity of material for elaboration, no culture has failed to seize upon the conspicuous facts of age and sex in some way, whether it be the convention of one Philippine tribe that no man can keep a secret, the Manus assumption that only men enjoy playing with babies, the Toda prescription of almost all domestic work as too sacred for women, or the Arapesh insistence that women's heads are stronger than men's. In the division of labour, in dress, in manners, in social and religious functioning—sometimes in only a few of these respects, sometimes in all—men and women are socially differentiated, and each sex, as a sex, forced to conform to the role assigned to it. In some societies, these socially defined roles are mainly expressed in dress or occupation, with no insistence upon innate temperamental differences. Women wear long hair and men wear short hair, or men wear curls and women shave their heads; women wear skirts and men wear trousers, or women wear trousers and men wear skirts. Women weave and men do not, or men weave and women do not. Such simple tie-ups as these between dress or occupation and sex are easily taught to every child and make no assumptions to which a given child cannot easily conform.

It is otherwise in societies that sharply differentiate the behaviour of men and women in terms which assume a genuine difference in temperament. Among the Dakota Indians of the Plains, the importance of an ability to stand any degree of danger or hardship was frantically insisted upon as a masculine characteristic. From the time that a boy was five or six, all the conscious educational effort of the household was bent towards shaping him into an indubitable male.

In such a society it is not surprising to find the *berdache,* the man who had voluntarily given up the struggle to conform to the masculine role and who wore female attire and followed the occupations of a woman.

The invert who lacks any discernible physical basis for his inversion has long puzzled students of sex, who when they can find no observable glandular abnormality turn to theories of early conditioning or identification with a parent of opposite sex. In the course of this investigation, we shall have occasion to examine the "masculine" woman and the "feminine" man as they occur in these different tribes, to inquire whether it is always a woman of dominating nature who is conceived as masculine, or a man who is gentle, submissive, or fond of children or embroidery who is conceived as feminine.

Two of these tribes have no idea that men and women are different in temperament. They allow them different economic and religious roles, different skills, different vulnerabilities to evil magic and supernatural influences. The Arapesh believe that painting in colour is appropriate only to men, and the Mundugumor consider fishing an essentially feminine task. But any idea that temperamental traits of the order of dominance, bravery, aggressiveness, objectivity, malleability, are inalienably associated with one sex (as opposed to the other) is entirely lacking. This may seem strange to a civilization which in its sociology, its medicine, its slang, its poetry, and its obscenity accepts the socially defined differences between the sexes as having an innate basis in temperament and explains any deviation from the socially determined role as abnormality of native endowment or early maturation. It came as a surprise to me because I too had been accustomed to use in my thinking such concepts as "mixed type," to think of some men as having "feminine" temperaments, of some women as having "masculine" minds.

෴ ෴ ෴

I was innocent of any suspicion that the temperaments which we regard as native to one sex might instead be mere variations of human temperament, to which the members of either or both sexes may, with more or less success in the case of different individuals, be educated to approximate.

Mead is not arguing, as she has sometimes been mistakenly interpreted, that there are no natural sex differences. On the contrary, she believes that biological sex differences are obvious and relatively immutable. Her claim, rather, is that sex differences themselves are not *naturally* tied to any *social* distinctions at all. In other words, cultural distinctions are cultural, even though sex distinctions are not, and therefore these two realms of distinctions among human beings should be considered separately by the scientist or anthropologist. For instance, while it is obvious that men and women have different sexual organs, it is not necessary on that account, that the different sexes take different roles, say aggressive and yielding, in sexual relations. All societies, claims Mead, must make some cultural distinctions—perhaps very elaborate ones—in order to function as a society, and all societies use to some extent the natural marks available to them—age, sex, and temperament—in order to organize these distinctions. Not all societies, however, align sex differences with differences in temperament in their social organization. Since our society does align sex and temperament, it is this last claim that Mead expects to have to support, and she does so in her reports on the three societies.

CONCLUSION

It is in the conclusion to *Sex and Temperament,* after she has delivered up the data from these cultures, that Mead speculates about the wisdom of any culture's attaching sex to temperament in its social design. She outlines three different ways a society can go about organizing itself. Her evaluation of each method and comparison of it to its competitors leads Mead to advocate the separation of natural sex differences from natural differences of temperament, and the attribution of social distinctions to different temperaments instead of to the different sexes.

The knowledge that the personalities of the two sexes are socially produced is congenial to every programme that looks forward towards a planned order of society. It is a two-edged sword that can be used to hew a more flexible, more varied society than the human race has ever built, or merely to cut a narrow path down which one sex or both sexes will be forced to march, regimented, looking neither to the right nor to the left. It makes possible a Fascist programme of education in which women are forced back into a mould that modern Europe had fatuously believed to be broken forever. It makes possible a Communist programme in which the two sexes are treated as nearly alike as their different physiological functions permit. Because it is social conditioning that is determinative, it has been possible for America, without conscious plan but none the less surely, partially to reverse the European tradition of male dominance, and to breed a generation of women who model their lives on the pattern of their school-teachers and their aggressive, directive mothers. Their brothers stumble about in a vain attempt to preserve the myth of male dominance in a society in which the girls have come to consider dominance their natural right.

⌒ ⌒ ⌒

. . . The result is an increasing number of American men who feel they must shout in order to maintain their vulnerable positions, and an increasing number of American women who clutch unhappily at a dominance that their society has granted them—but without giving them a charter of rules and regulations by which they can achieve it without damage to themselves, their husbands, and their children.

There are at least three courses open to a society that has realized the extent to which male and female personality are socially produced. Two of these courses have been tried before, over and over again, at different times in the long, irregular, repetitious history of the race. The first is to standardize the personality of men and women as clearly contrasting, complementary, and antithetical, and to make every institution in the society congruent with this standardization. If the society declared that woman's sole function was motherhood and the teaching and care of young children, it could so arrange matters that every woman who was not physiologically debarred should become a mother and be supported in the exercise of this function.

⌒ ⌒ ⌒

Such a system would be wasteful fo the gifts of many women who could exercise other functions far better than their ability to bear children in an already overpopulated world. It would be wasteful of the gifts of many men who could exercise their special personality gifts far better in the home than in the market-place. It would be wasteful, but it would be clear. It could attempt to guarantee to each individual the role for which society insisted upon training him or her, and such a system would penalize only those individuals who, in spite of all the training, did not display the approved personalities. There are millions of persons who would gladly return to such a standardized method of treating the relationship between the sexes.

⌒ ⌒ ⌒

The waste, if this occurs, will be not only of many women, but also of as many men, because regimentation of one sex carries with it, to greater or less degree, the regimentation of the other also. Every parental behest that defines a way of sitting, a response to a rebuke or a threat, a game, or an attempt to draw or sing or dance or paint, as feminine, is moulding the personality of each little girl's brother as well as moulding the personality of the sister. There can be no society which insists that women follow one special personality-pattern, defined as feminine, which does not do violence also to the individuality of many men.

Alternatively, society can take the course that has become especially associated with the plans of most radical groups: admit that men and women are capable of being moulded to a single pattern as easily as to a diverse one, and cease to make any distinction in the approved personality of both sexes. Girls can be trained exactly as boys are trained, taught the same code, the same forms of expression, the same occupations. This course might seem to be the logic which follows from the conviction that the potentialities which different societies label as either masculine or feminine are really potentialities of some members of each sex, and not sex-linked at all. If this is accepted, is it not reasonable to abandon the kind of artificial standardizations of sex-differences that have been so long characteristic of European society, and admit that they are social fictions for which we have no longer any use?

            ⬠ ⬠ ⬠

In evaluating such a programme as this, however, it is necessary to keep in mind the nature of the gains that society has achieved in its most complex forms. A sacrifice of distinctions in sex-personality may mean a sacrifice in complexity. The Arapesh recognize a minimum of distinction in personality between old and young, between men and women, and they lack categories of rank or status. We have seen that such a society at the best condemns to personal frustration, and at the worst to maladjustment, all of those men and women who do not conform to its simple emphases.

            ⬠ ⬠ ⬠

. . . The imaginative, highly intelligent person who is essentially in tune with the values of his society may also suffer by the lack of range and depth characteristic of too great simplicity. The active mind and intensity of one Arapesh boy whom I knew well was unsatisfied by the laissez-faire solutions, the lack of drama in his culture.

            ⬠ ⬠ ⬠

Nor is it the individual alone who suffers. Society is equally the loser, and we have seen such an attenuation in the dramatic representations of the Mundugumor.

            ⬠ ⬠ ⬠

But the Mundugumor developed a kind of personality for both men and women to which exclusion from any part of life was interpreted as a deadly insult. And as more and more Mundugumor women have demanded and been given the right of initiation, it is not surprising that the Mundugumor ceremonial life has dwindled, the actors have lost their audience, and one vivid artistic element in the life of the Mundugumor community is vanishing. The sacrifice of sex-differences has meant a loss in complexity to the society.

So in our own society. To insist that there are no sex-differences in a society that has always believed in them and depended upon them may be as subtle a form of standardizing personality as to insist that there are many sex-differences.

Take, for instance, the current assumption that women are more opposed to war than men, that any outspoken approval of war is more horrible, more revolting, in women than in men.

. . . This belief that women are naturally more interested in peace is undoubtedly artificial, part of the whole mythology that considers women to be gentler than men. But in contrast let us consider the possibility of a powerful minority that wished to turn a whole society wholeheartedly towards war. One way of doing this would be to insist that women's motives, women's interests, were identical with men's, that women should take as bloodthirsty a delight in preparing for war as ever men do.

Such a standardized society, in which men, women, children, priests, and soldiers were all trained to an undifferentiated and coherent set of values, must of necessity create the kind of deviant that we found among the Arapesh and the Mundugumor, the individual who, regardless of sex or occupation, rebels because he is temperamentally unable to accept the one-sided emphasis of his culture. The individuals who were specifically unadjusted in terms of their psycho-sexual role would, it is true, vanish, but with them would vanish the knowledge that there is more than one set of possible values.

To the extent that abolishing the differences in the approved personalities of men and women means abolishing any expression of the type of personality once called exclusively feminine, or once called exclusively masculine, such a course involves a social loss. Just as a festive occasion is the gayer and more charming if the two sexes are dressed differently, so it is in less material matters.

To the extent that a society insists upon different kinds of personality so that one age-group or class or sex-group may follow purposes disallowed or neglected in another, each individual participant in that society is the richer. The arbitrary assignment of set clothing, set manners, set social responses, to individuals born in a certain class, of a certain sex, or of a certain colour, to those on a certain day of the week, to those born with a certain complexion, does violence to the individual endowment of individuals, but permits the building of a rich culture.

Furthermore, when we consider the position of the deviant individual in historical cultures, those who are born into a complex society in the wrong sex or class for their personalities to have full sway are in a better position than those who are born into a simple society which does not use in any way their special temperamental gifts. The violent woman in a society that permits violence to men only, the strongly emotional member of an aristocracy in a culture that permits downright emotional expression only in the peasantry, the ritualistically inclined individual who is bred a Protestant in a country which has also Catholic institutions—each one of these can find expressed in some other group in the society the emotions that he or she is forbidden to manifest. He is given a certain kind of support by the mere existence of these values, values so congenial to him and so inaccessible because of an accident of birth. For those who are content with a vicarious spectator-role, or with materials upon which to feast the creative imagination, this may be almost enough. They may be content to experience from the sidewalks during a parade, from the audience of a theatre or from the nave of a church, those emotions the direct expression of which is denied to them. The crude compensations offered by the moving pictures to those whose lives are emotionally starved are offered in subtler forms by the art and literature of a complex society to the individual who is out of place in his sex or his class or his occupational group.

Could not the beauty that lies in contrast and complexity be obtained in some other way? If the social insistence upon different personalities for the two sexes results in so much confusion, so many unhappy deviants, so much disorientation, can we imagine a society that abandons these distinctions without abandoning the values that are at present dependent upon them?

Let us suppose that, instead of the classification laid down on the "natural" bases of sex and race, a society had decreed that all blue-eyed people were gentle, submissive, and responsive to the needs of others, and all brown-eyed people were arrogant, dominating, self-centred, and purposive. In this case two complementary social themes would be woven together—the culture, in its art, its religion, its formal personal relations, would have two threads instead of one. There would be blue-eyed men, and blue-eyed women, which would mean that there were gentle, "maternal" women, and gentle, "maternal" men. A blue-eyed man might marry a woman who had been bred to the same personality as himself, or a brown-eyed woman who had been bred to the contrasting personality.

. . . The individual would still suffer a mutilation of his temperamental preferences, for it would be the unrelated fact of eye-colour that would determine the attitudes which he was educated to show. Every blue-eyed person would be forced into submissiveness and declared maladjusted if he or she showed any traits that it had been decided were only appropriate to the brown-eyed. The greatest social loss, however, in the classification of personality on the basis of sex would not be present in this society which based its classification on eye-colour. Human relations, and especially those which involve sex, would not be artificially distorted.

But such a course, the substitution of eye-colour for sex as a basis upon which to educate children into groups showing contrasting personalities, while it would be a definite advance upon a classification by sex, remains a parody of all the attempts that society has made through history to define an individual's role in terms of sex, or colour, or date of birth, or shape of head.

However, the only solution of the problem does not lie between an acceptance of standardization of sex-differences with the resulting cost in individual happiness and adjustment, and the abolition of these differences with the consequent loss in social values. A civilization might take its cues not from such categories as age or sex, race or hereditary position in a family line, but instead of specializing personality along such simple lines recognize, train, and make a place for many and divergent temperamental endowments. It might build upon the different potentialities that it now attempts to extirpate artificially in some children and create artificially in others.

Historically the lessening of rigidity in the classification of the sexes has come about at different times, either by the creation of a new artificial category, or by the recognition of real individual differences. Sometimes the idea of social position has transcended sex-categories. In a society that recognizes gradations in wealth or rank, women of rank or women of wealth have been permitted an arrogance which was denied to both sexes among the lowly or the poor.

To break down one line of division, that between the sexes, and substitute another, that between classes, is no real advance.

If our aim is greater expression for each individual temperament, rather than any partisan interest in one sex or its fate, we must see these historical developments which have aided in freeing some women as nevertheless a kind of development that also involved major social losses.

The second way in which categories of sex-differences have become less rigid is through a recognition of genuine individual gifts as they occurred in either sex. Here a real distinction has been substituted for an artificial one, and the gains are tremendous for society and for the individual. Where writing is accepted as a profession that may be pursued by either sex with perfect suitability, individuals who have the ability to write need not be debarred from it by their sex, nor need they, if they do write, doubt their essential masculinity or femininity. An occupation that has no basis in sex-determined gifts can now recruit its ranks from twice as many potential artists. And it is here that we can find a ground-plan for building a society that would substitute real differences for arbitrary ones. We must recognize that beneath the superficial classifications of sex and race the same potentialities exist, recurring generation after generation, only to perish because society has no place for them. Just as society now permits the practice of an art to members of either sex, so it might also permit the development of many contrasting temperamental gifts in each sex. It might abandon its various attempts to make boys fight and to make girls remain passive, or to make all children fight, and instead shape our educational institutions to develop to the full the boy who shows a capacity for maternal behaviour, the girl who shows an opposite capacity that is stimulated by fighting against obstacles. No skill, no special aptitude, no vividness of imagination or precision of thinking would go unrecognized because the child who possessed it was of one sex rather than the other. No child would be relentlessly shaped to one pattern of behaviour, but instead there should be many patterns, in a world that had learned to allow to each individual the pattern which was most congenial to his gifts.

Such a civilization would not sacrifice the gains of thousands of years during which society has built up standards of diversity. The social gains would be conserved, and each child would be encouraged on the basis of his actual temperament. Where we now have patterns of behaviour for women and patterns of behaviour for men, we would then have patterns of behaviour that expressed the interests of individuals with many kinds of endowment. There would be ethical codes and social symbolisms, an art and a way of life, congenial to each endowment.

Historically our own culture has relied for the creation of rich and contrasting values upon many artificial distinctions, the most striking of which is sex. It will not be by the mere abolition of these distinctions that society will develop patterns in which individual gifts are given place instead of being forced into an ill-fitting mould. If we are to achieve a richer culture, rich in contrasting values, we must recognize the whole gamut of human potentialities, and so weave a less arbitrary social fabric, one in which each diverse human gift will find a fitting place.

In a sense, Mead provides in her conclusion a utopian vision, similarly to Gilman and also to Plato in Book V of his *Republic,* excerpted in Part Two. For Mead, while every society must somehow mark temperamental differences so as to distribute and regulate them within it, the best society should mark these differences according to the different talents and interest that happen naturally to arise in the individuals of that society. In this way, the most possible variation and talent can be accommodated, while creating the least and smallest range of restrictions on individual's pursuits of happy lives.

7. JEAN-PAUL SARTRE
(French, 1905–1980)

Sartre was one of the best known and most active intellectuals of the post–World War II era. Captured and imprisoned by the Germans during the war, Sartre joined the French Resistance after his release, and in all his writing—journalism, fiction, drama, and philosophy—Sartre championed individual freedom and personal responsibility in the face of the life-threatening challenges posed by the conditions of the twentieth century. But Sartre's existentialist philosophy (which develops some lines of thought from Nietzsche and Kierkegaard, excerpted in the last chapter) is also an ageless investigation. Sartre argued that human character was a result—not a cause—of human choice and action, and that therefore human beings should recognize the vast extent of their freedom. For Sartre, we are almost entirely what we make ourselves.

BEING AND NOTHINGNESS (1956)

The very long and often very technical *Being and Nothingness* is Sartre's major philosophical work. In it, he pursues the question of existence "phenomenologically," meaning that he gets at the question of what exists through a detailed description of consciousness. His study of consciousness develops the claim that "existence is prior to essence," or in other words that the sheer fact of consciousness exists and confronts us prior to any identifying feature of an individual human consciousness, like a particular idea or a particular feeling or character trait. Therefore, Sartre claims, consciousness constructs its own identity from its own raw, not-yet-rational, power. This it does by the process of "negation," the use of the concept of nothingness to delineate existent entities from each other. For instance, the concept of the Self, claims Sartre, is really a name one puts on the negation of the Other; or rather, self-consciousness is really consciousness of the not-other. But to be conscious of the not-other of course requires at the same time a consciousness of the Other, which is negated. Thus, according to Sartre, the concept of the Self, or of the human being, is really just a default upon which consciousness falls in its efforts not to be subsumed by the Other, of which it is always aware.

This relationship between Self and Other is of course reminiscent of Hegel's dialectic of Master and Slave—a battle in consciousness for the winning identity. Sartre acknowledges and relies on this similarity to Hegel, adding to it a rich lexicon of states of consciousness that result from the internal conflict between being and nothingness. One of these states of consciousness, which Sartre believes is fundamental to what we call "humanity," is a state he calls "Bad Faith." "Bad Faith" is essentially a self-delusion, the delusion upon which the very concept of the self relies for its existence. Thus, the Self amounts ultimately to a kind of lie consciousness tells itself about the Other. Through the beliefs that the Other is weak, unpleasant, immoral, unimportant, or otherwise non-threatening to or already vanquished by consciousness, consciousness gains a notion of its own identity, individuality, strength, and goodness.

But in order to benefit in these ways from these beliefs, consciousness must convince itself of their objective truth—it must pretend to itself that it was not the agent responsible for negating the Other, but rather that "nature" or "truth" or "God" has made the Other the Other and the Self the Self. In this way, the Self, which has acted as a free agent in all this, denies its own freedom and responsibility and pretends to itself that it is bound in its beliefs and actions by this "truth" or "nature." Sartre describes this as consciousness's tendency to deny its own "transcendence"—its freedom to construct the world, and the lines of distinction within it that mark off entities from each other—and to attribute its actions falsely to its "facticity"—unchangeable natural elements that behave in wholly determined ways. Sartre believed that actually very little of human nature is factical—the time and place one was born, maybe one's height, but little else. This denial of one's transcendence, then, is Bad Faith. For Sartre, Bad Faith is not the product of thought; it is the product of our actions and choices, which have an impact on consciousness's awareness of the world. When one acts in Bad Faith, one changes the landscape of consciousness such that the borders between the Self and the Other, between determined and free action, are reinforced.

"THE DATE" AND BAD FAITH

In the second section of Chapter Two of the first part of *Being and Nothingness,* titled "Patterns of Bad Faith," Sartre analyzes several typical examples of a consciousness in Bad Faith. One of the most memorable is the situation of "The Date," in which a young woman denies her own sexual feelings and responsibilities, by projecting them onto a young man.

II. PATTERNS OF BAD FAITH

. . . Take the example of a woman who has consented to go out with a particular man for the first time. She knows very well the intentions which the man who is speaking to her cherishes regarding her. She knows also that it will be necessary sooner or later for her to make a decision. But she does not want to realize the urgency; she concerns herself only with what is respectful and discreet in the attitude of her companion. She does not apprehend this conduct as an attempt to achieve what we call "the first approach"; that is, she does not want to see possibilities of temporal development which his conduct presents. She restricts this behavior to what is in the present; she does not wish to read in the phrases which he addresses to her anything other than their explicit meaning. If he says to her, "I find you so attractive!" she disarms this phrase of its sexual background; she attaches to the conversation and to the behavior of the speaker, the immediate meanings, which she imagines as objective qualities. The man who is speaking to her appears to her sincere and respectful as the table is round or square, as the wall coloring is blue or gray. The qualities thus attached to the person she is listening to are in this way fixed in a permanence like that of things, which is no other than the projection of the strict present of the qualities into the temporal flux. This is because she does not quite know what she wants. She is profoundly aware of the desire which she inspires, but the desire cruel and naked would humiliate and horrify her. Yet she would find no charm in a respect which would be only respect. In order to satisfy her, there must be a feeling which is addressed wholly to her *personality*—i.e., to her full freedom— and which would be a recognition of her freedom. But at the same time this feeling must be wholly desire; that is, it must address itself to her body as object. This time then she refuses to apprehend the desire for what it is; she does not even give it a name; she recognizes it only to the extent that it transcends itself toward admiration, esteem, respect and that it is wholly absorbed in the more refined forms which it produces, to the extent of no longer figuring anymore as a sort of warmth and density. But then suppose he takes her hand. This act of her companion risks changing the situation by calling for an immediate decision. To leave the hand there is to consent in herself to flirt, to engage herself. To withdraw it is to break the troubled and unstable harmony which gives the hour its charm. The aim is to postpone the moment of decision as long as possible. We know what happens next; the young woman leaves her hand there, but she *does not notice* that she is leaving it. She does not notice because it happens by chance that she is at this moment all intellect. She draws her companion up to the most lofty regions of sentimental speculation; she speaks of Life, of her life, she shows herself in her essential aspect—a personality, a consciousness. And during this time the divorce of the body from the soul is accomplished; the hand rests inert between the warm hands of her companion—neither consenting nor resisting—a thing.

We shall say that this woman is in bad faith. But we see immediately that she uses various procedures in order to maintain herself in this bad faith. She has disarmed the actions of her companion by reducing them to being only what they are; that is, to existing in the mode of the in-itself. But she permits herself to enjoy his desire, to the extent that she will apprehend it as not being what it is, will recognize its transcendence. Finally while sensing profoundly the presence of her own body—to the point of being aroused, perhaps—she realizes herself as *not being* her own body, and she contemplates it as though from above as a passive object to which events can *happen* but which can neither provoke them nor avoid them because all its possibilities are outside of it. What unity do we find in these various aspects of bad faith? It is a certain art of forming contradictory concepts which unite in themselves both an idea and the negation of that idea. The basic concept which is thus engendered utilizes the double property of the human being, who is at once a *facticity* and a *transcendence*. These two aspects of human reality are and ought to be capable of a valid coordination. But bad faith does not wish either to coordinate them or to surmount them in a synthesis. Bad faith seeks to affirm their identity while preserving their differences. It must affirm facticity as being transcendence and transcendence as *being* facticity, in such a way that at the instant when a person apprehends the one, he can find himself abruptly faced with the other.

Essentially, Sartre is arguing in this example that a woman's belief in her own virtue and in men's sexual aggressiveness, that her belief in the romance of a situation that is really calculated by both parties, is nothing but a Bad Faith effort to achieve sexual pleasure without taking responsibility for sexual desire. It is a microcosm, for Sartre, of the whole false edifice of morality, particularly sexual morality. We can also see from the example that Sartre means to challenge our ordinary intuitions that sexual morality is built upon or built to protect "natural" sex differences in "temperament" or "sexual drive." He implies here that sex differences are really just the products of a moral mythology that is maintained through the Bad Faith of self-conscious individuals. Sex-differences, at least those of sexual styles or temperaments, he indicates, are a part of our free transcendence, and are not factical at all. This is a bold claim, which has pleased some feminists and angered others. How should we understand, for instance, Sartre's attribution of responsibility to the woman in this case? Has it minimized the responsibility we should attribute to her date?

THE LOOK

The Sartrian image of most interest to later feminists—again with mixed reception—is his discussion of "the look" in section four of Chapter One of Part Three of *Being and Nothingness.* In Part Three, titled "Being-For-Others," Sartre gives a phenomenological analysis of human interrelationships. The look, according to Sartre, is the vehicle of consciousness's awareness of the Other-as-Other.

IV. THE LOOK

This woman whom I see coming toward me, this man who is passing by in the street, this beggar whom I hear calling before my window, all are for me *objects*—of that there is no doubt. Thus it is true that at least one of the modalities of the Other's presence to me is *object-ness.* But we have seen that if this relation of object-ness is the fundamental relation between the Other and myself, then the Other's existence remains purely conjectural. Now it is not only conjectural but *probable* that this voice which I hear is that of a man and not a song on a phonograph; it is infinitely *probable* that the passerby whom I see is a man and not a perfected robot. This means that without going beyond the limits of probability and indeed because of this very probability, my apprehension of the Other as an object essentially refers me to a fundamental apprehension of the Other in which he will not be revealed to me as an object but as a "presence in person."

⌐ ⌐ ⌐

. . . This relation which I call "being-seen-by-another," far from being merely one of the relations signified by the word *man,* represents an irreducible fact which can not be deduced either from the essence of the Other-as-object, or from my being-as-subject. On the contrary, if the concept of the Other-as-object is to have any meaning, this can be only as the result of the conversion and the degradation of that original relation. In a word, my apprehension of the Other in the world as *probably being* a man refers to my permanent possibility of *being-seen-by-him;* that is, to the permanent possibility that a subject who sees me may be substituted for the object seen by me. "Being-seen-by-the-Other" is the *truth* of "seeing-the-Other." Thus the notion of the Other can not under any circumstances aim at a solitary, extra-mundane consciousness which I can not even think. The man is defined by his relation to the world and by his relation to myself. He is that object in the world which determines an internal flow of the universe, an internal hemorrhage. He is the subject who is revealed to me in that flight of myself toward objectivation. But the original relation of myself to the Other is not only an absent truth aimed at across the concrete presence of an object in my universe; it is also a concrete, daily relation which at each instant I experience. At each instant the Other *is looking at me*. It is easy therefore for us to attempt with concrete examples to describe this fundamental connection which must form the basis of any theory concerning the Other. If the Other is on principle the *one who looks at me,* then we must be able to explain the meaning of the Other's look.

Every look directed toward me is manifested in connection with the appearance of a sensible form in our perceptive field, but contrary to what might be expected, it is not connected with any determined form. Of course what *most often* manifests a look is the convergence of two ocular globes in my direction. But the look will be given just as well on occasion when there is a rustling of branches, or the sound of a footstep followed by silence, or the slight opening of a shutter, or a light movement of a curtain. During an attack men who are crawling through the brush apprehend as a *look to be avoided,* not two eyes, but a white farmhouse which is outlined against the sky at the top of a little hill. It is obvious that the object thus constituted still manifests the look as being probable. It is only probable that behind the bush which has just moved there is someone hiding who is watching me. But this probability need not detain us for the moment; we shall return to this point later. What is important first is to define the look in itself. Now the bush, the farmhouse are not the look; they only represent the *eye,* for the eye is not at first apprehended as a sensible organ of vision but as the support for the look. They never refer therefore to the actual eye of the watcher hidden behind the curtain, behind a window in the farmhouse. In themselves they are already eyes. On the other hand neither is the look one quality among others of the object which functions as an eye, nor is it the total form of that object, nor a "worldly" relation which is established between that object and me. On the contrary, far from perceiving the look *on* the objects which manifest it, my apprehension of a look turned toward me appears on the ground of the destruction of the eyes which "look at me." If I apprehend the look, I cease to perceive the eyes; they are there, they remain in the field of my perception as pure *presentations,* but I do not make any use of them; they are neutralized, put out of play.

⌒ ⌒ ⌒

Let us imagine that moved by jealousy, curiosity, or vice I have just glued my ear to the door and looked through a keyhole. I am alone and on the level of a non-thetic self-consciousness. This means first of all that there is no self to inhabit my consciousness, nothing therefore to which I can refer my acts in order to qualify them. They are in no way *known; I am my acts* and hence they carry in themselves their whole justification. I am a pure consciousness *of* things, and things, caught up in the circuit of my selfness, offer to me their potentialities as the proof of my non-thetic consciousness (of) my own possibilities. This means that behind that door a spectacle is presented as "to be seen," a conversation as "to be heard." The door, the keyhole are at once both instruments and obstacles; they are presented as "to be handled with care"; the keyhole is given as "to be looked through close by and a little to one side," *etc.* Hence from this moment "I do what I have to do." No transcending view comes to confer upon my acts the character of a *given* on which a judgment can be brought to bear. My consciousness sticks to my acts, it *is* my acts; and my acts are commanded only by the ends to be attained and by the instruments to be employed. My attitude, for example, has no "outside"; it is a pure process of relating the instrument (the keyhole) to the end to be attained (the spectacle to be seen), a pure mode of losing myself in the world, of causing myself to be drunk in by things as ink is by a blotter in order that an instrumental-complex oriented toward an end may be synthetically detached on the ground of the world. The order is the reverse of causal order. It is the end to be attained which organizes all the moments which precede it. The end justifies the means; the means do not exist for themselves and outside the end.

ᗫ ᗫ ᗫ

But all of a sudden I hear footsteps in the hall. Someone is looking at me! What does this mean? It means that I am suddenly affected in my being and that essential modifications appear in my structure—modifications which I can apprehend and fix conceptually by means of the reflective *cogito.*

First of all, I now exist as *myself* for my unreflective consciousness. It is this irruption of the self which has been most often described: I see *myself* because *somebody* sees me—as it is usually expressed. This way of putting it is not wholly exact. But let us look more carefully. So long as we considered the for-itself in its isolation, we were able to maintain that the unreflective consciousness can not be inhabited by a self; the self was given in the form of an object and only for the reflective consciousness. But here the self comes to haunt the unreflective consciousness. Now the unreflective consciousness is a consciousness *of* the world. Therefore for the unreflective consciousness the self exists on the level of objects in the world; this role which devolved only on the reflective consciousness—the making-present of the self—belongs now to the unreflective consciousness. Only the reflective consciousness has the self directly for an object. The unreflective consciousness does not apprehend the *person* directly or as *its* object; the person is presented to consciousness *in so far as the person is an object for the Other.* This means that all of a sudden I am conscious of myself as escaping myself, not in that I am the foundation of my own nothingness but in that I have my foundation outside myself. I am for myself only as I am a pure reference to the Other.

ᗫ ᗫ ᗫ

. . . For the Other *I am seated* as this inkwell *is on* the table; for the Other, *I am leaning over* the keyhole as this tree *is bent* by the wind. Thus for the Other I have stripped myself of transcendence.

ᕽ ᕽ ᕽ

. . . My original fall is the existence of the Other. Shame—like price—is the apprehension of myself as a nature although that very nature escapes me and is unknowable as such. Strictly speaking, it is not that I perceive myself losing my freedom in order to become a *thing,* but my nature is—over there, outside my lived freedom—as a given attribute of this being which I am for the Other.

I grasp the Other's look at the very center of my *act* as the solidification and alienation of my own possibilities. In fear or in anxious or prudent anticipation, I perceive that these possibilities which I *am* and which are the condition of my transcendence are given also to another, given as about to be transcended in turn by his own possibilities. The Other as a look is only that—my transcendence transcended. Of course I still *am* my possibilities in the mode of non-thetic consciousness (of) these possibilities. But at the same time the look alienates them from me.

ᕽ ᕽ ᕽ

. . . Thus the appearance of the look is apprehended by me as the upsurge of an ekstatic relation of being, of which one term is the "me" as for-itself which is what it is not and which is not what it is, and of which the other term is still the "me" but outside my reach, outside my action, outside my knowledge. This term, since it is directly connected with the infinite possibilities of a free Other, is itself an infinite and inexhaustible synthesis of unrevealed properties. Through the Other's look I *live* myself as fixed in the midst of the world, as in danger, as irremediable. But I *know* neither what I am nor what is my place in the world, nor what face this world in which I am turns toward the Other.

ᕽ ᕽ ᕽ

At the same time I experience the Other's infinite freedom. It is for and by means of a freedom and only for and by means of it that my possibles can be limited and fixed. A material obstacle can not fix my possibilities; it is only the occasion for my projecting myself toward other possibles and can not confer upon them an *outside.* To remain at home because it is raining and to remain at home because one has been forbidden to go out are by no means the same thing.

The picture Sartre paints is not a happy one: through the look one first becomes conscious of oneself—but consciousness of oneself is thereby shown to be inherently secondary, negative, slavish, humiliated. One comes to consciousness of oneself only through one's consciousness of the judgment of oneself by others. This judgment, which is the vehicle of human identity, according to Sartre, is generically characterized by "looking," but may, as he states, occur in other ways as well.

The look, as Sartre renders it, does not appear to be associated with either sex; it is a generically human, humanizing, act. In the instant of the look, the Other objectifies the Self, who is only a free and conscious subject when he or she loses sight of the self in an act of awareness of something. Here, absorbed in the activities on the other side of the door, the keyhole-peeper is neither self or other. The judgment of the other, however, objectifies the keyhole-peeper, who in his or her recognition of this judgment, subjects him or herself to it. Hence the shame and embarrassment that he or she feels: a shame that Sartre believes is inherent in the concept of Self. The humiliation that the Self feels under the gaze of the Other is, for Sartre, equally masculine or feminine. Some later feminists, however, have modeled their analysis of women's position in society and in relationships with men on this image, claiming that women's secondary, negatively defined position is achieved in the way Sartre describes here, through the judgment of men. Consequently, the giving of the "look" has sometimes been identified with masculinity. Since woman has also been associated with the existentialists' notion of the Other, however (as we will see, for instance, in the selection from deBeauvoir), this identification can become quite complicated. Is the human self, objectified and humiliated by the "look" of the Other, most typically male or female? The look, and the relations it establishes, are similar to Hegel's description of the "fight to the death" between the master and the slave—one is humbled in the same instant that the other is placed in a position of power over him or her—and it shares with the Hegelian hypothesis an oft-used but ambiguous place in the discussion of the relation between the sexes.

8. SIMONE DE BEAUVOIR
(French, 1908–1986)

A somewhat unintentional leader in postwar feminism, Simone deBeauvoir was well known as a writer and journalist, particularly in France, even before the publication of her books associated with women's issues. After the publication of *The Second Sex,* from which all the passages here are taken, however, deBeauvoir became an established heroine for women around the world and for the women's movement. While today her work is less of a polemical force than it once was, deBeauvoir is still regarded by many feminists as the founding figure in recent feminism.

DeBeauvoir, the life-long companion of Jean-Paul Sartre, was also associated with existentialism, approaching the question of woman from the point of view of the individual woman's consciousness of herself as such. This accounts, in part, for her rare status as a woman philosopher of the first rank. Hers is a broad-ranging critical examination of the state of woman's consciousness.

THE SECOND SEX (1949, U.S. TRANS. 1952)

A long, complex, and highly intellectual work, *The Second Sex* investigates the notion and state of woman from a variety of perspectives—philosophical argument, historical analysis, literary criticism, psychology of development, and sociological analysis. We cannot hope here to provide any of deBeauvoir's more detailed discussions, and so will limit the passages included to those from the Introduction—which is more general in its approach—and the Conclusion—which is more philosophical.

INTRODUCTION

In the Introduction, deBeauvoir puts forward her famous thesis, "woman is the Other." By this, she means something similar to Sartre's notion, as given in his *Being and Nothingness,* some relevant passages of which appeared earlier. But deBeauvoir's notion of "Otherness," even in this initial discussion, is fleshed out very concretely, with a realistic representation of women's actual experience in the world.

> For a long time I have hesitated to write a book on woman. The subject is irritating, especially to women; and it is not new. Enough ink has been spilled in the quarreling over feminism, now practically over, and perhaps we should say no more about it. It is still talked about, however, for the voluminous nonsense uttered during the last century seems to have done little to illuminate the problem. After all, is there a problem? And if so, what is it? Are there women, really? Most assuredly the theory of the eternal feminine still has its adherents who will whisper in your ear: "Even in Russia women still are *women*"; and other erudite persons—sometimes the very same—say with a sigh: "Woman is losing her way, woman is lost." One wonders if women still exist, if they will always exist, whether or not it is desirable that they should, what place they occupy in this world, what their place should be. "What has become of women?" was asked recently in an ephemeral magazine.
>
> But first we must ask: what is a woman? . . . All agree in recognizing the fact that females exist in the human species; today as always they make up about one half of humanity. And yet we are told that femininity is in danger; we are exhorted to be women, remain women, become women. It would appear, then, that every female human being is not necessarily a woman; to be so considered she must share in that mysterious and threatened reality known as femininity.

> If her functioning as a female is not enough to define woman, if we decline also to explain her through "the eternal feminine," and if nevertheless we admit, provisionally, that women do exist, then we must face the question: what is a woman?
>
> To state the question is, to me, to suggest, at once, a preliminary answer. The fact that I ask it is in itself significant. A man would never get the notion of writing a book on the peculiar situation of the human male. But if I wish to define myself, I must first of all say: "I am a woman"; on this truth must be based all further discussion. A man never begins by presenting himself as an individual of a certain sex; it goes without saying that he is a man. The terms *masculine* and *feminine* are used symmetrically only as a matter of form, as on

legal papers. In actuality the relation of the two sexes is not quite like that of two electrical poles, for man represents both the positive and the neutral, as is indicated by the common use of *man* to designate human beings in general; whereas woman represents only the negative, defined by limiting criteria. without reciprocity. In the midst of an abstract discussion it is vexing to hear a man say: "You think thus and so because you are a woman"; but I know that my only defense is to reply: "I think thus and so because it is true," thereby removing my subjective self from the argument. It would be out of the question to reply: "And you think the contrary because you are a man," for it is understood that the fact of being a man is no peculiarity. A man is in the right in being a man; it is the woman who is in the wrong. It amounts to this: just as for the ancients there was an absolute vertical with reference to which the oblique was defined, so there is an absolute human type, the masculine. Woman has ovaries, a uterus; these peculiarities imprison her in her subjectivity, circumscribe her within the limits of her own nature. It is often said that she thinks with her glands. Man superbly ignores the fact that his anatomy also includes glands, such as the testicles, and that they secrete hormones. He thinks of his body as a direct and normal connection with the world, which he believes he apprehends objectively, whereas he regards the body of woman as a hindrance, a prison, weighed down by everything peculiar to it. "The female is a female by virtue of a certain *lack* of qualities," said Aristotle; "we should regard the female nature as afflicted with a natural defectiveness." And St. Thomas for his part pronounced woman to be an "imperfect man," an "incidental" being. This is symbolized in Genesis where Eve is depicted as made from what Bossuet called "a supernumerary bone" of Adam.

Thus humanity is male and man defines woman not in herself but as relative to him; she is not regarded as an autonomous being. . . . And she is simply what man decrees; thus she is called "the sex," by which is meant that she appears essentially to the male as a sexual being. For him she is sex—absolute sex, no less. She is defined and differentiated with reference to man and not he with reference to her; she is the incidental, the inessential as opposed to the essential. He is the Subject, he is the Absolute—she is the Other.

The category of the *Other* is as primordial as consciousness itself. In the most primitive societies, in the most ancient mythologies, one finds the expression of a duality—that of the Self and the Other. This duality was not originally attached to the division of the sexes; it was not dependent upon any empirical facts. It is revealed in such works as that of Granet on Chinese thought and those of Dumézil on the East Indies and Rome. The feminine element was at first no more involved in such pairs as Varuna-Mitra, Uranus-Zeus, Sun-Moon, and Day-Night than it was the contrasts between Good and Evil, lucky and unlucky auspices, right and left, God and Lucifer. Otherness is a fundamental category of human thought.

Thus it is that no group ever sets itself up as the One without at once setting up the Other over against itself. If three travelers chance to occupy the same compartment, that is enough to make vaguely hostile "others" out of all the rest of the passengers on the train. In small-town eyes all persons not belonging to the village are "strangers" and suspect; to the native of a country all who inhabit other countries are "foreigners"; Jews are "different" for the anti-Semite, Negroes are "inferior" for American racists, aborigines are "natives" for colonists, proletarians are the "lower class" for the privileged.

Lévi-Strauss, at the end of a profound work on the various forms of primitive societies, reaches the following conclusion: "Passage from the state of Nature to the state of Culture is marked by man's ability to view biological relations as a series of contrasts; duality, alternation, opposition, and symmetry, whether under definite or vague forms, constitute not so much phenomena to be explained as fundamental and immediately given data of social reality." These phenomena would be incomprehensible if in fact human society were simply a *Mitsein* or fellowship based on solidarity and friendliness. Things become clear, on the contrary, if, following Hegel, we find in consciousness itself a fundamental hostility toward every other consciousness; the subject can be posed only in being opposed—he sets himself up as the essential, as opposed to the other, the inessential, the object.

But the other consciousness, the other ego, sets up a reciprocal claim. The native traveling abroad is shocked to find himself in turn regarded as a "stranger" by the natives of neighboring countries. As a matter of fact, wars, festivals, trading, treaties, and contests among tribes, nations, and classes tend to deprive the concept *Other* of its absolute sense and to make manifest its relativity; willy-nilly, individuals and groups are forced to realize the reciprocity of their relations. How is it, then, that this reciprocity has not been recognized between the sexes, that one of the contrasting terms is set up as the sole essential, denying any relativity in regard to its correlative and defining the latter as pure otherness? Why is it that women do not dispute male sovereignty? No subject will readily volunteer to become the object, the inessential; it is not the Other who, in defining himself as the Other, establishes the One. The Other is posed as such by the One in defining himself as the One. But if the Other is not to regain the status of being the One, he must be submissive enough to accept this alien point of view. Whence comes this submission in the case of woman?

There are, to be sure, other cases in which a certain category has been able to dominate another completely for a time. Very often this privilege depends upon inequality of numbers—the majority imposes its rule upon the minority or persecutes it. But women are not a minority, like the American Negroes or the Jews; there are as many women as men on earth.

☞ ☞ ☞

. . . Throughout history they have always been subordinated to men, and hence their dependency is not the result of a historical event or a social change—it was not something that *occurred*. The reason why otherness in this case seems to be an absolute is in part that it lacks the contingent or incidental nature of historical facts. A condition brought about at a certain time can be abolished at some other time, as the Negroes of Haiti and others have proved;

but it might seem that a natural condition is beyond the possibility of change. In truth, however, the nature of things is no more immutably given, once for all, than is historical reality. If woman seems to be the inessential which never becomes the essential, it is because she herself fails to bring about this change. Proletarians say "We"; Negroes also. Regarding themselves as subjects, they transform the bourgeois, the whites, into "others." But women do not say "We," except at some congress of feminists or similar formal demonstration; men say "women," and women use the same word in referring to themselves. They do not authentically assume a subjective attitude. The proletarians have accomplished the revolution in Russia, the Negroes in Haiti, the Indo-Chinese are battling for it in Indo-China; but the women's effort has never been anything more than a symbolic agitation. They have gained only what men have been willing to grant; they have taken nothing, they have only received.

The reason for this is that women lack concrete means for organizing themselves into a unit which can stand face to face with the correlative unit. They have no past, no history, no religion of their own; and they have no such solidarity of work and interest as that of the proletariat. They are not even promiscuously herded together in the way that creates community feeling among the American Negroes, the ghetto Jews, the workers of Saint-Denis, or the factory hands of Renault. They live dispersed among the males, attached through residence, housework, economic condition, and social standing to certain men— fathers or husbands—more firmly than they are to other women. If they belong to the bourgeoisie, they feel solidarity with men of that class, not with proletarian women; if they are white, their allegiance is to white men, not to Negro women. The proletariat can propose to massacre the ruling class, and a sufficiently fanatical Jew or Negro might dream of getting sole possession of the atomic bomb and making humanity wholly Jewish or black; but woman cannot even dream of exterminating the males. The bond that unites her to her oppressors is not comparable to any other. The division of the sexes is a biological fact, not an event in human history. Male and female stand opposed within a primordial *Mitsein,* and woman has not broken it. The couple is a fundamental unity with its two halves riveted together, and the cleavage of society along the line of sex is impossible. Here is to be found the basic trait of woman: she is the Other in a totality of which the two components are necessary to one another.

☙ ☙ ☙

. . . [T]he master does not make a point to the need that he has for the other; he has in his grasp the power of satisfying this need through his own action; whereas the slave, in his dependent condition, his hope and fear, is quite conscious of the need he has for his master. Even if the need is at bottom equally urgent for both, it always works in favor of the oppressor and against the oppressed. That is why the liberation of the working class, for example, has been slow.

Now, woman has always been man's dependent, if not his slave; the two sexes have never shared the world in equality.

⌐ ⌐ ⌐

. . . To decline to be the Other, to refuse to be a party to the deal—this would be for women to renounce all the advantages conferred upon them by their alliance with the superior caste. Man-the-sovereign will provide woman-the-liege with material protection and will undertake the moral justification of her existence; thus she can evade at once both economic risk and the metaphysical risk of a liberty in which ends and aims must be contrived without assistance. Indeed, along with the ethical urge of each individual to affirm his subjective existence, there is also the temptation to forgo liberty and become a thing. This is an inauspicious road, for he who takes it—passive, lost, ruined—becomes henceforth the creature of another's will, frustrated in his transcendence and deprived of every value. But it is an easy road; on it one avoids the strain involved in undertaking an authentic existence. When man makes of woman the *Other,* he may, then, expect her to manifest deep-seated tendencies toward complicity. Thus, woman may fail to lay claim to the status of subject because she lacks definite resources, because she feels the necessary bond that ties her to man regardless of reciprocity, and because she is often very well pleased with her role as the *Other.*

But it will be asked at once: how did all this begin? It is easy to see that the duality of the sexes, like any duality, gives rise to conflict. And doubtless the winner will assume the status of absolute. But why should man have won from the start? It seems possible that women could have won the victory; or that the outcome of the conflict might never have been decided. How is it that this world has always belonged to the men and that things have begun to change only recently? Is this change a good thing? Will it bring about an equal sharing of the world between men and women?

These questions are not new, and they have often been answered. But the very fact that woman *is the Other* tends to cast suspicion upon all the justifications that men have ever been able to provide for it. These have all too evidently been dictated by men's interest. A little-known feminist of the seventeenth century, Poulain de la Barre, put it this way: "All that has been written about women by men should be suspect, for the men are at once judge and party to the lawsuit." Everywhere, at all times, the males have displayed their satisfaction in feeling that they are the lords of creation. " Blessed be God . . . that He did not make me a woman," say the Jews in their morning prayers, while their wives pray on a note of resignation: "Blessed be the Lord, who created me according to His will." The first among the blessings for which Plato thanked the gods was that he had been created free, not enslaved; the second, a man, not a woman. But the males could not enjoy this privilege fully unless they believed it to be founded on the absolute and the eternal; they sought to make the fact of their supremacy into a right.

⌐ ⌐ ⌐

Legislators, priests, philosophers, writers, and scientists have striven to show that the subordinate position of woman is willed in heaven and advantageous on earth. The religions invented by men reflect this wish for domination. In the legends of Eve and Pandora men have taken up arms against women. They have made use of philosophy and theology, as the quotations from Aristotle and St. Thomas have shown. Since ancient times satirists and moralists have delighted in showing up the weaknesses of women.

⤶ ⤶ ⤶

. . . Sometimes what is going on is clear enough. For instance, the Roman law limiting the rights of woman cited "the imbecility, the instability of the sex" just when the weakening of family ties seemed to threaten the interests of male heirs.

⤶ ⤶ ⤶

It was only later, in the eighteenth century, that genuinely democratic men began to view the matter objectively. Diderot, among others, strove to show that woman is, like man, a human being. Later John Stuart Mill came fervently to her defense. But these philosophers displayed unusual impartiality. In the nineteenth century the feminist quarrel became again a quarrel of partisans. One of the consequences of the industrial revolution was the entrance of women into productive labor, and it was just here that the claims of the feminists emerged from the realm of theory and acquired an economic basis, while their opponents became the more aggressive. Although landed property lost power to some extent, the bourgeoisie clung to the old morality that found the guarantee of private property in the solidity of the family. Woman was ordered back into the home the more harshly as her emanciaption became a real menace. Even within the working class the men endeavored to restrain woman's liberation, because they began to see the women as dangerous competitors—the more so because they were accustomed to work for lower wages.

In proving woman's inferiority, the antifeminists then began to draw not only upon religion, philosophy, and theology, as before, but also upon science— biology, experimental psychology, etc. At most they were willing to grant "equality in difference" to the *other* sex. That profitable formula is most significant; it is precisely like the "equal but separate" formula of the Jim Crow laws aimed at the North American Negroes. As is well known, this so-called equalitarian segregation has resulted only in the most extreme discrimination. The similarity just noted is in no way due to chance, for whether it is a race, a caste, a class, or a sex that is reduced to a position of inferiority, the methods of justification are the same. "The eternal feminine" corresponds to "the black soul" and to "the Jewish character." True, the Jewish problem is on the whole very different from the other two—to the anti-Semite the Jew is not so much an inferior as he is an enemy for whom there is to be granted no place on earth, for whom annihilation is the fate desired. But there are deep similarities between the situation of woman and that of the Negro. Both are being emancipated today from a like paternalism, and the former master class wishes to "keep them in their place"—that is, the place chosen for them. In both cases the former masters lavish more or less sincere eulogies, either on the virtues of "the good Negro" with his dormant, childish, merry soul—the submissive Negro—or on the merits of the woman who is "truly feminine"—that is, frivolous, infantile, irresponsible—the submissive woman. In both cases the dominant class bases its argument on a state of affairs that it has itself created.

↶ ↶ ↶

This vicious circle is met with in all analogous circumstances; when an individual (or a group of individuals) is kept in a situation of inferiority, the fact is that he *is* inferior. But the significance of the verb *to be* must be rightly understood here; it is in bad faith to give it a static value when it really has the dynamic Hegelian sense of "to have become." Yes, women on the whole *are* today inferior to men; that is, their situation affords them fewer possibilities. The question is: should that state of affairs continue?

Many men hope that it will continue; not all have given up the battle. The conservative bourgeoisie still see in the emancipation of women a menace to their morality and their interests. Some men dread feminine competition. Recently a male student wrote in the *Hebdo-Latin:* "Every woman student who goes into medicine or law robs us of a job." He never questioned his rights in this world. And economic interests are not the only ones concerned. One of the benefits that oppression confers upon the oppressors is that the most humble among them is made to *feel* superior; thus, a "poor white" in the South can console himself with the thought that he is not a "dirty nigger"—and the more prosperous whites cleverly exploit this pride.

Similarly, the most mediocre of males feels himself a demigod as compared with women.

↶ ↶ ↶

. . . Here is miraculous balm for those afflicted with an inferiority complex, and indeed no one is more arrogant toward women, more aggressive or scornful, than the man who is anxious about his virility. Those who are not fear-ridden in the presence of their fellow men are much more disposed to recognize a fellow creature in woman; but even to these the myth of woman, the Other, is precious for many reasons. They cannot be blamed for not cheerfully relinquishing all the benefits they derive from the myth, for they realize what they would lose in relinquishing woman as they fancy her to be, while they fail to realize what they have to gain from the woman of tomorrow. Refusal to pose oneself as the Subject, unique and absolute, requires great self-denial. Furthermore the vast majority of men make no such claim explicitly. They do not *postulate* woman as inferior, for today they are too thoroughly imbued with the ideal of democracy not to recognize all human beings as equals.

↶ ↶ ↶

So it is that many men will affirm as if in good faith that women *are* the equals of man and that they have nothing to clamor for, while *at the same time* they will say that women can never be the equals of man and that their demands are in vain. It is, in point of fact, a difficult matter for man to realize the extreme importance of social discriminations which seem outwardly insignificant but which produce in woman moral and intellectual effects so profound that they appear to spring from her original nature. The most sympathetic of men never fully comprehend woman's concrete situation. And there is no reason to put much trust in the men when they rush to the defense of privileges whose full extent they can hardly measure. We shall not, then, permit ourselves to be intimidated by the number and violence of the attacks launched against women, nor to be entrapped by the self-seeking eulogies bestowed on the "true woman," nor to profit by the enthusiasm for woman's destiny manifested by men who would not for the world have any part of it.

We should consider the arguments of the feminists with no less suspicion, however, for very often their controversial aim deprives them of all real value. If the "woman question" seems trivial, it is because masculine arrogance has made of it a "quarrel"; and when quarreling, one no longer reasons well. People have tirelessly sought to prove that woman is superior, inferior, or equal to man. Some say that, having been created after Adam, she is evidently a secondary being; others say on the contrary that Adam was only a rough draft and that God succeeded in producing the human being in perfection when He created Eve. Woman's brain is smaller; yes, but it is relatively larger. Christ was made a man; yes, but perhaps for his greater humility. Each argument at once suggests its opposite, and both are often fallacious. If we are to gain understanding, we must get out of these ruts; we must discard the vague notions of superiority, inferiority, equality which have hitherto corrupted every discussion of the subject and start afresh.

Very well, but just how shall we pose the question? And, to begin with, who are we to propound it at all? Man is at once judge and party to the case; but so is woman. What we need is an angel—neither man nor woman—but where shall we find one? Still, the angel would be poorly qualified to speak, for an angel is ignorant of all the basic facts involved in the problem. With a hermaphrodite we should be no better off, for here the situation is most peculiar; the hermaphrodite is not really the combination of a whole man and a whole woman, but consists of parts of each and thus is neither. It looks to me as if there are, after all, certain women who are best qualified to elucidate the situation of woman. Let us not be misled by the sophism that because Epimenides was a Cretan he was necessarily a liar; it is not a mysterious essence that compels men and women to act in good or in bad faith, it is their situation that inclines them more or less toward the search for truth. Many of today's women, fortunate in the restoration of all the privileges pertaining to the estate of the human being, can afford the luxury of impartiality—we even recognize its necessity. We are no longer like our partisan elders; by and large we have won the game.

⌐ ⌐ ⌐

. . . It is significant that books by women on women are in general animated in our day less by a wish to demand our rights than by an effort toward clarity and understanding. As we emerge from an era of excessive controversy, this book is offered as one attempt among others to confirm that statement.

⌒ ⌒ ⌒

. . . Every subject plays his part as such specifically through exploits or projects that serve as a mode of transcendence; he achieves liberty only through a continual reaching out toward other liberties. There is no justification for present existence other than its expansion into an indefinitely open future. Every time transcendence falls back into immanence, stagnation, there is a degradation of existence into the "*en-soi*"—the brutish life of subjection to given conditions—and of liberty into constraint and continence. This downfall represents a moral fault if the subject consents to it; if it is inflicted upon him, it spells frustration and oppression. In both cases it is an absolute evil. Every individual concerned to justify his existence feels that his existence involves an undefined need to transcend himself, to engage in freely chosen projects.

Now, what peculiarly signalizes the situation of woman is that she—a free and autonomous being like all human creatures—nevertheless finds herself living in a world where men compel her to assume the status of the Other. They propose to stabilize her as object and to doom her to immanence since her transcendence is to be overshadowed and forever transcended by another ego (*conscience*) which is essential and sovereign. The drama of woman lies in this conflict between the fundamental aspirations of every subject (*ego*)—who always regards the self as the essential—and the compulsions of a situation in which she is the inessential. How can a human being in woman's situation attain fulfillment? What roads are open to her? Which are blocked? How can independence be recovered in a state of dependency? What circumstances limit woman's liberty and how can they be overcome? These are the fundamental questions on which I would fain throw some light. This means that I am interested in the fortunes of the individual as defined not in terms of happiness but in terms of liberty.

Like Sartre, deBeauvoir advocates a freedom that is exhibited in and consists of action. Where Sartre seems at least implicitly to associate this active, free consciousness with men, deBeauvoir puts forward such a consciousness as a real possibility for women, proceeding to show how it is that women's subjective consciousness has been undermined. "Otherness," as she understands it, is a secondary status, one which the subject or Self posits by negation and out of a sense of inadequacy; and women share that status with any group that has been so negated. Here, deBeauvoir relies on Hegel, as well as anticipates contemporary arguments in which an analogy among oppressed peoples is drawn in order to demonstrate the unfairness of women's treatment by men.

DeBeauvoir is generally regarded as an "inessentialist," as her existentialist leanings would imply. She seems to believe that there is no natural, or factical, sex difference whatsoever—that all the differences which have been recognized throughout history are the creations of angry or defensive self-consciousness. Indeed, that deBeauvoir's leading question is "What is a woman?" indicates how strong is her belief in the transcendent nature of human consciousness: without the creation of feminine consciousness, over history and by men, she argues, there would be no such thing as woman, at all. Thus, in her more utopian discussion of the Conclusion to *The Second Sex,* deBeauvoir envisions a "woman" whose consciousness has overcome these distinctions.

CONCLUSION

The free consciousness of deBeauvoir's "new woman" is not at all like the "woman" of today; she is neither Other nor Self, but a consciousness unbound by the dichotomous dictates of the master/slave relation.

> The woman who is shut up in immanence endeavors to hold man in that prison also; thus the prison will be confused with the world, and woman will no longer suffer from being confined there: mother, wife, sweetheart are the jailers. Society, being codified by man, decrees that woman is inferior: she can do away with this inferiority only by destroying the male's superiority. She sets about mutilating, dominating man, she contradicts him, she denies his truth and his values. But in doing this she is only defending herself; it was neither a changeless essence nor a mistaken choice that doomed her to immanence, to inferiority. They were imposed upon her. All oppression creates a state of war. And this is no exception. The existent who is regarded as inessential cannot fail to demand the re-establishment of her sovereignty.
>
> Today the combat takes a different shape; instead of wishing to put man in a prison, woman endeavors to escape from one; she no longer seeks to drag him into the realms of immanence but to emerge, herself, into the light of transcendence. Now the attitude of the males creates a new conflict: it is with a bad grace that the man lets her go. He is very well pleased to remain the sovereign subject, the absolute superior, the essential being; he refuses to accept his companion as an equal in any concrete way. She replies to his lack of confidence in her by assuming an aggressive attitude. It is no longer a question of a war between individuals each shut up in his or her sphere: a caste claiming its rights goes over the top and it is resisted by the privileged caste. Here two transcendences are face to face; instead of displaying mutual recognition, each free being wishes to dominate the other.
>
> This difference of attitude is manifest on the sexual plane as on the spiritual plane. The "feminine" woman in making herself prey tries to reduce man, also, to her carnal passivity; she occupies herself in catching him in her trap, in enchaining him by means of the desire she arouses in him in submissively making herself a thing. The emancipated woman, on the contrary, wants to be active, a taker, and refuses the passivity man means to impose on her. Thus Elise and her emulators deny the values of the activities of virile type; they put the flesh above the spirit, continence above liberty, their routine wisdom above creative audacity. But the "modern" woman accepts masculine values: she prides herself on thinking, taking action, working, creating, on the same terms as men; instead of seeking to disparage them, she declares herself their equal.

෧ ෧ ෧

Woman is the victim of no mysterious fatality; the peculiarities that identify her as specifically a woman get their importance from the significance placed upon them. They can be surmounted, in the future, when they are regarded in new perspectives. Thus, as we have seen, through her erotic experience woman feels—and often detests—the domination of the male; but this is no reason to conclude that her ovaries condemn her to live forever on her knees. Virile aggressiveness seems like a lordly privilege only within a system that in its entirety conspires to affirm masculine sovereignty; and woman *feels* herself profoundly passive in the sexual act only because she already *thinks* of herself as such. Many modern women who lay claim to their dignity as human beings still envisage their erotic life from the standpoint of a tradition of slavery: since it seems to them humiliating to lie beneath the man, to be penetrated by him, they grow tense in frigidity. But if the reality were different, the meaning expressed symbolically in amorous gestures and postures would be different, too: a woman who pays and dominates her lover can, for example, take pride in her superb idleness and consider that she is enslaving the male who is actively exerting himself. And here and now there are many sexually well-balanced couples whose notions of victory and defeat are giving place to the idea of an exchange.

As a matter of fact, man, like woman, is flesh, therefore passive, the plaything of his hormones and of the species, the restless prey of his desires. And she, like him, in the midst of the carnal fever, is a consenting, a voluntary gift, an activity; they live out in their several fashions the strange ambiguity of existence made body. In those combats where they think they confront one another, it is really against the self that each one struggles, projecting into the partner that part of the self which is repudiated; instead of living out the ambiguities of their situation, each tries to make the other bear the abjection and tries to reserve the honor for the self. If, however, both should assume the ambiguity with a clear-sighted modesty, correlative of an authentic pride, they would see each other as equals and would live out their erotic drama in amity. The fact that we are human beings is infinitely more important than all the peculiarities that distinguish human beings from one another; it is never the given that confers superiorities: "virtue," as the ancients called it, is defined at the level of "that which depends on us." In both sexes is played out the same drama of the flesh and the spirit, of finitude and transcendence; both are gnawed away by time and laid in wait for by death, they have the same essential need for one another; and they can gain from their liberty the same glory. If they were to taste it, they would no longer be tempted to dispute fallacious privileges, and fraternity between them could then come into existence.

I shall be told that all this is utopian fancy, because woman cannot be "made over" unless society has first made her really the equal of man.

෧ ෧ ෧

. . . The fact is that oppressors cannot be expected to make a move of gratuitous generosity; but at one time the revolt of the oppressed, at another time even the very evolution of the privileged caste itself, creates new situations; thus men have been led, in their own interest, to give partial emancipation to woman: it remains only for women to continue their ascent, and the successes they are obtaining are an encouragement for them to do so. It seems almost certain that sooner or later they will arrive at complete economic and social equality, which will bring about an inner metamorphosis.

However this may be, there will be some to object that if such a world is possible it is not desirable. When woman is "the same" as her male, life will lose its salt and spice. This argument, also, has lost its novelty: those interested in perpetuating present conditions are always in tears about the marvelous past that is about to disappear, without having so much as a smile for the young future. It is quite true that doing away with the slave trade meant death to the great plantations, manificent with azaleas and camellias, it meant ruin to the whole refined Southern civilization.

. . . One can appreciate the beauty of flowers, the charm of women, and appreciate them at their true value; if these treasures cost blood or misery, they must be sacrificed.

It is nonsense to assert that revelry, vice, ecstasy, passion, would become impossible if man and woman were equal in concrete matters; the contradictions that put the flesh in opposition to the spirit, the instant to time, the swoon of immanence to the challenge of transcendence, the absolute of pleasure to the nothingness of forgetting, will never be resolved; in sexuality will always be materialized the tension, the anguish, the joy, the frustration, and the triumph of existence. To emancipate woman is to refuse to confine her to the relations she bears to man, not to deny them to her; let her have her independent existence and she will continue none the less to exist for him *also*: mutually recognizing each other as subject, each will yet remain for the other an *other.* The reciprocity of their relations will not do away with the miracles—desire, possession, love, dream, adventure—worked by the division of human beings into two separate categories; and the words that move us—giving, conquering, uniting—will not lose their meaning. On the contrary, when we abolish the slavery of half of humanity, together with the whole system of hypocrisy that it implies, then the "division" of humanity will reveal its genuine significance and the human couple will find its true form.

The case could not be better stated. It is for man to establish the reign of liberty in the midst of the world of the given. To gain the supreme victory, it is necessary, for one thing, that by and through their natural differentiation men and women unequivocally affirm their brotherhood.

In this conclusion, deBeauvoir, like Gilman and Mead and many others before her, anticipates an entirely new and utopian social organization, in which all dichotomous and oppressive power relations are overcome, one in which human consciousness is no longer that of a humiliated Self absurdly battling against the judgment of others, but instead a happy consciousness lost in the experience of life. In this vision—and in her belief that it can be achieved through feminist political action—deBeauvoir has become a wellspring for later feminists of various sorts.

SUGGESTED READINGS—PART FIVE

Anderson, Thomas C. *The Foundation and Structure of Sartrian Ethics.* Laurence: Regents Press, 1979.

Badinter, Elisabeth. *Mother Love: Myth and Reality.* New York: Macmillan, 1981.

Barnes, Hazel E. *An Existentialist Ethics.* New York: Knopf, 1967.

———. "Sartre and Sexism." *Philosophy and Literature* 14: 340–347, 1990.

deBeauvoir, Simone. *The Second Sex.* H.M. Parshley (trans). New York: Vintage, 1952.

Bell, Linda C. *Sartre's Ethics of Authenticity.* Tuscaloosa: University of Alabama Press, 1989.

Berger, Milton M. (ed). *Women Beyond Freud: New Concepts in Feminine Psychology.* New York: Brunener-Mazel, 1994.

Berghoffen, Debra. "The Look as Bad Faith." *Philosophy Today* 36: 221–227, 1992.

Bohannan, Paul and Mark Glazer (eds). *Highpoints in Anthropology.* New York: Knopf, 1973.

Booth, Allison. *Greatness Engendered: George Eliot and Virginia Woolf.* Ithaca: Cornell University Press, 1992.

———. *Camus and Sartre: Crisis and Commitment.* New York: Delta, 1972.

Brennan, Theresa. *The Interpretation of Flesh.* New York: Routledge, 1992.

Bukala, C.R. "Personal Objectification: Beyond Sartre's Theory of the Gaze." *The Modern Schoolman* 57: 99–120, 1980.

Cannon, Betty. *Sartre and Psychoanalysis.* Lawrence: University Press of Kansas, 1991.

Chassequet-Smirgel, Janine. *Female Sexuality: New PsychoanalyticViews.* Ann Arbor: University of Michigan Press, 1970.

Clement, Catherine. *The Weary Sons of Freud.* N. Ball (trans). London: Verso, 1987.

Crosland, Margaret. *Simone deBeauvoir: The Woman and her Work.* London: Heinemann, 1992.

Dahlberg, Frances (ed).*Woman the Gatherer.* New Haven: Yale University Press, 1981.

Dallery, Arleen B. "Sexual Embodiment: Beauvoir and French Feminism." *Hypatia* 3: 197–202, 1989.

Freeman, Derek. *Margaret Mead and Samoa: The Making and Unmaking of an Anthropological Myth.* Cambridge: Harvard University Press, 1983.

Freud, Sigmund. "Femininity." (*New Introductory Lectures On Psychoanalysis,* Lecture XXXIII) *The Standard Edition of the Complete Psychological Works of Sigmund Freud* 22 James Strachey (trans). London: The Hogarth Press and the Institute for Psychoanalysis, 1964.

———. "Hysterical Phantasies and their Relation to Bisexuality." *The Standard Edition of the Complete Psychological Works of Sigmund Freud Vol 9.* James Strachey (trans). London: The Hogarth Press and the Institute for Psychoanalysis, 1959.

———. *Introductory Lectures on Psychoanalysis.* James Strachey (trans). New York: Norton, 1966.

―――. "On Narcissism: An Introduction." *The Standard Edition of the Complete Psychological Works of Sigmund Freud Vol. 14.* James Strachey (trans). London: The Hogarth Press and the Institute for Psychoanalysis, 1957.

―――. "Three Essays on Sexuality." *The Standard Edition of the Complete Psychological Works of Sigmund Freud Vol. 7.* James Strachey (trans). London: The Hogarth Press and the Institute for Psychoanalysis, 1953.

Frey-Rohn, Liliane. *From Freud to Jung.* F. Engreen and E. Engreen (trans). New York: Putnam, 1974.

Gallop, J. *Feminism and Psychoanalysis: The Daughter's Seduction.* London: Macmillan, 1982.

Garrison, D. "Karen Horney and Feminism."*Signs* 6: 681–690, 1981.

Gilman, Charlotte Perkins. *The Living of Charlotte Perkins Gilman.* New York: D. Appleton-Century, 1935.

―――. *The Man-Made World or Our Androcentric Culture.* New York: Charlton, 1911.

―――. *Women and Economics.* New York: Harper Torchbook, 1966.

―――. "The Yellow Wallpaper." *The New England Magazine,* Jan. 1892.

Gohlke, Madelon S. *The Spectral Mother: Freud, Feminism and Psychoanalysis.* Ithaca: Cornell University Press, 1990.

Goodman, Richard. *Mead's Coming of Age in Samoa: A Dissenting View.* Oakland: Pipperine Press, 1983.

Greene, Naomi. "Sartre, Sexuality and the Second Sex."*Philosophy and Literature* 4: 199–211, 1980.

Hill, Mary A. *Charlotte Perkins Gilman: The Making of a Radical Feminist.* Philadelphia: Temple University Press, 1980.

Holt, David. *The Psychology of Carl Jung: Essays in Application and Deconstruction.* Lewiston: E. Mellon Press, 1992.

Homans, Margaret (ed). *Virginia Woolf: A Collection of Critical Essays.* Englewood Cliffs: Prentice-Hall, 1993.

Horney, Karen. *Feminine Psychology.* Harold Kelman, M.D. (ed). New York: Norton, 1973.

Howells, Christina (ed). *The Cambridge Companion to Sartre.* Cambridge: Cambridge University Press, 1992.

―――. *Sartre: The Necessity of Freedom.* Cambridge: Cambridge University Press, 1988.

Isaac, Jeffrey. *Arendt, Camus and Modern Rebellion.* New Haven: Yale University Press, 1992.

Jung, Carl Gustave, *Aion: Researches Into the Phenomenology of the Self. The Collected Works of C. G. Jung, Vol. 9.* New York: Pantheon, 1959.

Karpinski, Joanne B. (ed). *Critical Essays on Charlotte Perkins Gilman.* New York: G. K. Hall, 1992.

Kofman, Sarah. *The Enigma of Woman: Woman in Freud's Writings.* C. Porter (trans). Ithaca: Cornell University Press, 1985.

Kittay, Eva Feder. "Rereading Freud on 'Femininity'." *Hypatia* 2: 385–391, 1984.

Knapp, Bettina (ed). *Critical Essays on Albert Camus.* Boston: G. K. Hall, 1988.

Kruks, Sonya. "Simone deBeauvoir and the Limits to Freedom." *Social Text* 17, 1987.

Kurzweil, Edith. *Freudians and Feminists.* Boulder: Westview, 1995.

Leak, Andrew N. *The Perverted Consciousness: Sexuality and Sartre.* New York: St. Martin's, 1989.

LeGuin, Ursula. *Dispossessed.* New York: HarperCollins, 1991.

MacNabb, Elizabeth L. *The Fractured Family: The Second Sex and its (Dis)Connected Daughters.* New York: P. Lang, 1993.

Marcus, Jane (ed). *Virginia Woolf: A Feminist Slant.* Lincoln: University of Nebraska Press, 1983.

———.*Virginia Woolf and the Languages of Patriarchy.* Bloomington: Indiana University Press, 1987.

Marks, E. (ed). *Critical Essays on Simone deBeauvoir.* Oxford: Blackwell, 1990.

McBride, Joseph. *Albert Camus: Philosopher and Literateur.* New York: St. Martin's Press, 1992.

McBride, William L. *Sartre's Political Theory.* Bloomington: Indiana University Press, 1991.

Mead, Margaret. *Coming of Age in Samoa.* New York: William Morrow, 1971.

———. *Sex and Temperament in Three Primitive Societies.* New York: William Morrow, 1963.

Mitchell, Juliet. *Psychoanalysis and Feminism.* New York: Vintage, 1975.

Moi, Toril. *Feminist Theory and Simone deBeauvoir.* Oxford: Blackwell, 1990.

Murdoch, Iris. *Sartre: Romantic Rationalist.* Hammondworth: Penguin, 1989.

Murphy, Julien S. "The Look in Sartre and Rich." *Hypatia* 2: 113–124, 1987.

Papadopolous, Renos (ed). *Carl Gustave Jung: Critical Assessments.* New York: Routledge, 1992.

Paris, Bernard J. *Karen Horney: A Psychoanalyst's Search for Self Understanding.* New Haven: Yale University Press, 1994.

Sanday, P. R. and R. G. Goodenough (eds). *Beyond the Second Sex: New Directions in the Anthropology of Gender.* Philadelphia: University of Pennsylvania Press, 1990.

Sartre, Jean-Paul. *Being and Nothingness.* Hazel E. Barnes (trans). New York: Pocket Books, 1966.

———. *No Exit and Three Other Plays.* New York: Vintage, 1955.

Sayers, Janet. *Mothers of Psychoanalysis: Helene Deutsch, Karen Horney, Anna Freud and Melanie Klein.* New York: Norton, 1991.

Schlipp, Paul A. (ed). *The Philosophy of Jean-Paul Sartre.* LeSalle: Open Court, 1981.

Schwartz, Theodore (ed). *Socialization as Cultural Communication: Development of a Theme in the Work of Margaret Mead.* Berkeley: University of California Press, 1980.

Simons, Margaret (ed). *Feminist Interpretations of Simone deBeauvoir.* University Park: Penn State University Press, 1995.

Slipp, Samuel. *The Freudian Mystique: Freud, Women and Feminism.* New York: NYU Press, 1995.

Smith, Joseph H. (ed). *Psychoanalysis, Feminism and the Future of Gender.* Baltimore: Johns Hopkins University Press, 1994.

Sprintzen, David. *Camus: A Critical Examination.* Philadelphia: Temple University Press, 1988.

Tarrow, Susan. *Exile From the Kingdom: A Political Rereading of Albert Camus.* Tuscaloosa: University of Alabama Press, 1985.

Theunissen, Michael. *The Other: Studies in the Social Ontology of Husserl, Heidegger, Sartre and Buber.* C. Macann (trans). Cambridge: MIT Press, 1984.

Transne, Pamela J. *Virginia Woolf and the Politics of Style.* Albany: State University of New York Press, 1986.

Wehr, Demaris S. *Jung and Feminism: Liberating Archetypes.* Boston: Beacon, 1989.

Westkott, Marcia. *The Feminist Legacy of Karen Horney.* New Haven: Yale University Press, 1986.

Woolf, Leonard (ed). *A Writer's Diary: Being Extracts from the Diary of Virginia Woolf.* San Diego: Harcourt Brace, 1973.

Woolf, Virginia. *A Room of One's Own.* San Diego: Harcourt Brace, 1989.

———. *Orlando: A Biography.* San Diego: Harcourt Brace, 1979.

———. *Three Guineas.* San Diego: Harcourt Brace, 1963.

Young-Breuhl, Elisabeth (ed). *Freud On Women: A Reader.* New York: Norton, 1990.

PART SIX

THE LATE TWENTIETH CENTURY:
A POLITICS OF WORDS

Millett, Ortner, Foucault, Irigaray,
Cixous, Gilligan

INTRODUCTION

THE DISINTEGRATION OF THE SELF

During the postwar period that led up to the rebellious 1960s, certain residuals of the Second World War seeped into the habitual consciousness of ordinary individuals. The threat of nuclear war, the constant vigil of the cold war, the development of military intelligence into the secret intelligence agencies, the explosion of mass media—particularly television—and the increasing use of advertising within it, the economic prosperity resulting from the peacetime use of military productive forces, the development of rocketry and its subsequent use in the space program, the increasing use of computers in civil services and private industries: these and other after-effects of the war not only changed people's daily habits but also haunted their thoughts. The world of the 1960s seemed constitutionally unstable and unsafe, not just shaken by war, but inherently untrustworthy. It seemed vast in its dimensions— far beyond the comprehension or control of even the most capable individual. The daily life of individuals seemed increasingly at the mercy of unseen political and economic forces, the battle against which might already have been lost.

In such a climate, the notion of the individual self was increasingly difficult to articulate. The plethora of images on television and in advertisements; daily personal interaction with computers; the shifting demography that resulted from international expansion of private industry, from the improved technology of communication and travel, and from the emigration of the middle class from

557

the cities to the suburbs—all of these greatly threatened the coherence of the individual citizen's personality. Increasingly human nature seemed a confused—if not obsolete—concept, at least to the academics who wrote about the spirit of the age. The literature of the self depicted it increasingly as a bundle of disparate functions and dysfunctions, torn in its alliances, alienated from its traditions and ancestry, constantly pulled in different directions by the forces of fashion, political rhetoric, and corporate culture.

Many thinkers from different disciplines and perspectives—physiology and artificial intelligence, but also literary criticism and market analysis—modeled the human subject on the machine. Rather than an individual with conflicted parts made coherent by a history, a rational order, or a soul—as earlier thinkers had depicted the self—the human subject of the late twentieth century is more often than not characterized as a scattered mass of feelings, memories, and images, whose cohesion depends on a myth of selfhood provided by a seemingly arbitrary intellectual canon. Some contemporary thinkers advocate adherence to such a tradition for the sake of the maintenance of the identity of the self, some advocate abandoning it and dispersing the subject into new realms, and many contemporary thinkers fall somewhere in between. But there remains a pervasive characterization of the human being in our era as a disintegrated, unbounded group of ideas, cast among an incoherent play of external forces.

Writing in 1972, Gilles Deleuze and Felix Guattari, leading figures in French "postmodernism" (Deleuze as a philosopher and Guattari as a practicing psychoanalyst) characterized contemporary life as the interplay of "desiring machines"; essentially a happy assemblage of paranoid schizophrenics:

> *What a mistake to have ever said* the *id. Everywhere* it *is machines—real ones, not figurative ones: machines driving other machines, machines being driven by other machines, with all the necessary couplings and connections. An organ-machine is plugged into an energy-source-machine: the one produces a flow that the other interrupts. The breast is a machine that produces milk, and the mouth a machine coupled to it. . . . Hence we are all handymen: each with his little machines. For every organ-machine, an energy-machine: all the time, flows and interruptions. . . . Something is produced: the effects of a machine, not mere metaphors.*
>
> *A schizophrenic out for a walk is a better model than a neurotic lying on the analyst's couch. . . . There is no such thing as either man or nature now, only a process that produces the one within the other and couples the machines together. Producing-machines, desiring machines everywhere, schizophrenic machines, all species of life: the self and the non-self, outside and inside, no longer have any meaning whatsoever.*[1]

---

[1] Gilles Deleuze and Felix Guattari, *Anti-Oedipus: Capitalism and Schizophrenia.* Translated by Robert Hurley, Mark Seem, and Helen R. Lane. (Minneapolis: University of Minnesota Press, 1983 (1987)), pp. 1-2.

POLITICS, THE SELF, AND THE TEXT

Within this morass of confusion, academic discourse has perhaps of necessity undergone a change since the 1960s. A large number of disciplines have oriented themselves to the study of language—mathematical and computer languages, the rhetoric of advertising and politics, the study of literature, etc. In artificial intelligence and logic, it is posited that thinking is a primarily linguistic enterprise, significantly like a computer language. In a politics and business increasingly dependent on images and advertising, "sound-bites," and polls, the rhetorical presentation of ideas begins to function independently of the ideas themselves, and often with greater effect on the political life of citizens. In academia, recognition of the dependence of the various disciplines on the particular canon of books which comprise their histories, and on the very different uses and interpretations to which these works have been subjected, have given texts a kind of moral or political status, as the very stuff of Western intellectual history. The spectre of meaninglessness that hovers over late–twentieth century thought has led people in every discipline to investigate the notion of "meaning," and many have started from the assumption that "meaning" is a property of language.

Thus, where the nineteenth and early twentieth century might be characterized as primarily involved in technological endeavors, the late twentieth century can be characterized as involved in primarily critical, interpretive ones. Analysis and interpretation are the shared guiding principles today of very disparate schools of thought. Philosophy, in particular, has dispersed itself into specializations that ally it in one instance with computer science, in another with semantic analysis, and in another with literary criticism, specialties among which there seems to be little similarity but which in actuality share an interest in analysis and criticism of texts or statements. As you will see, the very different selections that appear in this chapter all involve themselves in one way or another in this sort of linguistic endeavor.

We may understand this trend also by reference to its historical development since the Second World War. During the fifties and early sixties there emerged, especially in France, a school of thought called "structuralism, " primarily in the disciplines of anthropology and linguistics. The structuralists claimed that certain social and psychological systems were best understood on the model of language, where a language is taken to be a closed system of placeholders for meaningful terms. According to the structuralist linguist Ferdinand Saussure, for instance, the structure of a meaningful sentence is given by the grammar of the language in which it appears—only verbs can fit in certain places in a sentence, only nouns elsewhere. Within this syntactic structure, meaning is achieved through a binary system of absence and presence—for instance, given that only a verb can appear in a particular place in a sentence, the particular verb that actually appears in that place has as its meaning "not-the-other-verbs-in-this-language." According to Saussure, all meaning ultimately amounts only to a negation of all but one possibility for significance—in other words, all meaning in any language is given by the structure of the language itself, and not by the world the language pretends to describe. The search for meaning, then, is figured as a wholly linguistic study, independent of any relation of language to the world that we might call "truth."

The method of "deconstruction," mentioned in the introduction of this book, has since the late 1960s increasingly been applied in various academic disciplines: it is basically a response to structuralism. As such, it is very much indebted to the structuralist viewpoint, many aspects of which it retains. The deconstructionists, sometimes called "post-structuralists," accepted that meaning was a function of language and not of the world, going so far as to imply that the world, or the objects of knowledge, *only* appear to us *in* language. Consequently, any academic study is and can only be an interpretation of a linguistic entity (whether an actual text or some unwritten interplay of signs). The deconstructionists, however, did not accept the analysis of language offered by the structuralists. First, deconstruction did not take language to be a closed system in which meanings could be unambiguously derived from grammar; rather, deconstruction saw language as a play of marks or signs of nearly infinite meaning and therefore with nearly infinite possibilities for interpretation. Second, deconstruction, while it accepted that meaning in a language was always given through binary oppositions, characterized this as an inherent flaw of language, inherently inegalitarian and violent. For instance, to define *x* within a language as merely *not-not-x* is to implicitly subordinate *not-x* to the primary term, *x:* to the extent that "night" just means "not-day," "day" is taken as the primary term, and "night" as secondary. Similarly, then, for the deconstructionists, meaning is found only within, or on the surface of, language itself—and not outside it. To commandeer page space or time in a conversation for one term is to actually obliterate that which is signified by the other term. Hence, use of language, though unavoidable, is thought by the deconstructionists always to do a kind of violence to the world.

Jacques Derrida, the leading figure in deconstruction, sums this uncomfortable late–twentieth century engulfment in language in a famous 1968 essay, "Differance."

> *Let us start . . . from the problematic of the sign and of writing. The sign is usually said to be put in the place of the thing itself, the present thing . . . The sign represents the present in its absence. It takes the place of the present. When we cannot grasp or show the thing, state the present . . . we signify, we go through the detour of the sign. We take or give signs. We signal. The sign, in this sense, is deferred presence. Whether we are concerned with the verbal or the written sign, with the monetary sign, or with electoral delegation and political representation, the circulation of signs defers the moment in which we can encounter the thing itself, make it ours, consume or expend it, touch it, see it, intuit its presence. What I am describing here in order to define it is the classically determined structure of the sign in all the banality of its characteristics—signification as the* differance *of temporization.*[2]

This post-structuralist focus on language accompanies the new, loosely integrated vision of the self discussed previously. While the words "mind" or "self" seem to represent unified entities, it is clear that the linguistic play that goes on within the mind, thus conceived, is far more disjointed. Therefore, for the

---

[2] Jacques Derrida, "Differance," from *Margins of Philosophy.* Translated by Alan Bass. (Chicago: University of Chicago Press, 1982), p. 9.

deconstructionists and those following them, the notion of the human subject itself is just a certain strategic spin on an interplay of disparate images. As such, the human being stands to be reinterpreted, played with, strategically reoriented or dismantled. As a coherent notion indicating an essential trait of a certain species it is, for the deconstructionists, dead.

The disintegration of the human being is seen by and large to be associated with a kind of "mental democracy," a kind of political diversity within the consciousness that reflects the diversity of the late–twentieth century democratic society. In this way, deconstruction—essentially a literary-critical enterprise—was gradually associated with a political discourse advocating diversity by questioning the existence of essential characteristics, or a "politics of identity." A person's intimate construction of his or her own subjective identity, and the reading of fictional and philosophical literature that guide that endeavor, have since deconstruction been figured as political activities, making the "personal political."

All these strains are implicated in Derrida's 1968 essay, "The Ends of Man." The title itself, of course, is a play on words, indicating at once the death of the notion of the human subject, the multiplicity that it is hoped may replace that notion, the historical evolution of another "species," a farcical Freudian allusion to heads and feet, anuses and penises, and a gesture towards something, perhaps "feminine," lying beyond the borders of "man." The essay begins with the claim that "Every philosophical colloquium necessarily has a political significance," and ends "Perhaps we are between . . . these two ends of Man [the guard surrounding and closing it and the daybreak opening onto something else]. But who, we?"[3] In these plays of language, then, these literary-critical exercises, late–twentieth century thinkers are hoping to do progressive political work, and to base that work on a new kind of human consciousness.

FEMINISM AND CRITICISM

Even for the feminists not explicitly associated with deconstruction or with other postmodern literary criticism, readers can discern the influence of this literary, linguistic turn, with its interest in uncovering and overcoming the binary oppositions inherent in language. Several of the authors in this chapter, for instance, Luce Irigaray and Helene Cixous, will go so far as to say that language as it is currently practiced is inherently masculine—and as such, sex-discriminatory. Kate Millett argues that much of the fiction written by men is inherently sexist, and that as the imaginative inspiration of our time, these works contribute to a sexist politic. Several of the following authors propose or expose new or alternative "feminine" languages or logics with which they hope to replace what they see as the patriarchal structure of culture. Some, like Carol Gilligan, are involved in a more conciliatory enterprise, distinguishing and presenting the features of "masculine" and "feminine" language or moral logic, so as to facilitate understanding between the sexes, and the happiness of men and women.

---

[3] Jacques Derrida, "The Ends of Man," from *Margins of Philosophy,* p. 134.

In addition, thinking about gender in the late twentieth century has allied itself more and more with an academic feminism that opposes itself to what it sees as a masculine intellectual tradition. Thus, in this chapter more than in earlier ones, the majority of the selections will be feminist in their orientation. Though very different in their intellectual foci and political goals, recent works on gender have tended to do feminist political and moral work through academic critical analyses of existing theories, practices, and/or traditions. This seems to be the legacy upon which our thoughts about gender in the next century will have to rely.

1. KATE MILLETT
(American, 1934–)

A sculptor, literary critic, and feminist activist, Kate Millett ushered in a new kind of feminist theory with her now classic *Sexual Politics,* from which all the following passages are taken. Millett was among the first to posit the existence of a system of patriarchy that subordinated women to men in the sexual, political, social, cultural, and psychological realms all at once. Her work does not specialize; in *Sexual Politics* as well as in her more recent work, Millett gives intellectual analyses that stretch across many disciplines. Still writing and giving shows of her visual artwork, Millett now lives in New York City.

SEXUAL POLITICS (1970)

Describing her method in the preface to this work, Millett claims, "It has been my conviction that the adventure of literary criticism . . . is capable of seizing upon the larger insights which literature affords into the life it describes, or interprets, or even distorts. This essay, composed of equal parts of literary and cultural criticism, is something of an anomaly, a hybrid, possibly a new mutation altogether."[4] Indeed it was such a new mutation, one that set a trend for the decades to come. *Sexual Politics* combines a fairly detailed political theory with an analysis of the history of the women's movement and with textual analyses of the fiction of D.H. Lawrence, Henry Miller, Norman Mailer, and Jean Genet. All the excerpts have been taken from the second chapter, in which Millett outlines her general theory, and which she describes as "in my opinion the most important in the book."[5]

THEORY OF SEXUAL POLITICS

This chapter, divided into subsections on the "ideological," "biological," "sociological," "class," "economic and educational," "force," "anthropological'" and

---

[4] Kate Millett, *Sexual Politics*. (Garden City: 1970), p. xii.

[5] Ibid., p. xi.

"psychological" bases of patriarchy, gives an analysis of the effects of each on the lives of women and a criticism of their use in the support of patriarchy.

> . . . Coitus can scarcely be said to take place in a vacuum; although of itself it appears a biological and physical activity, it is set so deeply within the larger context of human affairs that it serves as a charged microcosm of the variety of attitudes and values to which culture subscribes. Among other things, it may serve as a model of sexual politics on an individual or personal plane.

> But of course the transition from such scenes of intimacy to a wider context of political reference is a great step indeed. In introducing the term "sexual politics," one must first answer the inevitable question "Can the relationship between the sexes be viewed in a political light at all?" The answer depends on how one defines politics. This essay does not define the political as that relatively narrow and exclusive world of meetings, chairmen, and parties. The term "politics" shall refer to power-structured relationships, arrangements whereby one group of persons is controlled by another.

> The word "politics" is enlisted here when speaking of the sexes primarily because such a word is eminently useful in outlining the real nature of their relative status, historically and at the present. It is opportune, perhaps today even mandatory, that we develop a more relevant psychology and philosophy of power relationships beyond the simple conceptual framework provided by our traditional formal politics. Indeed, it may be imperative that we give some attention to defining a theory of politics which treats of power relationships on grounds less conventional than those to which we are accustomed. I have therefore found it pertinent to define them on grounds of personal contact and interaction between members of well-defined and coherent groups: races, castes, classes, and sexes. For it is precisely because certain groups have no representation in a number of recognized political structures that their position tends to be so stable, their oppression so continuous.

> In America, recent events have forced us to acknowledge at last that the relationship between the races is indeed a political one which involves the general control of one collectivity, defined by birth, over another collectivity, also defined by birth. Groups who rule by birthright are fast disappearing, yet there remains one ancient and universal scheme for the domination of one birth group by another—the scheme that prevails in the area of sex. The study of racism has convinced us that a truly political state of affairs operates between the races to perpetuate a series of oppressive circumstances. The subordinated group has inadequate redress through existing political institutions, and is deterred thereby from organizing into conventional political struggle and opposition.

> Quite in the same manner, a disinterested examination of our system of sexual relationship must point out that the situation between the sexes now, and throughout history, is . . . a relationship of dominance and subordinance. What goes largely unexamined, often even unacknowledged (yet is institutionalized

nonetheless) in our social order, is the birthright priority whereby males rule females. Through this system a most ingenious form of "interior colonization" has been achieved. It is one which tends moreover to be sturdier than any form of segregation, and more rigorous than class stratification, more uniform, certainly more enduring. However muted its present appearance may be, sexual dominion obtains nevertheless as perhaps the most pervasive ideology of our culture and provides its most fundamental concept of power.

This is so because our society, like all other historical civilizations, is a patriarchy. The fact is evident at once if one recalls that the military, industry, technology, universities, science, political office, and finance—in short every avenue of power within the society, including the coercive force of the police, is entirely in male hands. As the essence of politics is power such realization cannot fail to carry impact.

⌐ ⌐ ⌐

I IDEOLOGICAL

. . . Sexual politics obtains consent through the "socialization" of both sexes to basic patriarchal polities with regard to temperament, role, and status. As to status, a pervasive assent to the prejudice of male superiority guarantees superior status in the male, inferior in the female. The first item, temperament, involves the formation of human personality along stereotyped lines of sex category ("masculine" and "feminine"), based on the needs and values of the dominant group and dictated by what its members cherish in themselves and find convenient in subordinates: aggression, intelligence, force, and efficacy in the male; passivity, ignorance, docility, "virtue," and ineffectuality in the female. This is complemented by a second factor, sex role, which decrees a consonant and highly elaborate code of conduct, gesture and attitude for each sex. In terms of activity, sex role assigns domestic service and attendance upon infants to the female, the rest of human achievement, interest, and ambition to the male. The limited role allotted the female tends to arrest her at the level of biological experience. Therefore, nearly all that can be described as distinctly human rather than animal activity (in their own way animals also give birth and care for their young) is largely reserved for the male. Of course, status again follows from such an assignment. Were one to analyze the three categories one might designate status as the political component, role as the sociological, and temperament as the psychological—yet their interdependence is unquestionable and they form a chain. Those awarded higher status tend to adopt roles of mastery, largely because they are first encouraged to develop temperaments of dominance. That this is true of caste and class as well is self-evident.

II BIOLOGICAL

Patriarchal religion, popular attitude, and to some degree, science as well assumes these psycho-social distinctions to rest upon biological differences between the sexes, so that where culture is acknowledged as shaping behavior, it is said to do no more than cooperate with nature. Yet the temperamental distinctions created in patriarchy ("masculine" and "feminine" personality traits) do not appear to originate in human nature, those of role and status still less.

The heavier musculature of the male, a secondary sexual characteristic and common among manuals, is biological in origin but is also culturally encouraged through breeding, diet and exercise. Yet it is hardly an adequate category on which to base political relations *within civilization.* Male supremacy, like other political creeds, does not finally reside in physical strength but in the acceptance of a value system which is not biological. Superior physical strength is not a factor in political relations—vide those of race and class. Civilization has always been able to substitute other methods (technic, weaponry, knowledge) for those of physical strength, and contemporary civilization has no further need of it.

So much for the evanescent delights afforded by the game of origins. The question of the historical origins of patriarchy—whether patriarchy originated primordially in the male's superior strength, or upon a later mobilization of such strength under certain circumstances—appears at the moment to be unanswerable.

Unfortunately, as the psycho-social distinctions made between the two sex groups which are said to justify their present political relationship are not the clear, specific, measurable and neutral ones of the physical sciences, but are instead of an entirely different character—vague, amorphous, often even quasi-religious in phrasing—it must be admitted that many of the generally understood distinctions between the sexes in the more significant areas of role and temperament, not to mention status, have in fact, essentially cultural, rather than biological, bases.

Not only is there insufficient evidence for the thesis that the present social distinctions of patriarchy (status, role, temperament) are physical in origin, but we are hardly in a position to assess the existing differentiations, since distinctions which we know to be culturally induced at present so outweigh them. Whatever the "real" differences between the sexes may be, we are not likely to know them until the sexes are treated differently, that is alike. And this is very far from being the case at present. Important new research not only suggests that the possibilities of innate temperamental differences seem more remote than ever, but even raises questions as to the validity and permanence of psycho-sexual identity. In doing so it gives fairly concrete positive evidence of the overwhelmingly *cultural* character of gender, i.e. personality structure in terms of sexual category.

Because of our social circumstances, male and female are really two cultures and their life experiences are utterly different—and this is crucial. Implicit in all the gender identity development which takes place through childhood is the sum total of the parents', the peers', and the culture's notions of what is appropriate to each gender by way of temperament, character, interests, status, worth, gesture, and expression. Every moment of the child's life is a clue to how he or she must think and behave to attain or satisfy the demands which gender places upon one. In adolescence, the merciless task of conformity grows to crisis proportions, generally cooling and settling in maturity.

Since patriarchy's biological foundations appear to be so very insecure, one has some cause to admire the strength of a "socialization" which can continue a universal condition "on faith alone," as it were, or through an acquired value system exclusively. What does seem decisive in assuring the maintenance of the temperamental differences between the sexes is the conditioning of early childhood. Conditioning runs in a circle of self-perpetuation and self-fulfilling prophecy. To take a simple example: expectations the culture cherishes about his gender identity encourage the young male to develop aggressive impulses, and the female to thwart her own or turn them inward. The result is that the male tends to have aggression reinforced in his behavior, often with significant anti-social possibilities. Thereupon the culture consents to believe the possession of the male indicator, the testes, penis, and scrotum, in itself characterizes the aggressive impulse, and even vulgarly celebrates it in such encomiums as "that guy has balls." The same process of reinforcement is evident in producing the chief "feminine" virtue of passivity.

⌒ ⌒ ⌒

. . . The usual hope of such line of reasoning is that "nature," by some impossible outside chance, might still be depended upon to rationalize the patriarchal system. An important consideration to be remembered here is that in patriarchy, the function of norm is unthinkingly delegated to the male—were it not, one might as plausibly speak of "feminine" behavior as active, and "masculine" behavior as hyperactive or hyperaggressive.

⌒ ⌒ ⌒

. . . Politically, the fact that each group exhibits a circumscribed but complementary personality and range of activity is of secondary importance to the fact that each represents a status or power division. In the matter of conformity patriarchy is a governing ideology without peer; it is probable that no other system has ever exercised such a complete control over its subjects.

III SOCIOLOGICAL

Patriarchy's chief institution is the family. It is both a mirror of and a connection with the larger society; a patriarchal unit within a patriarchal whole. Mediating between the individual and the social structure, the family effects control and conformity where political and other authorities are insufficient. As the fundamental instrument and the foundation unit of patriarchal society the family and its roles are prototypical. Serving as an agent of the larger society, the family not only encourages its own members to adjust and conform, but acts as a unit in the government of the patriarchal state which rules its citizens through its family heads. Even in patriarchal societies where they are granted legal citizenship, women tend to be ruled through the family alone and have little or no formal relation to the state.

As co-operation between the family and the larger society is essential, else both would fall apart, the fate of three patriarchal institutions, the family, society, and the state are interrelated. In most forms of patriarchy this has generally led to the granting of religious support in statements such as the Catholic precept that "the father is head of the family," or Judaism's delegation of quasi-priestly authority to the male parent. Secular governments today also confirm this, as in census practices of designating the male as head of household, taxation, passports etc. Female heads of household tend to be regarded as undesirable; the phenomenon is a trait of poverty or misfortune. The Confucian prescription that the relationship between ruler and subject is parallel to that of father and children points to the essentially feudal character of the patriarchal family (and conversely, the familial character of feudalism) even in modern democracies.

In contemporary patriarchies the male's *de jure* priority has recently been modified through the granting of divorce protection, citizenship, and property to women. Their chattel status continues in their loss of name, their obligation to adopt the husband's domicile, and the general legal assumption that marriage involves an exchange of the female's domestic service and (sexual) consortium in return for financial support.

The chief contribution of the family in patriarchy is the socialization of the young (largely through the example and admonition of their parents) into patriarchal ideology's prescribed attitudes toward the categories of role, temperament, and status. Although slight differences of definition depend here upon the parents' grasp of cultural values, the general effect of uniformity is achieved, to be further reinforced through peers, schools, media, and other learning sources, formal and informal. While we may niggle over the balance of authority between the personalities of various houeholds, one must remember that the entire culture supports masculine authority in all areas of life and— outside of the home—permits the female none at all.

Although there is no biological reason why the two central functions of the family (socialization and reproduction) need be inseparable from or even take place within it, revolutionary or utopian efforts to remove these functions from the family have been so frustrated, so beset by difficulties, that most experiments so far have involved a gradual return to tradition. This is strong evidence of how basic a form patriarchy is within all societies, and of how pervasive its effects upon family members. It is perhaps also an admonition that change undertaken without a thorough understanding of the socio-political institution to be changed is hardly productive. And yet radical social change cannot take place without having an effect upon patriarchy. And not simply because it is the political form which subordinates such a large percentage of the population (women and youth) but because it serves as a citadel of property and traditional interests. Marriages are financial alliances, and each household operates as an economic entity much like a corporation.

≈ ≈ ≈

IV CLASS

It is in the area of class that the castelike status of the female within patriarchy is most liable to confusion, for sexual status often operates in a superficially confusing way within the variable of class. In a society where status is dependent upon the economic, social, and educational circumstances of class, it is possible for certain females to appear to stand higher than some males. Yet not when one looks more closely at the subject. This is perhaps easier to see by means of analogy: a black doctor or lawyer has higher social status than a poor white sharecropper. But race, itself a caste system which subsumes class, persuades the latter citizen that he belongs to a higher order of life, just as it oppresses the black professional in spirit, whatever his material success may be. In much the same manner, a truck driver or butcher has always his "manhood" to fall back upon. Should this final vanity be offended, he may contemplate more violent methods. The literature of the past thirty years provides a staggering number of incidents in which the caste of virility triumphs over the social status of wealthy or even educated women. In literary contexts one has to deal here with wish-fulfillment. Incidents from life (bullying, obscene, or hostile remarks) are probably another sort of psychological gesture of ascendancy. Both convey more hope than reality, for class divisions are generally quite impervious to the hostility of individuals. And yet while the existence of class division is not seriously threatened by such expressions of enmity, the existence of sexual hierarchy has been re-affirmed and mobilized to "punish" the female quite effectively.

The function of class or ethnic mores in patriarchy is largely a matter of how overtly displayed or how loudly enunciated the general ethic of masculine supremacy allows itself to become. Here one is confronted by what appears to be a paradox: while in the lower social strata, the male is more likely to claim authority on the strength of his sex rank alone, he is actually obliged more often to share power with the women of his class who are economically productive; whereas in the middle and upper classes, there is less tendency to assert a blunt patriarchal dominance, as men who enjoy such status have more power in any case.

ᗑ ᗑ ᗑ

. . . The fairly blatant male chauvinism which was once a province of the lower class or immigrant male has been absorbed and taken on a certain glamour through a number of contemporary figures, who have made it, and a certain number of other working-class male attitudes, part of a new, and at the moment, fashionable life style. So influential is this working-class ideal of brute virility (or more accurately, a literary and therefore middle-class version of it) become in our time that it may replace more discreet and "gentlemanly" attitudes of the past.

One of the chief effects of class within patriarchy is to set one woman against another, in the past creating a lively antagonism between whore and matron, and in the present between career woman and housewife. One envies the other her "security" and prestige, while the envied yearns beyond the confines of respectability for what she takes to be the other's freedom, adventure, and contact with the great world. Through the multiple advantages of the double standard, the male participates in both worlds, empowered by his superior social and economic resources to play the estranged women against each other as rivals. One might also recognize subsidiary status categories among women: not only is virtue class, but beauty and age as well.

Perhaps, in the final analysis, it is possible to argue that women tend to transcend the usual class stratifications in patriarchy, for whatever the class of her birth and education, the female has fewer permanent class association than does the male. Economic dependency renders her affiliations with any class a tangential, vicarious, and temporary matter. Aristotle observed that the only slave to whom a commoner might lay claim was his woman, and the service of an unpaid domestic still provides working-class males with a "cushion" against the buffets of the class system which incidentally provides them with some of the psychic luxuries of the leisure class. Thrown upon their own resources, few women rise above working class in personal prestige and economic power, and women as a group do not enjoy many of the interests and benefits any class many offer its male members. Women have therefore less of an investment in the class system. But it is important to understand that as with any group whose existence is parasitic to its rulers, women are a dependency class who live on surplus. And their marginal life frequently renders them conservative, for like all persons in their situation (slaves are a classic example here) they identify their own survival with the prosperity of those who feed them. The hope of seeking liberating radical solutions of their own seems too remote for the majority to dare contemplate and remains so until consciousness on the subject is raised.

ᗑ ᗑ ᗑ

V ECONOMIC AND EDUCATIONAL

One of the most efficient branches of patriarchal government lies in the agency of its economic hold over its female subjects. In traditional patriarchy, women, as non-persons without legal standing, were permitted no actual economic existence as they could neither own nor earn in their own right. Since women have always worked in patriarchal societies, often at the most routine or strenuous tasks, what is at issue here is not labor but economic reward. In modern reformed patriarchal societies, women have certain economic rights, yet the "woman's work" in which some two thirds of the female population in most developed countries are engaged is work that is not paid for. In a money economy where autonomy and prestige depend upon currency, this is a fact of great importance. In general, the position of women in patriarchy is a continuous function of their economic dependence. Just as their social position is vicarious and achieved (often on a temporary or marginal basis) through males, their relation to the economy is also typically vicarious or tangential.

In modern capitalist countries women also function as a reserve labor force, enlisted in times of war and expansion and discharged in times of peace and recession. In this role American women have replaced immigrant labor and now compete with the racial minorities. In socialist countries the female labor force is generally in the lower ranks as well, despite a high incidence of women in certain professions such as medicine. The status and rewards of such professions have declined as women enter them, and they are permitted to enter such areas under a rationale that society or the state (and socialist countries are also patriarchal) rather than woman is served by such activity.

Since woman's independence in economic life is viewed with distrust, prescriptive agencies of all kinds (religion, psychology, advertising, etc.) continuously admonish or even inveigh against the employment of middle-class women, particularly mothers.

. . . Women who are employed have two jobs since the burden of domestic service and child care is unrelieved either by day care or other social agencies, or by the co-operation of husbands. The invention of labor-saving devices has had no appreciable effect on the duration, even if it has affected the quality of their drudgery.

In terms of industry and production, the situation of women is in many ways comparable both to colonial and to pre-industrial peoples. Although they achieved their first economic autonomy in the industrial revolution and now constitute a large and underpaid factory population, women do not participate directly in technology or in production. What they customarily produce (domestic and personal service) has no market value and is, as it were, pre-capital. Nor, where they do participate in production of commodities through employment, do they own or control or even comprehend the process in which they participate. An example might make this clearer: the refrigerator is a machine all women use, some assemble it in factories, and a very few with scientific education understand its principles of operation. Yet the heavy industries which roll its steel and produce the dies for its parts are in male hands. The same is true of the typewriter, the auto, etc. Now, while knowledge is fragmented even among the male population, collectively they could reconstruct any technological device. But in the absence of males, women's distance from technology today is sufficiently great that it is doubtful that they could replace or repair such machines on any significant scale. Woman's distance from higher technology is even greater: large-scale building construction; the development of computers; the moon shot, occur as further examples. If knowledge is power, power is also knowledge, and a large factor in their subordinate position is the fairly systematic ignorance patriarchy imposes upon women.

As patriarchy enforces a temperamental imbalance of personality traits between the sexes, its educational institutions, segregated or co-educational, accept a cultural programing toward the generally operative division between "masculine" and "feminine" subject matter, assigning the humanities and certain social sciences (at least in their lower or marginal branches) to the female—and science and technology, the professions, business and engineering to the male. Of course the balance of employment, prestige and reward at present lie with the latter. Control of these fields is very eminently a matter of political power.

VI FORCE

. . . Just as under other total ideologies (racism and colonialism are somewhat analogous in this respect) control in patriarchal society would be imperfect, even inoperable, unless it had the rule of force to rely upon, both in emergencies and as an ever-present instrument of intimidation.

Historically, most patriarchies have institutionalized force through their legal systems.

Indirectly, one form of "death penalty" still obtains even in America today. Patriarchal legal systems in depriving women of control over their own bodies drive them to illegal abortions; it is estimated that between two and five thousand women die each year from this cause.

Excepting a social license to physical abuse among certain class and ethnic groups, force is diffuse and generalized in most contemporary patriarchies. Significantly, force itself is restricted to the male who alone is psychologically and technically equipped to perpetrate physical violence. Where differences in physical strength have become immaterial through the use of arms, the female is rendered innocuous by her socialization. Before assault she is almost universally defenseless both by her physical and emotional training. Needless to say, this has the most far-reaching effects on the social and psychological behavior of both sexes.

Patriarchal force also relies on a form of violence particularly sexual in character and realized most completely in the act of rape. The figures of rapes reported represent only a fraction of those which occur, as the "shame" of the event is sufficient to deter women from the notion of civil prosecution under the public circumstances of a trial. Traditionally rape has been viewed as an offense one male commits upon another—a matter of abusing "his woman."

Patriarchal societies typically link feelings of cruelty with sexuality, the latter often equated both with evil and with power. This is apparent both in the sexual fantasy reported by psychoanalysis and that reported by pornography. The rule here associates sadism with the male ("the masculine role") and victimization with the female ("the feminine role"). Emotional response to violence against women in patriarchy is often curiously ambivalent; references to wife-beating, for example, invariably produce laughter and some embarrassment. Exemplary atrocity, such as the mass murders committed by Richard Speck, greeted at one level with a certain scandalized, possibly hypocritical indignation, is capable of eliciting a mass response of titillation at another level. At such times one even hears from men occasional expressions of envy or amusement. In view of the sadistic character of such public fantasy as caters to male audiences in pornography or semi-pornographic media, one might expect that a certain element of identification is by no means absent from the general response. Probably a similar collective *frisson* sweeps through racist society when its more "logical" members have perpetrated a lynching. Unconsciously, both crimes may serve the larger group as a ritual act, cathartic in effect.

Hostility is expressed in a number of ways. One is laughter. Misogynist literature, the primary vehicle of masculine hostility, is both an hortatory and comic genre. Of all artistic forms in patriarchy it is the most frankly propagandistic. Its aim is to reinforce both sexual factions in their status.

Since the abatement of censorship, masculine hostility (psychological or physical) in specifically *sexual* contexts has become far more apparent. Yet as masculine hostility has been fairly continuous, one deals here probably less with a matter of increase than with a new frankness in expressing hostility in specifically sexual contexts.

In the foregoing sections, Millett concentrates her analyses on what we might call the "real world," looking at the actual practices of various societies, and of men and women. In the following sections, however, she turns her attention to more amorphous territory, giving her own interpretations of two of the crucially important ancient Western myths (which happen to be excerpted in the first chapter of this book). Note that in Millett's reading, these myths are through and through evidence of patriarchy.

VII ANTHROPOLOGICAL: MYTH AND RELIGION

Evidence from anthropology, religious and literary myth all attests to the
politically expedient character of patriarchal convictions about women.

⌒ ⌒ ⌒

. . . Under patriarchy the female did not herself develop the symbols by which
she is described. As both the primitive and the civilized worlds are male worlds,
the ideas which shaped culture in regard to the female were also of male design.
The image of women as we know it is an image created by men and fashioned to
suit their needs. These needs spring from a fear of the "otherness" of woman.
Yet this notion itself presupposes that patriarchy has already been established
and the male has already set himself as the human norm, the subject and referent
to which the female is "other" or alien. Whatever its origin, the function of the
male's sexual antipathy is to provide a means of control over a subordinate
group and a rationale which justifies the inferior station of those in a lower
order, "explaining" the oppression of their lives.

The feeling that woman's sexual functions are impure is both world-wide and
persistent. One sees evidence of it everywhere in literature, in myth, in primitive
and civilized life. It is striking how the notion persists today. The event of
menstruation, for example, is a largely clandestine affair, and the psycho-social
effect of the stigma attached must have great effect on the female ego. There is a
large anthropological literature on menstrual taboo; the practice of isolating
offenders in huts at the edge of the village occurs throughout the primitive
world. Contemporary slang denominates menstruation as "the curse." There is
considerable evidence that such discomfort as women suffer during their period
is often likely to be psychosomatic, rather than physiological, cultural rather
than biological, in origin. That this may also be true to some extent of labor and
delivery is attested to by the recent experiment with "painless childbirth."
Patriarchal circumstances and beliefs seem to have the effect of poisoning the
female's own sense of physical self until it often truly becomes the burden it is
said to be.

Primitive peoples explain the phenomenon of the female's genitals in terms
of a wound, sometimes reasoning that she was visited by a bird or snake and
mutilated into her present condition. Once she was wounded, now she bleeds.
Contemporary slang for the vagina is "gash." The Freudian description of the
female genitals is in terms of a "castrated" condition.

⌒ ⌒ ⌒

Nearly all patriarchies enforce taboos against women touching ritual objects
(those of war or religion) or food. In ancient and preliterate societies women are
generally not permitted to eat with men. Women eat apart today in a great
number of cultures, chiefly those of the Near and Far East. Some of the
inspiration of such custom appears to lie in fears of contamination, probably
sexual in origin.

⌒ ⌒ ⌒

All patriarchies have hedged virginity and defloration in elaborate rites and interdictions. Among preliterates virginity presents an interesting problem in ambivalence. On the one hand, it is, an in every patriarchy, a mysterious good because a sign of property received intact. On the other hand, it represents an unknown evil associated with the mana of blood and terrifyingly "other."

⌒ ⌒ ⌒

. . . Although any physical suffering endured in defloration must be on the part of the female (and most societies cause her—bodily and mentally—to suffer anguish), the social interest, institutionalized in patriarchal ritual and custom, is exclusively on the side of the male's property interest, prestige, or (among preliterates) hazard.

Patriarchal myth typically posits a golden age before the arrival of women, while its social practices permit males to be relieved of female company.

⌒ ⌒ ⌒

Primitive society practices its misogyny in terms of taboo and mana which evolve into explanatory myth. In historical cultures, this is transformed into ethical, then literary, and in the modern period, scientific rationalizations for the sexual politic. Myth is, of course, a felicitous advance in the level of propaganda, since it so often bases its arguments on ethics or theories of origins. The two leading myths of Western culture are the classical tale of Pandora's box and the Biblical story of the Fall. In both cases earlier man's concepts of feminine evil have passed through a final literary phase to become highly influential ethical justifications of things as they are.

⌒ ⌒ ⌒

The pandora myth is one of two important Western archetypes which condemn the female through her sexuality and explain her position as her well-deserved punishment for the primal sin under whose unfortunate consequences the race yet labors. Ethics have entered the scene, replacing the simplicities of ritual, taboo, and mana. The more sophisticated vehicle of myth also provides official explanations of sexual history. In Hesiod's tale, Zeus, a rancorous and arbitrary father figure, in sending Epimentheus evil in the form of female genitalia, is actually chastising him for adult heterosexual knowledge and activity. In opening the vessel she brings (the vulva or hymen, Pandora's "box") the male satisfies his curiosity but sustains the discovery only by punishing himself at the hands of the father god with death and the assorted calamities of postlapsarian life. The patriarchal trait of male rivalry across age or status line, particularly those of powerful father and rival son, is present as well as the ubiquitous maligning of the female.

The myth of the Fall is a highly finished version of the same themes. As the central myth of the Judeo-Christian imagination and therefore of our immediate cultural heritage, it is well that we appraise and acknowledge the enormous power it still holds over us even in a rationalist era which has long ago given up literal belief in it while maintaining its emotional assent intact. This mythic version of the female as the cause of human suffering, knowledge, and sin is still the foundation of sexual attitudes, for it represents the most crucial argument of the patriarchal tradition in the West.

The Israelites lived in a continual state of war with the fertility cults of their neighbors; these latter afforded sufficient attraction to be the source of constant defection, and the figure of Eve, like that of Pandora, has vestigial traces of a fertility goddess overthrown.

☞ ☞ ☞

. . . Adam is forbidden to eat of the fruit of life or of the knowledge of good and evil, the warning states explicitly what should happen if he tastes of the latter: "in that day that thou eatest thereof thou shalt surely die." He eats but fails to die (at least in the story), from which one might infer that the serpent told the truth.

But at the moment when the pair eat of the forbidden tree they awake to their nakedness and feel shame. Sexuality is clearly involved, though the fable insists it is only tangential to a higher prohibition against disobeying orders in the matter of another and less controversial appetite for food.

☞ ☞ ☞

. . . To blame the evils and sorrows of life—loss of Eden and the rest—on sexuality, would all too logically implicate the male, and such implication is hardly the purpose of the story, designed as it is expressly in order to blame all this world's discomfort on the female. Therefore it is the female who is tempted first and "beguiled" by the penis, transformed into something else, a snake. Thus Adam has "beaten the rap" of sexual guilt, which appears to be why the sexual motive is so repressed in the Biblical account. Yet the very transparency of the serpent's universal phallic value shows how uneasy the mythic mind can be about its shifts. Accordingly, in her inferiority and vulnerability the woman takes and eats, simple carnal thing that she is, affected by flattery even in a reptile. Only after this does the male fall, and with him, humanity—for the fable has made him the racial type, whereas Eve is a mere sexual type and, according to tradition, either expendable or replaceable.

☞ ☞ ☞

VIII PSYCHOLOGICAL

The aspects of patriarchy already described have each an effect upon the psychology of both sexes. Their principal result is the interiorization of patriarchal ideology. Status, temperament, and role are all value systems with endless psychological ramifications for each sex. Patriarchal marriage and the family with its ranks and division of labor play a large part in enforcing them. The male's superior economic position, the female's inferior one have also grave implications. The large quantity of guilt attached to sexuality in patriarchy is overwhelmingly placed upon the female, who is, culturally speaking, held to be the culpable or the more culpable party in nearly any sexual liaison, whatever the extenuating circumstances. A tendency toward the reification of the female makes her more often a sexual object than a person.

☞ ☞ ☞

. . . Woman is still denied sexual freedom and the biological control over her body through the cult of virginity, the double standard, the prescription against abortion, and in many places because contraception is physically or psychically unavailable to her.

The continual surveillance in which she is held tends to perpetuate the infantilization of women even in situations such as those of higher education. The female is continually obliged to seek survival or advancement through the approval of males as those who hold power. She may do this either through appeasement or through the exchange of her sexuality for support and status.

☞ ☞ ☞

. . . With the Indo-European languages this is a nearly inescapable habit of mind, for despite all the customary pretense that "man" and "humanity" are terms which apply equally to both sexes, the fact is hardly obscured that in practice, general application favors the male far more often than the female as referent, or even sole referent, for such designations.

When in any group of persons, the ego is subjected to such invidious versions of itself through social beliefs, ideology, and tradition, the effect is bound to be pernicious. This coupled with the persistent though frequently subtle denigration women encounter daily through personal contacts, the impressions gathered from the images and media about them, and the discrimination in matters of behavior, employment, and education which they endure, should make it no very special cause for surprise that women develop group characteristics common to those who suffer minority status and a marginal existence.

☞ ☞ ☞

What little literature the social sciences afford us in this context confirms the presence in women of the expected traits of minority status: group self-hatred and self-rejection, a contempt both for herself and for her fellows—the result of that continual, however subtle, reiteration of her inferiority which she eventually accepts as a fact.

☞ ☞ ☞

. . . It is a common trait of minority status that a small percentage of the fortunate are permitted to entertain their rulers. (That they may entertain their fellow subjects in the process is less to the point.) Women entertain, please, gratify, satisfy and flatter men with their sexuality. In most minority groups athletes or intellectuals are allowed to emerge as "stars," identification with whom should content their less fortunate fellows. In the case of women both such eventualities are discouraged on the reasonable grounds that the most popular explanations of the female's inferior status ascribe it to her physical weakness or intellectual inferiority. Logically, exhibitions of physical courage or agility are indecorous, just as any display of serious intelligence tends to be out of place.

Perhaps patriarchy's greatest psychological weapon is simply its universality and longevity. A referent scarcely exists with which it might be contrasted or by which it might be confuted. While the same might be said of class, patriarchy has a still more tenacious or powerful hold through its successful habit of passing itself off as nature.

2. SHERRY B. ORTNER
(American)

Trained as an anthropologist, Ortner's primary work has been the study of the Nepalese Sherpas. The following article, however, has obtained a status as a classic in philosophy as well as in anthropology and sociology.

"IS FEMALE TO MALE AS NATURE IS TO CULTURE?" (1974)

The article is an investigation of this deceptively simple question. The terms, "nature" and "culture," as we have seen in earlier chapters, are integral to the philosophical and literary conceptions of gender, but they have nonetheless remained ambiguous. Ortner begins with a working hypothesis: that there is such a thing as "culture" in itself, which delivers the framework within which individual and perhaps very different cultures negotiate their own traditions. Having laid this groundwork for her reflections, Ortner investigates the possibility that within this framework, there is a universal cultural association of femininity and "nature."

> . . . The secondary status of woman in society is one of the true universals, a pan-cultural fact. Yet within that universal fact, the specific cultural conceptions and symbolizations of woman are extraordinarily diverse and even mutually contradictory. Further, the actual treatment of women and their relative power and contribution vary enormously from culture to culture, and over different periods in the history of particular cultural traditions. Both of these points—the universal fact and the cultural variation—constitute problems to be explained.

> We may differentiate three levels of the problem:
>
> 1. The universal fact of culturally attributed second-class status of woman in every society. Two questions are important here. First, what do we mean by this; what is our evidence that this is a universal fact? And second, how are we to explain this fact, once having established it?

2. Specific ideologies, symbolizations, and socio-structural arrangements pertaining to women that vary widely from culture to culture. The problem at this level is to account for any particular cultural complex in terms of factors specific to that group—the standard level of anthropological analysis.

3. Observable on-the-ground details of women's activities, contributions, powers, influence, etc., often at variance with cultural ideology (although always constrained within the assumption that women may never be officially preeminent in the total system). This is the level of direct observation, often adopted now by feminist-oriented anthropologists.

This paper is primarily concerned with the first of these levels, the problem of the universal devaluation of women.

⌒ ⌒ ⌒

THE UNIVERSALITY OF FEMALE SUBORDINATION

What do I mean when I say that everywhere, in every known culture, women are considered in some degree inferior to man? First of all, I must stress that I am talking about *cultural* evaluations; I am saying that each culture, in its own way and on its own terms, makes this evaluation. But what would constitute evidence that a particular culture considers women inferior?

Three types of data would suffice: (1) elements of cultural ideology and informants' statements that *explicitly* devalue women, according them, their roles, their tasks, their products, and their social milieux less prestige than are accorded men and the male correlates; (2) symbolic devices, such as the attribution of defilement, which may be interpreted as *implicitly* making a statement of inferior valuation; and (3) social-structural arrangements that exclude women from participating in or contact with some realm in which the highest powers of the society are felt to reside. These three types of data may all of course be interrelated in any particular system, though they need not necessarily be. Further, any one of them will usually be sufficient to make the point of female inferiority in a given culture. Certainly, female exclusion from the most sacred rite or the highest political council is sufficient evidence. Certainly, explicit cultural ideology devaluing women (and their tasks, roles, products, etc.) is sufficient evidence. Symbolic indicators such as defilement are usually sufficient, although in a few cases in which, say, men and women are equally polluting to one another, a further indicator is required—and is, as far as my investigations have ascertained, always available.

On any or all of these counts, then, I would flatly assert that we find women subordinated to men in every known society. The search for a genuinely egalitarian, let alone matriarchal, culture has proved fruitless.

⌒ ⌒ ⌒

NATURE AND CULTURE

How are we to explain the universal devaluation of women? We could of course rest the case on biological determinism. There is something genetically inherent in the male of the species, so the biological determinists would argue, that makes them the naturally dominant sex; that "something" is lacking in females, and as a result women are not only naturally subordinate but in general quite satisfied with their position, since it affords them protection and the opportunity to maximize maternal pleasures, which to them are the most satisfying experiences of life. Without going into a detailed refutation of this position, I think it fair to say that it has failed to be established to the satisfaction of almost anyone in academic anthropology. This is to say, not that biological facts are irrelevant, or that men and women are not different, but that these facts and differences only take on significance of superior/inferior within the framework of culturally defined value systems.

If we are unwilling to rest the case on genetic determinism, it seems to me that we have only one way to proceed. We must attempt to interpret female subordination in light of other universals, factors built into the structure of the most generalized situation in which all human beings, in whatever culture, find themselves.

I translate the problem, in other words, into the following simple question. What could there be in the generalized structure and conditions of existence, common to every culture, that would lead every culture to place a lower value upon women? Specifically, my thesis is that woman is being identified with—or, if you will, seems to be a symbol of—something that every culture devalues, something that every culture defines as being of a lower order of existence than itself. Now it seems that there is only one thing that would fit that description, and that is "nature" in the most generalized sense. Every culture, or, generically, "culture," is engaged in the process of generating and sustaining systems of meaningful forms (symbols, artifacts, etc.) by means of which humanity transcends the givens of natural existence, bends them to its purposes, controls them in its interest. We may thus broadly equate culture with the notion of human consciousness, or with the products of human consciousness (i.e., systems of thought and technology), by means of which humanity attempts to assert control over nature.

One realm of cultural thought in which these points are often articulated is that of concepts of purity and pollution. Virtually every culture has some such beliefs, which seem in large part (though not, of course, entirely) to be concerned with the relationship between culture and nature (see Ortner, 1973, n.d.). A well-known aspect of purity/pollution beliefs cross-culturally is that of the natural "contagion" of pollution; left to its own devices, pollution (for these purposes grossly equated with the unregulated operation of natural energies) spreads and overpowers all that it comes in contact with.

ↄ ↄ ↄ

In any case, my point is simply that every culture implicitly recognizes and asserts a distinction between the operation of nature and the operation of culture (human consciousness and its products); and further, that the distinctiveness of culture rests precisely on the fact that it can under most circumstances transcend natural conditions and turn them to its purposes. Thus culture (i.e. every culture) at some level of awareness asserts itself to be not only distinct from but superior to nature, and that sense of distinctiveness and superiority rests precisely on the ability to transform—to "socialize" and "culturalize"—nature.

Returning now to the issue of women, their pan-cultural second-class status could be accounted for, quite simply, by postulating that women are being identified or symbolically associated with nature, as opposed to men, who are identified with culture. Since it is always culture's project to subsume and transcend nature, if women were considered part of nature, then culture would find it "natural" to subordinate, not to say oppress, them. Yet although this argument can be shown to have considerable force, it seems to oversimplify the case. The formulation I would like to defend and elaborate on in the following section, then, is that women are seen "merely" as being *closer* to nature than men. That is, culture (still equated relatively unambiguously with men) recognizes that women are active participants in its special processes, but at the same time sees them as being more rooted in, or having more direct affinity with, nature.

Ortner is arguing against the commonplace that we have seen in earlier thinkers, that whatever is cross-cultural must be natural. Instead, Ortner claims that there are culturally based, yet universal concepts, and that the concept of "nature" is one of them. On this basis, she will then attempt to answer the question posed in the title of the essay, investigating in what sense this universal notion of "nature" is universally associated with femininity. Her conclusion is subtle and, she believes, explains a number of otherwise confusing cultural phenomena regarding the status of women. According to Ortner, the female is universally figured within culture as *closer* to nature than the male, mediating between the fully cultural human sphere and the designated "natural," non-human one.

WHY IS WOMAN SEEN AS CLOSER TO NATURE?

It all begins of course with the body and the natural procreative functions specific to women alone. We can sort out for discussion three levels at which this absolute physiological fact has significance: (1) woman's *body and its functions,* more involved more of the time with "species life," seem to place her closer to nature, in contrast to man's physiology, which frees him more completely to take up the projects of culture; (2) woman's body and its functions place her in *social roles* that in turn are considered to be at a lower order of the cultural process than man's; and (3) woman's traditional social roles, imposed because of her body and its functions, in turn give her a different *psychic structure,* which like her physiological nature and her social roles, is seen as being closer to nature. ...

1. *Woman's physiology seen as closer to nature.* This part of my argument has been anticipated, with subtlety, cogency, and a great deal of hard data, by de Beauvoir (1953). De Beauvoir reviews the physiological structure, development, and functions of the human female and concludes that "the female, to a greater extent than the male, is the prey of the species" (p. 60). She points out that many major areas and processes of the woman's body serve no apparent function for the health and stability of the individual; on the contrary, as they perform their specific organic functions, they are often sources of discomfort, pain, and danger.

In other words, woman's body seems to doom her to mere reproduction of life; the male, in contrast, lacking natural creative functions, must (or has the opportunity to) assert his creativity externally, "artificially," through the medium of technology and symbols. In so doing, he creates relatively lasting, eternal, transcendent objects, while the woman creates only perishables—human beings.

This formulation opens up a number of important insights. It speaks, for example, to the great puzzle of why male activities involving the destruction of life (hunting and warfare) are often given more prestige than the female's ability to give birth, to create life.

Thus if male is, as I am suggesting, everywhere (unconsciously) associated with culture and female seems closer to nature, the rationale for these associations is not very difficult to grasp, merely from considering the implications of the physiological contrast between male and female. At the same time, however, woman cannot be consigned fully to the category of nature, for it is perfectly obvious that she is a full-fledged human being endowed with human consciousness just as a man is; she is half of the human race, without whose cooperation the whole enterprise would collapse. She may seem more in the possession of nature than man, but having consciousness, she thinks and speaks; she generates, communicates, and manipulates symbols, categories, and values. She participates in human dialogues not only with other women but also with men.

Because of woman's greater bodily involvement with the natural functions surrounding reproduction, she is seen as more a part of nature than man is. Yet in part because of her consciousness and participation in human social dialogue, she is recognized as a participant in culture. Thus she appears as something intermediate between culture and nature, lower on the scale of transcendence than man.

2. *Woman's social role seen as closer to nature.* Woman's physiological functions, I have just argued, may tend in themselves to motivate a view of woman as closer to nature, a view she herself, as an observer of herself and the world, would tend to agree with. Woman creates naturally from within her own being, whereas man is free to, or forced to, create artificially, that is, through cultural means, and in such a way as to sustain culture. In addition, I now wish to show how woman's physiological functions have tended universally to limit her social movement, and to confine her universally to certain social contexts which *in turn* are seen as closer to nature.

꘍ ꘍ ꘍

I refer here of course to woman's confinement to the domestic family context, a confinement motivated, no doubt, by her lactation processes.

꘍ ꘍ ꘍

Woman's association with the domestic circle would contribute to the view of her as closer to nature in several ways. In the first place, the sheer fact of constant association with children plays a role in the issue; one can easily see how infants and children might themselves be considered part of nature. Infants are barely human and utterly unsocialized; like animals they are unable to walk upright, they excrete without control, they do not speak.

꘍ ꘍ ꘍

One finds implicit recognition of an association between children and nature in many cultural practices. For example, most cultures have initiation rites for adolescents (primarily for boys; I shall return to this point below), the point of which is to move the child ritually from a less than fully human state into full participation in society and culture; many cultures do not hold funeral rites for children who die at early ages, explicitly because they are not yet fully social beings. Thus children are likely to be categorized with nature, and woman's close association with children may compound her potential for being seen as closer to nature herself. It is ironic that the rationale for boys' initiation rites in many cultures is that the boys must be purged of the defilement accrued from being around mother and other women so much of the time, when in fact much of the woman's defilement may derive from her being around children so much of the time.

The second major problematic implication of women's close association with the domestic context derives from certain structural conflicts between the family and society at large in any social system.

꘍ ꘍ ꘍

. . . Although not every culture articulates a radical opposition between the domestic and the public as such, it is hardly contestable that the domestic is always subsumed by the public; domestic units are allied with one another through the enactment of rules that are logically at a higher level than the units themselves; this creates an emergent unit—society—that is logically at a higher level than the domestic units of which it is composed.

⌒ ⌒ ⌒

. . . The point seems more adequately formulated as follows: the family (and hence woman) represents lower-level, socially fragmenting, particularistic sorts of concerns, as opposed to interfamilial relations representing higher-level, integrative, universalistic sorts of concerns. Since men lack a "natural" basis (nursing, generalized to child care) for a familial orientation, their sphere of activity is defined at the level of interfamilial relations. And hence, so the cultural reasoning seems to go, men are the "natural" proprietors of religion, ritual, politics, and other realms of cultural thought and action in which universalistic statements of spiritual and social synthesis are made. Thus men are identified not only with culture, in the sense of all human creativity, as opposed to nature; they are identified in particular with culture in the old-fashioned sense of the finer and higher aspects of human thought—art, religion, law, etc.

⌒ ⌒ ⌒

In the first place, one must point out that woman not only feeds and cleans up after children in a simple caretaker operation; she in fact is the primary agent of their early socialization. It is she who transforms newborn infants from mere organisms into cultured humans, teaching them manners and the proper ways to behave in order to become full-fledged members of the culture. On the basis of her socializing functions alone, she could not be more a representative of culture.

⌒ ⌒ ⌒

. . . Belonging to culture, yet appearing to have stronger and more direct connections with nature, she is once again seen as situated between the two realms.

3. *Woman's psyche seen as closer to nature.* The suggestion that woman has not only a different body and a different social locus from man but also a different psychic structure is most controversial. I will argue that she probably *does* have a different psychic structure, but I will draw heavily on Chodorow's paper to establish first that her psychic structure need not be assumed to be innate; it can be accounted for, as Chodorow convincingly shows, by the facts of the probably universal female socialization experience.

⌒ ⌒ ⌒

It is important to specify what we see as the dominant and universal aspects of the feminine psyche. If we postulate emotionality or irrationality, we are confronted with those traditions in various parts of the world in which women functionally are, and are seen as, more practical, pragmatic, and this-worldly than men. One relevant dimension that does seem pan-culturally applicable is that of relative concreteness vs. relative abstractness: the feminine personality tends to be involved with concrete feelings, things, and people, rather than with abstract entities: it tends toward personalism and particularism. A second, closely related, dimension seems to be that of relative subjectivity vs. relative objectivity.

⌐ ⌐ ⌐

Chodorow argues that, because mother is the early socializer of both boys and girls, both develop "personal identification" with her, i.e. diffuse identification with her general personality, behavior traits, values, and attitudes. A son, however, must ultimately shift to a masculine role identity, which involves building an identification with the father. Since father is almost always more remote than mother (he is rarely involved in child care, and perhaps works away from home much of the day), building an identification with father involves a "positional identification," i.e. identification with father's male role as a collection of abstract elements, rather than a personal identification with father as a real individual.

⌐ ⌐ ⌐

For a young girl, in contrast, the personal identification with mother, which was created in early infancy, can persist into the process of learning female role identity. Because mother is immediate and present when the daughter is learning role identity, learning to be a woman involves the continuity and development of a girl's relationship to her mother, and sustains the identification with her as an individual; it does not involve the learning of externally defined role characteristics.

⌐ ⌐ ⌐

It is thus not difficult to see how the feminine personality would lend weight to a view of women as being "closer to nature." Yet at the same time, the modes of relating characteristic of women undeniably play a powerful and important role in the cultural process. For just as relatively unmediated relating is in some sense at the lower end of the spectrum of human spiritual functions, embedded and particularizing rather than transcending and synthesizing, yet that mode of relating also stands at the upper end of that spectrum. Consider the mother-child relationship. Mothers tend to be committed to their children as individuals, regardless of sex, age, beauty, clan affiliation, or other categories in which the child might participate. Now any relationship with this quality—not just mother and child but any sort of highly personal, relatively unmediated commitment— may be seen as a challenge to culture and society "from below," insofar as it represents the fragmentary potential of individual loyalties vis-à-vis the solidarity of the group. But it may also be seen as embodying the synthesizing agent for culture and society "from above," in that it represents generalized human values above and beyond loyalties to particular social categories. Every society must have social categories that transcend personal loyalties, but every society must also generate a sense of ultimate moral unity for all its members above and beyond those social categories. Thus that psychic mode seemingly typical of women, which tends to disregard categories and to seek "communion" (Chodorow, p. 55, following Bakan, 1966) directly and personally with others, although it may appear infracultural from one point of view, is at the same time associated with the highest levels of the cultural process.

THE IMPLICATIONS OF INTERMEDIACY

⌐ ⌐ ⌐

. . . This intermediacy has several implications for analysis, depending upon how it is interpreted. First, of course, it answers my primary question of why woman is everywhere seen as lower than man, for even if she is not seen as nature pure and simple, she is still seen as achieving less transcendence of nature than man. Here intermediate simply means "middle status" on a hierarchy of being from culture to nature.

Second, intermediate may have the significance of "mediating," i.e. performing some sort of synthesizing or converting function between nature and culture, here seen (by culture) not as two ends of a continuum but as two radically different sorts of processes in the world. The domestic unit—and hence woman, who in virtually every case appears as its primary representative—is one of culture's crucial agencies for the conversion of nature into culture, especially with reference to the socialization of children.

⌐ ⌐ ⌐

Finally, woman's intermediate position may have the implication of greater symbolic ambiguity. . . . Shifting our image of the culture/nature relationship once again, we may envision culture in this case as a small clearing within the forest of the larger natural system. For this point of view, that which is intermediate between culture and nature is located on the continuous periphery of culture's clearing; and though it may thus appear to stand both above and below (and beside) culture, it is simply outside and around it. We can begin to understand then how a single system of cultural thought can often assign to woman completely polarized and apparently contradictory meanings, since extremes, as we say, meet. That she often represents both life and death is only the simplest example one could mention.

For another perspective on the same point, it will be recalled that the psychic mode associated with women seems to stand at both the bottom and the top of the scale of human modes of relation.

⌐ ⌐ ⌐

. . . Thus we can account easily for both the subversive feminine symbols (witches, evil eye, menstrual pollution, castrating mothers) and the feminine symbols of transcendence (mother goddesses, merciful dispensers of salvation, female symbols of justice, and the strong presence of feminine symbolism in the realms of art, religion, ritual, and law). Feminine symbolism, far more often than masculine symbolism, manifests this propensity toward polarized ambiguity—sometimes utterly exalted, sometimes utterly debased, rarely within the normal range of human possibilities.

⌐ ⌐ ⌐

In short, the postulate that woman is viewed as closer to nature than man has several implications for further analysis, and can be interpreted in several different ways. If it is viewed simply as a *middle* position on a scale from culture down to nature, then it is still seen as lower than culture and thus accounts for the pan-cultural assumption that woman is lower than man in the order of things. If it is read as a *mediating* element in the culture-nature relationship, then it may account in part for the cultural tendency not merely to devalue woman but to circumscribe and restrict her functions, since culture must maintain control over its (pragmatic and symbolic) mechanisms for the conversion of nature into culture. And if it is read as an *ambiguous* status between culture and nature, it may help account for the fact that, in specific cultural ideologies and symbolizations, woman can occasionally be aligned with culture, and in any event is often assigned polarized and contradictory meanings within a single symbolic system. Middle status, mediating functions, ambiguous meaning—all are different readings, for different contextual purposes, of woman's being seen as intermediate between nature and culture.

3. MICHEL FOUCAULT
(French, 1926–1984)

Weaving together history, philosophy, sociology, literary criticism, and other methodologies, Foucault argued in all his work that supposedly timeless and absolute ideas are really pawns in the power struggles of history. For instance, in his *Madness and Civilization,* Foucault attempts to demonstrate that what counts in any particular time period as insane behavior is whatever behavior it serves the growth of social power to label "insane"; similarly for criminality in his *Discipline and Punish.* In *The History of Sexuality,* from which all the following selections are taken, he makes a similar argument about sexuality. It was his last work and, many believe, his greatest.

THE HISTORY OF SEXUALITY: VOLUME I (1976)

In this "revisionist" history of sexuality, Foucault argues against the received wisdom of our day, which he calls "the repressive hypothesis." According to this hypothesis—which Foucault claims is misguided—sexuality has been repressed in Western civil society ever since the seventeenth century, and it is consequently the obligation of progressive thinkers to seek sexual freedom. As Foucault understands it, however, Western society since the seventeenth century has merely been involved in a process of replacing sexual *behavior* with a more and more complex *discourse* of sex, in order to expand the horizons of social power.

THE REPRESSIVE HYPOTHESIS

In the first two parts of Volume I, Foucault introduces his thesis and investigates the sincerity of the current-day beliefs.

> For a long time, the story goes, we supported a Victorian regime, and we continue to be dominated by it even today. Thus the image of the imperial prude is emblazoned on our restrained, mute, and hypocritical sexuality.

> But twilight soon fell upon this bright day, followed by the monotonous nights of the Victorian bourgeoisie. Sexuality was carefully confined; it moved into the home. The conjugal family took custody of it and absorbed it into the serious function of reproduction. On the subject of sex, silence became the rule.

> This discourse on modern sexual repression holds up well, owing no doubt to how easy it is to uphold. A solemn historical and political guarantee protects it. By placing the advent of the age of repression in the seventeenth century, after hundreds of years of open spaces and free expression, one adjusts it to coincide with the development of capitalism: it becomes an integral part of the bourgeois order. The minor chronicle of sex and its trials is transposed into the ceremonious history of the modes of production; its trifling aspect fades from view.

> But there may be another reason that makes it so gratifying for us to define the relationship between sex and power in terms of repression: something that one might call the speaker's benefit. If sex is repressed, that is, condemned to prohibition, nonexistence, and silence, then the mere fact that one is speaking about it has the appearance of a deliberate transgression. A person who holds forth in such language places himself to a certain extent outside the reach of power; he upsets established law; he somehow anticipates the coming freedom. This explains the solemnity with which one speaks of sex nowadays. When they had to allude to it, the first demographers and psychiatrists of the nineteenth century thought it advisable to excuse themselves for asking their readers to dwell on matters so trivial and base. But for decades now, we have found it difficult to speak on the subject without striking a different pose: we are conscious of defying established power, our tone of voice shows that we know we are being subversive, and we ardently conjure away the present and appeal to the future, whose day will be hastened by the contribution we believe we are

making. Something that smacks of revolt, of promised freedom, of the coming age of a different law, slips easily into this discourse on sexual oppression. Some of the ancient functions of prophecy are reactivated therein. Tomorrow sex will be good again. Because this repression is affirmed, one can discreetly bring into coexistence concepts which the fear of ridicule or the bitterness of history prevents most of us from putting side by side: revolution and happiness, or revolution and a different body, one that is newer and more beautiful; or indeed revolution and pleasure.

~ ~ ~

Briefly, my aim is to examine the case of a society which has been loudly castigating itself for its hypocrisy for more than a century, which speaks verbosely of its own silence, takes great pains to relate in detail the things it does not say, denounces the powers it exercises, and promises to liberate itself from the very laws that have made it function. I would like to explore not only these discourses but also the will that sustains them and the strategic intention that supports them. The question I would like to pose is not, Why are we repressed? but rather, Why do we say, with so much passion and so much resentment against our most recent past, against our present, and against ourselves, that we are repressed? By what spiral did we come to affirm that sex is negated? What led us to show, ostentatiously, that sex is something we hide, to say it is something we silence? And we do all this by formulating the matter in the most explicit terms, by trying to reveal it in its most naked reality, by affirming it in the positivity of its power and its effects.

~ ~ ~

One can raise three serious doubts concerning what I shall term the "repressive hypothesis." First doubt: Is sexual repression truly an established historical fact? Is what first comes into view—and consequently permits one to advance an initial hypothesis—really the accentuation or even the establishment of a regime of sexual repression beginning in the seventeenth century? This is a properly historical question. Second doubt: Do the workings of power, and in particular those mechanisms that are brought into play in societies such as ours, really belong primarily to the category of repression? Are prohibition, censorship, and denial truly the forms through which power is exercised in a general way, if not in every society, most certainly in our own? This is a historico-theoretical question. A third and final doubt: Did the critical discourse that addresses itself to repression come to act as a roadblock to a power mechanism, that had operated unchallenged up to that point, or is it not in fact part of the same historical network as the thing it denounces (and doubtless misrepresents) by calling it "repression"? Was there really a historical rupture between the age of repression and the critical analysis of repression? This is a historico-political question. My purpose in introducing these three doubts is not merely to construct counterarguments that are symmetrical and contrary to those outlined above; it is not a matter of saying that sexuality, far from being repressed in captialist and bourgeois societies, has on the contrary benefitted from a regime of unchanging liberty; nor is it a matter of saying that power in societies such as ours is more tolerant than repressive, and that the critique of repression, while it may give itself airs of a rupture with the past, actually forms part of a much older process and, depending on how one chooses to understand this process, will appear either as a new episode in the lessening of prohibitions, or as a more devious and discreet form of power.

The doubts I would like to oppose to the repressive hypothesis are aimed less at showing it to be mistaken than at putting it back within a general economy of discourses on sex in modern societies since the seventeenth century. Why has sexuality been so widely discussed, and what has been said about it? What were the effects of power generated by what was said? What are the links between these discourses, these effects of power, and the pleasures that were invested by them? What knowledge (*savoir*) was formed as a result of this linkage? The object, in short, is to define the regime of power-knowledge-pleasure that sustains the discourse on human sexuality in our part of the world. The central issue, then (at least in the first instance), is not to determine whether one says yes or no to sex, whether one formulates prohibitions or permissions, whether one asserts its importance or denies its effects, or whether one refines the words one uses to designate it; but to account for the fact that it is spoken about, to discover who does the speaking, the positions and viewpoints from which they speak, the institutions which prompt people to speak about it and which store and distribute the things that are said.

≈ ≈ ≈

Let there be no misunderstanding: I do not claim that sex has not been prohibited or barred or masked or misapprehended since the classical age; nor do I even assert that it has suffered these things any less from that period on than before. I do not maintain that the prohibition of sex is a ruse; but it is a ruse to make prohibition into the basic and constitutive element from which one would be able to write the history of what has been said concerning sex starting from the modern epoch. All these negative elements—defenses, censorships, denials—which the repressive hypothesis groups together in one great central mechanism destined to say no, are doubtless only component parts that have a local and tactical role to play in a transformation into discourse, a technology of power, and a will to knowledge that are far from being reducible to the former.

≈ ≈ ≈

I THE INCITEMENT TO DISCOURSE

. . . Yet when one looks back over these last three centuries with their continual transformations, things appear in a very different light: around and apropos of sex, one sees a veritable discursive explosion. We must be clear on this point, however. It is quite possible that there was an expurgation—and a very rigorous one—of the authorized vocabulary. It may indeed be true that a whole rhetoric of allusion and metaphor was codified. Without question, new rules of propriety screened out some words: there was a policing of statements. A control over enunciations as well: where and when it was not possible to talk about such things became much more strictly defined; in which circumstances, among which speakers, and within which social relationships. Areas were thus established, if not of utter silence, at least of tact and discretion: between parents and children, for instance, or teachers and pupils, or masters and domestic servants. This almost certainly constituted a whole restrictive economy, one that was incorporated into that politics of language and speech—spontaneous on the one hand, concerted on the other—which accompanied the social redistributions of the classical period.

☞ ☞ ☞

. . . A twofold evolution tended to make the flesh into the root of all evil, shifting the most important moment of transgression from the act itself to the stirrings—so difficult to perceive and formulate—of desire. For this was an evil that afflicted the whole man, and in the most secret of forms:

☞ ☞ ☞

. . . But after all, the Christian pastoral also sought to produce specific effects on desire, by the mere fact of transforming it—fully and deliberately—into discourse: effects of mastery and detachment, to be sure, but also an effect of spiritual reconversion, of turning back to God, a physical effect of blissful suffering from feeling in one's body the pangs of temptation and the love that resists it. This is the essential thing: that Western man has been drawn for three centuries to the task of telling everything concerning his sex; that since the classical age there has been a constant optimization and an increasing valorization of the discourse on sex; and that this carefully analytical discourse was meant to yield multiple effects of displacement, intensification, reorientation, and modification of desire itself. Not only were the boundaries of what one could say about sex enlarged, and men compelled to hear it said; but more important, discourse was connected to sex by a complex organization with varying effects, by a development that cannot be adequately explained merely by referring it to a law of prohibition. A censorship of sex? There was installed rather an apparatus for producing an ever greater quantity of discourse about sex, capable of functioning and taking effect in its very economy.

☞ ☞ ☞

A few examples will suffice. One of the great innovations in the techniques of power in the eighteenth century was the emergence of "population" as an economic and political problem: population as wealth, population as manpower or labor capacity, population balanced between its own growth and the resources it commanded. Governments perceived that they were not dealing simply with subjects, or even with a "people," but with a "population," with its specific phenomena and its peculiar variables: birth and death rates, life expectancy, fertility, state of health, frequency of illnesses, patterns of diet and habitation.

☞ ☞ ☞

. . . At the heart of this economic and political problem of population was sex: it was necessary to analyze the birthrate, the age of marriage, the legitimate and illegitimate births, the precocity and frequency of sexual relations, the ways of making them fertile or sterile, the effects of unmarried life or of the prohibitions, the impact of contraceptive practices—of those notorious "deadly secrets" which demographers on the eve of the Revolution knew were already familiar to the inhabitants of the countryside.

☞ ☞ ☞

One could mention many other centers which in the eighteenth or nineteenth century began to produce discourses on sex. First there was medicine, via the "nervous disorders"; next psychiatry, when it set out to discover the etiology of mental illnesses, focusing its gaze first on "excess," then onanism, then frustration, then "frauds against procreation," but especially when it annexed the whole of the sexual perversions as its own province; criminal justice, too, which had long been concerned with sexuality, particularly in the form of "heinous" crimes and crimes against nature, but which, toward the middle of the nineteenth century, broadened its jurisdiction to include petty offenses, minor indecencies, insignificant perversions; and lastly, all those social controls, cropping up at the end of the last century, which screened the sexuality of couples, parents and children, dangerous and endangered adolescents—undertaking to protect, separate, and forewarn, signaling perils everywhere, awakening people's attention, calling for diagnoses, piling up reports, organizing therapies. These sites radiated discourses aimed at sex, intensifying people's awareness of it as a constant danger, and this in turn created a further incentive to talk about it.

As Foucault understands it, the sexual *behavior* for which sexual *discourse* has been progressively substituted since the seventeenth century was largely outside of the control of the powerful forces in society; it was—at least for the most part— genuinely free action. However discourse, according to Foucault—which is printed, or spoken by "experts" in certain intellectual fields, played out in law, scientific journals, social circles—is a controllable medium. Hence, he claims that the "incitement to discourse" should be understood as a strategy on the part of socially powerful forces to control a larger and larger territory—the whole amorphous, almost infinitely complex world of thought, accessible through language. For Foucault then, discourse about sex—perhaps even discourse about gender—is one important pathway through which individuals are oppressed by power. Since discourse about childbirth and childrearing are among the first to develop, we may assume that women became early vehicles of the oppression and control exerted by this explosion of discourse.

In the second chapter of Part Two, Foucault addresses the notion of "perversion," claiming that the acts to which that name is now applied were not thought perverse until those in positions of power invented "perversion" as a vehicle for infiltrating sexuality. The notion of perversity was used by the state such that simple laws against consanguine marriages became involved psychiatric investigations of unconscious incest taboos, "perverse" individuals were marked and studied as persons instead of just punished for their criminal behavior, sexual pleasures and sexual ill health became subjects of medical and scientific discourse, and all aspects of family and bodily life were given sexual overtones. In these ways—particularly the last two—public power invaded the intimate recesses of individual and family life, making the sex lives of individuals, and particularly those of women, subject to public scrutiny.

SCIENTIA SEXUALIS

In the third part of Volume I, Foucault compares two ways of "producing the truth of sex": 1) *ars erotica,* typical of the East, and of the ancient and medieval periods in the West; and 2) *scientia sexualis,* Foucault's name for the investigation of sex according to modern scientific principles. Erotic practice, he claims, is a way of increasing one's knowledge of sex by increasing one's ability to elicit the pleasures of sex. The science of sex, on the other hand, is power's way of getting at otherwise "hidden" processes, i.e., putting our private lives under the microscope of discourse. According to Foucault, there are five strategies of *scientia sexualis:*

PART THREE

Historically, there have been two great procedures for producing the truth of sex.
On the one hand, the societies—and they are numerous: China, Japan, India, Rome, the Arabo-Moslem societies—which endowed themselves with an *ars erotica.* In the erotic art, truth is drawn from pleasure itself, understood as a practice and accumulated as experience; pleasure is not considered in relation to an absolute law of the permitted and the forbidden, nor by reference to a criterion of utility, but first and foremost in relation to itself; it is experienced as pleasure, evaluated in terms of its intensity, its specific quality, its duration, its reverberations in the body and the soul. Moreover, this knowledge must be deflected back into the sexual practice itself, in order to shape it as though from within and amplify its effects. In this way, there is formed a knowledge that must remain secret, not because of an element of infamy that might attach to its object, but because of the need to hold it in the greatest reserve, since, according to tradition, it would lose its effectiveness and its virtue by being divulged.

◠ ◠ ◠

On the face of it at least, our civilization possesses no *ars erotica.* In return, it is undoubtedly the only civilization to practice a *scientia sexualis;* or rather, the only civilization to have developed over the centuries procedures for telling the truth of sex which are geared to a form of knowledge-power strictly opposed to the art of initiations and the masterful secret: I have in mind the confession.

Western man has become a confessing animal. Whence a metamorphosis in literature: we have passed from a pleasure to be recounted and heard, centering on the heroic or marvelous narration of "trials" of bravery or sainthood, to a literature ordered according to the infinite task of extracting from the depths of oneself, in between the words, a truth which the very form of the confession holds out like a shimmering mirage.

. . . How did this immense and traditional extortion of the sexual confession come to be constituted in scientific terms?

1. *Through a clinical codification of the inducement to speak.* Combining confession with examination, the personal history with the deployment of a set of decipherable signs, and symptoms; the interrogation, the exacting questionnaire, and hypnosis.

2. *Through the postulate of a general and diffuse causality.* Having to tell everything, being able to pose questions about everything, found their justification in the principle that endowed sex with an inexhaustible and polymorphous causal power.

The limitless dangers that sex carried with it justified the exhaustive character of the inquisition to which it was subjected.

3. *Through the principle of a latency intrinsic to sexuality.* If it was necessary to extract the truth of sex through the technique of confession, this was not simply because it was difficult to tell, or stricken by the taboos of decency, but because the ways of sex were obscure, it was elusive by nature; its energy and its mechanisms escaped observation and its causal power was partly clandestine.

4. *Through the method of interpretation.* If one had to confess, this was not merely because the person to whom one confessed had the power to forgive, console, and direct, but because the work of producing the truth was obliged to pass through this relationship if it was to be scientifically validated. The truth did not reside solely in the subject who, by confessing, would reveal it wholly formed. It was constituted in two stages: present but incomplete, blind to itself, in the one who spoke, it could only reach completion in the one who assimilated and recorded it. It was the latter's function to verify this obscure truth.

☞ ☞ ☞

5. *Through the medicalization of the effects of confession.* The obtaining of the confession and its effects were recodified as therapeutic operations. Which meant first of all that the sexual domain was no longer accounted for simply by the notions of error or sins, excess or transgression, but was placed under the rule of the normal and the pathological (which, for that matter, were the transposition of the former categories); a characteristic sexual morbidity was defined for the first time; sex appeared as an extremely unstable pathological field, a surface of repercussion for other ailments but also the focus of a specific nosography, that of instincts, tendencies, images, pleasure, and conduct. This implied furthermore that sex would derive its meaning and its necessity from medical interventions: it would be required by the doctor, necessary for diagnosis, and effective by nature in the cure. Spoken in time, to the proper party, and by the person who was both the bearer of it and the one responsible for it, the truth healed.

THE DEPLOYMENT OF SEXUALITY

In this, the longest section of Volume I, Foucault discusses how sexuality was put into the service of power. In the first part, "Objective," Foucault defines his notion of power, which he contrasts to the dichotomous, "repressive" (i.e., master/slave) notion of power that we have seen in earlier thinkers. Foucault claims that the master/slave model is both false and slavish—in other words, it implies that power is evil and bad instead of available and useful. In contrast to it, he proposes that power is polymorphous—strategizing, hiding, pursuing expression wherever it can. In the second section, "Method," Foucault proposes that power, properly understood, is not repressive at all; rather, it possesses, invades, and creates, by taking objects—by "deploying" itself. Hence, according to Foucault, power has created sexuality in order to invade it further. It is in the third section, called "Domain," that Foucault addresses the issue of gender most directly, claiming that power has deployed sex by invading four spheres of intimate human behavior.

What distinguishes the analysis made in terms of the repression of instincts from that made in terms of the law of desire is clearly the way in which they each conceive of the nature and dynamics of the drives, not the way in which they conceive of power. They both rely on a common representation of power which, depending on the use made of it and the position it is accorded with respect to desire, leads to two contrary results: either to the promise of a "liberation," if power is seen as having only an external hold on desire, or if it is constitutive of desire itself, to the affirmation; you are always-already trapped.

☞ ☞ ☞

Underlying both the general theme that power represses sex and the idea that the law constitutes desire, one encounters the same putative mechanics of power.

It is defined in a strangely restrictive way, in that, to begin with, this power is poor in resources, sparing of its methods, monotonous in the tactics it utilizes, incapable of invention, and seemingly doomed always to repeat itself.

. . . One remains attached to a certain image of power-law, of power-sovereignty, which was traced out by the theoreticians of right and the monarchic institution. It is this image that we must break free of, that is, of the theoretical privilege of law and sovereignty, if we wish to analyze power within the concrete and historical framework of its operation. We must construct an analytic of power that no longer takes law as a model and a code.

DOMAIN

Sexuality must not be described as a stubborn drive, by nature alien and of necessity disobedient to a power which exhausts itself trying to subdue it and often fails to control it entirely. It appears rather as an especially dense transfer point for relations of power: between men and women, young people and old people, parents and offspring, teachers and students, priests and laity, an administration and a population. Sexuality is not the most intractable element in power relations, but rather one of those endowed with the greatest instrumentality; useful for the greatest number of maneuvers and capable of serving as a point of support, as a linchpin, for the most varied strategies.

In a first approach to the problem, it seems that we can distinguish four great strategic unities which, beginning in the eighteenth century, formed specific mechanisms of knowledge and power centering on sex.

1. *A hysterization of women's bodies:* a threefold process whereby the feminine body was analyzed—qualified and disqualified—is being thoroughly saturated with sexuality, whereby it was integrated into the sphere of medical practices, by reason of a pathology intrinsic to it; whereby, finally, it was placed in organic communication with the social body (whose regulated fecundity it was supposed to ensure), the family space (of which it had to be a substantial and functional element), and the life of children (which it produced and had to guarantee, by virtue of a biologico-moral responsibility lasting through the entire period of the children's education): the Mother, with her negative image of "nervous woman," constituted the most visible form of this hysterization.
2. *A pedagogization of children's sex:* a double assertion that practically all children indulge or are prone to indulge in sexual activity; and that, being unwarranted, at the same time "natural" and "contrary to nature," this

sexual activity posed physical and moral, individual and collective dangers; children were defined as "preliminary" sexual beings, on this side of sex, yet within it, astride a dangerous dividing line. Parents, families, educators, doctors, and eventually psychologists would have to take charge, in a continuous way, of this precious and perilous, dangerous and endangered sexual potential: this pedagogization was especially evident in the war against onanism, which in the West lasted nearly two centuries.

3. *A socialization of procreative behavior:* an economic socialization via all the incitements and restrictions, the "social" and fiscal measures brought to bear on the fertility of couples; a political socialization achieved through the "responsibilization" of couples with regard to the social body as a whole (which had to be limited or on the contrary reinvigorated), and a medical socialization carried out by attributing a pathogenic value—for the individual and the species—to birth-control practices.

4. *A psychiatrization of perverse pleasure:* the sexual instinct was isolated as a separate biological and psychical instinct; a clinical analysis was made of all the forms of anomalies by which it could be afflicted—it was assigned a role of normalization or pathologization with respect to all behavior; and finally, a corrective technology was sought for these anomalies.

Four figures emerged from this preoccupation with sex, which mounted throughout the nineteenth century—four privileged objects of knowledge, which were also targets and anchorage points for the ventures of knowledge; the hysterical woman, the masturbating child, the Malthusian couple, and the perverse adult. Each of them corresponded to one of these strategies which, each in its own way, invested and made use of the sex of women, children, and men.

What was at issue in these strategies? . . . In actual fact, what was involved, rather, was the very production of sexuality. Sexuality must not be thought of as a kind of natural given which power tries to hold in check, or as an obscure domain which knowledge tries gradually to uncover. It is the name that can be given to a historical construct.

It is in the sexual "domains" that power, via science, has expanded its realm—the hysterization of women's bodies, the pedagogization of children's sex, the socialization of procreative behavior, and the psychiatrization of perverse pleasures—that Foucault most closely involves the issue of gender in the history of sex. Note that three of these four tactics use women; hence the whole explosion of sex and sexual discourse is weighted to the feminine. In this sense, according to Foucault, women through history have, despite their increased public and economic activity, been used in the service of the expansion of power.

However, Foucault also makes an important distinction in the preceding passages between a notion of power as "repressive"—which he calls the "juridico-discursive" model—and a notion of power as strategic, expansive, malleable, an "omnipresent" power into which individuals may tap in order to expand their own freedom and pleasure. Foucault reaches two conclusions: 1) the deployment of sexuality and its discourse is specifically characteristic of Bourgeois societies, and 2) the deployment of sexuality is not a radical change in the nature of power from that of the middle ages, it is just a tactical shift. The book closes on a hopeful note, however: Foucault there gives a somewhat utopian discussion of "The Right of Death and the Power over Life" that can be gained when his new notion of power is fully exploited by individuals. The implication is that power is ultimately a freeing force, which may eventually break down the very boundary between life and death.

4. LUCE IRIGARAY
(French)

The "seminal" figure in French Feminism, (influenced by Nietzsche, Freud, and Derrida), Irigaray was trained in Freudian psychoanalysis. Her 1974 *Speculum of the Other Woman,* however, set her at odds with Freudians, but it did catapult her to fame among academic feminists. With doctorates in both linguistics and philosophy, in addition to her practice, Irigaray gives her work a stunning interdisciplinary flavor, comfortably meandering through the traditional divisions following the question of woman wherever it leads her.

THIS SEX WHICH IS NOT ONE (1977)

In this collection of brief essays, Irigaray develops some of the themes raised in her provocative *Speculum of the Other Woman.* Her essentialist feminist challenges are raised against what she calls the "phallomorphism"—the masculine structure—of Freudian theory, Western academic discourse, and Western economic assumptions. Her hope is to unbalance these systems in order to make room for a language that is really "woman's."

THIS SEX . . .

The second chapter of the book shares its title with the work as a whole and lays out Irigaray's claim that what she calls "the feminine imaginary" has a plural, amorphous sexuality that is not adequately expressed in a traditional sexual imagery—or even in a traditional metaphysics—based on single, identifiable entities. This traditional imagery she calls "phallomorphic"—indicating that its objects (perhaps the very notion of an "object") take the phallus as their metaphorical base.

2 THIS SEX WHICH IS NOT ONE

Female sexuality has always been conceptualized on the basis of masculine parameters. Thus the opposition between "masculine" clitoral activity and "feminine" vaginal passivity, an opposition which Freud—and many others— saw as stages, or alternatives, in the development of a sexually "normal" woman, seems rather too clearly required by the practice of male sexuality.

For the clitoris is conceived as a little penis pleasant to masturbate so long as castration anxiety does not exist (for the boy child), and the vagina is valued for the "lodging" it offers the male organ when the forbidden hand has to find a replacement for pleasure-giving.

In these terms, woman's erogenous zones never amount to anything but a clitoris-sex that is not comparable to the noble phallic organ, or a hold-envelope that serves to sheathe and massage the penis in intercourse: a non-sex, or a masculine organ turned back upon itself, self-embracing.

About woman and her pleasure, this view of the sexual relation has nothing to say. Her lot is that of "lack," "atrophy" (of the sexual organ), and "penis envy," the penis being the only sexual organ of recognized value. Thus she attempts by every means available to appropriate that organ for herself: through her somewhat servile love of the father-husband capable of giving her one, through her desire for a child-penis, preferably a boy, through access to the cultural values still reserved by right to males alone and therefore always masculine, and so on. Woman lives her own desire only as the expectation that she may at last come to possess an equivalent of the male organ.

Yet all this appears quite foreign to her own pleasure, unless it remains within the dominant phallic economy. Thus, for example, woman's autoeroticism is very different from man's. In order to touch himself, man needs an instrument: his hand, a woman's body, language . . . And this self-caressing requires at least a minimum of activity. As for woman, she touches herself in and of herself without any need for mediation, and before there is any way to distinguish activity from passivity. Woman "touches herself" all the time, and moreover no one can forbid her to do so, for her genitals are formed of two lips in continuous contact. Thus, within herself, she is already two—but not divisible into one(s)—that caress each other.

☞ ☞ ☞

Woman, in this sexual imaginary, is only a more or less obliging prop for the enactment of man's fantasies. That she may find pleasure there in that role, by proxy, is possible, even certain. But such pleasure is above all a masochistic prostitution of her body to a desire that is not her own, and it leaves her in a familiar state of dependency upon man.

☞ ☞ ☞

. . . Woman's desire would not be expected to speak the same language as man's; woman's desire has doubtless been submerged by the logic that has dominated the West since the time of the Greeks.

Within this logic, the predominance of the visual, and of the discrimination and individualization of form, is particularly foreign to female eroticism. Woman takes pleasure more from touching than from looking, and her entry into a dominant scopic economy signifies, again, her consignment to passivity: she is to be the beautiful object of contemplation. While her body finds itself thus eroticized, and called to a double movement of exhibition and of chaste retreat in order to stimulate the drives of the "subject," her sexual organ represents *the horror of nothing to see.* A defect in this systematics of representation and desire. A "hole" in its scoptophilic lens. It is already evident in Greek statuary that this nothing-to-see has to be excluded, rejected, from such a scene of representation. Woman's genitals are simply absent, masked, sewn back up inside their "crack."

This organ which has nothing to show for itself also lacks a form of its own. And if woman takes pleasure precisely from this incompleteness of form which allows her organ to touch itself over and over again, indefinitely, by itself, that pleasure is denied by a civilization that privileges phallomorphism. The value granted to the only definable form excludes the one that is in play in female autoeroticism. The *one* of form, of the individual, of the (male) sexual organ, of the proper name, of the proper meaning ... supplants, while separating and dividing, that contact of *at least two* (lips) which keeps woman in touch with herself, but without any possibility of distinguishing what is touching from what is touched.

Whence the mystery that woman represents in a culture claiming to count everything, to number everything by units, to inventory everything as individualities. *She is neither one nor two.* Rigorously speaking, she cannot be identified either as one person, or as two. She resists all adequate definition. Further, she has no "proper" name. And her sexual organ, which is not *one* organ, is counted as *none.* The negative, the underside, the reverse of the only visible and morphologically designatable organ (even if the passage from erection to detumescence does pose some problems): the penis.

Perhaps it is time to return to that repressed entity, the female imaginary. So woman does not have a sex organ? She has at least two of them, but they are not identifiable as ones. Indeed, she has many more. Her sexuality, always at least double, goes even further: it is *plural.* Is this the way culture is seeking to characterize itself now? Is this the way texts write themselves/are written now? Without quite knowing what censorship they are evading? Indeed, woman's pleasure does not have to choose between clitoral activity and vaginal passivity, for example. The pleasure of the vaginal caress does not have to be substituted for that of the clitoral caress. They each contribute, irreplaceably, to woman's pleasure. Among other caresses . . . Fondling the breasts, touching the vulva, spreading the lips, stroking the posterior wall of the vagina, brushing against the mouth of the uterus, and so on. To evoke only a few of the most specifically female pleasures. Pleasures which are somewhat misunderstood in sexual difference as it is imagined—or not imagined, the other sex being only the indispensable complement to the only sex.

But *woman has sex organs more or less everywhere.* She finds pleasure almost anywhere. Even if we refrain from invoking the hystericization of her entire body, the geography of her pleasure is far more diversified, more multiple in its differences, more complex, more subtle, than is commonly imagined—in an imaginary rather too narrowly focused on sameness.

"She" is indefinitely other in herself. This is doubtless why she is said to be whimsical, incomprehensible, agitated, capricious . . . not to mention her language, in which "she" sets off in all directions leaving "him" unable to discern the coherence of any meaning. Hers are contradictory words, somewhat mad from the standpoint of reason, inaudible for whoever listens to them with ready-made grids, with a fully elaborated code in hand. For in what she says, too, at least when she dares, woman is constantly touching herself. She steps ever so slightly aside from herself with a murmur, an exclamation, a whisper, a sentence left unfinished... When she returns, it is to set off again from elsewhere. From another point of pleasure, or of pain. One would have to listen with another ear, as if hearing an *"other meaning" always in the process of weaving itself, of embracing itself with words, but also of getting rid of words in order not to become fixed, congealed in them.* For if "she" says something, it is not, is already no longer, identical with what she means. What she says is never identical with anything, moreover; rather, it is contiguous. *It touches (upon).* And when it strays too far from that proximity, she breaks off and starts over at "zero": her body-sex.

It is useless, then, to trap women in the exact definition of what they mean, to make them repeat (themselves) so that it will be clear; they are already elsewhere in that discursive machinery where you expected to surprise them. They have not turned within themselves. Which must not be understood in the same way as within yourself. They do not have the interiority that you have, the one you perhaps suppose they have. Within themselves means *within the intimacy of that silent, multiple, diffuse touch.* And if you ask them insistently what they are thinking about, they can only reply: Nothing. Everything.

Thus what they desire is precisely nothing, and at the same time everything. Always something more and something else besides that *one*—sexual organ, for example—that you give them, attribute to them. Their desire is often interpreted, and feared, as a sort of insatiable hunger, a voracity that will swallow you whole. Whereas it really involves a different economy more than anything else, one that upsets the linearity of a project, undermines the goal-object of a desire, diffuses the polarization toward a single pleasure, disconcerts fidelity to a single discourse . . .

⌒ ⌒ ⌒

Woman always remains several, but she is kept from dispersion because the other is already within her and is autoerotically familiar to her. Which is not to say that she appropriates the other for herself, that she reduces it to her own property. Ownership and property are doubtless quite foreign to the feminine.

At least sexually. But not *nearness*. Nearness so pronounced that it makes all discrimination of identity, and thus all forms of property, impossible. Woman derives pleasure from what is *so near that she cannot have it, nor have herself.* She herself enters into a ceaseless exchange of herself with the other without any possibility of identifying either. This puts into question all prevailing economies: their calculations are irremediably stymied by woman's pleasure, as it increases indefinitely from its passage in and through the other.

However, in order for woman to reach the place where she takes pleasure as woman, a long detour by way of the analysis of the various systems of oppression brought to bear upon her is assuredly necessary. And claiming to fall back on the single solution of pleasure risks making her miss the process of going back through a social practice that *her* enjoyment requires.

For woman is traditionally a use-value for man, an exchange value among men; in other words, a commodity. As such, she remains the guardian of material substance, whose price will be established, in terms of the standard of their work of their need/desire, by "subjects": workers, merchants, consumers. Women are marked phallically by their fathers, husbands, procurers. And this branding determines their value in sexual commerce. Woman is never anything but the locus of a more or less competitive exchange between two men, including the competition for the possession of mother earth.

How can this object of transaction claim a right to pleasure without removing her/itself from established commerce?

⁀ ⁀ ⁀

A woman's development, however radical it may seek to be, would thus not suffice to liberate woman's desire. And to date no political theory or political practice has resolved, or sufficiently taken into consideration, this historical problem, even though Marxism has proclaimed its importance. But women do not constitute, strictly speaking, a class, and their dispersion among several classes makes their political struggle complex, their demands sometimes contradictory.

There remains, however, the condition of underdevelopment arising from women's submission by and to a culture that oppresses them, uses them, makes of them a medium of exchange, with very little profit to them. Except in the quasi monopolies of masochistic pleasure, the domestic labor force, and reproduction. The powers of slaves? Which are not negligible powers, moreover. For where pleasure is concerned, the master is not necessarily well served. Thus to reverse the relation, especially in the economy of sexuality, does not seem a desirable objective.

Building upon deBeauvoir's claim (excerpted in Part Five) that "woman is the other," Irigaray claims that woman is "indefinitely other in herself." For Irigaray, woman's "plural" sense of herself and of the world, means that she is self-reliant—sexually as well as psychologically—because she contains within her many different ways of conducting and adapting herself. Following the Freudian methodology of identifying the psyche through its internal "language"—its system of metaphors and symbols—Irigaray interprets the male and female genitals themselves as symbols, each of which yields its own interpretive schema for approaching the world. Each such schema, then—one guided by the image of the penis and one guided by the image of the vagina, clitoris, and lips—orients a worldview which may be called "masculine" (or "phallomorphic") or "feminine," respectively.

Notably, and this follows the metaphor of the "speculum" in her earlier work, the "phallomorphic" worldview is for her associated with *visual* imagery, while the "feminine imaginary" is *audial* and *tactile*. As Irigaray seems to understand it, it is through vision that men's primary sexuality is drawn out, and it is through vision that we experience the world as a set of singular, identifiable objects in space. Women, on the other hand, Irigaray claims, are excited primarily by sound and touch, senses through which the world appears more like a shapeless set of movements and feelings; of waves, echoes and re-echoes, pleasures and pains. It is this multiple, constantly moving, and ambiguous experience of the world that Irigaray implies is femininity, and much of the rest of her work is devoted to exploring its logic and its possibilities.

THE "MECHANICS" OF FLUIDS

In the sixth essay, "The 'Mechanics' of Fluids," Irigaray attempts to describe in words this female, audio-tactile imaginary, to distinguish it from the "phallomorphic" imaginary, and to draw out the psychological, theoretical, and economic consequences of each.

> It is already getting around—at what rate? in what contexts? in spite of what resistances?—that women diffuse themselves according to modalities scarcely compatible with the framework of the ruling symbolics. Which doesn't happen without causing some turbulence, we might even say some whirlwinds, that ought to be reconfined within solid walls of principle, to keep them from spreading to infinity. Otherwise they might even go so far as to disturb that third agency designated as the real—a transgression and confusion of boundaries that it is important to restore to their proper order.
>
> ⌐ ⌐ ⌐
>
> But what division is being perpetuated here between a language that is always subject to the postulates of ideality and an empirics that has forfeited all symbolization? And how can we fail to recognize that with respect to this caesura, to the schism that underwrites the purity of logic, language remains necessarily meta- "something"? Not simply in its articulation, in its utterance, here and now, by a subject, but because, owing to his own structure and unbeknownst to him, that "subject" is already repeating normative "judgments" on a nature that is resistant to such a transcription.

And how are we to prevent the very unconscious (of the) "subject" from being prorogated as such, indeed diminished in its interpretation, by a systematics that re-marks a historical "inattention" to fluids? In other words: what structuration of (the) language does not maintain a *complicity of long standing between rationality and a mechanics of solids alone?*

                            ≈ ≈ ≈

While she waits for these divine rediscoveries, a woman serves (only) as a *projective map* for the purpose of guaranteeing the totality of the system—the excess factor of its "greater than all"; she serves as *a geometric prop* for evaluating the "all" of the extension of each of its "concepts" including those that are still undetermined, serves as fixed and congealed *intervals* between their definitions in "language," and as the possibility of *establishing individual relationships* among these concepts.

All this is feasible by virtue of her "fluid" character, which has deprived her of all possibility of identity with herself within such a logic. A woman—paradoxically?—would thus serve in the proposition as the *copulative link.* But this copula turns out to have been appropriated in advance for a project of exhaustive formalization, already subjected to the constitution of the discourse of the "subject" in set(s). And the possibility that there may be several systems modulating the order of truths (of the subject) in no way contradicts the postulate of a syntactic equivalence among these various systems. All of which have excluded from their mode of symbolization *certain properties of real fluids.*

                            ≈ ≈ ≈

Thus if every psychic economy is organized around the phallus (or Phallus), we may ask what this primacy owes to a teleology of reabsorption of fluid in a solidified form. The lapses of the penis do not contradict this: the penis would only be the empirical representative of a model of ideal functioning; all desire would tend toward being or having this ideal. Which is not to say that the phallus has a simple status as transcendental "object," but that it dominates, as a keystone, a system of the economy of desire marked by idealism.

And, to be sure, the "subject" cannot rid itself of it in a single thrust. Certain naive statements about (religious?) conversion—also a matter of language—to materialism are the proof and symptom of this.

From there to standardizing the psychic mechanism according to laws that subject sexuality to the absolute power of form. . . .

For isn't that what we are still talking about? And how, so long as this prerogative lasts, can any articulation of sexual difference be possible? *Since what is in excess with respect to form—for example, the feminine sex—is necessarily rejected as beneath or beyond the system currently in force.* .

                            ≈ ≈ ≈

And yet that woman–thing speaks. But not "like," not "the *same*," not "identical with itself" nor to any x, etc. Not a "subject," unless transformed by phallocratism. It speaks "fluid," even in the paralytic undersides of that economy. Symptoms of an "it can't flow any more, it can't touch itself . . ." Of which one may understand that she imputes it to the father, and to his morphology.

Yet one must know how to listen otherwise than in good form(s) to hear what it says. That it is continuous, compressible, dilatable, viscous, conductible, diffusable, . . . That it is unending, potent and impotent owing to its resistance to the countable; that it enjoys and suffers from a greater sensitivity to pressures; that it changes—in volume or in force, for example—according to the degree of heat; that it is, in its physical reality, determined by friction between two infinitely neighboring entities—dynamics of the near and not of the proper, movements coming from the quasi contact between two unities hardly definable as such (in a coefficient of viscosity measured in poises, from Poiseuille, *sic*), and not energy of a finite system; that it allows itself to be easily traversed by flow by virtue of its conductivity to currents coming from other fluids or exerting pressure through the walls of a solid; that it mixes with bodies of a like state, sometimes dilutes itself in them in an almost homogeneous manner, which makes the distinction between the one and the other problematical; and furthermore that it is already diffuse "in itself," which disconcerts any attempt at static identification . . .

In the idea of a physics of fluids, Irigaray offers an image that perhaps explains many things about femininity, including its seeming inscrutability, or inapplicability, to so much academic theory. For as Irigaray points out, a flow of water can certainly be very powerful and active, and yet its power and activity are not adequately understood, and may even be overlooked, by a non-fluid mechanics. Thus, Irigaray implies, women's power and activity may be overlooked by theories in which power is understood in terms of the masses of solid objects, or where activity is understood in terms of the velocity of solid objects. These latter interpretive frameworks, she implies, are founded in a familiarity with the structure and movements of the penis, making our traditional physics—and indeed our metaphysics, psychology, and economy—"phallomorphic."

5. HELENE CIXOUS
(French, 1937–)

Cixous is a "French Feminist" often associated with Irigaray and others influenced by Freud, Nietzsche, and Derrida. She differs from these other feminist thinkers primarily in her less academic, more polemical and flamboyant style. Bold and provocative, Cixous is ever interested in the physical and political power of writing, to which theme she has returned in many of her works, which include a work on

opera, an extensive analysis of James Joyce, and an epic play on the life of Prince
Sihanouk of Cambodia.

"THE LAUGH OF THE MEDUSA" (1976)

Essentially a manifesto for a feminine revolution through writing, this famous and
explosive essay attempts to identify the expressive power of women, even as it
claims that such power is amorphous and multiple. Cixous's exercise seems to be
founded in the claim that women do and must "write their *bodies*"—those movable,
multiple sources of energy that in the most fundamental sense define them as women.

> I shall speak about women's writing: about *what it will do*. Woman must write
> her self: must write about women and bring women to writing, from which they
> have been driven away as violently as from their bodies—for the same reasons,
> by the same law, with the same fatal goal. Woman must put herself into the
> text—as into the world and into history—by her own movement.

☞ ☞ ☞

Thus, as there are no grounds for establishing a discourse, but rather an arid
millennial ground to break, what I say has at least two sides and two aims: to
break up, to destroy, and to foresee the unforeseeable, to project.

I write this as a woman, toward women. When I say "woman," I'm speaking
of woman in her inevitable struggle against conventional man; and of a universal
woman subject who must bring women to their senses and to their meaning in
history. But first it must be said that in spite of the enormity of the repression
that has kept them in the "dark"—that dark which people have been trying to
make them accept as their attribute—there is, at this time, no general woman,
no one typical woman. What they have *in common* I will say. But what strikes
me is the infinite richness of their individual constitutions: you can't talk about
a female sexuality, uniform, homogeneous, classifiable into codes—any more
than you can talk about one unconscious resembling another. Women's
imaginary is inexhaustible, like music, painting, writing: their stream of
phantasms is incredible.

I have been amazed more than once by a description a woman gave me of a
world all her own which she had been secretly haunting since early childhood. A
world of searching, the elaboration of a knowledge, on the basis of a systematic
experimentation with the bodily functions, a passionate and precise interrogation
of her erotogeneity. This practice, extraordinarily rich and inventive, in
particular as concerns masturbation, is prolonged or accompanied by a
production of forms, a veritable aesthetic activity, each stage of rapture
inscribing a resonant vision, a composition, something beautiful. Beauty will no
longer be forbidden.

I wished that woman would write and proclaim this unique empire so that
other women, other unacknowledged sovereigns, might exclaim: I, too,
overflow; my desires have invented new desires, my body knows unheard-of

songs. Time and again I, too, have felt so full of luminous torrents that I could burst—burst with forms much more beautiful than those which are put up in frames and sold for a stinking fortune. And I, too, said nothing, showed nothing; I didn't open my mouth, I didn't repaint my half of the world. I was ashamed. I was afraid, and I swallowed my shame and my fear. I said to myself: You are mad! What's the meaning of these waves, these floods, these outbursts? Where is the ebullient, infinite woman who, immersed as she was in her naivete, kept in the dark about herself, led into self-disdain by the great arm of parental-conjugal phallocentrism, hasn't been ashamed of her strength? Who, surprised and horrified by the fantastic tumult of her drives (for she was made to believe that a well-adjusted normal woman has a . . . divine composure), hasn't accused herself of being a monster? Who, feeling a funny desire stirring inside her (to sing, to write, to dare, to speak, in short, to bring out something new), hasn't thought she was sick? Well, her shameful sickness is that she resists death, that she makes trouble.

And why don't you write? Write! Writing is for you, you are for you; your body is yours, take it. I know why you haven't written. (And why I didn't write before the age of twenty-seven.) Because writing is at once too high, too great for you, it's reserved for the great—that is, for "great men"; and it's "silly." Besides, you've written a little, but in secret. And it wasn't good, because it was in secret, and because you punished yourself for writing, because you didn't go all the way; or because you wrote, irresistible, as when we would masturbate in secret, not to go further, but to attenuate the tension a bit, just enough to take the edge off. And then as soon as we come, we go and make ourselves feel guilty— so as to be forgiven; or to forget, to bury it until the next time.

Write, let no one hold you back, let nothing stop you; not man; not the imbecilic capitalist machinery, in which publishing houses are the crafty, obsequious relayers of imperatives handed down by an economy that works against us and off our backs; and not *yourself.* Smug-faced readers, managing editors, and big bosses don't like the true texts of women—female-sexed texts. That kind scares them.

I write woman: woman must write woman. And man, man: So only an oblique consideration will be found here of man; it's up to him to say where his masculinity and femininity are at: this will concern us once men have opened their eyes and seen themselves clearly.

◠ ◠ ◠

Men have committed the greatest crime against women. Insidiously, violently, they have led them to hate women, to be their own enemies, to mobilize their immense strength against themselves, to be the executants of their virile needs. They have made for women an antinarcissism! A narcissism which loves itself only to be loved for what women haven't got! They have constructed the infamous logic of antilove.

We the precocious, we the repressed of culture, our lovely mouths gagged with pollen, our wind knocked out of us, we the labyrinths, the ladders, the trampled spaces, the bevies—we are black and we are beautiful.

We're stormy, and that which is ours breaks loose from us without our fearing any debilitation. Our glances, our smiles, are spent; laughs exude from all our mouths; our blood flows and we extend ourselves without ever reaching an end; we never hold back our thoughts, our signs, our writing; and we're not afraid of lacking.

What happiness for us who are omitted, brushed aside at the scene of inheritances; we inspire ourselves and we expire without running out of breath, we are everywhere!

From now on, who, if we say so, can say no to us? We've come back from always.

It is time to liberate the New Woman from the Old by coming to know her—by loving her for getting by, for getting beyond the Old without delay, by going out ahead of what the New Woman will be, as an arrow quits the bow with a movement that gathers and separates the vibrations musically, in order to be more than her self.

I say that we must, for, with a few rare exceptions, there has not yet been any writing that inscribes femininity; exceptions so rare, in fact, that, after plowing through literature across languages, cultures, and ages, one can only be startled at this vain scouting mission. It is well known that the number of women writers (while having increased very slightly from the nineteenth century on) has always been ridiculously small. This is a useless and deceptive fact unless from their species of female writers we do not first deduct the immense majority whose workmanship is in no way different from male writing, and which either obscures women or reproduces the classic representations of women (as sensitive—intuitive—dreamy, etc.)

Let me insert here a parenthetical remark. I mean it when I speak of male writing. I maintain unequivocally that there is such a thing as *marked* writing; that, until now, far more extensively and repressively than is ever suspected or admitted, writing has been run by a libidinal and cultural—hence political, typically masculine—economy; that this is a locus where the repression of women has been perpetuated, over and over, more or less consciously, and in a manner that's frightening since it's often hidden or adorned with the mystifying charms of fiction; that this locus has grossly exaggerated all the signs of sexual opposition (and not sexual difference), where woman has never *her* turn to speak—this being all the more serious and unpardonable in that writing is precisely *the very possibility of change,* the space that can serve as a springboard for subversive thought, the precursory movement of a transformation of social and cultural structures.

☞ ☞ ☞

But only the poets—not the novelists, allies of representationalism. Because poetry involves gaining strength through the unconscious and because the unconscious, that other limitless country, is the place where the repressed manage to survive: women, or as Hoffmann would say, fairies.

She must write her self, because this is the invention of a *new insurgent* writing which, when the moment of her liberation has come, will allow her to carry out the indispensable ruptures and transformations in her history, first at two levels that cannot be separated.

   a. Individually. By writing her self, woman will return to the body which has been more than confiscated from her, which has been turned into the uncanny stranger on display—the ailing or dead figure, which so often turns out to be the nasty companion, the cause and location of inhibitions. Censor the body and you censor breath and speech at the same time.

   Write your self. Your body must be heard. Only then will the immense resources of the unconscious spring forth. Our naphtha will spread, throughout the world, without dollars—black or gold—nonassessed values that will change the rules of the old game.

⌒ ⌒ ⌒

   b. An act that will also be marked by woman's *seizing* the occasion to *speak,* hence her shattering entry into history, which has always been based *on her suppression.* To write and thus to forge for herself the antilogos weapon. To become *at will* the taker and initiator, for her own right, in every symbolic system, in every political process.

   It is time for women to start scoring their feats in written and oral language.

⌒ ⌒ ⌒

   Listen to a woman speak at a public gathering (if she hasn't painfully lost her wind). She doesn't "speak," she throws her trembling body forward; she lets go of herself, she flies; all of her passes into her voice, and it's with her body that she vitally supports the "logic" of her speech. Her flesh speaks true. She lays herself bare. In fact, she physically materializes what she's thinking; she signifies it with her body. In a certain way she *inscribes* what she's saying, because she doesn't deny her drives the intractable and impassioned part they have in speaking. Her speech, even when "theoretical" or political, is never simple or linear or "objectified," generalized: she draws her story into history.

⌒ ⌒ ⌒

   In women's speech, as in their writing, that element which never stops resonating, which, once we've been permeated by it, profoundly and imperceptibly touched by it, retains the power of moving us—that element is the song: first music from the first voice of love which is alive in every woman. Why this privileged relationship with the voice? Because no woman stockpiles as many defenses for countering the drives as does a man. You don't build walls around yourself, you don't forgo pleasure as "wisely" as he. Even if phallic mystification has generally contaminated good relationships, a woman is never far from "mother" (I mean outside her role functions: the "mother" as nonname and as source of goods). There is always within her at least a little of that good mother's milk. She writes in white ink.

   Woman for women.—There always remains in woman that force which produces/is produced by the other—in particular, the other woman. *In* her, matrix, cradler; herself giver as her mother and child; she is her own sister-daughter. You might object, "What about she who is the hysterical offspring of a bad mother?" Everything will be changed once woman gives woman to the other woman. There is hidden and always ready in woman the source; the locus for the other. The mother, too, is a metaphor. It is necessary and sufficient that the best of herself be given to woman by another woman for her to be able to love herself and return in love the body that was "born" to her. Touch me, caress me, you the living no-name, give me self as myself. The relation to the "mother," in terms of intense pleasure and violence, is curtailed no more than the relation to childhood (the child that she was, that she is, that she makes, remakes, undoes, there at the point where, the same, she others herself). Text: my body—shot through with streams of song, I don't mean the overbearing, clutchy "mother" but, rather, what touches you, the equivoice that affects you, fills your breast with an urge to come to language and launches your force; the rhythm that laughs you; the intimate recipient who makes all metaphors possible and desirable; body (body? bodies?), no more describable than god, the soul, or the Other; that part of you that leaves a space between yourself and urges you to inscribe in language your woman's style. In women there is always more or less of the mother who makes everything all right, who nourishes, and who stands up against separation; a force that will not be cut off but will knock the wind out of the codes. We will rethink womankind beginning with every form and every period of her body. The Americans remind us, "We are all Lesbians"; that is, don't denigrate woman, don't make of her what men have made of you.

⌐ ⌐ ⌐

. . . As subject for history, woman always occurs simultaneously in several places. Woman un-thinks the unifying, regulating history that homogenizes and channels forces, herding contradictions into a single battlefield. In woman, personal history blends together with the history of all women, as well as national and world history.

⌐ ⌐ ⌐

The new history is coming; it's not a dream, though it does extend beyond men's imagination, and for good reason. It's going to deprive them of their conceptual orthopedics, beginning with the destruction of their enticement machine.

It is impossible to *define* a feminine practice of writing, and this is an impossibility that will remain, for this practice can never be theorized, enclosed, coded—which doesn't mean that it doesn't exist. But it will always surpass the discourse that regulates the phallocentric system; it does and will take place in areas other than those subordinated to philosophico-theoretical domination. It will be conceived of only by subjects who are breakers of automatisms, by peripheral figures that no authority can ever subjugate.

Hence the necessity to affirm the flourishes of this writing, to give form to its movement, its never and distant byways. Bear in mind to begin with (1) that sexual opposition, which has always worked for man's profit to the point of reducing writing, too, to his laws, is only a historico-cultural limit. There is, there will be more and more rapidly pervasive now, a fiction that produces irreducible effects of femininity. (2) That it is through ignorance that most readers, critics, and writers of both sexes hesitate to admit or deny outright the possibility or the pertinence of a distinction between feminine and masculine writing. It will usually be said, thus disposing of sexual difference: either that all writing, to the extent that it materializes, is feminine; or, inversely—but it comes to the same thing—that the act of writing is equivalent to masculine masturbation (and so the woman who writes cuts herself out a paper penis); or that writing is bisexual, hence neuter, which again does away with differentiation. To admit that writing is precisely working (in) the in-between, inspecting the process of the same and of the other without which nothing can live, undoing the work of death—to admit this is first to want the two, as well as both, the ensemble of the one and the other, not fixed in sequences of struggle and expulsion or some other from of death but infinitely dynamized by an incessant process of exchange from one subject to another. A process of different subjects knowing one another and beginning one another anew only from the living boundaries of the other: a multiple and inexhaustible course with millions of encounters and transformations of the same into the other and into the in-between, from which woman takes her forms (and man, in his turn; but that's his other history.)

෧ ෧ ෧

Too bad for them if they fall apart upon discovering that women aren't men, or that the mother doesn't have one. But isn't this fear convenient for them? Wouldn't the worst be, isn't the worst, in truth, that women aren't castrated, that they have only to stop listening to the Sirens (for the Sirens were men) for history to change its meaning? You only have to look at the Medusa straight on to see her. And she's not deadly. She's beautiful and she's laughing.

Men say that there are two unrepresentable things: death and the feminine sex. That's because they need femininity to be associated with death; it's the jitters that gives them a hard-on! for themselves! They need to be afraid of us. Look at the trembling Perseuses moving backward toward us, clad in apotropes. What lovely backs! Not another minute to lose. Let's get out of here.

Let's hurry: the continent is not impenetrably dark. I've been there often. I was overjoyed one day to run into Jean Genét. It was in *Pompes funèbres*. He had come there led by his Jean. There are some men (all too few) who aren't afraid of femininity.

෧ ෧ ෧

In body.—More so than men who are coaxed toward social success, toward sublimation, women are body. More body, hence more writing. For a long time it has been in body that women have responded to persecution, to the familial-conjugal enterprise of domestication, to the repeated attempts at castrating them.

Those who have turned their tongues 10,000 times seven times before not speaking are either dead from it or more familiar with their tongues and their mouths than anyone else. Now, I-woman am going to blow up the Law, an explosion henceforth possible and ineluctable; let it be done, right now, *in* language.

≈ ≈ ≈

A feminine text cannot fail to be more than subversive. It is volcanic; as it is written it brings about an upheaval of the old property crust, carrier of masculine investments; there's no other way. There's no room for her if she's not a he. If she's a her-she, it's in order to smash everything, to shatter the framework of institutions, to blow up the law, to break up the "truth" with laughter.

For once she blazes *her* trail in the symbolic, she cannot fail to make of it the chaosmos of the "personal"—in her pronouns, her nouns, and her clique of referents. And for good reason. There will have been the long history of gynocide. This is known by the colonized peoples of yesterday, the workers, the nations, the species off whose backs the history of men has made its gold; those who have known the ignominy of persecution derive from it an obstinate future desire for grandeur; those who are locked up know better than their jailers the taste of free air. Thanks to their history, women today know (how to do and want) what men will be able to conceive of only much later. I say woman overturns the "personal," for if, by means of laws, lies, blackmail, and marriage, her right to herself has been extorted at the same time as her name, she has been able, through the very movement of mortal alienation, to see more closely the inanity of "propriety," the reductive stinginess of the masculine-conjugal subjective economy, which she doubly resists.

≈ ≈ ≈

Besides, isn't it evident that the penis gets around in my texts, that I give it place and appeal? Of course I do. I want all. I want all of me with all of him. Why should I deprive myself of a part of us? I want all of us. Woman of course has a desire for a "loving desire" and not a jealous one. But not because she is gelded; not because she's deprived and needs to be filled out, like some wounded person who wants to console herself or seek vengeance: I don't want a penis to decorate my body with. But I do desire the other for the other, whole and entire, male or female; because living means wanting everything that is, everything that lives, and wanting it alive. Castration? Let others toy with it. What's a desire originating from a lack? A pretty meager desire.

≈ ≈ ≈

Other love.—In the beginning are our differences. The new love dares for the other, wants the other, makes dizzying, precipitous flights between knowledge and invention. The woman arriving over and over again does not stand still; she's everywhere, she exchanges, she is the desire-that-gives. (Not enclosed in the paradox of the gift that takes nor under the illusion of unitary fusion. We're past that.) She comes in, comes-in-between herself me and you, between the other me where one is always infinitely more than one and more than me, without the fear of ever reaching a limit; she thrills in our becoming. And we'll keep on becoming! She cuts through defensive loves, motherages, and devourations: beyond selfish narcissism, in the moving, open, transitional space, she runs her risks. Beyond the struggle-to-the-death that's been removed to the bed, beyond the love-battle that claims to represent exchange, she scorns at an Eros dynamic that would be fed by hatred. Hatred: a heritage, again, a remainder, a duping subservience to the phallus. To love, to watch-think-seek the other in the other, to despecularize, to unhoard. Does this seem difficult? It's not impossible, and this is what nourishes life—a love that has no commerce with the apprehensive desire that provides against the lack and stultifies the strange; a love that rejoices in the exchange that multiplies. Wherever history still unfolds as the history of death, she does not tread. Opposition, hierarchizing exchange, the struggle for mastery which can end only in at least one death (one master—one slave, or two nonmasters ≠ two dead)—all that comes from a period in time governed by phallocentric values. The fact that this period extends into the present doesn't prevent woman from starting the history of life somewhere else. Elsewhere, she gives. She doesn't "know" what she's giving, she doesn't measure it; she gives, though, neither a counterfeit impression nor something she hasn't got. She gives more, with no assurance that she'll get back even some unexpected profit from what she puts out. She gives that there may be life, thought, transformation. This is an "economy" that can no longer be put in economic terms. Wherever she loves, all the old concepts of management are left behind. At the end of a more or less conscious computation, she finds not her sum but her differences. I am for you what you want me to be at the moment you look at me in a way you've never seen me before: at every instant. When I write, it's everything that we don't know we can be that is written out of me, without exclusions, without stipulation, and everything we will be calls us to the unflagging, intoxicating, unappeasable search for love. In one another we will never be lacking.

Despite Cixous's insistence that there is women's writing, distinct from men's, and despite her claims that such writing consists in inscribing the woman's body in one's written work, she admits that there are men (the best example of which, she claims, is Jean Genet) who are able to write as women. The implication of this claim is that certain qualities—to be found in her writing, women's writing, and the writing of Genet, one presumes—are exemplary of the "universal woman."

The qualities we find in Cixous's writing—caprice and paradox, as well as sexuality, challenge, passion, laughter, etc.—she claims are necessary to the real-world dissolution of what she calls "phallocentric" culture and history. Influenced—perhaps most of all among the authors of our era—by the Derridean-type claim that everything in the "world" is a kind of text, defined only in and by a discourse, Cixous implies that to rewrite the formerly phallocentric history of civilization is actually to change that history and to redirect its influence on the future.

6. CAROL GILLIGAN
(American, 1936–   )

An academic psychologist, now Professor of Human Development at Harvard University, Gilligan has attempted in all her work to expand the psychological models and assumptions prevalent in her field, by reinterpreting the data regarding women. Though not without her critics, Gilligan has become standard required reading in the study of feminist ethics and the psychology of women.

IN A DIFFERENT VOICE (1982)

In this groundbreaking book, Gilligan challenges the prevailing psychological theories of moral development. She claims that Freud's, and particularly Kohlberg's, theories take male development and male moral reasoning as their norm. This standard she calls "an ethic of principle," i.e., reasoning according to abstract rules or laws.

Kohlberg—with whom Gilligan worked as a student—had claimed that an individual's moral reason developed in six stages, from one of absolute egocentrism (in infancy) to one of abstract moral principles of duty, right, and entitlement (in an exceptionally mature adult). Few people, Kohlberg admitted, ever reached the sixth stage of moral reasoning, but women in particular almost never developed past the intermediate stage of satisfying social expectations—or so Kohlberg's analysis indicated. Gilligan argues that the reasoning exhibited by women in response to moral dilemmas posed them is not adequately assessed on Kohlberg's model. Rather, she claims, women reason about moral questions according to an "ethics of care" or "personal responsibility."

WOMEN'S PLACE IN THE MAN'S LIFE CYCLE

The first chapter of *In A Different Voice* is engaged primarily with psychological theory, analyzing the extant literature on moral development.

INTRODUCTION

This book records different modes of thinking about relationships and the association of these modes with male and female voices in psychological and literary texts and in the data of my research. The disparity between women's experience and the representation of human development, noted throughout the psychological literature, has generally been seen to signify a problem in women's development. Instead, the failure of women to fit existing models of human growth may point to a problem in the representation, a limitation in the conception of human condition, an omission of certain truths about life.

The different voice I describe is characterized not by gender but theme. Its association with women is an empirical observation, and it is primarily through women's voices that I trace its development. But this association is not absolute, and the contrasts between male and female voices are presented here to highlight a distinction between two modes of thought and to focus a problem of interpretation rather than to represent a generalization about either sex. In tracing development, I point to the interplay of these voices within each sex and suggest that their convergence marks times of crisis and change. No claims are made about the origins of the differences described or their distribution in a wider population, across cultures, or through time. Clearly, these differences arise in a social context where factors of social status and power combine with reproductive biology to shape the experience of males and females and the relations between the sexes. My interest lies in the interaction of experience and thought, in different voices and the dialogues to which they give rise, in the way we listen to ourselves and to others, in the stories we tell about our lives.

〜 〜 〜

The penchant of developmental theorists to project a masculine image, and one that appears frightening to women, goes back at least to Freud (1905), who built his theory of psychosexual development around the experiences of the male child that culminate in the Oedipus complex. In the 1920s, Freud struggled to resolve the contradictions posed for his theory by the differences in female anatomy and the different configuration of the young girl's early family relationships. After trying to fit women into his masculine conception, seeing them as envying that which they missed, he came instead to acknowledge, in the strength and persistence of women's pre-Oedipal attachments to their mothers, a developmental difference. He considered this difference in women's development to be responsible for what he saw as women's developmental failure.

Having tied the formation of the superego or conscience to castration anxiety, Freud considered women to be deprived by nature of the impetus for a clear-cut Oedipal resolution. Consequently, women's superego—the heir to the Oedipus complex—was compromised.

〜 〜 〜

Writing against the masculine bias of psychoanalytic theory, Chodorow argues that the existence of sex differences in the early experiences of individuation and relationship "does not mean that women have 'weaker' ego boundaries than men or are more prone to psychosis." It means instead that "girls emerge from this period with a basis for 'empathy' built into their primary definition of self in a way that boys do not." Chodorow thus replaces Freud's negative and derivative description of female psychology with a positive and direct account of her own: "Girls emerge with a stronger basis for experiencing another's needs or feelings as one's own (or of thinking that one is so experiencing another's needs and feelings). Furthermore, girls do not define themselves in terms of the denial of preoedipal relational modes to the same extent as do boys. Therefore, regression to these modes tends not to feel as much a basic threat to their ego. From very early, then, because they are parented by a person of the same gender ... girls come to experience themselves as less differentiated than boys, as more continuous with and related to the external object-world, and as differently oriented to their inner object-world as well."

Consequently, relationships, and particularly issues of dependency, are experienced differently by women and men. For boys and men, separation and individuation are critically tied to gender identity since separation from the mother is essential for the development of masculinity. For girls and women, issues of femininity or feminine identity do not depend on the achievement of separation from the mother or on the progress of individuation. Since masculinity is defined through separation while femininity is defined through attachment, male gender identity is threatened by intimacy while female gender identity is threatened by separation. Thus males tend to have difficulty with relationships, while females tend to have problems with individuation. The quality of embeddedness in social interaction and personal relationships that characterizes women's lives in contrast to men's, however, becomes not only a descriptive difference but also a developmental liability when the milestones of childhood and adolescent development in the psychological literature are markers of increasing separation. Women's failure to separate then becomes by definition a failure to develop.

☞ ☞ ☞

Girls, Piaget observes, have a more "pragmatic" attitude toward rules, "regarding a rule as good as long as the game repaid it." Girls are more tolerant in their attitudes toward rules, more willing to make exceptions, and more easily reconciled to innovations. As a result, the legal sense, which Piaget considers essential to moral development, "is far less developed in little girls than in boys."

☞ ☞ ☞

To Piaget's argument that children learn the respect for rules necessary for moral development by playing rule-bound games, Lawrence Kohlberg (1969) adds that these lessons are most effectively learned through the opportunities for role-taking that arise in the course of resolving disputes. Consequently, the moral lessons inherent in girls' play appear to be fewer than in boys'. Traditional girls' games like jump rope and hopscotch are turn-taking games, where competition is indirect since one person's success does not necessarily signify another's failure. Consequently, disputes requiring adjudication are less likely to occur.

☞ ☞ ☞

The problem that female adolescence presents for theorists of human development is apparent in Erikson's scheme. Erikson (1950) charts eight stages of psychosocial development, of which adolescence is the fifth. The task at this stage is to forge a coherent sense of self, to verify an identity that can span the discontinuity of puberty and make possible the adult capacity to love and work. The preparation for the successful resolution of the adolescent identity crisis is delineated in Erikson's description of the crises that characterize the preceding four stages. . . . But about whom is Erikson talking?

Once again it turns out to be the male child. For the female, Erikson (1968) says, the sequence is a bit different. She holds her identity in abeyance as she prepares to attract the man by whose name she will be known, by whose status she will be defined, the man who will rescue her from emptiness and loneliness by filling "the inner space." While for men, identity precedes intimacy and generativity in the optimal cycle of human separation and attachment, for women these tasks seem instead to be fused. Intimacy goes along with identity, as the female comes to know herself as she is known, through her relationships with others.

⌒   ⌒   ⌒

Only the initial stage of trust versus mistrust suggests the type of mutuality that Erikson means by intimacy and generativity and Freud means by genitality. The rest is separateness, with the result that development itself comes to be identified with separation, and attachments appear to be developmental impediments, as is repeatedly the case in the assessment of women.

⌒   ⌒   ⌒

"It is obvious," Virginia Woolf says, "that the values of women differ very often from the values which have been made by the other sex." Yet, she adds, "it is the masculine values that prevail." As a result, women come to question the normality of their feelings and to alter their judgments in deference to the opinion of others. In the nineteenth century novels written by women, Woolf sees at work "a mind which was slightly pulled from the straight and made to alter its clear vision in deference to external authority." The same deference to the values and opinions of others can be seen in the judgments of twentieth century women. The difficulty women experience in finding or speaking publicly in their own voices emerges repeatedly in the form of qualification and self-doubt, but also in intimations of a divided judgment, a public assessment and private assessment which are fundamentally at odds.

Yet the deference and confusion that Woolf criticizes in women derive from the values she sees as their strength. Women's deference is rooted not only in their social subordination but also in the substance of their moral concern. Sensitivity to the needs of others and the assumption of responsibility for taking care lead women to attend to voices other than their own and to include in their judgment other points of view. Women's moral weakness, manifest in an apparent diffusion and confusion of judgment, is thus inseparable from women's moral strength, an overriding concern with relationships and responsibilities. The reluctance to judge may itself be indicative of the care and concern for others that infuse the psychology of women's development and are responsible for what is generally seen as problematic in its nature.

Thus women not only define themselves in a context of human relationship but also judge themselves in terms of their ability to care. Women's place in man's life cycle has been that of nurturer, caretaker, and helpmate, the weaver of those networks of relationships on which she in turn relies. But while women have thus taken care of men, men have, in their theories of psychological development, as in their economic arrangements, tended to assume or devalue that care. When the focus on individuation and individual achievement extends into adulthood and maturity is equated with personal autonomy, concern with relationships appears as a weakness of women rather than as a human strength (Miller, 1976).

The discovery now being celebrated by men in mid-life of the importance of intimacy, relationships, and care is something that women have known from the beginning. However, because that knowledge in women has been considered "intuitive" or "instinctive," a function of anatomy coupled with destiny, psychologists have neglected to describe its development. In my research, I have found that women's moral development centers on the elaboration of that knowledge and thus delineates a critical line of psychological development in the lives of both of the sexes. The subject of moral development not only provides the final illustration of the reiterative pattern in the observation and assessment of sex differences in the literature on human development, but also indicates more particularly why the nature and significance of women's development has been for so long obscured and shrouded in mystery.

Kohlberg's (1958, 1981) six stages that describe the development of moral judgment from childhood to adulthood are based empirically on a study of eighty-four boys whose development Kohlberg has followed for a period of over twenty years. Although Kohlberg claims universality for his stage sequence, those groups not included in his original sample rarely reach his higher states (Edwards, 1975: Holstein, 1976; Simpson, 1974). Prominent among those who thus appear to be deficient in moral development when measured by Kohlberg's scale are women, whose judgments seem to exemplify the third stage of his six-stage sequence. At this stage morality is conceived in interpersonal terms and goodness is equated with helping and pleasing others. This conception of goodness is considered by Kohlberg and Kramer (1969) to be functional in the lives of mature women insofar as their lives take place in the home. Kohlberg and Kramer imply that only if women enter the traditional arena of male activity will they recognize the inadequacy of this moral perspective and progress like men toward higher stages where relationships are subordinated to rules (stage four) and rules to universal principles of justice (stages five and six).

When one begins with the study of women and derives developmental constructs from their lives, the outline of a moral conception different from that described by Freud, Piaget, or Kohlberg begins to emerge and informs a different description of development. In this conception, the moral problem arises from conflicting responsibilities rather than from competing rights and requires for its resolution a mode of thinking that is contextual and narrative rather than formal and abstract. This conception of morality as concerned with the activity of care centers moral development around the understanding of responsibility and relationships, just as the conception of morality as fairness ties moral development to the understanding of rights and rules.

This different construction of the moral problem by women may be seen as the critical reason for their failure to develop within the constraints of Kohlberg's system. Regarding all constructions of responsibility as evidence of a conventional moral understanding, Kohlberg defines the highest stages of moral development as deriving from a reflective understanding of human rights. That the morality of rights differs from the morality of responsibility in its emphasis on separation rather than connection, in its consideration of the individual rather than the relationship as primary, is illustrated by two responses to interview questions about the nature of morality. The first comes from a twenty-five-year-old man, one of the participants in Kohlberg's study:

> [What does the word morality mean to you?] *Nobody in the world knows the answer. I think it is recognizing the right of the individual, the rights of other individuals, not interfering with those rights. Act as fairly as you would have them treat you. I think it is basically to preserve the human being's right to existence. I think that is the most important. Secondly, the human being's right to do as he pleases, again without interfering with somebody else's rights.*

☞ ☞ ☞

Kohlberg (1973) cites this man's response as illustrative of the principled conception of human rights that exemplifies his fifth and sixth stages.

☞ ☞ ☞

The second response comes from a woman who participated in the rights and responsibilities study. She also was twenty-five and, at the time, a third-year law student:

> [Is there really some correct solution to moral problems, or is everybody's opinion equally right?] *No, I don't think everybody's opinion is equally right. I think that in some situations there may be opinions that are equally valid, and one could conscientiously adopt one of several courses of action. But there are other situations in which I think there are right and wrong answers, that sort of inhere in the nature of existence, of all individuals here who need to live with each other to live. We need to depend on each other, and hopefully it is not only a physical need but a need of fulfillment in ourselves, that a person's life is enriched by cooperating with other people and striving to live in harmony with everybody else, and to that end, there are right and wrong, there are things which promote that end and that move away from it, and in that way it is possible to choose in certain cases among different courses of action that obviously promote or harm that goal.*

⮐ ⮐ ⮐

Thus it becomes clear why a morality of rights and noninterference may appear frightening to women in its potential justification of indifference and unconcern. At the same time, it becomes clear why, from a male perspective, a morality of responsibility appears inconclusive and diffuse, given its insistent contextual relativism. Women's moral judgments thus elucidate the pattern observed in the description of the developmental differences between the sexes, but they also provide an alternative conception of maturity by which these differences can be assessed and their implications traced. The psychology of women that has consistently been described as distinctive in its greater orientation toward relationships and interdependence implies a more contextual mode of judgment and a different moral understanding. Given the differences in women's conceptions of self and morality, women bring to the life cycle a different point of view and order human experience in terms of different priorities.

Using Nancy Chodorow's 1974 work (see the suggested readings at the end of this chapter) as a foundation for her reinterpretation of Freud, Gilligan argues that what may look like "narcissistic" behavior when viewed according to the standard of abstract principle, may be alternatively understood as behavior in which the agent aims to respond appropriately to other people. If, as Chodorow had claimed, little girls' identities are formed through association with their caretaker, or primary love object, while little boys' are formed by separation from this parent or care-taker, then as they grow into adulthood, young men and women will form different worldviews corresponding to their different sense of self. They will differently in-terpret the moral framework of society. This is exactly what Gilligan claims is the case, finding that boys and men tend to understand the moral sphere in terms of the abstract duties, rights, and entitlements of individuals while girls and women tend to understand it as a web of interconnected and interdependent lives, negotiated over time by one's responses to others.

IMAGES OF RELATIONSHIP

Throughout the rest of the book, Gilligan demonstrates her claims through an analysis of the results of several studies, in each of which men and women face moral dilemmas at a particular stage of life. The first such study is a readministra-tion of one designed by Kohlberg. By reproducing transcripts of the interviews with Amy and Jake, two eleven-year-old participants, Gilligan allows the reader to make his or her own direct comparison between them. This adds significantly to the per-suasiveness of Gilligan's interpretation.

In 1914, with his essay "On Narcissism," Freud swallows his distaste at the thought of "abandoning observation for barren theoretical controversy" and extends his map of the psychological domain. Tracing the development of the capacity to love, which he equates with maturity and psychic health, he locates its origins in the contrast between love for the mother and love for the self. But in thus dividing the world of love into narcissism and "object" relationships, he finds that while men's development becomes clearer, women's becomes increasingly opaque. The problem arises because the contrast between mother and self yields two different images of relationships. Relying on the imagery of men's lives in charting the course of human growth, Freud is unable to trace in women the development of relationships, morality, or a clear sense of self.

☞ ☞ ☞

The shift in imagery that creates the problem in interpreting women's development is elucidated by the moral judgments of two eleven-year-old children, a boy and a girl, who see, in the same dilemma, two very different moral problems. While current theory brightly illuminates the line and the logic of the boy's thought, it casts scant light on that of the girl. The choice of a girl whose moral judgments elude existing categories of developmental assessment is meant to highlight the issue of interpretation rather than to exemplify sex differences per se. Adding a new line of interpretation, based on the imagery of the girl's thought, makes it possible not only to see development where previously development was not discerned but also to consider differences in the understanding of relationships without scaling these differences from better to worse.

The two children were in the same sixth-grade class at school and were participants in the rights and responsibilities study, designed to explore different conceptions of morality and self. The sample selected for this study was chosen to focus the variables of gender and age while maximizing developmental potential by holding constant, at a high level, the factors of intelligence, education, and social class that have been associated with moral development, at least as measured by existing scales. The two children in question, Amy and Jake, were both bright and articulate and, at least in their eleven-year-old aspirations, resisted easy categories of sex-role stereotyping, since Amy aspired to become a scientist while Jake preferred English to math. Yet their moral judgments seem initially to confirm familiar notions about differences between the sexes, suggesting that the edge girls have on moral development during the early school years gives way at puberty with the ascendance of formal logical thought in boys.

The dilemma that these eleven-year-olds were asked to resolve was one in the series devised by Kohlberg to measure moral development in adolescence by presenting a conflict between moral norms and exploring the logic of its resolution. In this particular dilemma, a man named Heinz considers whether or not to steal a drug which he cannot afford to buy in order to save the life of his wife. In the standard format of Kohlberg's interviewing procedure, the description of the dilemma itself—Heinz's predicament, the wife's disease, the druggist's refusal to lower his price—is followed by the question, "Should Heinz steal the drug?" The reasons for and against stealing are then explored through a series of questions that vary and extend the parameters of the dilemma in a way designed to reveal the underlying structure of moral thought.

Jake, at eleven, is clear from the outset that Heinz should steal the drug. Constructing the dilemma, as Kohlberg did, as a conflict between the values of property and life, he discerns the logical priority of life and uses that logic to justify his choice:

> *For one thing, a human life is worth more than money, and if the druggist only makes $1,000, he is still going to live, but if Heinz doesn't steal the drug, his wife is going to die.*

⌒ ⌒ ⌒

. . . Considering the moral dilemma to be "sort of like a math problem with humans," he sets it up as an equation and proceeds to work out the solution. Since his solution is rationally derived, he assumes that anyone following reason would arrive at the same conclusion and thus that a judge would also consider stealing to be the right thing for Heinz to do.

⌒ ⌒ ⌒

. . . While this boy's judgments at eleven are scored as conventional on Kohlberg's scale, a mixture of stages three and four, his ability to bring deductive logic to bear on the solution of moral dilemmas, to differentiate morality from law, and to see how laws can be considered to have mistakes points toward the principled conception of justice that Kohlberg equates with moral maturity.

In contrast, Amy's response to the dilemma conveys a very different impression, an image of development stunted by a failure of logic, an inability to think for herself. Asked if Heinz should steal the drug, she replies in a way that seems evasive and unsure:

> *Well, I don't think so. I think there might be other ways besides stealing it, like if he could borrow the money or make a loan or something, but he really shouldn't steal the drug—but his wife shouldn't die either.*

Asked why he should not steal the drug, she considers neither property nor law but rather the effect that theft could have on the relationship between Heinz and his wife:

> *If he stole the drug, he might save his wife then, but if he did, he might have to go to jail, and then his wife might get sicker again, and he couldn't get more of the drug, and it might not be good. So, they should really just talk it out and find some other way to make the money.*

Seeing in the dilemma not a math problem with humans but a narrative of relationships that extends over time, Amy envisions the wife's continuing need for her husband and the husband's continuing concern for his wife and seeks to respond to the druggist's need in a way that would sustain rather than sever connection. Just as she ties the wife's survival to the preservation of relationships, so she considers the value of the wife's life in a context of relationships. saying that it would be wrong to let her die because, "if she died, it hurts a lot of people and it hurts her." Since Amy's moral judgments is grounded in the belief that, "if somebody has something that would keep somebody alive, then it's not right not to give it to them," she considers the problem in the dilemma to arise not from the druggist's assertion of rights but from his failure of response.

⌒ ⌒ ⌒

. . . Seeing a world comprised of relationships rather than of people standing alone, a world that coheres through human connection rather than through systems of rules, she finds the puzzle in the dilemma to lie in the failure of the druggist to respond to the wife. Saying that "it is not right for someone to die when their life could be saved," she assumes that if the druggist were to see the consequences of his refusal to lower his price, he would realize that "he should just give it to the wife and then have the husband pay back the money later." Thus she considers the solution to the dilemma to lie in making the wife's condition more salient to the druggist or, that failing, in appealing to others who are in a position to help.

Just as Jake is confident the judge would agree that stealing is the right thing for Heinz to do, so Amy is confident that, "if Heinz and the druggist had talked it out long enough, they could reach something besides stealing."

⌒ ⌒ ⌒

Just as he relies on the conventions of logic to deduce the solution to this dilemma, assuming these conventions to be shared, so she relies on a process of communication, assuming connection and believing that her voice will be heard. Yet while his assumptions about agreement are confirmed by the convergence in logic between his answers and the questions posed, her assumptions are belied by the failure of communication, the interviewer's inability to understand her response.

⌒ ⌒ ⌒

Amy's judgments contain the insights central to an ethic of care, just as Jake's judgments reflect the logic of the justice approach. Her incipient awareness of the "method of truth," the central tenet of nonviolent conflict resolution, and her belief in the restorative activity of care, lead her to see the actors in the dilemma arrayed not as opponents in a contest of rights but as members of a network of relationships on whose continuation they all depend. Consequently her solution to the dilemma lies in activating the network by communication, securing the inclusion of the wife by strengthening rather than severing connections.

⌒ ⌒ ⌒

The contrast between a self defined through separation and a self delineated through connection, between a self measured against an abstract ideal of perfection and a self assessed through particular activities of care, becomes clearer and the implications of this contrast extend by considering the different ways these children resolve a conflict between responsibility to others and responsibility to self. The question about responsibility followed a dilemma posed by a woman's conflict between her commitments to work and to family relationships. While the details of this conflict color the text of Amy's response, Jake abstracts the problem of responsibility from the context in which it appears, replacing the themes of intimate relationship with his own imagery of explosive connection:

JAKE   AMY

(When responsibility to oneself and responsibility
to others conflict, how should one choose?)

You go about one-fourth to the others and three-fourths to yourself.

Well, it really depends on the situation. If you have a responsibility with somebody else, then you should keep it to a certain extent, but to the extent that it is really going to hurt you or stop you from doing something that you really, really want, then I think maybe you should put yourself first. But if it is your responsibility to somebody really close to you, you've just got to decide in that situation which is more important, yourself or that person, and like I said, it really depends on what kind of person you are and how you feel about the other person or persons involved.

↢ ↢ ↢

Again Jake constructs the dilemma as a mathematical equation, deriving a formula that guides the solution: one-fourth to others, three-fourths to yourself. Beginning with his responsibility to himself, a responsibility that he takes for granted, he then considers the extent to which he is responsible to others as well. Proceeding from a premise of separation but recognizing that "you have to live with other people," he seeks rules to limit interference and thus to minimize hurt.

↢ ↢ ↢

. . . To her, responsibility signifies response, an extension rather than a limitation of action. Thus it connotes an act of care rather than the restraint of aggression. Again seeking the solution that would be most inclusive of everyone's needs, she strives to resolve the dilemma in a way that "will make everybody happier."

↢ ↢ ↢

. . . To Jake, responsibility means *not doing* what he wants because he is thinking of others; to Amy, it means *doing* what others are counting on her to do regardless of what she herself wants. Both children are concerned with avoiding hurt but construe the problem in different ways—he seeing hurt to arise from the expression of aggression, she from a failure of response.

⌒ ⌒ ⌒

If aggression is tied, as women perceive, to the fracture of human connection, then the activities of care, as their fantasies suggest, are the activities that make the social world safe, by avoiding isolation and preventing aggression rather than by seeking rules to limit its extent. In this light, aggression appears no longer as an unruly impulse that must be contained but rather as a signal of a fracture of connection, the sign of a failure of relationship. From this perspective, the prevalence of violence in men's fantasies, denoting a world where danger is everywhere seen, signifies a problem in making connection, causing relationships to erupt and turning separation into a dangerous isolation. Reversing the usual mode of interpretation, in which the absence of aggression in women is tied to a problem with separation, makes it possible to see the prevalence of violence in men's stories, its odd location in the context of intimate relationships, and its association with betrayal and deceit as indicative of a problem with connection that leads relationships to become dangerous and safety to appear in separation. Then rule-bound competitive achievement situations, which for women threaten the web of connection, for men provide a mode of connection that establishes clear boundaries and limits aggression, and thus appears comparatively safe.

⌒ ⌒ ⌒

The argument Freud builds centers on the "feeling of our self, of our own ego," which "appears to us as something autonomous and unitary, marked off distinctly from everything else."

⌒ ⌒ ⌒

. . . This distinction arises through the experience of frustration when external sources of sensations evade the infant, "most of all, his mother's breast—and only reappear as a result of his screaming for help." In this screaming for help, Freud sees the birth of the self, the separation of ego from object that leads sensation to be located inside the self while others become objects of gratification.

This disengagement of self from the world outside, however, initiates not only the process of differentiation but also the search for autonomy, the wish to gain control over the sources and objects of pleasure in order to shore up the possibilities for happiness against the risk of disappointment and loss. Thus connection—associated by Freud with "infantile helplessness" and "limitless narcissism," with illusion and the denial of danger—gives way to separation.

Consequently, assertion, linked to aggression, becomes the basis for relationships. In this way, a primary separation, arising from disappointment and fueled by rage, creates a self whose relations with others or "objects" must then be protected by rules, a morality that contains this explosive potential and adjusts "the mutual relationships of human beings in the family, the state and the society."

Yet there is an intimation on Freud's part of a sensibility different from his own, of a mental state different from that upon which he premises his psychology, the "single exception" to the "primary mutual hostility of human beings," to the "aggressiveness" that "forms the basis of every relation of affection and love among people," and this exception is located in women's experience, in "the mother's relation to her male child." Once again women appear as the exception to the rule of relationships, by demonstrating a love not admixed with anger, a love arising neither from separation nor from a feeling of being at one with the external world as a whole, but rather from a feeling of connection, a primary bond between other and self. But this love of the mother cannot, Freud says, be shared by the son, who would thus "make himself dependent in a most dangerous way on a portion of the external world, namely his chosen love-object, and expose himself to extreme suffering if he should be rejected by that object or lose it through unfaithfulness or death."

⌒ ⌒ ⌒

. . . Throughout Freud's work women remain the exception to his portrayal of relationships, and they sound a continuing theme, of an experience of love which, however described—as narcissistic or as hostile to civilization—does not appear to have separation and aggression at its base. In this alternate light, the self appears neither stranded in isolation screaming for help nor lost in fusion with the entire world as a whole, but bound in an indissoluble mode of relationship that is observably different but hard to describe.

⌒ ⌒ ⌒

While the truths of psychological theory have blinded psychologists to the truth of women's experience, that experience illuminates a world which psychologists have found hard to trace, a territory where violence is rare and relationships appear safe. The reason women's experience has been so difficult to decipher or even discern is that a shift in the imagery of relationships gives rise to a problem of interpretation. The images of hierarchy and web, drawn from the texts of men's and women's fantasies and thoughts, convey different ways of structuring relationships and are associated with different views of morality and self. But these images create a problem in understanding because each distorts the other's representation. As the top of the hierarchy becomes the edge of the web and as the center of a network of connection becomes the middle of a hierarchical progression, each image marks as dangerous the place which the other defines as safe. Thus the images of hierarchy and web inform different modes of assertion and response: the wish to be alone at the top and the consequent fear that others will get too close; the wish to be at the center of connection and the consequent fear of being too far out on the edge. These disparate fears of being stranded and being caught give rise to different portrayals of achievement and affiliation, leading to different modes of action and different ways of assessing the consequences of choice.

The reinterpretation of women's experience in terms of their own imagery of relationships thus clarifies that experience and also provides a nonhierarchical vision of human connection. Since relationships, when cast in the image of hierarchy, appear inherently unstable and morally problematic, their transposition into the image of web changes an order of inequality into a structure of interconnection. But the power of the images of hierarchy and web, their evocation of feelings and their recurrence in thought, signifies the embeddedness of both of these images in the cycle of human life. The experiences of inequality and interconnection, inherent in the relation of parent and child, then give rise to the ethics of justice and care, the ideals of human relationship—the vision that self and other will be treated as of equal worth, that despite differences in power, things will be fair; the vision that everyone will be responded to and included, that no one will be left alone or hurt. These disparate visions in their tension reflect the paradoxical truths of human experience—that we know ourselves as separate only insofar as we live in connection with others, and that we experience relationship only insofar as we differentiate other from self.

Note that Gilligan's analysis is qualitative; despite her allegiance to a tradition of scientific psychology, she approaches the transcribed statements of the children almost as if they were literary texts she were interpreting. As is discernable throughout the book (e.g., the quote from Virginia Woolf), Gilligan follows Freud in her style, as the late–twentieth century genre would have her do, interspersing analyses of data with analyses of literature. Here, she reads in Amy's responses to the "Heinz dilemma" a far less rigid, more flexible, and socially-oriented moral logic than that to be found in Jake's. This leads her, not so much to abandon Freud's—or even Kohlberg's—findings as to reinterpret them, finding an equal legitimacy and a certain nobility to the female data that had perplexed her predecessors. This tone of egalitarianism marks Gilligan's feminism throughout her work; her aim is not to denigrate either the "masculine" moral logic or the theorists who described it, but rather to clarify and legitimate the alternative moral logic that she believes is common to women.

VISIONS OF MATURITY

In the last chapter of *In A Different Voice,* Gilligan makes clear that hers is a conciliatory project, not a bald advocation of her feminine "ethics of care." She claims that both "genders" of ethical reasoning—an ethics of principle and an ethics of care—are requisite to the happy moral community; and that the recognition of each is requisite to an adequate moral psychology.

As we have listened for centuries to the voices of men and the theories of development that their experience informs, so we have come more recently to notice not only the silence of women but the difficulty in hearing what they say when they speak. Yet in the different voice of women lies the truth of an ethic of care, the tie between relationship and responsibility, and the origins of aggression in the failure of connection. The failure to see the different reality of women's lives and to hear the differences in their voices stems in part from the assumption that there is a single mode of social experience and interpretation. By positing instead two different modes, we arrive at a more complex rendition of human experience which sees the truth of separation and attachment in the lives of women and men and recognizes how these truths are carried by different modes of language and thought.

To understand how the tension between responsibilities and rights sustains the dialectic of human development is to see the integrity of two disparate modes of experience that are in the end connected. While an ethic of justice proceeds from the premise of equality—that everyone should be treated the same—an ethic of care rests on the premise of nonviolence—that no one should be hurt. In the representation of maturity, both perspectives converge in the realization that just as inequality adversely affects both parties in an unequal relationship, so too violence is destructive for everyone involved. This dialogue between fairness and care not only provides a better understanding of relations between the sexes but also gives rise to a more comprehensive portrayal of adult work and family relationships.

SUGGESTED READINGS—PART SIX

Aladjem, Terry K. "The Philosopher's Prism: Foucault, Feminism and Critique."*Political Theory* 19: 277–291, 1991.

Balbus, Isaac D. "Disciplining Women: Michel Foucault and the Power of Feminist Discourse." *Praxis International* 5: 466–483, 1986.

Ben-Habib, Seyla. *Gender, Community and Postmodernism in Contemporary Ethics.* New York: Routledge, 1992.

Ben-Habib, Seyla, and Drucilla Cornell (eds). *Feminism as Critique: On the Politics of Gender.* Minneapolis: University of Minnesota Press, 1987.

Biddy, Martin. "Feminist Criticism and Foucault." *New German Critique* 27: 3–30, 1982.

Bly, Robert. *Iron John: A Book About Men.* Reading: Addison-Wesley, 1990.

Breen, Dana (ed). *The Gender Conundrum: Contemporary Psychoanalytic Perspectives on Femininity and Masculinity.* New York: Routledge, 1993.

Brell, Carl D. "Justice and Caring and the Problem of Moral Relativism: Reframing the Gender Question in Ethics." *Journal of Moral Education* 18: 97–111, 1989.

Brod, Harry. "The New Men's Studies: From Feminist Theory to Gender Scholarship." *Hypatia* 2: 179–196, 1987.

Butler, Judith. "Variations on Sex and Gender: Beauvoir, Wittig and Foucault." *Praxis International* 5: 505–516, 1986.

Calhoun, Cheshire. "Justice, Care, Gender Bias." *Journal of Philosophy* 85: 451–463, 1988.

Chanter, Tina. *Ethics of Eros: Irigaray's Rewriting of the Philosophers.* New York: Routledge, 1995.

Chodorow, Nancy. "Family Structure and Feminine Personality," in *Woman, Culture & Society,* M. Z. Rosaldo and L. Lamphere (eds). Palo Alto: Stanford University Press, 1974.

———. *The Reproduction of Mothering.* Berkeley: University of California Press, 1978.

Cixous, Helene. "The Laugh of the Medusa," in *The Signs Reader.* E. Abel and E. K. Abel (eds). Chicago: University of Chicago Press, 1983.

Conley, Verena, A. *Helene Cixous.* Toronto: University of Toronto Press, 1992.

———. *Helene Cixous: Writing the Feminine.* Lincoln: University of Nebraska Press, 1991.

Davis, William V. (ed). *Critical Essays on Robert Bly.* New York: G.K. Hall, 1992.

Diamond, Irene and Lee Quimby (eds). *Feminism and Foucault: Reflections on Resistance.* Boston: Northeastern University Press, 1988.

Erikson, Erik H. *Childhood and Society.* New York: Norton, 1950.

———. *Identity: Youth and Crisis.* New York: Norton, 1968.

Farganis, Sondra. *The Social Reconstruction of the Feminine Character.* Tottowa: Roman & Littlefield, 1986.

Flanagan, Owen. "Virtue, Sex and Gender: Some Philosophical Reflections on the Moral Psychology Debate." *Ethics* 92: 499–512, 1982.

Flanagan, Owen, and Kathryn Jackson. "Justice, Care and Gender: The Kohlberg-Gilligan Debate Revisited." *Ethics* 97: 622–637, 1987.

Flanagan, Owen, and Amelie O. Rorty (eds). *Identity, Character and Morality: Essays in Moral Psychology.* Cambridge: MIT Press, 1990.

Foucault, Michel. *The History of Sexuality: Volume I: An Introduction.* New York: Vintage, 1980.

Gilligan, Carol. *In A Different Voice.* Cambridge: Harvard University Press, 1982.

——— (ed). *Mapping the Moral Domain.* Cambridge: Harvard University Press, 1988.

Grosz, Elizabeth. *Sexual Subversions: Three French Feminists.* Boston: Allen and Unwin, 1989.

Gutting, Gary (ed). *The Cambridge Companion to Foucault.* Cambridge: Cambridge University Press, 1994.

Haas, Lynda. "Of Waters and Women: The Philosophy of Luce Irigaray." *Hypatia* 8: 1 50–159, 1993.

Harding, Sandra. "Is Gender a Variable in Conceptions of Rationality: A Survey of Issues." *Dialectica* 36: 225–242, 1982.

Harris, Victoria F. *The Incorporative Consciousness of Robert Bly.* Carbondale: Southern Illinois University Press, 1992.

Hekman, Susan. *Moral Voices, Moral Selves: Carol Gilligan and Feminist Moral Theory.* University Park: Penn State University Press, 1995.

Holmland, Christine. "The Lesbian, the Mother, the Heterosexual Lover: Irigaray's Recodings of Difference." *Feminist Studies* 17: 283–308, 1991.

Holmstrom, Nancy. "Do Women Have a Distinct Nature?" *Philosophical Forum* 14: 25–42, 1982.

Irigaray, Luce. *Speculum of the Other Woman.* Gillian C. Hill (trans). Ithaca: Cornell University Press, 1985.

———. *This Sex Which is Not One.* Catherine Porte (trans). Ithaca: Cornell University Press, 1985.

Johnson, Robert A. *Transformation: Understanding the Three Levels of Masculine Consciousness.* San Fransisco: Harper, 1991.

Keen, Sam. *Fire in the Belly: On Being a Man.* New York: Bantam, 1991.

Keller, Evelyn Fox. "The Gender-Science System: Or, Is Sex to Gender as Nature is to Science?" *Hypatia* 2: 37–49, 1987.

———. *Reflections on Gender and Science.* New Haven: Yale University Press, 1985.

Keohane, Nannerl O. "Feminist Scholarship and Human Nature." *Ethics* 93: 102–113, 1982.

Kittay, E.F. and D.T. Meyers (eds).*Women and Moral Theory.* Tottowa: Rowman & Littlefield, 1987.

Kohlberg, Lawrence. "Stage and Sequence: The Cognitive-Development Approach to Socialization," in D.A. Goslin (ed). *Handbook of Socialization Theory and Research.* Chicago: Rand McNally, 1969.

———. "Moral Stages and Moralization: The Cognitive-Developmental Approach." in T. Lickona (ed). *Moral Development and Behavior: Theory, Research and Social Issues.* New York: Holt, Rinehart and Winston, 1976.

———. *The Philosophy of Moral Development.* San Francisco: Harper & Row, 1981.

Kundera. Milan. *The Unbearable Lightness of Being.* New York: Harper Colophon, 1984.

Larrabee, Mary J. (ed). *An Ethic of Care: Feminist and Interdisciplinary Perspectives.* New York: Routledge, 1993.

Lee, Donald and Carl Stern. "Philosophy and Masculinity." *Southwest Philosophical Studies* 3: 120–125, 1978.

Leland, Dorothy. "Lacanian Analysis and French Feminism: Toward an Adequate Political Psychology." *Hypatia* 3: 81–103, 1989.

Lisak, David. "Sexual Aggression, Masculinity and Fathers." *Signs* 16, 1991.

McNay, Lois. *Foucault and Feminism: Power, Gender and the Self.* Boston: Northeastern University Press, 1993.

Marks E., and DeCourtivron, I. *New French Feminisms: An Anthology.* New York: Schocken, 1987.

Meyers, Diana T. "Personal Autonomy and the Paradox of Feminine Socialization." *Journal of Philosophy* 84: 619–629, 1987.

———. *Subjection and Subjectivity: Psychoanalytic Feminism and Moral Philosophy.* New York: Routledge, 1993.

Millett, Kate. *Sexual Politics.* Garden City: Doubleday, 1970.

Mills, P.J. *Woman, Nature and Psyche.* New Haven: Yale University Press, 1987.

Moi, Toril. *French Feminist Thought: A Reader.* New York: Blackwell, 1987.

Morrow, Franz. *Unleashing Our Unknown Selves: An Inquiry Into the Future of Femininity and Masculinity.* New York: Praeger, 1991.

Nicholson, Linda J. (ed). *Feminism—Postmodernism.* New York: Routledge, 1990.

Noddings, Nel. *Caring: A Feminine Approach to Ethics and Moral Education.* Berkeley: University of California Press, 1984.

O'Brien, John. *Milan Kundera and Feminism: Dangerous Intersections.* New York: St, Martin's, 1995.

Okin, Susan Moller, "Reason and Feeling in Thinking About Justice." *Ethics* 99: 229–249, 1989.

Oliver, Kelly. *Reading Kristeva: Unraveling the Double Bind.* Bloomington, Indiana U. Press, 1993.

Ortner, Sherry B. "Is Female to Male as Nature Is to Culture?" in *Woman, Culture & Society,* M. Z. Rosaldo and L. Lamphere (eds). Palo Alto: Stanford University Press, 1974.

Ortner, Sherry B., and Harriet Whitehead. *Sexual Meanings: The Cultural Construction of Gender and Sexuality.* Cambridge: Cambridge University Press, 1981.

Pateman, Carole and Elizabeth Grosz (eds). *Feminist Challenges.* Boston: Northeastern University Press, 1986.

Piaget, Jean. *Six Psychological Studies.* New York: Viking Books, 1968.

———. *Structuralism.* New York: Basic Books, 1970.

Pleck, Joseph H. *The Myth of Masculinity.* Cambridge: MIT Press, 1981.

Plumwood, Val. "Do We Need a Sex/Gender Distinction?" *Radical Philosophy* 51: 2–11, 1989.

———. "Women, Humanity and Nature." *Radical Philosophy* 48: 16–24, 1988.

Rajchman, John. *Michel Foucault: The Freedom of Philosophy.* New York: Columbia University Press, 1985.

Ramazanoglu, Caroline (ed). *Up Against Foucault: Explorations of Some Tensions Between Foucault and Feminism.* New York: Routledge, 1993.

Rooney, Phyllis. "A Different Different Voice: On The Feminist Challenge in Moral Theory." *Philosophical Forum* 22: 335–361, 1991.

Rosaldo, Michelle Zimbalist and Louise Lamphere. *Woman, Culture & Society.* Calfornia: Stanford University Press, 1974.

Ross, Stephen David. *Plenishment in the Earth: An Ethic of Inclusion.* Albany: State University of New York Press, 1995.

Sawicki, Jana. *Discipling Foucault: Feminism, Power and the Body.* New York: Routledge, 1991.

Schoenewolf, Gerald. *Sexual Animosity Between Men and Women.* Northvale: Aronson, 1989.

Sher, George. "Our Preferences, Ourselves." *Philosophy and Public Affairs* 12: 34–50, 1983.

Simons, Jon. *Foucault and the Political.* New York: Routledge, 1995.

Tannen, Deborah. *That's Not What I Meant!* New York: Morrow, 1986.

———. *You Just Don't Understand.* New York: Ballantine Books, 1991.

Treblicot, J. (ed). *Mothering Essays in Feminine Theory.* Tottowa: Rowman and Allenheld, 1984.

Valverde, Mariane. "Beyond Gender Dangers and Private Pleasures: Theory and Ethics in the Sex Debates." *Feminist Studies* 15: 237–254, 1989.

Walker, Margaret Urban. "What Does the Different Voice Say: Gilligan's Women and Moral Psychology." *Journal of Value Inquiry* 23: 123–134, 1989.

Whitbeck, Caroline. "Theories of Sex Difference." *Philosophical Forum* 5: 54–80, 1973.

Whitford, Margaret. *Luce Irigaray: Philosophy In the Feminine.* New York: Routledge, 1991.

Whitford, Margaret, C. Burke and N. Shore (eds). *Engaging With Irigaray: Feminist Philosophy and Modern European Thought.* New York: Columbia University Press, 1994.

PERMISSIONS AND ACKNOWLEDGMENTS

The Works and Days; Theogony; The Shield of Herakles, by Hesiod, translated by Richard Lattimore, The University of Michigan Press.

Excerpts Totalling 12 Pages From *The Odyssey Of Homer* By Richmond Lattimore. Copyright ©1965, 1967 By Richmond Lattimore. Copyright Renewed. Reprinted by permission of HarperCollins Publishers, Inc.

Kenneth Sylvan Guthrie, *The Pythagorean Sourcebook and Library,* © 1988, Phanes Press. Reprinted by permission.

Reprinted by permission of the publishers from *Ancilla to the Pre-Socratic Philosophers* by Kathleen Freeman, Cambridge, Mass.: Harvard University Press, 1948.

Excerpts from *Oresteia,* by Aeschylus, trans./ed. by Hugh Lloyd-Jones. Copyright ©1979 Hugh Lloyd-Jones. Reprinted by permission of University of California Press.

Agamemnon, The Libation Bearers, The Eumenides, from *The Oresteia* by Aeschylus and Robert Fagles, translator, translated by Robert Fagles, Translation copyright ©1966, 1967, 1975 by Robert Fagles. Used by permission of Viking Penguin, a division of Penguin Books USA Inc.

Oedipus the King by Sophocles, *Antigone* by Sophocles, from *Three Theban Plays* by Sophocles, translated by Robert Fagles, translated by Robert Fagles, Translation copyright ©1982 by Robert Fagles. Used by permission of Viking Penguin, a division of Penguin Books USA Inc.

Plato, The Republic and Other Works, translated by B. Jowett. Garden City, New York: Anchor Books, 1973.

Plato, *Symposium,* trans. by Nehemas and Woodruff; Indianapolis, Indiana and Cambridge, Massachusetts: Hackett Publishing Company, 1989.

Plato, *Republic,* translated by G.M.A. Grube, revised by C.D.C. Reeve; Indianapolis, Indiana and Cambridge, Massachusetts: Hackett Publishing Company, 1992.

Plato, *Theaetetus,* translated by M.J. Levett, Ed. by Bernard Williams, revised by Myles Burnyeat; Indianapolis, Indiana and Cambridge, Massachusetts: Hackett Publishing Company, 1992.

Reprinted by permission of the publishers and the Loeb Classical Library from *The Collected Works of Aristotle, Book I* translated by Peck, *Book VIII* translated by Rackham, and *Book IX* translated by Balme, Cambridge, Mass.: Harvard University Press, 1942.

Reprinted from *The Politics of Aristotle* edited and translated by Ernest Barker (1946) by permission of Oxford University Press.

Descartes, *Meditations on First Philosophy,* 3rd ed., translated by Donald A. Cress; Indianapolis, Indiana and Cambridge, Massachusetts: Hackett Publishing Company, 1993.

Descartes, *The Passions of the Soul,* translator Stephen H. Voss; Indianapolis, Indiana and Cambridge, Massachusetts: Hackett Publishing Company, 1989.

Hobbes, *Leviathan,* Ed. Edwin Curley; Indianapolis, Indiana and Cambridge, Massachusetts: Hackett Publishing Company, 1994.

Rousseau, *The Basic Political Writings,* translated by Donald A. Cress; Indianapolis, Indiana and Cambridge, Massachusetts: Hackett Publishing Company, 1987.

John Stuart Mill (ed, Susan M. Olkin), *The Subjection of Women;* Indianapolis, Indiana and Cambridge, Massachusetts: Hackett Publishing Company, 1988.

Kierkegaard, Søren; *Either/Or.* Copyright 1944/1959 by Princeton University Press. Reprinted by permission of Princeton University Press.

From *The Basic Writings Of Nietzsche* by Friedrich Nietzsche, Translated by Walter Kaufmann. Copyright ©1967 by Walter Kaufmann. Reprinted by permission of Random House, Inc.

From *The Gay Science* by Friedrich Nietzsche, Translated by Walter Kaufmann. Copyright ©1974 by Walter Kaufmann. Reprinted by permission of Random House, Inc.

From *The Genealogy Of Morals* by Friedrich Nietzsche, Translated by Walter Kaufmann. Copyright ©1969 by Walter Kaufmann. Reprinted by Permission of Random House, Inc.

Friedrich Nietzsche, from *Beyond Good and Evil.* Reprinted by permission from Penguin UK.

Excerpts from *Three Essays on the Theory of Sexuality* by Sigmund Freud. Copyright ©1962 by Sigmund Freud Copyrights, Ltd. Reprinted by permission of BasicBooks, a division of HarperCollins Publishers, Inc.

Reprinted from *New Introductory Lectures in Psycho-Analysis* by Sigmund Freud, translated from the German by James Strachey, with the permission of W.W. Norton & Company, Inc. Copyright 1933 by Sigmund Freud, renewed ©1961 by W.J.H. Sprott. English by James Strachey.

Excerpts from *A Room of One's Own* by Virginia Woolf, copyright 1929 by Harcourt Brace & Company and renewed 1957 by Leonard Woolf, reprinted by permission of the publisher.

Jung, Carl; *Collected Works,* Vol. 9. Copyright ©1959 renewed by Princeton University Press. Reprinted by permission of Princeton University Press.

Excerpted from *Feminine Psychology* by Karen Horney, edited by Harold Kelman, with the permission of W.W. Norton & Company, Inc. Copyright ©1967 by W.W. Norton & Company, Inc.

INDEX